Usage and Style

Language
20 Writing to the World
21 Language That Builds Common Ground
22 Language Variety
23 Word Choice and Spelling
24 Glossary of Usage

pages 229–266

Sentence Style
25 Coordination, Subordination, and Emphasis
26 Consistency and Completeness
27 Parallelism
28 Shifts
29 Conciseness
30 Sentence Variety

pages 267–290

Sentence Grammar
31 Basic Grammar
32 Verbs
33 Subject-Verb Agreement
34 Pronouns
35 Adjectives and Adverbs
36 Modifier Placement
37 Comma Splices and Fused Sentences
38 Sentence Fragments

pages 291–354

Punctuation and Mechanics
39 Commas
40 Semicolons
41 End Punctuation
42 Apostrophes
43 Quotation Marks
44 Other Punctuation
45 Capital Letters
46 Abbreviations and Numbers
47 Italics
48 Hyphens

pages 355–400

Resources

MLA Documentation
49 The Basics of MLA Style
50 In-Text Citations
51 List of Works Cited
52 STUDENT RESEARCH ESSAY, MLA STYLE

pages 401–458

APA, *Chicago*, and CSE Documentation
53 APA Style
STUDENT ESSAY, APA STYLE
54 *Chicago* Style
STUDENT ESSAY, *CHICAGO* STYLE
55 CSE Style
STUDENT PROPOSAL, CSE STYLE

pages 459–536

For Multilingual Writers
56 Writing in U.S. Academic Genres
57 Clauses and Sentences
58 Nouns and Noun Phrases
59 Verbs and Verb Phrases
60 Prepositions and Prepositional Phrases

pages 537–564

Writing in the Disciplines
Applied Sciences
STUDENT LAB REPORT
65 Writing for Business
STUDENT DOCUMENTS

pages 565–606

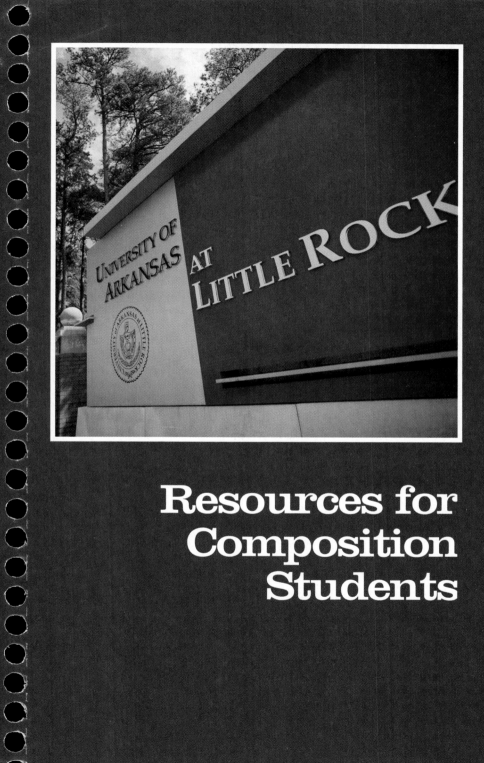

Resources for Composition Students

University of Arkansas at Little Rock

Letter to Students   *UALR-3*

UALR Resources for Composition Students

a Writing Program Administrators outcomes
statement   *UALR-5*

b Expectations for your composition course   *UALR-7*

c Resources for student writers   *UALR-9*

d Student responsibilities and rules of behavior   *UALR-13*

e Student acknowledgment   *UALR-15*

f Writing Program Administrators outcomes
statement journal   *UALR-19*

Cover Design: Joshua R. Johnson

Letter to Students

O n behalf of the Department of Rhetoric and Writing and the composition program, I want to welcome you to the University of Arkansas at Little Rock. We are pleased you are taking a composition course. You most likely purchased this University of Arkansas at Little Rock Edition of *The Everyday Writer* as a requirement for your composition course; however, you will find this handbook useful well beyond this course and into your professional career. This handbook will serve as a critical reference to support your growth as a writer.

In this book, you will find specific content to help you learn to evaluate audience, select genre and medium, think critically about sources and integrate them into your writing projects with proper documentation, engage in the writing process, clearly and effectively communicate your ideas, and attend to the surface issues of editing. These goals align with the learning outcomes for composition at UALR, which are adopted from the Writing Program Administrators Outcomes Statement (WPA OS). Universities and colleges across the country use the WPA OS. In the following pages, you will find a complete list of learning outcomes, and at the back of this book, you will find a guide to constructing portfolios titled *Portfolio Keeping*. Our program uses portfolios for individual student learning and programmatic assessment. A portfolio, unlike a test, allows you to demonstrate your learning over the duration of the semester in response to the learning outcomes.

Composition courses at UALR are offered during 15-week semesters and accelerated in both 8-week sessions during the academic year and 5-week sessions during the summer. Additionally, we offer face-to-face, online, and hybrid versions of our composition courses. Understanding how you learn will help you decide the best format and time frame for you. We encourage students to try hybrid courses before taking online courses or accelerated sessions. Accelerated and online courses require the same work as 15-week, face-to-face courses; the content is simply offered in an alternative format and/or time frame. Typically, students who are self-starters and who excel in writing do well in online and accelerated classes.

Taking advantage of UALR resources such as student counseling, career services, and the University Writing Center could be vital for you as a student writer. Additionally, utilizing the electronic resources that accompany this book, located at **bedfordstmartins.com/everydaywriter**, will serve you well. I strongly encourage you to know your instructor and reach out to him or her when you need clarification or support. You will find contact information for your instructor and course requirements in the syllabus. Participating in your class and submitting your writing assignments will be the key to your success in composition and beyond.

In the following pages you will find more information about resources to support your success in composition, ethical uses of sources, and UALR's policies on academic integrity. Because we want you to be successful in composition, we have provided some information about our expectations along with course descriptions. You also will find a journal for tracking your portfolio progress beginning on page UALR-19. In addition to the *Portfolio Keeping* supplement, following the index, this handbook also includes a section on *Understanding and Composing Multimodal Projects*, which will help you better understand multimodal composition.

Composition courses are offered through the Department of Rhetoric and Writing. As a department, our mission is to further your workplace, civic, and personal communication skills. Beyond composition, our department offers a variety of courses that will enhance your academic skills, including introductory research and persuasive writing courses. As a student of any major, you may be interested in taking upper-level writing courses such as Grant Writing, Writing for Publication, Document Design, or Technical Writing in order to become more competitive in the global marketplace. We also offer specialized courses on such topics as video game design, legal writing, reasoning and argument, and auto/biography to further your critical thinking and personal interests.

My door is always open. So, please come see me, or email me, if there is anything I can do to help you.

Sherry Rankins-Robertson, PhD

Director of Composition
Assistant Professor of Rhetoric and Writing
Office Location: Student Union-B, Room 104
sjrobertson@ualr.edu
(501) 569-3477

Resources for Composition Students UALR

UALRa Writing Program Administrators outcomes statement

RHETORICAL KNOWLEDGE

By the end of first year composition, students should:

- Focus on a purpose
- Respond to the needs of different audiences
- Respond appropriately to different kinds of rhetorical situations
- Use conventions of format and structure appropriate to a rhetorical situation
- Adopt appropriate voice, tone, and level of formality
- Understand how genres shape reading and writing
- Write in several genres

CRITICAL THINKING, READING, AND WRITING

By the end of first year composition, students should:

- Use writing and reading for inquiry, learning, thinking, and communicating
- Understand a writing assignment as a series of tasks, including finding, evaluating, analyzing, and synthesizing appropriate primary and secondary sources
- Integrate their own ideas with those of others
- Understand the relationships among language, knowledge, and power

PROCESSES

By the end of first year composition, students should:

- Be aware that it usually takes multiple drafts to create and complete a successful text
- Develop flexible strategies for generating, revising, editing, and proofreading
- Understand writing as an open process that permits writers to use later invention and rethinking to revise their work
- Understand the collaborative and social aspects of writing processes
- Learn to critique their own and others' works
- Learn to balance the advantages of relying on others with the responsibility of doing their part
- Use a variety of technologies to address a range of audiences

KNOWLEDGE OF CONVENTIONS

By the end of first year composition, students should:

- Learn common formats for different kinds of texts
- Develop knowledge of genre conventions ranging from structure and paragraphing to tone and mechanics
- Practice appropriate means of documenting their work
- Control such surface features as syntax, grammar, punctuation, and spelling

COMPOSING IN ELECTRONIC ENVIRONMENTS

As has become clear over the last twenty years, writing in the 21stcentury involves the use of digital technologies for several purposes, from drafting to peer reviewing to editing. Therefore, although the kinds of composing processes and texts expected from students vary across programs and institutions, there are nonetheless common expectations.

By the end of first year composition, students should:

- Use electronic environments for drafting, reviewing, revising, editing, and sharing texts
- Locate, evaluate, organize, and use research material collected from electronic sources, including scholarly library databases; other official databases (e.g., federal government databases); and informal electronic networks and Internet sources

- Understand and exploit the differences in the rhetorical strategies and in the affordances available for both print and electronic composing processes and texts

UALRb Expectations for your composition course

Courses taught in the composition program are often facilitated through a workshop setting, using small groups, and conferences with students both in collaborative teams and one-on-one between students and faculty members. Faculty members typically engage students through project-based learning and active learning strategies. Students are usually asked to generate several drafts of a writing project and seek feedback from classroom peers and interns in the University Writing Center prior to submission for a grade.

The types of writing you will be asked to produce in composition courses at UALR include multimodal composition. This handbook includes a variety of sources on multimedia assignments and a supplement titled *Understanding and Composing Multimodal Projects*, which follows the index, to support your success with selecting and using genres and media. The time needed to handle the workload for your composition course will vary based on the type of text you develop. So, you will want to allocate plenty of time for invention, production, and revision of genres in media unfamiliar to you (e.g., Web and sound projects). A typical college class requires three hours of classroom engagement and a minimum of six hours outside of class; therefore, you should plan to spend a minimum of nine hours a week to complete the work in your composition course. If you are striving for an A, you will want to invest additional time for your projects.

You should expect timely feedback about your progress and on your projects. Faculty feedback on projects typically addresses higher-order concerns (e.g., focus, audience, content, organization, and development) and helps students identify patterns of errors in lower-order concerns (e.g., grammar, mechanics, word choice, and spelling). This handbook addresses writing process strategies, including getting feedback from peers and comments from your instructor.

Overview of Composition Courses

RHET 0321: ACADEMIC LITERACY

This course offers practice in academic writing and reading with an emphasis on developing strategies and skills for college success: reading and writing fluency, editing techniques, reading comprehension, and vocabulary development. This fulfills the requirement for developmental reading and writing but does not fulfill a core curriculum requirement.

RHET 0310: COMPOSITION FUNDAMENTALS

The Composition Fundamentals course features practice in writing, with an emphasis on developing fluency and editing. This course does not fulfill the core curriculum requirement. RHET 0310 is cross-listed with RHET 1311: Composition I as part of UALR's Accelerated Learning Program for composition. Students must be jointly enrolled in each section.

RHET 1311: COMPOSITION I (FIRST SEMESTER SEQUENCE)

The first-semester course of composition is a research-intensive course. All writing projects are designed to help students understand how to locate, analyze, and integrate sources into their writing. Students will leave RHET 1311 with the ability to determine reliability and validity of sources, including the use of library databases and search engines. To facilitate this curriculum, assignments ask students to explore concepts and use research as support. RHET 1311 exposes students to academic conventions and writing for real-world audiences and purposes.

RHET 1312: COMPOSITION II (SECOND SEMESTER SEQUENCE)

The second-semester course of composition is an argument-based course that uses the Toulmin system of persuasion. All writing projects are designed to help students understand how to develop arguments with integrated sources. The course provides practice in rhetorical analysis, audience analysis, and examination of real-world rhetorical situations. Students will identify and avoid fallacies and learn uses for appeals and reasoning within the context of their writing. The course offers strategies in civil discourse and a foundation in information literacy. RHET 1312 exposes students to both academic conventions and writing for real-world audiences and purposes.

RHET 1320: HONORS COMPOSITION

Honors composition is a one-semester course of composition that accelerates students through composition. This course is designed for students who scored at least a 27 on the ACT, 610 on the SAT Writing, or 98 on the Compass and received at least a B grade in high school English. The course focuses on writing with sources, and students develop argumentative texts. RHET 1320 exposes students to both academic conventions and writing for real-world audiences and purposes.

UALRc   Resources for student writers

Faculty members are the front line for student success. You will find your faculty member's phone number, email, and office location on the first page of your course syllabus. Additionally, you will see available weekly office hours designated for individual student conferences. Many of our composition instructors can be found in Student Union-A, Room 100. On the Composition Program's Web site, located within the Department of Rhetoric and Writing Web site (**ualr.edu/rhetoric**), you will find maps and faculty contact information.

Beyond your instructor, there are a number of resources available at UALR to help you succeed as a writer. These include the Disability Resource Center, the University Writing Center, Career and Counseling Services, the Academic Success Center, available technology, and campus support for that technology.

The Disability Resource Center

LOCATION   Donaghey Student Center, Room 103

PHONE   (501) 569-3143

WEB   ualr.edu/disability

DIRECTOR   Sharon Downs
sadowns@ualr.edu

PURPOSE

The Disability Resource Center (DRC) collaborates with students, faculty, staff, and community members to create usable, equitable, inclusive, and sustainable environments. The DRC collaborates with faculty, staff, and students to make UALR accessible to everyone. The DRC works with the campus community to ensure that physical, curricular, and Web environments are designed to be barrier-free to the greatest extent possible. Some barriers to access can't be removed in a timely manner, and so that's when we work one-on-one with students to determine accommodations. This is a collaborative process between the DRC and the student, and when needed, with faculty.

University Writing Center

LOCATION	Student Union-B, Room 116
PHONE	(501) 569-8343
WEB	ualr.edu/writingcenter
DIRECTOR	Dr. Allison Holland
	adholland@ualr.edu

PURPOSE

The University Writing Center (UWC) is a student resource that is dedicated to helping writers of all ability levels to improve their skills at all stages of the writing process. The UWC emphasizes writing and the teaching of writing to UALR students and members of the community. The UWC provides a comfortable place to write, to receive training in working with writers, to use tools and resources in a community environment, and to receive encouragement.

Some of the UWC's many goals include:

- Providing high-quality guidance and organization to students for long-term writing improvement
- Reading work at any stage
- Discussing ways to make writing clearer and more effective
- Promoting positive personal attitudes about writing and academic achievement through writing growth
- Establishing a writing environment that consistently encourages honesty, integrity, personal development, and responsibility for writers at all ability levels
- Helping students identify error patterns, learn to use computers, and better understand assignments

Students interested in becoming interns in the UWC should contact their writing instructors or the UWC director.

Career and Counseling Services

LOCATION	Student Services Center, Room 119
PHONE	(501) 569-3185
WEB	ualr.edu/careerservices
	ualr.edu/personalcounseling
DIRECTOR	Dr. Mike Kirk
	hmkirk@ualr.edu

PURPOSE

Career Services provides services and programs designed to educate UALR students and alumni in the career development process, thus helping them gain a competitive advantage in a global economy. Additionally, personal counseling is available as a free service for UALR students.

College life can be challenging and stressful. Students experience challenges in a number of different ways: difficulties adjusting to college, confusion in deciding on an academic major, struggles in relationships, or problems getting along with a roommate. Students often feel anxious, depressed, confused, or overwhelmed at some point during their college experience and need help coping with feelings and problems that seem beyond their control.

For college students, help in dealing with these problems and feelings may come from friends, family members, or significant others, but in some cases, help is needed from a trained professional. Counseling is a process that helps individuals identify effective strategies to cope with difficult situations and to achieve personal goals.

Academic Success Center

LOCATION Speech Building, Room 101
PHONE (501) 569-3280
WEB ualr.edu/academicsuccess
DIRECTOR Kimberley Bright
sadowns@ualr.edu

PURPOSE

The Academic Success Center (ASC) houses four specialized programs: the Collegiate Success Program, the Program for Enhanced Learning, TRiO Ronald McNair Scholars, and TRiO Student Support Services. All programs offer enriching services designed to foster holistic success of students. The ASC offers valuable workshops on topics such as study skills, time and stress management, conflict resolution, and goal setting.

Computers Labs

LOCATION Ottenheimer Library, Room 104
PHONE (501) 569-3123
WEB ualr.edu/itservices/catalog/computer-labs

PURPOSE

There are several computer labs on campus for student use. One of the most convenient computer labs is on the first floor of the Ottenheimer Library. Another location where students will find computers to use for writing courses is the University Writing Center. Additionally, there are several departmental labs available across campus for students within corresponding majors. Check with the department linked to your major for information on technology available for student use.

UALR Digital Access

LOCATION   Ottenheimer Library, Room 104

PHONE   (501) 683-7602

WEB   ualr.edu/blackboard/contact

PURPOSE

Every student will inevitably take a course in which they are required to use UALR's learning management system, Blackboard. Each student must log in to Blackboard using a NetID that will be assigned to them when they become a student at UALR. Step-by-step instructions for logging in with screenshots can be found on the Blackboard Web site, located at **ualr.edu/blackboard/welcome/login**.

At UALR, students are digitally identified by their usernames. For example, Jordan A. Michelson would be issued the username jamichelson. This username would be used to log into computers on campus. Additionally, Jordan's email would be **jamichelson @ualr.edu** (username@ualr.edu).

A NetID is used to access the single sign-on myUALR, which includes all of the platforms for student engagement: Blackboard, UALR email, and BOSS. You may want to write down your information in the following format so you are able to log into UALR systems.

▶ MY UALR LOGIN INFORMATION

Jordan A. Michelson

NetID = jamX

Username = jamichelsonX

e-mail = jamichelsonX@ualr.edu

Note: X is a number assigned by UALR. The number may not exist if Jordan is the first user with the first initial "J" and last name "Michelson.

UALRd   Student responsibilities and rules of behavior

The *UALR Student Handbook* contains the Code of Student Rights, Responsibilities and Behavior under Section VI. As discussed in the handbook, students may not disturb classroom procedures with distracting or disruptive behavior. Any student who is involved in such disturbances may be subject to disciplinary action, including ejection from class. Examples of disruptive behavior and misconduct as outlined in the *Statement of Student Behavior* are:

- Conduct inappropriate for an academic setting
- Disrespect for authority
- Lewd, indecent, and obscene behavior
- Pattern of arriving late or leaving early
- Use of profanity
- Inappropriate use of electronic devices
- Bringing children or guests to class without prior approval
- Verbal, written, or electronic threats
- Refusal to follow a directive
- Harassment of faculty, students, or staff
- Usage or possession of intoxicants and/or illegal substances
- Possession of firearms or other weapons
- Behavior deemed disruptive by the instructor

Faculty members have the right to eject any student from class who exhibits or participates in behavior that inhibits student learning. A student who is ejected from a composition class is required to meet with the Director of Composition to gain reentry to the course. Depending on the severity of the student's misconduct, a student may be removed from the course and be required to meet with a representative from the Office of the Dean of Students.

Student responsibility for source use

Academic dishonesty cannot be condoned or tolerated in the university community. Such behavior is considered a student conduct violation, and students found responsible for committing an academic offense will be disciplined by the university. In a writing class, students may be found responsible for the following violations of academic integrity:

PLAGIARISM

To adopt and reproduce as one's own, to appropriate to one's own use and incorporate in one's own work without acknowledgement, ideas or passages from the writings and works of others.

COLLUSION

To obtain from another party, without specific approval in advance by an instructor, assistance in the production of work offered for credit to the extent that the work reflects the ideas or skills of the party consulted rather than those of the person in whose name the work is submitted.

DUPLICITY

To offer for credit identical or substantially unchanged work in two or more courses without specific advance approval of the professor(s) involved.

Course grades, withdrawals, and grade appeals

Composition courses (RHET 1311, RHET 1312, and RHET 1320) are essential to your education at UALR. In order to be successful in upper-level courses, you must have writing and argumentation skills that allow you to engage the subject matter and communicate well-reasoned ideas. For these reasons, UALR requires that students pass composition courses RHET 1311, RHET 1312, and RHET 1320 with a grade of C or better as core requirements for any degree. If a grade of C or better is not earned by a student, he or she will receive a grade of No Credit (NC) and will be required to retake the course.

INCOMPLETE

In accordance with UALR's policy on Incomplete grades, an instructor grants a grade of Incomplete when circumstances beyond the student's control have prevented him or her from completing all of the work required for a course. *The composition program typically will only consider a request for an Incomplete grade when a student has completed more than 60 percent of the semester's coursework and has a passing grade.*

It is the student's responsibility to contact the instructor and request an Incomplete grade. A contract in writing between the student and instructor is required and should include a statement of the work to be completed and the required completion date. This contract must be filed with the Director of Composition prior to the submission of an Incomplete on a final grade roster. Work must be completed and the Incomplete converted to the appropriate grade within 90 days of final grade submission. If not, the Incomplete grade will convert to a grade of NC.

GRADE APPEAL

Upon completion of a course, students may choose to appeal a course grade. Individual assignment grades cannot be disputed. The process for a course grade appeal can be found in the *UALR Student Handbook*, located in Section VIII: Appeals Procedures. Prior to initiating a formal appeal, attempts to resolve the grievance, including meeting the faculty member, Director of Composition, and the Department Chair are required.

We encourage you to familiarize yourself with the UALR Student Handbook for additional policies and procedures.

UALRe Student acknowledgment

You will need to sign and submit the student acknowledgment form for student rights and responsibilities within the University of Arkansas at Little Rock's composition program on page UALR-17 before your instructor will accept any work in your composition course.

Writing Program Administrators outcomes statement journal

Use this journal to track your growth in response to the learning outcomes throughout your career in composition courses at UALR.

Rhetorical knowledge

Focus on purpose.	
What does this mean?	
Why is it important?	
Where does it appear in my work?	

Respond to the needs of different audiences.	
What does this mean?	
Why is it important?	
Where does it appear in my work?	

Use conventions of format and structure appropriate to the rhetorical situation.	
What does this mean?	
Why is it important?	
Where does it appear in my work?	

Adopt appropriate voice, tone, and level of formality.	
What does this mean?	
Why is it important?	
Where does it appear in my work?	

Understand how genres shape reading and writing.	
What does this mean?	
Why is it important?	
Where does it appear in my work?	

Write in several genres.	
What does this mean?	
Why is it important?	
Where does it appear in my work?	

Critical thinking, reading, and writing

Use writing and reading for inquiry, learning, thinking, and communicating.	
What does this mean?	
Why is it important?	
Where does it appear in my work?	

Understand a writing assignment as a series of tasks, including finding, evaluating, analyzing, and synthesizing appropriate primary and secondary sources.	
What does this mean?	
Why is it important?	
Where does it appear in my work?	

Integrate your own ideas with those of others.	
What does this mean?	
Why is it important?	
Where does it appear in my work?	

Understand the relationships among language, knowledge, and power.	
What does this mean?	
Why is it important?	
Where does it appear in my work?	

Processes

Be aware that it usually takes multiple drafts to create and complete a successful text.	
What does this mean?	
Why is it important?	
Where does it appear in my work?	

Develop flexible strategies for generating, revising, editing, and proofreading.	
What does this mean?	
Why is it important?	
Where does it appear in my work?	

Understand writing as an open process that permits you to use later invention and rethinking to revise your work.	
What does this mean?	
Why is it important?	
Where does it appear in my work?	

Understand the collaborative and social aspects of writing processes.	
What does this mean?	
Why is it important?	
Where does it appear in my work?	

Learn to critique your own and others' works.	
What does this mean?	
Why is it important?	
Where does it appear in my work?	

Learn to balance the advantages of relying on others with the responsibility of doing your part.	
What does this mean?	
Why is it important?	
Where does it appear in my work?	

Use a variety of technologies to address a range of audiences.	
What does this mean?	
Why is it important?	
Where does it appear in my work?	

Knowledge of conventions

Learn common formats for different kinds of texts.	
What does this mean?	
Why is it important?	
Where does it appear in my work?	

Develop knowledge of genre conventions ranging from structure and paragraphing to tone and mechanics.	
What does this mean?	
Why is it important?	
Where does it appear in my work?	

Practice appropriate means of documenting your work.	
What does this mean?	
Why is it important?	
Where does it appear in my work?	

Control surface features such as syntax, grammar, punctuation, and spelling.

What does this mean?	
Why is it important?	
Where does it appear in my work?	

Composing in electronic environments

Use electronic environments for drafting, reviewing, editing, and sharing texts.

What does this mean?	
Why is it important?	
Where does it appear in my work?	

Locate, evaluate, organize, and use research material collected from electronic sources, including scholarly library databases; other official databases; and informal electronic networks and Internet sources.

What does this mean?	
Why is it important?	
Where does it appear in my work?	

Understand and exploit the differences in the rhetorical strategies and in the affordances available for both print and electronic composing processes and texts.

What does this mean?	
Why is it important?	
Where does it appear in my work?	

5TH EDITION

The Everyday Writer

Andrea A. Lunsford
STANFORD UNIVERSITY

A section for multilingual writers with

Paul Kei Matsuda
ARIZONA STATE UNIVERSITY

Christine M. Tardy
DEPAUL UNIVERSITY

Bedford / St. Martin's

BOSTON ◆ NEW YORK

For Bedford/St. Martin's

Executive Editor: Carolyn Lengel
Senior Production Editor: Harold Chester
Assistant Production Manager: Joe Ford
Marketing Manager: Scott Berzon
Editorial Assistant: Nicholas McCarthy
Copy Editor: Wendy Polhemus-Annibell
Indexer: Melanie Belkin
Photo Researcher: Connie Gardner
Permissions Manager: Kalina K. Ingham
Art Director: Lucy Krikorian
Text Design: Anne Carter; Claire Seng-Niemoeller
Illustrator: GB Tran
Cover Design: Donna Dennison
Composition: Graphic World
Printing and Binding: Quad Graphics

President, Bedford/St. Martin's: Denise B. Wydra
Presidents, Macmillan Higher Education: Joan E. Feinberg and Tom Scotty
Editor in Chief: Karen S. Henry
Director of Development: Erica T. Appel
Director of Marketing: Karen R. Soeltz
Production Director: Susan W. Brown
Associate Production Director: Elise S. Kaiser
Managing Editor: Shuli Traub

Library of Congress Control Number: 2012939678

7   6   5   4   3
f   e   d   c   b

For information, write: Bedford/St. Martin's, 75 Arlington Street, Boston, MA 02116   (617-399-4000)

ISBN 978-1-4576-0004-3 (Student edition, plastic comb)
ISBN 978-1-4576-1269-5 (Student edition, spiral)
ISBN 978-1-4576-1266-4 (Instructor's edition)

Acknowledgments

How to Use This Book

The Everyday Writer provides a "short and sweet" writing reference you can use easily on your own—at work, in class, even on the run. Small enough to tuck into a backpack or briefcase, this text has been designed to help you find information quickly, efficiently, and easily. I hope that this book will prove to be an everyday reference—and that the following tips will lead you to any information you need.

You'll find many more free resources—videos, tutorials, and research help—and access to e-books and other premium content on the book's companion Web site at **bedfordstmartins.com/everydaywriter**.

The Quick Access Menu on the inside front cover offers a brief overview of the book's contents, divided into twelve color-coded sections that correspond to the book's tabs. If you're looking for a particular chapter or a general topic, this is the simplest place to start. (You can also use the Contents on the inside back cover, which gives chapter titles and most major headings.)

On the back of each tabbed divider, you'll also find the tab contents listed in depth.

The tab contents gives a page number for the beginning of each section, but you can also flip through using the page headers to find the content you're looking for.

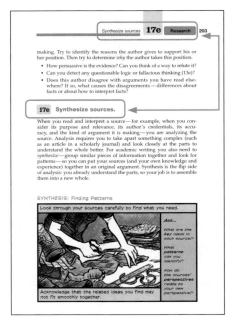

More ways into the book

Directories At the end of the book, you'll find several directories to help you locate special categories of content quickly, including a Directory of Storyboard Art to help you think in new ways about the writing process, a Directory of Student Writing in the book (with more on the Web site), directories of Chapters of Advice and Boxed Tips for multilingual writers, and directories to the "Considering Disabilities" and "Talking the Talk" boxes.

User-Friendly Index The index lists everything covered in the book. You can look up a topic either by its formal name (*ellipses*, for example) or, if you're not sure what the formal name is, by a familiar word you use to describe it (such as *dots*). Important concepts are defined in the index, too, so if you're just looking for a definition, you can find it immediately.

Guide to the Top Twenty Chapter 1 provides guidelines for recognizing, understanding, and editing the most commonly identified issues in student writing today. This section includes brief explanations, hand-edited examples, and cross-references to other places in the book where you'll find more detail on each topic.

Clear Guides to Research and Documentation   Easy-to-follow source maps walk you step-by-step through the processes of selecting, evaluating, using, and citing sources. Documentation models appear in two tabbed sections—gold for MLA style and white for APA, *Chicago*, and CSE styles—with the different documentation styles color-coded in these sections. Most models are also color-coded.

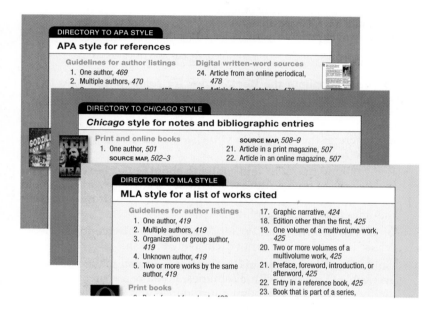

Revision Symbols   If your instructor uses revision symbols to mark your drafts, you can consult the list of symbols at the back of the book and its cross-references to places in the book where you'll find more help.

Glossary of Usage   Chapter 24 gives quick advice on commonly confused and misused words.

Hand-Edited Examples   Many examples are hand-edited in blue, allowing you to see the text and its revision at a glance. Pointers and boldface type make examples easy to spot on the page.

▶ When ~~him~~ *he* and Zelda were first married, they lived in New York.

▶ The boss invited ~~she~~ *her* and her family to dinner.

Color-Coded Examples Many examples that point out sentence construction or grammar issues use color-coding to focus your attention.

Helping verbs (also called auxiliary verbs) combine with other verbs (often called main verbs) to create verb phrases. Helping verbs include the various forms of *be, do, have* (which can also function as main verbs) and the words *can, could, may, might, must, shall, should, will,* and *would.*

▶ **You do need some sleep tonight!**
▶ **I could have danced all night.**
▶ **She would prefer to learn Italian rather than Spanish.**

See Chapters 32 and 33 for a complete discussion of verbs.

Boxed Tips throughout the Book Look for color-coded boxes to get focused help:

- Green "At a Glance" boxes at the beginning of most chapters (and elsewhere in the book) help you check your drafts with a critical eye and revise or edit.
- Red "Talking the Talk" and "Talking about Style" boxes help you make sense of how writing works in the academic world and help you make stylistic choices for various kinds of writing—in communities, jobs, and disciplines.
- Blue "For Multilingual Writers" boxes offer advice for students whose home language is not exclusively English.
- Gold "Considering Disabilities" boxes help you make your work accessible to readers with disabilities. If you're a writer with a disability, these boxes also point out resources and strategies you may want to use.

Storyboard Art Comic-style art throughout the green-tabbed sections helps you look at the writing process with fresh eyes—and reflect on how your process works. The storyboards are designed so you can think them through on your own. A complete list of storyboards appears in the directory at the back of the book. Exercises to focus your thinking on the storyboards can be found in *The Everyday Writer with Exercises* and on the Web site at **bedfordstmartins .com/everydaywriter**.

RHETORICAL SITUATIONS: Choose Your Topic

Browse around for a topic you care about.

Ask...

What interesting topic will meet the requirements for your assignment and context?

What do you know about the topic? What else do you need to find out?

What message do you want to convey?

Make sure your topic is manageable and suits your purpose....

Cross-References to the Web Site *The Everyday Writer* Web site expands the book's coverage. The cross-references in the book point you toward practical online resources—tutorials, interactive exercises, model student writing, research and documentation help, and more.

 bedfordstmartins.com/everydaywriter
Student Writing

A tutorial on using *The Everyday Writer*, Fifth Edition

For this book to serve you well, you need to get to know it — to know what's inside and how to find it. The following tutorial is designed to help you familiarize yourself with *The Everyday Writer*; the answers appear on the pages following the tutorial.

Getting Started with *The Everyday Writer*

1. Where will you find advice on revising a rough draft of an essay?
2. Where will you find quick information on identifying and fixing sentence fragments?
3. Where will you find guidelines on documenting electronic sources, such as information found on a Web site?
4. Where will you find advice for multilingual writers?

Planning and Drafting

5. Where in *The Everyday Writer* can you find general guidelines on planning and drafting an essay?
6. Where can you find information about how to make and support a claim?
7. Your instructor wants you to give an oral presentation based on a print essay you've written. Where would you find information about planning the presentation?

Doing Research

8. You have a topic but don't know where to begin your research. How can *The Everyday Writer* help you narrow down your options?
9. You've found Web sites related to your topic, but you aren't sure how reliable they are. Where can you find help in evaluating them?
10. Your instructor asks you to become a more critical reader of the sources you have found for your writing project. What section of the handbook will help you understand what to do?
11. You have misplaced the page number of a quotation from an article you want to use in your final project. Can you omit it? Where can you find the answer in *The Everyday Writer*?
12. Your instructor has asked you to use MLA style. How do you document information obtained from a DVD source?

Editing

13. As you edit a final draft, you stop at the following sentence: *Winning may be the name of the game but it isn't a name I care for very much.* Should you put a comma before *but*? How and where do you find this answer?

14. You speak several languages, and you still confuse the English prepositions *in* and *on*. Where can you find help?

15. Your instructor has written *ref* next to this sentence: *Transmitting video signals by satellite is a way of overcoming the problem of scarce airwaves and limiting how they are used.* Where do you look in your handbook for help responding to your instructor's comment?

16. You have spell-checked your document. Do you still need to proofread it? What information does *The Everyday Writer* provide?

Meeting Your Instructors' Expectations

17. You have gotten a draft of your essay back from your instructor with the comment *underdeveloped*. How can your handbook help you find out what you need to do to revise?

18. You want to let your instructor know that you will need to miss class the following day. What advice can *The Everyday Writer* give you about sending a message to someone you don't know very well?

19. You turned in a revised draft, but your instructor says you have only corrected minor errors. Where can you find information on doing thorough revisions?

20. You have been asked to look at a classmate's draft and make suggestions. How can you find out more about reviewing the work of your peers?

Writing in Any Discipline

21. You have a paper due in political science. You've never before written a political science paper, so you're not sure how to proceed. Do political science papers follow any set format? Where can you look for help?

22. You need to write a lab report for your chemistry class. Is there a model in *The Everyday Writer*?

23. For a literature course, you're writing an essay interpreting a poem by Emily Dickinson. Where can you find help?

24. You need to submit a reflective essay to complete the portfolio for your writing class. Where in *The Everyday Writer* can you find information about what to include and how to present the work?

Answers to the tutorial

1. Chapter 10.
2. Chapter 38, on sentence fragments.
3. The gold tab covers documenting sources, including electronic sources, in MLA style; the white tab covers documenting sources in APA, *Chicago*, and CSE styles.

4. The first blue tab includes five chapters (Chapters 56–60) that cover language issues of special interest to students who speak languages in addition to English. At the back of the book you will find a directory to all the materials for multilingual writers.

5. Chapters 6–7 offer guidelines on exploring, planning, and drafting.

6. Looking up *claim* in the index leads you to Chapter 13, on analyzing arguments, and to Chapter 14, on constructing an effective argument.

7. Looking in the directory of student writing points you toward the excerpts from a student presentation in 3c.

8. Chapter 16, "Doing Research," includes section 16b, "Use the library to get started."

9. Skimming the table of contents leads you to Chapter 17, on evaluating sources, and in particular to 17c, on evaluating usefulness and credibility, and to 17d, on reading sources critically.

10. Looking in the index under *reading* or *critical reading* — or checking the table of contents — should lead you to Chapter 12, "Critical Reading," which outlines steps in a critical reading process with examples for various kinds of texts.

11. Consulting the index under *sources* takes you to Chapter 18, "Integrating Sources and Avoiding Plagiarism," where you will find that you must include all of the necessary elements of a citation. "The Top Twenty" in Chapter 1 points out that incomplete documentation is one of the three most common problems in student writing today.

12. The table of contents leads you to the gold tab, which provides a full discussion of MLA documentation conventions. The directory to MLA style, in Chapter 51, points you to the model for citing a DVD.

13. You could turn directly to Chapter 39, on using commas, and look for examples of how to use commas in similar sentences. Looking at "The Top Twenty" in Chapter 1 will show you that omitting a comma in a compound sentence is one of the most common errors students make.

14. The table of contents tells you that Chapter 60 covers prepositions; 60a includes a set of strategies for using prepositions idiomatically, including several examples of sentences using *in* and *on*.

15. A list of revision symbols appears at the back of *The Everyday Writer*. Consulting this list tells you that *ref* refers to "unclear pronoun reference" and that this subject is discussed in 34g.

16. Looking up *proofreading* in the index will take you to an entry on spell checkers and proofreading. The information in section 23e points out that spell checkers miss many kinds of mistakes — there is no substitute for careful proofreading!

17. Looking up *instructor comments* in the index or skimming the table of contents will lead you to section 10c, which includes a chart on learning from instructor comments.

18. The table of contents shows you that section 2e, "Use media to communicate effectively," offers guidelines for sending formal messages, such as an email to an instructor.

19. In the index, you'll find an entry for *reviewing drafts* that directs you to a "Talking the Talk" box in Chapter 10. A directory to all the book's "Talking the Talk" boxes, which answer frequently asked questions about academic work, appears at the back of the book.

20. Looking under *peer review* in the index, or scanning the table of contents, will lead you to section 10b, a detailed look at how to act as a peer reviewer — and how to react when your work is under review.

21. Chapters 61–65 cover academic and professional writing in general, and Chapter 63 covers social science subjects.

22. Consulting the student directory at the back of the book will lead you to a chemistry lab report in Chapter 64, on writing for the natural and applied sciences.

23. Chapter 62, on writing for the humanities, provides guidelines for close readings of literature and a student paper comparing two poems by E. E. Cummings. (On the book's Web site, at **bedfordstmartins.com /everydaywriter**, you can also find a glossary of literary terms.)

24. Looking up *portfolios* in the index or skimming the table of contents will take you to Chapter 11, which includes material on planning a portfolio.

Preface

Today, we are in the midst of a literacy revolution the likes of which we haven't seen in at least two thousand years — or perhaps ever. One hallmark of this revolution is that students today are no longer just consumers of information; rather, they are active producers of knowledge. More than ever before, students today are *writers* — every day, every night, all the time; writing is all around them, like the air they breathe, so much so that they don't even notice. From contributing entries to Wikipedia to blogging, texting, tweeting, and posting to YouTube and Facebook, student writers are participating widely in what philosopher Kenneth Burke calls "the conversation of humankind." As access to new writing spaces grows, so too do the potential audiences: many writers, for example, are in daily contact with people around the world, and their work goes out to millions. In such a time, writers need to think more carefully than ever about how to craft effective messages and how best to represent themselves to others.

These ever-expanding opportunities for writers, as well as the challenges that inevitably come with them, have inspired this edition of *The Everyday Writer* — from the focus on thinking carefully about audience and purposes for writing and on attending to the "look" of writing; to an emphasis on moving smoothly between informal, social-media writing and academic writing; to a focus on writing to make something happen in the world; to an emphasis on the ways writing works across disciplines; to the questions that new genres and forms of writing raise about citing and documenting sources and about understanding and avoiding plagiarism. What remains constant is the focus on the "every-dayness" of writing and on down-to-earth, practical advice for how to write well in a multitude of situations as well as across a range of genres and media.

What also remains constant is the focus on rhetorical concerns. In a time of such challenging possibilities, taking a rhetorical perspective is particularly important. Why? Because a rhetorical perspective rejects either/or, right/wrong, black/white approaches to writing in favor of asking what choices will be most appropriate, effective, and ethical in a given writing situation. A rhetorical perspective also means paying careful attention to the purposes we want to achieve and the audiences we want to address. Writers today need to maintain such a rhetorical perspective every single day, and *The Everyday Writer*, Fifth Edition, provides them with the tools for doing so.

What's different about this edition?

The Literacy Revolution Has Arrived Students today are writing more than ever to communicate with friends and reach a wider public. The literacy revolution has brought with it opportunities for student writers to make their voices heard by audiences never before accessible to them; to create texts that include images, sound, and video as well as words; and to present these texts across a range of genres, from brochures and posters to blogs and Web-based reports. My research shows that students often make well-informed decisions in their everyday writing—so *The Everyday Writer* includes new features to help students understand the skills they already have as social writers and use those skills in their academic writing.

A Focus on Bridging Social and Academic Writing   *The Everyday Writer* shows students how to use the rhetorical strategies that they employ in their extracurricular writing—including an intuitive understanding of audience and purpose—to create more effective academic writing. Examples throughout show student writers using social media effectively, and advice in several chapters helps students consider the differences between social and academic writing.

An Awareness That Today's Academic Writing Goes Beyond Print Rhetorical advice in *The Everyday Writer* never assumes that students are producing only traditional print products. In addition to new coverage that specifically addresses the rhetorical considerations of tasks such as planning an online text and turning a print text into a presentation, advice throughout the book aims to help students create rhetorically effective texts for any situation.

More Student Writing in More Genres   Many students define good writing as active and participatory; they tell me that their most important writing aims to "make something happen in the world." Sample student writing in *The Everyday Writer* reflects the writing students are doing today, both in and out of class—from tweets and event promotions to reports and literary analyses. A new chapter on public writing, Chapter 4, "Writing to Make Something Happen in the World," helps students understand how to reach their communities with various kinds of texts.

New Attention to Critical Reading — and an Awareness That Students Today Must Respond to Many Kinds of Texts   A completely updated chapter on critical reading highlights the wide range of texts that students want, and are asked, to read (or view or listen to) today. Examples in the chapter analyze speeches, blog posts, and photos as well as literary works.

A Focus on the "Why" as Well as the "How" of Documenting Sources   New coverage of the basics of various documentation styles helps students understand why academic work calls for more specific citation than popular writing, how to tell the difference between a work from a database and a work online, why medium matters, and more. And additional visual help (including color-coding) with documentation models makes it easy to see what information writers should include in citations.

New Illustrations by *Vietnamerica* Artist GB Tran   Because of my own interest in graphic texts and in the ways words and images make meaning together, I'm thrilled that GB Tran, author of *Vietnamerica*, contributed illustrations to this book. In addition to the beautiful part opener and chapter opener images and other illustrations he created, he and I worked together on six multipanel series on crucial aspects of the writing process (on analyzing rhetorical situations, crafting a working thesis, reading critically, revising and editing, managing peer review, and synthesizing sources). Exercises that ask students to closely examine these panel illustrations appear in *The Everyday Writer with Exercises* and on the Web site at **bedfordstmartins.com /everydaywriter**.

What hasn't changed?

Attention to Good Writing, Not Just to Surface Correctness   *The Everyday Writer* helps students understand that effective texts in every genre and medium follow conventions that always depend on their audience, situation, and discipline.

Help for the Most Common Writing Problems   A nationwide study that I conducted with Karen Lunsford—revisiting the original 1986 research that Bob Connors and I did on student writing—shows the problems

U.S. college students are most likely to have in their writing today. This book's first chapter presents a quick guide to troubleshooting the Top Twenty—with examples, explanations, and information on where to turn in the book for more detailed information.

Up-to-Date Advice on Research and Documentation As best practices for research continue to evolve, so does *The Everyday Writer*. In this edition, you'll find integrated coverage of library and online research to help students find authoritative and credible information in any medium, plus advice on integrating sources, avoiding plagiarism, using social bookmarking tools for research, and citing sources in MLA, APA, *Chicago*, and CSE documentation styles. Visual source maps in all four documentation sections show students how to evaluate, use, and document print and online sources.

Comprehensive Coverage of Critical Thinking and Argument Because first-year writing assignments increasingly call for argument, *The Everyday Writer* provides all the information student writers need to respond effectively to their writing assignments, including practical advice on critical reading and analysis of all kinds of texts, instruction on composing arguments, and two complete student essays.

Essential Help for Writing in the Disciplines Along with strategies for understanding discipline-specific assignments, vocabulary, style, and use of evidence, this edition offers more student writing samples than ever before, including tweets and Facebook posts, an analysis of a graphic novel in both print-essay and multimodal-presentation form, research projects (in MLA, APA, *Chicago*, and CSE styles), business documents, sample writing from introductory courses in other disciplines, and writing for the public.

Unique Coverage of Language and Style Unique chapters on language help students think about language in context and about the consequences that language choices have on writers and readers. Boxed tips throughout the book help students communicate effectively across cultures—and use varieties of language both wisely and well.

An Inviting Design *The Everyday Writer* makes information easy to find and appealing to read.

A User-Friendly, All-in-One Index Entries include both everyday words (such as *that* or *which*) and grammatical terms (such as *pronoun*, which is defined in the index), so students can find what they're looking for quickly and easily.

Available in many formats with a wide array of ancillaries

Print, digital, and integrated media formats

The Everyday Writer, Fifth Edition
- **Comb** binding   ISBN 978-1-4576-0004-3
- **Spiral** binding   ISBN 978-1-4576-1269-5

The Everyday Writer with Exercises, Fifth Edition
Comb-bound book integrated with **LearningCurve adaptive online quizzing** that focuses students on grammar and style topics
ISBN 978-1-4576-1267-1

Visit **bedfordstmartins.com/everydaywriter/LC** for instructor access to LearningCurve.

The Everyday Writer, Fifth Edition, e-books
Assign the *e-Book for The Everyday Writer*, an interactive online e-book with extra tools and content that allow you to easily customize the book for your course and see student progress, or let students choose a downloadable e-book for their computer, tablet, or e-reader.

Customizable online or downloadable e-book formats: **bedfordstmartins .com/everydaywriter/formats**

CompClass for The Everyday Writer
Bedford's online course space integrates the tools and content that writers — and their teachers — need to develop and assess their work. *CompClass for The Everyday Writer* includes a dedicated writing and peer review space, LearningCurve adaptive online quizzing, an interactive e-book, and more.
ISBN 978-1-4576-2284-7

Resources for instructors

The Everyday Writer, Fifth Edition, Coursepacks
Free content for your course management system: **bedfordstmartins
.com/coursepacks**

Teaching with Lunsford Handbooks, 2013 Update
ISBN 978-1-4576-1268-8

**From Theory to Practice: A Selection of Essays,
Third Edition, by Andrea A. Lunsford**
ISBN 978-0-312-56729-3

Teacher to Teacher, Andrea Lunsford's channel
on the award-winning Bedford Bits blog at
bedfordbits.com

Visit **LunsfordHandbooks.com** for these and additional instructor
resources, including downloadable answer keys for *The Everyday Writer
with Exercises* and for the supplemental exercise book available with *The
Everyday Writer.*

Like **Andrea Lunsford on Facebook** to keep up with her research and
travels, and follow **@LunsfordHandbks on Twitter**.

Resources for students

✅ **LearningCurve packaged with *The Everyday Writer***
LearningCurve adaptive online quizzing is available as a package with *The Everyday Writer* (version without exercises). To order an access card packaged with the print book, use ISBN 978-1-4576-4370-5 (for comb-bound) or ISBN 978-1-4576-4369-9 (for spiral-bound). Students can also purchase access to LearningCurve at **bedfordstmartins.com /everydaywriter/LC**.

***Student Site for The Everyday Writer*, Fifth Edition**
Go to **bedfordstmartins.com/everydaywriter** for free resources — tutorials, exercises, documentation help, and more—plus optional premium content.

***Supplemental Exercises for The Everyday Writer*, Fifth Edition**
ISBN 978-1-4576-2251-9

Acknowledgments

As always, I am most grateful to Carolyn Lengel, my editor for this and two other handbooks as well: her patience, fortitude, and sheer hard work, her astute judgment, her wellspring of good ideas, her meticulous attention to detail, and most of all her great wit and sense of humor are gifts that just keep on giving. I am also thankful to Stephanie Butler and Adam Whitehurst for their help with planning the overall project and their advice on handbook media; to Karrin Varucene for her work on the teaching tab of the Instructor's Edition and for keeping the blog and Facebook pages on track; to Nick McCarthy for editorial assistance; to Claire Seng-Niemoeller and Anna Palchik for their brilliant contributions to art and design; to Donna Dennison for cover art; to Wendy Annibell for her meticulous copyediting; to Sarah Ferguson for her work on the book's new media components; and to Harold Chester, our diligent project editor.

Many thanks, also, to the unfailingly generous and supportive members of the Bedford/St. Martin's team: Joan Feinberg, Denise Wydra, Erica Appel, Karen Henry, Nancy Perry, Jimmy Fleming, Karen Soeltz, Scott Berzon, Shuli Traub, Nick Carbone, and Joe Ford.

For this edition, I am especially grateful to GB Tran, comics artist and author of *Vietnamerica*, whose simple, elegant, yet "everyday" drawings add immeasurably to the visual appeal of *The Everyday Writer*. I am also indebted to Paul Kei Matsuda and Christine Tardy for their extraordinarily helpful additions to the multilingual writer sections of this book; to Lisa Ede for her ongoing support and advice; and to Lisa Dresdner at Norwalk Community College for her fine work on *Teaching with Lunsford Handbooks*. I have also benefited greatly from the excellent advice of some very special colleagues: Colin Gifford Brooke, Syracuse University; Patrick Clauss, Butler University; Dànielle Nicole DeVoss, Michigan State University; Barbara Fister, Gustavus Adolphus College; Beverly Moss, Ohio State University; Arnold Zwicky, Stanford University; and Marilyn Moller.

I owe special thanks to the group of student writers whose work appears in and enriches this book and its companion Web site: Michelle Abbott, Carina Abernathy, Milena Ateyea, Julie Baird, Jennifer Bernal, Valerie Bredin, Taurean Brown, Tessa Cabello, Ben Canning, Leah Clendening, David Craig, Kelly Darr, Allyson Goldberg, Tara Gupta, Joanna Hays, Dana Hornbeak, Ajani Husbands, Bory Kea, James Kung, Emily Lesk, Nastassia Lopez, Heather Mackintosh-Sims, Merlla McLaughlin, Alicia Michalski, Laura Montgomery, Elva Negrete, Katie Paarlberg, Shannan Palma, Stephanie Parker, Teal Pfeifer, Amrit K. Rao, Heather Ricker, Amanda Rinder, Dawn Rodney, Rudy Rubio, Melissa Schraeder, Bonnie Sillay, Shuqiao Song, Jessica Thrower, Dennis Tyler, and Caroline Warner.

Once again, I have been guided by a group of hardworking and meticulous reviewers, including Teresa Aggen, Pikes Peak Community College; Tom Amorose, Seattle Pacific University; Christopher Baarstad, California State Polytechnic University, Pomona; Michelle Baptiste, University of California, Berkeley; Daisy L. Breneman, James Madison University; Matthew Bryan, University of Central Florida; William Carney, Cameron University; Rebecca Chapman, Vanderbilt University; Karen Culver, University of Miami; Cheryl H. Duffy, Fort Hays State University; Heidi Estrem, Boise State University; Susan Gebhardt-Burns, Norwalk Community College; Angela L. Glover, Simpson College; Melissa A. Goldthwaite, Saint Joseph's University; Andrew Green, University of Miami; Joy A. Hagen, University of California, Santa Cruz; Michelle Hager, San José State University; Chad Hammett, Texas State University, San Marcos; James Harger, Colorado Christian University; Kimberly Harrison, Florida International University; Kristy K. Hodson, California State Polytechnic University; Sarah Klotz, University of California, Davis; Mary R. Lamb, Clayton State University; Tom Lindsley, Iowa State University; Mary M. Mackie, Rogers State University; Anne McCarthy, North Carolina Central University; Molly McClennen, Marshall University; Holly McSpadden, Missouri Southern State University; Gina Merys, Creighton University; Jennifer Metsker, University of Michigan; Lyle W. Morgan, Pittsburg State University; Beverly Neiderman, Kent State University; Gary Olson, University of Washington; Susan Pagnac, Iowa State University; Shelley Harper Palmer, Rowan-Cabarrus Community

College; Jonathan Purkiss, Pulaski Technical College; Carolee Ritter, Southeast Community College; Kathleen J. Ryan, University of Montana; Robert Saba, Florida International University; Charlene Schauffler, Kent State University; Marti Singer, Georgia State University; Rachelle M. Smith, Emporia State University; Mary Tripp, University of Central Florida; Erik Turkman, University of Maryland; Samuel Waddell, York College of Pennsylvania; and Susan Zabowski, University of Miami.

Finally, and always, I continue to learn—from my students, who serve as the major inspiration for just about everything I do; from the very best sisters, nieces, and nephews anyone has ever had; and from my spectacular grand-nieces, Audrey and Lila: this book is for all of you.

Andrea A. Lunsford

Writing for College and Beyond

A mind that is stretched by a new experience
can never go back to its old dimensions.

— OLIVER WENDELL HOLMES

Writing for College and Beyond

1 **The Top Twenty: A Quick Guide to Troubleshooting Your Writing** *3*

2 **Expectations for College Writing** *12*
   a Move between social and academic writing *12*
   b Position yourself as an academic writer *14*
   c Read actively *16*
   d Plan research *17*
   e Use media to communicate effectively *17*

3 **Multimodal Assignments** *20*
   a Plan online assignments *20*
   b Join class discussions *24*
   c Prepare for presentations *25*
      STUDENT POWERPOINT PRESENTATION *31*

4 **Writing to Make Something Happen in the World** *36*
   a Decide what should happen *37*
   b Connect with your audience *37*
   c SAMPLE WRITING THAT MAKES SOMETHING HAPPEN IN THE WORLD *38*

For visual analysis Look carefully at the illustration on the front of this tab. What do you think this image suggests about writing for college and beyond?

The Top Twenty: A Quick Guide to Troubleshooting Your Writing

1

Surface errors—grammar, punctuation, word choice, and other small-scale matters—don't always disturb readers. Whether your instructor marks an error in any particular assignment will depend on personal judgments about how serious and distracting it is and about what you should be focusing on in the draft. In addition, not all surface errors are consistently viewed as errors: some of the patterns identified in the research for this book are considered errors by some instructors but as stylistic options by others. Such differing opinions don't mean that there is no such thing as correctness in writing—only that *correctness always depends on some context,* on whether the choices a writer makes seem appropriate to readers.

Research for this book reveals a number of changes that have occurred in student writing over the past twenty-plus years. First, writing assignments in first-year composition classes now focus less on personal narrative and much more on research essays and argument. As a result, students are now writing longer essays than they did twenty years ago and working much more often with sources, both print and digital. Thus it's no surprise that students today are struggling with the conventions for using and citing sources, a problem that did not show up in most earlier studies of student writing.

What else has changed? For starters, wrong-word errors are *by far the most common* errors among first-year student writers today. Twenty years ago, spelling errors were most common by a factor of more than three to one. The use of spell checkers has reduced the number of spelling errors in student writing—but spell checkers' suggestions may also be responsible for some (or many) of the wrong words students are using.

All writers want to be considered competent and careful. You know that your readers judge you by your control of the conventions you have agreed to use, even if the conventions change from time to time. To help you in producing writing that is conventionally correct, you should become familiar with the twenty most common error patterns among U.S. college students today, listed here in order of frequency. A brief explanation and examples of each error are provided in the following sections, and each error pattern is cross-referenced to other places in this book where you can find more detailed information and additional examples.

 bedfordstmartins.com/everydaywriter
Top Twenty

AT A GLANCE

The Top Twenty

1. Wrong word
2. Missing comma after an introductory element
3. Incomplete or missing documentation
4. Vague pronoun reference
5. Spelling (including homonyms)
6. Mechanical error with a quotation
7. Unnecessary comma
8. Unnecessary or missing capitalization
9. Missing word
10. Faulty sentence structure
11. Missing comma with a nonrestrictive element
12. Unnecessary shift in verb tense
13. Missing comma in a compound sentence
14. Unnecessary or missing apostrophe (including *its/it's*)
15. Fused (run-on) sentence
16. Comma splice
17. Lack of pronoun-antecedent agreement
18. Poorly integrated quotation
19. Unnecessary or missing hyphen
20. Sentence fragment

---

1   **Wrong word**

> *precedence*
> Religious texts, for them, take ~~prescience~~ over other kinds of sources.
>   ^

Prescience means "foresight," and precedence means "priority."

> *allergy*
> **The child suffered from a severe ~~allegory~~ to peanuts.**

Allegory is a spell checker's replacement for a misspelling of *allergy*.

> *of*
> **The panel discussed the ethical implications ~~on~~ the situation.**

Wrong-word errors can involve using a word with the wrong shade of meaning, using a word with a completely wrong meaning, or using a wrong preposition or another wrong word in an idiom. Selecting a word from a thesaurus without knowing its meaning, or allowing a spell checker to correct spelling automatically, can lead to wrong-word errors, so use these tools with care. If you have trouble with prepositions and idioms, memorize the standard usage. (See Chapter 23 on word choice and spelling and Chapter 60 on prepositions and idioms.)

2   Missing comma after an introductory element

> **Determined to get the job done, we worked all weekend.**

> **Although the study was flawed, the results may still be useful.**

Readers usually need a small pause—signaled by a comma—between an introductory word, phrase, or clause and the main part of the sentence. Use a comma after every introductory element. When the introductory element is very short, you don't always need a comma, but including it is never wrong. (See 39a.)

3   Incomplete or missing documentation

> *(263).*
> **Satrapi says, "When we're afraid, we lose all sense of analysis and reflection."**

This quotation comes from a print source, so a page number is needed.

> **Some experts agree that James Joyce wrote two of the five best novels**
> *("100 Best Novels").*
> **of all time.**

The source of this information should be indentified (this online source has no page numbers).

Cite each source you refer to in the text, following the guidelines of the documentation style you are using. (The preceding examples follow MLA style — see Chapters 49–52; for other styles, see Chapters 53–55.) Omitting documentation can result in charges of plagiarism (see Chapter 18).

4 Vague pronoun reference

POSSIBLE REFERENCE TO MORE THAN ONE WORD

▶ Transmitting radio signals by satellite is a way of overcoming the
  the airwaves
  problem of scarce airwaves and limiting how ~~they~~ are used.

In the original sentence, *they* could refer to the signals or to the airwaves.

REFERENCE IMPLIED BUT NOT STATED
                                    a policy
▶ The company prohibited smoking, ~~which~~ many employees resented.

What does *which* refer to? The editing clarifies what employees resented.

A pronoun should refer clearly to the word or words it replaces (called the *antecedent*) elsewhere in the sentence or in a previous sentence. If more than one word could be the antecedent, or if no specific antecedent is present, edit to make the meaning clear. (See Chapter 34.)

5 Spelling (including homonyms)

   Reagan
▶ Ronald ~~Regan~~ won the election in a landslide.

Everywhere
▶ ~~Every where~~ we went, we saw crowds of tourists.

The most common misspellings today are those that spell checkers cannot identify. The categories that spell checkers are most likely to miss include homonyms, compound words incorrectly spelled as separate words, and proper nouns, particularly names. After you run the spell checker, proofread carefully for errors such as these — and be sure to run the spell checker to catch other kinds of spelling mistakes. (See 23e.)

6 Mechanical error with a quotation

▶ "I grew up the victim of a disconcerting confusion~~,~~", Rodriguez says (249).

The comma should be placed *inside* the quotation marks.

Follow conventions when using quotation marks with commas (39h), colons (44d), and other punctuation (43f). Always use quotation marks in pairs, and follow the guidelines of your documentation style for block quotations (43b). Use quotation marks for titles of short works (43c), but use italics for titles of long works (47a).

7 Unnecessary comma

BEFORE CONJUNCTIONS IN COMPOUND CONSTRUCTIONS THAT ARE NOT COMPOUND SENTENCES

▶ **This conclusion applies to the United States/ and to the rest of the world.**

No comma is needed before *and* because it is joining two phrases that modify the same verb, *applies*.

WITH RESTRICTIVE ELEMENTS

▶ **Many parents/ of gifted children/ do not want them to skip a grade.**

No comma is needed to set off the restrictive phrase *of gifted children*, which is necessary to indicate which parents the sentence is talking about.

Do not use commas to set off restrictive elements that are necessary to the meaning of the words they modify. Do not use a comma before a coordinating conjunction (*and, but, for, nor, or, so, yet*) when the conjunction does not join parts of a compound sentence. Do not use a comma before the first or after the last item in a series, between a subject and verb, between a verb and its object or complement, or between a preposition and its object. (See 39j.)

8 Unnecessary or missing capitalization

      traditional   *medicines*   *ephedra*
▶ **Some ~~Traditional~~ Chinese ~~Medicines~~ containing ~~Ephedra~~ remain legal.**

Capitalize proper nouns and proper adjectives, the first words of sentences, and important words in titles, along with certain words indicating directions and family relationships. Do not capitalize most other words. When in doubt, check a dictionary. (See Chapter 45.)

9 Missing word

               against
▶ **The site foreman discriminated women and promoted men with less experience.**

Proofread carefully for omitted words, including prepositions (60a), parts of two-part verbs (60b), and correlative conjunctions (31h). Be particularly careful not to omit words from quotations.

10 Faulty sentence structure

▶ ~~The information which~~ *High* ~~high~~ school athletes are presented with
~~mainly includes~~ information on what credits *they* needed to graduate,
~~and thinking about the college~~ which ~~athletes are trying~~ *colleges to try* to play for,
and apply. *how to*

A sentence that starts out with one kind of structure and then changes to another kind can confuse readers. Make sure that each sentence contains a subject and a verb (31b), that subjects and predicates make sense together (26b), and that comparisons have clear meanings (26e). When you join elements (such as subjects or verb phrases) with a coordinating conjunction, make sure that the elements have parallel structures (see Chapter 27).

11 Missing comma with a nonrestrictive element

▶ Marina, who was the president of the club, was first to speak.

The clause *who was the president of the club* does not affect the basic meaning of the sentence: Marina was first to speak.

A nonrestrictive element gives information not essential to the basic meaning of the sentence. Use commas to set off a nonrestrictive element (39c).

12 Unnecessary shift in verb tense

▶ Priya was watching the great blue heron. Then she *slipped* slips and *fell* falls into the swamp.

Verbs that shift from one tense to another with no clear reason can confuse readers (28a).

13 Missing comma in a compound sentence

► Meredith waited for Samir‚ and her sister grew impatient.

Without the comma, a reader may think at first that Meredith waited for both Samir and her sister.

A compound sentence consists of two or more parts that could each stand alone as a sentence. When the parts are joined by a coordinating conjunction, use a comma before the conjunction to indicate a pause between the two thoughts (39b).

14 Unnecessary or missing apostrophe (including *its/it's*)

child's
► Overambitious parents can be very harmful to a ~~childs~~ well-being.

its   *It's*
► The car is lying on ~~it's~~ side in the ditch. ~~Its~~ a white 2004 Passat.

To make a noun possessive, add either an apostrophe and an -s (*Ed's book*) or an apostrophe alone (*the boys' gym*). Do not use an apostrophe in the possessive pronouns *ours*, *yours*, and *hers*. Use *its* to mean *belonging to it*; use *it's* only when you mean *it is* or *it has*. (See Chapter 42.)

15 Fused (run-on) sentence

but
► Klee's paintings seem simple‚ they are very sophisticated.

Although she
► ~~She~~ doubted the value of meditation‚ she decided to try it once.

A fused sentence (also called a *run-on*) joins clauses that could each stand alone as a sentence with no punctuation or words to link them. Fused sentences must either be divided into separate sentences or joined by adding words or punctuation. (See Chapter 37.)

16 Comma splice

for
► I was strongly attracted to her, she was beautiful and funny.

> *that*
> ▶ We hated the meat loaf/ ~~the cafeteria served it~~ every Friday.
>   ^

A comma splice occurs when only a comma separates clauses that could each stand alone as a sentence. To correct a comma splice, you can insert a semicolon or period, connect the clauses with a word such as *and* or *because*, or restructure the sentence. (See Chapter 37.)

17   Lack of pronoun-antecedent agreement

> *All students*   *uniforms.*
> ▶ ~~Every student~~ must provide their own ~~uniform.~~
>   ^   ^
>
>   *its*
> ▶ Each of the puppies thrived in ~~their~~ new home.
>   ^

Pronouns must agree with their antecedents in gender (male or female) and in number (singular or plural). Many indefinite pronouns, such as *everyone* and *each*, are always singular. When a singular antecedent can refer to a man or a woman, either rewrite the sentence to make the antecedent plural or to eliminate the pronoun, or use *his or her*, *he or she*, and so on. When antecedents are joined by *or* or *nor*, the pronoun must agree with the closer antecedent. A collective noun such as *team* can be either singular or plural, depending on whether the members are seen as a group or as individuals. (See 34f.)

18   Poorly integrated quotation

> *showed how color affects taste:*
> ▶ Schlosser cites a 1970s study that ~~"~~Once it became apparent that the
>   ^
>
>   steak was actually blue and the fries were green, some people
>
>   became ill" (Schlosser 565).
>
>   *According to Lars Eighner,*
> ▶ "Dumpster diving has serious drawbacks as a way of life" (~~Eighner~~ 383).
>   ^
>
>   Finding edible food is especially tricky.

Quotations should fit smoothly into the surrounding sentence structure. They should be linked clearly to the writing around them (usually with a signal phrase) rather than dropped abruptly into the writing. (See 18b.)

AT A GLANCE

Taking a Writing Inventory

One way to learn from your mistakes is to take a writing inventory. It can help you think critically and analytically about how to improve your writing skills.

1. Collect two or three pieces of your writing to which either your instructor or other students have responded.

2. Read through these writings, adding your own comments about their strengths and weaknesses. How do your comments compare with those of others?

3. Group all the comments into three categories — *broad content issues* (use of evidence and sources, attention to purpose and audience, and overall impression), *organization and presentation* (overall and paragraph-level organization, sentence structure and style, and formatting), and *surface errors* (problems with spelling, grammar, punctuation, and mechanics).

4. Make an inventory of your own strengths in each category.

5. Study your errors. Mark every instructor and peer comment that suggests or calls for an improvement, and put all these comments in a list. Consult the relevant part of this book or speak with your instructor if you don't understand a comment.

6. Make a list of the top problem areas you need to work on. How can you make improvements? Then note at least two strengths that you can build on in your writing. Record your findings in a writing log that you can add to as the class proceeds.

19 Unnecessary or missing hyphen

▶ This paper looks at fictional and real‸life examples.

A compound adjective modifying a noun that follows it requires a hyphen.

▶ The buyers want to fix⁀up the house and resell it.

A two-word verb should not be hyphenated.

A compound adjective that appears before a noun needs a hyphen. However, be careful not to hypenate two-word verbs or word groups that serve as subject complements. (See Chapter 48.)

20 Sentence fragment

NO SUBJECT

▶ Marie Antoinette spent huge sums of money on herself and her favorites.

Her extravagance
~~And~~ helped bring on the French Revolution.

NO COMPLETE VERB

was
▶ The old aluminum boat sitting on its trailer.

BEGINNING WITH A SUBORDINATING WORD

where
▶ We returned to the drugstore./, ~~Where~~ we waited for our buddies.

A sentence fragment is part of a sentence that is written as if it were a complete sentence. Reading your draft out loud, backwards, sentence by sentence, will help you spot sentence fragments. (See Chapter 38.)

> **bedfordstmartins.com/everydaywriter**
> **Taking a Writing Inventory**

---

2 Expectations for College Writing

Your college instructors—and your future colleagues and supervisors—will expect you to demonstrate your ability to think critically, to consider ethical issues, to find as well as solve problems, to do effective research, to work productively with people of widely different backgrounds, and to present the knowledge you construct in a variety of ways and in a variety of genres and media. Your success will depend on communicating clearly and on making appropriate choices for the context.

2a Move between social and academic writing.

Social connection today involves so much writing—text messages, tweets, Facebook posts, blogs, YouTube videos, and the like—that you probably do more writing out of class than in class. In fact, Web 2.0

and social networking have opened doors for writers like never before. Writing on social networking sites allows writers to get almost instant feedback, and anticipating responses from an audience often has the effect of making online writers very savvy: they know the importance of analyzing the audience and of using an appropriate style, level of formality, and tone to suit the online occasion.

As you know, writers on Twitter tell followers what's going on in short bursts of no more than 140 characters. Here are two representative tweets from the Twitter feed of Stephanie Parker, a college student whose interests include technology and Korean pop culture.

sparker2

Rain's over, going to Trader Joe's to buy some healthy stuff to fight this cold. . suggestions?

Watching Queen Seon Duk/선덕여왕 on @dramafever, love it so far! http://www.dramafever.com/drama/56/ #nowplaying

In these tweets, Stephanie shows a keen awareness both of her audiences on Twitter and of two very common purposes for this kind of informal writing—to seek information (in the first tweet, about foods to fight off a cold) and to share information (in the second tweet, about her view of a Korean drama, with a link so readers can check it out for themselves).

Facebook and similar sites allow for fast-paced conversation between writers. This status update from Alicia Michalski got a response in the form of a link to a YouTube video (of a man exercising to a song called "You Can Do It"), to which Alicia then replied—all in the space of twelve minutes.

Alicia Michalski Long, long day ahead of me. And the toughest won't even be my classes.
Yesterday at 8:14am • Comment • Like

Ryan Sundheimer http://www.youtube.com/watch?v=rCvtldLxu1Y
Tell me that doesn't inspire you!
Yesterday at 8:23am

Alicia Michalski If I had you at work yelling that to me, then yes, it'd be pretty inspiring! I'll just loop it on the speakers there!!
Yesterday at 8:26am

TALKING THE TALK

Conventions

"Aren't conventions just rules with another name?" Not entirely. Conventions — agreed-on language practices of grammar, punctuation, and style — convey a kind of shorthand information from writer to reader. In college writing, you will want to follow the conventions of standard academic English unless you have a good reason to do otherwise. But unlike hard-and-fast rules, conventions are flexible; a convention appropriate for one time or situation may be inappropriate for another. You may even choose to ignore conventions to achieve a particular effect. (You might, for example, write a sentence fragment rather than a full sentence, such as the *Not entirely* near the beginning of this box.) As you become more experienced and confident in your writing, you will develop a sense of which conventions to apply in different writing situations.

Like Stephanie and Alicia, many young writers today are adept at informal social writing across a range of genres and media. You may not think very hard about the audience you'll reach in a tweet or Facebook post, or about your purpose for writing in such spaces, but you are probably more skilled than you give yourself credit for when it comes to making appropriate choices for your informal writing.

Of course, informal writing is not the only writing skill a student needs to master. You'll also need to move back and forth between informal social writing and formal academic writing, and to write across a whole range of genres and media. Look closely at your informal writing: What do you assume about your audience? What is your purpose? How do you achieve a particular tone? In short, why do you write the way you do in these situations? Analyzing the choices you make in a given writing context will help you develop the ability to make good choices in other contexts as well—an ability that will allow you to move between social and academic writing.

2b Position yourself as an academic writer.

If you're like most students, you probably have less familiarity with academic writing contexts than you do with informal contexts. You may not have written anything much longer than five pages of formal academic writing before coming to college, and you may have done only minimal research. The contexts for your college writing will require you to face new challenges; you may be asked, for example, to create a persuasive Web site or to research, write, and deliver a multimedia presentation. You can begin the process of learning by figuring out what your instructors expect from you. Of course, expectations about academic writing vary considerably in different courses and different disciplines (see Chapters 61–65), but becoming familiar with widespread conventions will prepare you well for most academic situations.

Establishing authority

In the United States, most college instructors expect student writers to begin to establish their own authority—to become constructive critics who can analyze and interpret the work of others. But what does establishing authority mean in practice?

- Assume that your opinions count (as long as they are informed rather than tossed out with little thought) and that your audience expects you to present them in a well-reasoned manner.
- Show your familiarity with the ideas and works of others, both from the assigned course reading and from good points your instructor and classmates have made.

Being direct and clear

Your instructors will most often expect you to get to the point quickly and to be direct throughout an essay or other project. Research for this book confirms that readers depend on writers to organize and present their material—using sections, paragraphs, sentences, arguments, details, and source citations—in ways that aid understanding. Good academic writing prepares readers for what is coming next, provides definitions, and includes topic sentences. (See 20c for a description of the organization that instructors often prefer in student essays.) To achieve directness in your writing, try the following strategies:

- State your main point early and clearly.
- Avoid overqualifying your statements. Instead of writing *I think the facts reveal*, come right out and say *The facts reveal*.
- Avoid digressions. If you use an anecdote or example from personal experience, be sure it relates directly to the point you are making.
- Use appropriate evidence, such as examples and concrete details, to support each point.
- Make transitions from point to point obvious and clear. The first sentence of a new paragraph should reach back to the paragraph before and then look forward to what is to come (see Chapter 8).

- Follow logical organizational patterns (see Chapter 8).
- Design and format the project appropriately for the audience and purpose you have in mind (see Chapter 9).
- If your project is lengthy, you may also want to use brief summary statements between sections, but avoid unnecessary repetition.

AT A GLANCE

U.S. Academic Style

- Consider your purpose and audience carefully, making sure that your topic is appropriate to both. (Chapter 5)
- State your claim or thesis explicitly, and support it with examples, statistics, anecdotes, and authorities of various kinds. (Chapter 7)
- Carefully document all of your sources. (Chapters 49–55)
- Make explicit links between ideas. (Chapter 8)
- Consistently use the appropriate level of formality. (Chapter 23)
- Use conventional formats for academic genres. (Chapters 3–4 and 61–64)
- Use conventional grammar, spelling, punctuation, and mechanics. (Chapters 31–48)
- Use an easy-to-read type size and typeface, conventional margins, and double spacing. (Chapter 9)

2c Read actively.

Your instructors expect you to be an active reader—to offer informed opinions on what readings say. Stating your opinion doesn't require you to be negative or combative, just engaged with the class and the text. The following strategies will help you read actively:

- Note the name of the author and the date and place of publication; these items can give you clues to the writer's purpose and intended audience.
- Understand the overall content of a piece well enough to summarize it (12c).
- Formulate critical questions about the text, and bring these questions up in class.
- Understand each sentence, and make direct connections between sentences and paragraphs. Keep track of repeated themes or images, and figure out how they contribute to the entire piece.

- Note the author's attitude toward and assumptions about the topic. Then you can speculate on how the attitude and assumptions may have affected the author's thinking.
- Note the writer's sources: what evidence does the writer rely on, and why?
- Distinguish between the author's stance and the author's reporting on the stances of others. Watch for key phrases an author uses to signal an opposing argument: *while some have argued that, in the past,* and so on.
- Go beyond content to notice organizational patterns, use of sources, and choice of words.
- Consider annotating your readings, especially if they are very important (12b). Make notes in the margins that record your questions, challenges, or counter-examples to the text.
- If the readings are interactive — that is, if they allow you to post a comment — take advantage of this opportunity to get your voice into the conversation.

2d Plan research.

Much of the work you do in college may turn an informal curiosity into various kinds of more formal research: you might start by wondering how many students on your campus are vegetarians, for example, and end up with a research project for a sociology class that then becomes part of a multimedia presentation for a campus organization. Many of your writing assignments will require extensive formal research with a wide range of sources from various media as well as information drawn from observations, interviews, or surveys.

Research can help you find important information that you didn't know, even if you know a topic very well. And no matter what you discover, college research is an important tool for establishing credibility with your audience members and thus gaining their confidence. Often, what you write will be only as good as the research on which it is based. (For more on research, see Chapters 15–19.)

2e Use media to communicate effectively.

Your instructors will probably expect you to communicate both in and out of class using a variety of media. You may be asked to post to course management systems, lists, blogs, and wikis, and you may respond to the work of others on such sites. In addition, you will probably contact your instructor and classmates using email and text messages. Because electronic communication is so common, it's easy to fall into the habit of writing very informally. If you forget to adjust style and voice for different occasions and readers, you may undermine your own intentions.

Best practices for formal messages and posts

Email was once seen as highly informal, but you will probably use it today mainly for more formal purposes, particularly to communicate for work and for school. When writing most academic and professional messages, then, or when posting to a public list that may be read by people you don't know well, follow the conventions of standard academic English (2b), and be careful not to offend or irritate your audience—remember that jokes may be read as insults and that ALL CAPS may look like shouting. Finally, proofread to make sure your message is clear and free of errors, and that it is addressed to your intended audience, before you hit SEND.

EMAIL

- Use a subject line that states your purpose clearly.
- Use a formal greeting and closing (*Dear Ms. Aulie* rather than *Hey*).
- Keep messages as concise as possible.
- Conclude your message with your name and email address.
- Ask for permission before forwarding a sensitive message from someone else.
- Consider your email messages permanent and always findable, even if you delete them. Many people have been embarrassed (or worse, prosecuted) because of email trails.
- Make sure that the username on the email account you use for formal messages does not present a poor impression. If your username is *Party2Nite*, consider changing it, or use your school account for academic and professional communication.

DISCUSSION LISTS AND FORUMS

- Avoid unnecessary criticism of others' spelling or language. If a message is unclear, ask politely for a clarification. If you disagree with an assertion, offer what you believe to be the correct information, but don't insult the writer.

- If you think you've been insulted, give the writer the benefit of the doubt. Replying with patience establishes your credibility and helps you appear mature and fair.
- For email discussion lists, decide whether to reply off-list to the sender of a message or to the whole group, and be careful to use REPLY or REPLY ALL accordingly to avoid potential embarrassment.
- Keep in mind that because many discussion forums and email lists are archived, more people than you think may be reading your messages.

Best practices for informal situations

Sometimes audiences expect informality. When you write in certain situations—Twitter posts, for example, and most text messages—you can play with (or ignore) the conventions you would probably follow in formal writing. Most people receiving text messages expect shorthand such as *u* for "you," but be cautious about using such shortcuts with an employer or instructor. You may want to stick to a more formal method of contact if your employer or instructor has not explicitly invited you to send text messages—or texted you first.

Even when you think the situation calls for an informal tone, be attuned to your audience's needs and your purpose for writing. And when writing for any online writing space that allows users to say almost anything about themselves or to comment freely on the postings of others, bear in mind that anonymity sometimes makes online writers feel less inhibited than they would be in a face-to-face discussion. Don't say anything you want to remain private, and even if you disagree with another writer, avoid personal attacks.

bedfordstmartins.com/everydaywriter
Writing with Digital Media

3 Multimodal Assignments

As Clive Thompson noted in *Wired* magazine in 2009, "Before the Internet came along, most Americans never wrote anything, ever, that wasn't a school assignment." Times have indeed changed. More and more Americans are reading and writing for social purposes and for their jobs and communities, not just for school. Your "life writing" is increasingly likely to include blogs, online videos, PowerPoint presentations, and other texts incorporating not just words but images, sound, and video. And college writing classes are increasingly likely to require you to shift gears in similar ways—from writing posts on class forums and creating Web texts to making oral presentations with multimedia support. As one student explains, the multimodal realities of today's academic work require you to become "ambidextrous in the digital age."

3a Plan online assignments.

Writing assignments that your audiences will encounter online may repurpose your print-based work, or they may be entirely new, online-only texts that take advantage of the technology to include material that print texts can't offer, such as sound and video. Whether you are starting with work on a printed page or tackling an online assignment from

---

AT A GLANCE

Guidelines for Creating an Online Text

- Consider purpose, audience, and message. How can your text appeal to the right readers? How will it accomplish its purpose? (Chapter 5)
- Be realistic about the time available for the project, and plan accordingly.
- Think about the various types of online texts you can create, and determine which suits your needs based on what you want or need to do and what your audience expects: text, images, audio, video, or a combination? the latest updates first, or an index page? the ability to collaborate or comment? Make appropriate choices for your project and skills.
- Create an appealing design, or choose a template that follows basic design principles. (Chapter 9)
- Pay attention to user feedback, and make appropriate adjustments.

scratch, you will need to think just as carefully about your online context as you would about any other writing situation.

Rhetorical considerations of online texts

Early on, consider time and technical constraints carefully to make sure that your plan for an online text is manageable. But also remember to think about rhetorical concerns, such as your purpose for creating the text, the needs of your audience, and the main point or message you want to get across.

- Why are you creating this text (5d)? How do you want readers to use it? Considering purpose helps you determine what features your online text will need to incorporate.

- What potential audience (5e) can you identify? Considering audience will help you make good choices about tone, word choice, graphic style and design, level of detail, and many other factors. If your intended audience is limited to people you know (such as a wiki available only to members of your literature class), you may be able to make assumptions about their background, knowledge, and likely responses to your text. If you are covering a particular topic, you may have ideas about the type of audience you think you'll attract. Plan your text to appeal to the readers you expect— but remember that an online text may reach other, unanticipated audiences.

- What will you talk about? Your topic will also affect the content and design of your project. For example, if you want to write about the latest Hong Kong film releases, you might create a blog; if you want to explore the works of 1940s detective writers, you might produce a Web site. If you prefer to talk about or show information on your topic, you might consider creating an infographic or a video or audio text that you can post to an existing site.

- How do you relate to your subject matter? Your rhetorical stance (5d) determines how your audience will see you. Will you present yourself as an expert, a fan, or a novice seeking input from others? What information will make you seem credible and persuasive to your audience?

Types of online texts

Among the most common types of texts online are Web sites, blogs, wikis, and audio or video texts.

- Web sites and blogs are similar in appearance, and both usually include links to other parts of the site or to other sites. Both are relatively easy to update. Web sites are often organized as a cluster of associations. Readers expect blog content to be refreshed frequently (more often than the contents of a Web page), so blog posts are often time-stamped, and the newest content appears first. Blogs usually invite readers to comment publicly on each post, while Web sites often have a single contact link allowing readers to email the site's creator(s) directly.

- Wikis—collaborative online texts—create communities where all content is peer reviewed and evaluated by other members. They are powerful tools for sharing a lot of information because they draw on the collective knowledge of many contributors.

- Audio and video content can vary as widely as the content found in written-word media—audiobooks, video diaries, pop-culture mashups, radio shows, short documentaries, fiction films, and so on. Writers who create podcasts (which can be downloaded for playback) and streaming media (which can be played without downloading) may produce episodic content united by a common host or theme. Audio and video files can stand alone as online texts on sites such as YouTube, but they can also be embedded on a Web page or blog or included in a presentation to add dimension to still images and written words.

Features of online texts

Choose the features that will enable your audience to get the most from your online text.

- Online readers generally prefer short, manageable chunks of verbal text. If you are writing a long piece, consider breaking it up with headings and visuals. Include enough text to help readers make sense of your content, captions for visuals, sound transcripts (if you include audio files), and so on.

- Links to external sites are one method of documenting sources online. You can link to content that helps to prove a point—complex explanations, supporting statistics, bibliographies, referenced Web sites, or additional readings, for example. Links also help readers navigate from one part of a text to another. Each link should have a clear rhetorical purpose and be in an appropriate location. If it's important for users to read the whole paragraph, for instance, you may want to move the link to the end of it.

- Online texts—from blogs and video channels to online newspaper articles—often incorporate interactive features, such as "like" buttons, comments or forums, and a link to contact the writer.

- Online writers who give credit where credit is due have greater authority. If you have not created a verbal text, graphic, or audio or video clip yourself, provide a caption or link identifying the source, and ask permission to use it in a text for an online audience (see Chapter 18).

CONSIDERING DISABILITIES

Accessible Web Texts

Much on the Web remains hard to access and read for persons with disabilities. The Web site for the Americans with Disabilities Act provides guidelines on designing accessible sites, which include offering textual descriptions of any visuals and captions for any sound files. For details, visit www.ada.gov.

Time management

You already know that time management is crucial for your success in any writing situation. How well you can manage decisions will be affected both by your deadline and by how much time you can squeeze out of your other interests and responsibilities to meet that deadline. How much technical expertise do you have, and how much will you need to learn in order to create your text? Allow enough time for that learning to take place. Also consider how much research you will have to do and how long you will need to find, prepare, and seek permission (if needed—see Chapter 16) for any images, sound, or video files you want to use.

Design and organization of online texts

Ultimately, the organization and look of your text depend on what you are trying to achieve. You should make decisions about page length, color, visuals, multimedia, and interactive elements based on rhetorical choices (your audience, purpose, and message) and on practical constraints (the time and tools available). For more on design, see Chapter 9.

Just as you might outline an essay or create a storyboard for a video, you should develop a clear structure for your Web text. Some types of texts are organized in standard ways; others allow you to make choices about how to arrange materials. (For more on organizing a text, see 7d.) Choose a structure that makes sense for your purpose, audience, and message. Arrange your text to allow readers to find what they are looking for as quickly and intuitively as possible. Asking others to try out your site and give you feedback is a good way to learn what works and what doesn't.

3b Join class discussions.

Make sure your contributions to class discussions—whether live or online—are effective by following these guidelines:

- Be prepared.
- Follow the flow of conversation. Taking notes can help you listen purposefully in a classroom.
- Make sure your comments are relevant. Ask a key question, take the conversation in a new direction, or summarize or analyze what others have said.
- Be specific in your comments: *The passage in the middle of page 42 backs up what you're saying* is more useful than *I agree.*

FOR MULTILINGUAL WRITERS

Speaking Up in Class

Speaking up in class is viewed as inappropriate or even rude in some cultures. In the United States, however, doing so is expected and encouraged. Some instructors even assign credit for such class participation.

3c Prepare for presentations.

More and more students report that formal presentations are becoming part of their work both in and out of class. Good preparation is as necessary for a successful presentation as for any other writing assignment.

Considering your assignment, purpose, and audience for presentations

Begin preparing for a presentation as soon as you get the assignment. Think about how much time you have to prepare; how long the presentation is to be; whether you will use written-out text or note cards; whether visual aids, handouts, or other materials are called for; and what equipment you will need. If you are making a group presentation,

AT A GLANCE

Preparing for Presentations

- How can you ensure that your text meets the expectations of a live audience?
- How does your presentation fulfill your purpose, including the goals of the assignment?
- How do the introduction and conclusion hold the audience's attention?
- Is your organizational structure crystal clear? How do you guide listeners? Are your transitions and signpost language explicit? Do you effectively repeat key words or ideas?
- Have you marked the text you are using for pauses and emphasis?
- Have you prepared all necessary visuals, including presentation slides and other multimedia? Are they large enough to be seen? Would other visuals be helpful?
- Have you practiced your presentation and gotten response to it?

you will need time to divide duties and practice. Make sure that you understand the criteria for evaluation—how will the presentation be graded or assessed?

Consider the purpose of your presentation (5d). Are you to lead a discussion? teach a lesson? give a report? engage a group in an activity? Also consider the audience (5e). If your instructor is a member of the audience, what will he or she expect you to do—and do well? What do audience members know about your topic? What opinions do they already hold about it? What do they need to know to follow your presentation and perhaps accept your point of view?

Student Shuqiao Song got a two-part assignment for her writing class on graphic novels: she had to write an argument essay based on her research on a graphic novel, and then she had to turn that information into a script for a twelve-minute oral presentation with slides. After brainstorming and talking with her instructor, she chose Alison Bechdel's memoir *Fun Home: A Family Tragicomic* as her topic. She realized that although she wanted very much to earn a good grade, she also wanted to convince her classmates that Bechdel's book was complex and important—and she wanted to turn in a truly *impressive* performance in her presentation.

For Shuqiao Song's print essay, see 12e.

Making your introduction and conclusion memorable

Listeners, like readers, tend to remember beginnings and endings most readily, so work extra hard to make these elements memorable. Consider, for example, using a startling statement, opinion, or question; a dramatic anecdote; a powerful quotation; or a vivid image. Shifting language, especially into a variety of language that your audience will identify with, is another effective way to catch their attention (see Chapter 22). Whenever you can link your subject to the experiences and interests of your audience, do so.

Shuqiao Song began her presentation this way:

Welcome, everyone. I'm Shuqiao Song and I'm here today to talk about residents of a dysFUNctional *HOME*. We meet these residents in a graphic memoir called *Fun Home*.

(Here, Shuqiao showed a three-second video clip of author Alison Bechdel saying, "I love words, and I love pictures. But especially, I love them together—in a mystical way that I can't even explain.")

Student Writing

That was Alison Bechdel, author of *Fun Home*. In that clip, she conveniently introduces the topics of my presentation today: Words. Pictures. And the mystical way they work together.

CONSIDERING DISABILITIES

Accessible Presentations

Do all you can to make your presentations accessible.

- Do not rely on color or visuals alone to get across information — some individuals may be unable to pick up such cues.
- If you use video, provide captions to explain any sounds that won't be audible to some audience members.

Note that this presentation opened with a play on words ("dys*FUN*ctional *HOME*") and with a short, vivid video clip that summed up the main topic of the presentation. Also note the use of short sentences and fragments, special effects that act like drumbeats to get and hold the attention of the audience.

Using explicit structure and signpost language

Organize your presentation clearly and carefully, and give an overview of the main points at the outset. (You may want to recall these points toward the end of the talk.) Then, throughout your presentation, call attention to a new point by pausing before it and by using signpost language as an explicit transition: *The second crisis point in the breakup of the Soviet Union occurred shortly after the first* is more explicit than *Another thing went wrong.* (For a list of transitions, see 8e.) Repeated key words and ideas work as signposts, too.

At the end of Shuqiao's introduction, she set forth the structure of her presentation in a very clear, straightforward, and simple way to help her audience follow what came next:

> So, let me outline the rest of my presentation. First, I'll show how text is *insufficient*, but also why it is *necessary* in Bechdel's story.   **Student Writing**
>
> Second, I'll show how images can't be trusted yet why they are still necessary for Bechdel's purpose.
>
> Third and finally, I'll show how the interplay of text and image in *Fun Home* creates a more complex and comprehensive understanding of the story.

Choosing words and sentence structures

Avoid long, complicated sentences, and use straightforward sentence structure (subject-verb-object) as much as possible. Listeners prefer action verbs and concrete nouns to abstractions. You may need to deal with abstract ideas, but try to provide concrete examples for them (23c).

Shuqiao Song's presentation script included the following example:

Student Writing Now, to argue my second point, I'll begin with an image. This is a René Magritte painting. The text means, "This is not a pipe." Is this some surrealist Jedi mind trick? Not really. Now listen to the title of the painting to grasp Magritte's point. The painting is called *The Treason of Images*. Here Magritte is showing us that "this is not a pipe" because it is an *image* of a pipe.

Her short, straightforward sentences and vivid word choice ("Jedi mind trick") help make this passage easy on listeners.

Turning writing into a script for presentation

Even though you will rely on some written material, you will need to adapt it for speech. Depending on the assignment, the audience, and your personal preferences, you may even speak from a full script. If so, double- or triple-space it, and use print that is large enough to read. Try to end each page with the end of a sentence so that you won't have to pause while you turn a page. In addition, you may decide to mark spots where you want to pause and to highlight words you want to emphasize.

Take a look at this paragraph from Shuqiao Song's formal written essay on *Fun Home:*

A PARAGRAPH FROM A WRITTEN ESSAY

Student Writing

Finally, we can see how image and text function together. On the one hand, image and text support each other in that each highlights the subtleties of the other; but on the other hand, the more interesting interaction comes when there is some degree of distance between what is written and what is depicted. In *Fun Home*, there is no one-to-one closure that mentally connects text and image. Rather, Bechdel pushes the boundaries of mental closure between image and text. If the words and pictures match exactly, making the same point, the story would read like a children's book, and that would be too simple for what Bechdel is trying to accomplish. However, text and image can't be so mismatched that meaning completely eludes the readers. Bechdel crafts her story deliberately, leaving just enough mental space for the reader to solve the rest of the puzzle and resolve the cognitive dissonance. The reader's mental closure, which brings coherence to the text and images and draws together loose ends, allows for a more complex and sophisticated understanding of the story.

Now look at how she revised that paragraph into a script for oral presentation:

A PARAGRAPH REVISED FOR A LISTENING AUDIENCE

Student Writing

Finally, image and text can work together. They support each other: each highlights the subtleties of the other. But they are even more interesting when there's a gap — some distance between the story the words tell and the story the pictures tell. In *Fun Home*, text and image are never perfectly correlated. After all, if the words and pictures matched up exactly, the story would read like a kids' book. That would be way too simple for Bechdel's purposes. But we wouldn't want a complete disconnect between words and images either, since we wouldn't be able to make sense of them.

Still, Bechdel certainly pushes the boundaries that would allow us to bring closure between image and text. So what's the take-home point here? That in Bechdel's *Fun Home*, image and text are not just supporting actors of each other. Instead, each offers a *version* of the story. It's for us — the readers. We take these paired versions and weave them into a really rich understanding of the story.

Note that the revised paragraph presents the same information, but this time it is written to be heard, using helpful signpost language, some repetition, simple syntax, and informal varieties of English.

Speaking from notes

If you decide to speak from notes rather than from a full script, here are some tips for doing so effectively:

- In general, use one note card for each point in your presentation.
- Number the cards in case they get scrambled.
- On each card, start with the major point you want to make in large bold text. Include subpoints in a bulleted list below the main point, again printed large enough for you to see easily.
- Include signpost language on each note and use it to guide your listeners.
- Practice your presentation using the notes at least twice.
- Use color or brackets to mark material in your notes that you can skip if you run out of time.

The following note card for Shuqiao Song's introduction reminds her to emphasize her title and her three points. Notice how she has highlighted her signpost language as well as the card's number.

NOTECARD FOR AN ORAL PRESENTATION

> [Card 3]
>
> **Overview of the rest of the presentation**
> - First, text is insufficient but necessary
> - Second, images can't be trusted but are necessary
> - Finally, interplay of text and image creates complex, comprehensive understanding

Using visuals

Visuals are often an integral part of an oral presentation, carrying a lot of the message the speaker wants to convey. So think of your visuals not as add-ons but as a major means of getting your points across. Many speakers use presentation software (such as PowerPoint or Prezi) to help keep themselves on track and to guide the audience. In addition, posters, flip charts, chalkboards, or interactive whiteboards can also help you make strong visual statements.

SLIDES FROM A STUDENT POWERPOINT PRESENTATION

For her presentation, "Words, Images, and the Mystical Way They Work Together in Alison Bechdel's *Fun Home*," Shuqiao Song developed a series of very simple slides aimed at underscoring her points and keeping her audience focused on them. After introducing Bechdel and her book, Shuqiao provided an overview of the presentation as she clicked through the following slides:

So let me tell you, quickly, what I'll be doing in the rest of this presentation:

First, I'll show how text is *insufficient*, but also why it is *necessary* in Bechdel's story.

Second, I'll show how images can't be trusted yet why they are still necessary for Bechdel's purpose.

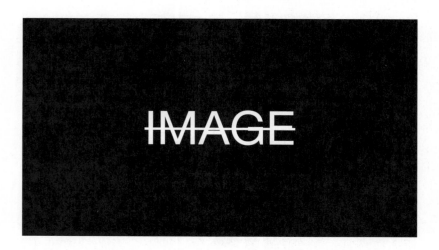

Third and finally, I'll show how the interplay of text and image in *Fun Home* works to create a more complex and comprehensive understanding of this magical story.

Each one of these slides—with simple text and punctuation—serves to emphasize Shuqiao's point and keep the audience's attention on the relationship between word and image.

When you work with visuals for your own presentation, remember that they must be large enough to be easily seen and read. Be sure the information is simple, clear, and easy to understand. And remember *not* to read from your visuals or turn your back on your audience as you refer to them. Most important, make sure your visuals engage and help your listeners rather than distract them from your message. Try out each visual on your classmates, friends, or roommates: if they do not clearly grasp the meaning and purpose of the visual, scrap it and try again.

You may also want to prepare handouts for your audience: pertinent bibliographies, for example, or text too extensive to be presented otherwise. Unless the handouts include material you want your audience to use while you speak, distribute them at the end of the presentation.

TIPS FOR USING PRESENTATION MEDIA

Before you begin designing your presentation, make sure that the equipment you need will be available. As you design presentation slides, keep some simple principles in mind (for more on design, see Chapter 9):

- Audiences can't read and listen to you at the same time, so make the slides support what you are saying as clearly and visually as possible. Just one or two words—or a visual without words—may back up what you are saying more effectively than a list of bullets.

- Never simply read the text of your slides.
- Use your media wisely, and respect your audience's time. If you feel that you need to include more than three or four bullet points (or more than fifty words of text) on a slide, you may be trying to convey information in a slideshow that would make more sense in a report. Rethink your presentation so that what you say and what you show work together to win over your audience.
- Use text on your slides to guide your audience — not as a teleprompter.
- Make sure any text or visual you show is big and clear enough to be visible, and create a clear contrast between text or illustration and background. In general, light backgrounds work better in a darkened room, and dark backgrounds in a lighted one.
- Make sure that sound or video clips are audible and that they relate directly to your topic. If you use sound as background, make sure it does not distract from what you are trying to say.
- Give credit for any visuals or audio that you have not created yourself.

Practicing your presentation

Prepare a draft of your presentation far enough in advance to allow for several run-throughs. Some speakers record their rehearsals and then revise based on the taped performance. Others practice in front of a mirror or in front of colleagues or friends, who can comment on content and style.

Make sure you will be heard clearly. If you are soft-spoken, concentrate on projecting your voice; if your voice tends to rise when you're in the spotlight, practice lowering the pitch. If you speak rapidly, practice slowing down. It's usually best to avoid sarcasm in favor of a tone that conveys interest in your topic and listeners.

Timing your run-throughs will tell you whether you need to cut (or expand) material to make the presentation an appropriate length.

Making your presentation

To calm your nerves and get off to a good start, know your material thoroughly and use the following strategies to good advantage before, during, and after your presentation:

- Visualize your presentation with the aim of feeling comfortable during it.

- Consider doing some deep-breathing exercises before the presentation, and concentrate on relaxing; avoid too much caffeine.
- Be sure you can access everything you need. Assume that microphones are always live, and don't say anything you don't want the audience to hear.
- Pause before you begin, concentrating on your opening lines.
- If possible, stand up. Most speakers make a stronger impression standing rather than sitting.
- Face your audience at all times, and make eye contact as much as possible.
- Allow time for the audience to respond and ask questions.
- Thank your audience at the end of your presentation.

> bedfordstmartins.com/everydaywriter
> **Student Writing > Multimedia Presentations**

4 Writing to Make Something Happen in the World

A large group of college students participating in a research study were asked, "What is good writing?" The researchers expected fairly straightforward answers like "writing that gets its message across," but the students kept coming back to one central idea: good writing "makes something happen in the world." They felt particular pride in the writing they did for family, friends, and community groups—and for many extracurricular activities that were meaningful to them. Furthermore, once these students graduated from college, they continued to create—and to value—these kinds of public writing.

At some point during your college years or soon after, you are highly likely to create writing that is not just something that you turn in for a grade but writing that you do because you want to make a difference. The writing that matters most to many students and citizens, then, is writing that has an effect in the world: writing that gets up off the page or screen, puts on its working boots, and marches out to get something done!

> **AT A GLANCE**
>
> ## Characteristics of Writing That Makes Something Happen
>
> - Public writing has a very clear *purpose* (to promote a local cause or event; to inform or explain an issue or problem; to persuade others to act; sometimes even to entertain).
> - It is intended for a specific *audience* and addresses those people directly.
> - It uses the *genre* most suited to its purpose and audience (a poster to alert people to an upcoming fund drive, a newsletter to inform members of a group, a brochure to describe the activities of a group, a letter to the editor to argue for a candidate or an issue), and it appears in a *medium* (print, online, or both) where the intended audience will see it.
> - It generally uses straightforward, everyday *language*.

4a Decide what should happen.

When you decide to write to make something happen, you'll generally have some idea of what effect you want that writing to have. Clarify what actions you want your readers to take in response to your writing, and then think about what people you most want to reach—audiences today can be as close as your immediate neighbors or as dispersed as global netizens. Who will be interested in the topic you are writing about? For example, if you are trying to encourage your elementary school to plant a garden, you might try to interest parents, teachers, and PTA members; if you are planning a voter registration drive, you might start with eighteen-year-olds on your campus.

4b Connect with your audience.

Once you have a target audience in mind, you'll need to think carefully about where and how you are likely to find them, how you can get their attention so they will read what you write, and what you can say to get them to achieve your purpose.

If you want to convince your neighbors to pool time, effort, and resources to build a local playground, then you have a head start: you know something about what they value and about what appeals would get their attention and convince them to join in this project. If you want to create a flash mob to publicize ineffective security at chemical plants near your city, on the other hand, you will need to reach as many people as possible, most of whom you will not know.

Genre and media

Even if you know the members of your audience, you still need to think about the genre and medium that will be most likely to reach them. To get neighbors involved in the playground project mentioned above, you might decide that a colorful print flyer delivered door to door and posted at neighborhood gathering places would work best. For a flash mob, however, an easily forwarded message—text, Twitter, or email—will probably work best.

Appropriate language

For all public writing, think carefully about the audience you want to reach—as well as *unintended* audiences your message might reach. Doing so can help you craft writing that will be persuasive without being offensive.

Timing

Making sure your text will appear in a timely manner is crucial to the success of your project. If you want people to plan to attend an event, present your text to them at least two weeks ahead of time. If you are issuing a newsletter or blog, make sure that you create posts or issues often enough to keep people interested (but not so often that readers can't or won't keep up). If you are reporting information based on something that has already happened, make it available as soon as possible so that your audience won't consider your report "old news."

4c   Sample writing that makes something happen in the world

On the following pages are some examples of the forms public writing can take.

POSTER

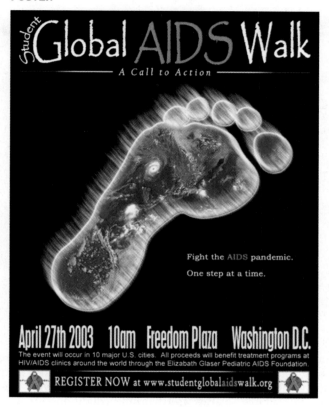

This poster, created by student Amrit Rao, has a very clear purpose: to attract participants to a walk aimed at raising money in support of AIDS research. In this case, Rao wanted to reach college students in the DC area; students, he felt, would be particularly aware of the need for such research and likely to respond by showing up for the walk. To reach as many students as possible, he decided to distribute the poster in both print and digital forms. He called on friends in the area to help place the poster in key locations on a dozen college campuses, and he emailed PDF versions of the poster to student body presidents on each campus, asking them to help spread the word.

FLYER

El Boletin de Trabajadores Temporales

Local 715 SEIU

Volume 1: Issue 3

Servicios educativos para sus hijos:

Necesitan mas ayuda sus niños con la tarea? o Quieren hacer algo despues de la escuela para divertirse? Informece sobre los varios programas que ofrece Stanford para niños que viven en la area cercana. Hay programas para niños de todos años desde la escuela primaria hasta la preparatoria. Ofrecen apoyo academico como ayuda con la tarea y tambien actividades Los programas son durante y despues de la escuela. Para aprender como puede inscribir sus hijos en uno de estos programas, llame a Leticia Rodriguez en la oficina de SEIU Local 715 al (650) 723-3680.

Preocupado por dinero?

Esta endeudado con tarjetas de credito? Quiere saber como obtener su reporte de credito? Nosotros podemos ayudarle a crear un presupuesto mensual, mejorar su puntuacion en su reporte de credito, reducir los intereses que paga en tarjetas de credito, y ahorrar dinero. Para citas gratuitas comuniquese con Araceli Rodriguez o Nancy Villareal a la oficina de SEIU, Local 715 al (650) 723-3680.

OPORTUNIDADES PARA TRABAJOS PERMANENTES

Según el acuerdo en el nuevo contracto de la unión, Stanford va a crear 40 posiciones permanentes en los próximos 4 años. Adicionalmente, trabajadores temporales que han trabajado 20 horas por semana por más de cuatro

CUENTO
PERSONAL

Student Anna Mumford created and posted copies of this flyer advocating for pay raises for campus workers. Again, her purpose is clear: she wants to raise awareness on her campus of what she views as highly inequitable salaries and working conditions for temporary workers. Her audience in this case is a local one that includes the temporary workers as well as the students, faculty, and administrators on her campus. Mumford did not have an easy way to distribute the information electronically to temporary workers, nor was she certain that all of them had access to computers, so she chose to produce a print flyer that would be easy to distribute across campus. She wrote in Spanish (on an English-speaking campus), the home language of most of the temporary workers, to reach her target audience more effectively.

NEWSLETTER

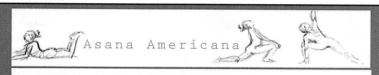

Asana Americana

Videos are up!
Joelle on About.com

I spent Memorial Day sequestered in Go Yoga shooting instructional videos for About.com. It was a hot day and my first time on film. (Second time was also this summer in a poet-bike messenger murder mystery set in NY--I play the role of a "senior editor." More about this next month!)

Some of the videos are now live. Take a look. Here's bow pose.

Thank you, Ann Pizer, former student, and current yoga adviser and blogger at About.com, for inviting me to do these videos. Read her blog post about the videos here.

After Labor Day
Back to Normal Teaching Schedule

I was fortunate to go on several retreats this summer. Thanks for your patience as I subbed out my classes. I'm now back to my normal schedule.

Curious about where I went?
I was at the Himalayan Institute, learning the magic of Tantra (it's not what you think!)--studies I'll continue over the next year. I was also in upstate New York at an inspired gathering of women called the Goddess Retreat, run by Kula teacher Alison Sinatra. Super heart-filled--and fun! And finally I attended Omega's Being Yoga conference in Rhinebeck, NY, to interview young PhD and yoga dynamo, Kelly McGonigal, who's developing compassion-based protocols sanctioned by the Dalai Lama.

My Recent Articles & Blog Posts

RECENT ARTICLES & BLOG POSTS:

YogaCityNYC
Interview with my teacher Gary Kraftsow Last Labor Day and again this summer, I interviewed Gary about his life as a student, teacher, and trainer of thousands. He was destined to become a great teacher--the stars foretold it--and has pioneered the field of yoga therapy in the US.

Anatomy Studies for Yoga Teachers: Jason R. Brown took the hard road to learn anatomy, but his new program (ASYT) makes the way much easier for the rest of us.

JOELLE'S YOGA
teaching & writing
NEWSLETTER

TEACHING SCHEDULE
Sunday, 10am open
Monday, 8:15pm basics

at Go Yoga
N6th at Berry, Williamsburg

Privates available by appointment or for trade

yoganation gmail com

INFO
If you have any questions, comments, or suggestions don't hesitate to get in touch.

Namaste!

photos of me by
timknoxphotography.com

As with the writers of the poster and flyer, yoga teacher Joelle Hann has a clear purpose in mind for her e-newsletter: to provide information to her audience—students and others interested in her yoga classes and developments in the yoga community. Emailing the newsletter to her subscribers allows Hann to reach an interested audience quickly and to provide links to more of the content she's discussing, and it also means that she can include photos, illustrations, and color to enhance her document's design impact.

EVENT INVITATION ON SOCIAL NETWORKING SITE

+ Select Guests to Invite

Pure Hell / The Bad Luck Charms / TV Tramps
• Share • Public Event

Time:	Saturday, October 16 · 6:00pm - 9:30pm
Location:	Europa
Created By:	Scenic Nyc, Bryan Swirsky
More Info:	All Ages (16+ with government issued ID, under 16 w/ parent, guardian) $8 adv, $10 day of. !!! Early show.

Pure Hell, one of the earliest all-black American punk-rock bands, formed in Philadelphia, Pennsylvania, in 1974, as punk rock was taking off and developing a following in nearby New York City. Discovered by Johnny Thunders during the heyday of the New York Dolls, the band moved to New York. In 1978, they toured Europe and released their only single ("These Boots are Made for Walking" b/w "No Rules"). Live performances by Pure Hell have been compared to the MC5, Sex Pistols, Dead Boys, Germs, and fellow Afropunks the Bad Brains, who identified Pure Hell as an influence. Their album (Noise Addiction), recorded in the late 1970s, was finally released this year. Pure Hell also has an unreleased album (The Black Box) produced in the mid 1990's by former members of L.A. Guns, Nine Inch Nails, and Lemmy Kilmister of Motorhead. Recent performances by Pure Hell in NYC showed that they still have what it takes!

Band promoter Bryan Swirsky used Facebook, where he has many friends who share his interest in punk rock, to reach an audience interested in seeing a reunion show by an all-black punk band that had a cult following in the 1970s. Those invited by Bryan could also invite their own interested friends, allowing news of the event to spread virally.

ONLINE REPORT

Less Trash, More Compost!
A report on a community partnership to reduce trash and promote composting and recycling at a summer camp

Funded in part by the New England Grassroots Environmental Fund

...When campers have something in their hand, they are very likely to ask where is the compost, where is the recycling... and that is exciting...

Counselor, Athol Area YMCA Day Camp

Deb Habib and Kaitlin Doherty
Seeds of Solidarity
November, 2007

Project Background and Goals

"Gross, but fun!" exclaims an eight-year old compost enthusiast, one of over 200 campers, plus counselors and staff at the Athol Area YMCA day camp in Orange, Massachusetts who worked together to successfully divert over one ton of their breakfast and lunch waste from the landfill to compost. And they won't mind telling you that they had fun doing it.

Seeds of Solidarity, a non-profit organization based in Orange, partnered with the summer food service director, the Athol Area YMCA, and a local hauler to implement a composting and recycling initiative, diverting the waste from approximately 3,600 meals at two sites over an eight-week period in the summer of 2007. This pilot project was inspired by success using biodegradable and compostable utensils and plates at the annual North Quabbin Garlic and Arts Festival, also sponsored by Seeds of Solidarity, which results in only two bags of trash for 10,000 people.

Athol and Orange are located in the North Quabbin region, where 20% of the children live below the federal poverty line. Food service director Sherry Fiske runs a state and federally funded summer food service program at 11 sites in Orange and Athol, providing free breakfast and lunch to children and families during the summer months. The YMCA camps based both at the Y site in Athol and Lake Selah in North Orange are among these summer food service sites. While school year lunch programs in the area utilize washable dishes and utensils, the summer food service program is held at temporary sites, resulting in heaping dumpsters of paper, plastic and polystyrene waste.

This report, created by Deb Habib and Kaitlin Doherty of the non-profit group Seeds of Solidarity, provides information about a successful experimental recycling and composting program at a Massachusetts camp. (Only the first page of the twenty-six-page PDF is shown.) Other sections include "Project Description," "Voices of Campers," "Successes and Challenges," "Summary of Key Considerations," and an appendix with additional documents (interviews with campers, letters to campers' parents before the program began, and graphs quantifying the outcomes). The report appears on the organization's Web site, which notes that Seeds of Solidarity "provid[es] people of all ages with the inspiration and practical tools to use renewable energy and grow food in their communities." While the report offers information about an experiment that has already taken place, the document also serves to encourage and inform others who might want to create a similar program.

The Writing Process

There may be people who like various aspects of the writing process. For some, it may be the excitement of facing a blank page. (Hate them!) For others, it could be a sense of getting a sentence just right. (Jerks!) There may be those who like the revision process, who can go over what they've produced with a cold eye and a keen ear and feel a satisfaction in making it better. (Liars!)

— RACHEL TOOR

The Writing Process

5 Rhetorical Situations *48*
  a Write to connect *48*
  b Make good choices for your rhetorical situation *48*
  c Plan your text's topic and message *49*
  d Consider your purpose and stance as a communicator *50*
  e Analyze your audience *52*
  f Consider other elements of the writing context *54*
  g A sample writing situation *56*

6 Exploring Ideas *58*
  a Try brainstorming *58*
  b Try freewriting or looping *58*
  c Try drawing or creating word pictures *59*
  d Try clustering *60*
  e Ask questions *61*
  f Browse sources *62*
  g Collaborate *62*

7 Planning and Drafting *64*
  a Narrow your topic *64*
  b Craft a working thesis *65*
  c Gather information to support your thesis *67*
  d Organize information *67*
  e Make a plan *71*
  f Create a draft *74*

8 Developing Paragraphs *75*
  a Focus on a main idea *75*
  b Provide details *77*
  c Use effective methods of development *79*
  d Consider paragraph length *85*
  e Make paragraphs flow *85*
  f Work on opening and closing paragraphs *88*

For visual analysis Look carefully at the illustration on the front of this tab. What do you think this image suggests about the writing process?

9   **Making Design Decisions**   *90*
  a   Plan a visual structure   *90*
  b   Choose appropriate formats   *92*
  c   Use headings appropriately   *95*
  d   Use visuals effectively   *96*

10   **Reviewing and Revising**   *100*
  a   Reread   *100*
  b   Get the most from peer review   *102*
  c   Consult instructor comments   *106*
  d   Revise   *109*

11   **Editing and Reflecting**   *112*
  a   Edit   *112*
  b   Reflect   *117*
    STUDENT REFLECTIVE STATEMENT   *119*

5 Rhetorical Situations

What do a documented essay on global warming research, a Facebook message objecting to the latest change to the site's privacy policy, a tweet to other students in your psychology class, a comment on a blog post, a letter to the editor of your local newspaper, and a Web site devoted to sustainability all have in common? To communicate effectively, the writers of these texts must analyze their particular situation and then respond to it in appropriate ways.

5a Write to connect.

If it is true that "no man [or woman!] is an island," then it is equally true that no piece of writing is an island, isolated and alone. Instead, writing is connected to a web of other writings as a writer extends, responds to, or challenges what others say. This has always been the case, but today it's especially important to remember that all writing exists within a rich and broad context and that all writers listen and respond to what others have said, even as they shape messages about particular topics and for particular purposes that help them connect to their audiences.

5b Make good choices for your rhetorical situation.

A *rhetorical situation* is the full set of circumstances surrounding any communication. When you communicate, whether you're posting on a social networking site, creating a video, or writing an essay for your psychology class, you need to consider and make careful choices about all the elements of your situation.

The rhetorical situation is often depicted as a triangle to present the idea that three important elements are closely connected — your *text*, including your topic and the message you want to convey (5c); your role as the *communicator*, including your purpose and your stance, or attitude toward the text (5d); and your *audience* (5e). If all the pieces making up the larger triangle don't work together, the communication will not be effective. But important as these elements are, they are connected to a *context* that shapes all the angles of the triangle. Considering context fully requires you to consider many other questions about the rhetorical situation, such as what kind of text you should create and what conventions you should follow to meet audience expectations for creating and delivering the text (5f).

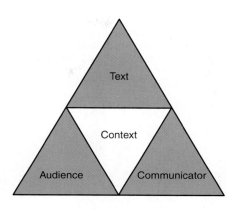

Informal and formal rhetorical situations

Most people are accustomed to writing in some rhetorical situations without analyzing them closely. When you post something on a friend's social networking page, for example, you probably spend little time pondering what your friend values or finds funny, how to phrase your words, which links or photos would best emphasize your point, or why you're taking the time to post. However, academic and other formal rhetorical situations may seem less familiar than the social writing you share with friends. Until you understand clearly what such situations demand of you, allow extra time to analyze the overall context, the topic and message, the purpose and stance, the audience, and other elements carefully.

5c Plan your text's topic and message.

An instructor or employer may tell you what topic to write about, but sometimes the choice will be yours. When the topic is left open, you may be tempted to put off getting started because you can't decide what to do. Experienced writers say that the best way to choose a topic is literally to let it choose you. Look to the topics that compel, puzzle, confuse, or pose a problem for you: these are likely to engage your interest and hence produce your best writing.

RHETORICAL SITUATIONS: Choose Your Topic

Browse around for a topic you care about.

Make sure your topic is manageable and suits your purpose....

Ask...

What *interesting* topic will meet the requirements for your assignment and context?

What do you know about the topic? What else do you need to find out?

What *message* do you want to convey?

Deciding on a broad topic is an essential step before beginning to write, but you need to go further than that to decide what you want to say about your topic and how you will shape what you want to say into a clear, powerful message.

5d Consider your purpose and stance as a communicator.

Whether you choose to communicate for purposes of your own or have that purpose set for you by an instructor or employer, you should consider the purpose for any communication carefully. For the writing you do that is not connected to a class or work assignment, your purpose may be very clear to you: you may want to convince neighbors to support a community garden, get others in your office to help keep the kitchen clean, or tell blog readers what you like or hate about your new phone. Even so, analyzing exactly what you want to accomplish and why can make you a more effective communicator.

Purposes for academic assignments

An academic assignment may clearly explain why, for whom, and about what you are supposed to write. But sometimes college assignments seem to come out of the blue, with no specific purpose, audience, or topic. Because comprehending the assignment fully and accurately

RHETORICAL SITUATIONS: Consider Your Purpose and Stance

Always keep your purpose in mind.

Ask...

Why are you writing?

What should the writing accomplish?

Where do you stand on your topic?

Think about how you want your audience to react....

is crucial to your success in responding to it, make every effort to understand what your instructor expects.

- What is the primary purpose of the piece of writing—to explain? to persuade? to entertain? some other purpose?
- What purpose did the person who gave you the assignment want to achieve—to make sure you have understood something? to evaluate your thinking and writing abilities? to test your ability to think outside the box?
- What are your own purposes in this piece of writing—to respond to a question? to learn about a topic? to communicate your ideas? to express feelings? How can you achieve these goals?
- What, exactly, does the assignment ask you to do? Look for such words as *analyze, classify, compare, define, describe, explain, prove,* and *survey.* Remember that these words may differ in meaning from discipline to discipline.

Stances for academic assignments

Thinking about your own position as a communicator and your attitude toward your text—your rhetorical stance—is just as important as making sure you communicate effectively.

- Where are you coming from on this topic? What is your overall attitude toward your topic? How strong are your opinions?

- What social, political, religious, personal, or other influences account for your attitude? Will you need to explain any of these influences?
- What is most interesting to you about the topic? Why do you care?
- What conclusions do you think you'll reach as you complete your text?
- How will you establish your credibility? How will you show you are knowledgeable and trustworthy?
- How will you convey your stance? Should you use words alone, combine words and images, include sound, or something else?

5e Analyze your audience.

Every communicator can benefit from thinking carefully about who the audience is, what the audience already knows or thinks, and what the audience needs and expects to find out. One of the characteristics of an effective communicator is the ability to write for a variety of audiences, using language, style, and evidence appropriate to particular readers, listeners, or viewers. Even if your text can theoretically reach people all over the world, focus your analysis on those you most want or need to reach and those who are most likely to take an interest.

RHETORICAL SITUATIONS: Imagine Your Audience

Think about a target audience for this text.

Ask...

Who are they? How are they like you? How are they different?

How will you reach this audience?

What do they already know and care about?

Remember to focus on getting your message across.

TALKING THE TALK

Assignments

"How do instructors come up with these assignments?" Assignments, like other kinds of writing, reflect particular rhetorical contexts that vary from instructor to instructor. Assignments also change over time. The assignment for an 1892 college writing contest was to write an essay "on coal." In the twentieth century, many college writing assignments asked students to write about their own experiences; in research conducted for this textbook in the 1980s, the most common writing assignment was a personal narrative. As expectations for college students — and the needs of society — change over time, assignments also change. Competing effectively in today's workforce calls for high-level thinking, for being able to argue convincingly, and for knowing how to do the research necessary to support a claim — so it's no surprise that college writing courses today give students assignments that allow them to develop such skills. A recent study of first-year college writing in the United States found that by far the most common assignment today asks students to compose a researched argument. (See Chapters 12–14.)

Informal and formal audiences

For some informal writing, you know exactly who your audience is, and communicating appropriately may be a simple matter. It's still worth remembering that when you post in a public space, you may not be aware of how large and varied your online audience can be. Can your friend's parents, or her prospective employer, see your posts on her Facebook page? (The answer depends partly on her privacy settings.) Who's reading the blogs you comment on?

Even if you write with intuitive ease in tweets and texts to friends, you may struggle when asked to write for an instructor or for a "general audience." You may wonder, for example, what a general audience might know about your topic, what they value, or what evidence they will find persuasive. When you are new to academic writing, making assumptions about such questions can be tricky. If you can identify samples of writing that appeal to a similar audience, look for clues about what that audience expects; if still in doubt, check with your instructor or drop by your campus writing center.

Appropriate language for an audience

- Is the language of your text as clear as it needs to be for your audience? If your readers can't understand what you mean, they're not likely to accept your points.
- For academic writing, should you use any specialized varieties of English along with standard academic English? any occupational,

---

FOR MULTILINGUAL WRITERS

Bringing in Other Languages

Even when you write in English, you may want or need to include words, phrases, or whole passages in another language. If so, consider whether your readers will understand that language and whether you need to provide a translation. See 22d for more on bringing in other languages.

---

professional, regional, or ethnic varieties? any words from a language other than English? any dialogue? (See Chapter 22.) How will these choices help you connect to your audience?

As you think about your audience, consider how you want them to respond to both the words and the images you use. And remember that images can evoke very strong responses in your audience and can affect the tone of your writing (5f), so choose them with special care.

5f   Consider other elements of the writing context.

After you have chosen a topic, shaped a message, and analyzed your purpose, stance, and audience in relation to your message, you still have other important decisions to make about the text you are developing.

Time and length

- How much time do you have to complete the text? Do you need to schedule research? Do you need to find or create images or media content? Be sure to allow time for revision and editing.

CONSIDERING DISABILITIES

Your Whole Audience

Remember that considering your whole audience means thinking about members with varying abilities and special needs. Approximately one in five Americans was living with a disability in the year 2000. All writers need to think carefully about how their words reach out and connect with such very diverse audiences.

- How long is the finished draft of the writing supposed to be? If you are writing a presentation, what time limits do you face for delivering it? If you are creating a work for the public, how much time can you expect the audience to devote to your work?

Genre, medium, and format

You may be assigned—or able to choose—to work in genres other than straightforward essays or in a medium other than print.

- What genre does your text call for—report? review? argument essay? research project? letter? blog posting? instructions for completing a task? promotional brochure? If you aren't familiar with the conventions of the genre, study examples created by others.
- What format or method of organization is expected for this genre? (See Chapter 7.) Should you conform to traditional formats, or will you gain from going in an unexpected direction?
- In what medium will the text appear—on the Internet? on a password-protected Web site? in a print essay submitted to your instructor? in a spoken presentation? Will your text use images, video, or audio? How will the media you use affect other choices you make?
- What design considerations should you keep in mind? (See Chapter 9.)

Tone and style

- What tone do you want to achieve—humorous? serious? impassioned? ironic? sincere? deeply knowledgeable?
- What words, sentence structures, and images or media will help you achieve this tone?
- Is the tone of the writing appropriate to your audience, purpose, and message? Do the words, images, or sounds you choose have the connotations you intend?

Remember that visual and audio elements can influence the tone of your writing as much as the words you choose. Such elements create associations in viewers' minds: one audience may react more positively than another to an element such as a rap or heavy metal soundtrack, for example—and a presentation with a heavy metal accompaniment will make a far different impression than the same presentation with an easy-listening soundtrack. Writers can influence the way their work is perceived by carefully analyzing their audience and choosing audio and visual elements that set a mood appropriate to the point they want to make.

Attitude and Point of View in Visuals

Images you choose to include in your work can help establish your credibility, but they always have a point of view and tone of their own. The postcard below, for instance, shows two physical perspectives — a photograph of a highway bridge and a road map showing its location — as well as a time perspective, from 1927, when the bridge was new. Images also reveal attitudes: this one, with the caption "America's Greatest Highway Bridge," sees the construction of the bridge as a triumph of technology, but the image might also convey nostalgia if readers know that the bridge became structurally unsound and had to be demolished in the 1970s. So when you choose an image, think hard about how well it fits in with your topic and purpose. What is the image's perspective and attitude — and do they serve the purpose of your writing?

5g A sample writing situation

Let's take an example of how one writer analyzes a rhetorical situation. Emily Lesk, a student in a first-year English course, gets an assignment that asks her to "explore the ways in which one or more media have affected an aspect of American identity." (More examples of Emily's work appear in the following chapters.) Because Emily is interested in advertising, she plans first to investigate how advertising might help shape American identity. Deciding that such a broad topic is not manageable in the time she has available, however, she shifts her focus to advertising for one company that seems particularly "American," Coca-Cola.

Since Emily's primary audience includes her instructor and her classmates, she needs to find ways to connect with them on an emotional as well as a logical level. She will do so, she decides, first by telling a story about being drawn into buying Coca-Cola products (even though she didn't really like the soft drink) because of the power of the advertising. She thinks that others in her audience may have had similar experiences. Here is a portion of her story and the visual she chose to illustrate it:

Even before setting foot in the Promised Land three years ago, I knew exactly where I could find the Coke T-shirt. **Student Writing**

The shop in the central block of Jerusalem's Ben Yehuda Street did offer other shirt designs, but the one with the bright white "Drink Coca-Cola Classic" written in Hebrew cursive across the chest was what drew in most of the dollar-carrying tourists. While waiting almost twenty minutes for my shirt (depicted in Fig. 1), I watched nearly everyone ahead of me say "the Coke shirt, *todah rabah* [thank you very much]."

Fig. 1. Hebrew Coca-Cola
T-shirt. Personal photograph.

At the time, I never thought it strange that I wanted one, too. Yet, I *had* absorbed sixteen years of Coca-Cola propaganda.

Thinking about how she relates to her audience brings Emily to reflect more deeply on herself as the writer: Why has she chosen this topic? What does it say about her beliefs and values? What is her attitude toward her topic and toward her audience? What does she need to do to establish her credentials to write on this topic and to this audience?

Finally, Emily knows she will need to pay careful attention to the context in which she is writing: the assignment is due in two weeks, so she needs to work fast; the assignment calls for an essay written in academic English, though she plans to include some dialogue and a number of visuals to keep it lively; and since she knows she tends to sound like a know-it-all, she determines to work carefully on her tone and style.

⊘ **bedfordstmartins.com/everydaywriter**
Student Writing

6 Exploring Ideas

T he point is so simple that we often forget it: we write best about topics we know well. So among the most important parts of the entire writing process are choosing a topic that will engage your interest, exploring that topic by surveying what you know about it, and determining what you need to find out. You can explore a topic in many ways; the goal is to find strategies that work well for you.

6a Try brainstorming.

One of the best ways to begin exploring a topic is also the most familiar: talk it over with others. Consider beginning with a brainstorming session. Brainstorming means tossing out ideas—often with other people, either in person or online. You can also brainstorm by yourself.

1. Within a time limit of five or ten minutes, list every word or phrase that comes to mind about the topic. Jot down key words and phrases, not sentences. No one has to understand the list but you. Don't worry about whether or not something will be useful—just list as much as you can in this brief span of time.
2. If little occurs to you, try coming up with thoughts about the opposite side of your topic. If you are trying, for instance, to think of reasons to raise tuition and are coming up blank, try concentrating on reasons to lower tuition. Once you start generating ideas in one direction, you'll find that you can usually move back to the other side fairly easily.
3. When the time is up, stop and read over the lists you have made. If anything else comes to mind, add it to your list. Then reread the list, looking for patterns of interesting ideas or one central idea.

6b Try freewriting or looping.

Freewriting is a method of exploring a topic by writing about it for a period of time *without stopping*.

1. Write for ten minutes or so. Think about your topic, and let your mind wander; write down whatever occurs to you. Don't worry about grammar or spelling. If you get stuck, write anything—just don't stop.

2. When the time is up, look at what you have written. You may discover some important insights and ideas.

If you like, you can continue the process by looping: find the central or most intriguing thought from your freewriting, and summarize it in a single sentence. Freewrite for five more minutes on the summary sentence, and then find and summarize the central thought from the second "loop." Keep this process going until you discover a clear angle or something about the topic that you can pursue.

CONSIDERING DISABILITIES

Freespeaking

If you are better at talking out than writing out your ideas, try freespeaking, which is basically the talking version of freewriting. Speak into a tape recorder or into a computer with voice-recognition software, and keep talking about your topic for at least seven to ten minutes. Say whatever comes to your mind — don't stop talking. You can then listen to or read the results of your freespeaking and look for an idea to pursue at greater length.

6c **Try drawing or creating word pictures.**

If you're someone who prefers visual thinking, you might either create a drawing about the topic or use figurative language—such as similes and metaphors—to describe what the topic resembles. Working with pictures or verbal imagery can sometimes also help illuminate the topic or uncover some of your unconscious ideas or preconceptions about it.

1. If you like to draw, try sketching your topic. What images do you come up with? What details of the drawing attract you most? What would you most like to expand on? A student planning to write an essay on her college experience began by thinking with pencils and pen in hand. Soon she found that she had drawn a vending machine several times, with different products

and different ways of inserting money to extract them (one of her drawings appears on p. 59). Her sketches led her to think about what it might mean to see an education as a product. Even abstract doodling can lead you to important insights about the topic and to focus your topic productively.

2. Look for figurative language—metaphors and similes—that your topic resembles. Try jotting down three or four possibilities, beginning with "My subject is _____" or "My subject is like _____." A student working on the subject of genetically modified crops came up with this: "Genetically modified foods are like empty calories: they do more harm than good." This exercise made one thing clear to this student writer: she already had a very strong bias that she would need to watch out for while developing her topic.

Play around a bit with your topic. Ask, for instance, "If my topic were a food (or a song or a movie or a video game), what would it be, and why?" Or write a Facebook status update about your topic, or send a tweet about why this topic appeals to you. Such exercises can get you out of the rut of everyday thinking and help you see your topic in a new light.

FOR MULTILINGUAL WRITERS

Using Your Native Language to Explore Ideas

For generating and exploring ideas — the work of much brainstorming, freewriting, looping, and clustering — you may be most successful at coming up with good ideas quickly and spontaneously if you work in your native language. Later in the process of writing, you can choose the best of these ideas and begin working with them in English.

6d Try clustering.

Clustering is a way of generating ideas using a visual scheme or chart. It is especially helpful for understanding the relationships among the parts of a broad topic and for developing subtopics. You may have a software program for clustering. If not, follow these steps:

1. Write down your topic in the middle of a blank piece of paper or screen and circle it.
2. In a ring around the topic circle, write what you see as the main parts of the topic. Circle each part, and then draw a line from it to the topic.

3. Think of more ideas, examples, facts, or other details relating to each main part. Write each of these near the appropriate part, circle each one, and draw a line from it to the part.
4. Repeat this process with each new circle until you can't think of any more details. Some trails may lead to dead ends, but you will still have many useful connections among ideas.

Here is an example of the clustering Emily Lesk did for her essay about Coca-Cola and American identity:

EMILY LESK'S CLUSTERING

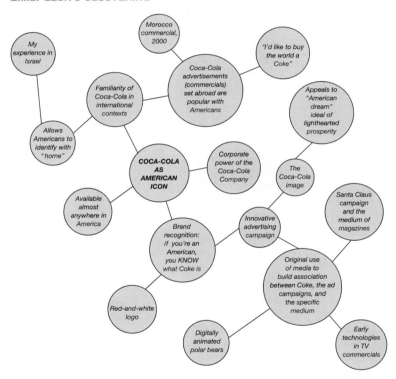

6e Ask questions.

Another basic strategy for exploring a topic and generating ideas is simply to ask and answer questions. Here are two widely used sets of questions to get you started.

Questions to describe a topic

Originally developed by Aristotle, the following questions can help you explore a topic by carefully and systematically describing it:

1. *What is it?* What are its characteristics, dimensions, features, and parts? What does it look like? What do other senses—taste, smell, touch, sound—tell you about it?
2. *What caused it?* What changes occurred to create your topic? How is it changing? How will it change?
3. *What is it like or unlike?* What features make your topic different from others? What comparisons can you make about your topic?
4. *What larger system is your topic a part of?* How does your topic fit into this system?
5. *What do people say about it?* What reactions does your topic arouse? What about the topic causes those reactions?

Questions to explain a topic

The well-known questions *who, what, when, where, why,* and *how,* widely used by news reporters, are especially helpful for explaining a topic.

1. *Who* is doing it?
2. *What* is at issue?
3. *When* does it take place?
4. *Where* is it happening?
5. *Why* does it occur?
6. *How* is it done?

6f Browse sources.

At the library and on the Internet, browse for a topic you want to learn more about. If you have a short list of ideas, do a quick check of reference works to get overviews of topics. You can begin with a general encyclopedia or a specialized reference work that focuses on a specific area, such as psychology (16c). You can also use Wikipedia as a starting point: look at entries that relate to your topic, especially noting the sources they cite. While you should never rely on Wikipedia alone, it is a highly accessible way to begin research.

6g Collaborate.

The texts you write are shaped in part by conversations with others. You might also consider using online tools that facilitate collaborative writing, such as Google Docs or wikis, to gather ideas and generate drafts. Writers often work together to come up with ideas, to respond to one another's drafts, or even to coauthor something. Here are some strategies for working with others:

1. Establish a regular meeting time and exchange contact information.
2. Establish ground rules for the group. Be sure every member has an equal opportunity—and responsibility—to contribute.
3. With final deadlines in mind, set an agenda for each group meeting.
4. Listen carefully to what each person says. If disagreements arise, try paraphrasing to see if everyone is hearing the same thing.
5. Use group meetings to work together on particularly difficult problems. If an assignment is complex, have each member explain one section to all the others. If the group has trouble understanding part of the task, check with whoever made the assignment.
6. Expect disagreement, and remember that the goal is not for everyone just to "go along." The challenge is to get a really spirited debate going and to argue through all possibilities.
7. If you are preparing a group-written document, divide up the drafting duties. Set reasonable deadlines for each stage of work. Schedule at least two meetings to iron out the final draft by reading it aloud and working for consistency of tone. Have everyone proofread the final draft, with one person making the corrections.
8. If the group will be making a presentation, be sure you know exactly how much time you will have. Decide how each member will contribute to the presentation. Leave time for at least two practice sessions.
9. Make a point of assessing the group's effectiveness. What has the group accomplished? What has it done best? What has it been least successful at? What has each member contributed? How could the group function more effectively?

7 Planning and Drafting

S ome writers just plunge right into their work and develop it as they go along. Others find that they work more effectively by making detailed blueprints before they begin drafting. Your planning and drafting may fall anywhere along this spectrum. As you plan and draft, you narrow your topic, decide on your thesis, organize materials to support that central idea, and sketch out a plan for your writing. As one student said, this is the time in the writing process "when the rubber meets the road."

7a Narrow your topic.

After exploring ideas, you may have found a topic that interests you and that you think would also be interesting to your readers. The topic, however, may be too large to be manageable. If that is the case, narrow your topic using any exploring technique that works for you (see Chapter 6).

Emily Lesk planned to discuss how advertising affects American identity, but she knew that such a topic was far too broad. After thinking about products that are pitched as particularly "American" in their advertising, she posted a Facebook status update asking friends to

WORKING THESIS: Plan Your Approach

Survey what you know about the topic.

Ask...

What is your connection to the topic?

What does your audience need to know?

How can you make your topic manageable?

Remember that there are many possible paths to approaching a topic.

"name products that seem super-American." She quickly got seventeen responses ranging from Hummers and Winchester rifles to "soft toilet paper," Spam, Wheaties, and apple pie. One friend identified Coca-Cola and Pepsi-Cola, two products that Emily associated with many memorable and well-documented advertising campaigns.

7b Craft a working thesis.

Academic and professional writing in the United States often contains an explicit thesis statement. The thesis functions as a promise to readers, letting them know what the writer will discuss. Your readers may (or may not) expect you to craft the thesis as a single sentence near the beginning of the text. If you want to suggest a thesis implicitly rather than stating one explicitly, if you plan to convey your main argument somewhere other than in your introduction, or if you prefer to make your thesis longer than a single sentence, consider whether the rhetorical situation allows such flexibility. For an academic project, also consult with your instructor about how to meet expectations.

Whether you plan to use an implicit or explicit thesis statement in your text, you should establish a tentative working thesis early in your writing process. The word *working* is important here because your thesis may well change as you write—your final thesis may be very different from the working thesis you begin with. Even so, a working thesis focuses your thinking and research, and helps keep you on track.

WORKING THESIS: Refine Your Topic

Match your approach to the requirements of the topic.

SCENIC DETOURS

SHORTCUT TO TOP

Ask...

How will your audience connect to your topic?

How can you help them see your perspective?

What is the most persuasive message for this context?

Remember that you are creating a *working* thesis that you can change as you go.

A working thesis should have two parts: a topic, which indicates the subject matter the writing is about, and a comment, which makes an important point about the topic.

▶ **In the graphic novel *Fun Home*, illustrations and words combine to make meanings that are more subtle than either words alone or images alone could convey.**

A successful working thesis has three characteristics:

1. It is potentially *interesting* to the intended audience.
2. It is as *specific* as possible.
3. It limits the topic enough to make it *manageable*.

You can evaluate a working thesis by checking it against each of these characteristics, as in the following examples:

▶ **Graphic novels combine words and images.**

INTERESTING?   The topic of graphic novels could be interesting, but this draft of a working thesis has no real comment attached to it—instead, it states a bare fact, and the only place to go from here is to more bare facts.

▶ **In graphic novels, words and images convey interesting meanings.**

SPECIFIC?   This thesis is not specific. What are "interesting meanings," exactly? How are they conveyed?

WORKING THESIS: Craft Your Message

Draft a working thesis.

Ask...

Should your thesis be *implicit* or *explicit* for this context and audience?

Are you conveying your own message—not just facts?

Does your working thesis help you understand where to go next?

Consider this a starting point for organizing and planning your draft....

▶ **Graphic novels have evolved in recent decades to become an important literary genre.**

> MANAGEABLE? This thesis would not be manageable for a short-term project because it would require research on several decades of history and on hundreds of texts from all over the world.

FOR MULTILINGUAL WRITERS

Stating a Thesis Explicitly

In some cultures, stating the main point explicitly may be considered rude or inelegant. In U.S. academic and business practices, however, readers often expect the writer to make key points and positions explicit. Unless your main point is highly controversial or hard for the reader to accept (such as a rejection letter), state your main point early — before presenting the supporting details.

7c Gather information to support your thesis.

Once you have a working thesis, consider whether you need to do research for your writing project. Your assignment may require research, or you may decide on your own to find out more about your topic or to locate examples and illustrations that will enhance your writing. You may even need to do research at more than one stage of the writing process as you define, narrow, and perhaps change your topic. Library research, online research, and field research can all help you find the information and visuals you need. (For more on conducting research and working with sources, see Chapters 16 and 17. For more on organizing your support into paragraphs, see Chapter 8.)

7d Organize information.

Remember to consider your audience, purpose, and topic as you think about how you will organize information to make it accessible and persuasive to your audience. At the simplest level, writers most often group information according to four principles — space, time, logic, and association.

Organizing according to space

The organizational principle of space refers to *where* bits of information occur within a setting. If the information you have gathered is descriptive, you may choose to organize it spatially. Using spatial organization allows the reader to "see" your information, to fix it in space.

INFORMATION ORGANIZED SPATIALLY

This photo shows the spatial arrangement described, with the darkened side areas for spectators and the brightly lighted front of the room. The photograph and writing together help readers see the scene vividly.

The scene was being filmed in a windowless building with a corrugated tin roof. We entered through the single side door and sat in folding chairs on a platform along one wall, separated from the rest of the room by beaded red curtains. Behind us was darkness. On the far wall, neon lights glowed dimly, illuminating a few unoccupied barstools on the other side of the room. But the front of the room was ablaze with light. Purple and white floodlights beamed down onto a circular dance floor, creating an almost supernatural glow. The film crew in the center of the room stood silhouetted against the light like an audience waiting for a show to begin.

Organizing according to time

The principle of time refers to *when* bits of information occur, usually chronologically. Chronological organization is the basic method used in cookbooks, lab reports, instruction manuals, and stories. Writers of these products organize information according to when it occurs in some process or sequence of events (narrative).

INFORMATION ORGANIZED CHRONOLOGICALLY

In July of 1877, Eadweard Muybridge photographed a horse in motion with a camera fast enough to capture clearly the split second when the horse's hooves were all off the ground—a moment never before caught on film. Throughout the fall of that year, newspapers were full of the news of Muybridge's achievement. His next goal was to photograph a sequence of such rapid images. In the summer of 1878, he set up a series of cameras along a track and snapped successive photos of a horse as it galloped past. Muybridge's technical achievement helped to pave the way for the first motion pictures a decade later.

This photo series shows the rapid passage of time, with each image capturing an instant too fast to see with the eye alone. The image and text together give readers a clear idea of Muybridge's achievement.

Organizing according to logic

The principle of logic refers to *how* bits of information are related logically. The most commonly used logical patterns include *illustration, definition, division and classification, comparison and contrast, cause and effect, problem and solution, use of analogies,* and *narration.* The example that follows organizes information logically, according to the principle of division. For other examples of paragraphs organized according to these logical patterns, see Chapter 8.

INFORMATION ORGANIZED LOGICALLY

Burns can be divided into three types based on the severity of tissue damage: (1) Superficial, or first-degree, burns damage only the top layer of skin (epidermis). They are red and painful, but not serious. (2) Partial thickness, or second-degree, burns damage both the epidermis and the layer just below it (dermis). Second-degree burns, which can be very painful, are characterized by blistering, swelling, and redness. (3) Full thickness, or third-degree, burns destroy both the epidermis and the dermis and damage underlying muscle and other tissues. They appear charred and black. The burn area itself is numb, but the surrounding area can be very painful. Third-degree burns can be fatal if the percentage of affected skin is sufficiently large.

The images are logically arranged to show burns of increasing severity.

Organizing according to association

The principle of association refers to how bits of information are related in terms of visuals, motifs, personal memories, and so on. Many contemporary essays are organized through a series of associations that grow directly out of the writer's memory or experience. Thus, associational organization is often used in personal narrative, where writers can use a chain of associations to render an experience vividly for readers.

INFORMATION ORGANIZED ASSOCIATIONALLY

This image works by association to emphasize the nostalgic charm of homemade ice cream.

Flying from San Francisco to Atlanta, I looked down to see the gentle roll of the Smoky Mountains begin to appear. Almost at once, I was back on my Granny's porch, sitting next to her drinking iced tea and watching all the grownups take turns cranking the ice-cream freezer. Finally the moment came when even the strongest arms could barely turn the churn. Granny lifted the cream can out of the wooden bucket, opened the lid, scooped the gleaming ice cream into a bowl, and topped it with ripe chopped peaches. I still haven't tasted anything better!

In much of your writing, you will want to use two or more principles of organization. In addition, you may want to include not only visuals but sound and other multimedia effects as well.

AT A GLANCE

Organizing Visuals

- Use images and visuals to capture your readers' attention and interest in a vivid way, to emphasize a point you make in your text, to present information that is difficult to convey in words, or to communicate with audiences with different language skills.
- Consider how the image works as an image and in combination with the text, and think about how readers are likely to respond to it.
- Place each visual as near as possible to the text it illustrates.
- Introduce each visual clearly: *As the map to the right depicts. . . .*
- Comment on the significance or effect of the visual: *Figure 1 corroborates the firefighters' statements. . . .*
- Label each visual appropriately, and cite the source.

7e Make a plan.

At this point, you will find it helpful to create an organizational plan or outline. To do so, simply begin with your thesis; review your exploratory notes, research materials, and visuals; and then list all the examples and other good reasons you have to support the thesis.

A sample organizational plan

One informal way to organize your ideas is to figure out what belongs in your introduction, body paragraphs, and conclusion. Here is how one student, who was writing about solutions to a problem, used this kind of plan:

WORKING THESIS

▶ **Increased motorcycle use demands the reorganization of campus parking lots.**

INTRODUCTION

give background and overview (motorcycle use up dramatically) and use a photograph of overcrowding in a lot

state purpose — to fulfill promise of thesis by offering solutions

BODY

describe the current situation (tell of my research at area parking lots)

describe the problem in detail (report on statistics; cars vs. cycles) and include a graph representing findings

present two possible solutions (enlarge lots or reallocate space)

CONCLUSION

recommend against first solution because of cost and space

recommend second solution, and summarize benefits of it

A formal outline

Even if you have made an informal written plan before drafting, you may also want—or be required—to prepare a formal outline, which can help you see exactly how the parts of your writing will fit together—how your ideas relate, where you need examples, and what the overall structure of your work will be. Most formal outlines follow a conventional format of numbered and lettered headings and subheadings, using roman numerals, capital letters, arabic numerals, and lowercase letters to show the levels of importance of the various ideas and their relationships. Each new level is indented to show its subordination to the preceding level.

Thesis statement
  I. First main idea
     A. First subordinate idea
        1. First supporting detail or point
        2. Second supporting detail
        3. Third supporting detail
     B. Second subordinate idea
        1. First supporting detail
        2. Second supporting detail

  II. Second main idea
     A. First subordinate idea
        1. First supporting detail
        2. Second supporting detail
     B. Second subordinate idea
        1. First supporting detail
        2. Second supporting detail
           a. First supporting detail
           b. Second supporting detail

Note that each level contains at least two parts, so there is no A without a B, no 1 without a 2. Also keep in mind that headings should be stated in parallel form—either all sentences or all grammatically parallel structures.

A storyboard

The technique of storyboarding—working out a narrative or argument in visual form—can be a good way to come up with an organizational plan, especially if you are developing a Web site or other multimedia project. For such projects you can even find storyboard templates online to help you get started.

For a typical college essay, however, you can create your own storyboard by using note cards or even sticky notes, taking advantage of different colors to keep track of threads of argument, subtopics, and so on. Remember that flexibility is a strong feature of storyboarding: you can move the cards and notes around, trying out different arrangements, until you find an organization that works well for your writing situation. Basic patterns for a storyboard include linear, hierarchical, and spoke-and-hub organization.

LINEAR ORGANIZATION

Use this when you want most readers to move in a particular order through your material. An online report might use the following linear organization:

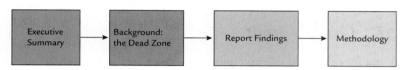

HIERARCHICAL ORGANIZATION

A hierarchy puts the most important material first, with subtopics branching out from the main idea. A multimedia presentation on dog bite prevention might be arranged like this:

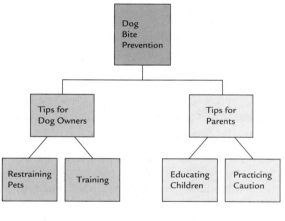

SPOKE-AND-HUB ORGANIZATION

A spoke-and-hub organization allows readers to move from place to place in no particular order. Many portfolio Web sites are arranged as shown at right:

Whatever form your plan takes, you may want or need to change it along the way. Writing has a way of stimulating thought, and the process of drafting may generate new ideas. Or you may find that you need to reexamine some data or information or gather more material.

7f Create a draft.

No matter how good your planning, investigating, and organizing have been, chances are you will need to do more work as you draft. This fact of life leads to the first principle of successful drafting: be flexible. If you see that your plan is not working, don't hesitate to alter it. If some information now seems irrelevant, leave it out—even if you went to great lengths to obtain it. Throughout the drafting process, you may need to refer to points you have already written about. You may learn that you need to do more research, that your whole thesis must be reshaped, or that your topic is still too broad and should be narrowed further. Very often you will continue planning, investigating, and organizing throughout the writing process.

AT A GLANCE

Drafting

- **Set up a computer folder or file for your essay**. Give the file a clear and relevant name, and save to it often. Number your drafts. If you decide to try a new direction, save the file as a new draft — you can always pick up with a previous one if the new version doesn't work out.

- **Have all your information close at hand and arranged according to your organizational plan**. Stopping to search for a piece of information can break your concentration or distract you.

- **Try to write in stretches of at least thirty minutes**. Writing can provide momentum, and once you get going, the task becomes easier.

- **Don't let small questions bog you down**. Just make a note of them in brackets — or in all caps — or make a tentative decision and move on.

- **Remember that first drafts aren't perfect**. Concentrate on getting all your ideas down, and don't worry about anything else.

- **Stop writing at a place where you know exactly what will come next**. Doing so will help you start easily when you return to the draft.

---

bedfordstmartins.com/everydaywriter
Student Writing

Developing Paragraphs 8

Paragraphs serve as signposts—pointers that help guide readers through a piece of writing. A look through a popular magazine will show paragraphs working this way: the first paragraph of an article almost always aims to get our attention and to persuade us to read on, and subsequent ones often indicate a new point or a shift in focus or tone.

Put most simply, a paragraph is a group of sentences or a single sentence set off as a unit. All the sentences in a paragraph usually revolve around one main idea.

8a Focus on a main idea.

An effective paragraph often focuses on one main idea. A good way to achieve such paragraph unity is to state the main idea clearly in one sentence and then relate all the other sentences in the paragraph to

AT A GLANCE

Editing Paragraphs

- What is the topic sentence of each paragraph? Is it stated or implied? Is the main idea of the paragraph clear? (8a)
- Does the first sentence of each paragraph let readers know what that paragraph is about? Does the last sentence in some way conclude that paragraph's discussion? If not, does it need to?
- Within each paragraph, how does each sentence relate to the main idea? Revise or eliminate any that do not. (8a)
- How completely does each paragraph develop its main idea? What details and images are included? Are they effective? Do any paragraphs need more detail? (8b)
- What other methods of development might make the paragraph more effective? (8c)
- Is each paragraph organized in a way that is easy to follow? Are sentences within each paragraph clearly linked? Do any of the transitions try to create links between ideas that do not really exist? (8e)
- Are the paragraphs clearly linked? Do any links need to be added? Are any of the transitions from one paragraph to another artificial? (8e)
- How does the introductory paragraph catch readers' interest? How does the last paragraph draw the piece to a conclusion? (8f)

FOR MULTILINGUAL WRITERS

Being Explicit

Native readers of English generally expect that paragraphs will have an explicitly stated main idea and that the connections between points in a paragraph will also be stated explicitly. Such step-by-step explicitness may strike you as unnecessary or ineffective, but it follows the traditional paragraph conventions of English.

that idea. The sentence that presents the main idea is called the topic sentence.

Announcing the main idea in a topic sentence

The following paragraph opens with a clear topic sentence, and the rest of the paragraph builds on the idea stated in that sentence:

> *Our friendship was the source of much happiness and many memories.* We grooved on every new recording from Jay-Z. We sweated together in the sweltering summer sun, trying to win the championship for our softball team. I recall the taste of pepperoni pizza as we discussed the highlights of our team's victory. Once we even became attracted to the same person, but luckily we were able to share his friendship.

A topic sentence does not always come at the beginning of a paragraph; it may come at the end. Occasionally a paragraph's main idea is so obvious that it need not be stated explicitly in a topic sentence.

Relating each sentence to the main idea

Whether the main idea of a paragraph is stated in a topic sentence or is implied, make sure that all other sentences in the paragraph contribute

TALKING THE TALK

Paragraph Length

"How long should a paragraph be?" In college writing, paragraphs should address a specific topic or idea and develop that idea with examples and evidence. There is no set rule about how many sentences are required to make a complete paragraph. So write as many sentences as you need — and no more.

to the main idea. In the preceding example about friendship, all of the sentences clearly relate to the point that is made in the first sentence. The result is a unified paragraph.

8b Provide details.

An effective paragraph develops its main idea by providing enough details—including visual details—to hold the reader's interest. Without such development, a paragraph may seem lifeless and abstract.

A POORLY DEVELOPED PARAGRAPH

> No such thing as human nature compels people to behave, think, or react in certain ways. Rather, from our infancy to our death, we are constantly being taught, by the society that surrounds us, the customs, norms, and mores of a distinct culture. Everything in culture is learned, not genetically transmitted.

This paragraph is boring. Although its main idea is clear and its sentences hold together, it fails to gain our interest or hold our attention because it lacks any specific examples or details. Now look at the paragraph revised to include needed specifics.

THE SAME PARAGRAPH, REVISED

> A child in Los Angeles decorates a Christmas tree with shiny red ornaments and sparkling tinsel. A few weeks later, a child in Beijing celebrates the Chinese New Year with feasting, firecrackers, and gift money in lucky red envelopes. It is not by instinct that one child knows how to decorate the tree while the other knows how to celebrate the New Year. No such thing as human nature compels people to behave, think, or react in certain ways. Rather, from the time of our infancy to our death, we are constantly being taught, by the society that surrounds us, the customs, norms, and mores of one or more distinct cultures. Everything in culture is learned, not genetically transmitted.

Though both paragraphs present the same point, only the second one comes to life. It does so by bringing in specific details *from* life, including images that show readers what the paragraph describes. We want to read this paragraph because it appeals to our senses (shiny red ornaments, firecrackers) and our curiosity (why are red envelopes considered lucky?).

Details in visual texts

Details are important in both written and visual texts. If you decide to use an image because of a particular detail, make sure your readers will notice what you want them to see. Crop out any unnecessary information, and clarify what's important about the image in your text or with a caption. The first image below shows the original photograph taken to illustrate a blog post about street food. The cropped second image, which appeared on the blog, makes the sandwich the center of the frame.

WEDNESDAY, APRIL 11, 2012

Fresh from the sea!

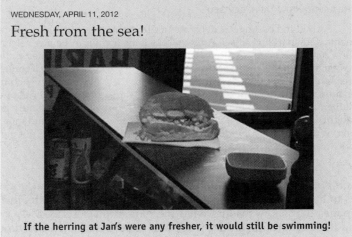

If the herring at Jan's were any fresher, it would still be swimming!

8c   Use effective methods of development.

As noted in 7d, there are several common methods of development. You can use them to develop paragraphs.

Narrative

A narrative paragraph uses the chronological elements of a story to develop a main idea. The following is one student's narrative paragraph that tells a personal story to support a point about the dangers of racing bicycles with flimsy alloy frames:

> People who have been exposed to the risk of dangerously designed bicycle frames have paid too high a price. I saw this danger myself in last year's Putney Race. An expensive graphite frame failed, and the rider was catapulted onto Vermont pavement at fifty miles per hour. The pack of riders behind him was so dense that other racers crashed into a tangled, sliding heap. The aftermath: four hospitalizations. I got off with some stitches, a bad road rash, and severely pulled tendons. My Italian racing bike was pretzeled, and my racing was over for that summer. Others were not so lucky. An Olympic hopeful, Brian Stone of the Northstar team, woke up in a hospital bed to find that his cycling was over—and not just for that summer. His kneecap had been surgically removed. He couldn't even walk.

Description

A descriptive paragraph uses specific details to create a clear impression. Notice how the following paragraph includes details to describe the appearance of the skyscraper and its effect on those who see it.

The Chrysler Building, completed in 1930, still attracts the eyes of tourists and New Yorkers alike with its shiny steel exterior. The Chrysler cars of the era are incorporated into the design: the eagle-head gargoyles on the upper vertices of the building are shaped like the automobiles' hood ornaments, and winged details imitate Chrysler radiator caps. At night, an elaborate lighting scheme spotlights the sleek, powerful eagles from below—turning them into striking silhouettes—and picks out each of the upper stories' famed triangular windows, arching up into the darkness like the rays of a stylized sun.

Definition

You may often need to write an entire paragraph in order to define a word or concept, as in the following example:

> Economics is the study of how people choose among the alternatives available to them. It's the study of little choices ("Should I take the chocolate or the strawberry?") and big choices ("Should we require a reduction in energy consumption in order to protect the environment?"). It's the study of individual choices, choices by firms, and choices by governments. Life presents each of us with a wide range of alternative uses of our time and other resources; economists examine how we choose among those alternatives.
> – TIMOTHY TREGARTHEN, *Economics*

Example

One of the most common ways of developing a paragraph is by illustrating a point with one or more examples.

> The Indians made names for us children in their teasing way. Because our very busy mother kept my hair cut short, like my brothers', they called me Short Furred One, pointing to their hair and making the sign for short, the right hand with fingers pressed close together, held upward, back out, at the height intended. With me this was about two feet tall, the Indians laughing gently at my abashed face. I am told that I was given a pair of

small moccasins that first time, to clear up my unhappiness at being picked out from the dusk behind the fire and my two unhappy shortcomings made conspicuous. — Mari Sandoz, "The Go-Along Ones"

Division and classification

Division breaks a single item into parts. Classification groups many separate items according to their similarities. A paragraph evaluating one history course might divide the course into several segments—textbooks, lectures, assignments—and examine each one in turn. A paragraph giving an overview of many history courses might classify the courses in a number of ways—by time periods, by geographic areas, by the kinds of assignments demanded, by the number of students enrolled, or by some other principle.

DIVISION

We all listen to music according to our separate capacities. But, for the sake of analysis, the whole listening process may become clearer if we break it up into its component parts, so to speak. In a certain sense, we all listen to music on three separate planes. For lack of a better terminology, one might name these: (1) the sensuous plane, (2) the expressive plane, (3) the sheerly musical plane. The only advantage to be gained from mechanically splitting up the listening process into these hypothetical planes is the clearer view to be had of the way in which we listen.
— Aaron Copland, *What to Listen For in Music*

CLASSIFICATION

Two types of people are seduced by fad diets. Those who have always been overweight turn to them out of despair; they have tried everything, and yet nothing seems to work. A second group of people to succumb appear perfectly healthy but are baited by slogans such as "look good, feel good." These slogans prompt self-questioning and insecurity—do I really look good and feel good?—and as a direct result, many healthy people fall prey to fad diets. With both types of people, however, the problems surrounding such diets are numerous and dangerous. In fact, these diets provide neither intelligent nor effective answers to weight control.

Comparison and contrast

When you compare two things, you look at their similarities; when you contrast two things, you focus on their differences. You can structure paragraphs that compare or contrast in two basic ways. One way is to present all the information about one item and then all the information about the other item, as in the following paragraph:

You could tell the veterans from the rookies by the way they were dressed. The knowledgeable ones had their heads covered by kerchiefs, so that if they were hired, tobacco dust wouldn't get in their hair; they had on clean dresses that by now were faded and shapeless, so that if they were hired they wouldn't get tobacco dust and grime on their best clothes. Those who were trying for the first time had their hair freshly done and wore attractive dresses; they wanted to make a good impression. But the dresses couldn't be seen at the distance that many were standing from the employment office, and they were crumpled in the crush.

– MARY MEBANE, "Summer Job"

Or you can switch back and forth between the two items, focusing on particular characteristics of each in turn.

Malcolm X emphasized the use of violence in his movement and employed the biblical principle of "an eye for an eye and a tooth for a tooth." King, on the other hand, felt that blacks should use nonviolent civil disobedience and employed the theme "turning the other cheek," which Malcolm X rejected as "beggarly" and "feeble." The philosophy of Malcolm X was one of revenge, and often it broke the unity of black Americans. More radical blacks supported him, while more conservative ones supported King. King thought that blacks should transcend their humanity. In contrast, Malcolm X thought they should embrace it and reserve their love for one another, regarding whites as "devils" and the "enemy." The distance between Martin Luther King Jr.'s thinking and Malcolm X's was the distance between growing up in the seminary and growing up on the streets, between the American dream and the American reality.

Analogy

Analogies (comparisons that explain an unfamiliar thing in terms of a familiar one) can also help develop paragraphs. In the following paragraph, the writer draws an unlikely analogy—between the human genome and Thanksgiving dinner—to help readers understand what scientists know about the human genome.

Think of the human genome as the ingredients list for a massive Thanksgiving dinner. Scientists long have had a general understanding of how the feast is cooked. They knew where the ovens were. Now, they also have a list of every ingredient. Yet much remains to be discovered. In most cases, no one knows exactly which ingredients are necessary for making, for example, the pumpkin pie as opposed to the cornbread. Indeed, many, if not most, of the recipes that use the genomic ingredients are missing, and there's little understanding why small variations in the quality of the ingredients can "cook up" diseases in one person but not in another.

– *USA TODAY*, "Cracking of Life's Genetic Code Carries Weighty Potential"

Cause and effect

You can often develop paragraphs by explaining the causes of something or the effects that something brings about. The following paragraph discusses how our desire for food that tastes good has affected history:

The human craving for flavor has been a largely unacknowledged and unexamined force in history. For millennia royal empires have been built, unexplored lands traversed, and great religions and philosophies changed by the spice trade. In 1492 Christopher Columbus set sail to find seasoning. Today the influence of flavor in the world marketplace is no less decisive. The rise and fall of corporate empires—of soft-drink companies, snack-food companies, and fast-food chains—is often determined by how their products taste.

– ERIC SCHLOSSER, *Fast Food Nation*

Process

Paragraphs that explain a process often use the principle of time or chronology to order the stages in the process.

By the late 20s, most people notice the first signs of aging in their physical appearance. Slight losses of elasticity in facial skin produce the first wrinkles, usually in those areas most involved in their characteristic facial expressions. As the skin continues to lose elasticity and fat deposits build up, the face sags a bit with age. Indeed, some people have drooping eyelids, sagging cheeks, and the hint of a double chin by age 40 (Whitbourne, 1985). Other parts of the body sag a bit as well, so as the years pass, adults need to exercise regularly if they want to maintain their muscle tone and body shape. Another harbinger of aging, the first gray hairs, is usually noticed in the 20s and can be explained by a reduction in the number of pigment-producing cells. Hair may become a bit less plentiful, too, because of hormonal changes and reduced blood supply to the skin.

– KATHLEEN STASSEN BERGER, *The Developing Person through the Life Span*

Problem and solution

Another way to develop a paragraph is to open with a topic sentence that states a problem or asks a question about a problem and then to offer a solution or answers in the sentences that follow—a technique used in this paragraph from a review of Ted Nordhaus and Michael Shellenberger's book *Break Through: From the Death of Environmentalism to the Politics of Possibility*:

> Unfortunately, at the moment growth means burning more fossil fuel. . . . How can that fact be faced? How to have growth that Americans want, but without limits that they instinctively oppose, and still reduce carbon emissions? [Nordhaus and Shellenberger's] answer is: investments in new technology. Acknowledge that America "is great at imagining, experimenting, and inventing the future," and then start spending. They cite examples ranging from the nuclear weapons program to the invention of the Internet to show what government money can do, and argue that too many clean-energy advocates focus on caps instead.
> – Bill McKibben, "Can Anyone Stop It?"

Reiteration

Reiteration is a method of development you may recognize from political speeches or some styles of preaching. In this pattern, the writer states the main point of a paragraph and then restates it, hammering home the point and often building in intensity as well. In the following passage from Barack Obama's 2004 speech at the Democratic National Convention, Obama contrasts what he identifies as the ideas of "those who are preparing to divide us" with memorable references to common ground and unity, including repeated references to the United States as he builds to his climactic point:

> Now even as we speak, there are those who are preparing to divide us—the spin masters, the negative ad peddlers who embrace the politics of anything goes. Well, I say to them tonight, there is not a liberal America and a conservative America—there is the United States of America. There is not a black America and a white America and Latino America and an Asian America—there's the United States of America. The pundits like to slice and dice our country into Red States and Blue States: Red States for Republicans, Blue States for Democrats. But I've got news for them, too. We worship an awesome God in the Blue States, and we don't like federal agents poking around in our libraries in the Red States. We coach Little League in the Blue States and yes, we've got some gay friends in the Red States. There are patriots who opposed the war in Iraq and there are patriots who supported the war in Iraq. We are one people, all of us pledging allegiance to the stars and stripes, all of us defending the United States of America.
> – Barack Obama

8d Consider paragraph length.

Paragraph length is determined by content and purpose. Paragraphs should develop an idea, create any desired effects (such as suspense or humor), and advance the larger piece of writing. Fulfilling these aims will sometimes require short paragraphs, sometimes long ones. For example, if you are writing a persuasive piece, you may put all your evidence into one long paragraph to create the impression of a solid, overwhelmingly convincing argument. In a story about an exciting event, on the other hand, you may use a series of short paragraphs to create suspense, to keep the reader rushing to each new paragraph to find out what happens next.

REASONS TO START A NEW PARAGRAPH

- to turn to a new idea
- to emphasize something (such as an idea or an example)
- to change speakers (in dialogue)
- to get readers to pause
- to take up a subtopic
- to start the conclusion

8e Make paragraphs flow.

A paragraph has coherence—or flows—if its details fit together clearly in a way that readers can easily follow. When you arrange information in a particular order (as described in 7d and 8c), you help readers move from one point to another. Regardless of your organization, however, be aware of several other ways to achieve paragraph coherence.

Repeating key words and phrases

Weaving in repeated key words and phrases—or pronouns that point to them—not only links sentences but also alerts readers to the importance of those words or phrases in the larger piece of writing. Notice in the following example how the repetition of the italicized key words and the use of pronouns that refer to those words help hold the paragraph together:

> Over the centuries, *shopping* has changed in function as well as in style. Before the Industrial Revolution, most consumer goods were sold in open-air *markets*, *customers* who went into an actual *shop* were expected to *buy* something, and *shoppers* were always expected to *bargain* for the best

possible *price*. In the nineteenth century, however, the development of the department *store* changed the relationship between buyers and sellers. Instead of visiting several *market* stalls or small *shops*, *customers* could now *buy* a variety of merchandise under the same roof; instead of feeling expected to *buy*, they were welcome just to look; and instead of *bargaining* with several merchants, they paid a fixed *price* for each *item*. In addition, *they* could return an *item* to the *store* and exchange *it* for a different one or get their money back. All of these changes helped transform *shopping* from serious requirement to psychological recreation.

Using parallelism

Parallel structures can help connect the sentences within a paragraph. As readers, we feel pulled along by the force of the parallel structures in the following example:

> William Faulkner's "Barn Burning" tells the story of a young boy trapped in a no-win situation. If he betrays his father, he loses his family. If he betrays justice, he becomes a fugitive. In trying to free himself from his trap, he does both.

Using transitions

Transitions are words such as *so*, *however*, and *thus* that signal relationships between sentences and paragraphs. Transitions help guide the reader from one idea to another. To understand how important transitions are in directing readers, try reading the following paragraph, from which all transitions have been removed.

A PARAGRAPH WITH NO TRANSITIONS

> In "The Fly," Katherine Mansfield tries to show us the real personality of the boss beneath his exterior. The fly helps her to portray this real self. The boss goes through a range of emotions and feelings. He expresses these feelings to a small but determined fly, whom the reader realizes he unconsciously relates to his son. The author basically splits up the story into three parts, with the boss's emotions and actions changing quite measurably. With old Woodifield, with himself, and with the fly, we see the boss's manipulativeness. Our understanding of him as a hard and cruel man grows.

If we work at it, we can figure out the relationship of these sentences to one another, for this paragraph is essentially unified by one major idea. But the lack of transitions results in an abrupt, choppy rhythm; the paragraph lurches from one detail to the next, dragging the confused reader behind. See how much easier the passage is to read and understand with transitions added.

THE SAME PARAGRAPH WITH TRANSITIONS

In "The Fly," Katherine Mansfield tries to show us the real personality of the boss beneath his exterior. The fly in the story's title helps her to portray this real self. In the course of the story, the boss goes through a range of emotions. At the end, he finally expresses these feelings to a small but determined fly, whom the reader realizes he unconsciously relates to his son. To accomplish her goal, the author basically splits up the story into three parts, with the boss's emotions and actions changing measurably throughout. First with old Woodifield, then with himself, and last with the fly, we see the boss's manipulativeness. With each part, our understanding of him as a hard and cruel man grows.

Commonly used transitions

TO SIGNAL SEQUENCE

again, also, and, and then, besides, finally, first . . . second . . . third, furthermore, last, moreover, next, still, too

TO SIGNAL TIME

after a few days, after a while, afterward, as long as, as soon as, at last, at that time, before, earlier, immediately, in the meantime, in the past, lately, later, meanwhile, now, presently, simultaneously, since, so far, soon, then, thereafter, until, when

TO SIGNAL COMPARISON

again, also, in the same way, likewise, once more, similarly

TO SIGNAL CONTRAST

although, but, despite, even though, however, in contrast, in spite of, instead, nevertheless, nonetheless, on the contrary, on the one hand . . . on the other hand, regardless, still, though, yet

TO SIGNAL EXAMPLES

after all, for example, for instance, indeed, in fact, of course, specifically, such as, the following example, to illustrate

TO SIGNAL CAUSE AND EFFECT

accordingly, as a result, because, consequently, for this purpose, hence, so, then, therefore, thereupon, thus, to this end

TO SIGNAL PLACE

above, adjacent to, below, beyond, closer to, elsewhere, far, farther on, here, near, nearby, opposite to, there, to the left, to the right

TO SIGNAL CONCESSION

although it is true that, granted that, I admit that, it may appear that, naturally, of course

TO SIGNAL SUMMARY, REPETITION, OR CONCLUSION

as a result, as has been noted, as I have said, as mentioned earlier, as we have seen, in any event, in conclusion, in other words, in short, on the whole, therefore, to summarize

8f Work on opening and closing paragraphs.

Opening paragraphs

Even a good piece of writing may remain unread if it has a weak opening paragraph. In addition to announcing your topic, an introductory paragraph must engage readers' interest and focus their attention on what is to follow. One common kind of opening paragraph follows a general-to-specific sequence, in which the writer opens with a general statement and then gets more and more specific, concluding with the thesis. The following paragraph illustrates such an opening:

> The human organism is adapted to function in face-to-face encounters. We know that face-to-face is the most effective way to pitch woo. And face-to-face is obviously the best way to transact an intimate relationship long term. But while we know this, there's much more to face-to-face interaction than meets the naked eye. And it is of grave importance. We risk losing a great deal in any heavy shift of social traffic onto exclusively electronic media. —MARIAM THALOS, "Why I Am Not a Friend"

In this paragraph, the opening sentence introduces a general subject, and the last sentence presents the thesis, which the rest of the essay will develop.

OTHER EFFECTIVE WAYS OF OPENING

- with a quotation: *There is a bumper sticker that reads, "Too bad ignorance isn't painful."* – NIKKI GIOVANNI, "Racism 101"
- with an anecdote: *Social networking pioneer Howard Rheingold begins his digital journalism course each year with a participatory experiment. Shut off your cell phones, he tells his students. Shut your laptop. Now, shut your eyes.* –CATHY DAVIDSON, *Now You See It*

- with a question: *Why are Americans terrified of using nuclear power as a source of energy?*
- with a strong opinion: *Men need a men's movement about as much as women need chest hair.* – JOHN RUSZKIEWICZ, *The Presence of Others*

Concluding paragraphs

A good conclusion wraps up a piece of writing in a satisfying and memorable way. A common and effective strategy for concluding is to restate the central idea (but not word for word), perhaps specifying it in several sentences, and then ending with a much more general statement.

> Lastly, and perhaps greatest of all, there was the ability, at the end, to turn quickly from war to peace once the fighting was over. Out of the way these two men [Generals Grant and Lee] behaved at Appomattox came the possibility of a peace of reconciliation. It was a possibility not wholly realized, in the years to come, but which did, in the end, help the two sections to become one nation again . . . after a war whose bitterness might have seemed to make such a reunion wholly impossible. No part of either man's life became him more than the part he played in this brief meeting in the McLean house at Appomattox. Their behavior there put all succeeding generations of Americans in their debt. Two great Americans, Grant and Lee—very different, yet under everything very much alike. Their encounter at Appomattox was one of the great moments of American history.
> – BRUCE CATTON, "Grant and Lee: A Study in Contrasts"

OTHER EFFECTIVE WAYS OF CONCLUDING

- with a quotation
- with a question
- with a vivid image
- with a call for action
- with a warning

9 Making Design Decisions

B ecause visual and design elements such as headings, lists, fonts, images, and graphics can help you get and keep a reader's attention, they bring a whole new dimension to writing — what some call *visual rhetoric.*

9a Plan a visual structure.

Effective writers consider the visual structure of any text they create. Their design decisions guide readers by making texts easier on the eyes and easier to understand.

Print and electronic options

One of your first design decisions will be choosing between print delivery and electronic delivery. In general, print documents are easily portable, easy to read without technical assistance, and relatively fast to produce. In addition, the tools for producing print texts are highly developed and stable. Electronic texts, on the other hand, can include sound, animation, and video; updates are easy to make; distribution is fast and efficient; and feedback can be swift. In many writing situations, the assignment will tell you whether to create a print document or an electronic text. Whether you are working to produce a text to be read in print or on a screen (or both), however, you should rely on some basic design principles.

Design principles

Designer Robin Williams, in her *Non-Designer's Design Book*, points out several very simple principles for designing effective texts—contrast, alignment, repetition, and proximity. These principles are illustrated in the examples shown on pp. 91–92.

CONTRAST

Contrast attracts your eye to elements on a page and guides you around it, helping you follow an argument or find information. You may achieve contrast through the use of color, icons, boldface or large type size, headings, and so on. Begin with a focus point—the dominant point, image, or words where you want your reader's eye to go first—and structure the flow of your visual information from this point.

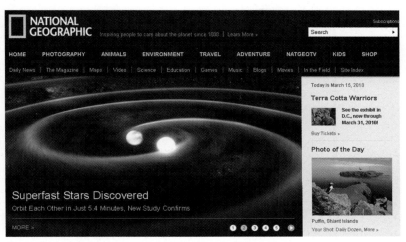

The National Geographic *Web site uses high-contrast yellow and white against a black background.*

ALIGNMENT

Alignment refers to the way visuals and text on a page are lined up, both horizontally and vertically. The overall guideline is not to mix alignments arbitrarily. That is, if you begin with a left alignment, stick with it for the major parts of your page. The result will be a cleaner and more organized look. In this book, for example, headings always align with the left margin.

REPETITION

Readers are guided by the repetition of key words and elements. Use a consistent design throughout your document for such elements as color, typeface, and images.

PROXIMITY

Parts of a text that are closely related should appear together (*proximate* to one another). Your goal is to position related points, text, and visuals near one another and to use clear headings to identify these clusters.

CONSISTENT OVERALL IMPRESSION

Aim for a design that creates the appropriate overall impression or mood for your text. For an academic essay, you will probably make conservative choices that strike a serious scholarly note. In a newsletter for a campus group, you might choose attention-getting images.

This flyer repeats images of generators and buildings to clarify key concepts, and it positions information about safe and unsafe locations for a generator next to illustrations of those locations.

9b Choose appropriate formats.

With so many options available, you should spend some time thinking about appropriate formatting elements for your text. Although the following guidelines often apply, remember that print documents, Web pages, slide shows, videos, and so on all have their own formatting conventions.

White space

Use white space, or negative space, to emphasize and direct readers to parts of the page. White space determines a page's density—the distance between information bits. You consider white space at the page level (margins), paragraph level (space between paragraphs), and sentence level

---

CONSIDERING DISABILITIES

Color for Contrast

Remember when you are using color that not everyone will see it as you do. Some individuals do not perceive color at all; others perceive color in a variety of ways, especially colors like blue and green, which are close together on the color spectrum. When putting colors next to one another, then, use those on opposite sides of the color spectrum, such as purple and gold, in order to achieve high contrast. Doing so will allow readers to see the contrast, if not the nuances, of color.

(space between sentences). Within the page, you can also use white space around particular content, such as a graphic or list, to make it stand out.

Color

Decisions about color depend to a large extent not only on the kind of equipment you are using—and, for printing, who's paying for the color ink cartridges—but also on the purpose(s) of your document and its intended audience. As you design your documents, keep in mind that some colors can evoke powerful responses, so take care that the colors you use match the message you are sending. Here are some other tips about the effective use of color:

- Use color to draw attention to elements you want to emphasize: headings, bullets, text boxes, or parts of charts or graphs.
- Be consistent in your use of color; use the same color for all sub-heads, for example.
- For most documents, keep the number of colors fairly small; too many colors can create a jumbled or confused look.
- Avoid colors that clash or that are hard on the eyes.

| Certain color combinations clash or are hard to read. | Other combinations are easier on the eyes. |

- Make sure all color visuals and text are legible in the format where they will be read. What appears readable on the screen—where colors can be sharper—may be less legible in a printed document.

Paper

The quality of the paper affects the overall look and feel of print documents. Although inexpensive paper is fine for your earlier drafts, use 8½″ × 11″ good-quality white bond paper for your final presentation.

FOR MULTILINGUAL WRITERS

Reading Patterns

In documents written in English and other Western languages, information tends to flow from left to right and top to bottom — since that is the way English texts are written. In some languages, which may be written from right to left or vertically, documents may be arranged from top right to bottom left. Understanding the reading patterns of the language you are working in will help you design your documents most effectively.

For résumés, you may wish to use parchment or cream-colored bond. For brochures and posters, colored paper may be appropriate as long as your text is still readable. Use the best-quality printer available to you for your final product.

Pagination

Your instructor may ask that you follow a particular pagination format for print texts (for MLA, APA, *Chicago,* and CSE styles, see Chapters 49–55); if not, beginning with the first page of text, place your last name and a number in the upper-right-hand corner of the page.

Type

Computers allow writers to choose among a great variety of type sizes and typefaces, or fonts. For most college writing, the easy-to-read 11- or 12-point type size is best.

> This is 12-point Times New Roman
> This is 11-point Times New Roman

A serif font, as is used in the main text of this book, is generally easier to read in print than a **sans serif font**. Although unusual fonts might seem attractive at first glance, readers may find such styles distracting and hard to read over long stretches of material.

Remember that typefaces help you create the tone of a document, so consider your audience and purpose when selecting type.

> *Different fonts convey different feelings.*
> **Different fonts convey different feelings.**
> **DIFFERENT FONTS CONVEY DIFFERENT FEELINGS.**
> Different fonts convey different feelings.

Most important, be consistent in the size and style of typeface you use, especially for the main part of your text. Unless you are striving for some special effect, shifting sizes and fonts within a document can give an appearance of disorderliness.

Spacing

Final drafts for most of your college writing should be double-spaced, with the first line of paragraphs indented one-half inch. Certain kinds of writing for certain disciplines may call for different spacing. Letters, memorandums, and online texts, for example, are usually single-spaced, with no paragraph indentation. Some long print reports may be printed with one-and-a-half-line spacing to save paper. Other kinds of documents, such as flyers and newsletters, may call for multiple columns. If in doubt, consult your instructor.

In general, leave one space after all punctuation except in the following cases:

- Leave no space before or after a dash (*Please respond — right away — to this message*).
- Leave no space before or after a hyphen (*a red-letter day*).
- Leave no space between punctuation marks ("*on my way,*").

Computers allow you to decide whether or not you want both side margins justified, or squared off—as they are on this page. Except in posters and other writing where you are trying to achieve a distinctive visual effect, you should always justify the left margin, though you may decide to indent lists and blocks of text that are set off. However, most readers—and many instructors—prefer the right margin to be "ragged," or unjustified.

9c   Use headings appropriately.

For brief essays and reports, you may need no headings at all. For longer documents, however, these devices call attention to the organization of the text and thus aid comprehension. Some kinds of reports use set headings (such as *Abstract* and *Summary*), which readers expect and writers therefore must provide; see 53d for an example. When you use headings, you need to decide on type size and style, wording, and placement.

Type size and style

This book, which is a long and complex document, uses various levels of headings. These levels of headings are distinguished by type sizes and fonts as well as by color.

In a college paper, you will usually distinguish levels of headings using only type—for example, all capitals for the first-level headings, capitals and lowercase boldface for the second level, capitals and lower-case italics for the third level, and so on.

FIRST-LEVEL HEADING
   Second-Level Heading
    Third-Level Heading

Consistent headings

Look for the most succinct and informative way to word headings. In general, state a topic in a single word, usually a noun (*Toxicity*); in a phrase, usually a noun phrase (*Levels of Toxicity*) or a gerund phrase (*Measuring Toxicity*); in a question that will be answered in the text (*How Can Toxicity Be Measured?*); or in an imperative that tells readers what steps to take (*Measure the Toxicity*). Whichever structure you choose, make sure you use it consistently for all headings of the same level.

Positioning

Be sure to position each level of heading consistently throughout the text. And remember not to put a heading at the very bottom of a page, since readers would have to turn to the next page to find the text that the heading is announcing.

9d Use visuals effectively.

Creating a visual design is more likely than ever before to be a part of your process of planning for a completed writing project. Visuals can help make a point more vividly and succinctly than words alone. In some cases, visuals may even be your primary text.

Selecting visuals

Consider carefully what you want visuals to do for your writing before making your selections. What will your audience want or need you to show? Try to choose visuals that will enhance your credibility, allow you to make your point more emphatically, and clarify your overall text. (See the following series of figures for advice on which visuals are best for particular situations.)

Effective visuals can come from many sources—your own drawings or photographs, charts or graphs you create on a computer, or materials created by others. If you are using a visual from another source, be sure to give appropriate credit and to get permission before using any visual that will be posted online or otherwise available to the public.

Use *pie charts* to compare parts to the whole.

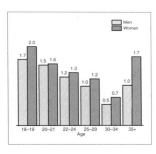

Use *bar graphs* and *line graphs* to compare one element with another, to compare elements over time, or to show correlations and frequency.

Use *tables* to draw attention to detailed numerical information.

Table 10: Commuter Rail Schedule: Reading/Haverhill Line, Boston 2004

	Train 223	Train 227	Train 231
North Station	3:00 pm	4:36 pm	5:15 pm
Reading	3:38 pm	4:54 pm	5:42 pm
Haverhill	4:04 pm	5:31 pm	6:21 pm

Use *diagrams* to illustrate textual information or to point out details of objects or places described.

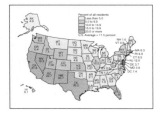

Use *maps* to show geographical locations and to emphasize spatial relationships.

Use *cartoons* to illustrate a point dramatically or comically.

Use *photographs* or *illustrations* to show particular people, places, objects, and situations described in the text or to help readers find or understand types of content.

Identifying visuals in your writing

Position visuals alongside or after the text that refers to them. Number your visuals (number tables separately from other visuals), and give them informative titles. In some instances, you may need to provide captions to give readers additional data as source information.

Figure 1. College Enrollment for Men and Women by Age, 2007 (in millions)

Table 1. Word Choice by Race: *Seesaw* and *Teeter-totter*, Chicago, 1986

Analyzing and altering visuals

Technical tools available to writers and designers today make it relatively easy to manipulate visuals. As you would with any source material, carefully assess any visuals you find for effectiveness, appropriateness, and validity. Here are tips for evaluating visuals:

- Check the context in which the visual appears. Is it part of an official government, school, or library site?
- If the visual is a photograph, are the date, time, place, and setting shown or explained? Is the information about the photo believable?
- If the visual is a chart, graph, or diagram, are the numbers and labels explained? Are the sources of the data given? Will the visual representation help readers make sense of the information, or could it mislead them? (See 18c.)

- Is biographical and contact information for the designer, artist, or photographer given?

At times, you may make certain changes to visuals that you use, such as cropping an image to show the most important detail or digitally brightening a dark image. Here, for example, are separate photos of a mountaintop cabin and a composite that digitally combines the originals into a single panoramic image to convey the setting more accurately. As long as the photograph is identified as a composite, the alteration is ethical.

Combining photos can sometimes be an appropriate choice.

This composite photo conveys the setting more effectively than the individual images.

To ensure that alterations to images are ethical, follow these guidelines:

- Do not attempt to mislead readers. Show things as accurately as possible.
- Tell your audience what changes you have made.
- Include all relevant information about the visual, including the source.

AT A GLANCE

Using Visuals Effectively

- Use visual elements for a specific purpose in your text — to illustrate something, to help prove a point, or to guide readers, for example.
- Tell the audience explicitly what the visual demonstrates, especially if it presents complex information. Do not assume readers will "read" the visual the way you do; your commentary on it is important.
- Number and title all visuals. Number and label tables and figures separately.
- Refer to each visual *before* it appears.
- Follow established conventions for documenting visual sources, and ask permission for use if your work will become available to the public. (18c and e)
- Get responses to your visuals in an early draft. If readers can't follow them or are distracted by them, revise accordingly.
- If you crop, brighten, or otherwise alter visuals to include them in your writing, be sure to do so ethically. (9d)

---

10 Reviewing and Revising

The ancient Roman poet Horace advised aspiring writers to get distance from their work by putting it away for *nine years*. Although impractical for most college writers, this advice still holds a nugget of truth: putting the draft away even for a day or two will clear your mind and give you more objectivity about your writing.

10a Reread.

After giving yourself and your draft a rest, review the draft by rereading it carefully for meaning; recalling your purpose and audience; reconsidering your stance; and evaluating your organization and use of visuals.

Meaning

When you pick up the draft again, don't sweat the small stuff. Instead, concentrate on your message and on whether you have expressed it clearly. Note any places where the meaning seems unclear.

Purpose

If you responded to an assignment, make sure that you have produced what was asked for. If you set out to prove something, have you succeeded? If you intended to propose a solution to a problem, have you set forth a well-supported solution rather than just an analysis of the problem?

Audience

How appropriately do you address your audience members, given their experiences and expectations? Will you catch their interest, and will they be able to follow your discussion?

Stance

Ask yourself one central question: where are you coming from in this draft? Consider whether your stance appropriately matches the stance you started out with, or whether your stance has legitimately evolved.

Organization

One way to check the organization of your draft is to outline it. After numbering the paragraphs, read through each one, jotting down its main idea. Do the main ideas clearly relate to the thesis and to one another? Can you identify any confusing leaps from point to point? Have you left out any important points?

Genre and media

You decided to write in a particular genre, so think again about why you made that choice. Is writing in this genre the best way to achieve your purpose and reach your audience? Does the draft fulfill the requirements of the genre? Would any content in your draft be more effective presented in another medium—for example, as a print handout instead of a Power-Point slide? Should you consider "translating" your work into another

---

FOR MULTILINGUAL WRITERS

Asking an Experienced Writer to Review Your Draft

One good way to make sure that your writing is easy to follow is to have someone else read it. You might ask someone who is experienced in the kind of writing you are working on to read over your draft and to point out any words or patterns that are unclear or ineffective.

medium (see Chapter 3)? Do you need to take any additional steps to make your work as effective as it can be in this medium?

Images and sound

Look closely at the images, audio, and video you have chosen to use. How do they contribute to your draft? Make sure that all visuals and media files are labeled with captions and sources, and remember to refer to visuals and media and to comment on their significance to the rest of your text. Would any information in your draft work better in visual than in verbal form?

10b Get the most from peer review.

In addition to your own critical appraisal and that of your instructor (10c), you will probably want to get responses to your draft from

---

AT A GLANCE

Guidelines for Peer Response

- *Initial thoughts.* What are the main strengths and weaknesses of the draft? What might confuse readers? What is the most important thing the writer says in the draft? What will readers want to know more about?
- *Assignment.* Does the draft carry out the assignment?
- *Title and introduction.* Do the title and introduction tell what the draft is about and catch readers' interest? How else might the draft begin?
- *Thesis and purpose.* Paraphrase the thesis: *In this paper, the writer will. . . .* Does the draft fulfill that promise?
- *Audience.* How does the draft interest and appeal to its audience?
- *Rhetorical stance.* Where does the writer stand? What words indicate the stance?
- *Supporting points.* List the main points, and review them one by one. How well does each point support the thesis? Do any need more explanation? Do any seem confusing or boring?
- *Visuals and design.* Do visuals, if any, add to the key points? Is the design clear and effective?
- *Organization and flow.* Is the writing easy to follow? How effective are transitions within sentences, between sentences, and between paragraphs?
- *Conclusion.* Does the draft conclude memorably? Is there another way it might end?

FOR MULTILINGUAL WRITERS
Understanding Peer Review

If you are not used to giving or receiving criticisms directly, you may be uneasy with a classmate's challenges to your work. However, constructive criticism is appropriate to peer review. Your peers will also expect you to offer your questions, suggestions, and insights.

friends, classmates, or colleagues. In a writing course, you may be asked to respond to the work of your peers as well as to seek responses from them.

Serving as a peer reviewer

One of the main goals of a peer reviewer is to help the writer see his or her draft differently. When you review a draft, you want to *show* the writer what does and doesn't work about particular aspects of the draft. Visually marking the draft can help the writer absorb at a glance the revisions you suggest.

PEER REVIEW: Work with a Writer

Give your full attention to offering as much help as you can.

Make sure that the writer can move forward when you're finished.

Ask...

What does the writer want you to *focus* on for this stage of the draft?

Can you restate the **main points** as you see them?

What **specific** suggestions do you think will improve the draft?

REVIEWING A PRINT DRAFT

When working with a hard copy of a draft, write compliments in the left margin and critiques, questions, and suggestions in the right margin. As long as you explain what your symbols mean, you can also use boxes, circles, single and double underlining, highlighting, or other visual annotations as shorthand for what you have to say about the draft.

REVIEWING A COMPUTER DRAFT

If the draft is an electronic file, the reviewer should save the document in a peer-review folder under an easy-to-recognize name. It's wise to include the writer's name, the assignment, the number of the draft, and the reviewer's initials. For example, the reviewer Ann G. Smith might name the file for the first draft of Javier Jabari's first essay *jabari.essay1.d1.ags*.

The reviewer can then use the word-processing program to add comments, questions, and suggestions to the text. Most such programs have a TRACK CHANGES tool that can show changes to the document in a different color and a COMMENT function that allows you to type a note in the margin. If your word processor doesn't have a COMMENT function, you can comment in footnotes instead.

Reviews of Emily Lesk's draft

On p. 105 are the first three paragraphs of Emily Lesk's draft, as reviewed electronically by two students, Beatrice Kim and Nastassia Lopez. (You'll find earlier appearances of Emily's work in 5g, 6d, and 7a.) Beatrice and Nastassia decided to use highlighting for particular purposes: green for material they found effective, yellow for language that seemed unclear, blue for material that could be expanded, and gray for material that could be deleted.

As this review shows, Nastassia and Bea agree on some of the major problems—and good points—in Emily's draft. The comments on the draft, however, reveal their different responses. You, too, will find that different readers do not always agree on what is effective or ineffective. In addition, you may find that you simply do not agree with their advice.

You can often proceed efficiently by looking first for areas of agreement (*everyone was confused by this sentence—I'd better review it*) or strong disagreement (*one person said my conclusion was "perfect," and someone else said it "didn't conclude"—better look carefully at that paragraph again*).

All-Powerful Coke

I don't drink Coke. Call me picky for disliking the soda's saccharine aftertaste. Call me cheap for choosing a water fountain over a twleve-ounce aluminum can that costs a dollar from a vending machine but only pennies to produce. Even call me unpatriotic for rejecting the potable god that over the last century has come to represent all the enjoyment and ease to be found in our American way of life. But don't call me a hypocrite when I admit that I still identify with Coke and the Coca-Cola culture.

I have a favorite T-shirt that says "Drink Coca-Cola Classic" in Hebrew. It's Israel's standard tourist fare, like little nested dolls in Russia or painted horses in Scandinavia, and before setting foot in the Promised Land three years ago I knew where I could find one. The T-shirt shop in the central block of a Jerusalem shopping center did offer other shirt designs ("Maccabee Beer" was a favorite), but that Coca-Cola shirt was what drew in most of the dollar-carrying tourists. I waited almost twenty minutes for mine, and I watched nearly everyone ahead of me say "the Coke shirt" (and "thanks" in Hebrew).

At the time, I never asked why I wanted the shirt. I do know, though, that the reason I wear it often, despite a hole in the right sleeve, has to do with its power as a conversation piece. Few people notice it without asking something like, "Does that say Coke?" I usually smile and nod. They mumble a compliment and we go our separate ways. But rarely does anyone want to know what language the world's most famous logo is written in. And why should they? Perhaps because Coca-Cola is a cultural icon that shapes American identity.

Comment: I'm not sure your title says enough about what your essay will argue. NL

Comment: The opening sentence is a good attention-getter. Wonder what will come next? NL

Comment: The beginning seems pretty abrupt. BK

Comment: What does this mean?? Will other members of your audience know? BK

Comment: The style of repeating the phrase "call me" is good, but I don't think the first three "call me" statements have much to do with the rest of the paper. NL

Comment: It would be cool to show this. BK

Comment: Not sure you need all these details. Is any of it going to be important later? NL

Comment: one of what? a doll or horse? NL

Comment: Say it in Hebrew? BK

Comment: This transition works really well. I wasn't sure before about where this was going, but the beginning of the paragraph here starts to clue me in. NL

Comment: good detail! Lots of people can relate to a "conversation piece" shirt. NL

Comment: I like the question — but is your next sentence really the answer? NL

Comment: Is this the thesis? Kind of comes out of nowhere. BK

bedfordstmartins.com/everydaywriter
Writing Resources > Working Online

PEER REVIEW: Work with Reviewers

Seek good advice about your draft.

Ask...

What issues do you want reviewers to focus on?

What do they think works and doesn't work in your draft?

Do you need more information to understand their suggestions?

Think about what reviewers want you to do next.

Getting help from peer reviewers

Remember that your reviewers should be acting as coaches, not judges, and that their job is to help you improve your essay as much as possible. Listen to and read their comments carefully. If you don't understand a particular suggestion, ask for clarification, examples, and so on. Remember, too, that reviewers are commenting on your writing, not on *you*, so be open and responsive to what they recommend. But you are the final authority on your essay; you will decide which suggestions to follow and which to disregard.

bedfordstmartins.com/everydaywriter
Student Writing

10c Consult instructor comments.

Instructor comments on any work that you have done can help you identify mistakes, particularly ones that you make repeatedly, and can point you toward larger issues that prevent your writing from being as effective as it could be. Whether or not you will have an opportunity to revise a particular piece of writing, you should look closely at the comments from your instructor.

In responding to student writing, however, instructors sometimes use phrases or comments that are a kind of shorthand—comments that are perfectly clear to the instructor but may be less clear to the students reading them. The instructor comments in the following chart, culled from over a thousand first-year student essays, are among those that you may find most puzzling. Alongside each comment you'll find information intended to allow you to revise as your instructor recommends. If your paper includes a puzzling comment that is not listed here, be sure to ask your instructor what the comment means and how you can fix the problem.

Instructor Comment	Actions to Take in Response
thesis not clear	Make sure that you have a main point, and state it directly. The rest of the paper will need to support the main point, too—this problem cannot be corrected by adding a sentence or two.
trying to do too much *covers too much ground*	Focus your main point more narrowly (7a) so that you can explain your topic fully in a project of the assigned length. You may need to cut back on some material and then provide evidence and details to expand what remains.
hard to follow *not logical* *incoherent* *jumps around* *parts not connected* *transition*	If overall organization is unclear, try mapping or outlining and rearranging your work. (7d) See if transitions and signals or additional explanation will solve the problem.
too general *vague*	Use concrete language and details, and make sure that you have something specific and interesting to say. (23c) If not, reconsider your topic.
underdeveloped *thin* *sparse*	Add examples and details, and be as specific as possible. (23c) You may need to do more research. (Chapters 15–17)
what about the opposition? *one-sided* *condescending* *overbearing*	Add information on why some people disagree with you, and represent their views fairly and completely before you refute them. Recognize that reasonable people may hold views that differ from yours. (14e)
repetitive *you've already said this*	Revise any parts of your writing that repeat an argument, point, word, or phrase; avoid using the same evidence over and over.

continued

Instructor Comment	Actions to Take in Response
awk *awkward*	Ask a peer or your instructor for suggestions about revising awkward sentences. (Chapters 25–30)
syntax *awkward syntax* *convoluted*	Read the sentence aloud to identify the problem; revise or replace the sentence. (Chapters 25–30)
unclear	Find another way to explain what you mean; add any background information or examples that your audience may need to follow your reasoning.
tone too conversational *not an academic voice* *too informal* *colloquial*	Consider your audience and genre, and revise material that may suggest that you are not serious about the topic, audience, or assignment. (Chapter 23)
pompous *stilted* *stiff*	Make sure you understand the connotations of the words you use. Revise material that adds nothing to your meaning, no matter how impressive it sounds. (23a and b)
set up quotation *integrate quotation*	Read the sentence containing the quotation aloud; revise it if it does not make sense as a sentence. Introduce every quotation with information about the source. Explain each quotation's importance to your work. (Chapter 18)
your words? *source?* *cite*	Mark all quotations clearly. Cite paraphrases and summaries of others' ideas. Give credit for help from others, and remember that you are responsible for your own work. (Chapters 17 and 18)
doc	Check the citations to be sure that you include all of the required information, that you punctuate correctly, and that you omit information not required by the documentation style. (Chapters 49–55)

10d Revise.

Approach comments from peer reviewers or from your instructor in several stages. First, read straight through the comments. Take a few minutes to digest the feedback and get some distance from your work. Then make a revision plan—as elaborate or as simple as you want—that prioritizes the changes needed in your next draft.

REVISION: Read All Comments Carefully

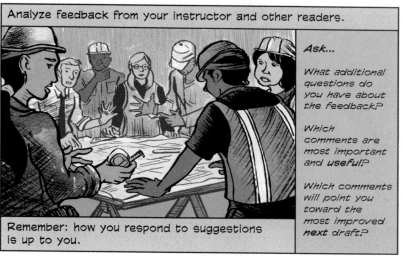

Analyze feedback from your instructor and other readers.

Ask...

What additional questions do you have about the feedback?

Which comments are most important and useful?

Which comments will point you toward the most improved next draft?

Remember: how you respond to suggestions is up to you.

If you have comments from more than one reviewer, you may want to begin by making two lists: (1) areas in which reviewers agree on needed changes, and (2) areas in which they disagree. You will then have to make choices about which advice to heed and which to ignore from both lists. Next, rank the suggestions you've chosen to address.

Focus on comments about your purpose, audience, stance, thesis, and support. Leave any changes to sentences, words, punctuation, and format for later in the process; your revision of bigger-picture issues comes first.

Prepare a file for your revised draft. Use your previous draft as a starting point, renaming it to indicate that it is a revision. (For example, Javier Jabari might rename his file *jabari essay1 d2*, using his name, assignment number, and draft number.)

In the new file, make the changes you identified in your revision plan. Be prepared to revise heavily, if necessary; if comments suggest that your thesis isn't working, for example, you may need to change the topic or the entire direction of your text. Heavy revision is not a sign that there's something wrong with your writing; on the contrary, major revision is a common feature of serious, goal-oriented writing.

Once you are satisfied that your revisions adequately address major concerns, make corrections to sentences, words, and punctuation.

REVISION: Plan Your Next Draft

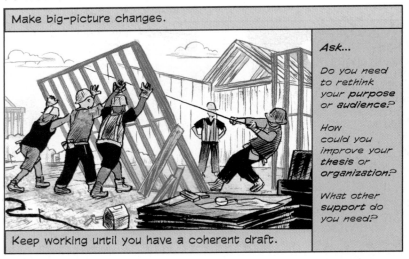

Make big-picture changes.

Ask...

Do you need to rethink your **purpose** or **audience?**

How could you improve your **thesis** or **organization?**

What other **support** do you need?

Keep working until you have a coherent draft.

Thesis

Make sure that your thesis states the topic clearly and comments on what is particularly significant about the topic (7b). In addition, ask yourself whether the thesis is narrowed and focused enough to be thoroughly proven. If not, take time now to refine or limit your thesis further.

When you revise your thesis, remember also to revise the rest of the draft accordingly.

Support

Make sure that each paragraph relates to or supports the thesis and that each paragraph has sufficient detail to support the point it is making. Eliminate unnecessary material, and identify sections that need further details or examples.

Organization

Should any sections or paragraphs be moved to clarify your point or support your thesis more logically? Are there any paragraphs or parts of paragraphs that don't fit with the essay now or that are unnecessary? Look for confusing leaps or omissions, and identify places where transitions would make the writing easier to follow.

Title, introduction, and conclusion

Does the title give information and draw readers in? Does the introduction attract their interest and present the topic in a way that makes them want to keep reading? Does the conclusion leave readers satisfied? Because readers notice beginnings and endings more than other parts of a piece of writing, pay special attention to how you introduce and conclude your work.

Visuals, media, and design

As you check what you've written about your topic, you also need to take a close look at the way your text looks and works. Do your visuals, audio, and video (if any) help you make your points? How can you make this content more effective? Do you use design effectively for your genre and medium? Is your text readable and inviting?

11   Editing and Reflecting

Whether you are writing a wedding invitation, an email to a client, or a history essay, make time to edit and proofread what you write. Editing involves fine-tuning the details of sentence structure, grammar, usage, punctuation, and spelling. Finally, careful proofreading aims at a perfect copy. For important writing, reflecting on how you accomplished the task can prepare you to achieve future writing goals.

11a   Edit.

Once you have revised a draft for content and organization, look closely at your sentences and words. Turning a "blah" sentence into a memorable one—or finding exactly the right word to express a thought—can result in writing that is really worth reading. As with life, variety is the spice of sentences. You can add variety to your sentences by looking closely at their length, structure, and opening patterns.

EDITING: Polish Your Draft

Don't forget the details.

Ask...

What does each **sentence** contribute to your purpose?

How can you choose **words** more effectively?

How can you improve your **tone** or **style**?

Follow appropriate conventions for your genre and audience.

Sentence length

Too many short sentences, especially one following another, can sound like a series of blasts on a car horn, whereas a steady stream of long sentences may tire or confuse readers. Most writers aim for some variety in length, breaking up a series of fairly long sentences with a very brief one.

In examining the following paragraph from her essay, Emily Lesk discovered that the sentences were all fairly long. In editing, she decided to shorten the second sentence, thereby offering a shorter sentence between two long ones.

Student Writing

In other words, Coca-Cola has hammered itself into our perceptions — both conscious and subconscious — of an American cultural identity by equating itself with media that define American culture. ~~When~~ *As* the omnipresent ~~general~~ magazine ~~that marked the earlier part of the century fell by the wayside under~~ *gave way to* television~~'s power,~~ Coke was there from the beginning. In its 1996 recap of the previous fifty years in industry history, the publication *Beverage Industry* cites Coca-Cola as a frontrunner in the very first form of television advertising: sponsorship of entire programs such as, in the case of Coke, *The Bob Dixon Show* and *The Adventures of Kit Carson.*

Sentence openings

Opening sentence after sentence in the same way results in a jerky, abrupt, or choppy rhythm. You can vary sentence openings by beginning with a dependent clause, a phrase, an adverb, a conjunctive adverb, or a coordinating conjunction (30b). Another paragraph in Emily Lesk's essay tells the story of how she got her Coke T-shirt in Israel. Before she revised, every sentence in the paragraph opened with the subject, so Emily decided to delete some examples and vary her sentence openings. The final version (which also appears in 5g) is a dramatic and easy-to-read paragraph.

~~I have a favorite T-shirt that says "Drink Coca-Cola Classic" in Hebrew. It's~~

~~Israel's standard tourist fare, like little nested dolls in Russia or painted horses in~~

Even ~~Seandinavia, and~~ before setting foot in ~~the Promised Land~~ *Israel* three years ago, I

exactly   *the Coke shirt.*   *'s Ben Yehuda Street*
knew where I could find ~~it.~~ The shop in the central block of a Jerusalem

~~shopping center~~ did offer other shirt designs, ("Macabee Beer" was a favorite),

but ~~that Coca-Cola shirt~~ was what drew in most of the dollar-carrying tourists.

While waiting   *my shirt,*
~~I waited~~ almost twenty minutes for ~~mine, and~~ I watched nearly everyone

todah rabah [thank you very much]."
ahead of me say "the Coke shirt," ~~(and "thanks" in Hebrew).~~

the one with a bright white "Drink Coca-Cola Classic"
written in Hebrew cursive across the chest

Opening with it *and* there

As you go over the opening sentences of your draft, look especially at those beginning with *it* or *there*. Sometimes these words can create a special emphasis, as in *It was a dark and stormy night*. But they can also appear too often. Another, more subtle problem with these openings is that they may be used to avoid taking responsibility for a statement. The following sentence can be improved by editing:

The university must
▶ ~~It is necessary to~~ raise student fees.

Tone

Tone refers to the attitude that a writer's language conveys toward the topic and the audience. In examining the tone of your draft, think about the nature of the topic, your own attitude toward it, and that of your intended audience. Does your language create the tone you want to achieve (humorous, serious, impassioned, and so on), and is that tone an appropriate one, given your audience and topic?

Word choice

Word choice—or diction—offers writers an opportunity to put their personal stamp on a piece of writing. Becoming aware of the kinds of words you use should help you get the most mileage out of each word. Check for connotations, or associations, of words and make sure you consider how any use of slang, jargon, or emotional language may affect your audience (see 23a–b).

Spell checkers

While these software tools won't catch every spelling error or identify all problems of style, they can be very useful. Most professional writers use their spell checkers religiously. Remember, however, that spell checkers are limited; they don't recognize most proper names, foreign words, or specialized language, and they do not recognize homonym errors (misspelling *there* as *their*, for example). (See 23e.)

Document design

Before you produce a copy for final proofreading, reconsider one last time the format and the "look" you want your document to have. This is one last opportunity to think carefully about the visual appearance of your final draft. (For more on document design, see Chapter 9. For more on the design conventions of different disciplines, see Chapters 61–65.)

AT A GLANCE

Word Choice

- Are the nouns primarily abstract and general or *concrete* and *specific*? Too many abstract and general nouns can result in boring prose.

- Are there too many nouns in relation to the number of verbs? This sentence is heavy and boring: *The effect of the overuse of nouns in writing is the placement of strain on the verbs.* Instead, say this: *Overusing nouns places a strain on the verbs.*

- How many verbs are forms of *be — be, am, is, are, was, were, being, been*? If *be* verbs account for more than about a third of your total verbs, you are probably overusing them.

- Are verbs *active* wherever possible? Passive verbs are harder to read and remember than active ones. Although the passive voice has many uses, your writing will gain strength and energy if you use active verbs.

- Are your words *appropriate*? Check to be sure they are not too fancy — or too casual.

Proofreading the final draft

Take time for one last, careful proofreading, which means reading to correct any typographical errors or other inconsistencies in spelling and punctuation. To proofread most effectively, read through the copy aloud, making sure that you've used punctuation marks correctly and consistently, that all sentences are complete (unless you've used intentional fragments or run-ons for special effects)—and that no words are missing. Then go through the copy again, this time reading backward so that you can focus on each individual word and its spelling.

A student's revised draft

Following are the first three paragraphs from Emily Lesk's edited and proofread draft that she submitted to her instructor. Compare these paragraphs with those from her reviewed draft in 10b.

Student Writer

Emily Lesk

Emily Lesk
Professor Arráez
Electric Rhetoric
November 15, 2011

Red, White, and Everywhere

America, I have a confession to make: I don't drink Coke. But don't call me a hypocrite just because I am still the proud owner of a bright red shirt that advertises it. Just call me an American.

Fig. 1. Hebrew Coca-Cola T-shirt.
Personal photograph.

Even before setting foot in Israel three years ago, I knew exactly where I could find the Coke shirt. The shop in the central block of Jerusalem's Ben Yehuda Street did offer other shirt designs, but the one with a bright white "Drink Coca-Cola Classic" written in Hebrew cursive across the chest was what drew in most of the dollar-carrying tourists. While waiting almost twenty minutes for my

shirt (depicted in Fig. 1), I watched nearly everyone ahead of me say "the Coke shirt, *todah rabah* [thank you very much]."

At the time, I never thought it strange that I wanted one, too. After having absorbed sixteen years of Coca-Cola propaganda through everything from NBC's Saturday morning cartoon lineup to the concession stand at Camden Yards (the Baltimore Orioles' ballpark), I associated the shirt with singing along to the "Just for the Taste of It" jingle and with America's favorite pastime, not with a brown fizzy beverage I refused to consume. When I later realized the immensity of Coke's corporate power, I felt somewhat manipulated, but that didn't stop me from wearing the shirt. I still don it often, despite the growing hole in the right sleeve, because of its power as a conversation piece. Few Americans notice it without asking something like "Does that say Coke?" I usually smile and nod. Then they mumble a one-word compliment, and we go our separate ways. But rarely do they want to know what language the internationally recognized logo is written in. And why should they? They are interested in what they can relate to as Americans: a familiar red-and-white logo, not a foreign language. Through nearly a century of brilliant advertising strategies, the Coca-Cola Company has given Americans not only a thirst-quenching beverage but a cultural icon that we have come to claim as our own.

 bedfordstmartins.com/everydaywriter
Student Writing

11b Reflect.

Research demonstrates a connection between careful reflection and learning: thinking back on what you've learned and assessing it help make that learning stick. As a result, first-year college writing courses are increasingly encouraging students to take time for such reflection. Whether or not your instructor asks you to write a formal reflection, whenever you finish a major piece of writing or a writing course, you should make time to think back over the experience and see what lessons you can learn from it.

Reflecting on your development as a writer

Here are some questions to get you started reflecting productively on your writing:

- What lessons have you learned from writing—from an individual piece of writing or from an entire writing course?
- From what you have learned, what can you apply to the work you will do in other classes?
- What about your writing do you feel most confident about—and why? When did you begin to develop this confidence?

- What about your writing do you find needs additional work, and what plans do you have for improving?
- What confusions did you have while writing, and what did you do to resolve them?
- What major questions do you still have about writing or about an individual piece of writing?
- How has writing helped to clarify your thinking, extend your knowledge, or deepen your understanding?
- Identify a favorite passage of your writing, and then try to articulate what about it pleases you. Can you apply what you learn from this analysis to other writing situations?
- How would you describe your development as a writer?

Portfolios

You may find it useful — or you may be required — to select samples for inclusion in a print or online portfolio of your written work. In preparing a portfolio, use these tips:

- *Consider your purpose and audience.* Do you want to fulfill course requirements for an instructor, show work to a prospective employer, keep a record of what you've done for personal reasons, or something else? Answering these questions will help you decide what to include in the portfolio and whether it should be in print or electronic form.
- *Based on the portfolio's purpose, decide on the number of entries.* You may decide to include a wide range of materials — from essays, problem sets, and photos to Web texts, multimedia presentations, a résumé, or anything else that is relevant — if readers can select only the pieces that interest them. For a portfolio that will be read from beginning to end, however, you should limit yourself to five to seven examples of your writing. You might include an academic essay that argues a claim, a personal essay, a brief report, writing based on research, significant correspondence, timed writing, or other work that you think shows your strengths as a writer.
- *Consider organization.* What arrangement — in chronological order, by genre, by topic — will make most sense to readers?
- *Think carefully about layout and design.* Will you include a menu, a table of contents, or appendices? How will you use color, font and type size, and other elements of design to enhance your portfolio (see Chapter 9)? Remember to label and date each piece of writing in the portfolio to help readers follow along easily. For print portfolios, number pages in consecutive order.

- *Edit and proofread* each piece in your portfolio and the reflective statement. Ask for responses from peers or an instructor.

Reflective statements

One of the most common writing assignments today is a reflective statement—often in the form of a letter, memo, or home page—that explains and analyzes the work a student has done in a writing course.

To create a reflective statement, think carefully about the impression it should give, and make sure your tone and style set the stage appropriately. Reflect on the strengths and weaknesses of your writing, using specific examples to provide evidence for each point you make. What are the most important things you have learned about writing—and about yourself as a writer—during the course?

If the reflective statement introduces your portfolio, follow your instructor's guidelines carefully. Unless asked to do otherwise, describe the portfolio's contents and explain why you have chosen each piece.

STUDENT REFLECTIVE STATEMENT

Here is a shortened version of the cover letter that James Kung wrote to accompany his first-year writing portfolio.

Student Writer

James Kung

December 6, 2011

Dear Professor Ashdown:

"Writing is difficult and takes a long time." This simple yet powerful statement has been uttered so many times in our class that it has essentially become our motto. During this class, my persuasive writing skills have improved dramatically, thanks to many hours spent writing, revising, polishing, and thinking about my topic. The various drafts, revisions, and other materials in my portfolio show this improvement.

I entered this first-quarter Writing and Rhetoric class with both strengths and weaknesses. I have always written fairly well-organized essays. However, despite this strength, I struggled throughout the term to narrow and define the various aspects of my research-based argument.

The first aspect of my essay that I had trouble narrowing and defining was my major claim, or my thesis statement. In my "Proposal for Research-Based

Argument," I proposed to argue about the case of Wen Ho Lee, the Los Alamos scientist accused of copying restricted government documents.

I stated, "The Wen Ho Lee incident deals with the persecution of not only one man, but of a whole ethnic group." You commented that the statement was a "sweeping claim" that would be "hard to support."

I spent weeks trying to rework that claim. Finally, as seen in my "Writer's Notebook 10/16/11," I realized that I had chosen the Lee case because of my belief that the political inactivity of Asian Americans contributed to the case against Lee. Therefore, I decided to focus on this issue in my thesis. Later I once again revised my claim, stating that the political inactivity did not cause but rather contributed to racial profiling in the Wen Ho Lee case.

I also had trouble defining my audience. I briefly alluded to the fact that my audience was a "typical American reader." However, I later decided to address my paper to an Asian American audience for two reasons. First, it would establish a greater ethos for myself as a Chinese American. Second, it would enable me to target the people the Wen Ho Lee case most directly affects: Asian Americans. As a result, in my final research-based argument, I was much more sensitive to the needs and concerns of my audience, and my audience trusted me more.

I hope to continue to improve my writing of research-based arguments.

Sincerely,

James Kung

James Kung

bedfordstmartins.com/everydaywriter
Writing Portfolios

Critical Thinking and Argument

To repeat what others have said requires
education; to challenge it requires brains.

— MARY PETTIBONE POOLE

Critical Thinking and Argument

12 Critical Reading *123*
  a Preview the text *123*
  b Read and annotate *125*
  c Summarize the main ideas *128*
  d Analyze the text *129*
  e STUDENT CRITICAL READING OF A TEXT (EXCERPT) *133*

13 Analyzing Arguments *136*
  a Think critically about argument *137*
  b Recognize cultural contexts *138*
  c Identify an argument's basic appeals *138*
  d Analyze the elements of argument *141*
  e Think critically about fallacies *144*
  f STUDENT RHETORICAL ANALYSIS *148*

14 Constructing Arguments *151*
  a Understand what counts as argument *151*
  b Make a claim and formulate a working thesis *153*
  c Examine your assumptions *154*
  d Shape your appeal to your audience *154*
  e Establish credibility through ethical appeals *154*
  f Use effective logical appeals *156*
  g Use appropriate emotional appeals *161*
  h Consult sources *163*
  i Organize your argument *164*
  j Consider design issues *166*
  k STUDENT ARGUMENT ESSAY *167*

For visual analysis Look carefully at the illustration on the front of this tab. What do you think this image suggests about critical thinking and argument?

Critical Reading **12**

F ilm critic Roger Ebert writes in a notebook as he watches movies, tearing out the pages as he fills them, until he "looks as though he's sitting on top of a cloud of paper," as an *Esquire* profile observed. Reading critically means questioning and commenting thoughtfully on a text—whether an assignment for a psychology class, a graphic novel, a business email, or a YouTube video. Any method you use to keep track of your questions and make yourself concentrate on a text can help you become a better critical reader.

12a Preview the text.

Find out all you can about a text before beginning to look closely at it, considering its context, author, subject, genre, and design.

PREVIEWING THE CONTEXT

- Where have you encountered the work? Are you encountering it in its original context? For example, an essay in a collection of readings may have been previously published in a magazine; a speech you watch on YouTube may have been delivered to a live or televised audience; a painting on a museum wall may have been created for a wealthy patron in a distant country centuries earlier.

- What can you infer from the original or current context of the work about its intended audience and purpose?

LEARNING ABOUT THE AUTHOR OR CREATOR

- What information can you find about the author or creator of the text?

- What purpose, expertise, and possible agenda might you expect this person to have? Where do you think the author or creator is coming from in this text?

CRITICAL READING: Preview

What do you expect to happen in this text?

Ask...

What does the title tell you? Who created this work?

When, where, and how are you encountering the text?

How do genre, media, and design affect your expectations?

Prepare to engage the text.

PREVIEWING THE SUBJECT

- What do you know about the subject of the text?
- What opinions do you have about the subject, and on what are your opinions based?
- What would you like to learn about the subject?
- What do you expect the main point to be? Why?

CONSIDERING THE TITLE, MEDIUM, GENRE, AND DESIGN

- What does the title (or caption or other heading) indicate?
- What do you know about the medium (or media) in which the work appears? Is it a text on the Web, a printed advertising brochure, a speech stored in iTunes, an animated cartoon on television, or some combination of media? What role does the medium play in achieving the purpose and connecting to the audience?
- What is the genre of the text—and what can it help illuminate about the intended audience or purpose? Why might the authors or creators have chosen this genre?
- How is the text presented? What do you notice about its formatting, use of color, visuals or illustrations, overall design, general appearance, and other design features?

TALKING THE TALK
Critical Thinking

"Are criticizing and thinking critically the same thing?" *Criticize* can sometimes mean "find fault with," and you certainly don't have to be relentlessly negative to think critically. Instead, critical thinking means, first and foremost, asking good questions — and not simply accepting what you see at face value. By asking not only what words and images mean, but also how meaning gets across, critical thinkers consider why a text makes a particular claim, what writers may be leaving out or ignoring, and how to tell whether evidence is accurate and believable. If you're considering questions like these, then you're thinking critically.

Sample preview of an assigned text

A student in a first-year composition class who had been asked to read and analyze Abraham Lincoln's Gettysburg Address made preview notes, a few of which are excerpted here.

> President Lincoln delivered the speech at a ceremony dedicating a national cemetery for Civil War soldiers. Crowds of people gathered in a field near Gettysburg, Pennsylvania, on November 19, 1863, to listen to him and other speakers. In July of that year, a Civil War battle that ended with 7,500 soldiers killed had taken place near where Lincoln spoke.
>
> My textbook has the most famous version of the speech — but nobody knows for sure exactly what Lincoln said 150 years ago. There's obviously no audio recording of him giving the speech! Newspapers at the time reported what listeners heard, but he didn't write the speech out until later.
>
> Lincoln gave this speech in the middle of the war, dedicating a national cemetery, so it must have been a pretty solemn occasion. He probably wanted his audience to think about why the war was worth fighting. He probably also thought that some of the dead soldiers' families might be there listening — as well as people who had seen the battle or its aftermath. Did he think about the possibility that future generations would read and think about this speech? As the leader of the Union, he was probably very interested in showing why the United States needed to stay together.

12b Read and annotate.

As you read a text for the first time, mark it up (if the medium allows you to do so) or take notes. Consider the text's content, author, intended audience, and genre and design.

CRITICAL READING: Read Carefully

What do you find out by going through the text from start to finish?

Get everything you can from your first reading.

Ask...

How does the text fit with your expectations?

What are the major points in the text? How are they supported?

How well do you understand the content?

READING FOR CONTENT

- What do you find confusing or unclear about the text? Where can you look for explanations or more information? Do you need background information in order to understand fully?
- What key terms and ideas—or key patterns—do you see? What key images stick in your mind?
- What sources or other works does this text cite, refer to, or allude to?
- How does the content fit with what you already know?
- Which points do you agree with? Which do you disagree with? Why?

READING FOR AUTHOR/CREATOR AND AUDIENCE

- Do the authors or creators present themselves as you anticipated in your preview?
- For what audience was this text created? Are you part of its intended audience?
- What underlying assumptions can you identify in the text?
- Are the medium and genre appropriate for the topic, audience, and purpose?

READING FOR DESIGN, COMPOSITION, AND STYLE

- Is the design appropriate for the subject and genre?
- Does the composition serve a purpose—for instance, does the layout help you see what is more and less important in the text?
- Do words, images, sound, and other media work together well?
- How would you describe the style of the text? What contributes to this impression—word choice? references to research or popular culture? formatting? color? something else?

Sample annotation of an assigned text

After previewing the context, author, subject, and other aspects of the following article from the online magazine *Good*, a student assigned to write about the article annotated the text as shown.

Is the Internet Warping Our Brains? ❶
CORD JEFFERSON, SENIOR EDITOR, *GOOD*

New research from Columbia University psychologist Betsy Sparrow ❷ suggests that Google, your favorite search engine turned email host turned social network, might actually be making you less likely to absorb information. Sparrow's study, "Google Effects on Memory: Cognitive Consequences of Having Information at Our Fingertips," found that people who were confident they could use the internet to access some bit of information in the future were less likely to recall that information themselves. ❸ However, they were more likely to recall how to go about accessing the information if necessary. Sparrow calls it "outsourcing data," letting the internet take care of some stuff so we can save our brains for things that can't be Googled, like parents' birthdays and coworkers' names. ❹

Is this a bad thing? ❺ Not necessarily, says Sparrow. For instance, for years people in the educational community have known that rote learning—that is, forcing children to memorize facts and dates—is a poor way to educate. ❻ If that's the case, allowing computers to do some of the memorizing for us might be a way to focus more on the more philosophical aspects of learning. ❼

"Perhaps ❽ those who teach in any context, be they college professors, doctors or business leaders, will become increasingly focused on imparting greater understanding of ideas and ways of thinking, and less focused on memorization," Sparrow told *Time*.

Of course, while you might think that this research suggests people on the internet are using less of their brains than those not online, you'd be wrong. Back in 2008, the neuroscientist Gary Small discovered the difference in brain activity between a person reading a book and a person searching for information on Google. According to Small, the person searching the internet was using a lot more of their mind than the person simply reading a book. **9** Like Sparrow, Small says he's not willing to say if the difference is bad or good, just that our minds react entirely differently when stimulated by the internet as opposed to other forms of media. **10**

[Video: Gary Small discusses "Your Brain on Google" (2:43)] **11**

1 This sounds like a leading question to me — makes me think the author's answer must be "yes."

2 Look for more information on this psychologist and her research.

3 How did the research show this? What were the participants asked to do?

4 Haven't we done this in other ways already — like taking notes so we don't have to remember?

5 Interesting question! Not sure how I would answer.

6 Check out this link to see what the arguments are against "rote learning."

7 This sounds right. But are we really going to become more philosophical if we don't have to remember things? What if we just get more distracted by trivia?

8 Or perhaps not! This seems pretty optimistic.

9 Wow! *Seems* like it should be a good thing to use more of our brain. But what does it really mean?

10 So the researchers here aren't ready to draw conclusions about what the differences mean for us. (Not that people would stop Googling if it turned out to be a bad thing.)

11 Watch a little of this to see if it might have important information to add.

12c Summarize the main ideas.

When you feel that you have read and thoroughly understood the text, try to summarize the contents in your own words. A summary *briefly* captures the main ideas of a text and omits information that is less important. Try to identify the key points in the text, find the essential evidence supporting those points, and explain the contents concisely and fairly, so that a reader unfamiliar with the original can make sense of it all. Deciding what to leave out can make summarizing a tricky task—but mastering this skill can serve you well in all the reading you do in your academic, professional, and civic life. To test your understanding—and to avoid unintentional plagiarism—it's wise to put the text aside while you write your summary. (For more information on writing a summary, see 17f.)

CRITICAL READING: Summarize

Sample summary of an assigned text

A student summarized the article "Is the Internet Warping Our Brains?" (12b) as shown below.

> The writer discusses two recent studies, one from 2011 and one from 2008, looking at how Internet use affects a person's mind. The 2011 study, by psychologist Betsy Sparrow, showed that if a person expects to be able to use Google to get information, then he or she is less likely to remember that information. Sparrow doesn't see this result as necessarily negative. She hopes that the widespread use of Google might lead educators to focus on "imparting greater understanding of ideas" rather than on "rote learning," which the writer says has been shown to be a bad way to teach students. (A link explains more about "rote learning.") The 2008 study, by neuroscientist Gary Small, shows that using the Internet actually activates more of a person's brain than reading a book. Like Sparrow, Small didn't draw conclusions about whether Internet use is therefore better or worse for a person's mind. It's just different.

12d Analyze the text.

When you feel that you understand the meaning of the text, move on to your analysis. You may want to begin the process by asking additional questions about the text.

CRITICAL READING: Analyze

How does the text get its meaning across?

Ask...

How does the text accomplish its purposes?

Are the text and its creator credible? Are their assumptions valid?

How effective are the evidence, support, and design?

Assess your overall impression.

ANALYZING IDEAS AND EXAMPLES

- What are the main points in this text? Are they implied or explicitly stated?
- Which points do you agree with? Which do you disagree with? Why?
- Does anything in the text surprise you? Why, or why not?
- What kind of examples does the text use? What other kinds of evidence does the text offer to back up the main points? Can you think of other examples or evidence that should have been included?
- Are viewpoints other than those of the author or creator included and treated fairly?
- How trustworthy are the sources the text cites or refers to?
- What assumptions does the text make? Are those assumptions valid? Why, or why not?

ANALYZING FOR OVERALL IMPRESSION

- Do the authors or creators achieve their purpose? Why, or why not?
- What intrigues, puzzles, or irritates you about the text? Why?
- What else would you like to know?

TALKING THE TALK

Visual Texts

"How can an image be a text?" In its traditional sense, a *text* involves words on paper. But we spend at least as much time reading and analyzing images — including moving images — as we spend on printed words. So it makes sense to broaden the definition of "text" to include anything that sends a message. That's why images, ads, videos, films, and the like are often called *visual texts*.

Sample analysis of a text

Following is a Pulitzer Prize–winning photograph (by Craig F. Walker of the *Denver Post*) and its caption. This image appeared as part of a series documenting the experiences of a Colorado teenager, Ian Fisher, who joined the U.S. Army to fight in Iraq.

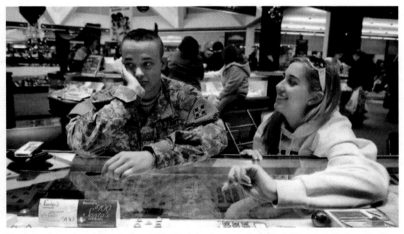

During a weekend home from his first assignment at Fort Carson, Colorado, Ian walked through a Denver-area mall with his new girlfriend, Kayla Spitzlberger, on December 15, 2007, and asked whether she wanted to go ring shopping. She was excited, but working out the financing made him nervous. They picked out the engagement ring in about five minutes, but Ian wouldn't officially propose until Christmas Day in front of her family. The couple had met in freshman math class but never really dated until now. She wrote to him during basic training and decided to give Ian a chance. The engagement would end before Valentine's Day.

A student's analysis of this photograph made the following points:

The couple are in the center of the photo—and at the center of our attention. But at this moment of choosing an engagement ring, they do not look "engaged" with each other. Kayla looks excited but uncertain, as if she knows that Ian feels doubts, but she hopes he will change his mind. She is looking right at him, with her body leaning toward him but her head leaning away: she looks very tentative. Ian is looking away from Kayla, and the expression on his face suggests that he's already having second thoughts about the expense of the ring (we see his wallet on the counter by his elbow) and perhaps even about asking Kayla to marry him. The accompanying caption helps us interpret the image, telling us about the couple's brief history together and noting that the engagement will last less than two months after this moment. But the message comes through pretty clearly without words.

Ian and Kayla look as if they're trying on roles in this photograph. She looks ready to take the plunge, and he is resisting. These attitudes conform to stereotypical gender roles for a man and woman considering marriage (or going shopping, for that matter). The woman is expected to want the marriage and the ring; the man knows that he shouldn't show too much enthusiasm about weddings and shopping. It's hard for the reader to tell whether Ian and Kayla really feel that they are making good or careful choices for their situation at this moment or whether they're just doing what they think they're supposed to do under the circumstances.

The reader also can't tell how the presence of the photographer, Craig F. Walker, affected the couple's actions. The photo is part of a series of images documenting Ian Fisher's life after joining the military, so Walker had probably spent a lot of time with Ian before this photo was taken. Did Ian want to give a particular impression of himself on this day? Were he and Kayla trying on "adult" roles in this situation? Were they feeling pressure to produce a memorable moment for the camera? And what was Walker thinking when he accompanied them to the mall and took this photograph? Did he foresee the end of their engagement when he captured this revealing moment? What was his agenda?

12e Student critical reading of a text (excerpt)

Following are excerpts from a student essay by Shuqiao Song based on her critical reading of Alison Bechdel's graphic memoir *Fun Home: A Family Tragicomic*. Shuqiao's critical reading involved looking closely at the words, at the images, and at how the words and images together create a complex story.

Student Writer

Shuqiao Song

For information on Shuqiao Song's PowerPoint presentation of this essay, see 3c.

bedfordstmartins.com/everydaywriter
Student Writing

Student Writing

Shuqiao Song

Dr. Andrea Lunsford

English 87N

13 March 2012

Residents of a Dys*FUN*ctional *HOME*

In a 2009 online interview, comic artist Alison Bechdel remarked, "I love words, and I love pictures. But especially, I love them together—in a mystical way that I can't even explain" ("Stuck"). Indeed, in her graphic novel memoir, *Fun Home: A Family Tragicomic,* text and image work together in a mystical way: text *and* image. But using both image and text results not in a simple summation but in a strange relationship—as strange as the relationship between Alison Bechdel and her father. These strange pairings have an alluring quality that makes Bechdel's *Fun Home* compelling; for her, both text and image are necessary. As Bechdel tells and shows us, alone, words can fail; alone, images deceive. Yet her life story ties both concepts inextricably to her memories and revelations such that only the interplay of text and image offers the reader the rich complexity, honesty, and possibilities in Bechdel's quest to understand the past. . . .

Song 3   Student Writing

The Bechdels' elaborately restored house is the gilded, but tense, context of young Alison's familial relationships and a metaphor for her father's deceptions. "He used his skillful artifice not to make things, but to make things appear to be what they were not," Bechdel notes alongside an image of her father taking a photo of their family, shown in Fig. 2 (*Fun* 16). The scene represents the nature of her father's artifice; her father is *posing* a photo, an image of their family.

Fig. 2. Alison Bechdel's father posing a family photo (Bechdel, *Fun* 16).

In that same scene, Bechdel also shows her own sleight of hand; she manipulates the scene and reverses her father's role and her own to show young Alison taking the photograph of the family and her father posing in Alison's place (Fig. 3). In the image, young Alison symbolizes Bechdel in the present— looking back through the camera lens to create a

Fig. 3. Alison and her father trade places (Bechdel, *Fun* 17).

Song 4

portrait of her family. But unlike her father, she isn't using false images to deceive. Bechdel overcomes the treason of images by confessing herself as an "artificer" to her audience (*Fun* 16). Bechdel doesn't villainize the illusory nature of images; she repurposes their illusory power to reinterpret her memories. . . .

Song 8

Works Cited

Bechdel, Alison. *Fun Home*. Boston: Houghton Mifflin, 2006. Print.

---. "Stuck in Vermont 109: Alison Bechdel." *YouTube*. YouTube, 13 Dec. 2008. Web. 6 Feb. 2009.

13 Analyzing Arguments

In one important sense, all language has an argumentative edge. When you greet friends, you wish to convince them that you're glad to see them; when advertisers pay for spots that appear alongside your social networking page, they want to persuade you to click and shop. Even apparently objective news reporting has strong argumentative overtones: when a news outlet highlights a particular story, for example, the editors are arguing that this subject is more important than others. Since argument is so pervasive, you need to be able to recognize and use it effectively — and to question your own arguments as well as those put forth by others.

AT A GLANCE

Analyzing an Argument

Here are some questions that can help you judge the effectiveness of an argument:

- What conclusions about the argument can you reach by playing both the believing and the doubting game? (13a)
- What cultural contexts inform the argument, and what do they tell you about where the writer is coming from? (13b)
- What emotional, ethical, and logical appeals is the writer making in support of the argument? (13c)
- How has the writer established credibility to write about the topic? (13c)
- What is the claim (or arguable statement)? Is the claim qualified in any way? (13d)
- What reasons and assumptions support and underlie the claim? (13d)
- What additional evidence backs up the assumption and claim? How current and reliable are the sources? (13d)
- How does the writer use images, graphics, or other visuals to support the argument?
- What fallacies can you identify, and what effect do they have on the argument's persuasiveness? (13e)
- What is the overall impression you get from analyzing the argument? Are you convinced?

13a Think critically about argument.

Critical thinking is a crucial component of argument, for it guides you in recognizing, formulating, and examining arguments. Here are some ways to think critically about argument:

- *Check understanding.* First, make sure you understand what is being argued and why. If you need to find out more about an unfamiliar subject to grasp the argument, do the research.
- *Play the believing—and the doubting—game.* Begin by playing the *believing game:* put yourself in the position of the person creating the argument to see the topic from that person's point of view as much as possible. Once you have given the argument sympathetic attention, play the *doubting game:* look skeptically at each claim, and examine each piece of evidence to see how well (or poorly) it supports the claim. Eventually, this process of believing and doubting will become natural.

- *Ask pertinent questions.* Whether you are thinking about others' ideas or your own, you should question unstated purposes and assumptions, the writer's qualifications, the context, the goal of the argument, and the evidence presented. What objections might be made to the argument?

- *Interpret and assess information.* All information that comes to you has a perspective—a spin. Your job is to identify the perspective and assess it, examining its sources and finding out what you can about its context.

- *Assess your own arguments.* The ultimate goal of all critical thinking is to reach your own conclusions. These, too, you must question and assess.

13b Recognize cultural contexts.

To understand as fully as possible the arguments of others, pay attention to clues to cultural context and to where the writer or creator is coming from. Put yourself in the position of the person creating the argument before looking skeptically at every claim and examining every piece of evidence. Above all, watch out for your own assumptions as you analyze what you read or see. For example, just because you assume that the use of statistics as support for your argument holds more water than, say, precedent drawn from religious belief, you can't assume that all writers agree with you. Take a writer's cultural beliefs into account before you begin to analyze an argument. (See Chapter 20.)

13c Identify an argument's basic appeals.

Aristotle categorized argumentative appeals into three types: emotional appeals that speak to readers' hearts and values (known to the ancient Greeks as *pathos*), ethical appeals that support the writer's character (*ethos*), and logical appeals that use facts and evidence (*logos*).

Emotional appeals

Emotional appeals stir your emotions and remind you of deeply held values. When politicians argue that the country needs more tax relief, they almost always use examples of one or more families they have met, stressing the concrete ways in which a tax cut would improve the quality of their lives. Doing so creates a strong emotional appeal. Some have criticized the use of emotional appeals in argument, claiming that they are a form of manipulation intended to mislead an audience. But emotional appeals are an important part of almost every argument. Critical readers are perfectly capable of "talking back" to such appeals by analyzing them, deciding which are acceptable and which are not.

The accompanying photo shows protesters at an Occupy Wall Street demonstration outside the New York Stock Exchange. The protesters' signs range from a simple logo for the United Auto Workers union to hand-painted cardboard slogans ("This is patriotic") to an American flag. To what emotions are the protesters appealing? Do you find this appeal effective, manipulative, or both? Would you accept this argument?

Ethical appeals

Ethical appeals support the credibility, moral character, and goodwill of the argument's creator. These appeals are especially important for critical readers to recognize and evaluate. We may respect and admire an athlete, for example, but should we invest in the mutual funds the athlete promotes? To identify ethical appeals in arguments, ask yourself these questions: How does the creator of the argument show that he or she has really done the homework on the subject and is knowledge-able and credible about it? What sort of character does he or she build, and how? More important, is that character trustworthy? What does the creator of the argument do to show that he or she has the best interests of an audience in mind? Do those best interests match your own, and, if not, how does that alter the effectiveness of the argument?

Logical appeals

Logical appeals are viewed as especially trustworthy: "The facts don't lie," some say. Of course, facts are not the only type of logical appeals, which also include firsthand evidence drawn from observations, inter-views, surveys and questionnaires, experiments, and personal experi-ence; and secondhand evidence drawn from authorities, the testimony of others, statistics, and other print and online sources. Critical readers need to examine logical appeals just as carefully as emotional and ethical ones. What is the source of the logical appeal—and is that source trustworthy? Are all terms defined clearly? Has the logical evidence presented been taken out of context, and, if so, does that change its meaning?

Analyzing appeals in a visual argument

The poster below, from TurnAround, an organization devoted to helping victims of domestic violence, is "intended to strike a chord with abusers as well as their victims." The dramatic combination of words

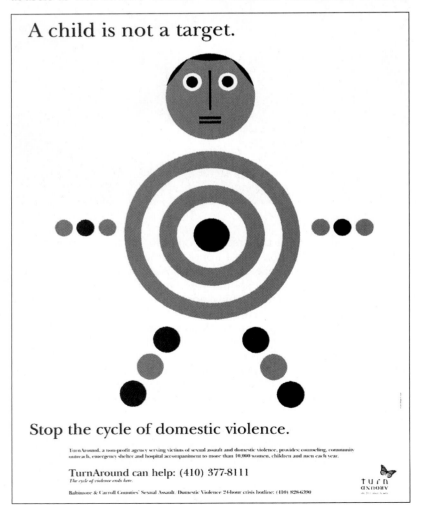

and image builds on an analogy between a child and a target and makes strong emotional and ethical appeals.

The bull's-eye that draws your attention to the center of the poster is probably the first thing you notice when you look at the image. Then you may observe that the "target" is, in fact, a child's body; it also has arms, legs, and a head with wide, staring eyes. The heading at the upper left, "A child is not a target," reinforces the bull's-eye/child connection.

This poster's stark image and headline appeal to viewers' emotions, offering the uncomfortable reminder that children are often the victims of domestic violence. The design causes viewers to see a target first and only afterward recognize that the target is actually a child—an unsettling experience. But the poster also offers ethical appeals ("Turn-Around can help") to show that the organization is credible and that it supports the worthwhile goal of ending "the cycle of domestic violence" by offering counseling and other support services. Finally, it uses the logical appeal of a statistic, noting that TurnAround has served "more than 10,000 women, children and men each year" and giving specific information about where to get help.

13d Analyze the elements of argument.

According to philosopher Stephen Toulmin's framework for analyzing arguments, most arguments contain common features: a *claim* or *claims*, *reasons* for the claim, *assumptions* (whether stated or unstated) that underlie the argument, *evidence* (facts, authoritative opinion, examples,

ELEMENTS OF A SAMPLE TOULMIN ARGUMENT

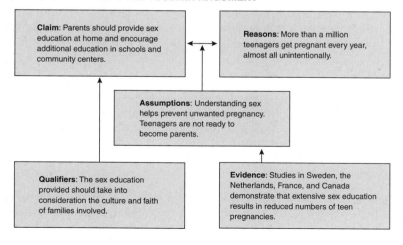

statistics, and so on), and *qualifiers* that limit the claim in some way. In the following discussion, we will examine each of these elements in more detail. The figure on p. 141 shows how these elements might be applied to an argument about sex education.

Claims

Claims (arguable statements) are statements of fact, opinion, or belief that form the backbone of arguments. Claims worthy of arguing are those that are debatable: to say "Ten degrees Fahrenheit is cold" is a claim, but it is probably not debatable—unless you are describing northern Alaska, where ten degrees might seem relatively balmy.

Reasons

A claim is only as good as the reasons explaining why the claim should be accepted. As you analyze claims, look for reasons drawn from facts, from authorities, from personal experience, and from examples. Test each reason by asking how directly it supports the claim, how timely it is, and what counter-reasons you could offer to question it.

Assumptions

Putting a claim and reasons together often results in what Aristotle called an *enthymeme*, an argument that rests on an assumption the writer expects the audience to hold. These assumptions (which Toulmin calls *warrants*) that connect claim and reasons are often the hardest to detect in an argument, partly because they are often unstated, sometimes masking a weak link. As a result, it's especially important to identify the assumptions in arguments you are analyzing. Once the assumption is identified, you can test it against evidence and your own experience before accepting it.

Evidence

As a critical reader, you must evaluate each piece of evidence (what Toulmin calls *backing*) the writer offers. Analyze how the evidence relates to the claim, whether it is appropriate and timely, and whether it comes from a credible source.

Qualifiers

Qualifiers offer a way of limiting or narrowing a claim so that it is as precise as possible. Words or phrases that signal a qualification include *few, often, in these circumstances, rarely, some, typically,* and so on.

Claims having no qualifiers can sometimes lead to overgeneralizations. For example, the statement *Grading damages learning* is less precise than *Grading can damage learning in some circumstances*. Look carefully for qualifiers in the arguments you analyze, since they will affect the strength and reach of the claim.

Analyzing elements of a visual argument

Visual arguments, too, can be analyzed using Toulmin's methods. Look at the accompanying advertising parody: it contains few words, yet it makes a subtle argument. A group of students discussed this advertisement, observing that the image intends to evoke a 1960s-era detergent commercial. They came up with several possible claims that the ad might be making.

POSSIBLE CLAIM   Pharmaceutical companies want to convince consumers that taking drugs to cure depression is no more serious than trying a new detergent.

POSSIBLE CLAIM   Consumers should beware of drug advertisements that make hard-to-prove claims aimed at getting customers to ask for a prescription.

POSSIBLE CLAIM   Buying products will not lead to greater happiness.

All of these claims can be supported by the ad. If you were to choose the first claim, for instance, you might word a reason like this: *This parody of a Prozac ad looks like a detergent commercial from the 1960s, but the product is a chemical that promises to "wash your blues away."* With some research into the actual dangers and benefits of antidepressants, you might find evidence that ads for such drugs sometimes minimize their downside and exaggerate their promise. You might also note that the ad's design takes viewers back to a decades-old scene of domestic happiness, suggesting that Prozac could return its users to some mythically perfect time in the past—and you would be well on your way to an analysis of this visual argument.

13e   Think critically about fallacies.

Fallacies have traditionally been viewed as serious flaws that damage the effectiveness of an argument. But arguments are ordinarily fairly complex in that they always occur in some specific rhetorical situation and in some particular place and time; thus what looks like a fallacy in one situation may appear quite different in another. The best advice is to learn to identify fallacies but to be cautious in jumping to quick conclusions about them. Rather than thinking of them as errors you can use to discredit an arguer, you might think of them as barriers to common ground and understanding, since they often shut off rather than engender debate.

Verbal fallacies

AD HOMINEM

Ad hominem charges make a personal attack rather than focusing on the issue at hand.

▶ **Who cares what that fat loudmouth says about the health care system?**

GUILT BY ASSOCIATION

Guilt by association attacks someone's credibility by linking that person with a person or activity the audience considers bad, suspicious, or untrustworthy.

▶ **She does not deserve reelection; her husband had extramarital affairs.**

FALSE AUTHORITY

False authority is often used by advertisers who show famous actors or athletes testifying to the greatness of a product about which they may know very little.

▶ **He's today's greatest NASCAR driver—and he banks at National Mutual!**

BANDWAGON APPEAL

Bandwagon appeal suggests that a great movement is underway and the reader will be a fool or a traitor not to join it.

▶ **This new phone is everyone's must-have item. Where's yours?**

FLATTERY

Flattery tries to persuade readers by suggesting that they are thoughtful, intelligent, or perceptive enough to agree with the writer.

▶ You have the taste to recognize the superlative artistry of Bling diamond jewelry.

IN-CROWD APPEAL

In-crowd appeal, a special kind of flattery, invites readers to identify with an admired and select group.

▶ Want to know a secret that more and more of Middletown's successful young professionals are finding out about? It's Mountainbrook Manor condominiums.

VEILED THREAT

Veiled threats try to frighten readers into agreement by hinting that they will suffer adverse consequences if they don't agree.

▶ If Public Service Electric Company does not get an immediate 15 percent rate increase, its services to you may be seriously affected.

FALSE ANALOGY

False analogies make comparisons between two situations that are not alike in important respects.

▶ The volleyball team's sudden descent in the rankings resembled the sinking of the *Titanic*.

BEGGING THE QUESTION

Begging the question is a kind of circular argument that treats a debatable statement as if it had been proved true.

▶ Television news covered that story well; I learned all I know about it by watching TV.

POST HOC FALLACY

The post hoc fallacy (from the Latin *post hoc, ergo propter hoc,* which means "after this, therefore caused by this") assumes that just because B happened *after* A, it must have been *caused* by A.

▶ We should not rebuild the town docks because every time we do, a big hurricane comes along and damages them.

NON SEQUITUR

A non sequitur (Latin for "it does not follow") attempts to tie together two or more logically unrelated ideas as if they were related.

▶ If we can send a spaceship to Mars, then we can discover a cure for cancer.

EITHER-OR FALLACY

The either-or fallacy insists that a complex situation can have only two possible outcomes.

▶ **If we do not build the new highway, businesses downtown will be forced to close.**

HASTY GENERALIZATION

A hasty generalization bases a conclusion on too little evidence or on bad or misunderstood evidence.

▶ **I couldn't understand the lecture today, so I'm sure this course will be impossible.**

OVERSIMPLIFICATION

Oversimplification claims an overly direct relationship between a cause and an effect.

▶ **If we prohibit the sale of alcohol, we will get rid of binge drinking.**

STRAW MAN

A straw-man argument misrepresents the opposition by pretending that opponents agree with something that few reasonable people would support.

▶ **My opponent believes that we should offer therapy to the terrorists. I disagree.**

Visual fallacies

Fallacies can also take the form of misleading images. The sheer power of images can make them especially difficult to analyze—people tend to believe what they see. Nevertheless, photographs and other visuals can be manipulated to present a false impression.

MISLEADING PHOTOGRAPHS

Faked or altered photos have existed since the invention of photography. On the following page, for example, is a photograph of Joseph Stalin, the Soviet Union's leader from 1929 to 1953, with his commissar Nikolai Yezhov. Stalin and the commissar had a political disagreement that resulted in Yezhov's execution in 1940. The second image shows the same photo after Stalin had it doctored to rewrite history.

Today's technology makes such photo alterations easier than ever. But photographs need not be altered to try to fool viewers. Think of all the photos that make a politician look misleadingly bad or good. In these cases, you should closely examine the motives of those responsible for publishing the images.

MISLEADING CHARTS AND GRAPHS

Facts and statistics, too, can be presented in ways that mislead readers. For example, the following bar graph purports to deliver an argument about how differently Democrats, on the one hand, and Republicans and Independents, on the other, felt about an issue:

DATA PRESENTED MISLEADINGLY

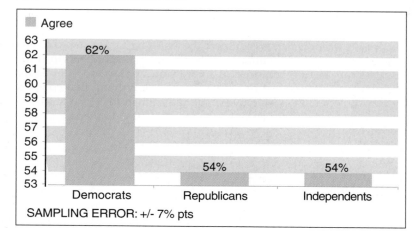

Look closely and you'll see a visual fallacy: the vertical axis starts not at zero but at 53 percent, so the apparently large difference between the groups is misleading. In fact, a majority of all respondents agree about the issue, and only eight percentage points separate Democrats from Republicans and Independents (in a poll with a margin of error of $+/-$ seven percentage points). Here's how the graph would look if the vertical axis began at zero:

DATA PRESENTED MORE ACCURATELY

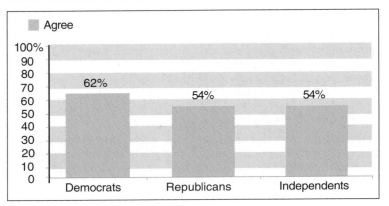

13f Student rhetorical analysis

Student Writer

Milena Ateyea

For a class assignment, Milena Ateyea was asked to analyze the emotional, ethical, and logical appeals in "Protecting Freedom of Expression at Harvard," an essay by Harvard president Derek Bok arguing that colleges should seek to persuade rather than to censor students who use speech or symbols that offend others.

bedfordstmartins.com/everydaywriter
Student Writing

A Curse and a Blessing

In 1991, when Derek Bok's essay "Protecting Freedom of Expression at Harvard" was first published in the *Boston Globe*, I had just come to America to escape the oppressive Communist regime in Bulgaria. Perhaps my background explains why I support Bok's argument that we should not put arbitrary limits on freedom of expression. Bok wrote the essay in response to a public display of Confederate flags and a swastika at Harvard, a situation that created a heated controversy among the students. As Bok notes, universities have struggled to achieve a balance between maintaining students' right of free speech and avoiding racist attacks. When choices must be made, however, Bok argues for preserving freedom of expression.

In order to support his claim and bridge the controversy, Bok uses a variety of rhetorical strategies. The author first immerses the reader in the controversy by vividly describing the incident: two Harvard students had hung Confederate flags in public view, thereby "upsetting students who equate the Confederacy with slavery" (51). Another student, protesting the flags, decided to display an even more offensive symbol—the swastika. These actions provoked heated discussions among students. Some students believed that school officials should remove the offensive symbols, whereas others suggested that the symbols "are a form of free speech and should be protected" (51). Bok establishes common ground between the factions: he regrets the actions of the offenders but does not believe we should prohibit such actions just because we disagree with them.

The author earns the reader's respect because of his knowledge and through his logical presentation of the issue. In partial support of his position, Bok refers to U.S. Supreme Court rulings, which remind us that "the display of swastikas or Confederate flags

---

Provocative title suggests mixed response to Bok

Connects article to her own experience to build credibility (ethical appeal)

Brief overview of Bok's argument

Identifies Bok's central claim

Links Bok's claim to strategies he uses to support it

Direct quotations show appeals to emotion through vivid description

Bok establishes common ground between two positions

Emphasizes Bok's credibility (ethical appeal)

Links Bok's credibility to use of logical appeals

clearly falls within the protection of the free-speech clause of the First Amendment" (52). The author also emphasizes the danger of the slippery slope of censorship when he warns the reader, "If we begin to forbid flags, it is only a short step to prohibiting offensive speakers" (52). Overall, however, Bok's work lacks the kinds of evidence that statistics, interviews with students, and other representative examples of controversial conduct could provide.

Comments critically on kinds of evidence Bok's argument lacks

Thus, his essay may not be strong enough to persuade all readers to make the leap from this specific situation to his general conclusion.

Reiterates Bok's credibility

Throughout, Bok's personal feelings are implied but not stated directly. As a lawyer who was president of Harvard for twenty years, Bok knows how to present his opinions respectfully without offending the feelings of the students. However, qualifying phrases like "I suspect that" and "Under the Supreme Court's rulings, as I read them" could weaken the effectiveness of his position.

Identifies qualifying phrases that may weaken claim

Analyzes weaknesses of Bok's proposed solution

Furthermore, Bok's attempt to be fair to all seems to dilute the strength of his proposed solution. He suggests that one should either ignore the insensitive deeds in the hope that students might change their behavior, or talk to the offending students to help them comprehend how their behavior is affecting other students.

Raises possibility that Bok's imperfect solution may work

Nevertheless, although Bok's proposed solution to the controversy does not appear at first reading to be very strong, it may ultimately be effective. There is enough flexibility in his approach to withstand various tests, and Bok's solution is general enough that it can change with the times and adapt to community standards.

Summarizes Bok's task

In writing this essay, Bok faced a challenging task: to write a short response to a specific situation that represents a very broad and controversial issue. Some people may find that freedom of expression is both a curse and a blessing because of the difficulties it creates. As one who has lived under a regime that permitted very

Ties conclusion back to title

Student Writing

limited, censored expression, I am all too aware that I could not have written this response in 1991 in Bulgaria. As a result, I feel, like Derek Bok, that freedom of expression is a blessing, in spite of any temporary problems associated with it.

Returns to own experience, which argues for accepting Bok's solution

Work Cited

Bok, Derek. "Protecting Freedom of Expression at Harvard." Rpt. in *Current Issues and Enduring Questions*. Ed. Sylvan Barnet and Hugo Bedau. 6th ed. Boston: Bedford, 2002. 51–52. *Boston Globe* 25 May 1991. Print.

Constructing Arguments   **14**

You respond to arguments all the time. When you see a stop sign and come to a halt, you've accepted the argument that stopping at such signs is a sensible thing to do. Unfortunately, constructing an effective argument of your own is not as easy as putting up a stop sign. Creating a thorough and convincing argument requires careful reasoning and attention to your audience and purpose.

14a Understand what counts as argument.

Although winning is an important purpose of argument, it is by no means the only purpose.

TO WIN The most traditional purpose of academic argument, arguing to win, is common in campus debating societies, in political debates, in trials, and often in business. The writer or speaker aims to present a position that will prevail over some other position.

Reviewing Your Argument

- What is the purpose of your argument — to win? to convince others? to explore an issue? (14a)
- Is the point you want to make arguable? (14a)
- Have you formulated a strong working thesis that includes a clear claim and good reasons? (14b)
- Have you considered your audience in shaping your appeals? (14d)
- How have you established your own credibility in the argument? (14e)
- How have you incorporated logical and emotional appeals into your argument? (14f and g)
- If you use sources, how effectively are they integrated into your argument? (14h)
- How is your argument organized? (14i)
- What design elements help you make your argument? (14j)

TO CONVINCE Often, out-and-out defeat of another's position is not only unrealistic but undesirable. Instead, the goal might be to convince another person to change his or her mind. Doing so calls on a writer to provide *compelling reasons* for an audience to accept some or all of the writer's conclusions.

TO EXPLORE AN ISSUE Argument to explore an issue or reach a decision seeks a sharing of information and perspectives in order to make informed choices.

TALKING THE TALK

Arguments

"Argument seems so negative — I don't want to attack anybody or contradict what someone else says." Sometimes — in law courts, for example — argument may call for attacking an opponent's credibility, and you may have used the word *argument* to describe a conversation in which the speakers said little more than "I did not!" and "You did, too!" But in college writing, argument usually means something much broader. Instead of attacking or contradicting, you will be expected to explore ideas and to work toward convincing yourself as well as others that these ideas are valuable.

Checking whether a statement can be argued

At school, at home, or on the job, you will often need to convince someone or decide something. To do so, start with an arguable statement, which should meet three criteria:

1. It attempts to convince readers of something, change their minds about something, or urge them to do something—or it explores a topic in order to make a wise decision.
2. It addresses a problem for which no easily acceptable solution exists or asks a question to which no absolute answer exists.
3. It presents a position that readers might realistically have varying perspectives on.

ARGUABLE STATEMENT Advertising in women's magazines contributes to the poor self-image that afflicts many young women.

This statement seeks to convince, addresses a problem—poor self-image among young women—that has no clear-cut solution, and takes a position many could disagree with.

UNARGUABLE Women's magazines earn millions of dollars
STATEMENT every year from advertising.

This statement does not present a position; it states a fact that can easily be verified and thus offers a poor basis for argument.

> **bedfordstmartins.com/everydaywriter**
> **Exercise Central > Critical Thinking and Argument**

14b Make a claim and formulate a working thesis.

Once you have an arguable statement, you need to develop it into a working thesis (7b). One way to do so is to identify the elements of an argument (13d): the claim or arguable statement; one or more reasons for the claim; and assumptions—sometimes unstated—that underlie the claim and reasons.

To turn a claim into a working thesis for an argument, include at least one good reason to support the arguable statement.

REASON Pesticides endanger the lives of farmworkers.

WORKING THESIS Because they endanger the lives of farmworkers,
(CLAIM WITH pesticides should be banned.
REASON ATTACHED)

14c Examine your assumptions.

Once you have a working thesis, examine your assumptions to help test your reasoning and strengthen your argument. Begin by identifying underlying assumptions that support the working thesis.

WORKING THESIS	Because they endanger the lives of farmworkers, pesticides should be banned.
ASSUMPTION 1	Workers have a right to a safe working environment.
ASSUMPTION 2	Substances that endanger the lives of workers deserve to be banned.

Once you have a working thesis, you may want to use qualifiers to make it more precise and thus less susceptible to criticism. The preceding thesis might be qualified in this way:

▶ Because they *often* endanger the lives of farmworkers, *most* pesticides should be banned.

14d Shape your appeal to your audience.

Arguments and the claims they make are effective only if they appeal to the appropriate audience. For example, if you want to argue for increased lighting in parking garages on campus, you might appeal to students by citing examples drawn from their experiences of the safety problems in such dimly lit garages. If you are writing to university administrators, however, you might focus on the negative publicity associated with past attacks in campus garages and evoke the anger that such attacks cause in parents, alumni, and other influential groups.

14e Establish credibility through ethical appeals.

To make your argument convincing, you must first gain the respect and trust of your readers, or establish credibility with them. In general, writers can establish credibility by making ethical appeals (13c) in four ways.

Demonstrating knowledge

A writer can establish credibility first by establishing credentials. To decide whether you know enough to argue an issue credibly, consider the following questions:

- Can you provide information about your topic from sources other than your own knowledge?
- How reliable are your sources?
- If sources contradict one another, can you account for or resolve the contradictions?
- Would a personal experience relating to the issue help support your claim?

These questions may well show that you must do more research, check sources, resolve contradictions, refocus your working thesis, or even change your topic.

Establishing common ground

Many arguments between people or groups are doomed to end without resolution because the two sides seem to occupy no starting point of agreement. The following questions can help you find common ground in presenting an argument. (See also Chapter 21.)

- On this issue, how can you discover opinions that differ from your own?
- What are the differing perspectives on the issue?
- What aspects of the issue can all sides agree on?
- How can you express such common ground clearly to all sides? Can you use other languages or varieties of English to establish common ground with those you address? (See Chapter 22.)

Demonstrating fairness

In arguing a position, writers must deal fairly with opposing arguments (also called counterarguments). Audiences are more inclined to listen to writers who seem to consider their opponents' views fairly than to those who ignore or distort such views. The following questions can

---

FOR MULTILINGUAL WRITERS

Counting Your Own Experience

You may have been told that your personal experience doesn't count in making academic arguments. If so, reconsider this advice, for showing an audience that you have relevant personal experience with a topic can carry strong persuasive appeal with many English-speaking readers.

help you discover ways of establishing yourself as open-minded and evenhanded:

- How can you show that you are taking into account all significant points of view?
- How can you demonstrate that you understand and sympathize with points of view other than your own?
- What can you do to show that you have considered evidence carefully, even when it does not support your position?

Some writers, instead of demonstrating fairness, may make unjustified attacks on an opponent's credibility. Avoid such attacks in your writing.

Visuals that make ethical appeals

In arguments and other kinds of writing, visuals can combine with text to help present a writer or an organization as trustworthy and credible.

Like businesses, many institutions and individuals are using logos and other images to brand themselves as they wish the public to see them. The Sustainable Food Laboratory logo, seen here, suggests that the organization is concerned about both food production and the environment.

Visuals that make ethical appeals add to your credibility and fairness as a writer. Just as you probably consider the impression your Facebook profile photo makes on your audience, you should think about what kind of case you're making for yourself when you choose images and design elements for your argument.

14f   Use effective logical appeals.

Credibility alone cannot and should not carry the full burden of convincing readers. Indeed, many are inclined to think that the logic of the argument—the reasoning behind it—is as important as its ethos.

Examples, precedents, and narratives

Just as a picture can sometimes be worth a thousand words, so can a well-conceived example be extremely valuable in arguing a point. Examples are used most often to support generalizations or to bring abstractions to life. In making the general statement that popular media send the message that a woman must be thin to be attractive; you might include these examples:

> At the supermarket checkout, a tabloid publishes unflattering photographs of a young singer and comments on her apparent weight gain in shocked captions that ask "What happened?!?" Another praises a star for quickly shedding "ugly pounds" after the recent birth of a child. The cover of *Cosmopolitan* features a glamorously made-up and airbrushed actress in an outfit that reveals her remarkably tiny waist and flat stomach. Every woman in every advertisement in the magazine is thin—and the context makes it clear that we're supposed to think that she is beautiful.

Precedents are examples taken from the past. If, as part of a proposal for increasing lighting in the library garage, you point out that the university has increased lighting in four other garages in the past year, you are arguing on the basis of precedent.

The following questions can help you check any use of example or precedent:

- How representative are the examples?
- Are they sufficient in strength or number to lead to a generalization?
- In what ways do they support your point?
- How closely does a precedent relate to the point you're trying to make? Are the situations really similar?
- How timely is the precedent? (What would have been applicable in 1920 is not necessarily applicable today.)

Because storytelling is universal, *narratives* can be very persuasive in helping readers understand and accept the logic of an argument. Narratives that use video and audio to capture the faces and voices of the people involved are often particularly compelling. In *As We Sow*, a documentary arguing against corporate pork production methods, the farmers shown here tell stories of their struggle to continue raising animals as their families have for generations.

Stories drawn from your own experience can appeal particularly to readers, for they not only help make your point in true-to-life, human terms but also help readers know you better and therefore identify with you more closely.

When you include stories in an argument, ask yourself the following questions:

- Does the narrative support your thesis?
- Will the story's significance to the argument be clear to your readers?
- Is the story one of several good reasons or pieces of evidence—or does it have to carry the main burden of the argument?

In research writing, you must identify your sources for any examples, precedents, or narratives not based on your own knowledge.

Authority and testimony

Another way to support an argument logically is to cite an authority. The use of authority has figured prominently in the controversy over smoking. Since the U.S. surgeon general's 1964 announcement that smoking is hazardous to health, many Americans have quit smoking, largely persuaded by the authority of the scientists offering the evidence.

Ask the following questions to be sure you are using authorities effectively:

- Is the authority *timely*? (The argument that the United States should pursue a policy that was supported by Thomas Jefferson will probably fail since Jefferson's time was so radically different from ours.)
- Is the authority *qualified* to judge the topic at hand? (To cite a movie star in an essay on linguistics may not help your argument.)
- Is the authority likely to be *known and respected* by readers? (To cite an unfamiliar authority without identification will reduce the impact of the evidence.)
- Are the authority's *credentials* clearly stated and verifiable? (Especially with Web-based sources, it is crucial to know whose authority guarantees the reliability of the information.)

Testimony—the evidence that an authority presents in support of a claim—is a feature of much contemporary argument. If testimony is timely, accurate, representative, and provided by a respected authority, then it, like authority itself, can add powerful support.

In research writing (see Chapters 15–19), you should cite your sources for authority and for testimony not based on your own knowledge.

Causes and effects

Showing that one event is the cause or the effect of another can help support an argument. Suppose you are trying to explain, in a petition to change your grade in a course, why you were unable to take the final examination. You would probably trace the causes of your failure to appear—your illness or the theft of your car, perhaps—so that the committee reading the petition would reconsider the effect—your not taking the examination.

Tracing causes often lays the groundwork for an argument, particularly if the effect of the causes is one we would like to change. In an environmental science class, for example, a student may argue that a national law regulating smokestack emissions from utility plants is needed because (1) acid rain on the East Coast originates from emissions at utility plants in the Midwest, (2) acid rain kills trees and other vegetation, (3) utility lobbyists have prevented midwestern states from passing strict laws controlling emissions from such plants, and (4) if such laws are not passed, acid rain will soon destroy most eastern forests. In this case, the fourth point ties all of the previous points together to provide an overall argument from effect: if X, then Y.

Inductive and deductive reasoning

Traditionally, logical arguments are classified as using either inductive or deductive reasoning; in practice, the two almost always work together. Inductive reasoning is the process of making a generalization based on a number of specific instances. If you find you are ill on ten occasions after eating seafood, for example, you will likely draw the inductive generalization that seafood makes you ill. It may not be an absolute certainty that seafood is to blame, but the probability lies in that direction.

Deductive reasoning, on the other hand, reaches a conclusion by assuming a general principle (known as a major premise) and then applying that principle to a specific case (the minor premise). In practice, this general principle is usually derived from induction. The inductive generalization *Seafood makes me ill*, for instance, could serve as the major premise for the deductive argument *Since all seafood makes me ill, the shrimp on this buffet is certain to make me ill*.

Deductive arguments have traditionally been analyzed as syllogisms—reasoning that contains a major premise, a minor premise, and a conclusion.

MAJOR PREMISE	All people die.
MINOR PREMISE	I am a person.
CONCLUSION	I will die.

Syllogisms, however, are too rigid and absolute to serve in arguments about questions that have no absolute answers, and they often lack any appeal to an audience. Aristotle's simpler alternative, the enthymeme, asks the audience to supply the implied major premise. Consider the following example:

> Since violent video games can be addictive and cause psychological harm, players and their parents must carefully evaluate such games and monitor their use.

You can analyze this enthymeme by restating it in the form of two premises and a conclusion.

MAJOR PREMISE　　Games that cause harm to players should be evaluated and monitored.

MINOR PREMISE　　Violent video games can cause psychological harm to players.

CONCLUSION　　These games should be evaluated and monitored.

Note that the major premise is one the writer can count on an audience agreeing with or supplying: safety and common sense demand that potentially harmful games be used with great care. By implicitly asking an audience to supply this premise to an argument, a writer engages the audience's participation.

Toulmin's system (13d) looks for claims, reasons, and assumptions instead of major and minor premises.

CLAIM　　Parents should not allow children to play violent video games.

REASON　　Exposure to violent video games may make children more indifferent to violence.

ASSUMPTION　　Parents do not want their children to be indifferent to violence.

Whether it is expressed as a syllogism, an enthymeme, or a claim, a deductive conclusion is only as strong as the premise or reasons on which it is based.

Visuals that make logical appeals

Visuals that make logical appeals can be especially useful in arguments, since they present factual information that can be taken in at a glance. *Mother Jones* used the following simple chart to carry a big message about income distribution in the United States. Consider how long it would take to explain all the information in this chart with words alone.

A VISUAL THAT MAKES A LOGICAL APPEAL

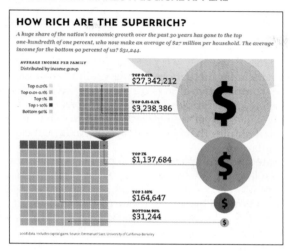

HOW RICH ARE THE SUPERRICH?

A huge share of the nation's economic growth over the past 30 years has gone to the top one-hundredth of one percent, who now make an average of $27 million per household. The average income for the bottom 90 percent of us? $31,244.

AVERAGE INCOME PER FAMILY
Distributed by income group

Top 0.01%
Top 0.01-0.1%
Top 1%
Top 1-10%
Bottom 90%

TOP 0.01%
$27,342,212

TOP 0.01-0.1%
$3,238,386

TOP 1%
$1,137,684

TOP 1-10%
$164,647

BOTTOM 90%
$31,244

2008 data; includes capital gains. Source: Emmanuel Saez, University of California-Berkeley

14g Use appropriate emotional appeals.

Most successful arguments appeal to our hearts as well as to our minds—as is vividly demonstrated by the campaign to curb the AIDS epidemic in Africa. Facts and figures (logical appeals) convince us that the problem is real and serious. What elicits an outpouring of support, however, is the arresting emotional power of stories and images of people living with the disease. But credible writers take particular care when they use emotional appeals; audiences can easily begin to feel manipulated when an argument tries too hard to appeal to their pity, anger, or fear.

Concrete descriptive details

Like photographs, vivid words can bring a moving immediacy to any argument. A student may amass facts and figures, including diagrams and maps, to illustrate the problem of wheelchair access to the library. But only when the student asks a friend who uses a wheelchair to accompany her to the library does the student writer discover the concrete details necessary to move readers. The student can then write, "Marie inched her heavy wheelchair up the steep entrance ramp, her arms straining, her face pinched with the sheer effort."

Figurative language

Figurative language, or figures of speech, can paint a detailed and vivid picture by making striking comparisons between something you are writing about and something else that helps a reader visualize, identify with, or understand it (23d).

Figures of speech include metaphors, similes, and analogies. Most simply, metaphors compare two things directly: *Richard the Lion-Hearted; old age is the evening of life.* Similes make comparisons using *like* or *as: Richard is as brave as a lion; old age is like the evening of life.* Analogies are extended metaphors or similes that compare an unfamiliar concept or process to a more familiar one.

Visuals can also create vivid comparisons. The panels below come from a cartoon from Tom Tomorrow's comic strip, *This Modern World*, called "If Real Life Were More Like the Internet." Tomorrow, whose work appears regularly online, suggests in these panels that digital content has value, just as physical products and services do—and that those who create such content should be able to earn a living from it. Tomorrow adds emotional weight to the comparison by making the cartoon characters who want free content seem selfish and blind to the needs of those who serve them.

A VISUAL THAT CREATES A VIVID COMPARISON

Visuals that make emotional appeals

Visuals that make emotional appeals can also add substance to your argument. To make sure that such visual appeals will enhance your argument, test them out with several potential readers to see how they

A VISUAL THAT MAKES AN EMOTIONAL APPEAL

interpret the appeal. Consider, for example, the photograph above, which shows a funeral arranged by an American Legion post in Florida to honor four U.S. military veterans who died homeless. Some readers might see this image as an indictment of the government, which allowed soldiers who had fought for their country to end up without a place to live—but others might view it instead (or also) as confirmation that patriots come from every walk of life or that veterans honor their own even when others fail to do so.

14h Consult sources.

In constructing an academic argument, it is often essential to use sources. The key to persuading people to accept your argument is providing good reasons; and even if your assignment doesn't specify that you must consult outside sources, they are often the most effective way of finding and establishing these reasons. Sources can help you to do the following:

- provide background information on your topic
- demonstrate your knowledge of the topic to readers
- cite authority and testimony in support of your thesis
- find opinions that differ from your own, which can help you sharpen your thinking, qualify your thesis if necessary, and demonstrate fairness to opposing arguments

For a thorough discussion of finding, gathering, and evaluating sources, see Chapters 15–19.

14i   Organize your argument.

Once you have assembled good reasons and evidence in support of an argumentative thesis, you must organize your material to present the argument convincingly. Although there is no universally favored, one-size-fits-all organizational framework, you may find it useful to try one of the following patterns.

The classical system

The system of argument often followed by ancient Greek and Roman orators is now referred to as *classical*. You can adapt the ancient format to written arguments as follows:

1. Introduction
   - Gain readers' attention and interest.
   - Establish your qualifications to write about your topic.
   - Establish common ground with readers.
   - Demonstrate fairness.
   - State or imply your thesis.

2. Background
   - Present any necessary background information, including relevant personal narrative.

3. Lines of argument
   - Present good reasons (including logical and emotional appeals) in support of your thesis.
   - Present reasons in order of importance, with the most important ones generally saved for last.
   - Demonstrate ways your argument may be in readers' best interest.

4. Alternative arguments
   - Examine alternative points of view.
   - Note advantages and disadvantages of alternative views.
   - Explain why one view is better than other(s).

5. Conclusion
   - Summarize the argument if you choose.
   - Elaborate on the implication of your thesis.
   - Make clear what you want readers to think or do.
   - Reinforce your credibility.

The Toulmin system

This simplified form of the Toulmin system (13d and 14f) can help you organize an argumentative essay:

1. Make your claim (arguable statement).

▶ **The federal government should ban smoking.**

2. Qualify your claim if necessary.

▶ **The ban would be limited to public places.**

3. Present good reasons to support your claim.

▶ **Smoking causes serious diseases in smokers.**
▶ **Nonsmokers are endangered by others' smoke.**

4. Explain the assumptions that underlie your claim and your reasons. Provide additional explanations for any controversial assumptions.

ASSUMPTION	The Constitution was established to "promote the general welfare."
ASSUMPTION	Citizens are entitled to protection from harmful actions by others.
ADDITIONAL EXPLANATION	The United States is based on a political system that is supposed to serve the basic needs of its people, including their health.

5. Provide additional evidence to support your claim (facts, statistics, testimony, and other logical, ethical, or emotional appeals).

STATISTICS	Cite the incidence of deaths attributed to secondhand smoke.
FACTS	Cite lawsuits won against large tobacco companies, including one that awarded billions of dollars to states in reparation for smoking-related health care costs.
FACTS	Cite bans on smoking already imposed on indoor public spaces in many cities.
AUTHORITY	Cite the surgeon general.

6. Acknowledge and respond to possible counterarguments.

COUNTER-ARGUMENT	Smokers have rights, too.
RESPONSE	The suggested ban applies only to public places; smokers are free to smoke in private.

7. Finally, state your conclusion in the strongest way possible.

14j Consider design issues.

Most writers today create arguments that are carefully designed to make the best use of space, font style and type size, color, visuals, and technology. Chapter 9 provides extensive information on design issues, and it would be wise to consult that chapter as you design an argument. The following tips will get you thinking about how to produce and design an argument that will add to the ethical, logical, and emotional appeals you are making:

- Spend some time deciding on a distinct visual style for your argument, one that will appeal to your intended readers, set a clear voice or tone for your argument, and guide readers through your text.
- Check out any conventions that may be expected in the kind of argument you are writing. Look for examples of similar arguments, or ask your instructor for information about such conventions (5f).
- Consider the use of white space, titles, and headings and how each page will look. Choose titles, headings, and subheadings that will guide readers from point to point (9c). You may want to set off an especially important part of your argument (such as a list of essential evidence) in a box, carefully labeled.
- Make sure that your visual design is consistent. If you choose a particular color, font, or type style for a particular purpose, such as a second-level heading, make sure that you use the same color, font, or type style for that purpose throughout your paper.
- Be sure to choose readable fonts and font sizes (9b and c).
- Choose colors carefully, and make sure that you use color appropriately for the genre and medium.
- Place images close to the text they illustrate, and label each one clearly. Make sure that audio and video files appear in appropriate places and are identified for users.
- After you have a rough draft of your design, test it out on friends and classmates, asking them to describe how readable it is, how easy it is to follow, and what you need to change to make it more effective. Decide what adjustments you need to make—in format, spacing, alignment, use of color and fonts, and so on.

14k Student argument essay

In this essay, Teal Pfeifer argues that images in the media affect how women see themselves, and she offers a solution to a problem. Her essay has been annotated to point out the various parts of her argument as well as her use of good reasons, evidence, and appeals to logic and emotion.

Student Writer

Teal Pfeifer

 bedfordstmartins.com/everydaywriter
Student Writing

Pfeifer 1

Teal Pfeifer

Professor Rashad

English 102

13 April 2012

Devastating Beauty

Title uses play on words to pique interest

Collarbones, hipbones, cheekbones—so many bones. She looks at the camera with sunken eyes, smiling, acting beautiful. Her dress is Versace, or Gucci, or Dior, and it is revealing, revealing every bone and joint in her thin, thin body. She looks fragile and beautiful, as if I could snap her in two. I look at her and feel the soft cushion of flesh that surrounds my own joints, my own shoulders and hips that are broad, my own ribs surrounded by skin and muscle and fat. I am not nearly as fragile or graceful or thin. I look away and wonder what kind of self-discipline it takes to become beautiful like the model in my magazine.

Opening uses emotional appeals and tries to establish common ground with readers

By age seventeen a young woman has seen an average of 250,000 ads featuring a severely underweight woman whose body type is, for the most part, unattainable by any means, including extreme ones such as anorexia, bulimia, and drug use ("The Skinny"). The media promote clothing, cigarettes, fragrances, and even food with images like these. In a culture that has become increasingly visual, the images put out for public consumption feature women that are a smaller size than ever before. In 1950, the White Rock Mineral Water girl was 5'4" tall and weighed 140 pounds; now she is 5'10" tall and weighs only 110 pounds, signifying the growing deviation between the weight of models and that of the normal female population (Pipher 184).

Presents background information on the problem and cites sources

This media phenomenon has had a major effect on the female population as a whole, both young and old. Five to ten million women in America today suffer from an eating disorder related

Introduces problem: ads encourage women's poor body image

to poor self-image, and yet advertisements continue to prey on insecurities fueled by a woman's desire to be thin. Current research shows that "80 percent of American women are dissatisfied with their appearance" and that "45 percent of those are on a diet on any given day" ("Statistics"). Yet even the most stringent dieting will generally fail to create the paper-thin body so valued in the media, and continuing efforts to do so can lead to serious psychological problems such as depression.

> Good reason for thesis: stringent dieting can cause psychological problems

While many women express dissatisfaction with their bodies, they are not the only victims of the emaciated images so frequently presented to them. Young girls are equally affected by these images, if not more so. Eighty percent of girls under age ten have already been on a diet and expressed the desire to be thinner and more beautiful (*Slim Hopes*). Thus, from a young age, beauty is equated with a specific size. The message girls get is an insidious one: in order to be your best self, you should wear size 0 or 1. The pressure only grows more intense as girls grow up. According to results from the Kaiser Family Foundation Survey "Reflections of Girls in the Media," 16 percent of ten- to seventeen-year-old girls reported that they had dieted or exercised to look like a TV character. Yet two-thirds of teenage girls acknowledged that these thin characters were not an accurate reflection of "real life" (qtd. in Dittrich, "Children").

> Provides statistical evidence that problem extends across age groups

> Uses logical appeals

It is tragic to see so much of the American population obsessed with weight and reaching an ideal that is, for the most part, ultimately unattainable. Equally troubling is the role magazines play in feeding this obsession. When a researcher asked female students from Stanford University to flip through several magazines containing images of glamorized, super-thin models (see Fig. 1), 68 percent of the women felt significantly worse about themselves after viewing the magazine models (qtd. in Dittrich, "Media"). Another study showed that looking at models on a long-term basis leads to stress, depression, guilt, and

> Good reason for thesis: magazines feed obsession with dieting

> Backs up reasons with research and expert opinion

Fig. 1. Young women reading magazines. Personal
photograph by author.

lowered self-worth (qtd. in Dittrich, "Media"). As Naomi Wolf points
out in *The Beauty Myth*, thinking obsessively about fat and dieting has
actually been shown to change thought patterns and brain chemistry.

Considers and rejects alternative solutions

How do we reject images that are so harmful to the women
and young girls who view them? Legislation regarding what can
be printed and distributed is not an option because of First
Amendment rights. Equally untenable is the idea of appealing to
the industries that hire emaciated models. As long as the beauty
and clothing industries are making a profit from the physically
insecure girls and women who view their ads, nothing will change.

States working thesis: a boycott would effectively solve problem

What, however, might happen if women stopped buying the
magazines that print such destructive images? A boycott is the
most effective way to rid the print medium of emaciated models
and eliminate the harmful effects they cause. If women stopped
buying magazines that target them with such harmful advertising,
magazines would be forced to change the kinds of ads they print.
Such a boycott would send a clear message: women and girls
reject the victimization that takes place every time they look at

a skeletally thin model and then feel worse about themselves. Consumers can ultimately control what is put on the market: if we don't buy, funding for such ads will dry up fast.

In the past, boycotts have been effective tools for social change. Rosa Parks, often identified as the mother of the modern-day civil rights movement, played a pivotal role in the Montgomery bus boycott in December 1955. When Parks refused to give up her seat to a white bus rider, she was arrested, and this incident inspired the boycott. For more than a year, the vast majority of African Americans in Montgomery chose to walk instead of ride the buses. Many of them were terrorized or harassed, but the boycott was eventually successful: segregation on buses was declared illegal by the U.S. Supreme Court.

Between 1965 and 1973, Cesar Chavez also used boycotts successfully to change wage policies and working conditions for millions of Mexicans and Mexican Americans who were being exploited by growers of grapes and lettuce. In his boycott efforts, Chavez moved on two fronts simultaneously: he asked the workers to withhold their labor, and he asked consumers to refrain from purchasing table grapes (and later, lettuce) in order to show their support for the workers. In this situation, not only did the boycott force an industry to improve existing conditions, but it also made the public aware of pressing labor issues. Thus a bond was formed between the workers and the community their labor was benefiting.

As a society, we have much to learn from boycotts of the past, and their lessons can help us confront contemporary social ills. As I have shown, body-image dissatisfaction and eating disorders are rising at an alarming rate among young girls and women in American society. This growing desire for an unrealistically thin body affects our minds and our spirits, especially when we are pummeled dozens of times a day with glamorized images of emaciated and unhealthy women. The resulting anorexia and

Good reason: boycotts have been effective

Presents a precedent/ example as evidence

Presents a second precedent/ example as evidence

Appeals directly to audience by using "we" in conclusion

Student Writing

Reinforces severity of problem and appeals to emotion

Restates thesis as a call to action

bulimia that women suffer from are not only diseases that can be cured; they are also ones that can be prevented—if women will take a solid stand against such supporting advertisements and the magazines that publish them. This is where power lies—in the hands of those who hand over the dollars that support the glorification of unhealthy and unrealistic bodies. It is our choice to exert this power and to reject magazines that promote such images.

Works Cited

Dittrich, Liz. "About-Face Facts on the Children and the Media." *About-Face*. About-Face, 1996–2010. Web. 10 Mar. 2012.

---. "About-Face Facts on the Media." *About-Face*. About-Face, 1996–2010. Web. 10 Mar. 2012.

Pipher, Mary. *Reviving Ophelia: Saving the Selves of Adolescent Girls*. New York: Ballantine, 1994. Print.

"The Skinny on Media and Weight." *Common Sense Media*. Common Sense Media Inc., 27 Sept. 2005. Web. 15 Mar. 2012.

Slim Hopes. Dir. Sut Jhally. Prod. Jean Kilbourne. Media Education Foundation, 1995. Videocassette.

"Statistics." *National Eating Disorders Association*. National Eating Disorders Association, 2005. Web. 14 Mar. 2012.

Wolf, Naomi. *The Beauty Myth*. New York: Harper, 2002. Print.

Young women reading magazines. Personal photograph by author. 14 Mar. 2012.

Research

Research is formalized curiosity. It is
poking and prying with a purpose.

— ZORA NEALE HURSTON

Research

15 Preparing for a Research Project *175*

a Analyze the research assignment *175*
b Formulate a research question and hypothesis *178*
c Plan your research *178*
d Set up a research log *179*
e Move from hypothesis to working thesis *179*

16 Doing Research *180*

a Understand different kinds of sources *180*
b Use the library to get started *182*
c Find library resources *184*
d Search the Internet *189*
e Conduct field research *191*

17 Evaluating Sources and Taking Notes *193*

a Understand the purpose of sources *193*
b Create a working bibliography *194*
c Evaluate a source's usefulness and credibility *196*
d Read critically, and interpret sources *197*
e Synthesize sources *203*
f Take notes and annotate sources *205*

18 Integrating Sources and Avoiding Plagiarism *211*

a Decide whether to quote, paraphrase, or summarize *212*
b Integrate quotations, paraphrases, and summaries effectively *213*
c Integrate visuals and media effectively *215*
d Check for excessive use of source material *216*
e Understand why you should acknowledge your sources *217*
f Know which sources to acknowledge *217*
g Uphold your academic integrity and avoid plagiarism *218*

19 Writing a Research Project *220*

a Refine your writing plans *220*
b Organize and draft *222*
c Incorporate source materials *225*
d Review and get responses to your draft *225*
e Revise and edit your draft *225*
f Prepare a list of sources *227*
g Prepare and proofread your final copy *227*

For visual analysis Look carefully at the illustration on the front of this tab. What do you think this image suggests about ways to do effective research?

Preparing for a Research Project **15**

Your employer asks you to recommend the best software for a particular project. You want to plan a spring break trip to the beach. Your instructor assigns a term paper about a jazz musician. Each of these situations calls for research, for examining various kinds of sources. Preparing to begin your research means taking a long look at what you already know, the best way to proceed, and the amount of time you have to find out what you need to know. For success in college and beyond, you need to understand how to start the process of academic research.

15a Analyze the research assignment.

In an introductory writing course, you might receive an assignment like this one:

> Choose a subject of interest to you, and use it as the basis for a research essay of approximately two thousand words that makes and substantiates a claim. You should use a minimum of five credible, authoritative sources.

Topic

If your assignment doesn't specify a topic, consider the following questions (see also 5c):

- What subjects do you already know something about? Which of them would you like to explore more fully?
- What subjects do you care about? What might you like to become an expert on?
- What subjects evoke a strong reaction from you, whether positive or negative?

Be sure to get responses about your possible topic from your instructor, classmates, and friends. Ask them whether they would be interested in reading about the topic, whether it seems manageable, and whether they know of any good sources for information on the topic.

Situation

Be sure to consider the rhetorical situation (see Chapter 5) of any research project. Here are detailed questions to think about:

AUDIENCE

- Who will be the audience for your research project (5e)?
- Who will be interested in the information you gather, and why? What will they want to know? What will they already know?
- What do you know about their backgrounds? What assumptions might they hold about the topic?
- What response do you want from them?
- What kinds of evidence will you need to convince them?
- What will your instructor expect?

TALKING THE TALK

Reaching an Audience

"Isn't my audience just my teacher?" To write effectively, you must think of your writing as more than just an assignment you have to complete to get a grade. Recognize that you have something to say — and that in order to get others to pay attention, you have to think about who they are and how to reach them. Of course, your instructor is part of your audience. But who else will be interested in your topic and the unique perspective you bring to it? What does that audience need from you?

PURPOSE

- If you can choose the purpose, what would you like to accomplish (5d)?
- If you have been assigned a specific research project, keep in mind the key words in that assignment. Does the assignment ask that you *describe, survey, analyze, persuade, explain, classify, compare,* or *contrast*? What do such words mean in this field?

YOUR POSITION ON THE TOPIC (STANCE)

- What is your attitude toward your topic? Are you curious about it? critical of it? Do you like it? dislike it? find it confusing?
- What influences have shaped your position (5d)?

SCOPE

- How long is the project supposed to be? Base your research and writing schedule on the scale of the finished project (a short versus a long paper or presentation, a brief oral report or a longer multimedia presentation, a simple versus a complex Web site) and the amount of time you have to complete it.

- How many and what kind(s) of sources should you use (16a)? What kind(s) of visuals — charts, maps, photographs, and so on — will you need? Will you do any field research — interviewing, surveying, or observing (16e)?

Here is a sample schedule for a research project:

15b　Formulate a research question and hypothesis.

Once you have analyzed your task, chosen your topic, and narrowed the topic to make it manageable (see 7a), formulate a research question that you can tentatively answer with a hypothesis. The hypothesis, a statement of what you anticipate your research will show, needs to be manageable, interesting, and specific (see 7b). In addition, it must be a debatable proposition that you can prove or disprove with a reasonable amount of research evidence.

David Craig, the student whose research paper appears in Chapter 52, made the following move from general topic to a narrowed topic and then to a research question and hypothesis:

TOPIC	Electronic messaging
NARROWED TOPIC	The language of messaging
ISSUE	The effect of messaging on youth literacy
RESEARCH QUESTION	How has the popularity of messaging affected literacy among today's youth?
HYPOTHESIS	Messaging seems to have a negative influence on the writing skills of young people.

15c　Plan your research.

Once you have formulated a hypothesis, determine what you already know about your topic. Tap your memory for sources by listing everything you can remember about *where* you learned about your topic: the Internet, text messages, books, magazines, courses, conversations, television. What you know comes from somewhere, and that somewhere can serve as a starting point for your research. (See Chapter 6 for more strategies for exploring ideas and getting your initial thoughts about a topic down on paper.)

Next, develop a research plan by answering the following questions:

- What kinds of sources (books, journal articles, databases, Web sites, government documents, reference works, and so on) will you need to consult (16a)? How many sources should you consult?
- How current do your sources need to be? For topical issues, especially those related to science, current sources are usually most important. For historical subjects, older sources may offer the best information.

- How can you determine the location and availability of the kinds of sources you need?

One goal of your research plan is to build a strong working bibliography (17b). Carrying out systematic research and keeping careful notes on your sources will make developing your works-cited list or bibliography easier.

15d Set up a research log.

Keeping a research log will make the job of writing and documenting your sources more efficient and accurate. Use your research log to jot down ideas about possible sources and to keep track of materials. When you record an online source in your log, include the URL or other information that will help you find the source again.

Here are a few guidelines for setting up a research log:

1. Create a folder, and label it with a name that will be easy to identify, such as *Research Log for Project on Messaging*.
2. Within this folder, create subfolders that will help you manage your project. These subfolders might include *Notes on Hypothesis and Thesis, Background Information, Visuals, Draft 1, Working Bibliography*, and so on.

You might prefer to begin a blog for your research project. You can use it to record your thoughts on the reading you are doing and, especially, add links from there to Web sites, documents, and articles you have found online.

Whatever form your research log takes, you must clearly distinguish the notes and comments you make from quoted passages you record (see Chapter 17).

15e Move from hypothesis to working thesis.

As you gather information, search catalogs and databases, and read and evaluate sources, you will probably refine your research question and change your hypothesis significantly. Only after you have explored your hypothesis, tested it, and sharpened it by reading, writing, and talking with others does it become a working thesis.

David Craig, the student whose hypothesis appears in 15b, did quite a bit of research on messaging language, youth literacy, and the possible connection between the two. The more he read, the more he felt

For David Craig's research essay, see Chapter 52.

that the hypothesis suggested by his discussion with instructors—that messaging had contributed to a decline in youth literacy—did not hold up. Thus, he shifted his attention to the positive effects of messaging on communication skills and developed the following working thesis: "Although some educators criticize messaging, it may aid literacy by encouraging young people to use words and to write—even if messaging requires a different kind of writing."

In doing your own research, you may find that your interest shifts, that a whole line of inquiry is unproductive, or that your hypothesis is simply wrong. The process of research pushes you to learn more about your hypothesis and to make it more precise.

16 Doing Research

How would you find out where to get the best coffee in town, or how to find sources for a Web project on a 1930s film star? Whether you are researching pizza or Picasso, you need to be familiar with the kinds of sources you are likely to use, the searches you can perform, and the types of research you will do most often: library, Internet, and field research.

16a Understand different kinds of sources.

Sources can include data from interviews and surveys, books and articles in print and online, Web sites, film, video, images, and more. Consider these important differences among sources.

Primary and secondary sources

Primary sources provide firsthand knowledge, while secondary sources report on or analyze the research of others. Primary sources are basic sources of raw information, including your own field research; films, works of art, or other objects you examine; literary works you read; and eyewitness accounts, photographs, news reports, and historical documents (such as letters and speeches). Secondary sources are descriptions or interpretations of primary sources, such as researchers' reports, reviews, biographies, and encyclopedia articles. Often what constitutes a primary or secondary source depends on the purpose of your research. A critic's evaluation of a film, for instance, serves as a secondary source if you are writing about the film but as a primary source if you are studying the critic's writing.

Scholarly and popular sources

While nonacademic sources like magazines can help you get started on a research project, you will usually want to depend more heavily on authorities in a field, whose work generally appears in scholarly journals in print or online. The following list will help you distinguish scholarly and popular sources:

SCHOLARLY

POPULAR

Title often contains the word *Journal*

Journal usually does not appear in title

Source available mainly through libraries and library databases

Source generally available outside of libraries (at newsstands or from a home Internet connection)

(continued)

SCHOLARLY	POPULAR
Few commercial advertisements	Many advertisements
Authors identified with academic credentials	Authors are usually journalists or reporters hired by the publication, not academics or experts
Summary or abstract appears on first page of article; articles are fairly long	No summary or abstract; articles are fairly short
Articles cite sources and provide bibliographies	Articles may include quotations but do not cite sources or provide bibliographies

Older and more current sources

Most projects can benefit from both older, historical sources and more current ones. Some older sources are classics, essential for understanding later scholarship. Others are simply dated. Whether a source appeared hundreds of years ago or this morning, evaluate it carefully to determine how useful it will be for you.

16b   Use the library to get started.

Many beginning researchers are tempted to assume that all the information they could possibly need is readily available on the Internet from a home connection. However, it is a good idea to begin almost any research project with the sources available in your college library.

Reference librarians

The purpose of a college reference library is to help students find information—and the staff of your library, especially reference librarians, will willingly help you figure out how to get started, what resources to choose for your project, and how to research more effectively. When in doubt, ask your librarian! You can make an appointment to talk with a librarian about your research project and get specific recommendations about databases and other helpful places to begin your research. In addition, many libraries have online tours and chat environments where students can ask questions about their research.

Wikis as Sources

"Why doesn't my instructor want me to use Wikipedia as a source?" Wikis are sites that users can add to and edit as they see fit; as a result, their contents are not always reliable. It's true that Wikipedia, a hugely popular site, has such a large and enthusiastic audience that users are likely to catch mistakes and remove deliberately false information quickly. But you can never be certain that a wiki entry has not been tampered with. Use wikis as sources for preliminary research and then make sure that you double-check any information you find there.

Catalogs and databases

Your library's computers hold many resources not accessible to students except through the library's system. In addition to the library's own catalog of books and other holdings, most college libraries also subscribe to a large number of databases—electronic collections of information, such as indexes to journal and magazine articles, texts of news stories and legal cases, lists of sources on particular topics, and compilations of statistics—that students can access for free.

Reference works

Consulting general reference works is another good way to get started on a research project. These works are especially helpful for getting an overview of a topic, identifying subtopics, finding more specialized sources, and identifying useful keywords for electronic searches.

ENCYCLOPEDIAS

Encyclopedias offer general background on a subject and often include bibliographies that can point you to more specialized sources. Remember that encyclopedias will serve as a place to start your research—not as major sources for a research project.

BIOGRAPHICAL RESOURCES

The lives and historical settings of famous people are the topics of biographical dictionaries and indexes.

BIBLIOGRAPHIES

Bibliographies are collections of resources available on a subject—for example, Shakespeare or World War II. Bibliographies may be databases or bound collections, and they may list books alone, both books and articles, or media such as film or video. A bibliography may simply list or describe each resource it includes, or it may include analysis of the resources.

ALMANACS, YEARBOOKS, AND ATLASES

Almanacs and yearbooks contain data on current events and statistical information. Look in an atlas for maps and other geographic data.

16c   Find library resources.

The library is one of a researcher's best friends, especially in an age of digital communication. Your college library houses a great number of print materials and gives you access to electronic catalogs, indexes, and databases. Check your library's Web site or ask a librarian for an introduction to the available resources.

Search options

The most important tools your library offers are its online catalog and databases. Searching these tools will always be easier and more efficient if you use carefully chosen words to limit the scope of your research.

SUBJECT WORD SEARCHING

Catalogs and databases usually index their contents not only by author and title but also by subject headings—standardized words and phrases used to classify the subject matter of books and articles. (For books, most U.S. academic libraries use the *Library of Congress Subject Headings*, or LCSH, for this purpose.) When you search the catalog by subject, you need to use the exact subject words.

KEYWORD SEARCHING

Searches using keywords, on the other hand, make use of the computer's ability to look for any term in any field of the electronic record, including not just subject but also author, title, series, and notes. In article databases, a keyword search will look in abstracts and summaries of articles as well. Keyword searching is less restrictive, but it requires you to put some thought into choosing your search terms in order to get the best results.

ADVANCED SEARCHING

Many library catalogs and database search engines offer advanced search options (sometimes on a separate page) to help you combine keywords, search for an exact phrase, or exclude items containing

Advanced search page from a library catalog that incorporates Boolean operators

particular keywords. Often they limit your search in other ways as well, such as by date, language, country of origin, or location of the keyword within a site.

Many catalogs and databases offer a search option using the Boolean operators AND, OR, and NOT, and some allow you to use parentheses to refine your search or wildcards to expand it. Note that much Boolean decision making is done for you when you use an advanced search option (as on the advanced search page shown above). Note, too, that search engines vary in the exact terms and symbols they use to refine searches, so check before you search.

- AND *limits your search.* If you enter the terms *messaging* AND *language* AND *literacy*, the search engine will retrieve only those items that contain *all* the terms. Some search engines use a plus sign (+) instead of AND.

- OR *expands your search.* If you enter the terms *messaging* OR *language*, the computer will retrieve every item that contains the term *messaging* and every item that contains the term *language*.

- NOT *limits your search.* If you enter the terms *messaging* NOT *language*, the search engine will retrieve every item that contains *messaging* except those that also contain the term *language*. Some search engines use a minus sign (−) or AND NOT instead of NOT.

- *Parentheses customize your search.* Entering *messaging* AND (*literacy* OR *linguistics*), for example, will locate items that mention either of those terms in connection with messaging.

- *Wildcards expand your search.* Use a wildcard, usually an asterisk (*) or a question mark (?), to find related words that begin with the same letters. Entering *messag** will locate *message, messages,* and *messaging.*

- *Quotation marks narrow your search.* Most search engines interpret words within quotation marks as a phrase that must appear with the words in that exact order.

Books

The library catalog lists all the library's books.

CATALOG INFORMATION

Library catalogs follow a standard pattern of organization, with each holding identified by three kinds of entries: one headed by the *author's name*, one by the *title*, and one or (usually) more by the *subject*. If you can't find a particular source under any of these headings, you can search the catalog by using a combination of subject headings and keywords. Such searches may turn up other useful titles as well.

Catalog entries for books list not only the author, title, subject, and publication information but also a call number that indicates how the book is classified and where it is shelved. Many online catalogs allow you to save the information about the book while you continue searching and then retrieve the call numbers for all of the books you want to find in one list. Once you have the call number for a book, look for a library map or shelving plan to tell you where the book is housed. Take the time to browse through the books near the call number you are looking for. Often you will find other books related to your topic nearby.

Following is a page of results for noted linguist and author David Crystal. Many electronic catalogs indicate whether a book has been checked out and, if so, when it is due to be returned. Sometimes you must click on a link to check the availability of the book.

Results for author search in library catalog database

BOOK INDEXES

Indexes can help you quickly locate complete bibliographic information on a book when you know only one piece of it—the author's last name, perhaps, or the title. Indexes can also alert you to other works by a particular author or on a particular subject. If you are looking for an older book, you may find the information you need in a print index rather than in an electronic database.

REVIEW INDEXES

A review index will help you find reviews of books you are interested in so that you can check the relevance of a source or get a thumbnail sketch of its contents before you track it down. For reviews more than ten years old, you will generally need to consult the print version of the index.

Periodical articles

Titles of periodicals held by a library appear in its catalog, but the titles of individual articles do not. To find the contents of periodicals, you will need to use an index source.

PERIODICAL INDEXES

Periodical indexes are databases or print volumes that hold information about articles published in newspapers, magazines, and scholarly journals. Different indexes cover different groups of periodicals. Ask a reference librarian for guidance about the most relevant index for your topic.

General indexes of periodicals list articles from general-interest magazines (such as *Time* or *Newsweek*), newspapers, or a combination of these. General indexes usually provide current sources on a topic, but you may need to look further for in-depth articles.

Many disciplines have *specialized indexes and abstracts* to help researchers find detailed information. To use these resources most efficiently, ask a reference librarian for help.

Some electronic periodical indexes offer the full text of articles and some offer abstracts (short summaries) of the articles. Be sure not to confuse an abstract with a complete article. Full-text databases can be extremely convenient—you can read and print out articles directly from the computer, without the extra step of tracking down the periodical in question. However, don't limit yourself to full-text databases, which may not include the sources that would benefit your research most. Databases that offer abstracts give you an overview of the article's contents that can help you decide whether you need to spend time finding and reading the full text.

To locate an indexed article that seems promising for your research project, you can check the library catalog to see whether the periodical is available electronically and, if so, whether your library has access to it. Using the library computer network for access can help you avoid paying to view the text of the article that is available online only for subscribers or for a fee.

If the periodical is not available electronically (some scholarly journals, for example, are not), the library catalog also will tell you whether

Results of a database search

Article page with abstract

a print version is available in your library's periodicals room. This room probably has recent issues of hundreds or even thousands of newspapers, magazines, and scholarly journals, and it may also contain bound volumes of past issues and microfilm copies of older newspapers.

Bibliographies

Bibliographies (lists of sources) in books or articles you are using for your research can lead you to other valuable resources. In addition, check with a reference librarian to find out whether your library has more extensive bibliographies devoted to the area of your research.

Other library resources

In addition to books and periodicals, libraries give you access to many other useful materials that might be appropriate for your research.

- *Special collections and archives.* Your library may house archives (collections of valuable papers) and other special materials that are often available to student researchers.
- *Audio, video, multimedia, and art collections.* Many libraries have areas devoted to media and art, where they collect films, videos, paintings, and sound recordings.
- *Government documents.* Many libraries have collections of historical documents produced by local or state government offices. You can also look at the online version of the U.S. Government Printing Office (GPO Access) for electronic versions of government publications from the past decade or so.
- *Interlibrary loans.* To borrow books, videos, copies of journal articles, or audio materials from another library, use an interlibrary loan. Some loans can take time, so be sure to plan ahead.

16d Search the Internet.

The Internet is many college students' favorite way of accessing information, and it's true that much information — including authoritative sources identical to those your library provides — can be found online, sometimes for free. However, information in library databases comes from identifiable and professionally edited sources; because no one is responsible for regulating information on the Web, you need to take special care to find out which information online is reliable and which is not. (See Chapter 17 for more on evaluating sources.)

Internet searches

Research using a search tool such as Google usually begins with a key-word search. Because the Internet contains vastly more material than the largest library catalog or database, Internet searching requires care in the choice of keywords. For example, if you need information on legal issues regarding the Internet and enter *Internet* and *law* as key-words in a Google search, you will get over three million hits. You may find what you need on the first page of hits, but if not, you will need to choose new keywords that lead to more specific sources.

Bookmarking tools

Today's powerful bookmarking tools can help you browse, sort, and track resources online. Social bookmarking sites allow users to tag information and share it with others. Once you register on a social bookmarking site, you can tag an online resource with any words you choose. Users' tags are visible to all other users. If you find a helpful site, you can check to see how others have tagged it and quickly browse similar tags to find related information. You can sort and group information according to your tags. Fellow users whose tags you like and trust can become part of your network so that you can follow their sites of interest.

Web browsers can also help you bookmark and return to online resources that you have found. However, unlike the bookmarking tools in a Web browser, which are tied to one machine, social bookmarking tools are available from any computer with an Internet connection.

Authoritative sources online

You can find many sources online that are authoritative and reliable. For example, the Internet enables you to enter virtual libraries that allow access to some collections in libraries other than your own. Online collections housed in government sites can also be reliable and useful sources. The Library of Congress, the National Institutes of Health, and the U.S. Census Bureau, for example, have large online collections of articles. For current national news, consult online versions of reputable newspapers such as the *Washington Post* or the *Chicago Tribune*, or electronic sites for news services such as C-SPAN. To limit your searches to scholarly works, try Google Scholar.

Some scholarly journals (such as those from Berkeley Electronic Press) and general-interest magazines (including *Slate* and *Salon*) are published only on the Web, and many other publications, like *Newsweek*, the *New Yorker*, and the *New Republic*, make at least some of their contents available online for free.

16e   Conduct field research.

For many research projects, particularly those in the social sciences and business, you will need to collect field data. The "field" may be many things—a classroom, a church, a laboratory, or the corner grocery store. As a field researcher, you will need to discover *where* you can find relevant information, *how* to gather it, and *who* might be your best providers of information.

Interviewing

Some information is best obtained by asking direct questions of other people. If you can talk with an expert—in person, on the telephone, or via the Internet—you might get information you could not obtain through any other kind of research. In addition to getting an expert opinion, you might ask for firsthand accounts or suggestions of other places to look or other people to consult.

AT A GLANCE
Conducting an Interview

1. Determine your purpose, and be sure it relates to your research question and your hypothesis.
2. Set up the interview well in advance. Specify how long it will take, and if you wish to record the session, ask permission to do so.
3. Prepare a written list of factual and open-ended questions. Brainstorming or freewriting can help you come up with questions (6a and b). Leave plenty of space for notes after each question. If the interview proceeds in a direction that seems fruitful, do not feel that you have to ask all of your prepared questions.
4. Record the subject, date, time, and place of the interview.
5. Thank those you interview, either in person or in a letter or email.

Observing

Trained observers report that making a faithful record of an observation requires intense concentration and mental agility. Moreover, an observer is never neutral—he or she always has an angle on what is being observed.

Conducting an Observation

1. Determine the purpose of the observation, and be sure it relates to your research question and hypothesis.
2. Brainstorm about what you are looking for, but don't be rigidly bound to your expectations.
3. Develop an appropriate system for recording data. Consider using a split notebook or page: on one side, record your observations directly; on the other, record your thoughts and interpretations.
4. Record the date, time, and place of the observation.

Conducting surveys

Surveys usually depend on questionnaires. On any questionnaire, the questions should be clear and easy to understand and designed so that you can analyze the answers easily. Questions that ask respondents to say *yes* or *no* or to rank items on a scale are particularly easy to tabulate:

The parking facilities on our campus are adequate.

○ Strongly agree　　○ Somewhat agree　　○ Unsure　　○ Somewhat disagree　　○ Strongly disagree

---

Designing a Survey Questionnaire

1. Write out your purpose, and review your research question and hypothesis to determine the kinds of questions to ask.
2. Figure out how to reach the respondents you need.
3. Draft potential questions, and make sure that each question calls for a short, specific answer.
4. Test the questions on several people, and revise questions that seem unfair, ambiguous, too hard to answer, or too time consuming.
5. For a questionnaire that is to be mailed or emailed, draft a cover letter explaining your purpose.
6. On the final version of the questionnaire, leave adequate space for answers.
7. Proofread the questionnaire carefully.

*Analyzing, synthesizing, and interpreting data
from field research*

To make sense of your data, find a focus for your analysis, since you can't pay attention to everything. Then synthesize the data by looking for recurring words or ideas that fall into patterns. Establish a system for coding your information, labeling each pattern you identify—a plus sign for every positive response, for example. Finally, interpret your data by summing up the meaning of what you have found. What is the significance of your findings? Be careful not to make large generalizations.

Evaluating Sources and Taking Notes **17**

The difference between a useful source and a poor one depends to a great extent on your topic, purpose, and audience. On almost any topic you can imagine (Why do mosquitoes bite? Who reads fan fiction? What musicians influenced Sonic Youth?), you will need research—looking into sources, gathering data, and thinking critically about these sources—to answer the question. With most topics, in fact, your problem will not be so much finding sources as figuring out *which* sources to consult in the limited time you have available. Learning how to tell which sources are best for you allows you to use your time wisely, and taking effective notes allows you to put the sources to work for you.

17a Understand the purpose of sources.

Why do writers decide to use one source rather than another? Sources serve different purposes, so part of evaluating sources involves deciding what you need the source to provide for your research projects. You may need background information or context that your audience will need to follow your writing; explanations of concepts unfamiliar to your audience; verbal and visual emphasis for your points; authority or evidence for your claims, which can help you create your own authority; other perspectives on your topic; or counter-examples or counter-evidence that you need to consider.

As you begin to work with your sources, make notes in your research log about why you plan to use a particular source. You should also begin your working bibliography.

17b   Create a working bibliography.

A working bibliography is a list of sources that you may potentially use for your project. As you find and begin to evaluate research sources—articles, books, Web sites, and so on—you should record source information for every source you think you might use. (Relevant information includes everything you need to find the source again and cite it correctly; the information you will need varies based on the type of source, whether you found it in a library or not, and whether you consulted it in print or online.) The emphasis here is on *working* because the list will probably include materials that end up not being useful. For this reason, you don't absolutely need to put all entries into the documentation style you will use (see Chapters 49–55). If you do follow the required documentation style, however, that part of your work will be done when you prepare the final draft.

The following chart will help you keep track of the sorts of information you should try to find:

Type of Source	Information to Collect (if applicable)
Print book	Library call number, author(s) or editor(s), title and subtitle, place of publication, publisher, year of publication, any other information (translator, edition, volume)
Part of a book	Call number, author(s) of part, title of part, author(s) or editor(s) of book, title of book, place of publication, publisher, year of publication, inclusive page numbers for part
Print periodical article	Call number of periodical, author(s) of article, title of article, name of periodical, volume number, issue number, date of issue, inclusive page numbers for article
Electronic source	Author(s), title of document, title of site, editor(s) of site, sponsor of site, publication information for print version of source, name of database or online service, date of electronic publication or last update, date you accessed the source, URL

For other kinds of sources (films, recordings, visuals), you should also list the information required by the documentation style you are using (see Chapters 49–55), and note where you found the information.

TALKING THE TALK

Research with an Open Mind

"What's wrong with looking for sources that back up what I want to say?" When you start researching a topic, keep an open mind: investigate every important source, even if you think you won't agree with it. If all your sources take the same position you take, you may be doing some pretty selective searching — and you may be missing a big part of the picture. Who knows? You may change your position after learning more about the topic. Even if you don't, ignoring counterarguments and other points of view harms your credibility, suggesting that you haven't done your homework.

Annotated bibliography

You might wish to annotate your working bibliography to include your own description and comments as well as publishing information (whether or not annotations are required) because annotating can help you understand and remember what the source says. If your instructor requires an annotated bibliography, be sure to ask for the specific guidelines you are to follow in creating the bibliography.

Annotations can sometimes be very detailed and may include summaries of the main points in a source and evaluations of the source's usefulness. However, most annotations students do on their own include fairly brief descriptions and comments.

ANNOTATED BIBLIOGRAPHY ENTRY

Gere, Anne Ruggles. "Kitchen Tables and Rented Rooms: The Extracurriculum

    of Composition." *Literacy: A Critical Sourcebook*. Ed. Ellen Cushman,

    Eugene R. Kintgen, Barry M. Kroll, and Mike Rose. Boston: Bedford, 2001.

    275–89. Print. This history of writing instruction argues that people teach

    writing and learn to write—and always have—more often in informal

    places like kitchens than in traditional writing classrooms. Gere presents

    numerous examples and comments on their importance to the study of

    writing today.

 bedfordstmartins.com/everydaywriter
Student Writing

17c   Evaluate a source's usefulness and credibility.

Since you want the information and ideas you glean from sources to be reliable and persuasive, you must evaluate each potential source carefully. The following guidelines can help you assess the usefulness and credibility of sources you are considering:

- *Your purpose.* What will this source add to your research project? Does it help you support a major point, demonstrate that you have thoroughly researched your topic, or help establish your own credibility through its authority?

- *Relevance.* How closely related is the source to the narrowed topic you are pursuing? You may need to read beyond the title and opening paragraph to check for relevance.

- *Level of specialization and audience.* General sources can be helpful as you begin your research, but you may then need the authority or currency of more specialized sources. On the other hand, extremely specialized works may be very hard to understand. Who was the source originally written for — the general public? experts in the field? advocates or opponents? How does this fit with your concept of your own audience?

- *Credentials of the publisher or sponsor.* What can you learn about the publisher or sponsor of the source you are using? For example, is it a newspaper known for integrity, or is it a tabloid? Is it a popular source, or is it sponsored by a professional or governmental organization or academic institution? If you're evaluating a book, is the publisher one you recognize or can find described on its own Web site? No hard and fast rules exist for deciding what kind of source to use. But knowing the sponsor's or publisher's credentials can help you determine whether a source is appropriate for your research project.

- *Credentials of the author.* As you do your research, note names that come up from one source to another, since these references may indicate that the author is influential in the field. An author's credentials may also be presented in the article, book, or Web site, or you can search the Internet for information about the author. In U.S. academic writing, experts and those with significant experience in a field have more authority on the subject than others.

- *Date of publication.* Recent sources are often more useful than older ones, particularly in the sciences or other fields that change rapidly. However, in some fields — such as the humanities — the most authoritative works may be older ones. The publication dates of Internet sites can often be difficult to pin down. And even for sites that include dates of posting, remember that the material posted may have been composed some time earlier.

- *Accuracy of the source.* How accurate and complete is the information in the source? How thorough is the bibliography or list of works cited that accompanies the source? Can you find other sources that corroborate what your source is saying?
- *Stance of the source.* Identify the source's point of view or rhetorical stance, and scrutinize it carefully. Does the source present facts, or does it interpret or evaluate them? If it presents facts, what is included and what is omitted, and why? If it interprets or evaluates information that is not disputed, the source's stance may be obvious, but at other times, you will need to think carefully about the source's goals (17d). What does the author or sponsoring group want? to convince you of an idea? sell you something? call you to action in some way?
- *Cross-references to the source.* Is the source cited in other works? If you see your source cited by others, notice how they cite it and what they say about it to find additional clues to its credibility.

For more on evaluating Web sources and periodical articles, see the Source Maps on pp. 198–201.

17d Read critically, and interpret sources.

For those sources that you want to analyze more closely, reading with a critical eye can make your research process more efficient. Use the following tips to guide your critical reading.

Your research question

As you read, keep your research question in mind, and ask yourself the following questions:

- How does this material address your research question and support your hypothesis?
- What quotations from this source might help support your thesis?
- Does the source include counterarguments to your hypothesis that you will need to answer? If so, what answers can you provide?

SOURCE MAP: Evaluating Web Sources

Is the sponsor credible?

1 Who is the **sponsor or publisher** of the source? See what information you can get from the URL. The domain names for government sites may end in *.gov* or *.mil* and for educational sites in *.edu*. The ending *.org* may — but does not always — indicate a nonprofit organization. If you see a tilde (~) or percent sign (%) followed by a name, or if you see a word such as *users* or *members*, the page's creator may be an individual, not an institution. In addition, check the header and footer, where the sponsor may be identified. The page shown here, from the domain **niemanwatchdog.org**, is from a site sponsored by the nonprofit Nieman Foundation for Journalism at Harvard University.

2 Look for an *About* page or a link to a home page for background information on the sponsor. Is a mission statement included? What are the sponsoring organization's purpose and point of view? Does the mission statement seem balanced? What is the purpose of the site (to inform, to persuade, to advocate for a cause, to advertise, or something else)? Does the information on the site come directly from the sponsor, or is the material reprinted from another source? If it is reprinted, check the original.

Is the author credible?

3 What are the **author's credentials**? Look for information accompanying the material on the page. You can also run a search on the author to find out more. Does the author seem qualified to write about this topic?

Is the information credible and current?

4 When was the information **posted or last updated**? Is it recent enough to be useful?

5 Does the page document sources with **footnotes or links**? If so, do the sources seem credible and current? Does the author include any additional resources for further information? Look for ways to corroborate the information the author provides.

① Sponsor or Publisher

④ Posted or Last Updated

② *About* Page

⑤ Links

③ Author's Credentials

SOURCE MAP: Evaluating Articles

Determine the relevance of the source.

1 Look for an **abstract**, which provides a summary of the entire article. Is this source directly related to your research? Does it provide useful information and insights? Will your readers consider it persuasive support for your thesis?

Determine the credibility of the publication.

2 Consider the publication's **title**. Words in the title such as *Journal*, *Review*, and *Quarterly* may indicate that the periodical is a scholarly source. Most research projects rely on authorities in a particular field, whose work usually appears in scholarly journals. For more on distinguishing between scholarly and popular sources, see 16a.

3 Try to determine the **publisher or sponsor**. This journal is published by Johns Hopkins University Press. Academic presses such as this one generally review articles carefully before publishing them and bear the authority of their academic sponsors.

Determine the credibility of the author.

4 Evaluate the **author's credentials**. In this case, they are given in a note, which indicates that the author is a college professor and has written at least two books on related topics.

Determine the currency of the article.

5 Look at the **publication date**, and think about whether your topic and your credibility depend on your use of very current sources.

Determine the accuracy of the article.

6 Look at the **sources cited** by the author of the article. Here, they are documented in footnotes. Ask yourself whether the works the author has cited seem credible and current. Are any of these works cited in other articles you've considered?

In addition, consider the following questions:

- What is the article's stance or point of view? What are the author's goals? What does the author want you to know or believe?

- How does this source fit in with your other sources? Does any of the information it provides contradict or challenge other sources?

HUMAN RIGHTS QUARTERLY

② Title of Publication

Prisons and Politics in Contemporary Latin America

① Abstract

Mark Ungar*

④ Author's Credentials

ABSTRACT

Despite democratization throughout Latin America, massive human rights abuses continue in the region's prisons. Conditions have become so bad that most governments have begun to enact improvements, including new criminal codes and facility decongestion. However, once in place, these reforms are undermined by chaotic criminal justice systems, poor policy administration, and rising crime rates leading to greater detention powers for the police. After describing current prison conditions in Latin America and the principal reforms to address them, this article explains how political and administrative limitations hinder the range of agencies and officials responsible for implementing those changes.

I. INTRODUCTION

Prison conditions not only constitute some of the worst human rights violations in contemporary Latin American democracies, but also reveal fundamental weaknesses in those democracies. Unlike most other human rights problems, those in the penitentiary system cannot be easily explained with authoritarian legacies or renegade officials. The systemic killing, overcrowding, disease, torture, rape, corruption, and due process abuses all occur under the state's twenty-four hour watch. Since the mid-1990s,

* Mark Ungar is Associate Professor of Political Science at Brooklyn College, City University of New York. Recent publications include the books *Elusive Reform: Democracy and the Rule of Law in Latin America* (Lynne Rienner, 2002) and *Violence and Politics: Globalization's Paradox* (Routledge, 2001) as well as articles and book chapters on democratization, policing, and judicial access. He works with Amnesty International USA and local rights groups in Latin America.

Human Rights Quarterly 25 (2003) 909–934 © 2003 by The Johns Hopkins University Press

⑤ Publication Date

③ Publisher

---

n America   915

...an. In Venezuela, the ...er 100, but jumped to ...ice Ministry agency in ...ven prisoners, far from ...state alone, the number ...1997.[11] Inmates form ...la Capital (PCC)—with ...d prisoners. In the riots ...001—which began in ...hat amount, and spread ...000 inmates—the PCC ...cation of PCC leaders. ...all sizes and security ...—often at unaffordable ...country's largest, some ...mmed into tiny airless ...ren of inmates living in ...d many of those in the ...curity La Paz facility of ...al en la Lucha Contra el ...to nearly airless cells of ...s lack potable water, ...infested with rats and ...also bring in weapons ...r trade in cocaine and ...ouse by prison officials, ...the National Guard in ...e often face retribution. ...39 prisoners protesting ...colony of El

10. INSPECTOR GENERAL DE CÁRCELES, INFORME ANNUAL (Caracas: Ministerio de Justicia 1994).
11. *Overcrowding Main Cause of Riots in Latin American Prisons*, AFP, 30 Dec. 1997.
12. Interviews with inmates, speaking on condition of anonymity in San Pedro prison (19 July 2000); Interviews with inmates, speaking on condition of anonymity in La Paz FELCN Prison (20 July 2000).
13. Typhus, cholera, tuberculosis, and scabies run rampant and the HIV rate may be as high as 25 percent. The warden of Retén de la Planta, where cells built for one inmate house three or four, says the prisons "are collapsing" because of insufficient budgets to train personnel. "Things fall apart and stay that way." Interview, Luis A. Lara Roche, Warden of Retén de la Planta, Caracas, Venezuela, 19 May 1995. At El Dorado prison in Bolívar state, there is one bed for every four inmates, cells are infested with vermin, and inmates lack clean bathing water and eating utensils.
14. *La Crisis Penitenciaria*, EL NACIONAL (Caracas), 2 Sept. 1988, at D2. On file with author.

⑥ Sources Cited

AT A GLANCE

Guidelines for Examining Potential Sources

Looking quickly at the various parts of a source can provide useful information and help you decide whether to explore that particular source more thoroughly. You are already familiar with some of these basic elements: title and subtitle, title page and copyright page, home page, table of contents, index, footnotes, and bibliography. Be sure to check other items as well.

- *Abstracts* — concise summaries of articles and books — routinely precede journal articles and are often included in indexes and databases.
- A *preface* or *foreword* generally discusses the writer's purpose and thesis.
- *Subheadings* within the text can alert you to how much detail is given on a topic.
- A *conclusion* or *afterword* may summarize or draw the strands of an argument together.
- For a digital source, click on some of the *links* to see if they're useful, and see if the overall *design* of the site is easy to navigate.

The author's stance and tone

Even a seemingly factual report, such as an encyclopedia article, is filled with judgments, often unstated. Read with an eye for the author's overall rhetorical stance, or perspective, as well as for facts or explicit opinions. Also pay attention to the author's tone, the way his or her attitude toward the topic and audience is conveyed. The following questions can help:

- Is the author a strong advocate or opponent of something? a skeptical critic? a specialist in the field?
- Are there any clues to why the author takes this stance?
- How does this stance affect the author's presentation and your reaction to it?
- What facts does the author include? Can you think of any important fact that is omitted?
- What is the author's tone? Is it cautious, angry, flippant, serious, impassioned? What words indicate this tone?

The author's argument and evidence

Every piece of writing takes a position. Even a scientific report implicitly "argues" that we should accept it and its data as reliable. As you read, look for the main point or the main argument the author is making. Try to identify the reasons the author gives to support his or her position. Then try to determine *why* the author takes this position.

- How persuasive is the evidence? Can you think of a way to refute it?
- Can you detect any questionable logic or fallacious thinking (13e)?
- Does this author disagree with arguments you have read elsewhere? If so, what causes the disagreements — differences about facts or about how to interpret facts?

17e Synthesize sources.

When you read and interpret a source—for example, when you consider its purpose and relevance, its author's credentials, its accuracy, and the kind of argument it is making—you are analyzing the source. Analysis requires you to take apart something complex (such as an article in a scholarly journal) and look closely at the parts to understand the whole better. For academic writing you also need to *synthesize*—group similar pieces of information together and look for patterns—so you can put your sources (and your own knowledge and experience) together in an original argument. Synthesis is the flip side of analysis: you already understand the parts, so your job is to assemble them into a new whole.

SYNTHESIS: Finding Patterns

Look through your sources carefully to find what you need.

Ask...

What are the key ideas in each source?

What patterns can you identify?

How do the sources' perspectives relate to your own perspective?

Acknowledge that the related ideas you find may not fit smoothly together.

To synthesize sources for a research project, try the following tips:

- *Read the material carefully.* For tips on reading with a critical eye, see Chapter 12.
- *Determine the important ideas in each source.* Take notes on each source (17f). Identify and summarize the key ideas of each piece.
- *Formulate a position.* Review the key ideas of each source and figure out how they fit together. Look for patterns: discussions of causes and effects, specific parts of a larger issue, background information, and so on. Be sure to consider the complexity of the issue, and demonstrate that you have considered more than one perspective.
- *Summon evidence to support your position.* You might use paraphrases, summaries, or direct quotations from your sources as evidence (18a), or your personal experience or prior knowledge. Integrate quotations properly (see Chapter 18), and keep your ideas central to the piece of writing.
- *Deal with counterarguments.* You don't have to use every idea or every source available — some will be more useful than others. However, ignoring evidence that opposes your position makes your argument weaker. You should acknowledge the existence of valid opinions that differ from yours, and try to explain why they are incorrect or incomplete.
- *Combine your source materials effectively.* Be careful to avoid simply summarizing or listing your research. Think carefully

SYNTHESIS: Combining Ideas

Weave your sources into your text.

Ask...

Why are you using each source?

How do your sources fit with what you want to say?

How can you arrange your ideas and others' ideas for the best effect?

Make sure your sources support your own voice and message.

about how the ideas in your reading support your argument. Try to weave the various sources together rather than discussing your sources one by one.

17f Take notes and annotate sources.

Note-taking methods vary greatly from one researcher to another, so you may decide to use a computer file, a notebook, or index cards. Regardless of the method, however, you should (1) record enough information to help you recall the major points of the source; (2) put the information in the form in which you are most likely to incorporate it into your research essay, whether a summary, a paraphrase, or a quotation; and (3) note all the information you will need to cite the source accurately. The following example shows the major items a note should include:

ELEMENTS OF AN ACCURATE NOTE

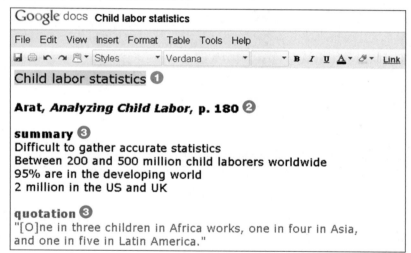

❶ *Use a subject heading.* Label each note with a brief but descriptive subject heading so that you can group similar subtopics together.

❷ *Identify the source.* List the author's name and a shortened title of the source, and a page number, if available. Your working-bibliography entry (17b) for the source will contain the full bibliographic information, so you don't need to repeat it in each note.

❸ *Indicate whether the note is a direct quotation, paraphrase, or summary.* Make sure quotations are copied accurately. Put square brackets around any change you make, and use ellipses if you omit material.

Taking complete notes will help you digest the source information as you read and incorporate the material into your text without inadvertently plagiarizing the source (see Chapter 18). Be sure to reread each note carefully, and recheck it against the source to make sure quotations, statistics, and specific facts are accurate.

Quoting

Some of the notes you take will contain quotations, which give the *exact words* of a source. Here, for example, is a note with a quotation that David Craig planned to use in his research paper:

QUOTATION NOTE

Google docs **Comments from educators**

File   Edit   View   Insert   Format   Table   Tools   Help

💾 🖨 ↶ ↷ 🖌 ▾ Styles ▾ Verdana ▾ ▾ **B** *I* U A ▾ ✎ ▾ Link

Comments from educators ❶

Jennifer 8. Lee, "I Think, Therefore IM" ❷
New York Times **(Web)**

quotation: ❸
Melanie Weaver was stunned by some of the term papers she received from a 10th-grade class she recently taught as part of an internship. "They would be trying to make a point in a paper, they would put a smiley face in the end," says Ms. Weaver, who teaches at Alvernia College in Reading, Pa. "If they were presenting an argument and they needed to present an opposite view, they would put in a frown."

---

❶ Subject heading

❷ Author and short title of source (no page number for electronic source)

❸ Direct quotation

AT A GLANCE

Guidelines for Taking Notes

- Copy quotations carefully, with punctuation, capitalization, and spelling *exactly* as in the original.
- Enclose the quotation in quotation marks; don't rely on your memory to distinguish your own words from those of the source.
- Use square brackets if you introduce words of your own into a quotation or make changes in it, and use ellipses if you omit material. If you later incorporate the quotation into your essay, copy it faithfully — brackets, ellipses, and all. (44b)
- Record the author's name, the shortened title, and the page number(s) on which the quotation appears. If the note refers to more than one page, use a slash (/) within the quotation to indicate where one page ends and another begins. For sources without page numbers, record the paragraph or other section number(s), if any.
- Make sure you have a corresponding working-bibliography entry with complete source information. (17b)
- Label the note with a subject heading, and identify it as a quotation.

Paraphrasing

A paraphrase accurately states all the relevant information from a passage *in your own words and sentence structures,* without any additional comments or elaborations. A paraphrase is useful when the main points of a passage, their order, and at least some details are important but — unlike passages worth quoting — the particular wording is not. Unlike a summary, a paraphrase always restates *all* the main points of a passage in the same order and often in about the same number of words.

ORIGINAL

Language play, the arguments suggest, will help the development of pronunciation ability through its focus on the properties of sounds and sound contrasts, such as rhyming. Playing with word endings and decoding the syntax of riddles will help the acquisition of grammar. Readiness to play with words and names, to exchange puns and to engage in nonsense talk, promotes links with semantic development. The kinds of dialogue interaction illustrated above are likely to have consequences for the development of conversational skills. And language play, by its nature, also contributes greatly to what in recent years has been called *metalinguistic awareness*, which is turning out to be of critical importance in the development of language skills in general and of literacy skills in particular.

– DAVID CRYSTAL, *Language Play* (180)

UNACCEPTABLE PARAPHRASE: STRAYING FROM THE AUTHOR'S IDEAS

Crystal argues that playing with language—creating rhymes, figuring out how riddles work, making puns, playing with names, using invented words, and so on—helps children figure out a great deal about language, from the basics of pronunciation and grammar to how to carry on a conversation. Increasing their understanding of how language works in turn helps them become more interested in learning new languages and in pursuing education (180).

This paraphrase starts off well enough, but it moves away from paraphrasing the original to inserting the writer's ideas; Crystal says nothing about learning new languages or pursuing education.

UNACCEPTABLE PARAPHRASE: USING THE AUTHOR'S WORDS

Crystal suggests that language play, including rhyme, helps children improve pronunciation ability, that looking at word endings and decoding the syntax of riddles allows them to understand grammar, and that other kinds of dialogue interaction teach conversation. Overall, language play may be of critical importance in the development of language and literacy skills (180).

Because the highlighted phrases are either borrowed from the original without quotation marks or changed only superficially, this paraphrase plagiarizes.

UNACCEPTABLE PARAPHRASE: USING THE AUTHOR'S SENTENCE STRUCTURES

Language play, Crystal suggests, will improve pronunciation by zeroing in on sounds such as rhymes. Having fun with word endings and analyzing riddle structure will help a person acquire grammar. Being prepared to play with language, to use puns and talk nonsense, improves the ability to use semantics. These playful methods of communication are likely to influence a person's ability to talk to others. And language play inherently adds enormously to what has recently been known as *metalinguistic awareness*, a concept of great magnitude in developing speech abilities generally and literacy abilities particularly (180).

Here is a paraphrase of the same passage that expresses the author's ideas accurately and acceptably:

ACCEPTABLE PARAPHRASE: IN THE STUDENT WRITER'S OWN WORDS

Crystal argues that playing with language—creating rhymes, figuring out riddles, making puns, playing with names, using invented words, and so on—helps children figure out a great deal, from the basics of pronunciation and grammar to how to carry on a conversation. This kind of play allows children to understand the overall concept of how language works, a concept that is key to learning to use—and read—language effectively (180).

AT A GLANCE

Guidelines for Paraphrasing

- Include all main points and any important details from the original source, in the same order in which the author presents them.
- State the meaning in your own words and sentence structures. If you want to include especially memorable language from the original, enclose it in quotation marks.
- Save your comments, elaborations, or reactions on another note.
- Record the author's name, the shortened title, and the page number(s) on which the original material appears. For sources without page numbers, record the paragraph, screen, or other section number(s), if any.
- Make sure you have a corresponding working-bibliography entry with complete source information. (17b)
- Label the note with a subject heading, and identify it as a paraphrase.

Summarizing

A summary is a significantly shortened version of a passage or even of a whole chapter or work that captures main ideas *in your own words.* Unlike a paraphrase, a summary uses just enough information to record the main points you wish to emphasize. To summarize a short passage, read it carefully and, without looking at the text, write a one- or two-sentence summary. Following is David Craig's note recording a summary of the Crystal passage on p. 207–8. Notice that it states the author's main points selectively—and without using his words.

SUMMARY NOTE

① Subject heading
② Author, title, page reference
③ Summary of source

For a long passage or an entire chapter, skim the headings and topic sentences, and make notes of each; then write your summary in a paragraph or two. For a whole book, you may want to refer to the preface and introduction as well as chapter titles, headings, and topic sentences—and your summary may take a page or more.

AT A GLANCE

Guidelines for Summarizing

- Include just enough information to recount the main points you want to cite. A summary is usually far shorter than the original.
- Use your own words. If you include any language from the original, enclose it in quotation marks.
- Record the author, shortened title, and page number(s) on which the original material appeared. For sources without page numbers, record the paragraph, screen, or other section number(s), if any.
- Make sure you have a corresponding working-bibliography entry with complete source information. (17b)
- Label the note with a subject heading, and identify it as a summary.

Identifying Sources

While some language communities and cultures expect audiences to recognize the sources of important documents and texts, thereby eliminating the need to cite them directly, conventions for writing in North America call for careful attribution of any quoted, paraphrased, or summarized material. When in doubt, explicitly identify your sources.

Annotating sources

Sometimes you may photocopy or print out a source you intend to use. In such cases, you can annotate the photocopies or printouts with your thoughts and questions and highlight interesting quotations and key terms.

You can copy online sources electronically, paste them into a computer file, and annotate them there. Try not to rely too heavily on copying or printing out whole pieces, however; you still need to read the material very carefully. And resist the temptation to treat copied material as notes, an action that could lead to inadvertent plagiarizing. (In a computer file, using a different color for text pasted from a source will help prevent this problem.)

Integrating Sources and Avoiding Plagiarism 18

In some ways, there really is nothing new under the sun, in writing and research as well as in life. Whatever writing you do has been influenced by what you have already read and experienced. As you work on your research project, you will be joining a scholarly conversation and responding to the work of others. Thus you will need to know how to use, integrate, and acknowledge the work of others.

Integrating sources into your writing can be quite a challenge. In fact, as a beginning researcher, you might do what Professor Rebecca Howard calls "patchwriting": that is, rather than integrate the sources smoothly and accurately, you patch together words, phrases, and even structures from sources into your own writing, sometimes without citation. The author of this textbook remembers doing just such "patchwriting" for a report in middle school on her hero, Dr. Albert Schweitzer.

AT A GLANCE

When to Quote, Paraphrase, or Summarize

QUOTE
- wording that is so memorable or powerful, or expresses a point so perfectly, that you cannot change it without weakening its meaning
- authors' opinions you wish to emphasize
- authors' words that show you are considering varying perspectives
- respected authorities whose opinions support your ideas
- authors whose opinions challenge or vary greatly from those of others in the field

PARAPHRASE
- passages you do not wish to quote but that use details important to your point

SUMMARIZE
- long passages in which the main point is important to your point but the details are not

Luckily, she had a teacher who sat patiently with her, showing her how to paraphrase and summarize and quote from the sources correctly and effectively. So it takes time and effort—and good instruction—to learn to integrate sources appropriately into your writing rather than patch-writing, which is sometimes considered plagiarism even if you didn't mean to plagiarize.

All writers need to understand current definitions of plagiarism (which have changed over time and differ from culture to culture) as well as the concept of intellectual property—the works protected by copyright and other laws—so they can give credit where credit is due.

18a   Decide whether to quote, paraphrase, or summarize.

You tentatively decided to quote, paraphrase, or summarize material when you took notes on your sources (17f). As you choose some of these sources for your research project and decide how to use them, however, you may reevaluate those decisions. The following guidelines can help you decide whether to quote, paraphrase, or summarize.

18b Integrate quotations, paraphrases, and summaries effectively.

Here are some general guidelines for integrating source materials into your writing.

Incorporating quotations

Quotations from respected authorities can help establish your credibility and show that you are considering various perspectives. However, because your essay is primarily your own work, limit your use of quotations.

BRIEF QUOTATIONS

Short quotations should run in with your text, enclosed by quotation marks (43a).

> In Miss Eckhart, Welty recognizes a character who shares with her "the love of her art and the love of giving it, the desire to give it until there is no more left" (10).

LONG QUOTATIONS

If you are following the style of the Modern Language Association (MLA), set off a prose quotation longer than four lines. If you are following the style of the American Psychological Association (APA), set off a quotation of more than forty words or more than one paragraph. If you are following *Chicago* style, set off a quotation of more than one hundred words or more than one paragraph. Begin such a quotation on a new line. For MLA style, indent every line one inch; for APA style, five to seven spaces; for *Chicago* style, indent the text or use a smaller font (check your instructor's preference). Quotation marks are unnecessary. Introduce long quotations with a signal phrase or a sentence followed by a colon.

The following long quotation follows MLA style:

A good seating arrangement can prevent problems; however, *withitness*, as defined by Woolfolk, works even better:

> Withitness is the ability to communicate to students that you are aware of what is happening in the classroom, that you "don't miss anything." With-it teachers seem to have "eyes in the back of their heads." They avoid becoming too absorbed with a few students, since this allows the rest of the class to wander. (359)

This technique works, however, only if students actually believe that their teacher will know everything that goes on.

INTEGRATING QUOTATIONS SMOOTHLY INTO YOUR TEXT

Carefully integrate quotations into your text so that they flow smoothly and clearly into the surrounding sentences. Use a signal phrase or verb, such as those identified in the following examples and listed below.

> As Eudora Welty notes, "learning stamps you with its moments. Childhood's learning," she continues, "is made up of moments. It isn't steady. It's a pulse" (9).

> In her essay, Haraway strongly opposes those who condemn technology outright, arguing that we must not indulge in a "demonology of technology" (181).

Notice that the examples alert readers to the quotations by using signal phrases that include the author's name. When you cite a quotation in this way, you need put only the page number in parentheses.

SIGNAL VERBS

acknowledges	concludes	emphasizes	replies
advises	concurs	expresses	reports
agrees	confirms	interprets	responds
allows	criticizes	lists	reveals
answers	declares	objects	says
asserts	describes	observes	states
believes	disagrees	offers	suggests
charges	discusses	opposes	thinks
claims	disputes	remarks	writes

BRACKETS AND ELLIPSES

In direct quotations, enclose in brackets any words you change or add, and indicate any deletions with ellipsis points (44f).

> "There is something wrong in the [Three Mile Island] area," one farmer told the Nuclear Regulatory Commission after the plant accident ("Legacy" 33).

> Economist John Kenneth Galbraith has pointed out that "large corporations cannot afford to compete with one another. . . . In a truly competitive market someone loses" (qtd. in Key 17).

Incorporating paraphrases and summaries

Introduce paraphrases and summaries clearly, usually with a signal phrase that includes the author of the source, as the highlighted words in this example indicate.

Professor of linguistics Deborah Tannen says that she offers her book *That's Not What I Meant!* to "women and men everywhere who are trying their best to talk to each other" (19). Tannen goes on to illustrate how communication between women and men breaks down and then to suggest that a full awareness of "genderlects" can improve relationships (297).

18c Integrate visuals and media effectively.

Choose visuals and media wisely, whether you use video, audio, photographs, illustrations, charts and graphs, or other kinds of images. Integrate all visuals and media smoothly into your text.

- *Does each visual or media file make a strong contribution to the written message?* Tangential or purely decorative visuals and media may weaken the power of your writing.
- *Is each visual or media file appropriate and fair to your subject?* An obviously biased perspective may seem unfair or manipulative to your audience.
- *Is each visual or media file appropriate for and fair to your audience?* Visuals and media should appeal to various members of your likely audience.

Whenever you post documents containing visuals or media to the Web, make sure you check for copyright information. While it is considered "fair use" to use such materials in an essay or other project for a college class, once that project is published on the Web, you might infringe on copyright protections if you do not ask the copyright holder for permission to use the visual or media file. U.S. copyright law considers the reproduction of works for purposes of teaching and scholarship to be "fair use" not bound by copyright, but the law is open to multiple intepretations. If you have questions about whether your work might infringe on copyright, ask your instructor for help.

Like quotations, paraphrases, and summaries, visuals and media need to be introduced and commented on in some way.

- Refer to the visual, audio, or video in the text (*As Fig. 3 demonstrates . . .*) and position it as close as possible after the first reference.
- Explain or comment on the relevance of the visual or media file. This can be done after the insertion point.
- Check the documentation system you are using to make sure you label visuals and media appropriately; MLA, for instance, asks that

you number and title tables and figures (*Table 1: Average Amount of Rainfall by Region*).

- If you are posting your document or essay on a Web site, make sure you have permission to use any visuals or media files that are covered by copyright.

For more on using visuals, see 9d.

18d Check for excessive use of source material.

Your text needs to synthesize your research in support of your own argument; it should not be a patchwork of quotations, paraphrases, and summaries from other people. You need a rhetorical stance that represents you as the author. If you cite too many sources, your own voice will disappear, a problem the following passage demonstrates:

> The United States is one of the countries with the most rapid population growth. In fact, rapid population increase has been a "prominent feature of American life since the founding of the republic" (Day 31). In the past, the cause of the high rate of population growth was the combination of large-scale immigration and a high birth rate. As Day notes, "Two facts stand out in the demographic history of the United States: first, the single position as a receiver of immigrants; second, our high rate of growth from natural increase" (31).
>
> Nevertheless, American population density is not as high as in most European countries. Day points out that the Netherlands, with a density of 906 persons per square mile, is more crowded than even the most densely populated American states (33).

TALKING THE TALK

Saying Something New

"What can I say about my topic that experts haven't already said?" All writers — no matter how experienced — face this problem. As you read more about your topic, you will soon see areas of disagreement among experts, who may not be as expert as they first appear. Notice what your sources say and, especially, what they don't say. Consider how your own interests and experiences give you a unique perspective on the topic. Slowly but surely you will identify a claim that you can make about the topic, one related to what others say but taking a new angle or adding something different to the discussion.

18e Understand why you should acknowledge your sources.

Acknowledging sources says to your reader that you have done your homework, that you have gained expertise on your topic, and that you are credible. Acknowledging sources can also demonstrate fairness—that you have considered several points of view. In addition, recognizing your sources can help provide background for your research by placing it in the context of other thinking. Most of all, you should acknowledge sources to help your readers follow your thoughts, understand how your ideas relate to the thoughts of others, and know where to go to find more information on your topic.

18f Know which sources to acknowledge.

As you carry out research, it is important to understand the distinction between materials that require acknowledgment (in in-text citations, footnotes, or endnotes; and in the works-cited list or bibliography) and those that do not.

Materials that do not require acknowledgment

- *Common knowledge.* If most readers already know a fact, you probably do not need to cite a source for it. You do not need to credit a source for the statement that Barack Obama was elected in 2008, for example.

- *Facts available in a wide variety of sources.* If a number of encyclopedias, almanacs, or textbooks include a certain piece of information, you usually need not cite a specific source for it.

- *Your own findings from field research.* If you conduct observations or surveys, simply announce your findings as your own. Acknowledge people you interview as individuals rather than as part of a survey.

Materials that require acknowledgment

Some of the information you use may need to be credited to a source.

- *Quotations, paraphrases, and summaries.* Whenever you use another person's words, ideas, or opinions, credit the source. Even though the wording of a paraphrase or summary is your own, you should still acknowledge the source.

- *Facts not widely known or claims that are arguable.* If your readers would be unlikely to know a fact, or if an author presents as fact a claim that may or may not be true, cite the source. If you are not sure whether a fact will be familiar to your readers or whether a statement is arguable, cite the source.

- *Visuals from any source.* Credit all visual and statistical material not derived from your own field research, even if you yourself create a graph or table from the data provided in a source.

- *Help provided by others.* If an instructor gave you a good idea or if friends responded to your draft or helped you conduct surveys, give credit.

18g   Uphold your academic integrity and avoid plagiarism.

One of the cornerstones of intellectual work is academic integrity. This principle accounts for our being able to trust those sources we use and to demonstrate that our own work is equally trustworthy. While there are many ways to damage academic integrity, two that are especially important are inaccurate or incomplete acknowledgment of sources in citations—sometimes called unintentional plagiarism—and plagiarism that is deliberately intended to pass off one writer's work as another's.

Whether it is intentional or not, plagiarism can result in serious consequences. At some colleges, students who plagiarize fail the course automatically; at others, they are expelled. Instructors who plagiarize, even inadvertently, have had their degrees revoked and their books

---

FOR MULTILINGUAL WRITERS

Plagiarism as a Cultural Concept

Many cultures do not recognize Western notions of plagiarism, which rest on a belief that language and ideas can be owned by writers. Indeed, in many countries other than the United States, and even within some communities in the United States, using the words and ideas of others without attribution is considered a sign of deep respect as well as an indication of knowledge. In academic writing in the United States, however, you should credit all materials except those that are common knowledge, that are available in a wide variety of sources, or that are your own creations (photographs, drawings, and so on) or your own findings from field research.

withdrawn from publication. And outside academic life, eminent political, business, and scientific leaders have been stripped of candidacies, positions, and awards because of plagiarism.

Inaccurate or incomplete citation of sources

If your paraphrase is too close to the wording or sentence structure of a source (even if you identify the source), if you do not identify the source of a quotation (even if you include the quotation marks), or if you fail to indicate clearly the source of an idea that you obviously did not come up with on your own, you may be accused of plagiarism even if your intent was not to plagiarize. Inaccurate or incomplete acknowledgment of sources often results either from carelessness or from not learning how to borrow material properly in the first place. Still, because the costs of even unintentional plagiarism can be severe, it's important to understand how it can happen and how you can guard against it.

As a writer of academic integrity, you will want to take responsibility for your research and for acknowledging all sources accurately. One easy way to keep track is to keep photocopies or printouts as you do your research; then you can identify needed quotations right on the copy.

Deliberate plagiarism

Deliberate plagiarism—handing in an essay written by a friend or purchased (or simply downloaded) from an essay-writing company; cutting and pasting passages directly from source materials without

---

AT A GLANCE

Avoiding Plagiarism

- Maintain an accurate and thorough working bibliography. (17b)
- Establish a consistent note-taking system, listing sources and page numbers and clearly identifying all quotations, paraphrases, summaries, statistics, and visuals. (17f)
- Identify all quotations with quotation marks — both in your notes and in your essay. Be sure your summaries and paraphrases use your own words and sentence structures. (18b)
- Give a citation or note for each quotation, paraphrase, summary, arguable assertion or opinion, statistic, and visual that is from a source. Prepare an accurate and complete list of sources cited according to the required documentation style. (See Chapters 49–55.)
- Plan ahead on writing assignments so that you can avoid the temptation to take shortcuts.

marking them with quotation marks and acknowledging your sources; failing to credit the source of an idea or concept in your text—is what most people think of when they hear the word *plagiarism*. This form of plagiarism is particularly troubling because it represents dishonesty and deception: those who intentionally plagiarize present the hard thinking and hard work of someone else as their own, and they claim knowledge they really don't have, thus deceiving their readers.

Deliberate plagiarism is also fairly simple to spot: your instructor will be well acquainted with your writing and likely to notice any sudden shifts in the style or quality of your work. In addition, by typing a few words from an essay into a search engine, your instructor can identify "matches" very easily.

> **bedfordstmartins.com/everydaywriter**
> **Research Tutorials**

19 Writing a Research Project

Everyday decisions often call for research and writing. In trying to choose between colleges in different towns, for example, one student made a long list of questions to answer: Which location had the lower cost of living? Which school offered more financial aid? Which program would be more likely to help graduates find a job? After conducting careful research, he was able to write a letter of acceptance to one place and a letter of regret to the other. In much the same way, when you are working on an academic project, there comes a time to draw the strands of your research together and articulate your conclusions in writing.

19a Refine your writing plans.

You should by now have notes containing facts, opinions, paraphrases, summaries, quotations, and other material; you probably have some images or media to include as well. You may also have ideas about how to synthesize these many pieces of information. And you should have some sense of whether your hypothesis has sufficient support. Now is the time to reconsider your purpose, audience, stance, and working thesis.

- What is your central purpose? What other purposes, if any, do you have?
- What is your stance toward your topic? Are you an advocate, a critic, a reporter, an observer?
- What audience(s) are you addressing?
- How much background information or context does your audience need?
- What supporting information will your readers find convincing— examples? quotations from authorities? statistics? graphs, charts, or other visuals? data from your field research?
- Should your tone be that of a colleague, an expert, a student?
- How can you establish common ground with your readers and show them that you have considered points of view other than your own? (See 14e and Chapter 21.)
- What is your working thesis trying to establish? Will your audience accept it?

Developing an explicit thesis

Writing out an explicit thesis statement allows you to articulate your major points and to see how well they carry out your purpose and appeal to your audience. Before you begin a full draft, then, try to develop your working thesis into an explicit statement.

David Craig developed the following explicit thesis statement:

> Instant messaging seems to be a positive force in the development of youth literacy because it promotes regular contact with words, the use of a written medium for communication, and the development of an alternative form of literacy.

FOR MULTILINGUAL WRITERS

Asking Experienced Writers to Review a Thesis

You might find it helpful to ask one or two classmates who have more experience with the particular type of academic writing to look at your explicit thesis. Ask if the thesis is as direct and clear as it can be, and revise accordingly.

Testing your thesis

Although writing out an explicit thesis will often confirm your research, you may find that your hypothesis is invalid, inadequately supported, or insufficiently focused. In such cases, you need to rethink your original research question and perhaps do further research. To test your thesis, consider the following questions:

- How can you state your thesis more precisely or more clearly (7b)? Should the wording be more specific?
- In what ways will your thesis interest your audience? What can you do to increase that interest?
- Will your thesis be manageable, given your limits of time and knowledge? If not, what can you do to make it more manageable?
- What evidence from your research supports each aspect of your thesis? What additional evidence do you need?

Considering design

As you move toward producing a draft, take some time to think about how you want your research essay or project to look. What font size will you use? Should you use color? Do you plan to insert text boxes, visuals, or media files? Will you need headings and subheadings? (See Chapter 9.)

19b Organize and draft.

Experienced writers differ considerably in the ways they go about organizing ideas and information, and you will want to experiment until you find a method that works well for you. (For more on organizational strategies, see 7d.)

Organizing by subject

You may find it useful to have physical notes to arrange—note cards or sticky notes, for example, or printouts of your slides or of notes you have been keeping online that you mark in some way to make the subject categories easy to identify. You can group the pieces around subject headings and reorder the parts until they seem to make sense. Shuqiao Song, whose critical analysis appears in 12e, organized the plans for her PowerPoint presentation (3c) by moving sticky notes around on her window, as shown in her photo on p. 223.

Sticky notes used to organize a presentation

Grouping your notes will help you see how well you can support your thesis and help you see if you have missed any essential points. Do you need to omit any ideas or sources? Do you need to find additional evidence for a main or supporting point? Once you have gathered everything together and organized your materials, you can see how the many small pieces of your research fit together. Make sure that your evidence supports your explicit thesis; if not, you may need to revise it or do additional research — or both.

Once you have established initial groups, skim through the notes and look for ways to organize your draft. Figure out what background your audience needs, what points you need to make first, how much detail and support to offer for each point, and so on.

Outlining

You can use outlines in various ways and at various stages. Some writers group their notes, write a draft, and then outline the draft to study its tentative structure. Others develop an informal working outline from their notes and revise it as they go along. Still other writers prefer to plot out their organization early on in a formal outline. (For more on outlines, see 7e.)

Drafting

For most college research projects, drafting should begin *at least* two weeks before the instructor's deadline in case you need to gather more

information or do more drafting. Set a deadline for having a complete draft, and structure your work with that date in mind. Gather your notes, outline, and sources, and read through them, getting involved in your topic. Most writers find that some sustained work (two or three hours at a time) pays off at this point. Begin drafting a section that you feel confident about. For example, if you are not sure how you want to introduce the draft but do know how you want to approach a particular point, begin with that, and return to the introduction later. The most important thing is to get started.

WORKING TITLE AND INTRODUCTION

The title and introduction play special roles, for they set the stage for what is to come. Ideally, the title announces the subject of the research essay or project in an intriguing or memorable way. The introduction should draw readers in and provide any background they will need to understand your discussion. Here are some tips for drafting an introduction to a research essay:

- It is often effective to *open with a question*, especially your research question. Next, you might explain what you will do to answer the question. Then *end with your explicit thesis statement* — in essence, the answer.
- Help readers by *forecasting your main points*.
- *Establish your own credibility* by revealing how you have become knowledgeable about the topic.
- A quotation can be a good attention-getter, but you may not want to open with a quotation if doing so will give that source too much emphasis.

CONCLUSION

A good conclusion to a research project helps readers know what they have learned. Its job is not to persuade (the body of the essay or project should already have done that) but to contribute to the overall effectiveness of your argument. Here are some strategies that may help:

- Refer to your thesis, and then expand to a more general conclusion that reminds readers of the significance of your discussion.

- If you have covered several main points, you may want to remind readers of them. Be careful, however, to provide more than a mere summary.
- Try to end with something that will have an impact—a provocative quotation or question, a vivid image, a call for action, or a warning. But guard against sounding preachy.

19c   Incorporate source materials.

When you reach the point of drafting your research project, a new task awaits: weaving your source materials into your writing. The challenge is to use your sources yet remain the author—to quote, paraphrase, and summarize other voices while remaining the major voice in your work. (See Chapter 18 for tips on integrating sources.)

19d   Review and get responses to your draft.

Once you've completed your draft, reread it slowly. As you do so, answer the following questions, and use them as a starting point for revision:

- What do you now see as its *purpose*? How does this compare with your original purpose? Does the draft do what your assignment requires?
- What *audience* does your essay address?
- What is your *stance* toward the topic?
- What is your *thesis*? Is it clearly stated?
- What *evidence* supports your thesis? Is the evidence sufficient?

Next, ask friends, classmates, and, if possible, your instructor to read and respond to your draft. Asking specific questions of your readers will result in the most helpful advice. (See Chapter 10.)

19e   Revise and edit your draft.

When you have considered your reviewers' responses and your own analysis, you can turn to revising and editing. See the box on p. 226 and sections 10d and 11a for more information.

AT A GLANCE

Guidelines for Revising a Research Project

- *Take responses into account.* Look at specific problems that review-ers think you need to solve or strengths you might capitalize on. For example, if they showed great interest in one point but no interest in another, consider expanding the first and deleting the second.

- *Reconsider your original purpose, audience, and stance.* Have you achieved your purpose? If not, consider how you can. How well have you appealed to your readers? Make sure you satisfy any special con-cerns of your reviewers. If your rhetorical stance toward your topic has changed, does your draft need to change, too?

- *Assess your research.* Think about whether you have investigated the topic thoroughly and consulted materials with more than one point of view. Have you left out any important sources? Are the sources you use reliable and appropriate for your topic? Have you synthesized your research findings and drawn warranted conclusions?

- *Assess your use of visuals and media,* making sure that each one sup-ports your argument, is clearly labeled, and is cited appropriately.

- *Gather additional material.* If you need to strengthen any points, first check your notes to see whether you already have the necessary infor-mation. In some instances, you may need to do more research.

- *Decide what changes you need to make.* List everything you must do to perfect your draft. With your deadline in mind, plan your revision.

- *Rewrite your draft.* Many writers prefer to revise first on paper rather than on a computer. However you revise, be sure to save copies of each draft. Begin with the major changes, such as adding content or reorga-nizing. Then turn to sentence-level problems and word choice. Can you sharpen the work's dominant impression?

- *Reevaluate the title, introduction, and conclusion.* Is your title specific and engaging? Does the introduction capture readers' attention and indicate what the work discusses? Does your conclusion help readers see the significance of your argument?

- *Check your documentation.* Make sure you've included a citation in your text for every quotation, paraphrase, summary, visual, and media file you incorporated, following your documentation style consistently.

- *Edit your draft.* Check grammar, usage, spelling, punctuation, and mechanics. Consider the advice of computer spell checkers (23e) and grammar checkers carefully before accepting it.

19f   Prepare a list of sources.

Once you have your final draft and source materials in place, you are ready to prepare a list of sources. Create an entry for each source used in your essay. Then double-check your essay against your list of sources cited; be sure that you have listed every source mentioned in the in-text citations or notes and that you have not listed any sources not cited in your essay. (For guidelines on documentation styles, see Chapters 49–55.)

19g   Prepare and proofread your final copy.

To make sure that the final version of your essay puts your best foot forward, proofread it carefully. Work with a hard copy, since reading on-screen often leads to inaccuracies and missed typos. Proofread once for typographical and grammatical errors and once again to make sure you haven't introduced new errors. (To locate examples of student writing in this book and on the Web site, see the Directory of Student Writing at the back of this book.)

Language

Many people think of language as a set
of rules; break them, and you're wrong.
But that's not how language works.

— ROBERT LANE GREENE

Language

20 Writing to the World *231*
  a Think about what seems "normal" *231*
  b Clarify meaning *232*
  c Meet audience expectations *233*

21 Language That Builds Common Ground *236*
  a Examine assumptions and avoid stereotypes *237*
  b Examine assumptions about gender *237*
  c Examine assumptions about race and ethnicity *238*
  d Consider other kinds of difference *239*

22 Language Variety *241*
  a Use standard varieties of English appropriately *242*
  b Use varieties of English to evoke a place or community *242*
  c Use varieties of English to build credibility with a community *244*
  d Bring in other languages appropriately *244*

23 Word Choice and Spelling *245*
  a Choose appropriate formality *246*
  b Consider denotation and connotation *249*
  c Use general and specific language effectively *249*
  d Use figurative language effectively *250*
  e Make spell checkers work for you *251*
  f Master spelling rules *254*

24 Glossary of Usage *256*

For visual analysis Look carefully at the illustration on the front of this tab. What do you think this image suggests about using language effectively?

Writing to the World **20**

People today often communicate instantaneously across vast distances and cultures. Businesspeople complete multinational transactions with a single click, students in Ohio take online classes at MIT or chat with hundreds of Facebook friends, and bloggers in Baghdad find readers in Atlanta.

Who will read what you write? What choices do you need to make in your writing to have the desired effect on your audience? When the whole world can potentially read your work, it's time to step back and think about how to communicate successfully with such a diverse group—how to become a world writer.

20a Think about what seems "normal."

Your judgment on what's "normal" may be based on assumptions you are not even aware of. But remember: behavior that is considered out of place in one context may appear perfectly normal in another. What's considered "normal" in a text message would be anything but in a request for an internship with a law firm. If you want to communicate with people across cultures, try to learn something about the norms in those cultures and be aware of the norms that guide your own behavior.

Like most people, you may tend to see your own way as the "normal" way to do things. How do your own values and assumptions guide your thinking and behavior? Keep in mind that if your ways seem inherently right, then—even without thinking about it—you may assume that other ways are somehow less than right.

- Know that most ways of communicating are influenced by cultural contexts and differ widely from one culture to the next.
- Pay close attention to the ways that people from cultures other than your own communicate, and be flexible.

AT A GLANCE

Communicating across Cultures

- Recognize what you consider "normal." Examine your own customary behaviors and assumptions, and think about how they may affect what you think and say (and write). (20a)
- Listen closely to someone from another culture, and ask for clarification if necessary. Carefully define your terms. (20b)
- Think about your audience's expectations. How much authority should you have? What kind of evidence will count most with your audience? (20c)
- Organize your writing with your audience's expectations in mind. If in doubt, use formal style. (20c)

- Pay attention to and respect the differences among individual people within a given culture. Don't assume that all members of a community behave in the same way or value the same things.
- Remember that your audience may be made up of people from many backgrounds who have very different concepts about what is appropriate or "normal." So don't assume unanimity!

20b   Clarify meaning.

When an instructor called for "originality" in his students' essays, what did he mean? A Filipina student thought *originality* meant going to an original source and explaining it; a student from Massachusetts thought *originality* meant coming up with an idea entirely on her own. The professor, however, expected students to read multiple sources and develop a critical point of their own about those sources. In subsequent classes, this professor defined *originality* as he was using it in his classes, and he gave examples of student work he judged original.
This brief example points to the challenges all writers face in trying to communicate across space, across languages, across cultures. While there are no foolproof rules, here are some tips for communicating with people from cultures other than your own:

- Listen carefully. Don't hesitate to ask people to explain or even repeat a point if you're not absolutely sure you understand.
- Take care to be explicit about the meanings of the words you use.

- Invite response—ask whether you're making yourself clear. This kind of back-and-forth is particularly easy (and necessary) in email.
- Remember that sometimes a picture is worth a thousand words. A visual may help make your meaning absolutely clear.

20c Meet audience expectations.

When you do your best to meet an audience's expectations about how a text should work, your writing is more likely to have the desired effect. In practice, figuring out what audiences want, need, or expect can be difficult—especially when you are writing in public spaces online and your audiences can be composed of anyone, anywhere. If you do know something about your readers' expectations, use what you know to present your work effectively. If you know little about your potential audiences, however, carefully examine your assumptions about your readers.

Expectations about your authority as a writer

In the United States, students are often asked to establish authority in their writing—by drawing on certain kinds of personal experience, by reporting on research they or others have conducted, or by taking a position for which they can offer strong evidence and support. But this expectation about writerly authority is by no means universal. Indeed, some cultures view student writers as novices whose job is to reflect what they learn from their teachers. One Japanese student, for example, said he was taught that it's rude to challenge a teacher: "Are you ever so smart that you should challenge the wisdom of the ages?"

As this student's comment reveals, a writer's tone also depends on his or her relationship with listeners and readers. As a world writer, you need to remember that those you're addressing may hold a wide range of attitudes about authority.

- What is your relationship to those you are addressing?
- What knowledge are you expected to have? Is it appropriate for or expected of you to demonstrate that knowledge—and, if so, how?
- What is your goal—to answer a question? to make a point? to agree? something else?
- What tone is appropriate? If in doubt, show respect: politeness is rarely if ever inappropriate.
- What level of control do you have over your writing? In a report, you may have the final say. But if you are writing on a wiki, where you share control with others, sensitivity to communal standards is key.

Expectations about persuasive evidence

How do you decide what evidence will best support your ideas? The answer depends, in large part, on the audience you want to persuade. American academics generally give great weight to factual evidence.

Differing concepts of what counts as evidence can lead to arguments that go nowhere. Consider, for example, how rare it is for a believer in creationism to be persuaded by what the theory of evolution presents as evidence—or for a supporter of evolutionary theory to be convinced by what creationists present as evidence. Think carefully about how you use evidence in writing, and pay attention to what counts as evidence to members of other groups you are trying to persuade.

- Should you rely on facts? concrete examples? firsthand experience? religious or philosophical texts? other sources?
- Should you include the testimony of experts? Which experts are valued most, and why?
- Should you use analogies as support? How much will they count?
- When does evidence from unedited Web sites such as blogs offer credible support, and when should you question or reject it?

Once you determine what counts as evidence in your own thinking and writing, think about where you learned to use and value this kind of evidence. You can ask these same questions about the use of evidence by members of other cultures.

Expectations about organization

As you make choices about how to organize your writing, remember that the patterns you find pleasing are likely to be ones that are deeply embedded in your own culture. For example, the organizational pattern favored by U.S. engineers, highly explicit and leaving little or nothing unsaid or unexplained, is probably familiar to most U.S. students: introduction and thesis, necessary background, overview of the parts to follow, systematic presentation of evidence, consideration of other viewpoints, and conclusion. If a piece of writing follows this pattern, American readers ordinarily find it well organized and coherent.

In the United States, many audiences (especially those in the academic and business worlds) expect a writer to get to the point as directly as possible and to take on the major responsibility of articulating that point efficiently and unambiguously. But not all audiences have such expectations. For instance, a Chinese student with an excellent command of English heard from her U.S. teachers that her writing was "vague," with too much "beating around the bush." As it turned out, her teachers in China had prized this kind of indirectness, expecting audiences to read between the lines.

When writing for audiences who may not share your expectations, then, think about how you can organize material to get your message across effectively. There are no hard and fast rules to help you organize your writing for effectiveness across cultures, but here are a few options to consider:

- Determine when to state your thesis—at the beginning? at the end? somewhere else? not at all?

- Consider whether digressions are a good idea, a requirement, or best avoided with your intended audience.

- Remember that electronic communication may call for certain ways of organizing. In messages or postings, you need to place the most important information first and be as succinct as possible. Or you may need to follow a template, as in submitting a résumé online.

Expectations about style

As with beauty, good style is most definitely in the eye of the beholder—and thus is always affected by language, culture, and rhetorical tradition. In fact, what constitutes effective style varies broadly across cultures and depends on the rhetorical situation—purpose, audience, and so on (see Chapter 5). Even so, there is one important style question to consider when writing across cultures: what level of formality is most appropriate? In most writing to a general audience in the United States, a fairly informal style is often acceptable, even appreciated. Many cultures, however, tend to value a more formal approach. When in doubt, it may be wise to err on the side of formality in writing to people from other cultures, especially to elders or to those in authority.

- Be careful to use proper titles:

    Dr. Atul Gawande   Professor Jaime Mejía

- Avoid slang and informal structures such as fragments.

- Do not use first names of people you do not know in correspondence (even in text messages) unless invited to do so. Note, however, that an invitation to use a first name could come indirectly; if someone signs a message to you with his or her first name, you are implicitly invited to use the first name as a term of address. (See 2e for more on electronic communication.)

- For business correspondence, use complete sentences and words; avoid contractions. Open with the salutation "Dear Mr. / Ms. " or the person's title, if you know it. Write dates with the day before the month, and spell out the name of the month: *7 June 2010.*

Beyond formality, other stylistic preferences vary widely, and context matters. Long, complex sentences and ornate language may be exactly what some audiences are looking for. On Twitter, on the other hand, writers have to limit their message to 140 characters—so using abbreviated words, symbols, and fragments is expected, even desirable.

World writers, then, should take very little about language for granted. To be an effective world writer, aim to recognize and respect stylistic differences as you move from community to community and to meet expectations whenever you can.

21 Language That Builds Common Ground

The golden rule of language use might be "Speak to others the way you want them to speak to you." The words we select have power: they can praise, delight, inspire — and also hurt, offend, or even destroy. Words that offend prevent others from identifying with you and thus damage your credibility. Few absolute guidelines exist for using words that respect differences and build common ground. Two rules, however, can help: consider carefully the sensitivities and preferences of others, and watch for words that betray your assumptions, even when you have not directly stated them.

AT A GLANCE

Using Language That Builds Common Ground

- Check for stereotypes and other assumptions that might come between you and your readers. Look, for instance, for language implying approval or disapproval and for the ways you use *we*, *you*, and *they*. (21a)
- Avoid potentially sexist language. (21b)
- Make sure your references to race, religion, sexual orientation, and so on are relevant or necessary to your discussion. If they are not, leave them out. (21c and d)
- Check that the terms you use to refer to groups are accurate and acceptable. (21c and d)

21a Examine assumptions and avoid stereotypes.

Unstated assumptions that enter into thinking and writing can destroy common ground by ignoring important differences between others and ourselves. For example, a student in a religion seminar who uses *we* to refer to Christians and *they* to refer to members of other religions had better be sure that everyone in the class identifies as Christian, or some may feel left out of the discussion.

At the same time, don't overgeneralize about or stereotype a group of people. Because stereotypes are often based on half-truths, misunderstandings, and hand-me-down prejudices, they can lead to intolerance, bias, and bigotry.

Sometimes stereotypes and assumptions lead writers to call special attention to a group affiliation when it is not relevant to the point, as in *a woman plumber* or *a white basketball player*. Even positive stereotypes — for example, *Jewish doctors are the best* — or neutral ones — *all college students like pizza* — can hurt, for they inevitably ignore the uniqueness of an individual. Careful writers make sure that their language doesn't stereotype any group or individual.

21b Examine assumptions about gender.

Powerful gender-related words can subtly affect our thinking and our behavior. For instance, at one time many young women were discouraged from pursuing careers in medicine or engineering at least partially because speakers commonly referred to hypothetical doctors or engineers as *he* (and then labeled a woman who worked as a doctor *a woman doctor*, as if to say, "She's an exception; doctors are normally men"). Similarly, a label like *male nurse* may offend by reflecting stereotyped assumptions about proper roles for men. Equally problematic is the traditional use of *man* and *mankind* to refer to people of both sexes and the use of *he* and *him* to refer generally to any human being. Because such usage ignores half of the people on earth, it hardly helps a writer build common ground.

Sexist language, those words and phrases that stereotype or ignore members of either sex or that unnecessarily call attention to gender, can usually be revised fairly easily. There are several alternatives to using masculine pronouns to refer to persons whose gender is unknown to the writer. One option is to recast the sentence using plural forms.

      Lawyers   *they*
▶ A lawyer must pass the bar exam before he can begin to practice.

Another option is to substitute pairs of pronouns such as *he or she*, *him or her*, and so on.

▶ A lawyer must pass the bar exam before he ^*or she* can begin to practice.

Yet another way to revise the sentence is to eliminate the pronouns.

▶ A lawyer must pass the bar exam before ~~he can begin~~ ^*beginning* to practice.

Beyond the pronoun issue, try to eliminate sexist nouns from your writing.

INSTEAD OF	TRY USING
anchorman, anchorwoman	anchor
businessman	businessperson, business executive
chairman, chairwoman	chair, chairperson
congressman	member of Congress, representative
fireman	firefighter
mailman	mail carrier
male nurse	nurse
man, mankind	humans, human beings, humanity, the human race, humankind
manpower	workers, personnel
mothering	parenting
policeman, policewoman	police officer
salesman	salesperson, sales associate
woman engineer	engineer

21c Examine assumptions about race and ethnicity.

In building common ground, writers must watch for any words that ignore differences not only among individual members of a race or ethnic group but also among subgroups. Writers must be aware, for instance, of the many nations to which American Indians belong and of the diverse places from which Americans of Spanish-speaking ancestry have emigrated.

Preferred terms

Identifying preferred terms is sometimes not an easy task, for they can change often and vary widely.

The word *colored*, for example, was once widely used in the United States to refer to Americans of African ancestry. By the 1950s, the preferred term had become *Negro*. This changed in the 1960s, however, as *black* came to be preferred by most, though certainly not all, members of that community. Then, in the late 1980s, some leaders of the American black community urged that *black* be replaced by *African American*.

The word *Oriental*, once used to refer to people of East Asian descent, is now often considered offensive. At the University of California at Berkeley, the Oriental Languages Department is now known as the East Asian Languages Department. One advocate of the change explained that *Oriental* is appropriate for objects—like rugs—but not for people.

Once widely preferred, the term *Native American* is being challenged by those who argue that the most appropriate way to refer to indigenous people is by the specific name of the tribe or pueblo, such as *Chippewa* or *Tesuque*. In Alaska and parts of Canada, many indigenous peoples once referred to as *Eskimos* now prefer *Inuit* or a specific term such as *Tlingit*. It has also become fairly common for tribal groups to refer to themselves as *Indians* or *Indian tribes*.

Among Americans of Spanish-speaking descent, the preferred terms of reference are many: *Chicano/Chicana, Hispanic, Latin American, Latino/Latina, Mexican American, Dominican*, and *Puerto Rican*, to name but a few.

Clearly, then, ethnic terminology changes often enough to challenge even the most careful writers — including writers who belong to the groups they are writing about. The best advice may be to consider your words carefully, to *listen* for the way members of groups refer to themselves (or *ask* about preferences), and to check any term you're unsure of in a current dictionary.

21d   Consider other kinds of difference.

Age

Mention age if it is relevant, but be aware that age-related terms (*matronly, well-preserved*, and so on) can carry derogatory connotations. Describing Mr. Fry as *elderly but still active* may sound polite to you, but chances are Mr. Fry would prefer being called *an active seventy-eight-year-old* — or just *a seventy-eight-year-old*, which eliminates the unstated assumption of surprise that he is active at his age.

Class

Take special care to examine your words for assumptions about class. As a writer, you should not assume that all your readers share your background or values — that your classmates all own cars, for instance. And avoid using any words — *redneck*, *blueblood*, and the like — that might alienate members of an audience.

Geographical area

You should not assume that geography determines personality or lifestyle. New Englanders are not all thrifty and tight-lipped; people in "red states" may hold liberal views; midwesterners are not always polite. Be careful not to make simplistic assumptions.

Check also that you use geographical terms accurately.

AMERICA, AMERICAN Although many people use these words to refer to the United States alone, such usage will not necessarily be acceptable to people from Canada, Mexico, and Central or South America.

BRITISH, ENGLISH Use *British* to refer to the island of Great Britain, which includes England, Scotland, and Wales, or to the United Kingdom of Great Britain and Northern Ireland. In general, do not use *English* for these broader senses.

ARAB This term refers only to people of Arabic-speaking descent. Note that Iran is not an Arab nation; its people speak Farsi, not Arabic. Note also that *Arab* is not synonymous with *Muslim* or *Moslem* (a believer in Islam). Most (but not all) Arabs are Muslim, but many Muslims (those in Pakistan, for example) are not Arab.

Physical ability or health

When writing about a person with a serious illness or physical disability, ask yourself whether mentioning the disability is relevant to your discussion and whether the words you use carry negative connotations. You might choose, for example, to say someone *uses* a wheelchair rather than to say he or she is *confined to* one. Similarly, you might note a subtle but meaningful difference in calling someone a *person with AIDS* rather than an *AIDS victim*. Mentioning the person first and the disability second, such as referring to a *child with diabetes* rather than a *diabetic child* or a *diabetic*, is always a good idea.

Religion

Assumptions about religious groups are very often inaccurate and unfair. For example, Roman Catholics hold a wide spectrum of views on abortion, Muslim women do not all wear veils, and many Baptists are not fundamentalists. In fact, many people do not believe in or practice a religion at all, so be careful of such assumptions. As in other cases, do not use religious labels without considering their relevance to your point.

Sexual orientation

If you wish to build common ground, do not assume that readers all share one sexual orientation. As with any label, reference to sexual orientation should be governed by context. Someone writing about Representative Barney Frank's legislative record would probably have little if any reason to refer to his sexual orientation. On the other hand, someone writing about diversity in U.S. government might find it important to note that Frank was the first U.S. congressman to voluntarily make his homosexuality public.

 bedfordstmartins.com/everydaywriter
Exercise Central > Language That Builds Common Ground

Language Variety 22

Comedian Dave Chappelle has said, "Every black American is bilingual. We speak street vernacular, and we speak job interview." As Chappelle understands, English comes in many varieties that differ from one another in pronunciation, vocabulary, usage, and grammar. You probably already adjust the variety of language you use depending on how well — and how formally — you know the audience you are addressing. Adding language variety to your writing can improve your communication with your audience if you think carefully about the effect you want to achieve.

AT A GLANCE

Language Variety

You can use different varieties of language to good effect for the following purposes:

- to repeat someone's exact words
- to evoke a person, place, or activity
- to establish your credibility and build common ground
- to make a strong point
- to connect with an audience

22a   Use standard varieties of English appropriately.

How do writers decide when to use another language or switch from one variety of English to another? Even writers who are perfectly fluent in several languages must think for a moment before switching linguistic gears. The key to shifting among varieties of English and among languages is appropriateness: you need to consider when such shifts will help your audience appreciate your message and when shifts may be a mistake. Used appropriately and wisely, *any* variety of English can serve a good purpose.

One variety of English, often referred to as the "standard" or "standard academic," is that taught prescriptively in schools, represented in this and most other textbooks, used in the national media, and written and spoken widely by those wielding social and economic power. As the language used in business and most public institutions, standard English is a variety you will want to be completely familiar with. Standard English, however, is only one of many effective varieties of English and itself varies according to purpose and audience, from the more formal style used in academic writing to the informal style characteristic of casual conversation.

22b   Use varieties of English to evoke a place or community.

> "Ever'body says words different," said Ivy. "Arkansas folks says 'em different from Oklahomy folks says 'em different. And we seen a lady from Massachusetts, an' she said 'em differentest of all. Couldn' hardly make out what she was sayin'." —JOHN STEINBECK, *The Grapes of Wrath*

Using the language of a local community is an effective way to evoke a character or place. Author and radio host Garrison Keillor, for example, peppers his tales of his native Minnesota with the homespun English

Global Varieties of English

Like other world languages, English is used in many countries, so it has many global varieties. For example, British English differs somewhat from U.S. English in certain vocabulary (*bonnet* for hood of a car), syntax (*to hospital* rather than *to the hospital*), spelling (*centre* rather than *center*), and pronunciation. If you have learned a non-American variety of English, you will want to recognize, and to appreciate, the ways in which it differs from the variety widely used in U.S. academic settings.

spoken there: "I once was a tall dark heartbreaker who, when I slouched into a room, women jumped up and asked if they could get me something, and now they only smile and say, 'My mother is a big fan of yours. You sure are a day-brightener for her. You sure make her chuckle.'"

Weaving together regionalisms and standard English can also be effective in creating a sense of place. Here, an anthropologist writing about one Carolina community takes care to let the residents speak their minds—and in their own words:

> For Roadville, schooling is something most folks have not gotten enough of, but everybody believes will do something toward helping an individual "get on." In the words of one oldtime resident, "Folks that ain't got no schooling don't get to be nobody nowadays."
>
> –Shirley Brice Heath, *Ways with Words*

Varieties of language can also help writers evoke other kinds of communities. In this panel from *One! Hundred! Demons!*, Lynda Barry uses playground language to present a vivid image of remembered childhood games. See how kids' use of slang ("Dag") and colloquialisms ("Whose up is it?") helps readers join in the experience.

22c Use varieties of English to build credibility
with a community.

Whether you are American Indian or trace your ancestry to Europe, Asia, Latin America, Africa, or elsewhere, your heritage lives on in the diversity of the English language.

See how one Hawaiian writer uses a local variety of English to paint a picture of young teens hearing a "chicken skin" story from their grandmother.

> "—So, rather dan being rid of da shark, da people were stuck with many little ones, for dere mistake."
>
> Then Grandma Wong wen' pause, for dramatic effect, I guess, and she wen' add, "Dis is one of dose times. . . . Da time of da sharks."
>
> Those words ended another of Grandma's chicken skin stories. The stories she told us had been passed on to her by her grandmother, who had heard them from her grandmother. Always skipping a generation.
>
> —RODNEY MORALES, "When the Shark Bites"

Notice how the narrator of the story uses both standard and nonstandard varieties of English—presenting information necessary to the story line mostly in standard English and using a local, ethnic variety to represent spoken language. One important reason for the shift from standard English is to demonstrate that the writer is a member of the community whose language he is representing and thus to build credibility with others in the community.

Take care, however, in using the language of communities other than your own. When used inappropriately, such language can have an opposite effect, perhaps destroying credibility and alienating your audience.

22d Bring in other languages appropriately.

You might use a language other than English for the same reasons you might use different varieties of English: to represent the actual words of a speaker, to make a point, to connect with your audience, or to get their attention. See how Gerald Haslam uses Spanish to capture his great-grandmother's words and to make a point about his relationship to her.

"*Expectoran su sangre!*" exclaimed Great-grandma when I showed her the small horned toad I had removed from my breast pocket. I turned toward my mother, who translated: "They spit blood."

"*De los ojos,*" Grandma added. "From their eyes," mother explained, herself uncomfortable in the presence of the small beast.

I grinned, "Awwwwwww."

But my Great-grandmother did not smile. "*Son muy tóxicos,*" she nodded with finality. Mother moved back an involuntary step, her hands suddenly busy at her breast. "Put that thing down," she ordered.

"His name's John," I said.

– GERALD HASLAM, *California Childhood*

Word Choice and Spelling **23**

Deciding which word is the right word can be a challenge. It's not unusual to find many words that have similar but subtly different meanings, and each makes a different impression on your audience. For instance, the "pasta with marinara sauce" presented in a restaurant may look and taste much like the "macaroni and gravy" served at an Italian family dinner, but the choice of one label rather than the other tells us not only about the food but also about the people serving it and the people they expect to serve it to.

AT A GLANCE

Editing for Appropriate Language and Spelling

- Check to see that your language reflects the appropriate level of formality for your audience, purpose, and topic. (23a)
- Unless you are writing for a specialized audience that will understand jargon, either define technical terms or replace them with words that are easy to understand. (23a)
- Consider the connotations of words carefully. If you say someone is *pushy*, be sure you mean to be critical; otherwise, use a word like *assertive*. (23b)
- Use both general and specific words. If you are writing about the general category *beds*, for example, do you give enough concrete detail (*an antique four-poster bed*)? (23c)
- Look for clichés, and replace them with fresher language. (23d)
- Use spell checkers with care. (23e)

Ensuring that you choose the correct spelling for the word you want to use is also important. Spell checkers can help you avoid some errors, but they can also make other mistakes more likely, including word choice errors, so use them with care (see 23e).

23a Choose appropriate formality.

Choose a level of formality that matches your audience, purpose, and topic. In an email or letter to a friend or close associate, informal language is often appropriate. For most academic and professional writing, however, more formal language is appropriate because you are addressing people you do not know well. Compare the following responses to a request for information about a job candidate:

EMAIL TO SOMEONE YOU KNOW WELL

Maisha is great — hire her if you can!

LETTER OF RECOMMENDATION TO SOMEONE YOU DO NOT KNOW

I am pleased to recommend Maisha Fisher. She will bring good ideas and extraordinary energy to your organization.

Slang and colloquial language

Slang, or extremely informal language, is often confined to a relatively small group and usually becomes obsolete rather quickly, though some slang gains wide use (*workaholic, duh*). Colloquial language, such as *a lot*, *in a bind*, or *snooze*, is less informal, more widely used, and longer lasting than most slang.

Writers who use slang and colloquial language run the risk of not being understood or of not being taken seriously. If you are writing for

---

TALKING THE TALK

Texting Abbreviations

"Can I use text-message slang when I contact my teacher?" In a chat or text message, abbreviations such as *u* for *you* may be conventional, but using such shortcuts when communicating with an instructor can be a mistake. At least some of your instructors are likely to view them as disrespectful, unprofessional, or simply sloppy writing. Unless you are working to create a special effect for a special purpose and audience, keep to the conventions of standard English for college writing—and for contacting your instructor.

a general audience about gun-control legislation, for example, and you use the term *gat* to refer to a weapon, some readers may not know what you mean, and others may be irritated by what they see as a frivolous reference to a deadly serious subject.

Jargon

Jargon is the special vocabulary of a trade or profession, enabling members to speak and write concisely to one another. Reserve jargon for an audience that will understand your terms. The example that follows, from a blog about fonts and typefaces, uses jargon appropriately for an interested and knowledgeable audience.

The Modern typeface classification is usually associated with Didones and display faces that often have too much contrast for text use. The Ingeborg family was designed with the intent of producing a Modern face that was readable at any size. Its roots might well be historic, but its approach is very contemporary. The three text weights (Regular, Bold, and Heavy) are functional and discreet while the Display weights (Fat and Block) catch the reader's eye with a dynamic form and a whole lot of ink on the paper. The family includes a boatload of extras like unicase alternates, swash caps, and a lined fill.

—FONTSHOP.COM BLOG

Depending on the needs of the audience, jargon can be irritating and incomprehensible—or extremely helpful. Terms that begin as jargon for specialists (such as *asynchronous* or *vertical integration*) can quickly become part of the mainstream if they provide a useful shorthand for an otherwise lengthy explanation. Before you use technical jargon, remember your readers: if they will not understand the terms, or if you don't know them well enough to judge, then say what you need to say in everyday language.

Pompous language, euphemisms, and doublespeak

Stuffy or pompous language is unnecessarily formal for the purpose, audience, or topic. It often gives writing an insincere or unintentionally humorous tone, making a writer's ideas seem insignificant or even unbelievable.

Avoiding Fancy Language

In writing standard academic English, which is fairly formal, students are often tempted to use many "big words" instead of simple language. Although learning impressive words can be a good way to expand your vocabulary, it is usually best to avoid flowery or fancy language in college writing. Academic writing at U.S. universities tends to value clear, concise prose.

POMPOUS

Pursuant to the August 9 memorandum regarding the increased unit cost of automotive fuels, it is incumbent upon us to endeavor to make maximal utilization of electronic or telephonic communication in lieu of personal visitation.

REVISED

As noted in the August 9 memo, higher gasoline prices require us to email or telephone whenever possible rather than make personal visits.

As these examples illustrate, some writers use words in an attempt to sound expert, and these puffed-up words can easily backfire.

INSTEAD OF	TRY USING	INSTEAD OF	TRY USING
ascertain	find out	optimal	best
commence	begin	parameters	boundaries
finalize	finish, complete	peruse	look at
impact (as verb)	affect	ramp up	increase
methodology	method	utilize	use

Euphemisms are words and phrases that make unpleasant ideas seem less harsh. *Your position is being eliminated* seeks to soften the blow of being fired or laid off. Other euphemisms include *pass on* or *pass away* for *die* and *plus-sized* for *fat*. Although euphemisms can sometimes appeal to an audience by showing that you are considerate of people's feelings, they can also sound insincere or evasive.

Doublespeak is language used to hide or distort the truth. During massive layoffs and cutbacks in the business world, companies speak of firings as *employee repositioning* or *proactive downsizing,* and of unpaid time off as a *furlough.* The public — and particularly those who lose their jobs — recognize these terms for what they are.

23b Consider denotation and connotation.

Thinking of a stone tossed into a pool and ripples spreading out from it can help you understand the distinction between *denotation,* the dictionary meaning of a word (the stone), and *connotation,* the associations that accompany the word (the ripples). The words *enthusiasm, passion,* and *obsession,* for instance, all carry roughly the same denotation. But the connotations are quite different: an *enthusiasm* is a pleasurable and absorbing interest; a *passion* has a strong emotional component and may affect someone positively or negatively; an *obsession* is an unhealthy attachment that excludes other interests.

Note the differences in connotation among the following three statements:

► **Students Against Racism (SAR) erected a temporary barrier on the campus oval. They say it symbolizes "the many barriers to those discriminated against by university policies."**

► **Left-wing agitators threw up an eyesore on the oval to stampede the university into giving in to their demands.**

► **Supporters of human rights for all students challenged the university's investment in racism by erecting a protest barrier on campus.**

The first statement is the most neutral, merely stating facts; the second, using words with negative connotations (*agitators, eyesore, stampede*), is strongly critical; the third, using a phrase with positive connotations (*supporters of human rights*) and presenting assertions as facts (*the university's investment in racism*), gives a favorable slant to the story.

23c Use general and specific language effectively.

Effective writers balance general words, which name or describe groups or classes, with specific words, which identify individual and particular things. Some general words are abstract; they refer to things we cannot perceive through our five senses. Specific words are often concrete; they name things we can see, hear, touch, taste, or smell. We can seldom draw a clear-cut line between general or abstract words on the one hand and specific or concrete words on the other. Instead, most words fall somewhere in between.

GENERAL	LESS GENERAL	SPECIFIC	MORE SPECIFIC
book	dictionary	abridged dictionary	the fourth edition of *The American Heritage College Dictionary*

ABSTRACT	LESS ABSTRACT	CONCRETE	MORE CONCRETE
culture	visual art	painting	van Gogh's *Starry Night*

Strong writing usually provides readers with both an overall picture and specific examples or concrete details to fill in that picture. In the following passage, the author might have simply made a general statement — *their breakfast was always liberal and good* — or simply given the details of the breakfast. Instead, he is both general and specific.

> There would be a brisk fire crackling in the hearth, the old smoke-gold of morning and the smell of fog, the crisp cheerful voices of the people and their ruddy competent morning look, and the cheerful smells of breakfast, which was always liberal and good, the best meal that they had: kidneys and ham and eggs and sausages and toast and marmalade and tea.
> — THOMAS WOLFE, *Of Time and the River*

23d Use figurative language effectively.

Figurative language, or figures of speech, can paint pictures in a reader's mind, allowing one to "see" a point readily and clearly. Far from being merely decorative, such language can be crucial to understanding.

Similes, metaphors, and analogies

Similes use *like, as, as if,* or *as though* to make explicit the similarity between two seemingly different things.

> ► You can tell the graphic-novels section in a bookstore from afar, by the young bodies sprawled around it like casualties of a localized disaster.
> — PETER SCHJELDAHL

> ► The comb felt as if it was raking my skin off.
> — MALCOLM X, "My First Conk"

Metaphors are implicit comparisons, omitting the *like, as, as if,* or *though* of similes.

> ► The Internet is the new town square. — JEB HENSARLING

Mixed metaphors make comparisons that are inconsistent.

> ► The lectures were like brilliant comets streaking through the night sky,
>
> *dazzling*   *flashes*
> ~~showering~~ listeners with a ~~torrential rain~~ of insights.

The images of streaking light and heavy precipitation are inconsistent; in the revised sentence, all of the images relate to light.

Analogies compare similar features of two dissimilar things; they explain something unfamiliar by relating it to something familiar.

▶ One way to establish that peace-preserving threat of mutual assured destruction is to commit yourself beforehand, which helps explain why so many retailers promise to match any competitor's advertised price. Consumers view these guarantees as conducive to lower prices. But in fact offering a price-matching guarantee should make it less likely that competitors will slash prices, since they know that any cuts they make will immediately be matched. It's the retail version of the doomsday machine.
— James Surowiecki

▶ One Hundred and Twenty-fifth Street was to Harlem what the Mississippi was to the South, a long traveling river always going somewhere, carrying something. — Maya Angelou, *The Heart of a Woman*

FOR MULTILINGUAL WRITERS
Learning Idioms
Why do you wear a diamond *on* your finger but *in* your ear? See 60a.

Clichés

A cliché is a frequently used expression such as *busy as a bee*. By definition, we use clichés all the time, especially in speech, and many serve usefully as shorthand for familiar ideas or as a way of connecting to an audience. But if you use too many clichés in your writing, readers may conclude that what you are saying is not very new or interesting — or true. To check for clichés, use this rule of thumb: if you can predict exactly what the next word in a phrase will be, the phrase stands a good chance of being a cliché.

⊙ bedfordstmartins.com/everydaywriter
Exercise Central > Appropriate Language

23e Make spell checkers work for you.

Research conducted for this textbook shows that spelling errors have changed dramatically in the past twenty years — and the reason is spell checkers. Although these programs have weeded out many once-common misspellings, they are not foolproof. Spell checkers still allow typical kinds of errors that you should look out for.

Common errors with spell checkers

- *Homonyms.* Spell checkers cannot distinguish between words such as *affect* and *effect* that sound alike but are spelled differently.

- *Proper nouns.* A spell checker cannot tell you when you have misspelled a proper name. Proofread names with special care.
- *Compound words written as two words.* Spell checkers will not see a problem if *nowhere* is incorrectly written as *no where.* When in doubt, check a dictionary.
- *Typos.* The spell checker will not flag *heat* even if you meant to type *heart.*

Spell checker use

To make spell checkers work best for you, you need to learn to adapt them to your own needs.

- Always proofread carefully, even after you have used the spell checker. The more important the message or document, the more careful you should be about its accuracy and clarity.
- Use a dictionary to look up any word the spell checker highlights that you are not sure of.
- If your spell checker's dictionary allows you to add new words, enter proper names, non-English words, or specialized language you use regularly and have trouble spelling. Be careful to enter the correct spelling!
- If you know that you mix up certain homonyms, such as *there* and *their*, check for them after running your spell checker.
- Remember that spell checkers are not sensitive to capitalization. If you write "the united states," the spell checker won't question it.
- Do *not* automatically accept the spell checker's suggestions: you may end up with a word you don't really want.

TALKING THE TALK

Spell Checkers and Wrong-Word Errors

"Can I trust spell checkers to correct a word I've spelled wrong?" In a word, no. The spell checker may suggest bizarre substitutes for many proper names and specialized terms (even when you spell them correctly) and for certain typographical errors, thus introducing wrong words into your paper if you accept its suggestions automatically. For example, a student who had typed *fantic* instead of *frantic* found that the spell checker's first choice was to substitute *fanatic* — a replacement that made no sense. Wrong-word errors are the most common surface error in college writing today (see Chapter 1), and spell checkers are partly to blame. So be careful not to take a spell checker's recommendation without paying careful attention to the replacement word.

Homonyms

A relatively small number of homonyms — just eight groups — cause writers the most frequent trouble.

accept (to take or receive)	to (in the direction of)
except (to leave out)	too (in addition; excessive)
affect (an emotion; to have an influence)	two (number between *one* and *three*)
effect (a result; to cause to happen)	weather (climatic conditions)
	whether (if)
its (possessive of *it*)	who's (contraction of *who is* or *who has*)
it's (contraction of *it is* or *it has*)	
their (possessive of *they*)	whose (possessive of *who*)
there (in that place)	your (possessive of *you*)
they're (contraction of *they are*)	you're (contraction of *you are*)

If you tend to confuse particular homonyms, try creating a special memory device to help you remember the differences. For example, "*We* all complain about the *weather*" will remind you that *weather* (the climate) starts with *we*.

In addition, pay close attention to homonyms that may be spelled as one word or two, depending on the meaning.

▶ **Of course, they did not wear** *everyday* **clothes** *every day.*

▶ **Before the six lawyers were** *all ready* **to negotiate, it was** *already* **May.**

▶ **The director** *may be* **on time. But** *maybe* **she'll be late.**

For additional advice on commonly confused words, see the glossary of usage in Chapter 24.

FOR MULTILINGUAL WRITERS

Recognizing American Spellings

Different varieties of English often use different spelling conventions. If you have learned British or Indian English, for example, you will want to be aware of some of the more common spelling differences in American English. For example, words ending in *–yse* or *–ise* in British/Indian English (*analyse, criticise*) usually end in *–yze* or *–ize* in American English (*analyze, criticize*); words ending in *–our* in British/Indian English (*labour, colour*) usually end in *–or* in American English (*labor, color*); and words ending in *–re* in British/Indian English (*theatre, centre*) usually end in *–er* in American English (*theater, center*).

23f Master spelling rules.

General spelling rules can help writers enormously, but many rules have exceptions. When in doubt, consult a dictionary.

i *before* e *except after* c

Here is a slightly expanded version of the "*i* before *e*" rule:

I BEFORE *E*	ach*ie*ve, br*ie*f, f*ie*ld, fr*ie*nd
EXCEPT AFTER *C*	c*ei*ling, rec*ei*pt, perc*ei*ve
OR WHEN PRONOUNCED *AY*	*ei*ghth, n*ei*ghbor, r*ei*gn, w*ei*gh
OR IN WEIRD EXCEPTIONS	*ei*ther, for*ei*gn, h*ei*ght, l*ei*sure, n*ei*ther, s*ei*ze

Word endings (suffixes)

FINAL SILENT *E*

Drop the final silent *e* when you add an ending that starts with a vowel.

imagine + -able = imaginable   exercise + -ing = exercising

Generally, keep the final *e* if the ending starts with a consonant. Common exceptions include *argument, judgment, noticeable,* and *truly.*

force + -ful = forceful   state + -ly = stately

FINAL *Y*

When adding an ending to a word that ends in a consonant plus *y,* change the *y* to an *i* in most cases.

try, tried   busy, busily

Keep the *y* if it is part of a proper name or if the ending begins with *i.*

Kennedy, Kennedyesque   dry, drying

FINAL CONSONANTS

When adding an ending beginning with a vowel to a word that ends with a vowel and a consonant, double the final consonant if the original word is one syllable or if the accent is on the same syllable in both the original and the new word.

stop, stopped   begin, beginner   refer, referral

Otherwise, do not double the final consonant.

bait, baiting   start, started   refer, reference

Plurals

ADDING -*S* OR -*ES*

For most nouns, add -*s*. For words ending in *s*, *ch*, *sh*, *x*, or *z*, add -*es*.

pencil, pencils   church, churches   bus, buses

In general, add -*s* to nouns ending in *o* if the *o* is preceded by a vowel. Add -*es* if the *o* is preceded by a consonant.

rodeo, rodeos   patio, patios   potato, potatoes   hero, heroes

For some nouns ending in *f* or *fe*, change *f* to *v*, and add -*s* or -*es*.

calf, calves   life, lives   hoof, hooves

For compound nouns written as separate or hyphenated words, make the most important part plural, whether or not it is the last part of the compound.

lieutenant governors   brothers-in-law

For plurals of numbers and words used as terms, see 42c.

CONSIDERING DISABILITIES

Spelling

Spelling is especially difficult for people who have trouble processing letters and sounds in sequence. Technology can help: "talking pens" can scan words and read them aloud, and voice-recognition programs can transcribe dictated text.

⊙ **bedfordstmartins.com/everydaywriter**
Exercise Central > Spelling

24   Glossary of Usage

Conventions of usage might be called the "good manners" of discourse. And just as manners vary from culture to culture and time to time, so do conventions of usage. Matters of usage, like other language choices you must make, depend on what your purpose is and on what is appropriate for a particular audience at a particular time.

a, an   Use *a* with a word that begins with a consonant (*a book*), a consonant sound such as "y" or "w" (*a euphoric moment, a one-sided match*), or a sounded *h* (*a hemisphere*). Use *an* with a word that begins with a vowel (*an umbrella*), a vowel sound (*an X-ray*), or a silent *h* (*an honor*).

accept, except   The verb *accept* means "receive" or "agree to." *Except* is usually a preposition that means "aside from" or "excluding." *All the plaintiffs except Mr. Kim decided to accept the settlement.*

advice, advise   The noun *advice* means "opinion" or "suggestion"; the verb *advise* means "offer advice." *Doctors advise everyone not to smoke, but many people ignore the advice.*

affect, effect   As a verb, *affect* means "influence" or "move the emotions of"; as a noun, it means "emotions" or "feelings." *Effect* is a noun meaning "result"; less commonly, it is a verb meaning "bring about." *The storm affected a large area. Its effects included widespread power failures. The drug effected a major change in the patient's affect.*

aggravate   The formal meaning is "make worse." *Having another mouth to feed aggravated their poverty.* In academic and professional writing, avoid using *aggravate* to mean "irritate" or "annoy."

all ready, already   *All ready* means "fully prepared." *Already* means "previously." *We were all ready for Lucy's party when we learned that she had already left.*

all right, alright   Avoid the spelling *alright*.

all together, altogether   *All together* means "all in a group" or "gathered in one place." *Altogether* means "completely" or "everything considered." *When the board members were all together, their mutual distrust was altogether obvious.*

allude, elude   *Allude* means "refer indirectly." *Elude* means "avoid" or "escape from." *The candidate did not even allude to her opponent. The suspect eluded the police for several days.*

allusion, illusion   An *allusion* is an indirect reference. An *illusion* is a false or misleading appearance. *The speaker's allusion to the Bible created an illusion of piety.*

a lot   Avoid the spelling *alot*.

already   See *all ready, already*.

alright   See *all right, alright*.

altogether   See *all together, altogether*.

among, between   In referring to two things or people, use *between*. In referring to three or more, use *among*. *The relationship between the twins is different from that among the other three children.*

amount, number   Use *amount* with quantities you cannot count; use *number* for quantities you can count. *A small number of volunteers cleared a large amount of brush.*

an   See *a, an*.

and/or   Avoid this term except in business or legal writing. Instead of *fat and/or protein*, write *fat, protein*, or *both*.

any body, anybody, any one, anyone   *Anybody* and *anyone* are pronouns meaning "any person." *Anyone* [or *anybody*] *would enjoy this film. Any body* is an adjective modifying a noun. *Any body of water has its own ecology. Any one* is two adjectives or a pronoun modified by an adjective. *Customers could buy only two sale items at any one time. The winner could choose any one of the prizes.*

anyplace   In academic and professional discourse, use *anywhere* instead.

anyway, anyways   In writing, use *anyway*, not *anyways*.

apt, liable, likely   *Likely to* means "probably will," and *apt to* means "inclines or tends to." In many instances, they are interchangeable. *Liable* often carries a more negative sense and is also a legal term meaning "obligated" or "responsible."

as   Avoid sentences in which it is not clear if *as* means "when" or "because." For example, does *Carl left town as his father was arriving* mean "at the same time as his father was arriving" or "because his father was arriving"?

as, as if, like   In academic and professional writing, use *as* or *as if* instead of *like* to introduce a clause. *The dog howled as if* [not *like*] *it were in pain. She did as* [not *like*] *I suggested.*

assure, ensure, insure   *Assure* means "convince" or "promise"; its direct object is usually a person or persons. *She assured voters she would not raise taxes. Ensure* and *insure* both mean "make certain," but *insure* usually refers specifically to protection against financial loss. *When the city rationed water to ensure that the supply would last, the Browns could no longer afford to insure their car-wash business.*

as to   Do not use *as to* as a substitute for *about*. *Karen was unsure about* [not *as to*] *Bruce's intentions.*

at, where   See *where*.

awhile, a while   Always use *a while* after a preposition such as *for, in*, or *after*. *We drove awhile and then stopped for a while.*

bad, badly   Use *bad* after a linking verb such as *be, feel*, or *seem*. Use *badly* to modify an action verb, an adjective, or another verb. *The hostess felt bad because the dinner was badly prepared.*

bare, bear   Use *bare* to mean "uncovered" and *bear* to refer to the animal or to mean "carry" or "endure": *The walls were bare. The emptiness was hard to bear.*

because of, due to   Use *due to* when the effect, stated as a noun, appears before the verb *be*. *His illness was due to malnutrition.* (*Illness*, a noun, is the effect.) Use *because of* when the effect is stated as a clause. *He was sick because of malnutrition.* (*He was sick*, a clause, is the effect.)

being as, being that In academic or professional writing, use *because* or *since* instead of these expressions. *Because* [not *being as*] *Romeo killed Tybalt, he was banished to Padua.*

beside, besides *Beside* is a preposition meaning "next to." *Besides* can be a preposition meaning "other than" or an adverb meaning "in addition." *No one besides Francesca would sit beside him.*

between See *among, between.*

brake, break *Brake* means "to stop" and also refers to a stopping mechanism: *Check the brakes. Break* means "fracture" or an interruption: *The coffee break was too short.*

breath, breathe *Breath* is a noun; *breathe,* a verb. *"Breathe,"* said the nurse, so *June took a deep breath.*

bring, take Use *bring* when an object is moved from a farther to a nearer place; use *take* when the opposite is true. *Take the box to the post office; bring back my mail.*

but that, but what Avoid using these as substitutes for *that* in expressions of doubt. *Hercule Poirot never doubted that* [not *but that*] *he would solve the case.*

but yet Do not use these words together. *He is strong but* [not *but yet*] *gentle.*

can, may *Can* refers to ability and *may* to possibility or permission. *Since I can ski the slalom well, I may win the race.*

can't hardly *Hardly* has a negative meaning; therefore, *can't hardly* is a double negative. This expression is commonly used in some varieties of English but is not used in academic English. *Tim can* [not *can't*] *hardly wait.*

can't help but This expression is redundant. Use *I can't help going* rather than *I can't help but go.*

censor, censure *Censor* means "remove that which is considered offensive." *Censure* means "formally reprimand." *The newspaper censored stories that offended advertisers. The legislature censured the official for misconduct.*

compare to, compare with *Compare to* means "regard as similar." *Jamie compared the loss to a kick in the head. Compare with* means "examine to find differences or similarities." *Compare Tim Burton's films with David Lynch's.*

complement, compliment *Complement* means "go well with." *Compliment* means "praise." *Guests complimented her on how her earrings complemented her gown.*

comprise, compose *Comprise* means "contain." *Compose* means "make up." *The class comprises twenty students. Twenty students compose the class.*

conscience, conscious *Conscience* means "a sense of right and wrong." *Conscious* means "awake" or "aware." *Lisa was conscious of a guilty conscience.*

consensus of opinion Use *consensus* instead of this redundant phrase. *The family consensus was to sell the old house.*

consequently, subsequently *Consequently* means "as a result"; *subsequently* means "then." *He quit, and subsequently his wife lost her job; consequently, they had to sell their house.*

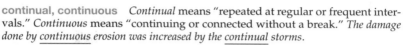

continual, continuous *Continual* means "repeated at regular or frequent intervals." *Continuous* means "continuing or connected without a break." *The damage done by* continuous *erosion was increased by the* continual *storms.*

could of *Have,* not *of,* should follow *could, would, should,* or *might. We could* have [not *of*] *invited them.*

criteria, criterion *Criterion* means "standard of judgment" or "necessary qualification." *Criteria* is the plural form. *Image is the wrong* criterion *for choosing a president.*

data *Data* is the plural form of the Latin word *datum,* meaning "fact." Although *data* is used informally as either singular or plural, in academic or professional writing, treat *data* as plural. *These* data *indicate that fewer people are smoking.*

different from, different than *Different from* is generally preferred in academic and professional writing, although both phrases are widely used. *Her lab results were no* different from [not *than*] *his.*

discreet, discrete *Discreet* means "tactful" or "prudent." *Discrete* means "separate" or "distinct." *The leader's* discreet *efforts kept all the* discrete *factions unified.*

disinterested, uninterested *Disinterested* means "unbiased." *Uninterested* means "indifferent." *Finding* disinterested *jurors was difficult. She was* uninterested *in the verdict.*

distinct, distinctive *Distinct* means "separate" or "well defined." *Distinctive* means "characteristic." *Germany includes many* distinct *regions, each with a* distinctive *accent.*

doesn't, don't *Doesn't* is the contraction for *does not.* Use it with *he, she, it,* and singular nouns. *Don't* stands for *do not;* use it with *I, you, we, they,* and plural nouns.

due to See *because of, due to.*

each other, one another Use *each other* in sentences involving two subjects and *one another* in sentences involving more than two.

effect See *affect, effect.*

elicit, illicit The verb *elicit* means "draw out." The adjective *illicit* means "illegal." *The police* elicited *from the criminal the names of others involved in* illicit *activities.*

elude See *allude, elude.*

emigrate from, immigrate to *Emigrate from* means "move away from one's country." *Immigrate to* means "move to another country." *We* emigrated *from Norway in 1999. We* immigrated *to the United States.*

ensure See *assure, ensure, insure.*

enthused, enthusiastic Use *enthusiastic* rather than *enthused* in academic and professional writing.

equally as good Replace this redundant phrase with *equally good* or *as good.*

every day, everyday *Everyday* is an adjective meaning "ordinary." *Every day* is an adjective and a noun, meaning "each day." *I wore* everyday *clothes almost* every day.

every one, everyone *Everyone* is a pronoun. *Every one* is an adjective and a pronoun, referring to each member of a group. *Because he began after everyone else, David could not finish every one of the problems.*

except See *accept, except.*

explicit, implicit *Explicit* means "directly or openly expressed." *Implicit* means "indirectly expressed or implied." *The explicit message of the ad urged consumers to buy the product, while the implicit message promised popularity if they did so.*

farther, further *Farther* refers to physical distance. *How much farther is it to Munich? Further* refers to time or degree. *I want to avoid further delays.*

fewer, less Use *fewer* with nouns that can be counted. Use *less* with general amounts that you cannot count. *The world needs fewer bombs and less hostility.*

finalize *Finalize* is a pretentious way of saying "end" or "make final." *We closed* [not *finalized*] *the deal.*

firstly, secondly, etc. *First, second*, etc., are more common in U.S. English.

flaunt, flout *Flaunt* means to "show off." *Flout* means to "mock" or "scorn." *The drug dealers flouted authority by flaunting their wealth.*

former, latter *Former* refers to the first and *latter* to the second of two things previously mentioned. *Kathy and Anna are athletes; the former plays tennis, and the latter runs.*

further See *farther, further.*

good, well *Good* is an adjective and should not be used as a substitute for the adverb *well. Gabriel is a good host who cooks well.*

good and *Good and* is colloquial for "very"; avoid it in academic and professional writing.

hanged, hung *Hanged* refers to executions; *hung* is used for all other meanings.

hardly See *can't hardly.*

herself, himself, myself, yourself Do not use these reflexive pronouns as subjects or as objects unless they are necessary. *Jane and I* [not *myself*] *agree. They invited John and me* [not *myself*].

he/she, his/her Better solutions for avoiding sexist language are to write out *he or she*, to eliminate pronouns entirely, or to make the subject plural. Instead of writing *Everyone should carry his/her driver's license*, try *Drivers should carry their licenses* or *People should carry their driver's licenses.*

himself See *herself, himself, myself, yourself.*

hisself Use *himself* instead in academic or professional writing.

hopefully *Hopefully* is often used informally to mean "it is hoped," but its formal meaning is "with hope." *Sam watched the roulette wheel hopefully* [not *Hopefully, Sam will win*].

hung See *hanged, hung.*

illicit See *elicit, illicit.*

illusion See *allusion, illusion.*

immigrate to See *emigrate from, immigrate to.*

impact   Some readers object to the colloquial use of *impact* or *impact on* as a verb meaning "affect." *Population control may reduce* [not *impact*] *world hunger.*

implicit   See *explicit, implicit.*

imply, infer   To *imply* is to suggest indirectly. To *infer* is to guess or conclude on the basis of an indirect suggestion. *The note implied they were planning a small wedding; we inferred we would not be invited.*

inside of, outside of   Use *inside* and *outside* instead. *The class regularly met outside* [not *outside of*] *the building.*

insure   See *assure, ensure, insure.*

interact, interface   *Interact* is a vague word meaning "do something that somehow involves another person." *Interface* is computer jargon; when used as a verb, it means "discuss" or "communicate." Avoid both verbs in academic and professional writing.

irregardless, regardless   *Irregardless* is a double negative. Use *regardless.*

is when, is where   These vague expressions are often incorrectly used in definitions. *Schizophrenia is a psychotic condition in which* [not *is when* or *is where*] *a person withdraws from reality.*

its, it's   *Its* is the possessive form of *it. It's* is a contraction for *it is* or *it has. It's important to observe the rat before it eats its meal.*

kind, sort, type   These singular nouns should be modified with *this* or *that*, not *these* or *those*, and followed by other singular nouns, not plural nouns. *Wear this kind of dress* [not *those kind of dresses*].

kind of, sort of   Avoid these colloquialisms. *Amy was somewhat* [not *kind of*] *tired.*

know, no   Use *know* to mean "understand." *No* is the opposite of *yes.*

later, latter   *Later* means "after some time." *Latter* refers to the second of two items named. *Juan and Chad won all their early matches, but the latter was injured later in the season.*

latter   See *former, latter* and *later, latter.*

lay, lie   *Lay* means "place" or "put." Its main forms are *lay, laid, laid.* It generally has a direct object, specifying what has been placed. *She laid her books on the desk. Lie* means "recline" or "be positioned" and does not take a direct object. Its main forms are *lie, lay, lain. She lay awake until two.*

leave, let   *Leave* means "go away." *Let* means "allow." *Leave alone* and *let alone* are interchangeable. *Let me leave now, and leave* [or *let*] *me alone from now on!*

lend, loan   In academic and professional writing, do not use *loan* as a verb; use *lend* instead. *Please lend me your pen so that I may fill out this application for a loan.*

less   See *fewer, less.*

let   See *leave, let.*

liable   See *apt, liable, likely.*

lie   See *lay, lie.*

like   See *as, as if, like.*

likely   See *apt, liable, likely.*

literally *Literally* means "actually" or "exactly as stated." Use it to stress the truth of a statement that might otherwise be understood as figurative. Do not use *literally* as an intensifier in a figurative statement. *Mirna was literally at the edge of her seat* may be accurate, but *Mirna is so hungry that she could literally eat a horse* is not.

loan See *lend, loan*.

loose, lose *Lose* is a verb meaning "misplace." *Loose* is an adjective that means "not securely attached." *Sew on that loose button before you lose it.*

lots, lots of Avoid these informal expressions meaning "much" or "many" in academic or professional discourse.

man, mankind Replace these terms with *people, humans, humankind, men and women,* or similar wording.

may See *can, may*.

may be, maybe *May be* is a verb phrase. *Maybe* is an adverb that means "perhaps." *He may be the head of the organization, but maybe someone else would handle a crisis better.*

media *Media* is the plural form of the noun *medium* and takes a plural verb. *The media are* [not *is*] *obsessed with scandals.*

might of See *could of*.

moral, morale A *moral* is a succinct lesson. *The moral of the story is that generosity is rewarded. Morale* means "spirit" or "mood." *Office morale was low.*

myself See *herself, himself, myself, yourself*.

no See *know, no*.

nor, or Use *either* with *or* and *neither* with *nor*.

number See *amount, number*.

off, of Use *off* without *of*. *The spaghetti slipped off* [not *off of*] *the plate.*

OK, O.K., okay All are acceptable spellings, but avoid the term in academic and professional discourse.

on account of Use this substitute for *because of* sparingly or not at all.

one another See *each other, one another*.

or See *nor, or*.

outside of See *inside of, outside of*.

owing to the fact that Avoid this and other wordy expressions for *because*.

passed, past Use *passed* to mean "went by" or "received a passing grade": *The marching band passed the reviewing stand.* Use *past* to refer to a time before the present: *Historians study the past.*

per Use the Latin *per* only in standard technical phrases such as *miles per hour.* Otherwise, find English equivalents. *As mentioned in* [not *As per*] *the latest report, the country's average food consumption each day* [not *per day*] *is only 2,000 calories.*

percent, percentage Use *percent* with a specific number; use *percentage* with an adjective such as *large* or *small*. *Last year, 80 percent of the members were female. A large percentage of the members are women.*

plenty *Plenty* means "enough" or "a great abundance." *They told us America was a land of plenty.* Colloquially, it is used to mean "very," a usage you should avoid in academic and professional writing. *He was very [not plenty] tired.*

plus *Plus* means "in addition to." *Your salary plus mine will cover our expenses.* In academic writing, do not use *plus* to mean "besides" or "moreover." *That dress does not fit me. Besides [not Plus], it is the wrong color.*

precede, proceed *Precede* means "come before"; *proceed* means "go forward." *Despite the storm that preceded the ceremony, the wedding proceeded on schedule.*

pretty Except in informal situations, avoid using *pretty* as a substitute for "rather," "somewhat," or "quite." *Bill was quite [not pretty] disagreeable.*

principal, principle When used as a noun, *principal* refers to a head official or an amount of money; when used as an adjective, it means "most significant." *Principle* means "fundamental law or belief." *Albert went to the principal and defended himself with the principle of free speech.*

proceed See *precede, proceed.*

quotation, quote *Quote* is a verb, and *quotation* is a noun. *He quoted the president, and the quotation [not quote] was preserved in history books.*

raise, rise *Raise* means "lift" or "move upward." (Referring to children, it means "bring up.") It takes a direct object; someone raises something. *The guests raised their glasses to toast. Rise* means "go upward." It does not take a direct object; something rises by itself. *She saw the steam rise from the pan.*

rarely ever Use *rarely* by itself, or use *hardly ever. When we were poor, we rarely went to the movies.*

real, really *Real* is an adjective, and *really* is an adverb. Do not substitute *real* for *really.* In academic and professional writing, do not use *real* or *really* to mean "very." *The old man walked very [not real or really] slowly.*

reason is because Use either *the reason is that* or *because* — not both. *The reason the copier stopped is that [not is because] the paper jammed.*

reason why This expression is redundant. *The reason [not reason why] this book is short is market demand.*

regardless See *irregardless, regardless.*

respectfully, respectively *Respectfully* means "with respect." *Respectively* means "in the order given." *Karen and David are, respectively, a juggler and an acrobat. The children treated their grandparents respectfully.*

rise See *raise, rise.*

set, sit *Set* usually means "put" or "place" and takes a direct object. *Sit* refers to taking a seat and does not take an object. *Set your cup on the table, and sit down.*

should of See *could of.*

since Be careful not to use *since* ambiguously. In *Since I broke my leg, I've stayed home,* the word *since* might be understood to mean either "because" or "ever since."

sit See *set, sit.*

so In academic and professional writing, avoid using *so* alone to mean "very." Instead, follow *so* with *that* to show how the intensified condition leads to a result. *Aaron was so tired that he fell asleep at the wheel.*

someplace Use *somewhere* instead in academic and professional writing.

some time, sometime, sometimes *Some time* refers to a length of time. *Please leave me some time to dress. Sometime* means "at some indefinite later time." *Sometime I will take you to London. Sometimes* means "occasionally." *Sometimes I eat sushi.*

sort See *kind, sort, type.*

sort of See *kind of, sort of.*

stationary, stationery *Stationary* means "standing still"; *stationery* means "writing paper." *When the bus was stationary, Pat took out stationery and wrote a note.*

subsequently See *consequently, subsequently.*

supposed to, used to Be careful to include the final *-d* in these expressions. *He is supposed to attend.*

sure, surely Avoid using *sure* as an intensifier. Instead, use *certainly. I was certainly glad to see you.*

take See *bring, take.*

than, then Use *than* in comparative statements. *The cat was bigger than the dog.* Use *then* when referring to a sequence of events. *I won, and then I cried.*

that, which A clause beginning with *that* singles out the item being described. *The book that is on the table is a good one* specifies the book on the table as opposed to some other book. A clause beginning with *which* may or may not single out the item, although some writers use *which* clauses only to add more information about an item being described. *The book, which is on the table, is a good one* contains a *which* clause between the commas. The clause simply adds extra, nonessential information about the book; it does not specify which book.

theirselves Use *themselves* instead in academic and professional writing.

then See *than, then.*

thorough, threw, through *Thorough* means "complete": *After a thorough inspection, the restaurant reopened. Threw* is the past tense of *throw,* and *through* means "in one side and out the other": *He threw the ball through a window.*

to, too, two *To* generally shows direction. *Too* means "also." *Two* is the number. *We, too, are going to the meeting in two hours.* Avoid using *to* after *where. Where are you flying* [not *flying to*]?

two See *to, too, two.*

type See *kind, sort, type.*

uninterested See *disinterested, uninterested.*

unique Some people argue that *unique* means "one and only" and object to usage that suggests it means merely "unusual." In formal writing, avoid constructions such as *quite unique.*

used to See *supposed to, used to.*

very Avoid using *very* to intensify a weak adjective or adverb; instead, replace the adjective or adverb with a stronger, more precise, or more colorful word. Instead of *very nice,* for example, use *kind, warm, sensitive, endearing,* or *friendly.*

way, ways   When referring to distance, use *way*. *Graduation was a long way* [not *ways*] *off*.

well   See *good, well*.

where   Use *where* alone, not with words such as *at* and *to*. *Where are you going* [not *going to*]?

which   See *that, which*.

who, whom   Use *who* if the word is the subject of the clause and *whom* if the word is the object of the clause. *Monica, who smokes incessantly, is my godmother.* (*Who* is the subject of the clause; the verb is *smokes*.) *Monica, whom I saw last winter, lives in Tucson.* (*Whom* is the object of the verb *saw*.)

who's, whose   *Who's* is a contraction for *who is* or *who has*. *Who's on the patio? Whose* is a possessive form. *Whose sculpture is in the garden? Whose is on the patio?*

would of   See *could of*.

yet   See *but yet*.

your, you're   *Your* shows possession. *Bring your sleeping bag along. You're* is the contraction for *you are*. *You're in the wrong sleeping bag.*

yourself   See *herself, himself, myself, yourself*.

Sentence Style

Look: wear your black some days, and
wear your purple others. There is no
other rule besides pulling it off.

— ZADIE SMITH

Sentence Style

25 **Coordination, Subordination, and Emphasis** *269*
  a Use coordination to relate equal ideas *270*
  b Use subordination to distinguish main ideas *271*
  c Use closing and opening positions for emphasis *274*

26 **Consistency and Completeness** *275*
  a Revise faulty sentence structure *276*
  b Match up subjects and predicates *276*
  c Use elliptical structures carefully *277*
  d Check for missing words *278*
  e Make comparisons complete, consistent, and clear *278*

27 **Parallelism** *279*
  a Make items in a series parallel *279*
  b Make paired ideas parallel *280*
  c Include all necessary words *281*

28 **Shifts** *281*
  a Revise unnecessary shifts in verb tense *282*
  b Revise unnecessary shifts in mood *282*
  c Revise unnecessary shifts in voice *282*
  d Revise unnecessary shifts in person and number *282*
  e Revise shifts between direct and indirect discourse *283*
  f Revise shifts in tone and word choice *283*

29 **Conciseness** *284*
  a Eliminate unnecessary words *285*
  b Eliminate redundant words *285*
  c Eliminate empty words *286*
  d Replace wordy phrases *286*
  e Simplify sentence structure *287*

30 **Sentence Variety** *288*
  a Vary sentence length *288*
  b Vary sentence openings *288*

For visual analysis Look carefully at the illustration on the front of this tab. What do you think this image suggests about using style effectively?

Coordination, Subordination, and Emphasis 25

C oordination and subordination are ways of joining ideas in sentences that show relationships between ideas and emphasize more important ideas. In speech, people tend to use *and* and *so* as all-purpose connectors.

> I'm leaving now, and I'll see you later.

The meaning of this sentence may be perfectly clear in speech, which provides clues with voice, facial expressions, and gestures. But in writing, the sentence could have multiple meanings, including these:

> Although I'm leaving now, I'll see you later.

> I'm leaving now because I'll see you later.

A coordinating conjunction such as *and* gives ideas equal emphasis, and a subordinating conjunction such as *although* or *because* emphasizes one

---

AT A GLANCE

Editing for Coordination, Subordination, and Emphasis

How do your ideas flow from one sentence to another? Do they connect smoothly and clearly? Are the more important ideas given more emphasis than less important ones?

- Look for strings of short sentences that might be combined to join related ideas. (25a)

  > The report was short/, ~~It~~ *but it* was persuasive/, ~~It~~ *it* changed my mind.

- If you use *and* excessively, decide whether all the ideas are equally important. If they are not equal, edit to subordinate the less important ones. (25b)

continued

- Make sure that the most important ideas appear in independent clauses that can stand alone as complete sentences. (25b)

  Even though the
  ▶ ~~The~~ report was short, ~~even though~~ it changed my mind.

- Identify the word or words you want to receive special emphasis. If those words are buried in the middle of a sentence, edit the sentence to change their position. The end and the beginning are generally the most emphatic. (25c)

- If a sentence includes a series of three or more words, phrases, or clauses, try to arrange the items in the series in climactic order, with the most important item last. (25c)

idea more than another. Choosing appropriate conjunctions also allows a writer to specify how the ideas are related.

25a   Use coordination to relate equal ideas.

When used well, coordination relates separate but equal ideas. The element that links the ideas, usually a coordinating conjunction (*and, but, for, nor, or, so, yet*) or a semicolon, makes the precise relationship clear. The following sentences by N. Scott Momaday all use coordination, but the relationship between independent clauses differs in each sentence:

▶ They acquired horses, **and** their ancient nomadic spirit was suddenly free of the ground.

▶ There is perfect freedom in the mountains, **but** it belongs to the eagle and the elk, the badger and the bear.

▶ No longer were they slaves to the simple necessity of survival**;** they were a lordly and dangerous society of fighters and thieves, hunters and priests of the sun.

–N. Scott Momaday, The Way to Rainy Mountain

Momaday uses coordination in these sentences carefully in order to achieve very specific effects. In the first sentence, for example, the use of *and* gives a sense of adding on: "They acquired horses" *and*, of equal importance, "their ancient nomadic spirit was suddenly free." Momaday might have made other, equally correct choices, but they would have resulted in slightly different sentences. Compare these altered versions with Momaday's sentences. How do the changes affect your understanding?

▶ They acquired horses, so their ancient nomadic spirit was suddenly free of the ground.

▶ There is perfect freedom in the mountains; it belongs to the eagle and the elk, the badger and the bear.

In your own writing, think about exactly what information you want to convey with coordination. You, too, may have several correct options—so make the choice that works best for your situation and audience.

Coordination can help make explicit the relationship between two ideas.

▶ Generations have now grown up with *The Simpsons*; Bart, Lisa, and Maggie never get older, but today's college students may have been watching the show since before they could talk.

Connecting these two sentences with a semicolon strengthens the connection between two closely related ideas.

When you connect ideas within a sentence, make sure the relationship between the ideas is clear.

▶ Watching television is a common way to spend leisure time, and it *but* makes viewers apathetic.

What does television's being a common form of leisure have to do with viewers' being apathetic? Changing *and* to *but* better relates the two ideas.

25b Use subordination to distinguish main ideas.

Subordination allows you to distinguish major points from minor points or to bring in supporting details. If, for instance, you put your main idea in an independent clause—words that could stand alone as a sentence (31m)—you might then put any less significant ideas in dependent clauses, phrases, or even single words. The following sentence highlights the subordinated point:

▶ Mrs. Viola Cullinan was a plump woman who lived in a three-bedroom house somewhere behind the post office.
— Maya Angelou, "My Name Is Margaret"

The dependent clause adds important information about Mrs. Cullinan, but it is subordinate to the independent clause.

Notice that the choice of what to subordinate rests with the writer and depends on the intended meaning. Angelou might have given the same basic information differently.

▶ **Mrs. Viola Cullinan, a plump woman, lived in a three-bedroom house somewhere behind the post office.**

Subordinating the information about Mrs. Cullinan's size to that about her house would suggest a slightly different meaning, of course. When you write, think carefully about what you want to emphasize and subordinate information accordingly.

Subordination also establishes logical relationships among ideas. These relationships are often specified by relative pronouns—such as *which*, *who*, and *that*—and by subordinating conjunctions.

COMMON SUBORDINATING CONJUNCTIONS

after	if	though
although	in order that	unless
as	once	until
as if	since	when
because	so that	where
before	than	while
even though		

The following sentence highlights the subordinate clause and underlines the subordinating word:

▶ **She usually rested her smile until late afternoon <u>when</u> her women friends dropped in and Miss Glory, the cook, served them cold drinks on the closed-in porch.** — MAYA ANGELOU, "My Name Is Margaret"

Using too many coordinate structures can be monotonous and can make it hard for readers to recognize the most important ideas. Subordinating lesser ideas can help highlight the main ideas.

▶ **Many people check email in the evening, and so they turn on**

Though they
the computer. ~~They~~ may intend to respond only to urgent messages,

which
a friend sends a link to a blog post, ~~and~~ they decide to read ~~it~~

Eventually,
for just a short while/. ~~and~~ they get engrossed in Facebook, and they

end up spending the whole evening in front of the screen.

Determining what to subordinate

Although our
► ~~Our~~ new boss can be difficult, ~~although~~ she has revived and maybe
even saved the division.

The editing puts the more important information—that she has saved part
of the company—in an independent clause and subordinates the rest.

Avoiding excessive subordination

When too many subordinate clauses are strung together, readers may
have trouble keeping track of the main idea.

TOO MUCH SUBORDINATION

► Philip II sent the Spanish Armada to conquer England, which was
ruled by Elizabeth, who had executed Mary because she was plotting to
overthrow Elizabeth, who was a Protestant, whereas Mary and Philip
were Roman Catholics.

TALKING ABOUT STYLE

Subordination

Carefully used subordination can create powerful effects. Some particularly fine examples come from Martin Luther King Jr.

Perhaps it is easy for those who have never felt the stinging darts
of segregation to say, "Wait." But *when* you have seen vicious
mobs lynch your mothers and fathers at will and drown your sisters
and brothers at whim; *when* you have seen hate-filled policemen
curse, kick, and even kill your black brothers and sisters; . . . *when*
you have to concoct an answer for a five-year-old son who is asking: "Daddy, why do white people treat colored people so mean?";
when you take a cross-country drive and find it necessary to sleep
night after night in the uncomfortable corners of your automobile
because no motel will accept you; . . . *when* your first name becomes "nigger," your middle name becomes "boy" (however old
you are) and your last name becomes "John," and your wife and
mother are never given the respected title "Mrs."; . . . *when* you are
forever fighting a degenerating sense of "nobodiness"—then you
will understand why we find it difficult to wait.

– MARTIN LUTHER KING JR., "Letter from Birmingham Jail"

REVISED

▶ **Philip II sent the Spanish Armada to conquer England, which was ruled by Elizabeth, a Protestant. She had executed Mary, a Roman Catholic like Philip, because Mary was plotting to overthrow her.**

Putting the facts about Elizabeth executing Mary into an independent clause makes key information easier to recognize.

⟳ **bedfordstmartins.com/everydaywriter**
Exercise Central > Coordination and Subordination

25c **Use closing and opening positions for emphasis.**

When you read a sentence, the part you are most likely to remember is the ending. This part of the sentence should move the writing forward by providing new information, as it does in the following example:

▶ **Employers today expect college graduates to have excellent writing skills.**

A less emphatic but still important position in a sentence is the opening, which often connects the new sentence with what has come before.

▶ **Today's employers want a college-educated workforce that can communicate well. Excellent writing skills are high on the list of qualifications.**

If you place relatively unimportant information in the memorable closing position of a sentence, you may undercut what you want to emphasize or give more emphasis to the closing words than you intend.

Last month, she   *$500,000.*
▶ ~~She gave~~ **$500,000 to the school capital campaign** ~~last month.~~
   ^   ^

Moving *$500,000* to the end of the sentence emphasizes the amount.

Using climactic order to emphasize important ideas

When you arrange ideas in order of increasing importance, power, or drama, your writing builds to a climax. By saving its most dramatic item for last, the following sentence makes its point forcefully and memorably:

▶ **After they've finished with the pantry, the medicine cabinet, and the attic, [neat people] will throw out the red geranium (too many leaves), sell the dog (too many fleas), and send the children off to boarding school (too many scuffmarks on the hardwood floors).**

— SUSANNE BRITT, "Neat People vs. Sloppy People"

The original version of the next sentence fails to achieve strong emphasis because its verbs are not sequenced in order of increasing power; the editing provides climactic order.

▶ Violent video games ~assault our eyes,~ ~damage our brains~/. *offend our ears,* ~and~ *and* ~offend our ears.~

TALKING ABOUT STYLE

Anticlimax and Humor

Sometimes it's fun to turn the principle of climactic order upside down, opening with grand or exaggerated language only to end anticlimactically, with everyday words.

> He is a writer for the ages — the ages of four to eight.
> — DOROTHY PARKER

Parker builds up high expectations at the beginning of the sentence — only to undercut them unexpectedly by shifting the meaning of *ages*. Having led readers to expect something dramatic, she makes us laugh, or at least smile, with words that are decidedly undramatic.

---

bedfordstmartins.com/everydaywriter
Exercise Central > Emphasis

Consistency and Completeness **26**

In conversation, you will hear inconsistent and incomplete structures all the time. For instance, during an interview with journalist Bill Moyers, Jon Stewart discussed the supposed objectivity of news reporting.

> But news has never been objective. It's always . . . what does every newscast start with? "Our top stories tonight." That's a list. That's a subjective . . . some editor made a decision: "Here's our top stories. Number one: There's a fire in the Bronx."

Because Stewart is talking casually, some of his sentences begin one way but then move in another direction. The mixed structures pose no problem for the viewer — they sound like conversations we hear every day — but sentences such as these can be confusing in writing.

26a Revise faulty sentence structure.

One inconsistency that poses problems for writers and readers is a mixed structure, which results from beginning a sentence with one grammatical pattern and then switching to another one.

MIXED   The fact that I get up at 5:00 AM, a wake-up time that explains why I'm always tired in the evening.

The sentence starts out with a subject (*The fact*) followed by a dependent clause (*that I get up at 5:00 AM*). The sentence needs a predicate to complete the independent clause, but instead it moves to another phrase followed by a dependent clause (*a wake-up time that explains why I'm always tired in the evening*), and what results is a fragment.

REVISED   The fact that I get up at 5:00 AM explains why I'm always tired in the evening.

Deleting *a wake-up time that* changes the rest of the sentence into a predicate.

REVISED   I get up at 5:00 AM, a wake-up time that explains why I'm always tired in the evening.

Deleting *The fact that* turns the beginning of the sentence into an independent clause.

(For information about subjects and predicates, see 31j and k; for information about independent and dependent clauses, see 31m.)

26b Match up subjects and predicates.

Another kind of mixed structure, called faulty predication, occurs when a subject and predicate do not fit together grammatically or simply do not make sense together. Many cases of faulty predication result from using forms of *be* when another verb would be stronger.

▶ A characteristic that I admire is ~~a person who is generous~~. *generosity.*

A person is not a characteristic.

▶ The rules of the corporation ~~expect~~ employees to be on time. *require*

Rules cannot expect anything.

AT A GLANCE

Editing for Consistency and Completeness

- If you find an especially confusing sentence, check to see whether it has a subject and a predicate. If not, revise as necessary. (26a) If you find both a subject and a predicate, and you are still confused, see whether the subject and verb make sense together. (26b)

- Revise any *is when*, *is where*, and *reason . . . is because* constructions. (26b)

  > *the practice of sending*
  > ► Spamming is ~~where companies~~ send electronic junk mail.
  >   ^

- Check all comparisons for completeness. (26e)

  > *we like*
  > ► We like Lisa better than Margaret.
  >   ^

Is when, is where, *and the reason . . . is because*

Constructions using *is when*, *is where*, and *the reason . . . is because* are used frequently in informal contexts, but they may be inappropriate in academic writing because they describe a noun using an adverb clause (31m).

> *an unfair characterization of*
> ► A stereotype is ~~when someone characterizes~~ a group. ~~unfairly.~~
>   ^   ^

> *a place*
> ► A confluence is where two rivers join to form one.
>   ^

> ► ~~The reason~~ I like to play soccer ~~is because~~ it provides aerobic exercise.

26c Use elliptical structures carefully.

Sometimes writers omit a word in a compound structure. This type of structure, known as an elliptical structure, is appropriate when the word omitted later in the compound is exactly the same as the word earlier in the compound.

> ► That bell belonged to the figure of Miss Duling as though it grew directly out of her right arm, as wings grew out of an angel or a tail [grew] out of the devil. — EUDORA WELTY, *One Writer's Beginnings*

If the omitted word does not match a word in the other part of the compound, readers might be confused, so the omission is inappropriate in formal writing.

▶ His skills are weak, and his performance ^is^ only average.

The verb *is* does not match the verb in the other part of the compound (*are*), so the writer needs to include it.

26d Check for missing words.

The best way to catch inadvertent omissions is to proofread carefully.

▶ The new Web site makes it easier to look ^at^ and choose from the company's inventory.

26e Make comparisons complete, consistent, and clear.

When you compare two or more things, the comparison must be complete, logically consistent, and clear.

▶ I was embarrassed because my parents were so different ^*from my friends' parents.*^

Different from what? Adding *from my friends' parents* tells readers with what the comparison is being made.

UNCLEAR	Aneil always felt more affection for his brother than his sister.
CLEAR	Aneil always felt more affection for his brother than his sister did.
CLEAR	Aneil always felt more affection for his brother than he did for his sister.

> **bedfordstmartins.com/everydaywriter**
> **Exercise Central > Consistency and Completeness**

Parallelism 27

P arallel grammatical structures show up in many familiar phrases: *sink or swim, rise and shine, shape up or ship out.* If you look and listen for these structures, you will see parallelism in everyday use. Bumper stickers often use parallel grammatical structures to make their messages memorable (*Minds are like parachutes; both work best when open*), but the pleasing effects of parallel structures can benefit any kind of writing.

27a Make items in a series parallel.

Parallelism makes a series both graceful and easy to follow.

▶ In the eighteenth century, armed forces could fight in open fields and on the high seas. Today, they can clash on the ground anywhere, on the sea, under the sea, and in the air.

— DONALD SNOW AND EUGENE BROWN, *The Contours of Power*

The parallel phrases, as well as the parallel structure of the sentences themselves, highlight the contrast between warfare in the eighteenth century and warfare today.

AT A GLANCE

Editing for Parallelism

- Look for any series of three or more items, and make all of the items parallel in structure. (27a)
- Be sure items in lists and in related headings are parallel. (27a)
- Check for places where two ideas are paired in the same sentence. Often these ideas will appear on either side of *and, but, or, nor, for, so,* or *yet,* or after each part of *both . . . and, either . . . or, neither . . . nor, not only . . . but also, whether . . . or,* or *just as . . . so.* Edit to make the two ideas parallel in structure. (27b)
- Check parallel structures to be sure that you have included all necessary words — prepositions, the *to* of the infinitive, and so on. (27c)

In the following sentences, note how the revisions make all items in the series parallel:

▶ The quarter horse skipped, pranced, and ~~was sashaying.~~ *sashayed.*

▶ The children ran down the hill, skipped over the lawn, and into the *jumped* swimming pool.

▶ The duties of the job include babysitting, housecleaning, and ~~preparation of~~ *preparing* meals.

Items in a list, on a formal outline (p. 71), and in headings in a paper (p. 95) should be parallel.

▶ Kitchen rules: (1) Coffee to be made only by library staff. (2) Coffee

service to be closed at 4:00 PM. (3) Doughnuts to be kept in cabinet.

Coffee materials not to be handled by faculty.
(4) ~~No faculty members should handle coffee materials.~~

27b Make paired ideas parallel.

Parallel structures can help you pair two ideas effectively. The more nearly parallel the two structures are, the stronger the connection between the ideas will be.

▶ History became popular, and historians became alarmed.

— WILL DURANT

▶ I type in one place, but I write all over the house.

— TONI MORRISON

▶ Writers are often more interesting on the page than they are in ~~person.~~ *the flesh.*

In these examples, the parallel structures help readers see an important contrast between two ideas or acts.

With coordinating conjunctions

When you link ideas with a coordinating conjunction—*and, but, or, nor, for, so,* or *yet*—try to make the ideas parallel in structure.

▶ Consult a friend in your class or *who is* good at math.

> *accepts*
> ► The wise politician promises the possible and ~~should accept~~ the
> inevitable.
> ^

In both sentences, the editing links the two ideas by making them parallel.

With correlative conjunctions

Use the same structure after both parts of a correlative conjunction: *either . . . or, both . . . and, neither . . . nor, not . . . but, not only . . . but also, just as . . . so,* and *whether . . . or.*

> *live in*
> ► I wanted not only to go away to school but also to New England.
> ^

Balancing *to go* with *to live* links the two ideas and makes the sentence easier to read.

27c Include all necessary words.

In addition to making parallel elements grammatically similar, be sure to include any words—prepositions, articles, verb forms, and so on—that are necessary for clarity, grammar, or idiom.

> *in*
> ► We'll move to a town in the Southwest or Mexico.
> ^

To a town in Mexico or to Mexico in general? The editing makes the meaning clear.

---

bedfordstmartins.com/everydaywriter
Exercise Central > Parallelism

Shifts 28

A shift in writing is an abrupt change that results in inconsistency. Sometimes a writer or speaker will shift deliberately, as linguist Geneva Smitherman does in this passage from *Word from the Mother*: "There are days when I optimistically predict that Hip Hop will survive—and thrive. . . . In the larger realm of Hip Hop culture, there is cause for optimism as we witness Hip Hop younguns tryna git they political activist game togetha."

Smitherman's shift from formal academic language to vernacular speech calls out for and holds our attention. Although writers make shifts for good rhetorical reasons, unintentional shifts in verb tenses, pronouns, and tone can be confusing to readers.

28a   Revise unnecessary shifts in verb tense.

If the verbs in a passage refer to actions occurring at different times, they may require different tenses. Be careful, however, not to change tenses for no reason.

> A few countries produce almost all of the world's illegal drugs, but
>   *affects*
> addiction ~~affected~~ many countries.
>   ^

28b   Revise unnecessary shifts in mood.

Be careful not to shift from one mood to another without good reason. The mood of a verb can be indicative (he *closes* the door), imperative (*close* the door), or subjunctive (if the door *were closed*) (32h).

> Keep your eye on the ball, and ~~you should~~ bend your knees.

28c   Revise unnecessary shifts in voice.

Do not shift without reason between the active voice (she *sold* it) and the passive voice (it *was sold*). Sometimes a shift in voice is justified, but often it only confuses readers (32g).

>   *me*
> Two youths approached me/ and ~~I was~~ asked for my wallet.
>   ^

> The original sentence shifts from the active (*youths approached*) to the passive (*I was asked*), so it is unclear who asked for the wallet. Making both verbs active clears up the confusion.

28d   Revise unnecessary shifts in person and number.

Unnecessary shifts in point of view among first person (*I*, *we*), second person (*you*), and third person (*he, she, it, they*), or between singular and plural subjects can be very confusing to readers.

> **AT A GLANCE**
>
> ## Confusing Shifts
>
> - Make sure you have a reason for shifting from one verb tense to another. (28a)
> - Revise any shifts in mood — perhaps from an indicative statement to an imperative — that are not necessary. (28b)
> - Check for shifts from active (*She asks questions*) to passive voice (*Questions are asked*). Are they intentional? (28c)
> - Make sure you have good reasons for any shifts in person or number — from *we* to *you*, for example. (28d)
> - Check your writing for consistency in tone and word choice. (28f)

    You

▶ ~~Someone~~ can do well on this job if you budget your time.

Is the writer making a general statement or giving advice? Eliminating the shift eliminates this confusion.

28e   Revise shifts between direct and indirect discourse.

When you quote someone's exact words, you are using direct discourse: *She said, "I'm an editor."* When you report what someone says without repeating the exact words, you are using indirect discourse: *She says she is an editor.* Shifting between direct and indirect discourse in the same sentence can cause problems, especially with questions.

    he

▶ Viet asked what could he do to help?.

The editing eliminates an awkward shift by reporting Viet's question indirectly. It could also be edited to quote Viet directly: *Viet asked, "What can I do to help?"*

28f   Revise shifts in tone and word choice.

Tone, a writer's attitude toward a topic or audience, is related to word choice and to overall formality or informality. Watch out for tone or diction shifts that can confuse readers and leave them wondering what your real attitude is (5f).

FOR MULTILINGUAL WRITERS

Shifting Tenses in Reported Speech

If Al said to Maria, "I will marry you," why did she then correctly tell her mom, "He said that he *would* marry me"? For guidelines on reporting speech, see 59b.

INCONSISTENT TONE

> The question of child care forces a society to make profound decisions about its economic values. Can most families with young children actually live adequately on only one salary? If some conservatives had their way, June Cleaver would still be stuck in the kitchen baking cookies for Wally and the Beaver and waiting for Ward to bring home the bacon, except that, with only one income, the Cleavers would be lucky to afford hot dogs.

In this version, the first two sentences set a serious, formal tone by discussing child care in fairly general, abstract terms. But in the third sentence, the writer shifts suddenly to sarcasm, to references to television characters of an earlier era, and to informal language like *stuck* and *bring home the bacon*. Readers cannot tell whether the writer is presenting a serious analysis or preparing for a humorous satire. The revision makes the tone consistently formal.

REVISED

> The question of child care forces a society to make profound decisions about its economic values. Can most families with young children actually live adequately on only one salary? Some conservatives believe that women with young children should not work outside the home, but many mothers are forced to do so for financial reasons.

bedfordstmartins.com/everydaywriter
Exercise Central > Shifts

29 Conciseness

If you have a Twitter account, you know a lot about being concise—that is, about getting messages across without wasting words (Twitter limits writers to 140 characters). Recently, *New York Times* editor Bill Keller decided to start a discussion by tweeting, "Twitter makes you stupid. Discuss." That little comment drew a large number of responses, including one from his wife that read, "I don't know if Twitter makes you stupid, but it's making you late for dinner. Come home."

No matter how you feel about the effects of Twitter on the brain (or stomach!), you can make any writing more effective by using clear structures and choosing words that convey exactly what you mean to say.

AT A GLANCE

Editing for Conciseness

- Look for redundant words. If you are unsure about a word, read the sentence without it; if meaning is not affected, leave the word out. (29a and b)
- Take out empty words — words like *aspect* or *factor*, *definitely* or *very*. (29c)
- Replace wordy phrases with a single word. Instead of *because of the fact that*, try *because*. (29d)
- Reconsider any sentences that begin with *it is* or *there is/are*. Unless they create special emphasis, try recasting the sentences without these words. (29e)

29a Eliminate unnecessary words.

Usually you'll want to make your point in the fewest possible words.

WORDY   One thing that her constant and continual use of vulgar expressions or four-letter words indicated to the day-care workers was that she might really have a great deal of trouble in terms of her ability to get along in a successful manner with other six-year-olds in her age group.

Why write that sentence when you could instead write the following?

REVISED   Her constant use of four-letter words told the day-care workers she might have trouble getting along with other six-year-olds.

29b Eliminate redundant words.

Sometimes writers say that something is large *in size* or red *in color* or that two ingredients should be *combined together*. Such words are redundant, or unnecessary for meaning, as are the deleted words in the following examples:

> *Attendance*
> ~~Compulsory attendance~~ at assemblies is required.
>   ^

> Many different forms of hazing occur, such as physical ~~abuse~~ and
> mental abuse.

29c   Eliminate empty words.

Empty words are so general or overused that they contribute no real meaning to a sentence.

EMPTY WORDS

angle, area, aspect, case, character, element, factor, field, kind, nature, scope, situation, thing, type

Many modifiers are so common that they have become empty words.

MEANINGLESS MODIFIERS

absolutely, awesome, awfully, central, definitely, fine, great, literally, major, quite, really, very

When you cannot simply delete empty words, think of a more specific way to say what you mean.

> *Housing*   *strongly influence*
> ~~The housing situation~~ can ~~have a really significant impact on the~~
>   ^   ^
>   *social*
> ~~social aspect of~~ a student's life.
>   ^

29d   Replace wordy phrases.

Wordy phrases can be reduced to a word or two with no loss in meaning.

WORDY	CONCISE
at all times	always
at that point in time	then
at the present time	now / today
due to the fact that	because
for the purpose of	for
in order to	to
in spite of the fact that	although
in the event that	if

29e   Simplify sentence structure.

Using the simplest grammatical structures possible can tighten and strengthen your sentences considerably.

▶ Hurricane Katrina, ~~which was certainly~~ one of the most powerful storms
  widespread
  ever to hit the Gulf Coast, caused damage. ~~to a very wide area.~~

Reducing a clause to an appositive, deleting unnecessary words, and replacing five words with one tighten the sentence and make it easier to read.

Using strong verbs

Be verbs (*is, are, was, were, been*) often result in wordiness.

  harms
▶ A high-fat, high-cholesterol diet ~~is bad for~~ your heart.

Avoiding there is, there are, *and* it is

Sometimes expletive constructions—*there is, there are,* and *it is*—can introduce a topic effectively; often, however, your writing will be better without them.

  Many
▶ ~~There are many~~ people ~~who~~ fear success because they believe they do
  not deserve it.

  Presidential   *need*
▶ ~~It is necessary for presidential~~ candidates to perform well on television.

Using active voice

Some writing situations call for the passive voice (32g), but it is always wordier than the active—and often makes for dull or even difficult reading.

  Gower
▶ ~~In Gower's research, it was~~ found that pythons often dwell in trees.

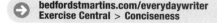
bedfordstmartins.com/everydaywriter
Exercise Central > Conciseness

30 Sentence Variety

Row upon row of trees identical in size and shape may appeal to our sense of orderliness, but in spite of that appeal, the rows soon become boring. Constant uniformity in anything, in fact, soon gets tiresome. Variety is important in sentence structures because too much uniformity results in dull, listless prose. This chapter examines ways to revise sentences by creating variety in length and in openings.

AT A GLANCE

Editing for Sentence Variety

- Count the words in each of your sentences. If the difference between the longest and shortest sentences is fairly small — say, five words or fewer — try revising your sentences to create greater variety. (30a)
- If many sentences have fewer than ten words, consider whether any of them need more detail or should be combined with other sentences.
- How do your sentences open? If all or most of them open with a subject, try recasting some sentences to begin with a transition, a phrase, or a dependent clause. (30b)

30a Vary sentence length.

Is there a "just right" length for a particular sentence or idea? The answer depends partly on your purpose, intended audience, and topic. But note that after one or more long sentences with complex ideas or images, the punch of a short sentence can be refreshing.

▶ To become a doctor, you spend so much time in the tunnels of preparation—head down, trying not to screw up, just going from one day to the next—that it is a shock to find yourself at the other end, with someone offering you a job. **But the day comes.** – ATUL GAWANDE, *Better*

30b Vary sentence openings.

If sentence after sentence begins with a subject, a passage may become monotonous or hard to read.

TALKING ABOUT STYLE

Technical Writing

For some types of writing, varying sentence structure and length is not always appropriate. Many technical writers, particularly those who write manuals that will be translated into other languages, must follow stringent rules for sentence structure and length. One computer company, for example, requires writers to adhere to a strict subject-verb-object order and limit all sentences to no more than fifteen words. Learn the style conventions of your field as fully as possible, and bring them to bear on your own sentence revisions.

▶ The way football and basketball are played is as interesting as the

Because football   *each*

players. ~~Football~~ is a game of precision/, ~~Each~~ play is diagrammed to

however,

accomplish a certain goal. Basketball, is a game of endurance.

In fact, a

~~A~~ basketball game looks like a track meet; the team that drops of

exhaustion first, loses. Basketball players are often compared to artists/;

their

~~The players'~~ moves and slam dunks are their masterpieces.

The editing adds variety by using a subordinating word (*Because*) and a prepositional phrase (*In fact*) and by linking sentences. Varying sentence openings prevents the passage from seeming to jerk or lurch along.

You can add variety to your sentence openings by using transitions, various kinds of phrases, and dependent clauses.

TRANSITIONAL EXPRESSIONS

▶ In contrast, our approach will save time and money.

▶ Nevertheless, the show must go on.

PHRASES

▶ Before dawn, tired commuters drink their first cups of coffee.

▶ Frustrated by the delays, the drivers started honking their horns.

▶ To qualify for flight training, one must be in good physical condition.

▶ Our hopes for victory dashed, we started home.

DEPENDENT CLAUSES

▶ **What they want** is a place to call home.

▶ **Because the hills were dry,** the fire spread rapidly.

bedfordstmartins.com/everydaywriter
Exercise Central > Sentence Variety

Sentence Grammar

Most of us don't know a gerund from
a gerbil and don't care, but we'd like to
speak and write as though we did.

— PATRICIA T. O'CONNER

Sentence Grammar

31 Basic Grammar 294

  a The basic grammar of sentences *294*

PARTS OF SPEECH

  b Verbs *295*
  c Nouns *296*
  d Pronouns *296*
  e Adjectives *298*
  f Adverbs *299*
  g Prepositions *299*
  h Conjunctions *300*
  i Interjections *302*

PARTS OF SENTENCES

  j Subjects *303*
  k Predicates *304*
  l Phrases *306*
  m Clauses *308*

TYPES OF SENTENCES

  n Grammatical classifications *309*
  o Functional classifications *310*

32 Verbs *311*

  a Understand the five forms of verbs *312*
  b Use helping (auxiliary) verbs appropriately *313*
  c Use appropriate forms of irregular verbs *313*
  d Choose between *lie* and *lay*, *sit* and *set*, *rise* and *raise* *316*
  e Use verb tenses appropriately *317*
  f Sequence verb tenses effectively *320*
  g Use active and passive voice effectively *321*
  h Use mood effectively *322*

33 Subject-Verb Agreement *323*

  a Match verb forms with third-person singular subjects *324*
  b Check subjects and verbs separated by other words *325*
  c Make verbs agree with compound subjects *325*
  d Make verbs agree with collective-noun subjects *326*
  e Make verbs agree with indefinite-pronoun subjects *327*
  f Make verbs agree with antecedents of *who*, *which*, and *that* *327*
  g Use appropriate forms of linking verbs *328*

For visual analysis Look carefully at the illustration on the front of this tab. What do you think this image suggests how grammar works?

h Make verbs agree with subjects that are plural in form but singular in meaning *328*
i Make verbs agree with subjects that follow verbs *329*
j Make verbs agree with titles and words used as words *329*

34 Pronouns *329*
a Consider a pronoun's role in the sentence *330*
b Use *who*, *whoever*, *whom*, and *whomever* appropriately *332*
c Consider case in compound structures *334*
d Consider case in elliptical constructions *334*
e Use *we* and *us* appropriately before a noun *335*
f Make pronouns agree with antecedents *335*
g Make pronouns refer to clear antecedents *337*

35 Adjectives and Adverbs *339*
a Use adjectives after linking verbs *339*
b Use adverbs to modify verbs, adjectives, and adverbs *340*
c Choose appropriate comparative and superlative forms *341*

36 Modifier Placement *343*
a Revise misplaced modifiers *344*
b Revise disruptive modifiers *345*
c Revise dangling modifiers *346*

37 Comma Splices and Fused Sentences *347*
a Separate the clauses into two sentences *347*
b Link the clauses with a comma and a coordinating conjunction *349*
c Link the clauses with a semicolon *349*
d Rewrite the clauses as one independent clause *350*
e Rewrite one independent clause as a dependent clause *350*
f Link the two clauses with a dash *351*

38 Sentence Fragments *352*
a Revise phrase fragments *353*
b Revise compound-predicate fragments *354*
c Revise dependent-clause fragments *354*

31 Basic Grammar

The grammar of our first language comes to us almost automatically, without our thinking much about it or even being aware of it. Listen in, for instance, on a conversation between a six-year-old and her sister.

> AUDREY: My new bike that Daddy got me has a pink basket and a loud horn, and I love it.
>
> LILA: Can I ride it?
>
> AUDREY: Sure, as soon as you get big enough.

This simple conversation features sophisticated grammar used effortlessly. Every language has grammar (basic structures), and native speakers understand and use these structures long before they learn what to call parts of a sentence or the different options for putting the pieces of sentences together effectively. Thinking carefully about the basic structures of English can help you make wise choices for your audience and your rhetorical situation.

31a The basic grammar of sentences

A sentence is a grammatically complete group of words that expresses a thought. In standard English, a grammatically complete sentence must contain a subject, which identifies what the sentence is about, and a predicate, which says or asks something about the subject or tells the subject to do something.

SUBJECT	PREDICATE
I	have a dream.
The rain in Spain	stays mainly in the plain.
Stephen Colbert, who hosts a cable TV show,	pretends to be a conservative.

Some sentences have only a one-word predicate with an implied, or understood, subject (for example, *Stop!*). Most sentences, however, contain additional words that expand the basic subject and predicate. In the preceding example, for instance, the subject might have been simply *Stephen Colbert*; the words *who hosts a cable TV show* tell us more about the subject. Similarly, the predicate of that sentence could grammatically be *pretends*; the words *to be a conservative* expand the predicate by telling us what Colbert pretends.

Parts of Speech

All English words belong to one or more of eight grammatical categories called parts of speech: verbs, nouns, pronouns, adjectives, adverbs, prepositions, conjunctions, and interjections. Many English words regularly function as more than one part of speech. Take the word *book*, for example: when you *book a flight*, it is a verb; when you *take a good book to the beach*, it is a noun; and when you *have book knowledge*, it is an adjective.

TALKING THE TALK

Grammatical Terms

"I never learned any grammar." You may lack *conscious* knowledge of grammar and grammatical terms (and if so, you are not alone — American students today rarely study English grammar). But you probably understand the ideas that grammatical terms such as *auxiliary verb* and *direct object* represent, even if the terms themselves are unfamiliar. Brushing up on the terms commonly used to talk about grammar will make it easier for you and your instructor — as well as other readers and reviewers — to share a common language when you want to discuss the best ways to get your ideas across clearly and with few distractions.

31b Verbs

Verbs are among the most important words because they move the meanings of sentences along. Verbs show actions of body or mind (*skip, speculate*), occurrences (*become, happen*), or states of being (*be, seem*). They can also change form to show *time, person, number, voice,* and *mood.*

TIME	we work, we worked
PERSON	I work, she works
NUMBER	one person works, two people work
VOICE	she asks, she is asked
MOOD	we see, if we saw

Helping verbs (also called auxiliary verbs) combine with other verbs (often called main verbs) to create verb phrases. Helping verbs include the various forms of *be*, *do*, and *have* (which can also function as main verbs) and the words *can*, *could*, *may*, *might*, *must*, *shall*, *should*, *will*, and *would*.

▶ You **do need** some sleep tonight!

▶ I **could have danced** all night.

▶ She **would prefer** to learn Italian rather than Spanish.

See Chapters 32 and 33 for a complete discussion of verbs.

31c   Nouns

A noun names a person (*aviator, child*), place (*lake, library*), thing (*truck, suitcase*), or concept (*happiness, balance*). Proper nouns name specific people, places, things, and concepts: *Bill, Iowa, Supreme Court, Buddhism.* Collective nouns name groups: *team, flock, jury* (33d).

You can change most nouns from singular (one) to plural (more than one) by adding *-s* or *-es*: *horse, horses; kiss, kisses.* Some nouns, however, have irregular plural forms: *woman, women; alumnus, alumni; mouse, mice; deer, deer.* Noncount nouns—such as *dust, peace,* and *prosperity*—do not have a plural form because they name something that cannot easily be counted (58a).

To show ownership, nouns take the possessive form by adding an apostrophe plus *-s* to a singular noun or just an apostrophe to a plural noun: *the horse's owner, the boys' dilemma* (42a).

FOR MULTILINGUAL WRITERS

Using Count and Noncount Nouns

Do people conduct *research* or *researches*? See 58a for a discussion of count and noncount nouns.

31d   Pronouns

Pronouns often take the place of nouns, other pronouns, or other words functioning as a noun. Pronouns serve as short forms so that you do not have to repeat a word or group of words you have already mentioned. A word or group of words that a pronoun replaces or refers to is called the antecedent of the pronoun. (See Chapter 34.)

ANTECEDENT   PRONOUN
▶ *Caitlin* refused the invitation even though *she* wanted to go.

Here are the categories of pronouns:

PERSONAL PRONOUNS

Personal pronouns refer to specific persons or things.

I, me, you, he, she, him, her, it, we, us, they, them

▶ When Keisha saw the dogs, she called them, and they ran to her.

POSSESSIVE PRONOUNS

Possessive pronouns are personal pronouns that indicate ownership.

my, mine, your, yours, her, hers, his, its, our, ours, their, theirs

▶ My roommate lost her keys.

REFLEXIVE PRONOUNS

Reflexive pronouns refer back to the subject of the sentence and end in *-self* or *-selves*.

myself, yourself, himself, herself, itself, oneself, ourselves, yourselves, themselves

▶ The seals sunned themselves on the warm rocks.

INTENSIVE PRONOUNS

Intensive pronouns have the same form as reflexive pronouns. They emphasize a noun or another pronoun.

▶ He decided to paint the apartment himself.

INDEFINITE PRONOUNS

Indefinite pronouns do not refer to specific nouns, although they may refer to identifiable persons or things. The following is a partial list:

all, another, anybody, both, each, either, everything, few, many, most, neither, none, no one, nothing, one, some, something

▶ Everybody screamed, and someone fainted, when the lights went out.

DEMONSTRATIVE PRONOUNS

Demonstrative pronouns point to specific nouns.

this, that, these, those

▶ These are Peter's books.

INTERROGATIVE PRONOUNS

Interrogative pronouns are used to ask questions.

> *who, which, what*

> ▶ **Who can help set up the chairs for the meeting?**

RELATIVE PRONOUNS

Relative pronouns introduce dependent clauses and relate the information to the rest of the sentence (31m). The interrogative pronoun *who* and the relative pronouns *who* and *whoever* have different forms depending on how they are used in a sentence (34b).

> *who, which, that, what, whoever, whichever, whatever*

> ▶ **Maya, who hires interns, is the manager whom you should contact.**

RECIPROCAL PRONOUNS

Reciprocal pronouns refer to individual parts of a plural antecedent.

> *each other, one another*

> ▶ **The business failed because the partners distrusted each other.**

31e　Adjectives

Adjectives modify nouns and pronouns, usually by describing, identifying, or limiting those words. Some people refer to the identifying or quantifying adjectives as *determiners* (58c).

> ▶ **The red Corvette ran off the road.** [describes]
> ▶ **That Corvette needs to be repaired.** [identifies]
> ▶ **We saw several Corvettes race by.** [quantifies]

In addition to their basic forms, most descriptive adjectives have other forms that allow you to make comparisons: *small, smaller, smallest; foolish, more foolish, most foolish, less foolish, least foolish* (35c). Many words that function in some sentences as pronouns (31d) can function as identifying adjectives when they are followed by a noun.

> ▶ **That is a dangerous intersection.** [pronoun]
> ▶ **That intersection is dangerous.** [identifying adjective]

Adjectives usually precede the words they modify, though they may follow linking verbs: *The car was defective*.

Other kinds of identifying or quantifying adjectives are articles (*a, an, the*) and numbers (*three, sixty-fifth*).

Proper adjectives are adjectives formed from or related to proper nouns (*British, Emersonian*). Proper adjectives are capitalized (45b).

FOR MULTILINGUAL WRITERS

Deciding When Articles Are Necessary

Do you say "I'm working on *a* paper" or "I'm working on *the* paper"? Deciding when to use the articles *a*, *an*, and *the* can be challenging for multilingual writers since many languages have nothing directly comparable to them. For help using articles, see 58d.

31f Adverbs

Adverbs modify verbs, adjectives, other adverbs, or entire clauses. They often answer the questions *when? where? why? to what extent?* Many adverbs have an *-ly* ending, though some do not (*always, never, very, well*), and some words that end in *-ly* are not adverbs but adjectives (*scholarly, lovely*). One of the most common adverbs is *not*.

▶ **Jabari recently visited his roommate's family in Maine.** [modifies the verb *visited*]

▶ **It was an unexpectedly exciting trip.** [modifies the adjective *exciting*]

▶ **The visit ended too soon.** [modifies the adverb *soon*]

▶ **Frankly, he would have liked to stay another month.** [modifies the independent clause that makes up the rest of the sentence]

Many adverbs, like many adjectives, take other forms when making comparisons: *forcefully, more forcefully, most forcefully, less forcefully, least forcefully* (35c).

Conjunctive adverbs modify an entire clause and help connect the meaning between that clause and the preceding clause (or sentence). Examples of conjunctive adverbs include *however, furthermore, therefore,* and *likewise* (31h).

31g Prepositions

Prepositions are important structural words that express relationships—in time, space, or other senses—between nouns or pronouns and other words in a sentence.

▶ We did not want to leave **during** the game.

▶ The contestants waited nervously **for** the announcement.

▶ Drive **across** the bridge, and go **down** the avenue **past** three stoplights.

SOME COMMON PREPOSITIONS

about	at	down	near	since
above	before	during	of	through
across	behind	except	off	toward
after	below	for	on	under
against	beneath	from	onto	until
along	beside	in	out	up
among	between	inside	over	upon
around	beyond	into	past	with
as	by	like	regarding	without

SOME COMPOUND PREPOSITIONS

according to	except for	instead of
as well as	in addition to	next to
because of	in front of	out of
by way of	in place of	with regard to
due to	in spite of	

Research for this book shows that many writers today—including native speakers of English—have trouble using prepositions correctly. If you aren't sure which preposition to use, consult a dictionary.

31h Conjunctions

Conjunctions connect words or groups of words to each other and tell something about the relationship between these words.

Coordinating conjunctions

Coordinating conjunctions (25a) join equivalent structures—two or more nouns, pronouns, verbs, adjectives, adverbs, prepositions, conjunctions, phrases, or clauses.

▶ A strong **but** warm breeze blew across the desert.

▶ Please print **or** type the information on the application form.

▶ Taiwo worked two shifts today, **so** she is tired tonight.

COORDINATING CONJUNCTIONS

and	for	or	yet
but	nor	so	

Correlative conjunctions

Correlative conjunctions join equal elements, and they come in pairs.

▶ **Both** Bechtel **and** Kaiser submitted bids on the project.
▶ Jeff **not only** sent a card **but also** visited me in the hospital.

CORRELATIVE CONJUNCTIONS

both . . . and	just as . . . so	not only . . . but also
either . . . or	neither . . . nor	whether . . . or

Subordinating conjunctions

Subordinating conjunctions introduce adverb clauses and signal the relationship between an adverb clause and another clause. For instance, in the following sentence, the subordinating conjunction *while* signals that the two events in the sentence happened simultaneously:

▶ Sweat ran down my face **while** I frantically searched for my child.

SOME SUBORDINATING CONJUNCTIONS

after	if	unless
although	in order that	until
as	once	when
as if	since	where
because	so that	whether
before	than	while
even though	though	

Conjunctive adverbs

Conjunctive adverbs signal a logical relationship between parts of a sentence and, when used with a semicolon, can link independent clauses (31m).

▶ The cider tasted bitter; **however,** each of us drank a tall glass of it.
▶ The cider tasted bitter; each of us, **however,** drank a tall glass of it.

SOME CONJUNCTIVE ADVERBS

also	however	moreover	similarly
anyway	incidentally	namely	still
besides	indeed	nevertheless	then
certainly	instead	next	therefore
finally	likewise	now	thus
furthermore	meanwhile	otherwise	undoubtedly

31i   Interjections

Interjections express surprise or emotion: *oh, ouch, ah, hey.* Interjections often stand alone. Even when interjections are part of a sentence, they do not relate grammatically to the rest of the sentence.

▶ **Hey, no one suggested that we would find an easy solution.**

Parts of Sentences

Knowing a word's part of speech helps you understand how to use that word. But you also need to look at the part the word plays in a particular sentence. Consider, for instance, the word *description.*

SUBJECT
▶ **This *description* conveys the ecology of the Everglades.**

DIRECT OBJECT
▶ **I read a *description* of the ecology of the Everglades.**

Description is a noun in both sentences, yet in the first it serves as the subject of the verb *conveys,* while in the second it serves as the direct object of the verb *read.*

AT A GLANCE

Basic Sentence Patterns

1. subject/verb

       S   V
   ▶   **Babies drool.**

2. subject/verb/subject complement

       S   V   SC
   ▶   **Babies smell sweet.**

continued

3. subject/verb/direct object

     S V DO
▶ **Babies drink milk.**

4. subject/verb/indirect object/direct object

     S   V   IO   DO
▶ **Babies give grandparents pleasure.**

5. subject/verb/direct object/object complement

     S V DO OC
▶ **Babies keep parents awake.**

31j Subjects

The subject of a sentence identifies what the sentence is about. The simple subject consists of one or more nouns or pronouns; the complete subject consists of the simple subject with all its modifiers.

▶ **Baseball is a summer game.**

  ┌────── COMPLETE SUBJECT ──────┐
▶ **Sailing over the fence, the ball crashed through Mr. Wilson's window.**

  ┌────── COMPLETE SUBJECT ──────┐
▶ **Those who sit in the bleachers have the most fun.**

A compound subject contains two or more simple subjects joined with a coordinating conjunction (*and, but, or*) or a correlative conjunction (*both . . . and, either . . . or, neither . . . nor*). (See 31h.)

▶ **Baseball and softball developed from cricket.**
▶ **Both baseball and softball developed from cricket.**

The subject usually comes before the predicate, or verb, but sometimes writers reverse this order to achieve a special effect.

▶ **Up to the plate stepped Casey.**

In imperative sentences, which express requests or commands, the subject *you* is usually implied but not stated.

▶ **(You) Keep your eye on the ball.**

In questions and certain other constructions, the subject usually appears between the auxiliary verb (31b) and the main verb.

▶ **Did Casey save the game?**

In sentences beginning with *there* or *here* followed by a form of *be*, the subject always follows the verb. *There* and *here* are never the subject.

▶ **There was no joy in Mudville.**

31k Predicates

In addition to a subject, every sentence has a predicate, which asserts or asks something about the subject or tells the subject to do something. The hinge, or key word, of a predicate is the verb. The simple predicate of a sentence consists of the main verb and any auxiliaries (31b); the complete predicate includes the simple predicate plus any modifiers of the verb and any objects or complements and their modifiers.

      ⌐———— COMPLETE PREDICATE ————⌐
▶ **Both of us are planning to major in history.**

A compound predicate contains two or more verbs that have the same subject, usually joined by a coordinating or a correlative conjunction.

      ⌐————— COMPOUND PREDICATE —————⌐
▶ **Omar shut the book, put it back on the shelf, and sighed.**

      ⌐———— COMPOUND PREDICATE ————⌐
▶ **The Amish neither drive cars nor use electricity.**

On the basis of how they function in predicates, verbs can be divided into three categories: linking, transitive, and intransitive.

Linking verbs

A linking verb links, or joins, a subject with a subject complement (sc), a word or group of words that identifies or describes the subject.

    ⌐———— SC ————⌐
▶ **Nastassia is a single mother.**

    ⌐— SC —⌐
▶ **She is patient.**

If it identifies the subject, the complement is a noun or pronoun (*a single mother*). If it describes the subject, the complement is an adjective (*patient*).

    The forms of *be*, when used as main verbs rather than as auxiliary verbs, are linking verbs (like *are* in this sentence). Other verbs—such as *appear*, *become*, *feel*, *grow*, *look*, *make*, *seem*, *smell*, and *sound*—can also function as linking verbs, depending on the sense of the sentence.

Transitive verbs

A transitive verb expresses action that is directed toward a noun or pronoun, called the direct object (DO) of the verb.

```
                ┌─── DO ───┐
```
▶ He **peeled** all the rutabagas.

In the preceding example, the subject and verb do not express a complete thought. The direct object completes the thought by saying *what* he peeled.

A direct object may be followed by an object complement, a word (C) or word group that describes or identifies the direct object. Object complements may be adjectives, as in the next example, or nouns, as in the second example.

```
    ┌────────────────── DO ──────────────────┐┌── OC ──┐
```
▶ I **find** cell-phone conversations in restaurants very annoying.

```
            ┌── DO ──┐  ┌── OC ──┐
```
▶ Alana **considers** Keyshawn her best friend.

A transitive verb may also be followed by an indirect object, which tells to whom or what, or for whom or what, the verb's action is done. You might say the indirect object is the recipient of the direct object.

```
              IO ┌──── DO ────┐
```
▶ The sound of the traffic **gave** me a splitting headache.

Intransitive verbs

An intransitive verb expresses action that is not directed toward an object. Therefore, an intransitive verb does not have a direct object.

▶ The Red Sox **persevered**.
▶ Their fans **watched** anxiously.

The verb *persevered* has no object (it makes no sense to ask, *persevered what?*), and the verb *watched* has an object that is implied but not expressed.

Some verbs that express action can be only transitive or only intransitive, but most can be used either way, with or without a direct object.

```
                            ┌─ DO ─┐
```
▶ A maid wearing a uniform **opened** the door.

The verb *opened* is transitive here.

▶ The door **opened** silently.

The verb *opened* is intransitive here.

311 Phrases

A phrase is a group of words that lacks either a subject or a predicate or both.

Noun phrases

A noun phrase consists of a noun and all its modifiers. In a sentence, a noun phrase can play the role of a subject, object, or complement.

> ┌─────── SUBJECT ───────┐
> ▶ **Delicious, gooey peanut butter** is surprisingly healthful.

> ┌─ OBJECT ─┐
> ▶ Dieters prefer **green salad**.

> ┌─ COMPLEMENT ─┐
> ▶ A tuna sandwich is **a popular lunch**.

Verb phrases

A main verb and its auxiliary verbs make up a verb phrase, which can function only one way in a sentence: as a predicate.

> ▶ I **can swim** for a long time.
> ▶ His headaches **might have been caused** by tension.

Prepositional phrases

A prepositional phrase includes a preposition, a noun or pronoun (called the object of the preposition), and any modifiers of the object. Prepositional phrases usually serve as adjectives or adverbs.

ADJECTIVE Our house in Maine is a cabin.

ADVERB From Cadillac Mountain, you can see the Northern Lights.

Verbal phrases

Verbals are verb forms that do not function as verbs. Instead, they stand in for nouns, adjectives, or adverbs. A verbal phrase is made up of a verbal and any modifiers, objects, or complements. There are three kinds of verbals: participles, gerunds, and infinitives.

PARTICIPIAL PHRASES

A participial phrase always functions as an adjective and can include either a present participle (the *crying* child) or a past participle (the *spoken* word).

▶ A dog howling at the moon kept me awake.

▶ Irritated by the delay, Louise complained.

GERUND PHRASES

A gerund has the same form as a present participle, ending in *-ing*. But a gerund or a gerund phrase always functions as a noun.

⌈ SUBJECT ⌉
▶ Recycling is not always easy.

⌈————— DIRECT OBJECT —————⌉
▶ He ignored the loud wailing from the sandbox.

INFINITIVE PHRASES

An infinitive phrase can function as a noun, adjective, or adverb. The infinitive is the *to* form of a verb: *to be, to write.*

⌈——— ADJECTIVE ———⌉
▶ A vote would be a good way to end the meeting.

⌈——— ADVERB ———⌉
▶ To perfect a draft, always proofread carefully.

⌈——— NOUN ———⌉
▶ My goal is to be a biology teacher.

Absolute phrases

An absolute phrase usually includes a noun or pronoun and a participle. It modifies an entire sentence rather than a particular word and is usually set off from the rest of the sentence with commas (39a).

▶ I stood on the deck, the wind whipping my hair.
▶ My fears laid to rest, I climbed into the plane for my first solo flight.

Appositive phrases

A noun phrase that renames the noun or pronoun immediately preceding it is called an appositive phrase.

▶ The report, a hefty three-volume work, included sixty recommendations.
▶ A single desire, to change the corporation's policies, guided our actions.

31m Clauses

A clause is a group of words containing a subject and a predicate. There are two kinds of clauses: independent and dependent.

Independent clauses (also known as main clauses) can stand alone as complete sentences: *The window is open.* Pairs of independent clauses may be joined with a comma and a coordinating conjunction (*and*, *but*, *for*, *or*, *nor*, *so*, or *yet*).

▶ **The window is open,** *so* **we'd better be quiet.**

Like independent clauses, dependent clauses (also known as subordinate clauses) contain a subject and a predicate, but they cannot stand alone as complete sentences because they begin with a subordinating word (25b). Dependent clauses function as nouns, adjectives, or adverbs.

▶ **Because the window is open, the room feels cool.**

In this combination, the subordinating conjunction *because* transforms the independent clause *the window is open* into a dependent clause. In doing so, it indicates a causal relationship between the two clauses.

Noun clauses

Noun clauses can function as subjects, direct objects, subject complements, or objects of prepositions. A noun clause is always contained within another clause. Noun clauses usually begin with a relative pronoun (*that*, *which*, *what*, *who*, *whom*, *whose*, *whatever*, *whoever*, *whomever*, *whichever*) or with *when*, *where*, *whether*, *why*, or *how*.

$$\overline{\qquad\text{S}\qquad}$$
▶ **That she had a good job was important to him.**

$$\overline{\qquad\text{DO}\qquad}$$
▶ **He asked where she went to college.**

$$\overline{\qquad\text{SC}\qquad}$$
▶ **The real question was why he wanted to know.**

$$\overline{\qquad\text{OBJ OF PREP}\qquad}$$
▶ **He was looking for whatever information was available.**

Notice that in each of these sentences the noun clause is an integral part of the independent clause that makes up the sentence. For example, in the second sentence, the independent clause is not just *he asked* but *he asked where she went to college.*

Adjective clauses

Adjective clauses modify nouns and pronouns in other clauses. Usually adjective clauses immediately follow the words they modify. Most of these clauses begin with the relative pronoun *who, whom, whose, that,* or *which.* Some begin with *when, where,* or *why.*

▶ The surgery, which took three hours, was a complete success.

▶ It was performed by the surgeon who had developed the procedure.

▶ The hospital was the one where I was born.

Sometimes the relative pronoun introducing an adjective clause may be omitted.

▶ That is one book [that] I intend to read.

Adverb clauses

Adverb clauses modify verbs, adjectives, or other adverbs. They begin with a subordinating conjunction (31h) and, like adverbs, they usually tell when, where, why, how, or to what extent.

▶ We hiked where there were few other hikers.

▶ My backpack felt heavier than it ever had.

▶ I climbed as swiftly as I could under the weight of my backpack.

Types of Sentences

Like words, sentences can be classified in different ways: grammatically and functionally.

31n Grammatical classifications

Grammatically, sentences may be classified as simple, compound, complex, and compound-complex.

Simple sentences

A simple sentence consists of one independent clause and no dependent clause.

┌─────────────── INDEPENDENT CLAUSE ───────────────┐
▶ **The trailer is surrounded by a wooden deck.**

┌─────────────── INDEPENDENT CLAUSE ───────────────┐
▶ **Both my roommate and I left our keys in the room.**

Compound sentences

A compound sentence consists of two or more independent clauses and no dependent clause. The clauses may be joined by a comma and a co-ordinating conjunction (*and, but, or, nor, for, so, yet*) or by a semicolon.

┌──────────── IND CLAUSE ────────────┐   ┌──── IND CLAUSE ────┐
▶ **Occasionally, a car goes up the dirt trail, and dust flies everywhere.**

┌──────── IND CLAUSE ────────┐ ┌──────── IND CLAUSE ────────┐
▶ **Angelo is obsessed with soccer; he eats, breathes, and lives the game.**

Complex sentences

A complex sentence consists of one independent clause and at least one dependent clause.

┌──── IND CLAUSE ────┐ ┌──── DEP CLAUSE ────┐
▶ **Many people believe that anyone can earn a living.**

Compound-complex sentences

A compound-complex sentence consists of two or more independent clauses and at least one dependent clause.

┌──── IND CLAUSE ────┐ ┌──── DEP CLAUSE ────┐   ┌──── IND CLAUSE ────┐
▶ **I complimented Luis when he finished the job, and he seemed pleased.**

┌──────────── IND CLAUSE ────────────┐   ┌──── IND CLAUSE ────┐
▶ **Sister Lucy tried her best to help Martin, but he was an undisciplined**

┌─┐ ┌──────── DEP CLAUSE ────────┐
boy who drove many teachers to despair.

310 Functional classifications

In terms of function, sentences can be classified as declarative (making a statement), interrogative (asking a question), imperative (giving a command), or exclamatory (expressing strong feeling).

DECLARATIVE	He sings with the Grace Church Boys' Choir.
INTERROGATIVE	How long has he sung with them?
IMPERATIVE	Comb his hair before the performance starts.
EXCLAMATORY	What voices those boys have!

bedfordstmartins.com/everydaywriter
Exercise Central > Basic Grammar

Verbs **32**

Restaurant menus often spotlight verbs in action. One famous place in Boston, for instance, offers to bake, broil, pan-fry, deep-fry, poach, sauté, fricassée, blacken, or scallop any of the fish entrées on its menu. To someone ordering—or cooking—at this restaurant, the important distinctions lie entirely in the verbs.

When used skillfully, verbs can be the heartbeat of prose, moving it along, enlivening it, carrying its action. (See Chapter 33 for advice on subject-verb agreement and Chapter 59 for more about verbs for multilingual writers.)

AT A GLANCE

Editing the Verbs in Your Own Writing

- Check verb endings that cause you trouble. (32a and c)
- Double-check forms of *lie* and *lay*, *sit* and *set*, *rise* and *raise*. See that the words you use are appropriate for your meaning. (32d)
- If you are writing about a literary work, remember to refer to the action in the work in the present tense. (32e)
- If you have problems with verb tenses, use the guidelines on p. 320 to check your verbs.
- Check all uses of the passive voice for appropriateness. (32g)
- Check all verbs used to introduce quotations, paraphrases, and summaries. If you rely on *say*, *write*, and other very general verbs, try substituting more vivid, specific verbs (*claim*, *insist*, and *wonder*, for instance).

32a Understand the five forms of verbs.

Except for *be*, all English verbs have five forms.

BASE FORM	PAST TENSE	PAST PARTICIPLE	PRESENT PARTICIPLE	-S FORM
talk	talked	talked	talking	talks
adore	adored	adored	adoring	adores

BASE FORM	We often go to Legal Sea Foods.
PAST TENSE	Grandpa always ordered bluefish.
PAST PARTICIPLE	Grandma has tried the oyster stew.
PRESENT PARTICIPLE	Juanita is getting the shrimp platter.
-S FORM	The chowder needs salt and pepper.

-s *and* -es *endings*

Except with *be* and *have*, the *-s* form consists of the base form plus *-s* or *-es*. In standard English, this form indicates action in the present for third-person singular subjects. All singular nouns; the personal pronouns *he*, *she*, and *it*; and many other pronouns (such as *this, anyone, everything*, and *someone*) are third-person singular.

	SINGULAR	PLURAL
FIRST PERSON	I wish	we wish
SECOND PERSON	you wish	you wish
THIRD PERSON	he/she/it wishes	they wish
	Joe wishes	children wish
	someone wishes	many wish

TALKING ABOUT STYLE

Everyday Use of *Be*

Spoken varieties of English may follow rules for the use of *be* that differ from the rules in standard English. For instance, you may have heard speakers say sentences like "She ain't here now" (instead of the standard English *She isn't here now*) or "He be at work every Saturday" (instead of the standard English *He is at work every Saturday*). You may sometimes want to quote dialogue featuring such spoken usages of *be* when you write. In most academic and professional writing, however, you will want to follow the conventions of standard English. (For help on using varieties of English appropriately, see Chapter 22.)

Forms of be

Be has three forms in the present tense and two in the past tense.

BASE FORM	be
PAST PARTICIPLE	been
PRESENT PARTICIPLE	being
PRESENT TENSE	I am, he/she/it is, we/you/they are
PAST TENSE	I/he/she/it was, we/you/they were

32b Use helping (auxiliary) verbs appropriately.

Use helping (auxiliary) verbs with a base form, present participle, or past participle to form verb tenses, questions, and negatives. The most common helping verbs are forms of *be, do,* and *have.*

▶ We **have considered** all viewpoints.
▶ The problem **is ranking** them fairly.
▶ **Do** you **know** the answer? No, I **do not know** it.

A special set of helping verbs known as auxiliaries—*can, could, might, may, must, ought to, shall, will, should, would*—indicate future actions, possibility, necessity, obligation, and so on.

▶ You **can see** three states from the top of the mountain.
▶ She **should visit** this spot more often.

FOR MULTILINGUAL WRITERS

Using Modal Auxiliaries

Why do we not say "Alice can to read Latin"? For a discussion of *can* and other modal auxiliaries, see 59b.

32c Use appropriate forms of irregular verbs.

A verb is regular when its past tense and past participle are formed by adding *-ed* or *-d* to the base form.

BASE FORM	PAST TENSE	PAST PARTICIPLE
love	loved	loved
honor	honored	honored
obey	obeyed	obeyed

A verb is irregular when it does not follow the *-ed* or *-d* pattern. If you are not sure whether a verb form is regular or irregular, or what the correct form is, consult the following list or a dictionary. Dictionaries list any irregular forms under the entry for the base form.

Some common irregular verbs

BASE FORM	PAST TENSE	PAST PARTICIPLE
arise	arose	arisen
be	was/were	been
beat	beat	beaten
become	became	become
begin	began	begun
bite	bit	bitten, bit
blow	blew	blown
break	broke	broken
bring	brought	brought
broadcast	broadcast	broadcast
build	built	built
burn	burned, burnt	burned, burnt
burst	burst	burst
buy	bought	bought
catch	caught	caught
choose	chose	chosen
come	came	come
cost	cost	cost
dig	dug	dug
dive	dived, dove	dived
do	did	done
draw	drew	drawn
dream	dreamed, dreamt	dreamed, dreamt
drink	drank	drunk
drive	drove	driven
eat	ate	eaten
fall	fell	fallen
feel	felt	felt
fight	fought	fought

BASE FORM	PAST TENSE	PAST PARTICIPLE
find	found	found
fly	flew	flown
forget	forgot	forgotten, forgot
freeze	froze	frozen
get	got	gotten, got
give	gave	given
go	went	gone
grow	grew	grown
hang (suspend)[1]	hung	hung
have	had	had
hear	heard	heard
hide	hid	hidden
hit	hit	hit
keep	kept	kept
know	knew	known
lay	laid	laid
lead	led	led
leave	left	left
lend	lent	lent
let	let	let
lie (recline)[2]	lay	lain
lose	lost	lost
make	made	made
mean	meant	meant
meet	met	met
prove	proved	proved, proven
put	put	put
read	read	read
ride	rode	ridden
ring	rang	rung
rise	rose	risen

---

[1]*Hang* meaning "execute by hanging" is regular: *hang, hanged, hanged.*
[2]*Lie* meaning "tell a falsehood" is regular: *lie, lied, lied.*

BASE FORM	PAST TENSE	PAST PARTICIPLE
run	ran	run
say	said	said
see	saw	seen
send	sent	sent
set	set	set
shake	shook	shaken
shoot	shot	shot
show	showed	showed, shown
shrink	shrank	shrunk
sing	sang	sung
sink	sank	sunk
sit	sat	sat
sleep	slept	slept
speak	spoke	spoken
spend	spent	spent
spring	sprang, sprung	sprung
stand	stood	stood
steal	stole	stolen
strike	struck	struck, stricken
swim	swam	swum
swing	swung	swung
take	took	taken
tear	tore	torn
throw	threw	thrown
wake	woke, waked	waked, woken
wear	wore	worn
write	wrote	written

32d Choose between *lie* and *lay*, *sit* and *set*, *rise* and *raise*.

These pairs of verbs cause confusion because both verbs in each pair have similar-sounding forms and related meanings. In each pair, one of the verbs is transitive, meaning that it is followed by a direct object

(*I laid the cloth on the table*). The other is intransitive, meaning that it does not have an object (*He lay on the floor when his back ached*). The best way to avoid confusing these verbs is to memorize their forms and meanings.

BASE FORM	PAST TENSE	PAST PARTICIPLE	PRESENT PARTICIPLE	-S FORM
lie (recline)	lay	lain	lying	lies
lay (put)	laid	laid	laying	lays
sit (be seated)	sat	sat	sitting	sits
set (put)	set	set	setting	sets
rise (get up)	rose	risen	rising	rises
raise (lift)	raised	raised	raising	raises

► The doctor asked the patient to l̲a̲y̲ on his side. *lie*

► She s̲a̲t̲ the vase on the table. *set*

► He r̲a̲i̲s̲e̲d̲ up in bed and glared at us. *rose*

32e Use verb tenses appropriately.

Verb tenses show when the action takes place. The three simple tenses are the present tense, the past tense, and the future tense.

PRESENT TENSE	I ask, write
PAST TENSE	I asked, wrote
FUTURE TENSE	I will ask, will write

More complex aspects of time are expressed through progressive, perfect, and perfect progressive forms of the simple tenses.

PRESENT PROGRESSIVE	she is asking, is writing
PAST PROGRESSIVE	she was asking, was writing
FUTURE PROGRESSIVE	she will be asking, will be writing
PRESENT PERFECT	she has asked, has written
PAST PERFECT	she had asked, had written
FUTURE PERFECT	she will have asked, will have written
PRESENT PERFECT PROGRESSIVE	she has been asking, has been writing

| PAST PERFECT PROGRESSIVE | she had been asking, had been writing |
| FUTURE PERFECT PROGRESSIVE | she will have been asking, will have been writing |

The simple tenses locate an action only within the three basic time frames of present, past, and future. Progressive forms express continuing actions; perfect forms express actions completed before another action or time in the present, past, or future; perfect progressive forms express actions that continue up to some point in the present, past, or future.

Present tense

SIMPLE PRESENT

Use the simple present to indicate actions occurring now and those occurring habitually.

▶ I **eat** breakfast every day at 8:00 AM.

▶ Love **conquers** all.

Use the simple present when writing about action in literary works.

　　　　　　　　　　realizes　　　　*is*
▶ Ishmael slowly ~~realized~~ all that ~~was~~ at stake in the search for
　 the white whale.

General truths or scientific facts should be in the simple present, even when the predicate of the sentence is in the past tense.

　　　　　　　　　　　　　　　　　　　　　　　makes
▶ Pasteur demonstrated that his boiling process ~~made~~ milk safe.

When you are quoting, summarizing, or paraphrasing a work, in general use the present tense.

　　　　　　　　writes
▶ Keith Walters ~~wrote~~ that the "reputed consequences and promised
　 blessings of literacy are legion."

But in an essay using APA (American Psychological Association) style, the reporting of your experiments or another researcher's work should be in the past tense (*wrote, noted*) or the present perfect (*has reported*). (See Chapter 53.)

　　　　　　noted
▶ Comer (1995) ~~notes~~ that protesters who deprive themselves of food
　 (for example, Gandhi) are seen not as dysfunctional but rather as
　 "caring, sacrificing, even heroic" (p. 5).

PRESENT PROGRESSIVE

Use the present progressive to indicate actions that are ongoing in the present: *You are driving too fast.*

PRESENT PERFECT

Use the present perfect to indicate actions begun in the past and either completed at some unspecified time in the past or continuing into the present: *Uncontrolled logging has destroyed many forests.*

PRESENT PERFECT PROGRESSIVE

Use the present perfect progressive to indicate an ongoing action begun in the past and continuing into the present: *The two sides have been trying to settle the case out of court.*

Past tense

SIMPLE PAST

Use the simple past to indicate actions that occurred at a specific time and do not extend into the present: *Germany invaded Poland on September 1, 1939.*

PAST PROGRESSIVE

Use the past progressive to indicate continuing actions in the past: *Lenin was living in exile in Zurich when the tsar was overthrown.*

PAST PERFECT

Use the past perfect to indicate actions that were completed by a specific time in the past or before some other past action occurred: *By the fourth century, Christianity had become the state religion.*

PAST PERFECT PROGRESSIVE

Use the past perfect progressive to indicate continuing actions in the past that began before a specific time or before some other past action began: *Carter had been planning a naval career until his father died.*

Future tense

SIMPLE FUTURE

Use the simple future to indicate actions that have yet to begin: *The Vermeer show will come to Washington in September.*

FUTURE PROGRESSIVE

Use the future progressive to indicate continuing actions in the future: *The loans will be coming due over the next two years.*

FUTURE PERFECT

Use the future perfect to indicate actions that will be completed by a specified time in the future: *In ten years, your investment will have doubled.*

FUTURE PERFECT PROGRESSIVE

Use the future perfect progressive to indicate continuing actions that will be completed by some specified time in the future: *In May, I will have been working at IBM for five years.*

AT A GLANCE

Editing Verb Tenses

If you have trouble with verb tense in standard English, make a point of checking for these common trouble spots as you proofread.

- Problems with verb form: writing *seen* for *saw*, for example, which confuses the past-participle and past-tense forms. (32c)
- Problems with tense: using the simple past (*Uncle Charlie arrived*) when meaning requires the present perfect (*Uncle Charlie has arrived*). (32e)
- Think carefully before using a regional or ethnic variety of English (*she nervous*) in situations calling for standard academic English (*she is nervous*). (See Chapter 22.)

32f Sequence verb tenses effectively.

Careful and accurate use of tenses is important for clear writing. Even the simplest narrative describes actions that take place at different times; when you use the appropriate tense for each action, readers can follow such time changes easily.

▶ By the time he **lent** her the money, she **had declared** bankruptcy.

Use an infinitive (*to* plus a base form: *to go*) to indicate actions occurring at the same time as or later than the action of the predicate verb.

▶ Each couple **hopes to win** the dance contest.

The hoping is in the present; the winning is in the future.

Use a present participle (base form plus *-ing*) to indicate actions occurring at the same time as that of the predicate verb.

▶ **Seeking to relieve unemployment,** Roosevelt established several public works programs.

A past participle or a present-perfect participle (*having* plus a past participle) indicates actions occurring before that of the predicate verb.

Flown
▶ ~~Flying~~ to the front, the troops joined their hard-pressed comrades.

The past participle *flown* shows that the flying occurred before the joining.

Having crushed
▶ ~~Crushing~~ all opposition at home, he launched a war of conquest.

He launched the war after he crushed the opposition.

One common error is to use *would* in both clauses of a sentence with an *if* clause. Use *would* only in one clause.

had
▶ If I ~~would have~~ played harder, I would have won.

32g Use active and passive voice effectively.

Voice tells whether a subject is acting (*He questions us*) or being acted upon (*He is questioned*). When the subject is acting, the verb is in the active voice; when the subject is being acted upon, the verb is in the passive voice. Most contemporary writers use the active voice as much as possible because it livens up their writing.

PASSIVE   Huge pine trees were uprooted by the storm.
ACTIVE   The storm uprooted huge pine trees.

The passive voice can work to good advantage in some situations. Newspaper reporters often use the passive voice to protect the confidentiality of their sources, as in the familiar expression *it is reported that*. You can also use the passive voice when you want to emphasize the recipient of an action rather than the performer of the action.

DALLAS, Nov. 22—President John Fitzgerald Kennedy was shot and killed by an assassin today.   – TOM WICKER, *New York Times*

Wicker uses the passive voice with good reason: to focus on Kennedy, not on who killed him.

To shift a sentence from passive to active voice, make the performer of the action the subject of the sentence.

destroyed his acting career.
▶ His acting career ~~was destroyed by his~~ unprofessional behavior on the set.

TALKING ABOUT STYLE

Technical and Scientific Writing

Much technical and scientific writing uses the passive voice effectively to highlight what is being studied rather than who is doing the studying.

The Earth's plates are created where they separate and are re-cycled where they collide, in a continuous process of creation and destruction.

– FRANK PRESS AND RAYMOND SIEVER, *Understanding Earth*

32h Use mood effectively.

The mood of a verb indicates the attitude of the writer. The indicative mood states facts or opinions and asks questions: *I did the right thing.* The imperative mood gives commands and instructions: *Do the right thing.* The subjunctive mood (used primarily in dependent clauses beginning with *that* or *if*) expresses wishes and conditions that are contrary to fact: *If I were doing the right thing, I'd know it.*

Forming and using the subjunctive

The present subjunctive uses the base form of the verb with all subjects.

▶ It is important that children **be** psychologically ready for a new sibling.

The past subjunctive is the same as the simple past except for the verb *be*, which uses *were* for all subjects.

▶ He spent money as if he **had** infinite credit.
▶ If the store **were** better located, it would attract more customers.

Because the subjunctive creates a rather formal tone, many people today tend to substitute the indicative mood in informal conversation.

▶ If the store *was* better located, it would attract more customers.

For academic or professional writing, use the subjunctive in the following contexts:

CLAUSES EXPRESSING A WISH

　　　　　　　　　　　　　　were
▶ He wished that his mother was still living nearby.
　　　　　　　　　　　　　　　^

THAT CLAUSES EXPRESSING A REQUEST OR DEMAND

> *be*
> ▶ The job demands that employees ~~are~~ in good physical condition.
>   ^

IF CLAUSES EXPRESSING A CONDITION THAT DOES NOT EXIST

> *were*
> ▶ If the federal government ~~was~~ to ban the sale of tobacco, tobacco
>   ^
> companies and distributors would suffer a great loss.

FOR MULTILINGUAL WRITERS

Using the Subjunctive

"If you were to practice writing every day, it would eventually seem much easier to you." For a discussion of this and other uses of the sub-junctive, see 57f.

⟳ **bedfordstmartins.com/everydaywriter**
   Exercise Central > Verbs

Subject-Verb Agreement **33**

S ubjects and verbs are at work in almost every statement you make, and you make them agree effortlessly most of the time. Look, for instance, at three sentences taken from a recent broadcast of a baseball game.

> The pitcher powers another blistering curveball over the plate.

> The Yanks move on to Milwaukee tomorrow.

> The duel of the no-hitters continues into the eighth.

Take time to listen to someone reporting an event—a play-by-play an-nouncer, perhaps, or an on-the-scene reporter. Note some of the subject-verb combinations. Do you find any that don't sound right, that might not agree?

33a Match verb forms with third-person singular subjects.

To make a verb in the present tense agree with a third-person singular subject, add *-s* or *-es* to the base form.

▶ **A vegetarian diet lowers the risk of heart disease.**

▶ **What you eat affects your health.**

In the preceding example, the subject is the noun clause *what you eat*. The clause is singular, so the base form of the verb *affect* takes an *-s*.

To make a verb in the present tense agree with any other subject, use the base form of the verb.

▶ **I miss my family.**

▶ **They live in another state.**

AT A GLANCE

Editing for Subject-Verb Agreement

- Identify the subject that goes with each verb. Cover up any words between the subject and the verb to identify agreement problems more easily. (33b)
- Check compound subjects. Those joined by *and* usually take a plural verb. With those subjects joined by *or* or *nor*, however, the verb agrees with the part of the subject closer or closest to the verb. (33c)
- Check collective-noun subjects. These nouns take a singular verb when they refer to a group as a single unit, but they take a plural verb when they refer to the multiple members of a group. (33d)
- Check indefinite-pronoun subjects. Most take a singular verb. *Both*, *few*, *many*, *others*, and *several* take a plural verb, and *all*, *any*, *enough*, *more*, *most*, *none*, and *some* can be either singular or plural. (33e)

Have and *be* do not follow the *-s* or *-es* pattern with third-person singular subjects. *Have* changes to *has*; *be* has irregular forms in both the present and past tenses (32a).

▶ **War is hell.**

▶ **The soldier was brave beyond the call of duty.**

33b Check subjects and verbs separated by other words.

Make sure the verb agrees with the subject and not with another noun that falls in between.

▶ A vase of flowers **makes** a room attractive.

have
▶ Many books on the best-seller list ~~has~~ little literary value.

The simple subject is *books*, not *list*.

Be careful when you use phrases beginning with *as well as, along with, in addition to, together with,* and similar prepositions. They do not make a singular subject plural.

was
▶ A passenger, as well as the driver, ~~were~~ injured in the accident.

Though this sentence has a grammatically singular subject, it suggests a plural subject. The sentence makes better sense with a compound subject: *The driver and a passenger were injured in the accident.*

33c Make verbs agree with compound subjects.

Subjects joined by *and* generally require a plural verb form.

were
▶ A backpack, a canteen, and a rifle ~~was~~ issued to each recruit.

When subjects joined by *and* are considered a single unit or refer to the same person or thing, they take a singular verb form.

▶ George W. Bush's older brother and political ally **was** the governor of Florida.

remains
▶ Drinking and driving ~~remain~~ a major cause of highway accidents
and fatalities.

In this sentence, *drinking and driving* is considered a single activity, and a singular verb is used.

If the word *each* or *every* precedes subjects joined by *and*, the verb form is singular.

▶ Each boy and girl **chooses** one gift to take home.

With subjects joined by *or* or *nor*, the verb agrees with the part closer or closest to the verb.

▶ **Either the witnesses or the defendant** *is* **lying.**

If you find this sentence awkward, put the plural noun closer to the verb: *Either the defendant or the witnesses are lying.*

33d Make verbs agree with collective-noun subjects.

Collective nouns—such as *family, team, audience, group, jury, crowd, band, class,* and *committee*—refer to a group. Collective nouns can take either singular or plural verbs, depending on whether they refer to the group as a single unit or to the multiple members of the group. The meaning of a sentence as a whole is your guide to whether a collective noun refers to a unit or to the multiple parts of a unit.

▶ **After deliberating, the jury** *reports* **its verdict.**

The jury acts as a single unit.

▶ **The jury still** *disagree* **on a number of counts.**

The members of the jury act as multiple individuals.

▶ **The family of ducklings** scatter**s** *(scatter)* **when the cat approaches.**

Family here refers to the many ducks; they cannot scatter as one.

Treat fractions that refer to singular nouns as singular and those that refer to plural nouns as plural.

▶ **Two-thirds of the park** *has* **burned.**

Two-thirds refers to the single portion of the park that burned.

▶ **Two-thirds of the students** *were* **commuters.**

Two-thirds here refers to the students who commuted as many individuals.

Even though *eyeglasses, scissors, pants,* and other such words refer to single items, they take plural verbs because they are made up of pairs.

▶ **Where** *are* **my reading glasses?**

Treat phrases starting with *the number of* as singular and with *a number of* as plural.

SINGULAR   The number of applicants for the internship *was* amazing.

PLURAL   A number of applicants *were* put on the waiting list.

33e Make verbs agree with indefinite-pronoun subjects.

Indefinite pronouns do not refer to specific persons or things. Most take singular verb forms.

SOME COMMON INDEFINITE PRONOUNS

another	each	much	one
any	either	neither	other
anybody	everybody	nobody	somebody
anyone	everyone	no one	someone
anything	everything	nothing	something

▶ Of the two jobs, neither holds much appeal.

        depicts
▶ Each of the plays depict a hero undone by a tragic flaw.

Both, few, many, others, and *several* are plural.

▶ Though many apply, few are chosen.

All, any, enough, more, most, none, and *some* can be singular or plural, depending on the noun they refer to.

▶ All of the cake *was* eaten.

▶ All of the candidates *promise* to improve the schools.

33f Make verbs agree with antecedents of *who*, *which*, and *that*.

When the relative pronouns *who, which,* and *that* are used as a subject, the verb agrees with the antecedent of the pronoun (see 31d and 34f).

▶ Fear is an ingredient that goes into creating stereotypes.

▶ Guilt and fear are ingredients that go into creating stereotypes.

Problems often occur with the words *one of the*. In general, *one of the* takes a plural verb, while *the only one of the* takes a singular verb.

> *work*
> ► Carla is one of the employees who always ~~works~~ overtime.

Some employees always work overtime. Carla is among them. Thus *who* refers to *employees*, and the verb is plural.

> *works*
> ► Ming is the only one of the employees who always ~~work~~ overtime.

Only one employee always works overtime, and that employee is Ming. Thus *one*, not *employees*, is the antecedent of *who*, and the verb form is singular.

33g Use appropriate forms of linking verbs.

A linking verb (31k) should agree with its subject, which usually precedes the verb, not with the subject complement, that follows it.

> *are*
> ► The three key treaties ~~is~~ the topic of my talk.

The subject is *treaties*, not *topic*.

> *was*
> ► Nero Wolfe's passion ~~were~~ orchids.

The subject is *passion*, not *orchids*.

33h Make verbs agree with subjects that are plural in form but singular in meaning.

Some words that end in *-s* appear plural but are singular in meaning and thus take singular verb forms.

> *strikes*
> ► Measles still ~~strike~~ many Americans.

Some nouns of this kind (such as *statistics* and *politics*) may be either singular or plural, depending on context.

SINGULAR   Statistics *is* a course I really dread.

PLURAL   The statistics in that study *are* highly questionable.

33i Make verbs agree with subjects that follow verbs.

In English, verbs usually follow subjects. When this order is reversed, make the verb agree with the subject, not with a noun that precedes it.

stand
▶ Beside the barn ~~stands~~ silos filled with grain.

The subject is *silos*; it is plural, so the verb must be *stand*.

In sentences beginning with *there is* or *there are* (or *there was* or *were*), *there* serves only as an introductory word; the subject follows the verb.

▶ There are five basic positions in classical ballet.

33j Make verbs agree with titles and words used as words.

describes
▶ *One Writer's Beginnings* ~~describe~~ Eudora Welty's childhood.

is
▶ *Steroids* ~~are~~ a little word that packs a big punch in the world of sports.

> bedfordstmartins.com/everydaywriter
> Exercise Central > Subject-Verb Agreement

Pronouns 34

As words that stand in for nouns, pronouns carry a lot of weight in everyday language. These directions show one of the reasons why it's important to use pronouns clearly:

> When you see a dirt road turning left off Winston Lane, follow it for two more miles.

The word *it* could mean either the dirt road or Winston Lane. Pronouns can improve understanding, but only when they're used carefully and accurately.

Editing Pronouns

- Are all pronouns after forms of the verb *be* in the subjective case? *It's me* is common in spoken English, but in formal writing use *It is I.* (34a)

- To check for use of *who* and *whom* (and *whoever* and *whomever*), try substituting *he* or *him*. If *he* is correct, use *who* (or *whoever*); if *him*, use *whom* or *whomever*. (34b)

- In compound structures, make sure any pronouns are in the same case they would be in if used alone (*She and Jake were living in Spain*). (34c)

- When a pronoun follows *than* or *as*, complete the sentence mentally. If the pronoun is the subject of an unstated verb, it should be subjective (*I like her better than he [likes her]*). If it is the object of an unstated verb, make it objective (*I like her better than [I like] him*). (34d)

- If you have used *he*, *his*, or *him* to refer to *everyone* or another singular indefinite pronoun that includes both males and females, revise the sentence. If you have used *they* to refer to a singular indefinite pronoun, rewrite the sentence. (34f)

- For each pronoun, identify a specific word that it refers to. If you cannot find one specific word, supply one. If the pronoun refers to more than one word, revise the sentence. (34g)

- Check each use of *it*, *this*, *that*, and *which* to be sure the pronoun refers to a specific word. (34g)

- Be sure that any use of *you* refers to your specific reader or readers. (34g)

34a   Consider a pronoun's role in the sentence.

Most speakers of English know intuitively when to use *I*, *me*, and *my*. Our choices reflect differences in case, the form a pronoun takes to indicate how it acts in a sentence. Pronouns acting as subjects are in the subjective case (*I*); those acting as objects are in the objective case (*me*); those acting as possessives are in the possessive case (*my*).

SUBJECTIVE PRONOUNS	OBJECTIVE PRONOUNS	POSSESSIVE PRONOUNS
I	me	my/mine
we	us	our/ours
you	you	your/yours
he/she/it	him/her/it	his/her/hers/its
they	them	their/theirs
who/whoever	whom/whomever	whose

Subjective case

A pronoun should be in the subjective case (*I, we, you, he/she/it, they, who, whoever*) when it is a subject, a subject complement, or an appositive renaming a subject or subject complement.

SUBJECT

She was passionate about recycling.

SUBJECT COMPLEMENT

The main supporter of the recycling program was she.

APPOSITIVE RENAMING A SUBJECT OR SUBJECT COMPLEMENT

Three colleagues — Peter, John, and she — worked on the program.

Americans routinely use the objective case for subject complements, especially in conversation: *Who's there? It's me.* If the subjective case for a subject complement sounds stilted or awkward (*It's I*), try rewriting the sentence using the pronoun as the subject (*I'm here*).

> *She was the*
> ▶ ~~The~~ first person to see Kishore after the awards. ~~was she.~~

Objective case

Use the objective case (*me, us, you, him/her/it, them*) when a pronoun functions as a direct or indirect object, an object of a preposition, an appositive renaming an object, or a subject of an infinitive.

DIRECT OBJECT

The boss surprised her with a big raise.

INDIRECT OBJECT

The owner gave him a reward.

OBJECT OF A PREPOSITION

Several friends went with me.

APPOSITIVE RENAMING AN OBJECT

The students elected two representatives, Joan and me.

SUBJECT OF AN INFINITIVE

The students convinced him to vote for the school bond.

Possessive case

Use the possessive case when a pronoun shows possession or owner-ship. The adjective forms of possessive pronouns (*my, our, your, his/her/its, their, whose*) are used before nouns or gerunds, and noun forms (*mine, ours, yours, his/hers/its, theirs, whose*) take the place of a possessive noun. Possessive pronouns do not include apostrophes (42a).

BEFORE A NOUN

The sound of her voice came right through the walls.

IN PLACE OF A POSSESSIVE NOUN

The responsibility is hers.

Pronouns before a gerund should be in the possessive case.

> *his*
> ▶ I remember ~~him~~ singing.
>   ^

His modifies the gerund *singing.*

34b   Use *who, whoever, whom,* and *whomever* appropriately.

A common problem with pronoun case is deciding whether to use *who* or *whom*. Even when traditional grammar requires *whom*, many Amer-icans use *who* instead, especially in speech. Nevertheless, you should understand the difference between *who* and *whom* so that you can make informed choices in situations such as formal college writing that may call for the use of *whom* (or *whomever*) in the objective case. The most common confusion with *who* and *whom* occurs when they begin a ques-tion and when they introduce a dependent clause.

In questions

You can determine whether to use *who* or *whom* at the beginning of a question by answering the question using a personal pronoun. If the answer is *he, she,* or *they,* use *who*; if it is *him, her,* or *them,* use *whom.*

> *Whom*
> ▶ ~~Who~~ did you visit?
>   ^

I visited *them. Them* is objective; thus *whom* is correct.

TALKING THE TALK

Correctness or Stuffiness?

"I think *Everyone has their opinion* sounds better than *Everyone has his or her opinion*. And nobody says *whom*. Why should I write that way?" Over time, the conventions governing certain usages — such as *who* versus *whom*, or *their* versus *his* or *her* when it refers to an indefinite pronoun like *everyone* — have become much more relaxed. To many Americans, *Whom did you talk to?* and *No one finished his or her test* — both of which are technically "correct" — sound unpleasantly fussy. However, other people object to less formal constructions such as *Who did you talk to?* and *No one finished their test*; to them, such usages signal a lack of discrimination. Unfortunately, you can't please everyone. Use whatever you are most comfortable with in speaking, but be more careful in formal writing. If you don't know whether your audience will prefer more or less formality, try recasting your sentence.

Who

▶ ~~Whom~~ do you think wrote the story?
  ^

I think *she* wrote the story. *She* is subjective; thus *who* is correct.

In dependent clauses

The case of a pronoun in a dependent clause is determined by its purpose in the clause, no matter how that clause functions in the sentence. If the pronoun acts as a subject or subject complement in the clause, use *who* or *whoever*. If the pronoun acts as an object in the clause, use *whom* or *whomever*.

                                          who
▶ Anyone can hypnotize someone ~~whom~~ wants to be hypnotized.
                                          ^

The verb of the clause is *wants*, and its subject is *who*.

Whomever

▶ ~~Whoever~~ the party suspected of disloyalty was executed.
  ^

Whomever is the object of *suspected* in the clause *whomever the party suspected of disloyalty*.

If you are not sure, try separating the dependent clause from the rest of the sentence and looking at it in isolation. Then rewrite the clause as a new sentence, and substitute a personal pronoun for *who(ever)* or *whom(ever)*. If you substitute *he, she,* or *they,* use *who* or *whoever*; if *him, her,* or *them* is correct, use *whom* or *whomever*.

▶ The minister grimaced at (*whoever/whomever*) made any noise.

Isolate the clause *whoever/whomever made any noise.* Substituting a personal pronoun gives you *they made any noise. They* acts as the subject; therefore, *The minister grimaced at* <u>whoever</u> *made any noise.*

▶ The minister smiled at (*whoever/whomever*) she greeted.

Isolate and rearrange the clause to get *she greeted whoever/whomever.* Substituting a personal pronoun gives you *she greeted them. Them* acts as an object; therefore, *The minister smiled at* <u>whomever</u> *she greeted.*

▶ The minister grimaced at *whoever* she thought made the noise.

Ignore such expressions as *he thinks* and *she says* when you isolate the clause.

34c Consider case in compound structures.

When a pronoun is part of a compound subject, complement, object, or appositive, put it in the same case you would use if the pronoun were alone.

▶ When ~~him~~ *he* and Zelda were first married, they lived in New York.

▶ The boss invited ~~she~~ *her* and her family to dinner.

▶ This morning saw yet another conflict between my sister and ~~I.~~ *me.*

▶ Both panelists—Javonne and ~~me,~~ *I*—were stumped.

To decide whether to use the subjective or objective case in a compound structure, mentally delete the rest of the compound and try the pronoun alone.

▶ Come to the park with Anh and ~~I.~~ *me.*

Mentally deleting *Anh and* results in *Come to the park with I.* Rewrite as *Come to the park with Anh and* <u>me</u>.

34d Consider case in elliptical constructions.

In elliptical constructions, some words are understood but left out. When an elliptical construction ends in a pronoun, put the pronoun in the case it would be in if the construction were complete.

▶ **His sister has always been more athletic than** *he* **[is].**

In some elliptical constructions, the case of the pronoun depends on the meaning intended.

▶ **Willie likes Lily more than** *she* **[likes Lily].**

She is the subject of the omitted verb *likes*.

▶ **Willie likes Lily more than [he likes]** *her*.

Her is the object of the omitted verb *likes*.

34e Use *we* and *us* appropriately before a noun.

If you are unsure about whether to use *we* or *us* before a noun, recast the sentence without the noun. Use whichever pronoun would be correct if the noun were omitted.

    We
▶ **U̲s fans never give up hope.**

Without *fans*, *we* would be the subject.

               us
▶ **The Rangers depend on we fans.**

Without *fans*, *us* would be the object of a preposition.

34f Make pronouns agree with antecedents.

The antecedent of a pronoun is the word the pronoun refers to. The antecedent usually appears before the pronoun—earlier in the sentence or in the prior sentence. Pronouns and antecedents are said to agree when they match up in person, number, and gender.

SINGULAR   The choirmaster raised his baton.

PLURAL   The boys picked up their music.

Compound antecedents

Compound antecedents joined by *and* require plural pronouns.

▶ **My parents and I tried to resolve our disagreement.**

When *each* or *every* precedes a compound antecedent, however, it takes a singular pronoun.

▶ **Every plant and animal has its own ecological niche.**

With a compound antecedent joined by *or* or *nor*, the pronoun agrees with the nearer or nearest antecedent. If the parts of the antecedent are of different genders, however, this kind of sentence can be awkward or ambiguous and may need to be revised.

> AWKWARD   Neither Annie nor Barry got *his* work done.
>
> REVISED   Annie didn't get *her* work done, and neither did Barry.

When a compound antecedent contains both singular and plural parts, the sentence may sound awkward unless the plural part comes last.

▶ **Neither the newspaper nor the radio stations would reveal *their* sources.**

Collective-noun antecedents

A collective noun that refers to a single unit (*herd, team, audience*) requires a singular pronoun.

▶ **The *audience* fixed *its* attention on center stage.**

When such an antecedent refers to the multiple parts of a unit, however, it requires a plural pronoun.

▶ **The director chose this *cast* for the play because *they* had experience in the roles.**

Indefinite-pronoun antecedents

Indefinite pronouns are those that do not refer to specific persons or things. Most indefinite pronouns are always singular; a few are always plural. Some can be singular or plural depending on the context.

▶ **One of the ballerinas lost *her* balance.**

▶ **Many in the audience jumped to *their* feet.**

> SINGULAR   *Some* of the furniture was showing *its* age.
>
> PLURAL   *Some* of the farmers abandoned *their* land.

> **AT A GLANCE**
>
> ## Editing Out Sexist Pronouns
>
> *Everyone should know* his *legal rights.*
>
> Here are three ways to express the same idea without *his*:
>
> 1. Revise to make the antecedent a plural noun.
>   *All citizens should know* their *legal rights.*
> 2. Revise the sentence altogether.
>   *Everyone should have some knowledge of basic legal rights.*
> 3. Use both masculine and feminine pronouns.
>   *Everyone should know* his or her *legal rights.*
>
> This third option, using both masculine and feminine pronouns, can be awkward, especially when repeated several times in a passage.

Sexist pronouns

Indefinite pronouns often serve as antecedents that may be either male or female. Writers used to use a masculine pronoun, known as the generic *he*, to refer to such indefinite pronouns. However, such wording ignores or even excludes females.

When the antecedent is *anybody, each,* or *everyone,* some people avoid the generic *he* by using a plural pronoun.

▶ *Everyone* **should know** *their* **legal rights.**

You will hear such sentences in conversation and even see them in writing, but many people in academic contexts still consider *anybody, each,* and *everyone* singular, and they think using *their* with singular antecedents is too informal. They prefer one of the solutions in the box.

34g Make pronouns refer to clear antecedents.

The antecedent of a pronoun is the word the pronoun substitutes for. If a pronoun is too far from its antecedent, readers will have trouble making the connection between the two.

Ambiguous antecedents

Readers have trouble when a pronoun can refer to more than one antecedent.

the bridge
▶ **The car went over the bridge just before it fell into the water.**

What fell into the water—the car or the bridge? The revision makes the meaning clear.

> Kerry told Ellen, ^{"I}̬ s̶h̶e̶ should be ready soon.["]

Reporting Kerry's words directly, in quotation marks, eliminates the ambiguity.

Vague use of it, this, that, *and* which

The words *it*, *this*, *that*, and *which* often function as a shortcut for referring to something mentioned earlier. But such shortcuts can cause confusion. Like other pronouns, each must refer to a specific antecedent.

> When the senators realized the bill would be defeated, they tried to
> *The entire effort*
> postpone the vote but failed. I̶t̶ was a fiasco.

> *and that news*
> Nancy just found out that she won the lottery, w̶h̶i̶c̶h̶ explains her
> sudden resignation from her job.

Indefinite use of you, it, *and* they

In conversation, we frequently use *you*, *it*, and *they* in an indefinite sense in such expressions as *you never know; in the paper, it said;* and *they say*. In academic and professional writing, however, use *you* only to mean "you, the reader," and *they* or *it* only to refer to a clear antecedent.

> *people*
> Commercials try to make y̶o̶u̶ buy without thinking.

> *The*
> O̶n̶ t̶h̶e̶ Weather Channel/ i̶t̶ reported that an earthquake devastated parts of Pakistan.

> *Many restaurants in France*
> I̶n̶ F̶r̶a̶n̶c̶e̶,̶ t̶h̶e̶y̶ allow dogs. i̶n̶ m̶a̶n̶y̶ r̶e̶s̶t̶a̶u̶r̶a̶n̶t̶s̶.̶

Possessive antecedents

A possessive may *suggest* a noun antecedent but does not serve as a clear antecedent.

> *her*   *Alexa*
> In A̶l̶e̶x̶a̶'̶s̶ formal complaint, s̶h̶e̶ showed why the test question was wrong.

Adjectives and Adverbs **35**

Adjectives and adverbs often bring indispensable differences in meaning to the words they modify. In basketball, for example, there is an important difference between a *flagrant* foul and a *technical* foul, a *layup* and a *reverse layup*, and an *angry* coach and an *abusively angry* coach. In each instance, the modifiers are crucial to accurate communication.

Adjectives modify nouns and pronouns; they answer the questions *which? how many?* and *what kind?* Adverbs modify verbs, adjectives, and other adverbs; they answer the questions *how? when? where?* and *to what extent?* Many adverbs are formed by adding *-ly* to adjectives (*slight, slightly*), but many adverbs are formed in other ways (*outdoors*) or have forms of their own (*very*).

AT A GLANCE

Editing Adjectives and Adverbs

- Scrutinize each adjective and adverb. Consider synonyms for each word to see whether you have chosen the best word possible.
- See if a more specific noun would eliminate the need for an adjective (*mansion* rather than *enormous house*, for instance). Do the same with verbs and adverbs.
- Look for places where you might make your writing more specific or vivid by adding an adjective or adverb.
- Check that adjectives modify only nouns and pronouns and that adverbs modify only verbs, adjectives, and other adverbs. (35b) Check especially for proper use of *good* and *well*, *bad* and *badly*, *real* and *really*. (35b and c)
- Make sure all comparisons are complete. (35c)
- If English is not your first language, check that adjectives are in the right order. (58e)

35a Use adjectives after linking verbs.

When adjectives come after linking verbs, they usually serve as a subject complement, to describe the subject: *I am patient.* Note that in specific sentences, some verbs may or may not be linking verbs—

appear, become, feel, grow, look, make, prove, seem, smell, sound, and *taste,* for instance. When a word following one of these verbs modifies the subject, use an adjective; when it modifies the verb, use an adverb.

ADJECTIVE   Fluffy looked *angry*.

ADVERB   Fluffy looked *angrily* at the poodle.

Linking verbs suggest a state of being, not an action. In the preceding examples, *looked angry* suggests the state of being angry; *looked angrily* suggests an angry action.

FOR MULTILINGUAL WRITERS

Using Adjectives with Plural Nouns

In Spanish, Russian, and many other languages, adjectives agree in number with the nouns they modify. In English, adjectives do not change number this way: *the kittens are cute* (not *cutes*).

35b Use adverbs to modify verbs, adjectives, and adverbs.

In everyday conversation, you will often hear (and perhaps use) adjectives in place of adverbs. For example, people often say *go quick* instead of *go quickly*. When you write in standard academic English, however, use adverbs to modify verbs, adjectives, and other adverbs.

▶ You can feel the song's meter if you listen careful. *carefully.*

▶ The audience was real disappointed by the show. *really*

Good, well, bad, *and* badly

The modifiers *good, well, bad,* and *badly* cause problems for many writers because the distinctions between *good* and *well* and between *bad* and *badly* are often not observed in conversation. Problems also arise because *well* can function as either an adjective or an adverb. *Good* and *bad* are always adjectives, and both can be used after a linking verb.

► The weather looks *good* today.

        well   *badly.*

► He plays the trumpet ~~good~~ and the trombone not ~~bad.~~

Badly is an adverb and can modify a verb, an adjective, or another adverb. After a linking verb, use *bad* instead.

    bad

► I feel ~~badly~~ for the Toronto fans.

The linking verb *feel* requires the adjective *bad*.

As an adjective, *well* means "in good health"; as an adverb, it means "in a good way" or "thoroughly."

ADJECTIVE   After a week of rest, Julio felt *well* again.

ADVERB   She plays *well* enough to make the team.

FOR MULTILINGUAL WRITERS

Determining Adjective Sequence

Should you write *these beautiful blue kitchen tiles* or *these blue beautiful kitchen tiles*? See 58e for guidelines on adjective sequence.

35c   Choose appropriate comparative and superlative forms.

Most adjectives and adverbs have three forms: positive, comparative, and superlative.

POSITIVE	COMPARATIVE	SUPERLATIVE
large	larger	largest
early	earlier	earliest
careful	more careful	most careful
happily	more happily	most happily

► Canada is larger than the United States.
► My son needs to be more careful with his money.
► They are the most happily married couple I know.

Form the comparative and superlative of most one- or two-syllable adjectives by adding *-er* and *-est*. With some two-syllable adjectives, longer adjectives, and most adverbs, use *more* and *most: scientific, more scientific, most scientific; elegantly, more elegantly, most elegantly.* If you are not sure, consult the dictionary entry for the simple form.

Irregular adjectives and adverbs

Some short adjectives and adverbs have irregular comparative and superlative forms.

POSITIVE	COMPARATIVE	SUPERLATIVE
good, well	better	best
bad, badly	worse	worst
little (quantity)	less	least
many, much, some	more	most

Comparatives vs. superlatives

Use the comparative to compare two things; use the superlative to compare three or more.

▶ Rome is a much **older** city than New York.

▶ Damascus is one of the ~~older~~ cities in the world.
          oldest

Double comparatives and superlatives

Double comparatives and superlatives are those that unnecessarily use both the *-er* or *-est* ending and *more* or *most.* Occasionally, these forms can act to build a special emphasis, as in the title of Spike Lee's movie *Mo' Better Blues.* In academic and professional writing, however, do not use *more* or *most* before adjectives or adverbs ending in *-er* or *-est.*

▶ Paris is the ~~most~~ loveliest city in the world.

Incomplete comparisons

In speaking, we sometimes state only part of a comparison because the context makes the meaning clear. For example, you might tell a friend "Your car is better," but the context makes it clear that you mean "Your car is better *than mine.*" In writing, take the time to check for incomplete comparisons—and to complete them if they are unclear.

▶ The patients taking the drug appeared healthier/
          than those receiving a placebo.

Absolute concepts

Some readers consider modifiers such as *perfect* and *unique* to be absolute concepts; according to this view, a construction such as *more unique* is illogical because a thing is either unique or it isn't, so modified forms of the concept don't make sense. However, many seemingly absolute words have multiple meanings, all of which are widely accepted as correct. For example, *unique* may mean *one of a kind* or *unequaled*, but it can also simply mean *distinctive* or *unusual*.

If you think your readers will object to a construction such as *more perfect* (which appears in the U.S. Constitution) or *somewhat unique* (which was used by J. D. Salinger), then avoid such uses.

> **TALKING ABOUT STYLE**
>
> ## Multiple Negation
>
> Speakers of English sometimes use more than one negative at a time (*I can't hardly see you*). Multiple negatives, in fact, have a long history in English and can be found in the works of Chaucer and Shakespeare. It was only in the eighteenth century, in an effort to make English more uniform, that double negatives came to be seen as incorrect. Emphatic double negatives — and triple, quadruple, and more — are used in many varieties of spoken English (*Don't none of you know nothing at all*).
>
> Even though multiple negatives occur in many varieties of English (and in many other languages), in academic or professional writing you will play it safe if you avoid them — unless you are quoting dialogue or creating a special effect.

⊙ **bedfordstmartins.com/everydaywriter**
Exercise Central > Adjectives and Adverbs

Modifier Placement **36**

Modifiers enrich writing by making it more concrete or vivid, often adding important or even essential details. To be effective, modifiers should refer clearly to the words they modify and be positioned close to those words. Consider, for example, a sign seen recently in a hotel:

DO NOT USE THE ELEVATORS IN CASE OF FIRE.

Should we really avoid the elevators altogether for fear of causing a fire? Repositioning the modifier *in case of fire* eliminates such confusion—and makes clear that we are to avoid the elevators only if there is a fire: IN CASE OF FIRE, DO NOT USE THE ELEVATORS. This chapter reviews the conventions of accurate modifier placement.

AT A GLANCE

Editing Misplaced or Dangling Modifiers

1. Identify all the modifiers in each sentence, and draw an arrow from each modifier to the word it modifies.
2. If a modifier is far from the word it modifies, try to move the two closer together. (36a)
3. Does any modifier seem to refer to a word other than the one it is intended to modify? If so, move the modifier so that it refers clearly to only the intended word. (36a)
4. If you cannot find the word to which a modifier refers, revise the sentence: supply such a word, or revise the modifier itself so that it clearly refers to a word already in the sentence. (36c)

36a   Revise misplaced modifiers.

Modifiers can cause confusion or ambiguity if they are not close enough to the words they modify or if they seem to modify more than one word in the sentence.

▶ She teaches a seminar this term ~~on voodoo~~ *on voodoo* at Skyline College.

The voodoo was not at the college; the seminar is.

▶ ~~Billowing from every window,~~ *He* saw clouds of smoke~~,~~ *billowing from every window.*

People cannot billow from windows.

▶ *After he lost the 1962 gubernatorial race,* Nixon told reporters that he planned to get out of politics. ~~after he lost the 1962 gubernatorial race.~~

The unedited sentence implies that Nixon planned to lose the race.

Limiting modifiers

Be especially careful with the placement of limiting modifiers such as *almost, even, just, merely,* and *only*. In general, these modifiers should be placed right before or after the words they modify. Putting them in other positions may produce not just ambiguity but a completely different meaning.

AMBIGUOUS	The court *only* hears civil cases on Tuesdays.
CLEAR	The court hears only civil cases on Tuesdays.
CLEAR	The court hears civil cases on Tuesdays only.

In the first sentence, placing *only* before *hears* makes the meaning ambiguous. Does the writer mean that civil cases are the only cases heard on Tuesdays or that those are the only days when civil cases are heard?

▶ The city ~~almost~~ spent $20 million on the new stadium.
  almost

The original sentence suggests the money was almost spent; moving *almost* makes clear that the amount spent was almost $20 million.

Squinting modifiers

If a modifier can refer to either the word before it or the word after it, it is a squinting modifier. Put the modifier where it clearly relates to only a single word.

SQUINTING	Students who practice writing *often* will benefit.
REVISED	Students who often practice writing will benefit.
REVISED	Students who practice writing will often benefit.

36b Revise disruptive modifiers.

Disruptive modifiers interrupt the connections between parts of a grammatical structure or a sentence, making it hard for readers to follow the progress of the thought.

▶ ~~Vegetables will, if they are cooked too long,~~ lose most of their nutritional value.
  If they are cooked too long, vegetables will

In general, do not place a modifier between the *to* and the verb of an infinitive (*to often complain*). Doing so makes it hard for readers to recognize that the two go together.

> *surrender*
> ▶ Hitler expected the British to fairly quickly. ~~surrender.~~

In some sentences, however, a modifier sounds awkward if it does not split the infinitive. In such cases, it may be best to reword the sentence to eliminate the infinitive altogether.

SPLIT   I hope *to* almost *equal* my last year's income.

REVISED   I hope that I will earn almost as much as I did last year.

36c Revise dangling modifiers.

Dangling modifiers modify nothing in particular in the rest of a sentence. They often *seem* to modify something that is implied but not actually present in the sentence. Dangling modifiers frequently appear at the beginnings or ends of sentences.

DANGLING   Driving nonstop, Salishan Lodge is located two hours from Portland.

REVISED   Driving nonstop from Portland, you can reach Salishan Lodge in two hours.

To revise a dangling modifier, often you need to add a subject that the modifier clearly refers to. In some cases, however, you have to revise the modifier itself, turning it into a phrase or a clause.

> *our family gave away*
> ▶ Reluctantly, the hound ~~was given away~~ to a neighbor.

In the original sentence, was the dog reluctant, or was someone else who is not mentioned reluctant?

> *When he was*
> ▶ As a young boy, his grandmother told stories of her years as a country schoolteacher.

His grandmother was never a young boy.

> *My*
> ▶ ~~Thumbing through the magazine,~~ my eyes automatically noticed the
> *as I was thumbing through the magazine.*
> perfume ads.

Eyes cannot thumb through a magazine.

Comma Splices and Fused Sentences **37**

A comma splice results from placing only a comma between clauses. We often see comma splices in advertising and other slogans, where they can provide a catchy rhythm.

> Dogs have owners, cats have staff.
> – BUMPER STICKER

Another related construction is a fused, or run-on, sentence, which results from joining two independent clauses with no punctuation or connecting word between them. The bumper sticker as a fused sentence would be "Dogs have owners cats have staff."

You will seldom profit from using comma splices or fused sentences in academic or professional writing. In fact, doing so will almost always draw an instructor's criticism.

37a Separate the clauses into two sentences.

The simplest way to revise comma splices or fused sentences is to separate them into two sentences.

COMMA SPLICE **My mother spends long hours every spring tilling the**
This
soil and moving manure/. this part of gardening is
nauseating.

FUSED SENTENCE **My mother spends long hours every spring tilling the**
This
soil and moving manure. this part of gardening is
nauseating.

If the two clauses are very short, making them two sentences may sound abrupt and terse, so some other method of revision is probably preferable.

AT A GLANCE

Editing for Comma Splices and Fused Sentences

Two independent clauses — groups of words that can stand alone as sentences — joined with no punctuation form a fused sentence. Two such clauses joined only by a comma form a comma splice. Here are six methods of editing comma splices and fused sentences. As you edit, look at the sentences around the ones you are revising to determine how a particular method will affect the rhythm of the passage.

1. Separate the clauses into two sentences. (37a)

   > *Education* is an elusive word,/. *It* it often means different things to different people.

2. Link the clauses with a comma and a coordinating conjunction (*and, but, or, nor, for, so,* or *yet*). (37b)

   > *Education* is an elusive word, *for* it often means different things to different people.

3. Link the clauses with a semicolon. (37c)

   > *Education* is an elusive word,/; it often means different things to different people.

   If the clauses are linked with only a comma and a conjunctive adverb — a word like *however, then, therefore* — add a semicolon.

   > *Education* is an elusive word,/; indeed, it often means different things to different people.

4. Recast the two clauses as one independent clause. (37d)

   > *An elusive word, education*
   > *Education* is an elusive word, it often means different things to different people.

5. Recast one independent clause as a dependent clause. (37e)

   > *Education* is an elusive word,/ *because* it often means different things to different people.

6. In informal writing, link the clauses with a dash. (37f)

   > *Education* is an elusive word,/ — its meaning varies.

37b Link the clauses with a comma and a coordinating conjunction.

If the two clauses are closely related and equally important, join them with a comma and a coordinating conjunction (*and, but, or, nor, for, so,* or *yet*). (See 25a.)

COMMA
SPLICE

I got up feeling bad,~ *and* I feel even worse now.

FUSED
SENTENCE

I should pay my tuition,~ *but* I need a new car.

37c Link the clauses with a semicolon.

If the ideas in the two clauses are closely related and you want to give them equal emphasis, link them with a semicolon.

COMMA
SPLICE

This photograph is not at all realistic/; it even uses dreamlike images to convey its message.

FUSED
SENTENCE

The practice of journalism is changing dramatically; advances in technology have sped up news cycles.

Be careful when you link clauses with a conjunctive adverb or a transitional phrase. You must precede such words and phrases with a semicolon (see Chapter 40), with a period, or with a comma combined with a coordinating conjunction (25a).

COMMA
SPLICE

Many developing countries have very high birthrates/; therefore, most of their citizens are young.

FUSED
SENTENCE

Many developing countries have very high birthrates.
T
~~t~~herefore, most of their citizens are young.

FUSED
SENTENCE

Many developing countries have very high birthrates, *and,*
therefore, most of their citizens are young.

SOME CONJUNCTIVE ADVERBS AND TRANSITIONAL PHRASES

also	in contrast	next
anyway	indeed	now
besides	in fact	otherwise
certainly	instead	similarly
finally	likewise	still
furthermore	meanwhile	then
however	moreover	therefore
in addition	namely	thus
incidentally	nevertheless	undoubtedly

FOR MULTILINGUAL WRITERS

Judging Sentence Length

In U.S. academic contexts, readers sometimes find a series of short sentences "choppy" and undesirable. If you want to connect two independent clauses into one sentence, be sure to join them using one of the methods discussed in this chapter so that you avoid creating a comma splice or fused sentence. Another useful tip for writing in American English is to avoid writing several very long sentences in a row. If you find this pattern in your writing, try breaking it up by including a shorter sentence occasionally. (See Chapter 30.)

37d Rewrite the clauses as one independent clause.

Sometimes you can reduce two spliced or fused independent clauses to a single independent clause.

> *Most*
> COMMA   A large part of my mail is advertisements/ most of the
> SPLICE   ^   *and*
> rest is bills.   ^

37e Rewrite one independent clause as a dependent clause.

When one independent clause is more important than the other, try converting the less important one to a dependent clause (25b).

COMMA
SPLICE

which reacted against mass production,
The arts and crafts movement, called for handmade
objects/. it reacted against mass production.

In the revision, the writer chooses to emphasize the first clause, the one describing what the movement advocated, and to make the second clause, the one describing what it reacted against, into a dependent clause.

FUSED
SENTENCE

Although
Zora Neale Hurston is regarded as one of America's
major novelists, she died in obscurity.

In the revision, the writer chooses to emphasize the second clause and to make the first one into a dependent clause by adding the subordinating conjunction *although*.

37f Link the two clauses with a dash.

In informal writing, you can use a dash to join the two clauses, especially when the second clause elaborates on the first clause.

COMMA
SPLICE

—
Exercise trends come and go/this year yoga is hot.

---

bedfordstmartins.com/everydaywriter
Exercise Central > Comma Splices and Fused Sentences

38 Sentence Fragments

S entence fragments are often used to make writing sound conversational, as in this Facebook status update:

> Realizing that there are no edible bagels in this part of Oregon. Sigh.

Fragments—groups of words that are punctuated as sentences but are not sentences—are often seen in intentionally informal writing and in public writing, such as advertising, that aims to attract attention or give a phrase special emphasis. But you should think carefully before using fragments in academic or professional writing, where some readers might regard them as errors.

AT A GLANCE

Editing for Sentence Fragments

A group of words must meet three criteria to form a complete sentence. If it does not meet all three, it is a fragment. Revise a fragment by combining it with a nearby sentence or by rewriting it as a complete sentence.

1. A sentence must have a subject. (31j)

2. A sentence must have a verb, not just a verbal. A verbal cannot function as a sentence's verb without an auxiliary verb. (31k and l)

   VERB   The terrier is *barking*.

   VERBAL The terrier *barking*.

3. Unless it is a question, a sentence must have at least one clause that does not begin with a subordinating word. (31h) Following are some common subordinating words:

although	if	when
as	since	where
because	that	whether
before	though	which
how	unless	who

38a Revise phrase fragments.

Phrases are groups of words that lack a subject, a verb, or both (311). When verbal phrases, prepositional phrases, noun phrases, and appositive phrases are punctuated like sentences, they become fragments. To revise these fragments, attach them to an independent clause, or make them a separate sentence.

▶ NBC is broadcasting the debates./ ~~With~~ discussions afterward.
with

> *With discussions afterward* is a prepositional phrase, not a sentence. The editing combines the phrase with an independent clause.

▶ The town's growth is controlled by zoning laws./ ~~A~~ strict set of
a

regulations for builders and corporations.

> *A strict set of regulations for builders and corporations* is an appositive phrase renaming the noun *zoning laws*. The editing attaches the fragment to the sentence containing that noun.

▶ Kamika stayed out of school for three months after Linda was born.

She did so to
~~To~~ recuperate and to take care of the baby.

> *To recuperate and to take care of the baby* includes verbals, not verbs. The revision—adding a subject (*she*) and a verb (*did*)—turns the fragment into a separate sentence.

Fragments beginning with transitions

If you introduce an example or explanation with one of the following transitions, be certain you write a sentence, not a fragment.

also	for example	like
as a result	for instance	such as
besides	instead	that is

▶ Joan Didion has written on many subjects./ ~~Such~~ as the Hoover Dam
such

and migraine headaches.

> The second word group is a phrase, not a sentence. The editing combines it with an independent clause.

38b   Revise compound-predicate fragments.

A compound predicate consists of two or more verbs, along with their modifiers and objects, that have the same subject. Fragments occur when one part of a compound predicate lacks a subject but is punctuated as a separate sentence. These fragments usually begin with *and*, *but*, or *or*. You can revise them by attaching them to the independent clause that contains the rest of the predicate.

▶ They sold their house./ ~~And~~ *and* moved into an apartment.

38c   Revise dependent-clause fragments.

Dependent clauses contain both a subject and a verb, but they cannot stand alone as sentences; they depend on an independent clause to complete their meaning. Dependent clauses usually begin with words such as *after*, *because*, *before*, *if*, *since*, *though*, *unless*, *until*, *when*, *where*, *while*, *who*, *which*, and *that*. You can usually combine dependent-clause fragments with a nearby independent clause.

▶ When I decided to work part-time/, I gave up a lot of my earning potential.

If you cannot smoothly attach a clause to a nearby independent clause, try deleting the opening subordinating word and turning the dependent clause into a sentence.

▶ The majority of injuries in automobile accidents occur in two ways.

~~When an~~ *An* occupant either is hurt by something inside the car or is

thrown from the car.

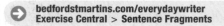

bedfordstmartins.com/everydaywriter
Exercise Central > Sentence Fragments

Punctuation and Mechanics

The function of most punctuation . . . is to add precision and complexity to meaning. It increases the information potential of strings of words.

— LOUIS MENAND

Punctuation and Mechanics

39 Commas *358*
- **a** Use commas to set off introductory words, phrases, and clauses *358*
- **b** Use commas with conjunctions that join clauses in compound sentences *359*
- **c** Use commas to set off nonrestrictive elements *360*
- **d** Use commas with items in a series *362*
- **e** Use commas to set off parenthetical and transitional expressions *363*
- **f** Use commas to set off contrasting elements, interjections, direct address, and tag questions *364*
- **g** Use commas with dates, addresses, titles, and numbers *364*
- **h** Use commas to set off most quotations *365*
- **i** Use commas to prevent confusion *366*
- **j** Eliminate unnecessary commas *366*

40 Semicolons *367*
- **a** Use semicolons to link independent clauses *368*
- **b** Use semicolons to separate items in a series containing other punctuation *369*
- **c** Revise misused semicolons *369*

41 End Punctuation *370*
- **a** Periods *370*
- **b** Question marks *371*
- **c** Exclamation points *372*

42 Apostrophes *372*
- **a** Use apostrophes appropriately to show possession *373*
- **b** Use apostrophes in contractions *374*
- **c** Avoid apostrophes in most plural forms *375*

43 Quotation Marks *375*
- **a** Use quotation marks to identify direct quotations *375*
- **b** Punctuate block quotations and poetry appropriately *376*
- **c** Use quotation marks for titles of short works *377*
- **d** Use quotation marks appropriately for definitions *378*
- **e** Use quotation marks to identify irony and invented terms *378*

For visual analysis Look carefully at the illustration on the front of this tab. How might it relate to the idea of punctuation and other mechanical features of writing?

f Follow conventions for other punctuation with quotation marks *378*

g Revise misused quotation marks *379*

44 Other Punctuation *380*
a Parentheses *380*
b Brackets *382*
c Dashes *382*
d Colons *383*
e Slashes *384*
f Ellipses *385*

45 Capital Letters *386*
a Capitalize the first word of a sentence or line of poetry *387*
b Capitalize proper nouns and proper adjectives *387*
c Capitalize titles of works *389*
d Revise unnecessary capitalization *389*

46 Abbreviations and Numbers *390*
a Abbreviate some titles before and all titles after proper names *391*
b Abbreviate years and hours appropriately *391*
c Abbreviate some business, government, and science terms *391*
d Use abbreviations in official company names *392*
e Use Latin abbreviations appropriately *392*
f Use symbols and unit abbreviations appropriately *392*
g Use other abbreviations according to convention *393*
h Spell out numbers expressed in one or two words *394*
i Spell out numbers that begin sentences *394*
j Use figures according to convention *394*

47 Italics *395*
a Italicize titles of long works *395*
b Italicize words, letters, and numbers used as terms *396*
c Italicize non-English words and phrases *396*

48 Hyphens *397*
a Use hyphens with compound words *397*
b Use hyphens with prefixes and suffixes *398*
c Avoid unnecessary hyphens *398*

39 Commas

Commas often play a crucial role in meaning. See how important the comma is in the following directions for making hot cereal:

Add Cream of Wheat slowly, stirring constantly.

That sentence tells the cook to *add the cereal slowly*. If the comma came before the word *slowly,* however, the cook might add all of the cereal at once and *stir slowly.* Using commas correctly can help you communicate more effectively.

39a Use commas to set off introductory words, phrases, and clauses.

▶ However, health care costs keep rising.

▶ In the end, only you can decide.

▶ Wearing new running shoes, Logan prepared for the race.

▶ To win the contest, Connor needed skill and luck.

▶ Pencil poised in anticipation, Audrey waited for the drawing contest to begin.

▶ While her friends watched, Lila practiced her gymnastics routine.

Some writers omit the comma if the introductory element is short and does not seem to require a pause after it.

▶ *At the racetrack* Henry lost his entire paycheck.

However, you will seldom be wrong if you use a comma after an introductory element.

AT A GLANCE

Editing for Commas

Research for this book shows that five of the most common errors in college writing involve commas. Check your writing for these errors:

1. Check every sentence that doesn't begin with the subject to see whether it opens with an introductory element (a word, phrase, or clause that describes the subject or tells when, where, how, or why the main action of the sentence occurs). Use a comma to separate the introductory material from the main part of the sentence. (39a)

2. Look at every sentence that contains one of the conjunctions *and, but, or, nor, for, so,* or *yet*. If the groups of words both before and after the conjunction function as complete sentences, you have a compound sentence. Make sure to use a comma before the conjunction. (39b)

3. Look at each adjective clause beginning with *which, who, whom, whose, when,* or *where*, and at each phrase and appositive. (31m) Is the element essential to the meaning of the sentence? If the sentence would be unclear without it, do not set off the element with commas. (39c)

4. Make sure that adjective clauses beginning with *that* are not set off with commas. (39c and j) Do not use commas between subjects and verbs, verbs and objects or complements, or prepositions and objects; to separate parts of compound constructions other than compound sentences; to set off restrictive clauses; or before the first or after the last item in a series. (39j)

5. Do not use a comma alone to separate sentences (see Chapter 37).

39b Use commas with conjunctions that join clauses in compound sentences.

A comma usually precedes a coordinating conjunction (*and, but, or, nor, for, so,* or *yet*) that joins two independent clauses in a compound sentence (31m).

▶ The title sounds impressive‚ but *administrative clerk* is just another word for *photocopier*.

▶ The show started at last‚ and the crowd grew quiet.

With very short clauses, you can sometimes omit the comma.

▶ She saw her chance and she took it.

Always use the comma if there is any chance the sentence will be mis-read without it.

▶ I opened the junk drawer, and the cabinet door jammed.

Use a semicolon rather than a comma when the clauses are long and complex or contain their own commas.

▶ **When these early migrations took place, the ice was still confined to the lands in the far north; but eight hundred thousand years ago, when man was already established in the temperate latitudes, the ice moved southward until it covered large parts of Europe and Asia.**
— ROBERT JASTROW, *Until the Sun Dies*

39c Use commas to set off nonrestrictive elements.

Nonrestrictive elements are word groups that do not limit, or restrict, the meaning of the noun or pronoun they modify. Setting nonrestrictive elements off with commas shows your readers that the information is not essential to the meaning of the sentence. Restrictive elements, on the other hand, *are* essential to meaning and should *not* be set off with commas. The same sentence may mean different things with and without the commas:

▶ **The bus drivers rejecting the management offer remained on strike.**
▶ **The bus drivers, rejecting the management offer, remained on strike.**

The first sentence says that only *some* bus drivers, the ones rejecting the offer, remained on strike. The second says that *all* the drivers did.

Since the decision to include or omit commas affects how readers interpret your sentence, you should think especially carefully about what you mean and use commas (or omit them) accordingly.

RESTRICTIVE   Drivers *who have been convicted of drunken driving* should lose their licenses.

In the preceding sentence, the clause *who have been convicted of drunken driving* is essential because it explains that only drivers who have been convicted of drunken driving should lose their licenses. Therefore, it is *not* set off with commas.

NONRESTRICTIVE   The two drivers involved in the accident, *who have been convicted of drunken driving,* should lose their licenses.

In the second sentence, however, the clause *who have been convicted of drunken driving* is not essential to the meaning because it merely provides more information about what it modifies, *The two drivers involved in the accident*. Therefore, the clause is set off with commas.

To decide whether an element is restrictive or nonrestrictive, read the sentence without the element, and see if the deletion changes the meaning of the rest of the sentence. If the deletion does change the meaning, the element is probably restrictive, and you should not set it off with commas. If it does not change the meaning, the element is probably nonrestrictive and requires commas.

Adjective and adverb clauses

An adjective clause that begins with *that* is always restrictive; do not set it off with commas. An adjective clause beginning with *which* may be either restrictive or nonrestrictive; however, some writers prefer to use *which* only for nonrestrictive clauses, which they set off with commas.

RESTRICTIVE CLAUSES

▶ **The claim** *that men like seriously to battle one another to some sort of finish* **is a myth.**   – JOHN MCMURTRY, "Kill 'Em! Crush 'Em! Eat 'Em Raw!"

The *that* clause is necessary to the meaning because it explains which claim is a myth; therefore, the clause is not set off with commas.

▶ **The man/ who rescued Jana's puppy/ won her eternal gratitude.**

The *who* clause is necessary to the meaning because only the man who rescued the puppy won the gratitude; therefore, the clause takes no commas.

NONRESTRICTIVE CLAUSES

▶ **I borrowed books from the rental library of Shakespeare and Company,** *which was the library and bookstore of Sylvia Beach at 12 rue de l'Odeon.*
     – ERNEST HEMINGWAY, *A Moveable Feast*

The clause describing Shakespeare and Company is not necessary to the meaning of the sentence and therefore is set off with a comma.

In general, set off an adverb clause that follows a main clause only if it begins with *although, even though, while,* or another subordinating conjunction expressing contrast.

▶ **He uses semicolons frequently, while she prefers periods and short sentences.**

The clause *while she prefers periods and short sentences* expresses contrast; therefore, it is set off with a comma.

Do *not* set off any other adverb clause that follows a main clause.

▶ **Remember to check your calculations/ before you submit the form.**

Phrases

Participial phrases may be restrictive or nonrestrictive. Prepositional phrases are usually restrictive, but sometimes they are not essential to the meaning of a sentence and are set off with commas (31l).

NONRESTRICTIVE PHRASES

▶ **Frédéric Chopin, in poor health, still composed prolifically.**

The phrase *in poor health* does not limit the meaning of *Frédéric Chopin* and so is set off with commas.

Appositives

An appositive renames a nearby noun (31l). When an appositive is not essential to identify what it renames, it is set off with commas.

NONRESTRICTIVE APPOSITIVES

▶ **Jon Stewart, the comic and news commentator, often pokes fun at political leaders.**

Jon Stewart's name identifies him; the appositive *the comic and news commentator* provides extra information.

RESTRICTIVE APPOSITIVES

▶ **Mozart's opera/ *The Marriage of Figaro*/ was considered revolutionary.**

The appositive is restrictive because Mozart wrote more than one opera.

39d Use commas with items in a series.

▶ **He has plundered our seas, ravaged our coasts, burnt our towns, and destroyed the lives of our people.**   – Declaration of Independence

You may see a series with no comma after the next-to-last item, particularly in newspaper writing. Occasionally, however, omitting the comma can cause confusion.

▶ **All the cafeteria's vegetables—broccoli, green beans, peas, and carrots— were cooked to a gray mush.**

Without the comma after *peas,* you wouldn't know if there were three choices (the third being a *mixture* of peas and carrots) or four.

When the items in a series contain commas of their own or other punctuation, separate them with semicolons rather than commas (40b).

Coordinate adjectives, those that relate equally to the noun they modify, should be separated by commas.

▶ **The long, twisting, muddy road led to a shack in the woods.**

In a sentence like *The cracked bathroom mirror reflected his face,* however, *cracked* and *bathroom* are not coordinate because *bathroom mirror* is the equivalent of a single word, which is modified by *cracked.* Hence, they are *not* separated by commas.

You can usually determine whether adjectives are coordinate by inserting *and* between them. If the sentence makes sense with the *and,* the adjectives are coordinate and should be separated by commas.

▶ **They are sincere *and* talented *and* inquisitive researchers.**

The sentence makes sense with the *and*s, so the adjectives should be separated by commas: *They are sincere, talented, inquisitive researchers.*

▶ **Byron carried an elegant *and* pocket watch.**

The sentence does not make sense with *and,* so the adjectives *elegant* and *pocket* should not be separated by commas: *Byron carried an elegant pocket watch.*

39e Use commas to set off parenthetical and transitional expressions.

Parenthetical expressions add comments or information. Because they often interrupt the flow of a sentence or digress, they are usually set off with commas.

▶ **Some studies have shown that chocolate, of all things, helps to prevent tooth decay.**

▶ **Roald Dahl's stories, it turns out, were often inspired by his own childhood.**

Transitional expressions, conjunctive adverbs (words such as *however* and *furthermore*), and other words and phrases used to connect parts of sentences are usually set off with commas (8e).

▶ **Ozone is a by-product of dry cleaning, for example.**

▶ **Ceiling fans are, moreover, less expensive than air conditioners.**

39f Use commas to set off contrasting elements, interjections, direct address, and tag questions.

CONTRASTING ELEMENTS

▶ On official business it was she, not my father, one would usually hear on the phone or in stores.

> – RICHARD RODRIGUEZ, "Aria: A Memoir of a Bilingual Childhood"

INTERJECTIONS

▶ My God, who wouldn't want a wife?   – JUDY BRADY, "I Want a Wife"

DIRECT ADDRESS

▶ Remember, sir, that you are under oath.

TAG QUESTIONS

▶ The governor did not veto the unemployment bill, did she?

39g Use commas with dates, addresses, titles, and numbers.

Dates

Use a comma between the day of the week and the month, between the day of the month and the year, and between the year and the rest of the sentence, if any.

▶ The attacks on the morning of Tuesday, September 11, 2001, took the United States by surprise.

Do not use commas with dates in inverted order or with dates consisting of only the month and the year.

▶ She dated the letter *26 August 2008.*
▶ Thousands of Germans swarmed over the wall in *November 1989.*

Addresses and place-names

Use a comma after each part of an address or place-name, including the state if there is no ZIP code. Do not precede a ZIP code with a comma.

▶ Forward my mail to the Department of English, The Ohio State University, Columbus, Ohio 43210.

▶ Portland, Oregon, is much larger than Portland, Maine.

Titles

Use commas to set off a title such as *MD* or *PhD* from the name preceding it and from the rest of the sentence. The titles *Jr.* and *Sr.,* however, often appear without commas.

▶ Oliver Sacks, MD, has written about the way the mind works.

▶ Martin Luther King Jr. was one of the twentieth century's greatest orators.

Numbers

In numerals of five digits or more, use a comma between each group of three, starting from the right.

▶ The city's population rose to 158,000 in the 2000 census.

The comma is optional within numerals of four digits but never occurs in four-digit dates, street addresses, or page numbers.

▶ The college had an enrollment of *1,789* [or *1789*] in the fall of 2008.

▶ My grandparents live at *2428* Loring Place.

▶ Turn to page *1566.*

39h Use commas to set off most quotations.

Commas set off a quotation from words used to introduce or identify the source of the quotation. A comma following a quotation goes inside the closing quotation mark. (See 44d for advice about using colons instead of commas to introduce quotations.)

▶ A German proverb warns, "Go to law for a sheep, and lose your cow."

▶ "All I know about grammar," said Joan Didion, "is its infinite power."

Do not use a comma after a question mark or exclamation point.

▶ "What's a thousand dollars?/" asks Groucho Marx in *Cocoanuts.*
"Mere chicken feed. A poultry matter."

▶ "Out, damned spot!/" cries Lady Macbeth.

Do not use a comma when you introduce a quotation with *that.*

▶ The writer of Ecclesiastes concludes that/ "all is vanity."

Do not use a comma before an indirect quotation—one that does not use the speaker's exact words.

▶ Patrick Henry declared/ that he wanted either liberty or death.

39i   Use commas to prevent confusion.

Sometimes commas are necessary to make sentences easier to read or understand.

▶ The members of the dance troupe strutted in, in matching costumes.

▶ Before, I had planned to major in biology.

39j   Eliminate unnecessary commas.

Excessive use of commas can spoil an otherwise fine sentence.

Around restrictive elements

Do not use commas to set off restrictive elements—elements that limit, or define, the meaning of the words they modify or refer to (39c).

▶ I don't let my children watch films/ that are violent.

▶ A law/ reforming campaign financing/ was passed in 2002.

▶ My only defense/ against my allergies/ is to stay indoors.

▶ The actor/ Philip Seymour Hoffman/ might win the award.

Between subjects and verbs, verbs and objects or complements, and prepositions and objects

Do not use a comma between a subject and its verb, a verb and its object or complement, or a preposition and its object. This rule holds true even if the subject, object, or complement is a long phrase or clause.

▶ Watching movies late at night/ is a way for me to relax.

▶ Parents must decide/ how much television their children may watch.

▶ The winner of/ the community-service award stepped forward.

In compound constructions

In compound constructions (other than compound sentences—see 39b), do not use a comma before or after a coordinating conjunction that joins the two parts.

▶ **Improved health care/ and more free trade were two of the administration's goals.**

The *and* here joins parts of a compound subject, which should not be separated by a comma.

▶ **Donald Trump was born rich/ and used his money to make money.**

The *and* here joins parts of a compound predicate, which should not be separated by a comma.

Before the first or after the last item in a series

▶ **The auction included/ furniture, paintings, and china.**

▶ **The swimmer took slow, elegant, powerful/ strokes.**

> **bedfordstmartins.com/everydaywriter**
> **Exercise Central > Commas**

Semicolons **40**

The following public-service announcement, posted in New York City subway cars, reminded commuters what to do with a used newspaper at the end of the ride:

> Please put it in a trash can; that's good news for everyone.

The semicolon in the subway announcement separates two clauses that could have been written as separate sentences. Semicolons, which create a pause stronger than that of a comma but not as strong as the full pause of a period, show close connections between related ideas.

AT A GLANCE

Editing for Semicolons

- If you use semicolons, be sure they appear only between independent clauses — groups of words that can stand alone as sentences (40a) — or between items in a series. (40b)
- If you find few or no semicolons in your writing, ask yourself whether you should add some. Would any closely related ideas in two sentences be better expressed in one sentence with a semicolon? (40a)

40a Use semicolons to link independent clauses.

Though a comma and a coordinating conjunction often join independent clauses, semicolons provide writers with subtler ways of signaling closely related clauses. The clause following a semicolon often restates an idea expressed in the first clause; it sometimes expands on or presents a contrast to the first.

▶ **Immigration acts were passed; newcomers had to prove, besides moral correctness and financial solvency, their ability to read.**
— Mary Gordon, "More Than Just a Shrine"

Gordon uses a semicolon to join the two clauses, giving the sentence an abrupt rhythm that suits the topic: laws that imposed strict requirements.

A semicolon should link independent clauses joined by conjunctive adverbs such as *therefore, however,* and *indeed* or transitional expressions such as *in fact, in addition,* and *for example* (31h).

▶ **The circus comes as close to being the world in microcosm as anything I know; in a way, it puts all the rest of show business in the shade.**
— E. B. White, "The Ring of Time"

If two independent clauses joined by a coordinating conjunction contain commas, you may use a semicolon instead of a comma before the conjunction to make the sentence easier to read.

▶ **Every year, whether the Republican or the Democratic party is in office, more and more power drains away from the individual to feed vast reservoirs in far-off places; and we have less and less say about the shape of events which shape our future.**
— William F. Buckley Jr., "Why Don't We Complain?"

40b Use semicolons to separate items in a series containing other punctuation.

Ordinarily, commas separate items in a series (39d). But when the items themselves contain commas or other marks of punctuation, using semicolons to separate the items will make the sentence clearer and easier to read.

▶ **Anthropology encompasses archaeology, the study of ancient civilizations through artifacts; linguistics, the study of the structure and development of language; and cultural anthropology, the study of language, customs, and behavior.**

40c Revise misused semicolons.

A comma, not a semicolon, should separate an independent clause from a dependent clause or phrase.

▶ **The police found fingerprints; which they used to identify the thief.**

▶ **The new system would encourage students to register for courses online; thus streamlining registration.**

A colon, not a semicolon, should introduce a series or list.

▶ **The reunion tour includes the following bands; Urban Waste, Murphy's Law, Rapid Deployment, and Ism.**

bedfordstmartins.com/everydaywriter
Exercise Central > Semicolons

41   End Punctuation

Periods, question marks, and exclamation points often appear in advertising to create special effects or draw readers along from line to line.

> You have a choice to make.
> Where can you turn for advice?
> Ask our experts today!

End punctuation tells us how to read each sentence—as a matter-of-fact statement, a query, or an emphatic request. Making appropriate choices with end punctuation allows readers to understand exactly what you mean.

AT A GLANCE

Editing for End Punctuation

- If all or almost all of your sentences end with periods, see if some of them might be phrased more effectively as questions or exclamations. (41a–c)
- Check to be sure you use question marks appropriately. (41b)
- If you use exclamation points, consider whether each is justified. Does the sentence call for extra emphasis? If in doubt, use a period instead. (41c)

41a   Periods

Use a period to close sentences that make statements or give mild commands.

▶ **All books are either dreams or swords.**   – AMY LOWELL

▶ **Don't use a fancy word if a simpler word will do.**
     – GEORGE ORWELL, "Politics and the English Language"

▶ **Please close the door.**

A period also closes indirect questions, which report rather than ask questions.

▶ **I asked how old the child was.**

▶ **We all wonder who will win the election.**

Until recently, periods have been used with most abbreviations in American English (see Chapter 46). However, more and more abbreviations are appearing without periods.

Mr.	MD	BC *or* B.C.
Ms.	PhD	BCE *or* B.C.E.
Mrs.	MBA	AD *or* A.D.
Jr.	RN	AM *or* a.m.
Dr.	Sen.	PM *or* p.m.

Some abbreviations rarely if ever appear with periods. These include the postal abbreviations of state names, such as *FL* and *TN* (though the traditional abbreviations, such as *Fla.* and *Tenn.*, do call for periods), and most groups of initials (*GE, CIA, AIDS, UNICEF*). If you are not sure whether a particular abbreviation should include periods, check a dictionary, or follow the style guidelines (such as those of the Modern Language Association) you are using in a research paper.

41b Question marks

Use question marks to close sentences that ask direct questions.

▶ **How is the human mind like a computer, and how is it different?**
— KATHLEEN STASSEN BERGER AND ROSS A. THOMPSON,
The Developing Person through Childhood and Adolescence

Question marks do not close *indirect* questions, which report rather than ask questions.

▶ **She asked whether I opposed his nomination.**

Do not use a comma or a period immediately after a question mark that ends a direct quotation.

▶ **"Am I my brother's keeper?/" Cain asked.**

▶ **Cain asked, "Am I my brother's keeper?/"**

Questions in a series may have question marks even when they are not separate sentences.

▶ **I often confront a difficult choice: should I go to practice? finish my homework? spend time with my friends?**

A question mark in parentheses indicates that a writer is unsure of a date, a figure, or a word.

▶ **Quintilian died in AD 96 (?).**

41c Exclamation points

Use an exclamation point to show surprise or strong emotion.

► **In those few moments of geologic time will be the story of all that has happened since we became a nation. And what a story it will be!**
— JAMES RETTIE, "But a Watch in the Night"

Use exclamation points very sparingly because they can distract your readers or suggest that you are exaggerating.

► **This university is so large, so varied, that attempting to tell someone**

everything about it would take three years!.
                                            ^

Do not use a comma or a period immediately after an exclamation point that ends a direct quotation.

► **On my last visit, I looked out the sliding glass doors and ran breathlessly to Connor in the kitchen: "There's a *huge* black pig in the backyard!"/**   — ELLEN ASHDOWN, "Living by the Dead"

> **bedfordstmartins.com/everydaywriter**
> **Exercise Central > End Punctuation**

42 Apostrophes

The little apostrophe can make a big difference in meaning. The following sign at a neighborhood swimming pool, for instance, says something different from what the writer probably intended:

> Please deposit your garbage (and your guests) in the trash receptacles before leaving the pool area.

The sign indicates that guests should be put in the trash. Adding a single apostrophe would offer a more neighborly statement: *Please deposit your garbage (and your guests') in the trash receptacles before leaving the pool area* asks that the guests' garbage, not the guests themselves, be thrown away.

AT A GLANCE

Editing for Apostrophes

- Check each noun that ends in -s and shows possession. Is the apostrophe in the right place, either before or after the -s? (42a)
- Check the possessive form of each indefinite pronoun, such as *someone's*. Be sure the apostrophe comes before the -s. (42a)
- Check each personal pronoun that ends with -s (*yours, his, hers, its, ours, theirs*) to make sure it does not include an apostrophe. (42a)
- Does each *it's* mean *it is* or *it has*? If not, remove the apostrophe. (42b)
- Make sure other contractions use apostrophes correctly. (42b)

42a Use apostrophes appropriately to show possession.

The possessive case denotes ownership or possession of one thing by another.

Singular nouns and indefinite pronouns

Add an apostrophe and -s to form the possessive of most singular nouns, including those that end in -s, and of indefinite pronouns (31d). Do not use apostrophes with the possessive forms of personal pronouns: *yours, his, hers, its, ours, theirs.*

- ▶ The **bus's** fumes overpowered her.
- ▶ *Star Wars* made George **Lucas's** fortune.
- ▶ **Anyone's** guess is as good as mine.

Plural nouns

To form the possessive case of plural nouns not ending in -s, add an apostrophe and -s.

- ▶ The **men's** department sells business attire.

For plural nouns ending in -s, add only the apostrophe.

- ▶ The three **clowns'** costumes were bright green and orange.

Compound nouns

For compound nouns, make the last word in the group possessive.

- ▶ The secretary of state's speech was televised.
- ▶ Both her daughters-in-law's birthdays fall in July.
- ▶ My in-laws' disapproval dampened our enthusiasm for the new house.

Two or more nouns

To signal individual possession by two or more owners, make each noun possessive.

- ▶ Great differences exist between Jerry Bruckheimer's and Ridley Scott's films.

  Bruckheimer and Scott have produced different films.

To signal joint possession, make only the last noun possessive.

- ▶ Wallace and Gromit's creator is Nick Park.

  Wallace and Gromit have the same creator.

42b Use apostrophes in contractions.

Contractions are two-word combinations formed by leaving out certain letters, which are indicated by an apostrophe.

it is, it has/it's	I would, I had/I'd	will not/won't
was not/wasn't	he would, he had/he'd	let us/let's
I am/I'm	would not/wouldn't	cannot/can't
he is, he has/he's	do not/don't	who is, who has/who's
you will/you'll	does not/doesn't	

Contractions are common in conversation and informal writing. Academic and professional work, however, often calls for greater formality.

Distinguishing it's and its

Its is the possessive form of *it*. *It's* is a contraction for *it is* or *it has*.

- ▶ This disease is unusual; its symptoms vary from person to person.
- ▶ It's a difficult disease to diagnose.

42c Avoid apostrophes in most plural forms.

Many style guides now advise against using apostrophes for any plurals.

▶ The gymnasts need marks of *8s* and *9s* to qualify for the finals.

Others use an apostrophe and –*s* to form the plural of numbers, letters, and words referred to as terms.

▶ The five *Shakespeare's* in the essay were spelled five different ways.

Check your instructor's preference.

> **bedfordstmartins.com/everydaywriter**
> **Exercise Central > Apostrophes**

Quotation Marks **43**

A s a way of bringing other people's words into your own, quotations can be a powerful writing tool.

> Mrs. Macken encourages parents to get books for their children, to read to them when they are "li'l," and when they start school to make certain they attend regularly. She holds herself up as an example of "a millhand's daughter who wanted to be a schoolteacher and did it through sheer hard work."
> – SHIRLEY BRICE HEATH, *Ways with Words*

The writer lets her subject speak for herself—and lets readers hear Mrs. Macken's voice.

43a Use quotation marks to identify direct quotations.

▶ President Obama asked Congress to "try common sense."
▶ She smiled and said, "Son, this is one incident that I will never forget."

Use quotation marks to enclose the words of each speaker within running dialogue. Mark each shift in speaker with a new paragraph.

"I want no proof of their affection," said Elinor; "but of their engagement I do."

"I am perfectly satisfied of both."

"Yet not a syllable has been said to you on the subject, by either of
them."   –Jane Austen, *Sense and Sensibility*

AT A GLANCE

Editing for Quotation Marks

- Use quotation marks around direct quotations and titles of short works.
  (43a and c)
- Do not use quotation marks around set-off quotations of more than
  four lines of prose or more than three lines of poetry, or around titles of
  long works. Consult a style guide, such as that of the Modern Language
  Association (MLA), for guidelines. (43b and c)
- Use quotation marks to signal irony and invented words, but do so sparingly. (43e)
- Check other punctuation used with closing quotation marks. (43f)

  Periods and commas should be *inside* the quotation marks.

  Colons, semicolons, and footnote numbers should be *outside*.

  Question marks, exclamation points, and dashes should be *inside* if
  they are part of the quoted material, *outside* if they are not.

- Never use quotation marks around indirect quotations. (43g)
- Do not use quotation marks just to add emphasis to words. (43g)

Single quotation marks

Single quotation marks enclose a quotation within a quotation. Open
and close the quoted passage with double quotation marks, and change
any quotation marks that appear *within* the quotation to single quotation marks.

> ▶ Baldwin says, "The title 'The Uses of the Blues' does not refer to music; I
> don't know anything about music."

43b   Punctuate block quotations and poetry appropriately.

If the prose passage you wish to quote is more than four typed lines, set
the quotation off by starting it on a new line and indenting it one inch
from the left margin. This format, known as block quotation, does not
require quotation marks.

In "Suspended," Joy Harjo tells of her first awareness of jazz as a child:

> My rite of passage into the world of humanity occurred then, via jazz.
> The music made a startling bridge between the familiar and strange
> lands, an appropriate vehicle, for . . . we were there when jazz was born.
> I recognized it, that humid afternoon in my formative years, as a way to
> speak beyond the confines of ordinary language. I still hear it. (84)

This block quotation, including the ellipsis dots and the page number in parentheses at the end, follows the style of the Modern Language Association (MLA). The American Psychological Association (APA) has different guidelines for setting off block quotations. (See Chapters 49 and 53.)

When quoting poetry, if the quotation is brief (fewer than four lines), include it within your text. Separate the lines of the poem with slashes, each preceded and followed by a space, in order to tell the reader where one line of the poem ends and the next begins.

> In one of his best-known poems, Robert Frost remarks, "Two roads diverged in a
> yellow wood, and I — / I took the one less traveled by / And that has made all
> the difference."

To quote more than three lines of poetry, indent the block one inch from the left margin. Do not use quotation marks. Take care to follow the spacing, capitalization, punctuation, and other features of the original poem.

> The duke in Robert Browning's poem "My Last Duchess" is clearly a jealous, vain
> person, whose arrogance is illustrated through this statement:
>> She thanked men — good! but thanked
>> Somehow — I know not how — as if she ranked
>> My gift of a nine-hundred-years-old name
>> With anybody's gift. (lines 31–34)

43c Use quotation marks for titles of short works.

Quotation marks are used to enclose the titles of short poems, short stories, articles, essays, songs, sections of books, and episodes of television and radio programs.

- ▶ **"Dover Beach" moves from calmness to sadness.** [poem]
- ▶ **Alice Walker's "Everyday Use" is about more than just quilts.** [short story]
- ▶ **The *Atlantic* published an article entitled "Illiberal Education."** [article]

▶ In "Photography," Susan Sontag considers the role of photography in our society. [essay]

▶ The *Nature* episode "Echo of the Elephants" portrays ivory hunters unfavorably. [television series episode]

Use italics rather than quotation marks for the titles of television series, magazines, movies, and other long works (see 47a).

43d Use quotation marks appropriately for definitions.

▶ In social science, the term *sample size* means "the number of individuals being studied in a research project."
— KATHLEEN STASSEN BERGER AND ROSS A. THOMPSON,
The Developing Person through Childhood and Adolescence

Use italics for words used as a term, like *sample size* above (see 47b).

43e Use quotation marks to identify irony and invented terms.

To show readers that you are using a word or phrase ironically or that you made it up, enclose it in quotation marks.

▶ The "banquet" consisted of dried-out chicken and canned vegetables.

The quotation marks suggest that the meal was anything but a banquet.

▶ Your whole first paragraph or first page may have to be guillotined in any case after your piece is finished: it is a kind of "forebirth."
— JACQUES BARZUN, "A Writer's Discipline"

The writer made up the term *forebirth*.

43f Follow conventions for other punctuation with quotation marks.

Periods and commas go *inside* closing quotation marks.

▶ "Don't compromise yourself," said Janis Joplin. "You are all you've got."

When you follow MLA style for documenting a short quotation, place the period *after* the parentheses with source information (see Chapter 50).

▶ In places, de Beauvoir "sees Marxists as believing in subjectivity" (Whitmarsh 63).

For more information on using a comma with a quotation, see 39h.

Colons, semicolons, and footnote numbers go *outside* closing quotation marks.

▶ I felt one emotion after finishing "Eveline": sorrow.

▶ Everything is dark, and "a visionary light settles in her eyes"; this vision, this light, is her salvation.

▶ Tragedy is defined by Aristotle as "an imitation of an action that is serious and of a certain magnitude."[1]

Question marks, exclamation points, and dashes go *inside* if they are part of the quoted material, *outside* if they are not.

PART OF THE QUOTATION

▶ The cashier asked, "Would you like to super-size that?"

▶ "Jump!" one of the firefighters shouted.

NOT PART OF THE QUOTATION

▶ What is the theme of "The Birth-Mark"?

▶ "Break a leg"—that phrase is supposed to bring good luck.

43g Revise misused quotation marks.

Do not use quotation marks for indirect quotations—those that do not use someone's exact words.

▶ Mother said that ⁄⁄she was sure she would never forget the incident.⁄⁄

Do not use quotation marks just to add emphasis to particular words or phrases.

▶ Michael said that his views might not be ⁄⁄politically correct⁄⁄ but that he wasn't going to change them for anything.

▶ Much time was spent speculating about their ⁄⁄relationship.⁄⁄

Do not use quotation marks around slang or colloquial language; they create the impression that you are apologizing for using those words. If you have a good reason to use slang or a colloquial term, use it without quotation marks.

▶ After our twenty-mile hike, we were ready to ⁄⁄turn in.⁄⁄

FOR MULTILINGUAL WRITERS

Quoting in American English

Remember that the way you mark quotations in American English (" ") may not be the same as in other languages. In French, for example, quotations are marked with *guillemets* (« »), while in German, quotations take split-level marks („ "). Writers of British English use single quotation marks first and, when necessary, double quotation marks for quotations within quotations. If you are writing for an American audience, be careful to follow the U.S. conventions governing quotation marks.

bedfordstmartins.com/everydaywriter
Exercise Central > Quotation Marks

44 Other Punctuation

Parentheses, brackets, dashes, colons, slashes, and ellipses are everywhere. Every URL includes colons and slashes, many sites use brackets or parentheses to identify updates and embedded media, and dashes and ellipses are increasingly common in writing that expresses conversational informality.

You can also use these punctuation marks for more formal purposes: to signal relationships among parts of sentences, to create particular rhythms, and to help readers follow your thoughts.

44a Parentheses

Use parentheses to enclose material that is of minor or secondary importance in a sentence—material that supplements, clarifies, comments on, or illustrates what precedes or follows it.

▶ Inventors and men of genius have almost always been regarded as fools at the beginning (and very often at the end) of their careers.
                                                            – FYODOR DOSTOYEVSKY

▶ During my research, I found problems with the flat-rate income tax (a single-rate tax with no deductions).

AT A GLANCE

Editing for Effective Use of Punctuation

- Be sure that any material enclosed in parentheses or set off with dashes requires special treatment — and that the parentheses or dashes don't make the sentence difficult to follow. Use parentheses to de-emphasize material they enclose and dashes to add emphasis. (44a and c)
- Use brackets to enclose parenthetical elements in material that is already within parentheses and to enclose words or comments inserted into a quotation. (44b)
- Use colons to introduce explanations, series, lists, and some quotations. Do not put a colon between a verb and its object or complement, between a preposition and its object, or after expressions like *such as*. (44d)
- Use slashes to mark line divisions in poetry quoted within your own text. (44e)
- Use ellipses (three equally spaced dots) to indicate omissions from quoted passages. (44f)

Enclosing textual citations

▶ Freud and his followers have had a most significant impact on the ways abnormal functioning is understood and treated **(Joseph, 1991)**.
— RONALD J. COMER, *Abnormal Psychology*

▶ Zamora notes that Kahlo referred to her first self-portrait, given to a close friend, as "your Botticelli" **(110)**.

The first in-text citation above shows the style of the American Psychological Association (APA); the second, the style of the Modern Language Association (MLA).

Enclosing numbers or letters in a list

▶ Five distinct styles can be distinguished: **(1)** Old New England, **(2)** Deep South, **(3)** Middle American, **(4)** Wild West, and **(5)** Far West or Californian. — ALISON LURIE, *The Language of Clothes*

With other marks of punctuation

A period may be placed either inside or outside a closing parenthesis, depending on whether the parenthetical text is part of a larger sentence. A comma, if needed, is always placed *outside* a closing parenthesis (and never before an opening one).

▶ Gene Tunney's single defeat in an eleven-year career was to a flamboyant and dangerous fighter named Harry Greb ("The Human Windmill"), who seems to have been, judging from boxing literature, the dirtiest fighter in history. — JOYCE CAROL OATES, "On Boxing"

Choosing among parentheses, commas, and dashes

In general, use commas when the material to be set off is least interruptive (39c, e, and f), parentheses when it is more interruptive, and dashes when it is the most interruptive (44c).

44b Brackets

Use brackets to enclose parenthetical elements in material that is itself within parentheses and to enclose explanatory words or comments that you are inserting into a quotation.

Setting off material within parentheses

▶ Eventually the investigation had to examine the major agencies (including the previously sacrosanct National Security Agency [NSA]) that were conducting covert operations.

Inserting material within quotations

▶ Massing notes that "on average, it [Fox News] attracts more than eight million people daily — more than double the number who watch CNN."

The bracketed words clarify *it* in the original quotation.

In the quotation in the following sentence, the artist Gauguin's name is misspelled. The bracketed word *sic*, which means "so," tells readers that the person being quoted — not the writer who has picked up the quotation — made the mistake.

▶ One admirer wrote, "She was the most striking woman I'd ever seen — a sort of wonderful combination of Mia Farrow and one of Gauguin's [*sic*] Polynesian nymphs."

44c Dashes

Dashes give more emphasis than parentheses to the material they enclose. Many word-processing programs automatically convert two typed hyphens into a solid dash.

▶ The pleasures of reading itself—who doesn't remember?—were like those of Christmas cake, a sweet devouring.

— EUDORA WELTY, "A Sweet Devouring"

Emphasizing explanatory material

▶ Indeed, several of modern India's greatest scholars—such as the Mughal historian Muzaffar Alam of the University of Chicago—are madrasa graduates.

— WILLIAM DALRYMPLE

Emphasizing material at the end of a sentence

▶ In the twentieth century it has become almost impossible to moralize about epidemics—except those which are transmitted sexually.

— SUSAN SONTAG, *AIDS and Its Metaphors*

Marking a sudden change in tone

▶ New York is a catastrophe—but a magnificent catastrophe.

— LE CORBUSIER

Introducing a summary or explanation

▶ In walking, the average adult person employs a motor mechanism that weighs about eighty pounds—sixty pounds of muscle and twenty pounds of bone.

— EDWIN WAY TEALE

Indicating hesitation in speech

▶ As the officer approached his car, the driver stammered, "What—what have I done?"

44d Colons

Use a colon to introduce explanations or examples and to separate some elements from one another.

Introducing an explanation, an example, or an appositive

▶ The men may also wear the getup known as Sun Belt Cool: a pale beige suit, open-collared shirt (often in a darker shade than the suit), cream-colored loafers and aviator sunglasses.

— ALISON LURIE, *The Language of Clothes*

Introducing a series, a list, or a quotation

▶ At the baby's one-month birthday party, Ah Po gave him the Four Valuable Things: ink, inkslab, paper, and brush.

— MAXINE HONG KINGSTON, *China Men*

▶ The teachers wondered: "Do boys and girls really learn differently?"

The preceding example could have taken a comma instead of a colon (see 39h). Use a colon rather than a comma to introduce a quotation when the lead-in is a complete sentence on its own.

▶ The State of the Union address contained one surprising statement: "America is addicted to oil."

Separating elements

SALUTATIONS IN FORMAL LETTERS

▶ Dear Dr. Chapman:

HOURS, MINUTES, AND SECONDS

▶ 4:59 PM

▶ 2:15:06

RATIOS

▶ a ratio of 5:1

BIBLICAL CHAPTERS AND VERSES

▶ I Corinthians 3:3–5

TITLES AND SUBTITLES

▶ *The Joy of Insight: Passions of a Physicist*

CITIES AND PUBLISHERS IN BIBLIOGRAPHIC ENTRIES

▶ Boston: Bedford, 2012

Editing for colons

Do not put a colon between a verb and its object or complement— unless the object is a quotation.

▶ Some natural fibers are:̸ cotton, wool, silk, and linen.

Do not put a colon between a preposition and its object or after such expressions as *such as, especially,* and *including.*

▶ In poetry, additional power may come from devices such as:̸ simile, metaphor, and alliteration.

44e   Slashes

Use a slash to separate alternatives.

▶ Then there was Daryl, the cabdriver/bartender.

— JOHN L'HEUREUX, *The Handmaid of Desire*

Use slashes to mark line divisions between two or three lines of poetry quoted within running text. When using a slash to separate lines of poetry, precede and follow it with a space (43b).

▶ **In Sonnet 29, the persona states, "For thy sweet love rememb'red such wealth brings / That then I scorn to change my state with kings."**

Slashes also separate parts of fractions and Internet addresses.

44f Ellipses

Ellipses, or ellipsis points, are three equally spaced dots. Ellipses usually indicate that something has been omitted from a quoted passage, but they can also signal a pause or hesitation in speech in the same way that a dash can.

Indicating omissions

Just as you should carefully use quotation marks around any material that you quote directly from a source, so you should carefully use ellipses to indicate that you have left out part of a quotation that otherwise appears to be a complete sentence.

The ellipses in the following example indicate two omissions—one in the middle of the sentence and one at the end. When you omit the last part of a quoted sentence, add a period after the ellipses, for a total of four dots. Be sure a complete sentence comes before and after the four points. If you are adding your own ellipses to a quotation that already has other ellipses, enclose yours in brackets.

ORIGINAL TEXT

▶ **The quasi-official division of the population into three economic classes called high-, middle-, and low-income groups rather misses the point, because as a class indicator the amount of money is not as important as the source.** — PAUL FUSSELL, "Notes on Class"

WITH ELLIPSES

▶ **As Paul Fussell argues, "The quasi-official division of the population into three economic classes . . . rather misses the point. . . ."**

If your shortened quotation ends with a source (such as a page number, a name, or a title), follow these steps:

1. Use three ellipsis points but no period after the quotation.
2. Add the closing quotation mark, closed up to the third ellipsis point.
3. Add the source documentation in parentheses.
4. Use a period to indicate the end of the sentence.

▶ Packer argues, "The Administration is right to reconsider its strategy . . ." (34).

Indicating hesitation

▶ Then the voice, husky and familiar, came to wash over us — "The winnah, and still heavyweight champeen of the world . . . Joe Louis."
— MAYA ANGELOU, *I Know Why the Caged Bird Sings*

⊙ **bedfordstmartins.com/everydaywriter**
Exercise Central > Other Punctuation

---

45   Capital Letters

C apital letters are a key signal in everyday life. Look around any store to see their importance: you can shop for Levi's or *any* blue jeans, for Coca-Cola or *any* cola, for Kleenex or *any* tissue. As these examples show, one of the most common reasons for capitalizing a word is to indicate that it is part of a name or title — of a brand, person, article, or something else.

AT A GLANCE

Editing for Capitalization

- Capitalize the first word of each sentence. If you quote a poem, follow its original capitalization. (45a)
- Check to make sure you have appropriately capitalized proper nouns and proper adjectives. (45b)
- Review where you have used titles of people or of works to be sure you have capitalized them correctly. (45b and c)
- Double-check the capitalization of geographical directions (*north* or *North*?), family relationships (*dad* or *Dad*?), and seasons of the year (*winter*, not *Winter*). (45d)
- In email, check to see that you have not capitalized whole words or phrases. (45d)

45a Capitalize the first word of a sentence or line of poetry.

Capitalize the first word of a sentence. If you are quoting a full sentence, capitalize the first word of the quotation.

▶ Kennedy said, "Let us never negotiate out of fear."

Capitalization of a sentence following a colon is optional.

▶ Gould cites the work of Darwin: The [*or* the] theory of natural selection incorporates the principle of evolutionary ties among all animals.

Capitalize a sentence within parentheses unless the parenthetical sentence is inserted into another sentence.

▶ Gould cites the work of Darwin. (Other researchers cite more recent evolutionary theorists.)
▶ Gould cites the work of Darwin (see page 150).

When citing poetry, follow the capitalization of the original poem. Though most poets capitalize the first word of each line in a poem, some poets do not.

▶ Morning sun heats up the young beech tree
leaves and almost lights them into fireflies

– JUNE JORDAN, "Aftermath"

45b Capitalize proper nouns and proper adjectives.

Capitalize proper nouns (those naming specific persons, places, and things) and most proper adjectives (those formed from proper nouns). All other nouns are common nouns and are not capitalized unless they begin a sentence or are used as part of a proper noun: *a street* or *the street where you live,* but *Elm Street.* The following list shows proper nouns and adjectives on the left and related common nouns and adjectives on the right.

PEOPLE

Ang Lee	the film's director
Nixonian	political

NATIONS, NATIONALITIES, ETHNIC GROUPS, AND LANGUAGES

Brazil, Brazilian	their native country, his citizenship
Italian American	an ethnic group

PLACES

Pacific Ocean	an ocean
Hawaiian Islands	tropical islands

STRUCTURES AND MONUMENTS

the Lincoln Memorial	a monument
the Eiffel Tower	a landmark

SHIPS, TRAINS, AIRCRAFT, AND SPACECRAFT

the *Queen Mary*	a cruise ship
the *City of New Orleans*	the 6:00 train

ORGANIZATIONS, BUSINESSES, AND GOVERNMENT INSTITUTIONS

United Auto Workers	a trade union
Library of Congress	certain federal agencies

ACADEMIC INSTITUTIONS AND COURSES

University of Maryland	a state university
Political Science 102	my political science course

HISTORICAL EVENTS AND ERAS

the Easter Uprising	a rebellion
the Renaissance	the fifteenth century

RELIGIONS AND RELIGIOUS TERMS

God	a deity
the Qur'an	a holy book
Catholicism, Catholic	a religion, their religious affiliation

TRADE NAMES

Nike	running shoes
Cheerios	cereal

Some contemporary companies use capitals called *InterCaps* in the middle of their own or their product's names. Follow the style you see in company advertising or on the product itself—*eBay, FedEx, iTunes.*

Titles of individuals

Capitalize titles used before a proper name. When used alone or following a proper name, most titles are not capitalized. One common exception is the word *president,* which many writers capitalize whenever it refers to the president of the United States.

Chief Justice Roberts	John Roberts, the chief justice
Professor Lisa Ede	my English professor
Dr. Edward A. Davies	Edward A. Davies, our doctor

45c Capitalize titles of works.

Capitalize most words in titles of books, articles, stories, speeches, essays, plays, poems, documents, films, paintings, and musical compositions. Do not capitalize an article (*a, an, the*), a preposition, a conjunction, or the *to* in an infinitive unless it is the first or last word in a title or subtitle.

Walt Whitman: A Life	Declaration of Independence
"As Time Goes By"	*Charlie and the Chocolate Factory*
"Shooting an Elephant"	*Rebel without a Cause*

45d Revise unnecessary capitalization.

Do not capitalize a compass direction unless the word designates a specific geographic region.

▶ Voters in the South and much of the West tend to favor socially conservative candidates.

▶ John Muir headed ~~West,~~ *west,* motivated by the need to explore.

Do not capitalize a word indicating a family relationship unless the word is used as part of the name or as a substitute for the name.

▶ I could always tell when Mother was annoyed with Aunt Rose.

▶ When she was a child, my ~~Mother~~ *mother* shared a room with my ~~Aunt.~~ *aunt.*

Do not capitalize seasons of the year and parts of the academic or financial year.

spring	fall semester
winter	winter term
autumn	third-quarter earnings

Do not capitalize whole words or phrases for emphasis in online writing, which comes across to readers as SHOUTING. Use italics,

---

FOR MULTILINGUAL WRITERS

Learning English Capitalization

Capitalization systems vary considerably among languages, and some languages (Arabic, Chinese, Hindi, and Hebrew, for example) do not use capital letters at all. English may be the only language to capitalize the first-person singular pronoun (*I*), but Dutch and German capitalize some forms of the second-person pronoun (*you*). German capitalizes all nouns; English used to capitalize more nouns than it does now (see, for instance, the Declaration of Independence).

---

boldface, underlining, or (if you can't format text) asterisks to add emphasis.

▶ **Sorry for the abrupt response, but I am *very* busy.**

> **bedfordstmartins.com/everydaywriter**
> **Exercise Central > Capitalization**

46 Abbreviations and Numbers

Any time you look up an address, you see an abundance of abbreviations and numbers, as in the following movie theater listing from a Google map of Berkeley, California:

Oaks Theater   1875 Solano Av   Brk

Abbreviations and numbers allow writers to present detailed information in a small amount of space.

AT A GLANCE

Editing Abbreviations and Numbers

- Use abbreviations and numbers according to the conventions of a specific field (see p. 393): for example, *57%* might be acceptable in a math paper, but *57 percent* may be more appropriate in a sociology essay. (46f)
- If you use an abbreviation readers might not understand, spell out the term the first time you use it, and give the abbreviation in parentheses. (46c)

46a Abbreviate some titles before and all titles after proper names.

Ms. Susanna Moller	Henry Louis Gates Jr.
Mr. Aaron Oforlea	Karen Lancry, MD
Dr. Cheryl Gold	Samuel Cohen, PhD

Other titles—including religious, academic, and government titles—should be spelled out in academic writing. In other writing, they can be abbreviated before a full name but should be written out when used with only a last name.

Rev. Fleming Rutledge	Reverend Rutledge
Prof. Jaime Mejía	Professor Mejía
Gen. Colin Powell	General Powell

Do not use both a title and an academic degree with a person's name. Use one or the other. Instead of *Dr. Beverly Moss, PhD,* write *Dr. Beverly Moss* or *Beverly Moss, PhD.* (Note that academic degrees such as *RN* and *PhD* often appear without periods; see 41a.)

46b Abbreviate years and hours appropriately.

You can use the following abbreviations with numerals. Notice that AD precedes the numeral; all other abbreviations follow the numeral. Today, BCE and CE are generally preferred over BC and AD, and periods in all four of these abbreviations are optional.

399 BCE ("before the common era") *or* 399 BC ("before Christ")

49 CE ("common era") *or* AD 49 (*anno Domini,* Latin for "year of our Lord")

11:15 AM (*or* a.m.)

9:00 PM (*or* p.m.)

For these abbreviations, you may use full-size capital letters or small caps, a typographical option in word-processing programs.

46c Abbreviate some business, government, and science terms.

As long as you can be sure your readers will understand them, use common abbreviations such as *PBS, NASA, DNA,* and *CIA.* If an abbreviation may be unfamiliar, however, spell out the full term the first time you use it, and give the abbreviation in parentheses. After that, you can use the abbreviation by itself.

▶ **The Comprehensive Test Ban (CTB) Treaty was first proposed in the 1950s. For those nations signing it, the CTB would bring to a halt all nuclear weapons testing.**

46d   Use abbreviations in official company names.

Use such abbreviations as *Co., Inc., Corp.,* and *&* if they are part of a company's official name. Do not, however, use these abbreviations in most other contexts.

▶ **Sears, Roebuck & Co. was the only large ~~corp.~~ in town.**
  corporation

▶ **Paola has a part-time job at the Warner ~~Brothers~~ store in the mall.**
  Bros.

46e   Use Latin abbreviations appropriately.

In general, avoid these Latin abbreviations except when citing sources:

cf.	compare (*confer*)
e.g.	for example (*exempli gratia*)
et al.	and others (*et alia*)
etc.	and so forth (*et cetera*)
i.e.	that is (*id est*)
N.B.	note well (*nota bene*)
P.S.	postscript (*postscriptum*)

▶ **Many firms have policies to help working parents—~~e.g.,~~ flexible hours,**
  for example,
  parental leave, and day care.

▶ **Before the conference began, Haivan unpacked the name tags, programs,**
  pens, ~~etc.~~
  and so forth.

46f   Use symbols and unit abbreviations appropriately.

Symbols such as %, +, $, and = are acceptable in charts and graphs. Dollar signs are acceptable with figures: *$11* (but not with words: *eleven*

TALKING ABOUT STYLE

Abbreviations and Numbers in Different Fields

Use of abbreviations and numbers varies in different fields. See a typical example from a biochemistry textbook:

> The energy of a green photon...is 57 kilocalories per mole (kcal/mol). An alternative unit of energy is the joule (J), which is equal to 0.239 calorie; 1 kcal/mol is equal to 4.184 kJ/mol.
> – LUBERT STRYER, *Biochemistry*

These two sentences demonstrate how useful figures and abbreviations can be; reading the same sentences would be very difficult if the numbers and units of measurement were all written out.

Become familiar with the conventions governing abbreviations and numbers in your field. The following reference books provide guidelines:

MLA Handbook for Writers of Research Papers for literature and the humanities

Publication Manual of the American Psychological Association for the social sciences

Scientific Style and Format: The CSE Manual for Authors, Editors, and Publishers for the natural sciences

The Chicago Manual of Style for the humanities

AIP Style Manual for physics and the applied sciences

---

dollars). Units of measurement can be abbreviated in charts and graphs (*4 in.*) but not in the body of a paper (*four inches*).

46g Use other abbreviations according to convention.

Some abbreviations required in notes and in source citations are not appropriate in the body of a paper.

CHAPTER AND PAGES	chapter, page, pages (*not* ch., p., pp.)
MONTHS	January, February (*not* Jan., Feb.)
STATES AND NATIONS	California, Mexico (*not* Calif., Mex.)
	Two exceptions are Washington, D.C., and U.S.

46h   Spell out numbers expressed in one or two words.

If you can write out a number in one or two words, do so. Use figures for longer numbers.

▶ Her screams were heard by 38 people, none of whom called the police.
thirty-eight

▶ A baseball is held together by ~~two hundred sixteen~~ red stitches.
216

If one of several numbers *of the same kind* in the same sentence requires a figure, you should use figures for all the numbers in that sentence.

▶ An audio system can range in cost from ~~one hundred dollars~~ to $2,599.
$100

46i   Spell out numbers that begin sentences.

When a sentence begins with a number, either spell out the number or rewrite the sentence.

▶ ~~119~~ years of CIA labor cost taxpayers sixteen million dollars.
One hundred nineteen

Most readers find it easier to read figures than three-word numbers; thus the best solution may be to rewrite this sentence: *Taxpayers spent sixteen million dollars for 119 years of CIA labor.*

46j   Use figures according to convention.

ADDRESSES	23 Main Street; 175 Fifth Avenue
DATES	September 17, 1951; 6 June 1983; 4 BCE; the 1860s
DECIMALS AND FRACTIONS	65.34; 8^1/$_2$
PERCENTAGES	77 percent (*or* 77%)
EXACT AMOUNTS OF MONEY	$7,348; $1.46 trillion; $2.50; thirty-five (*or* 35) cents
SCORES AND STATISTICS	an 8–3 Red Sox victory; a verbal score of 600; an average age of 22; a mean of 53
TIME OF DAY	6:00 AM (*or* a.m.)

FOR MULTILINGUAL WRITERS

Using the Term *Hundred*

The term *hundred* is used idiomatically in English. When it is linked with numbers like two, eight, and so on, the word *hundred* remains singular: *Eight hundred years have passed and still old animosities run deep.* Add the plural *-s* to *hundred* only when no number precedes the term: *Hundreds of priceless books were lost in the fire.*

➡ **bedfordstmartins.com/everydaywriter**
Exercise Central > Abbreviations and Numbers

Italics 47

The slanted type known as *italics* is more than just a pretty typeface. Indeed, italics give words special meaning or emphasis. In the sentence "Many people read *People* on the subway every day," the italics (and the capital letter) tell us that *People* is a publication. You may use your computer to produce italic type; if not, underline words that you would otherwise italicize.

AT A GLANCE

Editing for Italics

- Check that all titles of long works are italicized. (47a)
- If you use any words, letters, or numbers as terms, make sure they are in italics. (47b)
- Italicize any non-English words or phrases that are not in an English dictionary. (47c)

47a Italicize titles of long works.

In general, use italics for titles of long works; use quotation marks for shorter works (43c).

BOOKS	*Fun Home: A Family Tragicomic*
CHOREOGRAPHIC WORKS	Agnes de Mille's *Rodeo*

FILMS AND VIDEOS	*Avatar*
LONG MUSICAL WORKS	*Brandenburg Concertos*
LONG POEMS	*Bhagavad Gita*
MAGAZINES AND JOURNALS	*Ebony*, the *New England Journal of Medicine*
NEWSPAPERS	the *Cleveland Plain Dealer*
PAINTINGS AND SCULPTURE	Georgia O'Keeffe's *Black Iris*
PAMPHLETS	Thomas Paine's *Common Sense*
PLAYS	*Sweeney Todd*
RADIO SERIES	*All Things Considered*
RECORDINGS	*Slade Alive!*
SOFTWARE	*Dreamweaver*
TELEVISION SERIES	*The Wire*
WEB SITES	*Voice of the Shuttle*

47b Italicize words, letters, and numbers used as terms.

▶ On the back of his jersey was the famous 24.
▶ One characteristic of some New York speech is the absence of postvocalic *r*—for example, pronouncing the word *four* as "fouh."

47c Italicize non-English words and phrases.

Italicize words from other languages unless they have become part of English—like the French "bourgeois" or the Italian "pasta," for example. If a word is in an English dictionary, it does not need italics.

▶ At last one of the phantom sleighs gliding along the street would come to a stop, and with gawky haste Mr. Burness in his fox-furred *shapka* would make for our door.   – VLADIMIR NABOKOV, *Speak, Memory*

Hyphens **48**

H yphens are undoubtedly confusing to many
people — hyphen problems are now one
of the twenty most common surface errors in
student writing. The confusion is understandable. Over time, the conventions for hyphen
use in a given word can change (*tomorrow* was
once spelled *to-morrow*). New words, even compounds such as *firewall*, generally don't use hyphens, but controversy continues to rage over
whether to hyphenate *email* (or is it *e-mail*?). And some words are hyphenated when they serve one kind of purpose in a sentence and not
when they serve another.

48a Use hyphens with compound words.

Some compounds are one word (*rowboat, pickup*), some are separate
words (*hard drive*), and some require hyphens (*sister-in-law*). You should
consult a dictionary to be sure. However, the following conventions can
help you decide when to use hyphens with compound words.

Compound adjectives

Hyphenate most compound adjectives that precede a noun but not
those that follow a noun.

a *well-liked* boss	My boss is *well liked*.
a *six-foot* plank	The plank is *six feet long*.

AT A GLANCE

Editing for Hyphens

- Double-check compound words to be sure they are properly closed up,
  separated, or hyphenated. If in doubt, consult a dictionary. (48a)
- Check all terms that have prefixes or suffixes to see whether you need
  hyphens. (48b)
- Do not hyphenate two-word verbs or word groups that serve as subject
  complements. (48c)

In general, the reason for hyphenating compound adjectives is to facilitate reading.

▶ **Designers often use potted plants as living-room dividers.**

Without the hyphen, *living* may seem to modify *room dividers.*

Never hyphenate an *-ly* adverb and an adjective.

▶ **They used a widely⁄distributed mailing list.**

Fractions and compound numbers

Use a hyphen to write out fractions and to spell out compound numbers from twenty-one to ninety-nine.

one-seventh	thirty-seven
two and seven-sixteenths	three hundred fifty-four thousand

48b   Use hyphens with prefixes and suffixes.

Most words containing prefixes or suffixes are written without hyphens: *antiwar, gorillalike.* Here are some exceptions:

BEFORE CAPITALIZED BASE WORDS	un-American, non-Catholic
WITH FIGURES	pre-1960, post-1945
WITH CERTAIN PREFIXES AND SUFFIXES	all-state, ex-partner, self-possessed, quasi-legislative, mayor-elect, fifty-odd
WITH COMPOUND BASE WORDS	pre-high school, post-cold war
FOR CLARITY OR EASE OF READING	re-cover, anti-inflation, troll-like

Re-cover means "cover again"; the hyphen distinguishes it from *recover,* meaning "get well." In *anti-inflation* and *troll-like,* the hyphens separate confusing clusters of vowels and consonants.

48c   Avoid unnecessary hyphens.

Unnecessary hyphens are at least as common a problem as omitted ones. Do not hyphenate the parts of a two-word verb such as *depend on, turn off,* or *tune out* (60b).

▶ **Every player must pick‚up a medical form before football tryouts.**

The words *pick up* act as a verb and should not be hyphenated.

However, be careful to check that two words do indeed function as a verb in the sentence (31b); if they function as an adjective, a hyphen may be needed.

▶ **Let's sign up for the early class.**

The verb *sign up* should not have a hyphen.

▶ **Where is the sign-up sheet?**

The compound adjective *sign-up,* which modifies the noun *sheet,* needs a hyphen.

Do not hyphenate a subject complement—a word group that follows a linking verb (such as a form of *be* or *seem*) and describes the subject (31k).

▶ **Audrey is almost nine‚years‚old.**

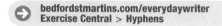

bedfordstmartins.com/everydaywriter
Exercise Central > Hyphens

MLA Documentation

Careful citation shows your reader that you've done your homework. . . . It amounts to laying your intellectual cards on the table.

— JACK LYNCH

MLA Documentation

49 **The Basics of MLA Style**   *403*
  a Think about what readers need from your citation   *403*
  b Identify the type of source you are using   *404*
  c Plan and connect your citations   *407*
  d Include notes as needed   *408*

50 **MLA Style for In-Text Citations**   *409*

51 **MLA Style for a List of Works Cited**   *416*

52 **A Student Research Essay, MLA Style**   *447*

For visual analysis Look carefully at the illustration on the front of this tab. What do you think this image suggests about the kinds of sources writers might document in MLA style?

The Basics of MLA Style **49**

Different rhetorical situations call for different approaches to citing sources—that is, for different ways of answering the question "Says who?" If you're reading a popular magazine, you probably won't expect the writer to provide careful source citations or a list of references at the end of an article. If you're posting material on a blog, you might follow conventions for citation by simply linking to the material you're talking about. But in other situations, including most academic writing, you will be expected to follow a more rigorous system for citing the information you use. Many courses in English ask writers to follow MLA style, the system developed by the Modern Language Association. For further reference, consult Chapters 50–52 or the *MLA Handbook for Writers of Research Papers*, Seventh Edition (2009).

49a Think about what readers need from your citation.

Why does academic work call for very careful citation practices when writing for the general public may not? The answer to that question is pretty easy: readers of your academic work (your instructor, other students, perhaps even researchers and professionals in your field) expect to get certain information from source citations:

- Source citations demonstrate that while you may not yet be a recognized expert on the topic you've nevertheless done your homework, and you are a part of the conversation surrounding it. You include sources that you find credible and that provide evidence and good reasons to back up your claims, as well as sources that you need to respond to or refute (see 17a). Careful citation shows your readers what you know, where you stand, and what you think is important.

- Source citations show that you understand the need to give credit when you make use of someone else's intellectual property.

Especially in academic writing, when it's better to be safe than sorry, include a citation for any source you think you might need to cite. (See Chapter 18 for details.)

- Source citations give explicit directions to guide readers who want to look for themselves at the works you're using.

The guidelines for MLA style (or APA, *Chicago,* or CSE—if you are asked to use these systems, see Chapters 53–55) help you with this last purpose, giving you instructions on exactly what information to include in your citation and how to format that information.

49b Identify the type of source you are using.

Before you can decide how to cite your source following MLA guidelines, you need to determine what kind of source you're using. This task can be surprisingly difficult. Citing a print book may seem relatively easy (though dizzying complications can arise—such as if the book has an editor or a translator, multiple editions, or chapters written by different people, to name a few possibilities). But citing digital sources may be especially mystifying. How, for instance, can you tell a Web site from a database you access online? What if your digital source reuses material from another source? Who publishes a digital text? Taking a step-by-step approach can help you solve such puzzles.

Print, digital, and other media sources

If your source has printed pages—a book or a newspaper, for instance—and you read the print version, you should look at the Directory to MLA Style on p. 416 for information on citing a print source. If the print source is a regularly issued journal, magazine, or newspaper (look for a date or seasonal information such as "Spring 2012" on the cover or first page), consider it a periodical rather than a book.

Be careful, however. If you access the digital version of a magazine or newspaper article, or if you read a book on an e-reader device such as a Kindle, then you should cite your source not as a print text but as a digital one. A digital version of a source may include updates or corrections that the print version lacks, so MLA guidelines require you to indicate your mode of access and to cite print and digital sources differently. Make sure to provide the correct information!

When you need to cite a source that consists mainly of material other than written words—such as a film, song, or artwork—you will need to provide additional information about how you encountered the material. See the Directory to MLA Style on p. 417 for more information on citing multimedia sources.

Articles from Web and database sources

Many students wonder how to distinguish between a Web source and a source from a database. Both, after all, can be reached from a computer (if you have home access to your school library's online resources, you may be able to reach databases from any wired location). But guidelines for citing articles from the two types of sources are different, and so are considerations for using each type of writing.

DATABASE SOURCES

You need a subscription to look through most databases, so individual researchers almost always gain access to articles in databases through the computer system of a school or community library that pays to subscribe. The easiest way to tell whether a source comes from a database, then, is that its information is *not* available for free to anyone with an Internet connection. Many databases are digital collections of articles that originally appeared in print periodicals. The articles generally have the same written-word content as they did in print form, without changes or updates (some databases omit illustrations that appear in the print versions of articles, but others upload articles as PDFs that show not just words and illustrations but also the original print layout and page numbering). Print periodicals have editors, and some journals are peer-reviewed by experts in a field, ensuring that an authority vouches for the accuracy of the information. Finding information in an article from a database does *not* guarantee its credibility, but such information often has more authority behind it than much of what you find for free on the Web.

David Craig, whose research writing appears in Chapter 52, found the following source in Academic Search Premier, a database he accessed through a library Web site. From this page he was able to click through to the full text of the article. He printed this computer screen in

A SOURCE FROM A DATABASE

① Author   **③** Periodical title   **⑤** Database name

② Article title   **④** Print publication data

case he needed to cite the article; the image includes all the information (other than his date of access) that he would need to create a complete MLA citation for an article from a database. Including the original print publication information for the article and the name of the database allows any reader who can access the database to locate the same article.

WEB SOURCES

Almost anyone can create a page on the Web, and information posted there often has not been verified by anyone. Therefore, MLA guidelines ask you to identify the publisher or sponsor for any work from a Web site that you cite in your writing. Information about sponsors and publishers often appears at the bottom of a page, on a home page, or in a separate "About" section on a reputable Web site (see pp. 198–99 in Chapter 17 for details on evaluating Web sources).

If the site doesn't identify a sponsor or publisher, you may still use it (see pp. 436–37), but you should do more digging to find out about the site's creator, and you would be wise to verify information on such a site before including it in your own text. David Craig looked at a Web site called "Text Message 101" while doing his preliminary research; although no author was identified, the information seemed useful. But when he noticed that the site's sponsor was a cell phone provider using the site to sell phone plans, he decided against using the source in his writing project.

Teal Pfeifer, whose paper on how media messages affect body image appears in Chapter 14, downloaded this article by Dr. Sut Jhally, a professor of media studies, from the author's personal Web site.

A WORK FROM A WEB SITE

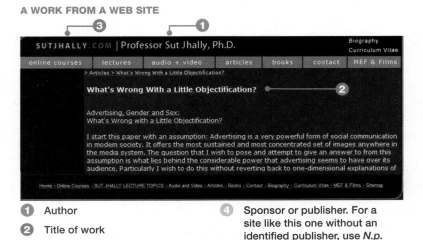

① Author

② Title of work

③ Title of Web site

④ Sponsor or publisher. For a site like this one without an identified publisher, use *N.p.*

⑤ Date of publication. For undated material such as this, use *n.d.*

Web sources for content beyond the written word

Many sources used in academic writing consist mainly of written words, presented either in print or in digital form. But you may also want to include sources in which images and other media are at least as important as written words. Figuring out which model to follow for media sources that appear online can pose additional questions.

While researching her PowerPoint presentation on Alison Bechdel's graphic memoir *Fun Home* (see Chapter 3), Shuqiao Song came across a brief video interview with Bechdel on YouTube that she wanted to play for her audience. However, the YouTube post noted that the interview had originally appeared on a video log called *Stuck in Vermont* and that this interview grew out of, and included passages from, a print interview from a small local print publication. (This kind of complicated backstory is by no means unusual for online media.) Shuqiao had to decide whether the video clip was most like a video, an interview, a work from a Web site, or something else entirely. After consulting with her instructor, she decided to give the full citation for the source as a work from a Web site (see the source map on pp. 436–37), since a YouTube citation seemed likely to make the source most accessible to those who saw her presentation. (For advice on making such decisions when no exact model is available, see the box on p. 440.)

49c Plan and connect your citations.

MLA citations appear in two parts—the brief in-text citation, usually in parentheses in the body of your written text, and the full citation in the list of works cited, to which the in-text citation directs your readers. The most straightforward in-text citations include the author's name and the page number, but many variations on this basic format are discussed in Chapter 50.

In the text of his research essay (see Chapter 52), David Craig includes a paraphrase of material from the print book *Language Play* by linguist David Crystal. As shown here, he cites the book page on which the original information appears in a parenthetical reference that points readers to the entry for "Crystal, David" in his list of works cited. He also cites statistics from a report with four named authors that he found on a Web site sponsored by the nonprofit Pew Internet & American Life Project. The report, like many online texts, does not include page numbers. These examples show just two of the many ways to cite sources using in-text citations and a list of works cited. You'll need to make case-by-case decisions based on the types of sources you include. For more information on in-text citation practices, see Chapter 50; to find models of types of sources for the list of works cited, consult Chapter 51.

to David Crystal, an internationally recognized scholar of linguistics at the University of Wales, as young children develop and learn how words string together to express ideas, they go through many phases of language play. The singsong rhymes and nonsensical chants of preschoolers are vital to their learning language, and a healthy appetite for such wordplay leads to a better command of language later in life (182).

Craig 10

Year Trend in SAT Scores *Is Yielding Results: Reading and Writing Are Causes for Concern*. New York: College Board, 2002. Print.

College Board. "2011 SAT Trends." *Collegeboard.org*. College Board, 14 Sept. 2011. Web. 6 Dec. 2011.

Crystal, David. *Language Play*. Chicago: U of Chicago P, 1998. Print.

The Discouraging Word. "Re: Messaging and Literacy." Message to the author. 13 Nov. 2011. E-mail.

"Is Texting Destroying Kids' Writing Style?" *Curriculum Review* 48.1 (2008): 4-5. *Academic Search Premier*. Web. 7 Dec. 2011.

Leibowitz, Wendy R. "Technology Transforms Writing and the Teaching of Writing." *Chronicle of Higher Education* 26 Nov. 1999: A67-68. Print.

Lenhart, Amanda, Sousan Arafeh, Aaron Smith, and Alexandra Macgill. *Writing, Technology & Teens*. Washington: Pew Internet & Amer. Life Project, 2008. Web. 6 Dec. 2011.

the rise. According to the Pew Internet & American Life Project, 85 percent of those aged 12-17 at least occasionally write text messages, instant messages, or comments on social networking sites (Lenhart, Arafeh, Smith, and Macgill). In 2001, the most

eenage Life Online: The Rise of and the Internet's Impact on hips. Washington: Pew Internet . 6 Dec. 2011.

McCarroll, Christina. "Teens Ready to Prove Text-Messaging Skills Can Score SAT Points." *Christian Science Monitor* 11 Mar. 2005. Web. 10 Dec. 2011.

49d Include notes as needed.

MLA citation style asks you to include explanatory notes for information or comments that don't readily fit into your text but are needed for clarification or further explanation. In addition, MLA permits bibliographic notes for offering information about or evaluation of a source, or to list multiple sources that relate to a single point. Use superscript numbers in the text to refer readers to the notes, which may appear as endnotes (under the heading *Notes* on a separate page immediately before the list of works cited) or as footnotes at the bottom of each page where a superscript number appears.

Although messaging relies on the written word, many messagers disregard standard writing conventions. For example, here is a snippet from an IM conversation between two teenage girls:[1]

1. This transcript of an IM conversation was collected on 20 Nov. 2011. The teenagers' names are concealed to protect their privacy.

MLA Style for In-Text Citations   50

MLA style requires a citation in the text of an essay for every quotation, paraphrase, summary, or other material requiring documentation (see 18f). In-text citations document material from other sources with both signal phrases and parenthetical references. Parenthetical references should include the information your readers need to locate the full reference in the list of works cited at the end of the text. (See Chapter 51.) An in-text citation in MLA style gives the reader two kinds of information: (1) it indicates which source on the works-cited page the writer is referring to, and (2) it explains where in the source the material quoted, paraphrased, or summarized can be found, if the source has page numbers or other numbered sections.

The basic MLA in-text citation includes the author's last name either in a signal phrase introducing the source material (see 18b) or in parentheses at the end of the sentence. For print sources, it also includes the page number in parentheses at the end of the sentence.

DIRECTORY TO MLA STYLE

MLA style for in-text citations

1. Author named in a signal phrase, *410*
2. Author named in a parenthetical reference, *410*
3. Two or three authors, *411*
4. Four or more authors, *411*
5. Organization as author, *411*

DIRECTORY TO MLA STYLE

MLA style for in-text citations, continued

6. Unknown author, *411*
7. Author of two or more works cited in the same project, *411*
8. Two or more authors with the same last name, *411*
9. Indirect source (author quoting someone else), *412*
10. Multivolume work, *412*
11. Literary work, *412*
12. Work in an anthology or collection, *413*

13. Sacred text, *413*
14. Encyclopedia or dictionary entry, *413*
15. Government source with no author named, *413*
16. Electronic or nonprint source, *413*
17. Entire work, *414*
18. Two or more sources in one parenthetical reference, *414*
19. Visual included in the text, *414*

SAMPLE CITATION USING A SIGNAL PHRASE

In his discussion of Monty Python routines, Crystal notes that the group relished "breaking the normal rules" of language (107).

SAMPLE PARENTHETICAL CITATION

A noted linguist explains that Monty Python humor often relied on "bizarre linguistic interactions" (Crystal 108).

> bedfordstmartins.com/everydaywriter
> **Documenting Sources**

Note in the following examples where punctuation is placed in relation to the parentheses.

1. AUTHOR NAMED IN A SIGNAL PHRASE

The MLA recommends using the author's name in a signal phrase to introduce the material and citing the page number(s) in parentheses.

Lee claims that his comic-book creation, Thor, was "the first regularly published superhero to speak in a consistently archaic manner" (199).

2. AUTHOR NAMED IN A PARENTHETICAL REFERENCE

When you do not mention the author in a signal phrase, include the author's last name before the page number(s) in the parentheses. Use no punctuation between the author's name and the page number(s).

The word *Bollywood* is sometimes considered an insult because it implies that Indian movies are merely "a derivative of the American film industry" (Chopra 9).

3. TWO OR THREE AUTHORS

Use all the authors' last names in a signal phrase or in parentheses.

Gortner, Hebrun, and Nicolson maintain that "opinion leaders" influence other people in an organization because they are respected, not because they hold high positions (175).

4. FOUR OR MORE AUTHORS

Name all the authors in a signal phrase or in parentheses, or use the first author's name and *et al.* ("and others").

Similarly, as Belenky, Clinchy, Tarule, and Goldberger assert, examining the lives of women expands our understanding of human development (7).

Similarly, as Belenky et al. assert, examining the lives of women expands our understanding of human development (7).

5. ORGANIZATION AS AUTHOR

Give the group's full name or a shortened form of it in a signal phrase or in parentheses.

Any study of social welfare involves a close analysis of "the impacts, the benefits, and the costs" of its policies (Social Research Corporation iii).

6. UNKNOWN AUTHOR

Use the full title, if it is brief, in your text—or a shortened version of the title in parentheses.

One analysis defines *hype* as "an artificially engendered atmosphere of hysteria" ("Today's Marketplace" 51).

7. AUTHOR OF TWO OR MORE WORKS CITED IN THE SAME PROJECT

If your list of works cited has more than one work by the same author, include a shortened version of the title of the work you are citing in a signal phrase or in parentheses to prevent reader confusion.

Gardner shows readers their own silliness in his description of a "pointless, ridiculous monster, crouched in the shadows, stinking of dead men, murdered children, and martyred cows" (*Grendel* 2).

8. TWO OR MORE AUTHORS WITH THE SAME LAST NAME

Include the author's first *and* last names in a signal phrase or first initial and last name in a parenthetical reference.

Children will learn to write if they are allowed to choose their own subjects, James Britton asserts, citing the Schools Council study of the 1960s (37-42).

9. INDIRECT SOURCE (AUTHOR QUOTING SOMEONE ELSE)

Use the abbreviation *qtd. in* to indicate that you are quoting from someone else's report of a source.

As Arthur Miller says, "When somebody is destroyed everybody finally contributes to it, but in Willy's case, the end product would be virtually the same" (qtd. in Martin and Meyer 375).

10. MULTIVOLUME WORK

In a parenthetical reference, note the volume number first and then the page number(s), with a colon and one space between them.

Modernist writers prized experimentation and gradually even sought to blur the line between poetry and prose, according to Forster (3: 150).

If you name only one volume of the work in your list of works cited, include only the page number in the parentheses.

11. LITERARY WORK

Because literary works are often available in many different editions, cite the page number(s) from the edition you used followed by a semi-colon, and then give other identifying information that will lead readers to the passage in any edition. Indicate the act and/or scene in a play (*37; sc. 1*). For a novel, indicate the part or chapter (*175; ch. 4*).

In utter despair, Dostoyevsky's character Mitya wonders aloud about the "terrible tragedies realism inflicts on people" (376; bk. 8, ch. 2).

For a poem, cite the part (if there is one) and line(s), separated by a period. If you are citing only line numbers, use the word *line(s)* in the first reference (*lines 33–34).*

Whitman speculates, "All goes onward and outward, nothing collapses, / And to die is different from what anyone supposed, and luckier" (6.129-30).

For a verse play, give only the act, scene, and line numbers, separated by periods.

The witches greet Banquo as "Lesser than Macbeth, and greater" (1.3.65).

12. WORK IN AN ANTHOLOGY OR COLLECTION

For an essay, short story, or other piece of prose reprinted in an anthology, use the name of the author of the work, not the editor of the anthology, but use the page number(s) from the anthology.

> Narratives of captivity play a major role in early writing by women in the
> United States, as demonstrated by Silko (219).

13. SACRED TEXT

To cite a sacred text such as the Qur'an or the Bible, give the title of the edition you used, the book, and the chapter and verse (or their equivalent) separated by a period. In your text, spell out the names of books. In parenthetical references, use abbreviations for books with names of five or more letters (*Gen.* for *Genesis*).

> He ignored the admonition "Pride goes before destruction, and a haughty
> spirit before a fall" (*New Oxford Annotated Bible,* Prov. 16.18).

14. ENCYCLOPEDIA OR DICTIONARY ENTRY

An entry from a reference work—such as an encyclopedia or dictionary—without an author will appear on the works-cited list under the entry's title. Enclose the title in quotation marks and place it in parentheses. Omit the page number for reference works that arrange entries alphabetically.

> The term *prion* was coined by Stanley B. Prusiner from the words
> *proteinaceous* and *infectious* and a suffix meaning *particle* ("Prion").

15. GOVERNMENT SOURCE WITH NO AUTHOR NAMED

Because entries for sources authored by government agencies will appear on your list of works cited under the name of the country (see Chapter 51, item 70), your in-text citation for such a source should include the name of the country as well as the name of the agency responsible for the source.

> To reduce the agricultural runoff into the Chesapeake Bay, the United States
> Environmental Protection Agency has argued that "[h]igh nutrient loading
> crops, such as corn and soybean, should be replaced with alternatives in
> environmentally sensitive areas" (2-26).

16. ELECTRONIC OR NONPRINT SOURCE

Give enough information in a signal phrase or in parentheses for readers to locate the source in your list of works cited. Many works found online or in electronic databases lack stable page numbers; you can omit the page number in such cases. However, if you are citing a work with stable pagination, such as an article in PDF format, include the page number in parentheses.

> As a *Slate* analysis has noted, "Prominent sports psychologists get praised for their successes and don't get grief for their failures" (Engber).

The source, an article on a Web site, does not have stable pagination.

> According to Whitmarsh, the British military had experimented with using balloons for observation as far back as 1879 (328).

The source, an online PDF of a print article, includes stable page numbers.

If the source includes numbered sections, paragraphs, or screens, include the abbreviation (*sec.*), paragraph (*par.*), or screen (*scr.*) number in parentheses.

> Sherman notes that the "immediate, interactive, and on-the-spot" nature of Internet information can make nondigital media seem outdated (sec. 32).

17. ENTIRE WORK

Include the reference in the text, without any page numbers.

> Jon Krakauer's *Into the Wild* both criticizes and admires the solitary impulses of its young hero, which end up killing him.

18. TWO OR MORE SOURCES IN ONE PARENTHETICAL REFERENCE

Separate the information with semicolons.

> Economists recommend that *employment* be redefined to include unpaid domestic labor (Clark 148; Nevins 39).

19. VISUAL INCLUDED IN THE TEXT

When you include an image in your text, number it and include a parenthetical reference in your text (*see Fig.* 2). Number figures (photos, drawings, cartoons, maps, graphs, and charts) and tables separately. Each visual should include a caption with the figure or table number and information about the source—either a complete citation or enough information to direct readers to the works-cited entry. (See 9d.)

> This trend is illustrated in a chart distributed by the College Board as part of its 2011 analysis of aggregate SAT data (see Fig. 1).

Soon after the preceding sentence, readers find the following figure and a caption referring them to the entry on the list of works cited (see Chapter 52 to read the student's entire research paper):

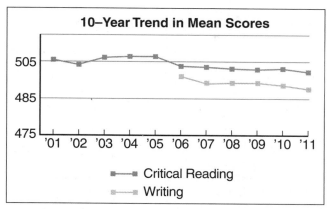

Fig. 1. Ten-year trend in mean SAT reading and writing scores (2001-2011). Source: College Board, "2011 SAT Trends."

An image that you create might appear with a caption like this (see 14k to see this example used in a student essay):

Fig. 4. Young women reading magazines. Personal photograph by author.

51 MLA Style for a List of Works Cited

A list of works cited is an alphabetical list of the sources you have referred to in your essay. (If your instructor asks you to list everything you have read as background, call the list *Works Consulted*.)

> bedfordstmartins.com/everydaywriter
> **Documenting Sources**

DIRECTORY TO MLA STYLE

MLA style for a list of works cited

Guidelines for author listings

1. One author, *419*
2. Multiple authors, *419*
3. Organization or group author, *419*
4. Unknown author, *419*
5. Two or more works by the same author, *419*

Print books

6. Basic format for a book, *420*
   SOURCE MAP, *422–23*
7. Author and editor both named, *420*
8. Editor, no author named, *420*
9. Anthology, *420*
10. Work in an anthology or chapter in a book with an editor, *421*
11. Two or more items from the same anthology, *421*
12. Translation, *421*
13. Book with both translator and editor, *421*
14. Translation of a section of a book, *421*
15. Translation of a book by an unknown author, *424*
16. Book in a language other than English, *424*

17. Graphic narrative, *424*
18. Edition other than the first, *425*
19. One volume of a multivolume work, *425*
20. Two or more volumes of a multivolume work, *425*
21. Preface, foreword, introduction, or afterward, *425*
22. Entry in a reference book, *425*
23. Book that is part of a series, *425*
24. Republication (modern edition of an older book), *425*
25. Publisher's imprint, *426*
26. Book with a title within the title, *426*
27. Sacred text, *426*

Print periodicals

28. Article in a print journal, *426*
29. Article in a print magazine, *426*
    SOURCE MAP, *428–29*
30. Article in a print newspaper, *427*
31. Article that skips pages, *427*
32. Editorial or letter to the editor, *427*
33. Review, *427*
34. Unsigned article, *430*

MLA style for a list of works cited, continued

Digital written-word sources

35. Work from a database, *431*
    SOURCE MAP, *432–33*
36. Article from the Web site of a journal, *431*
37. Article in a magazine on the Web, *431*
38. Article in a newspaper on the Web, *431*
39. Book on the Web, *434*
40. Poem on the Web, *434*
41. Editorial or letter in a Web periodical, *434*
42. Review in a Web periodical, *434*
43. Entry in a Web reference work, *435*
44. Work from a Web site, *435*
    SOURCE MAP, *436–37*
45. Entire Web site, *435*
46. Academic course Web site, *438*
47. Blog, *438*
48. Post or comment on a blog, *438*
49. Entry in a wiki, *438*
50. Posting to a discussion group or newsgroup, *439*
51. Posting to a social networking site, *439*
52. Email or message on social networking site, *439*
53. Tweet, *439*

Visual, audio, multimedia, and live sources

54. Film or DVD, *440*
55. Online video clip, *440*
56. Television or radio program, *440*
57. Broadcast interview, *441*
58. Unpublished or personal interview, *441*
59. Sound recording, *441*
60. Musical composition, *442*
61. Computer game, *442*
62. Lecture or speech, *442*
63. Live performance, *443*
64. Podcast (streaming), *443*
65. Digital file, *443*
66. Work of art or photograph, *443*
67. Map or chart, *444*
68. Cartoon or comic strip, *444*
69. Advertisement, *445*

Academic, government, and legal sources (including digital versions)

70. Report or pamphlet, *445*
71. Government publication, *445*
72. Published proceedings of a conference, *446*
73. Dissertation, *446*
74. Dissertation abstract, *446*
75. Published interview, *446*
76. Unpublished letter, *446*
77. Manuscript or other unpublished work, *447*
78. Legal source, *447*

Guidelines for author listings

The list of works cited is arranged alphabetically. The in-text citations in your writing point readers toward particular sources on the list (see Chapter 50).

NAME CITED IN SIGNAL PHRASE IN TEXT

Crystal explains. . . .

NAME IN PARENTHETICAL CITATION IN TEXT

. . . (Crystal 107).

BEGINNING OF ENTRY ON LIST OF WORKS CITED

Crystal, David.

AT A GLANCE

Formatting a List of Works Cited

- Start your list on a separate page after the text of your document and any notes.
- Continue the consecutive numbering of pages.
- Center the heading *Works Cited* (not italicized or in quotation marks) one inch from the top of the page.
- Begin each entry flush with the left margin, but indent subsequent lines one-half inch. Double-space the entire list.
- List sources alphabetically by the first word. Start with the author's name, if available; if not, use the editor's name, if available. If no author or editor is given, start with the title.
- List the author's last name first, followed by a comma and the first name. If a source has multiple authors, subsequent authors' names appear first name first (see model 2).
- Italicize titles of books and long works, but put titles of articles and other short works in quotation marks.
- In general, use a period and a space after each element of the entry; look at the models in this chapter for information on punctuating particular kinds of entries.
- For a book, list the city of publication (add a country abbreviation for non-U.S. cities that may be unfamiliar). Follow it with a colon and a shortened form of the publisher's name — omit *Co.* or *Inc.*, shorten names such as *Simon & Schuster* to *Simon*, and abbreviate *University Press* to *UP*.
- List dates of periodical publication or of access to electronic items in day, month, year order, and abbreviate months except for May, June, and July.
- Give a medium, such as *Print* or *Web*, for each entry.
- List inclusive page numbers for a part of a larger work.

Models 1–5 on p. 419 explain how to arrange author names. The information that follows the name of the author depends on the type of work you are citing—a book (models 6–27); a print periodical (models 28–34); a written text from a digital source, such as an article from a Web site or database (models 35–53); sources from art, film, comics, or other media, including live performances (models 54–69); and academic, government, and legal sources (models 70–78). Consult the model that most closely resembles the kind of source you are using.

1. ONE AUTHOR

Put the last name first, followed by a comma, the first name (and initial, if any), and a period.

Crystal, David.

2. MULTIPLE AUTHORS

List the first author with the last name first (see model 1). Give the names of any other authors with the first name first. Separate authors' names with commas, and include the word *and* before the last person's name.

Martineau, Jane, Desmond Shawe-Taylor, and Jonathan Bate.

For four or more authors, either list all the names, or list the first author followed by a comma and *et al.* ("and others").

Lupton, Ellen, Jennifer Tobias, Alicia Imperiale, Grace Jeffers, and Randi Mates.

Lupton, Ellen, et al.

3. ORGANIZATION OR GROUP AUTHOR

Give the name of the group, government agency, corporation, or other organization listed as the author.

Getty Trust.

United States. Government Accountability Office.

4. UNKNOWN AUTHOR

When the author is not identified, begin the entry with the title, and alphabetize by the first important word. Italicize titles of books and long works, but put titles of articles and other short works in quotation marks.

"California Sues EPA over Emissions."

New Concise World Atlas.

5. TWO OR MORE WORKS BY THE SAME AUTHOR

Arrange the entries alphabetically by title. Include the author's name in the first entry, but in subsequent entries, use three hyphens followed by a period. (For the basic format for citing a book, see model 6. For the basic format for citing an article from an online newspaper, see model 38.)

> Chopra, Anupama. "Bollywood Princess, Hollywood Hopeful." *New York Times*.
> New York Times, 10 Feb. 2008. Web. 13 Feb. 2008.
>
> ---. *King of Bollywood: Shah Rukh Khan and the Seductive World of Indian*
> *Cinema*. New York: Warner, 2007. Print.

Note: Use three hyphens only when the work is by *exactly* the same author(s) as the previous entry.

Print books

6. BASIC FORMAT FOR A BOOK

Begin with the author name(s). (See models 1–5.) Then include the title and subtitle, the city of publication, the publisher, the publication year, and the medium (*Print*). The source map on pp. 422–23 shows where to find this information in a typical book.

> Crystal, David. *Language Play*. Chicago: U of Chicago P, 1998. Print.

Note: Place a period and a space after the name, title, and date. Place a colon after the city and a comma after the publisher, and shorten the publisher's name—omit *Co.* or *Inc.,* and abbreviate *University Press* to *UP*.

7. AUTHOR AND EDITOR BOTH NAMED

> Bangs, Lester. *Psychotic Reactions and Carburetor Dung*. Ed. Greil Marcus.
> New York: Knopf, 1988. Print.

Note: To cite the editor's contribution instead, begin the entry with the editor's name.

> Marcus, Greil, ed. *Psychotic Reactions and Carburetor Dung*. By Lester Bangs.
> New York: Knopf, 1988. Print.

8. EDITOR, NO AUTHOR NAMED

> Wall, Cheryl A., ed. *Changing Our Own Words: Essays on Criticism, Theory, and*
> *Writing by Black Women*. New Brunswick: Rutgers UP, 1989. Print.

9. ANTHOLOGY

Cite an entire anthology the same way you would cite a book with an editor and no named author (see model 8).

> Walker, Dale L., ed. *Westward: A Fictional History of the American West*.
> New York: Forge, 2003. Print.

10. WORK IN AN ANTHOLOGY OR CHAPTER IN A BOOK WITH AN EDITOR

List the author(s) of the selection or chapter; its title, in quotation marks; the title of the book, italicized; *Ed.* and the name(s) of the editor(s); publication information; and the selection's page numbers.

> Komunyakaa, Yusef. "Facing It." *The Seagull Reader*. Ed. Joseph Kelly. New York: Norton, 2000. 126-27. Print.

Note: Use the following format to provide original publication information for a reprinted selection:

> Byatt, A. S. "The Thing in the Forest." *New Yorker* 3 June 2002: 80-89. Rpt. in *The O. Henry Prize Stories 2003*. Ed. Laura Furman. New York: Anchor, 2003. 3-22. Print.

11. TWO OR MORE ITEMS FROM THE SAME ANTHOLOGY

List the anthology as one entry (see model 9). Also list each selection separately with a cross-reference to the anthology.

> Estleman, Loren D. "Big Tim Magoon and the Wild West." Walker 391-404. Print.

> Salzer, Susan K. "Miss Libbie Tells All." Walker 199-212. Print.

12. TRANSLATION

> Bolaño, Roberto. *2666*. Trans. Natasha Wimmer. New York: Farrar, 2008. Print.

13. BOOK WITH BOTH TRANSLATOR AND EDITOR

List the editor's and translator's names after the title, in the order they appear on the title page.

> Kant, Immanuel. *"Toward Perpetual Peace" and Other Writings on Politics, Peace, and History*. Ed. Pauline Kleingeld. Trans. David L. Colclasure. New Haven: Yale UP, 2006. Print.

14. TRANSLATION OF A SECTION OF A BOOK

If different translators have worked on various parts of the book, identify the translator of the part you are citing.

> García Lorca, Federico. "The Little Mad Boy." Trans. W. S. Merwin. *The Selected Poems of Federico García Lorca*. Ed. Francisco García Lorca and Donald M. Allen. London: Penguin, 1969. Print.

MLA SOURCE MAP: Books

Take information from the book's title page and copyright page (on the reverse side of the title page), not from the book's cover or a library catalog.

1 **Author.** List the last name first. End with a period. For variations, see models 2–5.

2 **Title.** Italicize the title and any subtitle; capitalize all major words. End with a period.

3 **City of publication.** If more than one city is given, use the first one listed. For foreign cities, add an abbreviation of the country or province (*Cork, Ire.*). Follow it with a colon.

4 **Publisher.** Give a shortened version of the publisher's name (*Oxford UP* for *Oxford University Press*). Follow it with a comma.

5 **Year of publication.** If more than one copyright date is given, use the most recent one. End with a period.

6 **Medium of publication.** End with the medium (*Print*) followed by a period.

A citation for the book on p. 423 would look like this:

Patel, Raj. *The Value of Nothing: How to Reshape Market Society and Redefine Democracy.* New York: Picador, 2009. Print.

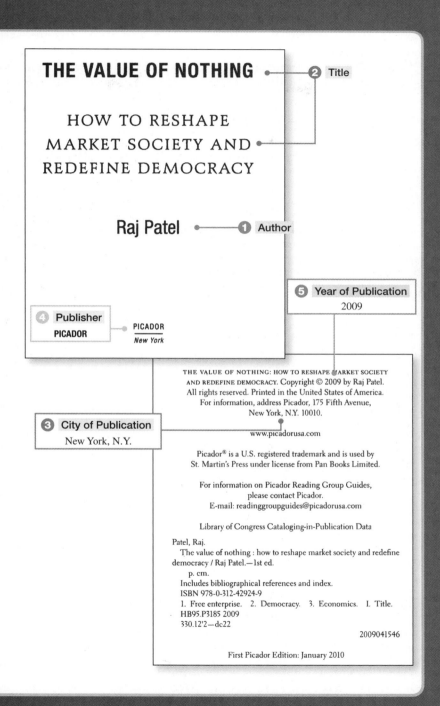

THE VALUE OF NOTHING

2 Title

HOW TO RESHAPE MARKET SOCIETY AND REDEFINE DEMOCRACY

Raj Patel

1 Author

5 Year of Publication
2009

4 Publisher
PICADOR

PICADOR
New York

THE VALUE OF NOTHING: HOW TO RESHAPE MARKET SOCIETY
AND REDEFINE DEMOCRACY. Copyright © 2009 by Raj Patel.
All rights reserved. Printed in the United States of America.
For information, address Picador, 175 Fifth Avenue,
New York, N.Y. 10010.

www.picadorusa.com

Picador® is a U.S. registered trademark and is used by
St. Martin's Press under license from Pan Books Limited.

For information on Picador Reading Group Guides,
please contact Picador.
E-mail: readinggroupguides@picadorusa.com

Library of Congress Cataloging-in-Publication Data

Patel, Raj.
    The value of nothing : how to reshape market society and redefine
democracy / Raj Patel.—1st ed.
        p. cm.
    Includes bibliographical references and index.
    ISBN 978-0-312-42924-9
    1. Free enterprise.   2. Democracy.   3. Economics.   I. Title.
    HB95.P3185 2009
    330.12'2—dc22

                                        2009041546

        First Picador Edition: January 2010

3 City of Publication
New York, N.Y.

AT A GLANCE

Combining Parts of Models

What should you do if your source doesn't match the model exactly? Suppose, for instance, that your source is a translated essay that appears in the fifth edition of an anthology.

- Identify a basic model to follow. If you decide that your source looks most like an essay in an anthology, you would start with a citation that looks like model 10.

- Look for models that show the additional elements in your source. For this example, you would need to add elements of model 14 (for the translation) and model 18 (for an edition other than the first).

- Add new elements from other models to your basic model in the order indicated.

- If you still aren't sure how to arrange the pieces to create a combination model, check the *MLA Handbook* or ask your instructor.

---

15. TRANSLATION OF A BOOK BY AN UNKNOWN AUTHOR

Grettir's Saga. Trans. Denton Fox and Hermann Palsson. Toronto: U of Toronto P, 1974. Print.

16. BOOK IN A LANGUAGE OTHER THAN ENGLISH

Include a translation of the title in brackets, if necessary.

Benedetti, Mario. *La borra del café [The Coffee Grind]*. Buenos Aires: Sudamericana, 2000. Print.

17. GRAPHIC NARRATIVE

If the words and images are created by the same person, cite a graphic narrative just as you would a book (model 6).

Bechdel, Alison. *Fun Home: A Family Tragicomic*. New York: Houghton, 2006. Print.

If the work is a collaboration, indicate the author or illustrator who is most important to your research before the title of the work. List other contributors after the title, in the order of their appearance on the title page. Label each person's contribution to the work.

Stavans, Ilan, writer. *Latino USA: A Cartoon History*. Illus. Lalo Arcaraz. New York: Basic, 2000. Print.

18. EDITION OTHER THAN THE FIRST

> Walker, John A. *Art in the Age of Mass Media*. 3rd ed. London: Pluto, 2001.
> Print.

19. ONE VOLUME OF A MULTIVOLUME WORK

Give the number of the volume cited after the title. Including the total number of volumes after the publication date is optional.

> Ch'oe, Yong-Ho, Peter Lee, and William Theodore De Barry, eds. *Sources of Korean Tradition*. Vol. 2. New York: Columbia UP, 2000. Print. 2 vols.

20. TWO OR MORE VOLUMES OF A MULTIVOLUME WORK

> Ch'oe, Yong-Ho, Peter Lee, and William Theodore De Barry, eds. *Sources of Korean Tradition*. 2 vols. New York: Columbia UP, 2000. Print.

21. PREFACE, FOREWORD, INTRODUCTION, OR AFTERWORD

After the writer's name, describe the contribution. After the title, indicate the book's author (with *By*) or editor (with *Ed.*).

> Atwan, Robert. Foreword. *The Best American Essays 2002*. Ed. Stephen Jay Gould.
> Boston: Houghton, 2002. viii-xii. Print.

> Moore, Thurston. Introduction. *Confusion Is Next: The Sonic Youth Story*. By Alec
> Foege. New York: St. Martin's, 1994. xi. Print.

22. ENTRY IN A REFERENCE BOOK

For a well-known encyclopedia, note the edition (if identified) and year of publication. If the entries are alphabetized, omit publication information and page number.

> Kettering, Alison McNeil. "Art Nouveau." *World Book Encyclopedia*. 2002 ed.
> Print.

23. BOOK THAT IS PART OF A SERIES

Cite the series name (and number, if any) from the title page.

> Nichanian, Marc, and Vartan Matiossian, eds. *Yeghishe Charents: Poet of the Revolution*. Costa Mesa: Mazda, 2003. Print. Armenian Studies Ser. 5.

24. REPUBLICATION (MODERN EDITION OF AN OLDER BOOK)

Indicate the original publication date after the title.

> Austen, Jane. *Sense and Sensibility*. 1813. New York: Dover, 1996. Print.

25. PUBLISHER'S IMPRINT

If the title page gives a publisher's imprint, hyphenate the imprint and the publisher's name.

> Hornby, Nick. *About a Boy*. New York: Riverhead-Penguin Putnam, 1998. Print.

26. BOOK WITH A TITLE WITHIN THE TITLE

Do not italicize a book title within a title. For an article title within a title, italicize as usual and place the article title in quotation marks.

> Mullaney, Julie. *Arundhati Roy's* The God of Small Things: *A Reader's Guide*.
> New York: Continuum, 2002. Print.

> Rhynes, Martha. *"I, Too, Sing America": The Story of Langston Hughes*.
> Greensboro: Morgan, 2002. Print.

27. SACRED TEXT

To cite individual published editions of sacred books, begin the entry with the title.

> *Qur'an: The Final Testament (Authorized English Version) with Arabic Text*. Trans.
> Rashad Khalifa. Fremont: Universal Unity, 2000. Print.

Print periodicals

Begin with the author name(s). (See models 1–5.) Then include the article title, the title of the periodical, the date or volume information, the page numbers, and the medium (*Print*). The source map on pp. 428–29 shows where to find this information in a sample periodical.

28. ARTICLE IN A PRINT JOURNAL

Follow the journal title with the volume number, a period, the issue number (if given), and the year (in parentheses).

> Gigante, Denise. "The Monster in the Rainbow: Keats and the Science of Life."
> *PMLA* 117.3 (2002): 433-48. Print.

29. ARTICLE IN A PRINT MAGAZINE

Provide the date from the magazine cover instead of volume or issue numbers.

> Surowiecki, James. "The Stimulus Strategy." *New Yorker* 25 Feb. 2008: 29. Print.

> Taubin, Amy. "All Talk?" *Film Comment* Nov.-Dec. 2007: 45-47. Print.

Formatting Print Periodical Entries

- Put titles of articles from periodicals in quotation marks. Place the period inside the closing quotation mark.
- Give the title of the periodical as it appears on the magazine's or journal's cover or newspaper's front page; omit any initial *A, An,* or *The.* Italicize the title.
- For journals, include the volume number, a period, the issue number, if given, and the year in parentheses.
- For magazines and newspapers, give the date in this order: day (if given), month, year. Abbreviate months except for May, June, and July.
- List inclusive page numbers if the article appears on consecutive pages. If it skips pages, give only the first page number and a plus sign.
- End with the medium (*Print*).

30. ARTICLE IN A PRINT NEWSPAPER

Include the edition (if listed) and the section number or letter (if listed).

> Longman, Jeré. "Kim Jong-il, Sportsman." *New York Times* 21 Dec. 2011, late ed.: B12. Print.

Note: For locally published newspapers, add the city in brackets after the name if it is not part of the name: *Globe and Mail [Toronto].*

31. ARTICLE THAT SKIPS PAGES

When an article skips pages, give only the first page number and a plus sign.

> Tyrnauer, Matthew. "Empire by Martha." *Vanity Fair* Sept. 2002: 364+. Print.

32. EDITORIAL OR LETTER TO THE EDITOR

Include the writer's name, if given, and the title, if any, followed by a label for the work.

> "California Dreaming." Editorial. *Nation* 25 Feb. 2008: 4. Print.

> Galbraith, James K. "JFK's Plans to Withdraw." Letter. *New York Review of Books* 6 Dec. 2007: 77-78. Print.

33. REVIEW

> Franklin, Nancy. "Teen Spirit." Rev. of *Glee,* by Ryan Murphy, Brad Falchuk, and Ian Brennan. *New Yorker* 10 May 2010: 72-73. Print.

MLA SOURCE MAP: Articles in Print Periodicals

1 **Author.** List the last name first. End with a period. For variations, see models 2–5.

2 **Article title.** Put the title and any subtitle in quotation marks; capitalize all major words. Place a period inside the closing quotation mark.

3 **Periodical title.** Italicize the title; capitalize all major words. Omit any initial *A, An,* or *The.*

4 **Volume and issue / Date of publication.** For journals, give the volume number and issue number (if any), separated by a period; then list the year in parentheses and follow it with a colon.

For magazines, list the day (if given), month, and year.

5 **Page numbers.** List inclusive page numbers. If the article skips pages, put the first page number and a plus sign. End with a period.

6 **Medium.** Give the medium (*Print*). End with a period.

A citation for the magazine article on p. 429 would look like this:

Quart, Alissa. "Lost Media, Found Media: Snapshots from the Future of Writing." *Columbia Journalism Review* May/June 2008: 30-34. Print.

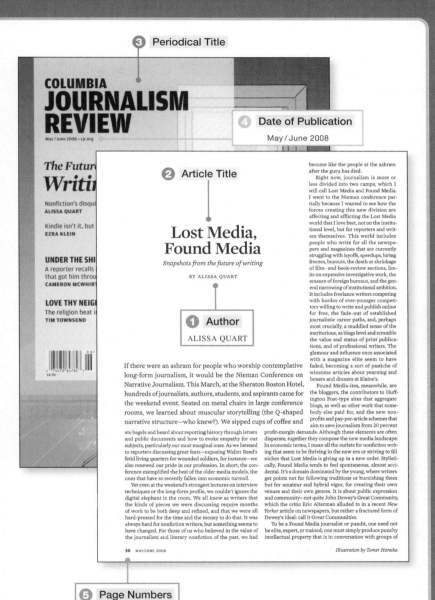

③ Periodical Title

COLUMBIA
JOURNALISM REVIEW
May / June 2008 · cjr.org

The Futur...
Writi...

Nonfiction's disqui...
ALISSA QUART

Kindle isn't it, but
EZRA KLEIN

UNDER THE SHI...
A reporter recalls
that got him throu...
CAMERON MCWHIRT...

LOVE THY NEIG...
The religion beat i...
TIM TOWNSEND

④ Date of Publication

May / June 2008

② Article Title

Lost Media, Found Media

Snapshots from the future of writing

BY ALISSA QUART

① Author

ALISSA QUART

If there were an ashram for people who worship contemplative long-form journalism, it would be the Nieman Conference on Narrative Journalism. This March, at the Sheraton Boston Hotel, hundreds of journalists, authors, students, and aspirants came for the weekend event. Seated on metal chairs in large conference rooms, we learned about muscular storytelling (the Q-shaped narrative structure—who knew?). We sipped cups of coffee and ate bagels and heard about reporting history through letters and public documents and how to evoke empathy for our subjects, particularly our most marginal ones. As we listened to reporters discussing great feats—exposing Walter Reed's fetid living quarters for wounded soldiers, for instance—we also renewed our pride in our profession. In short, the conference exemplified the best of the older media models, the ones that have recently fallen into economic turmoil.

Yet even at the weekend's strongest lectures on interview techniques or the long-form profile, we couldn't ignore the digital elephant in the room. We all knew as writers that the kinds of pieces we were discussing require months of work to be both deep and refined, and that we were all hard-pressed for the time and the money to do that. It was always hard for nonfiction writers, but something seems to have changed. For those of us who believed in the value of the journalism and literary nonfiction of the past, we had

become like the people at the ashram after the guru has died.

Right now, journalism is more or less divided into two camps, which I will call Lost Media and Found Media. I went to the Nieman conference partially because I wanted to see how the forces creating this new division are affecting and afflicting the Lost Media world that I love best, not on the institutional level, but for reporters and writers themselves. This world includes people who write for all the newspapers and magazines that are currently struggling with layoffs, speedups, hiring freezes, buyouts, the death or shrinkage of film- and book-review sections, limits on expensive investigative work, the erasure of foreign bureaus, and the general narrowing of institutional ambition. It includes freelance writers competing with hordes of ever-younger competitors willing to write and publish online for free, the fade-out of established journalistic career paths, and, perhaps most crucially, a muddled sense of the meritorious, as blogs level and scramble the value and status of print publications, and of professional writers. The glamour and influence once associated with a magazine elite seem to have faded, becoming a sort of pastiche of winsome articles about yearning and boxers and dinners at Elaine's.

Found Media-ites, meanwhile, are the bloggers, the contributors to Huffington Post-type sites that aggregate blogs, as well as other work that somebody else paid for, and the new non-profits and pay-per-article schemes that aim to save journalism from 20 percent profit-margin demands. Although these elements are often disparate, together they compose the new media landscape. In economic terms, I mean all the outlets for nonfiction writing that seem to be thriving in the new era or striving to fill niches that Lost Media is giving up in a new order. Stylistically, Found Media tends to feel spontaneous, almost accidental. It's a domain dominated by the young, where writers get points not for following traditions or burnishing them but for amateur and hybrid vigor, for creating their own venues and their own genres. It is about public expression and community—not quite John Dewey's Great Community, which the critic Eric Alterman alluded to in a recent *New Yorker* article on newspapers, but rather a fractured form of Dewey's ideal: call it Great Communities.

To be a Found Media journalist or pundit, one need not be elite, expert, or trained; one must simply produce punchy intellectual property that is in conversation with groups of

Illustration by Tomer Hanuka

⑤ Page Numbers

30

Schwarz, Benjamin. Rev. of *The Second World War: A Short History,* by R. A. C.
    Parker. *Atlantic Monthly* May 2002: 110-11. Print.

34. UNSIGNED ARTICLE

"Performance of the Week." *Time* 6 Oct. 2003: 18. Print.

Digital written-word sources

Digital sources such as Web sites differ from print sources in the ease
with which they can be—and frequently are—changed, updated, or
even eliminated. In addition, the various electronic media do not organize their works the same way. The most commonly cited electronic
sources are documents from Web sites and databases. For help determining which is which, see 49b.

AT A GLANCE

Citing Digital Sources

When citing sources accessed online or from an electronic database,
give as many of the following elements as you can find:

1. **Author.** Give the author's name, if available.
2. **Title.** Put titles of articles or short works in quotation marks. Italicize
   book titles.

For works from databases:

3. **Title of periodical,** italicized.
4. **Publication information.** After
   the volume/issue/year or date,
   include page numbers (or *n.
   pag.* if no page numbers are
   listed).
5. **Name of database,** italicized,
   if you used a subscription service such as Academic Search
   Premier.
6. **Medium of publication.** Use *Web.*
7. **Date of access.** Give the most recent date you accessed the source.

For works from the Web:

3. **Title of the site,** italicized.
4. **Name of the publisher or
   sponsor.** This information usually appears at the bottom of
   the page.
5. **Date of online publication
   or most recent update.** This
   information often appears at
   the bottom of the page. If no
   date is given, use *n.d.*

If you think your readers will have difficulty finding the source without
a URL, put it after the period following the date of access, inside angle
brackets, with a period after the closing bracket.

35. WORK FROM A DATABASE

The basic format for citing a work from a database appears in the source map on pp. 432–33.

For a periodical article that is available in print but that you access in an online database through a library subscription service such as Academic Search Premier, begin with the author's name (if given); the title of the work, in quotation marks; the title of the periodical, italicized; and publication information for the print version of the work (see models 28–34). Include the page numbers from the print version; if no page numbers are available, use *n. pag.* Then give the name of the online database, italicized; the medium (*Web*); and your most recent date of access.

> Collins, Ross F. "Cattle Barons and Ink Slingers: How Cow Country Journalists
>
> Created a Great American Myth." *American Journalism* 24.3 (2007): 7-29.
>
> *Communication and Mass Media Complete*. Web. 7 Feb. 2008.

36. ARTICLE FROM THE WEB SITE OF A JOURNAL

Begin an entry for an online journal article as you would one for a print journal article (see model 28). If an article does not have page numbers, use *n. pag.* End with the medium consulted (*Web*) and the date of access.

> Gallagher, Brian. "Greta Garbo Is Sad: Some Historical Reflections on the
>
> Paradoxes of Stardom in the American Film Industry, 1910-1960."
>
> *Images: A Journal of Film and Popular Culture* 3 (1997): n. pag. Web.
>
> 7 Aug. 2009.

37. ARTICLE IN A MAGAZINE ON THE WEB

See model 29 for print publication information if the article appears in print. After the name of the magazine, give the sponsor of the Web site, the date of publication, the medium (*Web*), and the date of access.

> Shapiro, Walter. "The Quest for Universal Healthcare." *Salon*. Salon Media Group,
>
> 21 Feb. 2008. Web. 2 Mar. 2008.

38. ARTICLE IN A NEWSPAPER ON THE WEB

After the name of the newspaper, give the publisher, publication date, medium (*Web*), and access date.

> Bustillo, Miguel, and Carol J. Williams. "Old Guard in Cuba Keeps Reins." *Los*
>
> *Angeles Times*. Los Angeles Times, 25 Feb. 2008. Web. 26 Feb. 2011.

MLA SOURCE MAP: Articles from Databases

Library subscriptions — such as EBSCOhost and Academic Search Premier — provide access to huge databases of articles.

1 **Author.** List the last name first. End with a period. For variations, see models 2–5.

2 **Article title.** Enclose the title and any subtitle in quotation marks.

3 **Periodical title.** Italicize it. Exclude any initial *A, An,* or *The.*

4 **Print publication information.** List the volume and issue number, if any; the date of publication, including the day (if given), month, and year, in that order; and the inclusive page numbers. If an article has no page numbers, write *n. pag.*

5 **Database name.** Italicize the name of the database.

6 **Medium.** For an online database, use *Web.*

7 **Date of access.** Give the day, month, and year, then a period.

A citation for the article on p. 433 would look like this:

Arnett, Robert P. *"Casino Royale* and Franchise Remix: James Bond as
    Superhero." *Film Criticism* 33.3 (2009): 1-16. *Academic Search Premier.*
    Web. 16 May 2011.

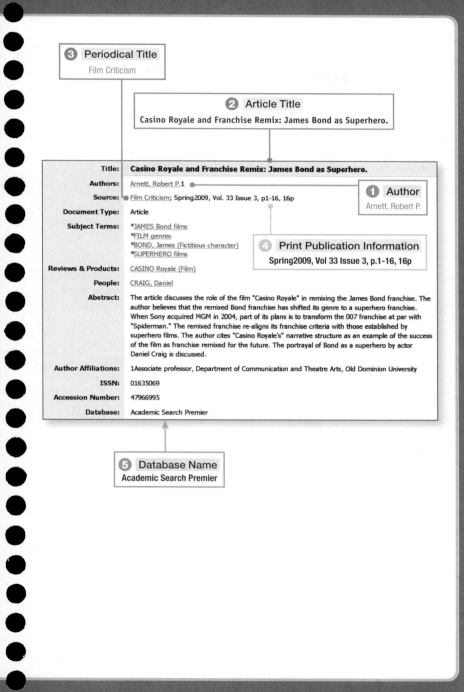

③ Periodical Title
Film Criticism

② Article Title
Casino Royale and Franchise Remix: James Bond as Superhero.

Title:	**Casino Royale and Franchise Remix: James Bond as Superhero.**
Authors:	Arnett, Robert P.1
Source:	Film Criticism; Spring2009, Vol. 33 Issue 3, p1-16, 16p
Document Type:	Article
Subject Terms:	*JAMES Bond films *FILM genres *BOND, James (Fictitious character) *SUPERHERO films
Reviews & Products:	CASINO Royale (Film)
People:	CRAIG, Daniel
Abstract:	The article discusses the role of the film "Casino Royale" in remixing the James Bond franchise. The author believes that the remixed Bond franchise has shifted its genre to a superhero franchise. When Sony acquired MGM in 2004, part of its plans is to transform the 007 franchise at par with "Spiderman." The remixed franchise re-aligns its franchise criteria with those established by superhero films. The author cites "Casino Royale's" narrative structure as an example of the success of the film as franchise remixed for the future. The portrayal of Bond as a superhero by actor Daniel Craig is discussed.
Author Affiliations:	1Associate professor, Department of Communication and Theatre Arts, Old Dominion University
ISSN:	01635069
Accession Number:	47966995
Database:	Academic Search Premier

① Author
Arnett, Robert P.

④ Print Publication Information
Spring2009, Vol 33 Issue 3, p.1-16, 16p

⑤ Database Name
Academic Search Premier

433

39. BOOK ON THE WEB

Provide information as for a print book (see models 6–27); then give the name of the Web site, the medium, and the date of access.

> Euripides. *The Trojan Women*. Trans. Gilbert Murray. New York: Oxford UP,
>
> 1915. *Internet Sacred Text Archive*. Web. 12 Oct. 2011.

Note: Cite a part of an online book as you would a part of a print book (see models 10 and 21). Give the print publication information (if any); the name of the site; the medium (*Web*); and the date of access.

> Riis, Jacob. "The Genesis of the Gang." *The Battle with the Slum*.
>
> New York: Macmillan, 1902. N. pag. *Bartleby.com: Great Books Online*.
>
> Web. 31 Mar. 2011.

40. POEM ON THE WEB

Include the poet's name, the title of the poem, and the print publication information (if any) as you would for part of an online book (model 39). End with the name of the site, the medium (*Web*), and the date of access.

> Dickinson, Emily. "The Grass." *Poems: Emily Dickinson*. Boston, 1891. N. pag.
>
> *Humanities Text Initiative American Verse Project*. Web. 6 Jan. 2011.

41. EDITORIAL OR LETTER IN A WEB PERIODICAL

Include the word *Editorial* or *Letter* after the author (if given) and title (if any). End with the periodical name, the sponsor of the Web site, the date of posting or most recent update, the medium, and the access date.

> "The Funding Gap." Editorial. *Washington Post*. Washington Post, 5 Nov. 2003.
>
> Web. 19 Oct. 2010.

> Moore, Paula. "Go Vegetarian." Letter. *New York Times*. New York Times, 25 Feb.
>
> 2008. Web. 25 Feb. 2011.

42. REVIEW IN A WEB PERIODICAL

Cite an online review as you would a print review (see model 33). End with the name of the Web site, the sponsor, the date of electronic publication, the medium, and the date of access.

> Seitz, Matt Zoller. "A Modern Horror Film." Rev. of *The Social Network*, dir. David
>
> Fincher. *Salon*. Salon Media Group, 4 Oct. 2010. Web. 24 May 2011.

43. ENTRY IN A WEB REFERENCE WORK

Cite the entry as you would an entry from a print reference work (see model 22). Follow with the name of the Web site, the sponsor, date of publication, medium, and date of access.

> "Tour de France." *Encyclopaedia Britannica Online.* Encyclopaedia Britannica,
>
> 2006. Web. 21 May 2006.

44. WORK FROM A WEB SITE

For basic information on citing a work from a Web site, see the source map on pp. 436–37. Include all of the following elements that are available: the author; the title of the work in quotation marks; the name of the Web site, italicized; the name of the publisher or sponsor (if none is available, use *N.p.*); the date of publication (if not available, use *n.d.*); the medium (*Web*); and the date of access.

> "America: A Center-Left Nation." *Media Matters for America.* Media Matters for
>
> America, 27 May 2009. Web. 31 May 2011.

> Stauder, Ellen Keck. "Darkness Audible: Negative Capability and Mark Doty's
>
> 'Nocturne in Black and Gold.'" *Romantic Circles Praxis Series.* U of Maryland,
>
> 2003. Web. 28 Sept. 2003.

45. ENTIRE WEB SITE

Follow the guidelines for a specific work from the Web, beginning with the name of the author, editor, compiler, director, narrator, or translator, followed by the title of the Web site, italicized; the name of the sponsor or publisher (if none, use *N.p.*); the date of publication or last update; the medium of publication (*Web*); and the date of access.

> Bernstein, Charles, Kenneth Goldsmith, Martin Spinelli, and Patrick Durgin, eds.
>
> *Electronic Poetry Corner.* SUNY Buffalo, 2003. Web. 26 Sept. 2006.

> *Weather.com.* Weather Channel Interactive, 2011. Web. 13 Mar. 2011.

For a personal Web site, include the name of the person who created the site; the title or (if there is no title) a description such as *Home page,* not italicized; the name of the larger site, if different from the personal site's title; the publisher or sponsor of the site (if none, use *N.p.*); the date of the last update; the medium of publication (*Web*); and the date of access.

> Ede, Lisa. Home page. *Oregon State.* Oregon State U, 2010. Web. 17 May
>
> 2010.

MLA SOURCE MAP: Works from Web Sites

You may need to browse other parts of a site to find some of the following elements, and some sites may omit elements. Uncover as much information as you can.

1 **Author.** List the last name first. End with a period. If no author is given, begin with the title. For variations, see models 2–5.

2 **Title of work.** Enclose the title and any subtitle of the work in quotation marks.

3 **Title of Web site.** Give the title of the entire Web site, italicized.

4 **Publisher or sponsor.** Look for the sponsor's name at the bottom of the home page. If no information is available, write *N.p.* Follow it with a comma.

5 **Date of publication or latest update.** Give the most recent date, followed by a period. If no date is available, use *n.d.*

6 **Medium.** Use *Web* and follow it with a period.

7 **Date of access.** Give the date you accessed the work. End with a period.

A citation for the work on p. 437 would look like this:

Tønnesson, Øyvind. "Mahatma Gandhi, the Missing Laureate." *Nobelprize.org.*
   Nobel Foundation, 1 Dec. 1999. Web. 4 May 2005.

1 Author
Øyvind Tønnesson

2 Title of Work

3 Title of Web Site

Nobelprize.org

Mahatma Gandhi, the Missing Laureate

by Øyvind Tønnesson
Nobelprize.org Peace Editor, 1998-2000
1 December 1999

5 Date of Publication
1 December 1999

4 Publisher or Sponsor
The Official Web Site of the Nobel Foundation

46. ACADEMIC COURSE WEB SITE

For a course site, include the name of the instructor, the title of the course in quotation marks, the title of the site in italics, the department (if relevant) and institution sponsoring the site, the date (or *n.d.*), the medium (*Web*), and the access date.

> Creekmur, Corey K., and Philip Lutgendorf. "Topics in Asian Cinema: Popular
>
> Hindi Cinema." *University of Iowa.* Depts. of English, Cinema, and
>
> Comparative Literature, U of Iowa, 2004. Web. 13 Mar. 2007.

For a department Web site, give the department name, the description *Dept. home page,* the institution (in italics), the site sponsor, the medium (*Web*), and the access information.

> English Dept. home page. *Amherst College.* Amherst Coll., n.d. Web. 5 Apr. 2011.

47. BLOG

For an entire blog, give the author's name; the title of the blog, italicized; the sponsor or publisher of the blog (if there is none, use *N.p.*); the date of the most recent update; the medium (*Web*); and the date of access.

> *Little Green Footballs.* Little Green Footballs, 23 Aug. 2011. Web. 23 Aug. 2011.

Note: To cite a blogger who writes under a pseudonym, begin with the pseudonym and then put the writer's real name (if you know it) in square brackets.

> Atrios [Duncan Black]. *Eschaton.* N.p., 27 June 2011. Web. 27 June 2011.

48. POST OR COMMENT ON A BLOG

Give the author's name; the title of the post or comment, in quotation marks (if there is no title, use the description *Web log post* or *Web log comment,* not italicized); the title of the blog, italicized; the sponsor of the blog (if there is none, use *N.p.*); the date of the most recent update; the medium (*Web*); and the date of access.

> Marcotte, Amanda. "Rights without Perfection." *Pandagon.* N.p., 16 May 2010.
>
> Web. 16 May 2010.

49. ENTRY IN A WIKI

Because wiki content is collectively edited, do not include an author. Treat a wiki as you would a work from a Web site (see model 44). Include the title of the entry; the name of the wiki, italicized; the sponsor or publisher of the wiki (use *N.p.* if there is no sponsor); the date of the latest update; the medium (*Web*); and the date of access. Check with your instructor before using a wiki as a source.

"Fédération Internationale de Football Association." *Wikipedia.* Wikimedia

Foundation, 27 June 2011. Web. 27 June 2011.

50. POSTING TO A DISCUSSION GROUP OR NEWSGROUP

Begin with the author's name and the title of the posting in quotation marks (or the words *Online posting*). Follow with the name of the Web site, the sponsor or publisher of the site (use *N.p.* if there is no sponsor), the date of publication, the medium (*Web*), and the date of access.

Daly, Catherine. "Poetry Slams." *Poetics Discussion List.* SUNY Buffalo,

29 Aug. 2003. Web. 1 Oct. 2005.

51. POSTING TO A SOCIAL NETWORKING SITE

To cite a posting on Facebook or another social networking site, include the writer's name, a description of the posting, the date of the posting, and the medium of delivery. (The MLA does not provide guidelines for citing postings on such sites; this model is based on the MLA's guidelines for citing email.)

Ferguson, Sarah. Status update. 6 Mar. 2008. Facebook posting.

52. EMAIL OR MESSAGE ON SOCIAL NETWORKING SITE

Include the writer's name; the subject line, in quotation marks (for email); *Message to* (not italicized or in quotation marks) followed by the recipient's name; the date of the message; and the medium of delivery (*E-mail*). (MLA style hyphenates *e-mail.*)

Harris, Jay. "Thoughts on Impromptu Stage Productions." Message to the

author. 16 July 2006. E-mail.

53. TWEET

Include the writer's real name, if known, with the user name (if different) in parentheses. If you don't know the real name, give just the user name. Include the entire tweet, in quotation marks. End with date and time of message and the medium (*Tweet*).

BedfordBits. "#4C12 'Think of citations as a guide for the engaged reader.'

Writing center tutor quoted by E. Kleinfeld. See http://citationproject.net/"

23 Mar. 2012, 4:01 p.m. Tweet.

Visual, audio, multimedia, and live sources

54. FILM OR DVD

If you cite a particular person's work, start with that name. If not, start with the title; then name the director, distributor, and year of release. Other contributors, such as writers or performers, may follow the director. If you cite a DVD instead of a theatrical release, include the original film release date and the label *DVD*. For material found on a Web site, give the name of the site or database, the medium (*Web*), and the access date.

> *Black Swan*. Dir. Darren Aronofsky. Perf. Natalie Portman. Fox Searchlight, 2010.
> Film.
>
> *Spirited Away*. Dir. Hayao Miyazaki. 2001. Walt Disney Video, 2003. DVD.
>
> Winner, Michael, dir. *Death Wish*. Perf. Charles Bronson. Paramount, 1974.
> *Netflix*. Web. 11 Nov. 2011.

55. ONLINE VIDEO CLIP

Cite a short online video as you would a work from a Web site (see model 44).

> Weber, Jan. "As We Sow, Part 1: Where Are the Farmers?" *YouTube*. YouTube, 15
> Mar. 2008. Web. 27 Sept. 2010.

56. TELEVISION OR RADIO PROGRAM

In general, begin with the title of the program, italicized. Then list important contributors (narrator, writer, director, actors); the network; the local station and city, if any; the broadcast date; and the medium. To cite

---

AT A GLANCE

Citing Sources without Models in MLA Style

To cite a source for which you cannot find a model, collect as much information as you can find — about the creator, title, sponsor, date of posting or latest update, the date you accessed the site and its location — with the goal of helping your readers find the source for themselves, if possible. Then look at the models in this section to see which one most closely matches the type of source you are using.

In an academic writing project, before citing an electronic source for which you have no model, also be sure to ask your instructor for help.

a particular person's work, begin with that name. To cite a particular episode from a series, begin with the episode title, in quotation marks.

> *The American Experience: Buffalo Bill.* Writ., dir., prod. Rob Rapley. PBS. WNET, New York, 25 Feb. 2008. Television.

> "The Suitcase." *Mad Men.* Writ. Matthew Weiner. Dir. Jennifer Getzinger. AMC, 5 Sept. 2010. Television.

Note: For a streaming version online, give the name of the Web site, italicized. Then give the publisher or sponsor, a comma, and the date posted. End with the medium (*Web*) and the access date.

> Limbaugh, Rush. *The Rush Limbaugh Show. RushLimbaugh.com.* Premier Radio Networks, 29 Feb. 2012. Web. 2 Apr. 2012.

57. BROADCAST INTERVIEW

List the person interviewed and then the title, if any. If the interview has no title, use the label *Interview* and name the interviewer, if relevant. Then identify the source. To cite a broadcast interview, end with information about the program, the date(s) the interview took place, and the medium.

> Revkin, Andrew. Interview with Terry Gross. *Fresh Air.* Natl. Public Radio. WNYC, New York, 14 June 2006. Radio.

Note: If you listened to an archived version online, provide the site's sponsor (if known), the date of the interview, the medium (*Web*), and the access date. For a podcast interview, see model 64.

> Revkin, Andrew. Interview with Terry Gross. *Fresh Air. NPR.org.* NPR, 14 June 2006. Web. 12 Jan. 2009.

58. UNPUBLISHED OR PERSONAL INTERVIEW

List the person interviewed; the label *Telephone interview, Personal interview,* or *E-mail interview*; and the date the interview took place.

> Freedman, Sasha. Personal interview. 10 Nov. 2011.

59. SOUND RECORDING

List the name of the person or group you wish to emphasize (such as the composer, conductor, or band); the title of the recording or composition; the artist, if appropriate; the manufacturer; and the year of issue. Give the medium (such as *CD, MP3 file,* or *LP*). If you are citing a particular song or selection, include its title, in quotation marks, before the title of the recording.

> Bach, Johann Sebastian. *Bach: Violin Concertos.* Perf. Itzhak Perlman and Pinchas Zukerman. English Chamber Orch. EMI, 2002. CD.

> Sonic Youth. "Incinerate." *Rather Ripped.* Geffen, 2006. MP3 file.

Note: If you are citing instrumental music that is identified only by form, number, and key, do not underline, italicize, or enclose it in quotation marks.

> Grieg, Edvard. Concerto in A minor, op. 16. Cond. Eugene Ormandy. Philadelphia Orch. RCA, 1989. LP.

60. MUSICAL COMPOSITION

When you are not citing a specific published version, first give the composer's name, followed by the title.

> Mozart, Wolfgang Amadeus. *Don Giovanni,* K527.

> Mozart, Wolfgang Amadeus. Symphony no. 41 in C major, K551.

Note: Cite a published score as you would a book. If you include the date the composition was written, do so immediately after the title.

> Schoenberg, Arnold. *Chamber Symphony No. 1 for 15 Solo Instruments, Op. 9.* 1906. New York: Dover, 2002. Print.

61. COMPUTER GAME

Include the version after the title, then the city and publisher, date, and medium.

> *Grand Theft Auto: Tales from Liberty City.* PlayStation 3 vers. New York: Rockstar Games, 2009. DVD-ROM.

Cite an online game as you would a work from a Web site (see model 44).

> *The Sims 3.* PC vers. *TheSims.com.* Electronic Arts, 2011. Web. 30 Nov. 2011.

62. LECTURE OR SPEECH

List the speaker; title, in quotation marks; sponsoring institution or group; place; and date. If the speech is untitled, use a label such as *Lecture.*

> Colbert, Stephen. Speech. White House Correspondents' Association Dinner. *YouTube.* YouTube, 29 Apr. 2006. Web. 20 May 2011.

Eugenides, Jeffrey. Portland Arts and Lectures. Arlene Schnitzer Concert Hall,

Portland, OR. 30 Sept. 2003. Lecture.

63. LIVE PERFORMANCE

List the title, appropriate names (such as writer or performer), the place, and the date. To cite a particular person's work, begin the entry with that name.

Anything Goes. By Cole Porter. Perf. Klea Blackhurst. Shubert Theater,

New Haven. 7 Oct. 2003. Performance.

64. PODCAST (STREAMING)

Include all of the following that are relevant and available: the speaker, the title of the podcast, the title of the program, the host or performers, the title of the site, the site's sponsor, the date of posting, the medium (*Web*), and the access date. (This model is based on MLA guidelines for a short work from a Web site. For a downloaded podcast, see model 65.)

"Seven Arrested in U.S. Terror Raid." *Morning Report.* Host Krishnan Guru-Murthy.

4 Radio. Channel 4 News, 23 June 2006. Web. 27 June 2010.

65. DIGITAL FILE

A citation for a file that you can download — one that exists independently, not only on a Web site — begins with citation information required for the type of source (a photograph or sound recording, for example). For the medium, indicate the type of file (*MP3 file, JPEG file*).

Officers' Winter Quarters, Army of Potomac, Brandy Station. Mar. 1864. Prints and

Photographs Div., Lib. of Cong. TIFF file.

"Return to the Giant Pool of Money." *This American Life.* Narr. Ira Glass. NPR, 25

Sept. 2009. MP3 file.

66. WORK OF ART OR PHOTOGRAPH

List the artist or photographer; the work's title, italicized; the date of composition (if unknown, use *n.d.*); and the medium of composition (*Oil on canvas, Bronze*). Then cite the name of the museum or other location and the city. To cite a reproduction in a book, add the publication information. To cite artwork found online, omit the medium of composition, and after the location, add the title of the database

---

AT A GLANCE

Citing Visuals That Appear in Your Text

If you choose to include images in your text, you need to cite and caption them correctly (see pp. 414–15).

- For a work that you have created, the works-cited entry should begin with a descriptive phrase from the image's caption ("Bus stop in Los Angeles"), a label ("Photograph by author"), and the date.

- For a visual reproduced from another source, you can include the complete citation information in the caption (see model 19 on p. 414), or you can indicate the source to allow readers to find it on the list of works cited. If you give the complete citation in the caption and do not cite the visual elsewhere in your text, you can omit the visual from your works-cited page.

---

or Web site, italicized; the medium consulted (*Web*); and the date of access.

> Chagall, Marc. *The Poet with the Birds*. 1911. Minneapolis Inst. of Arts. *artsmia.org*. Web. 6 Oct. 2011.

> *General William Palmer in Old Age*. 1810. Oil on canvas. National Army Museum, London. *White Mughals: Love and Betrayal in Eighteenth-Century India*. By William Dalrymple. New York: Penguin, 2002. 270. Print.

> Kahlo, Frida. *Self-Portrait with Cropped Hair*. 1940. Oil on canvas. Museum of Mod. Art, New York.

67. MAP OR CHART

Cite a map or chart as you would a book or a short work within a longer work and include the word *Map* or *Chart* after the title. Add the medium of publication. For an online source, end with the date of access.

> "Australia." Map. *Perry-Castañeda Library Map Collection*. U of Texas, 1999. Web. 4 Nov. 2010.

> *California*. Map. Chicago: Rand, 2002. Print.

68. CARTOON OR COMIC STRIP

List the artist's name; the title (if any) of the cartoon or comic strip, in quotation marks; the label *Cartoon* or *Comic strip*; and the usual publication information for a print periodical (see models 28–31) or a work from a Web site (model 44).

Johnston, Lynn. "For Better or Worse." Comic strip. *FBorFW.com.* Lynn Johnston
    Publications, 30 June 2006. Web. 20 July 2006.

Lewis, Eric. "The Unpublished Freud." Cartoon. *New Yorker* 11 Mar. 2002: 80. Print.

69. ADVERTISEMENT

Include the label *Advertisement* after the name of the item or organization being advertised.

Microsoft. Advertisement. *Harper's* Oct. 2003: 2-3. Print.

Microsoft. Advertisement. *New York Times.* New York Times, 11 Nov. 2003. Web.
    11 Nov. 2003.

Academic, government, and legal sources (including digital versions)

If an online version is not shown here, use the appropriate model for the source and then end with the medium and date of access.

70. REPORT OR PAMPHLET

Follow the guidelines for a print book (models 6–27) or an online book (model 39).

Allen, Katherine, and Lee Rainie. *Parents Online.* Washington: Pew Internet and
    Amer. Life Project, 2002. Print.

Environmental Working Group. *Dead in the Water.* Washington: Environmental
    Working Group, 2006. Web. 24 Apr. 2011.

71. GOVERNMENT PUBLICATION

Begin with the author, if identified. Otherwise, start with the name of the government, followed by the agency. For congressional documents, cite the number, session, and house of Congress (*S* for Senate, *H* for House of Representatives); the type (*Report, Resolution, Document*) in abbreviated form; and the number. End with the publication information. The print publisher is often the Government Printing Office (GPO). For online versions, follow the models for a work from a Web site (model 44) or an entire Web site (model 45).

Gregg, Judd. *Report to Accompany the Genetic Information Act of 2003.* US
    108th Cong., 1st sess. S. Rept. 108-22. Washington: GPO, 2003. Print.

Kinsella, Kevin, and Victoria Velkoff. *An Aging World: 2001.* US Bureau of the
    Census. Washington: GPO, 2001. Print.

United States. Environmental Protection Agency. Office of Emergency and

   Remedial Response. *This Is Superfund.* Jan. 2000. *Environmental*

   Protection Agency. Web. 16 Aug. 2002.

72. PUBLISHED PROCEEDINGS OF A CONFERENCE

Cite proceedings as you would a book.

Cleary, John, and Gary Gurtler, eds. *Proceedings of the Boston Area Colloquium in*

   Ancient Philosophy 2002. Boston: Brill Academic, 2003. Print.

73. DISSERTATION

Enclose the title in quotation marks. Add the label *Diss.*, the school, and
the year the work was accepted.

Paris, Django. "Our Culture: Difference, Division, and Unity in Multicultural Youth

   Space." Diss. Stanford U, 2008. Print.

Note: Cite a published dissertation as a book, adding the identification
Diss. and the university after the title.

74. DISSERTATION ABSTRACT

Cite as you would an unpublished dissertation (see model 73). For the
abstract of a dissertation using *Dissertation Abstracts International* (*DAI*),
include the *DAI* volume, year, and page number.

Huang-Tiller, Gillian C. "The Power of the Meta-Genre: Cultural, Sexual, and

   Racial Politics of the American Modernist Sonnet." Diss. U of Notre Dame,

   2000. *DAI* 61 (2000): 1401. Print.

75. PUBLISHED INTERVIEW

List the person interviewed; the title of the interview (if any) or the
label *Interview* and the interviewer's name, if relevant. Then provide information about the source, following the appropriate model.

Paretsky, Sara. Interview. *Progressive.* Progressive Magazine, 14 Jan. 2008. Web.

   12 Feb. 2011.

Taylor, Max. "Max Taylor on Winning." *Time* 13 Nov. 2000: 66. Print.

76. UNPUBLISHED LETTER

Cite a published letter as a work in an anthology (see model 10). If the
letter is unpublished, follow this form:

Anzaldúa, Gloria. Letter to the author. 10 Sept. 2002. MS.

77. MANUSCRIPT OR OTHER UNPUBLISHED WORK

List the author's name; the title (if any) or a description of the material; the form of the material (such as *MS* for manuscript) and any identifying numbers; and the name and location of the library or research institution housing the material, if applicable.

> Woolf, Virginia. "The Searchlight." N.d. TS. Ser. III, Box 4, Item 184. Papers of
>
> Virginia Woolf, 1902-1956. Smith Coll., Northampton.

78. LEGAL SOURCE

To cite a court case, give the names of the first plaintiff and defendant, the case number, the name of the court, and the date of the decision. To cite an act, give the name of the act followed by its Public Law (*Pub. L.*) number, the date the act was enacted, and its Statutes at Large (*Stat.*) cataloging number.

> Eldred v. Ashcroft. No. 01-618. Supreme Ct. of the US. 15 Jan. 2003. Print.
>
> Museum and Library Services Act of 2003. Pub. L. 108-81. 25 Sept. 2003. Stat.
>
> 117.991. Print.

Note: You do not need an entry on the list of works cited when you cite articles of the U.S. Constitution and laws in the U.S. Code.

52 A Student Research Essay, MLA Style

A brief research essay by David Craig appears on the following pages. David followed the MLA guidelines described in the preceding chapters. Note that this essay has been reproduced in a narrow format to allow for annotation.

Student Writer

David Craig

bedfordstmartins.com/everydaywriter
Student Writing

Craig 1

Name,
instructor,
course, date
aligned at left

David Craig

Professor Turkman

English 219

8 December 2011

Title centered

Messaging: The Language of Youth Literacy

Opens with
attention-
getting
statement

The English language is under attack. At least, that is what
many people seem to believe. From concerned parents to local
librarians, everyone seems to have a negative comment on the
state of youth literacy today. They fear that the current generation
of grade school students will graduate with an extremely low level
of literacy, and they point out that although language education
hasn't changed, kids are having more trouble reading and writing

Background on
the problem of
youth literacy

than in the past. When asked about the cause of this situation,
many adults pin the blame on technologies such as texting and
instant messaging, arguing that electronic shortcuts create and
compound undesirable reading and writing habits and discourage
students from learning conventionally correct ways to use language.

Thesis
statement

But although the arguments against messaging are passionate,
evidence suggests that they may not hold up.

The disagreements about messaging shortcuts are profound,
even among academics. John Briggs, an English professor at the

Quotation used
as evidence

University of California, Riverside, says, "Americans have always
been informal, but now the informality of precollege culture is so
ubiquitous that many students have no practice in using language
in any formal setting at all" (qtd. in McCarroll). Such objections
are not new; Sven Birkerts of Mount Holyoke College argued in
1999 that "[students] read more casually. They strip-mine what
they read" online and consequently produce "quickly generated,
casual prose" (qtd. in Leibowitz A67). However, academics are also
among the defenders of texting and instant messaging (IM), with
some suggesting that messaging may be a beneficial force in the

development of youth literacy because it promotes regular contact with words and the use of a written medium for communication.

Texting and instant messaging allow two individuals who are separated by any distance to engage in real-time, written communication. Although such communication relies on the written word, many messagers disregard standard writing conventions. For example, here is a snippet from an IM conversation between two teenage girls:[1]

> Teen One: sorry im talkinto like 10 ppl at a time
>
> Teen Two: u izzyful person
>
> Teen Two: kwel
>
> Teen One: hey i g2g

As this brief conversation shows, participants must use words to communicate via texting and messaging, but their words do not have to be in standard English.

The issue of youth literacy does demand attention because standardized test scores for language assessments, such as the verbal and writing sections of the College Board's SAT, have declined in recent years. This trend is illustrated in a chart distributed by the College Board as part of its 2011 analysis of aggregate SAT data (see Fig. 1).

The trend lines illustrate a significant pattern that may lead to the conclusion that youth literacy is on the decline. These lines display the ten-year paths (from 2001 to 2011) of reading and writing scores, respectively. Within this period, the average verbal score dropped a few points — and appears to be headed toward a further decline in the future.

Based on the preceding statistics, parents and educators appear to be right about the decline in youth literacy. And this

Definition and example of messaging

Writer considers argument that youth literacy is in decline

Figure explained in text and cited in parenthetical reference

Discussion of Figure 1

---

1. This transcript of an IM conversation was collected on 20 Nov. 2011. The teenagers' names are concealed to protect privacy.

Explanatory note; see 49d.

Craig 3

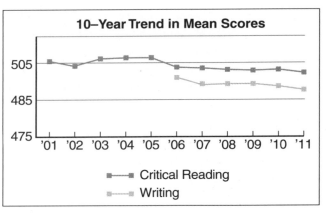

10–Year Trend in Mean Scores

505

485

475

'01 '02 '03 '04 '05 '06 '07 '08 '09 '10 '11

■ Critical Reading
■ Writing

Figure labeled, titled, and credited to source; inserted at appropriate point in text

Fig. 1. Ten-year trend in mean SAT reading and writing scores (2001-2011). Source: College Board, "2011 SAT Trends."

Writer acknowledges part of critics' argument; transition to next point

Statistical evidence cited

trend is occurring while electronic communication is on the rise. According to the Pew Internet & American Life Project, 85 percent of those aged 12-17 at least occasionally write text messages, instant messages, or comments on social networking sites (Lenhart, Arafeh, Smith, and Macgill). In 2001, the most conservative estimate based on Pew numbers showed that American youths spent, at a minimum, nearly three million hours per day on messaging services (Lenhart and Lewis 20). These numbers are now expanding thanks to texting and messaging on popular Web 2.0 sites — such as Facebook. What's more, young messengers seem to be using a new vocabulary.

Writer's field research introduced

In the interest of establishing the existence of a messaging language, I analyzed 11,341 lines of text from IM conversations between youths in my target demographic: U.S. residents aged twelve to seventeen. Young messengers voluntarily sent me chat logs, but they were unaware of the exact nature of my research. Once all of the logs had been gathered, I went through them, recording the number of times messaging language was used in place of conventional words and phrases. Then I generated graphs to display how often these replacements were used.

During the course of my study, I identified four types of messaging language: phonetic replacements, acronyms, abbreviations, and inanities. An example of phonetic replacement is using *ur* for *you are*. Another popular type of messaging language is the acronym; for a majority of the people in my study, the most common acronym was *lol*, a construction that means *laughing out loud*. Abbreviations are also common in messaging, but I discovered that typical IM abbreviations, such as *etc.*, are not new to the English language. Finally, I found a class of words that I call "inanities." These words include completely new words or expressions, combinations of several slang categories, or simply nonsensical variations of other words. My favorite from this category is *lolz*, an inanity that translates directly to *lol* yet includes a terminating *z* for no obvious reason.

Findings of field research presented

In the chat transcripts that I analyzed, the best display of typical messaging lingo came from the conversations between two thirteen-year-old Texan girls, who are avid IM users. Figure 2 is a graph showing how often they used certain phonetic replacements and abbreviations. On the *y*-axis, frequency of replacement is plotted, a calculation that compares the number of times a word or phrase is used in messaging language with the total number of times that it is communicated in any form. On the *x*-axis, specific messaging words and phrases are listed.

Figure introduced and explained

My research shows that the Texan girls use the first ten phonetic replacements or abbreviations at least 50 percent of the time in their normal messaging writing. For example, every

Craig 5

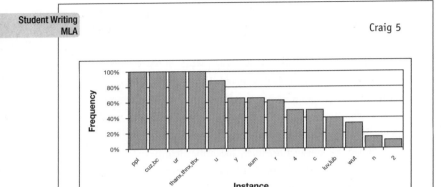

Fig. 2. Usage of phonetic replacements and abbreviations in messaging.

time one of them writes *see*, there is a parallel time when *c* is used in its place. In light of this finding, it appears that the popular messaging culture contains at least some elements of its own language. It also seems that much of this language is new: no formal dictionary yet identifies the most common messaging words and phrases. Only in the heyday of the telegraph or on the rolls of a stenographer would you find a similar situation, but these "languages" were never a popular medium of youth communication. Texting and instant messaging, however, are very popular among young people and continue to generate attention and debate in academic circles.

My research shows that messaging is certainly widespread, and it does seem to have its own particular vocabulary, yet these two factors alone do not mean it has a damaging influence on youth literacy. As noted earlier, however, some people claim that the new technology is a threat to the English language.

Jacquie Ream — a former teacher and author — told a reporter from *Curriculum Review,* "Text messaging is destroying the written word. The students aren't writing letters, they're typing into their cell phones one line at a time. Feelings aren't communicated with

Craig 6

words when you're texting; emotions are sideways smiley faces. Kids are typing shorthand jargon that isn't even a complete thought" (qtd. in "Is Texting Destroying?").

Parenthetical reference uses brief title, author unknown

The critics of messaging are numerous. But if we look to the field of linguistics, a central concept — metalinguistics — challenges these criticisms and leads to a more reasonable conclusion — that messaging has no negative impact on a student's development of or proficiency with traditional literacy.

Transition to support of thesis and refutation of critics

Scholars of metalinguistics offer support for the claim that messaging is not damaging to those who use it. As noted earlier, one of the most prominent components of messaging language is phonetic replacement, in which a word such as *everyone* becomes *every1*. This type of wordplay has a special importance in the development of an advanced literacy, and for good reason. According to David Crystal, an internationally recognized scholar of linguistics at the University of Wales, as young children develop and learn how words string together to express ideas, they go through many phases of language play. The singsong rhymes and nonsensical chants of preschoolers are vital to their learning language, and a healthy appetite for such wordplay leads to a better command of language later in life (182).

Linguistic authority cited in support of thesis

As justification for his view of the connection between language play and advanced literacy, Crystal presents an argument for metalinguistic awareness. According to Crystal, *metalinguistics* refers to the ability to "step back" and use words to analyze how language works:

> If we are good at stepping back, at thinking in a more abstract way about what we hear and what we say, then we are more likely to be good at acquiring those skills which depend on just such a stepping back in order to be successful — and this means, chiefly, reading

Block format for a quotation of more than four lines

Craig 7

Ellipses and brackets indicate omissions and changes in quotation

and writing. . . . [T]he greater our ability to play with language, . . . the more advanced will be our command of language as a whole. (Crystal 181)

If we accept the findings of linguists such as Crystal that metalinguistic awareness leads to increased literacy, then it seems reasonable to argue that the phonetic language of messaging can

Writer links Crystal's views to thesis

also lead to increased metalinguistic awareness and, therefore, increases in overall literacy. As messagers develop proficiency with a variety of phonetic replacements and other types of texting and messaging words, they should increase their subconscious knowledge of metalinguistics.

Another refutation of critics' assumptions

Metalinguistics also involves our ability to write in a variety of distinct styles and tones. Yet in the debate over messaging and literacy, many critics assume that either messaging or academic literacy will eventually win out in a person and that the two modes cannot exist side by side. This assumption is, however, false. Human beings ordinarily develop a large range of language abilities, from the formal to the relaxed and from the mainstream to the

Example from well-known work of literature used as support

subcultural. Mark Twain, for example, had an understanding of local speech that he employed when writing dialogue for *Huckleberry Finn*. Yet few people would argue that Twain's knowledge of this form of English had a negative impact on his ability to write in standard English.

However, just as Mark Twain used dialects carefully in dialogue, writers must pay careful attention to the kind of language they use in any setting. The owner of the language Web site *The Discouraging Word*, who is an anonymous English literature graduate student at the University of Chicago, backs up this idea in an e-mail to me:

Email correspondence cited in support of claim

What is necessary, we feel, is that students learn how to shift between different styles of writing — that, in other words, the abbreviations and shortcuts of messaging should be used online . . . but that they should not be used in an essay submitted to a teacher. . . . Messaging might even be considered . . . a different way of reading and writing, one that requires specific and unique skills shared by certain communities.

The analytical ability that is necessary for writers to choose an appropriate tone and style in their writing is, of course, metalinguistic in nature because it involves the comparison of two or more language systems. Thus, youths who grasp multiple languages will have a greater natural understanding of metalinguistics. More specifically, young people who possess both messaging and traditional skills stand to be better off than their peers who have been trained only in traditional or conventional systems. Far from being hurt by their online pastime, instant messagers can be aided in standard writing by their experience with messaging language.

Writer synthesizes evidence for claim

The fact remains, however, that youth literacy seems to be declining. What, if not messaging, is the main cause of this phenomenon? According to the College Board, which collects data on several questions from its test takers, course work in English composition and grammar classes decreased by 14 percent between 1992 and 2002 (Carnahan and Coletti 11). The possibility of messaging causing a decline in literacy seems inadequate when statistics on English education for US youths provide other evidence of the possible causes. Simply put, schools in the United States are not teaching English as much as they used to. Rather than blaming texting and messaging language alone for the decline in literacy and test scores, we must also look toward our schools' lack of focus on the teaching of standard English skills.

Transition to final point

Alternate explanation for decline in literacy

My findings indicate that the use of messaging poses virtually no threat to the development or maintenance of formal language skills among American youths aged twelve to seventeen. Diverse

Transition to conclusion

Concluding
paragraph
sums up
argument and
reiterates
thesis

language skills tend to increase a person's metalinguistic awareness and, thereby, his or her ability to use language effectively to achieve a desired purpose in a particular situation. The current decline in youth literacy is not due to the rise of texting and messaging. Rather, fewer young students seem to be receiving an adequate education in the use of conventional English. Unfortunately, it may always be fashionable to blame new tools for old problems, but in the case of messaging, that blame is not warranted. Although messaging may expose literacy problems, it does not create them.

Craig 10

Works Cited

Carnahan, Kristin, and Chiara Coletti. *Ten-Year Trend in SAT Scores Indicates Increased Emphasis on Math Is Yielding Results: Reading and Writing Are Causes for Concern*. New York: College Board, 2002. Print.

College Board. "2011 SAT Trends." *Collegeboard.org*. College Board, 14 Sept. 2011. Web. 6 Dec. 2011.

Crystal, David. *Language Play*. Chicago: U of Chicago P, 1998. Print.

The Discouraging Word. "Re: Messaging and Literacy." Message to the author. 13 Nov. 2011. E-mail.

"Is Texting Destroying Kids' Writing Style?" *Curriculum Review* 48.1 (2008): 4-5. *Academic Search Premier*. Web. 7 Dec. 2011.

Leibowitz, Wendy R. "Technology Transforms Writing and the Teaching of Writing." *Chronicle of Higher Education* 26 Nov. 1999: A67-68. Print.

Lenhart, Amanda, Sousan Arafeh, Aaron Smith, and Alexandra Macgill. *Writing, Technology & Teens*. Washington: Pew Internet & Amer. Life Project, 2008. Web. 6 Dec. 2011.

Lenhart, Amanda, and Oliver Lewis. *Teenage Life Online: The Rise of the Instant-Message Generation and the Internet's Impact on Friendships and Family Relationships*. Washington: Pew Internet & Amer. Life Project, 2001. Web. 6 Dec. 2011.

McCarroll, Christina. "Teens Ready to Prove Text-Messaging Skills Can Score SAT Points." *Christian Science Monitor* 11 Mar. 2005. Web. 10 Dec. 2011.

Heading centered

Report

Graph

Book

Email

Article from database

Print newspaper article

Online report

Subsequent lines of each entry indented

Online newspaper article

APA, *Chicago,* and CSE Documentation

Documentation styles in different disciplines vary according to
what information is valued most highly. Thus in the sciences and
social sciences, where timeliness of publication is crucial, the date
of publication comes up front, right after the author's name.

— ANDREA A. LUNSFORD

APA, *Chicago*, and CSE Documentation

53 APA Style *461*
   a The basics of APA style *461*
   b APA style for in-text citations *463*
   c APA style for a list of references *467*
   d A STUDENT RESEARCH ESSAY, APA STYLE *487*

54 *Chicago* Style *497*
   a The basics of *Chicago* style *497*
   b *Chicago* style for notes and bibliographic entries *500*
   c AN EXCERPT FROM A STUDENT RESEARCH ESSAY, *CHICAGO* STYLE *515*

55 CSE Style *521*
   a CSE style for in-text citations *521*
   b CSE style for a list of references *522*
   c AN EXCERPT FROM A STUDENT RESEARCH PROPOSAL, CSE STYLE *532*

For visual analysis Look carefully at the illustration on the front of this tab. What do you think this image suggests about the kinds of sources writers might document in various disciplines?

APA Style **53**

C hapter 53 discusses the basic formats prescribed by the American Psychological Association (APA), guidelines that are widely used in the social sciences. For further reference, consult the *Publication Manual of the American Psychological Association*, Sixth Edition (2010).

> **bedfordstmartins.com/everydaywriter**
> **Documenting Sources**

53a The basics of APA style

Why does academic work call for very careful citation practices when writing for the general public may not? The answer is that readers of academic work expect to get certain information from source citations:

- Source citations demonstrate that you've done your homework on your topic and that you are a part of the conversation surrounding it.
- Source citations show that you understand the need to give credit when you make use of someone else's intellectual property. (See Chapter 18 for details.)
- Source citations give explicit directions to guide readers who want to look for themselves at the works you're using.

The guidelines for APA style tell you exactly what information to include in your citation and how to format that information.

TYPES OF SOURCES

Look at the Directory to APA Style on p. 468 for guidelines on citing various types of sources—print books (or parts of print books), print periodicals (journals, magazines, or newspapers), and digital written-word sources (an online magazine or newspaper article, or a book on an e-reader). A digital version of a source may include updates or corrections that the print version of the same work lacks, so it's important to provide the correct information for readers. For sources that consist mainly of material other than written words—such as a film, song, or artwork—consult the "other sources" section of the directory. And if you can't find a model exactly like the source you've selected, see the box on p. 470.

ARTICLES FROM WEB AND DATABASE SOURCES

You need a subscription to look through most databases, so individual researchers almost always gain access to articles in databases through the computer system of a school or community library that pays to subscribe. The easiest way to tell whether a source comes from a database, then, is that its information is *not* generally available for free to anyone with an Internet connection. Many databases are digital collections of articles that originally appeared in edited print periodicals, ensuring that an authority has vouched for the accuracy of the information. Such sources often have more credibility than much of what is available for free on the Web.

Parts of citations

APA citations appear in two parts of your text—a brief in-text citation in the body of your written text and a full citation in the list of references, to which the in-text citation directs readers. The most straightforward in-text citations include the author's name, the publication year, and the page number, but many variations on this basic format are discussed in 53b.

　　In the text of her research essay (see 53d), Tawnya Redding includes a paraphrase of material from an online journal that she accessed through the publisher's Web site. She cites the authors' names and the year of publication in a parenthetical reference, pointing readers to the entry for "Baker, F., & Bor, W. (2008)" in her references list, shown on the next page.

Content notes

APA style allows you to use content notes, either at the bottom of the page or on a separate page at the end of the text, to expand or supplement your text. Indicate such notes in the text by superscript numerals (^{1}). Double-space all entries. Indent the first line of each note five spaces, but begin subsequent lines at the left margin.

SUPERSCRIPT NUMBER IN TEXT

The age of the children involved in the study was an important factor in the selection of items for the questionnaire.[1]

MOOD MUSIC 9

References

Baker, F., & Bor, W. (2008). Can music preference indicate mental

health status in young people? *Australasian Psychiatry, 16*(4),

284–288. Retrieved from http://www3.interscience.wiley.com/

journal/118565538/home

types of music can alter the mood of at-risk youth in a negative
way. This view of the correlation between music and suicide risk
is supported by a meta-analysis done by Baker and Bor (2008), in
which the authors assert that most studies reject the notion that
music is a causal factor and suggest that music preference is more

he association

ioral, and

ogy, 19(2),

y metal music

and adolescent suicidal risk. *Journal of Youth and Adolescence,*

30(3), 321–332.

Lai, Y. (1999). Effects of music listening on depressed women in

FOOTNOTE

[1]Marjorie Youngston Forman and William Cole of the Child Study Team
provided great assistance in identifying appropriate items for the questionnaire.

53b APA style for in-text citations

DIRECTORY TO APA STYLE

APA style for in-text citations

1. Basic format for a quotation, *464*
2. Basic format for a paraphrase or summary, *464*
3. Two authors, *464*
4. Three to five authors, *465*
5. Six or more authors, *465*
6. Corporate or group author, *465*
7. Unknown author, *465*
8. Two or more authors with the same last name, *465*
9. Two or more works by an author in a single year, *466*
10. Two or more sources in one parenthetical reference, *466*
11. Indirect source, *466*
12. Personal communication, *466*
13. Electronic document, *466*
14. Table or figure reproduced in the text, *467*

An in-text citation in APA style always indicates *which source* on the references page the writer is referring to, and it explains in what year the material was published; for quoted material, the in-text citation also indicates *where* in the source the quotation can be found.

Note that APA style generally calls for using the past tense or present perfect tense for signal verbs: *Baker (2003) showed* or *Baker (2003) has shown.* Use the present tense only to discuss results (*the experiment demonstrates*) or widely accepted information (*researchers agree*).

1. BASIC FORMAT FOR A QUOTATION

Generally, use the author's name in a signal phrase to introduce the cited material, and place the date, in parentheses, immediately after the author's name. The page number, preceded by *p.*, appears in parentheses after the quotation.

> Gitlin (2001) pointed out that "political critics, convinced that the media are rigged against them, are often blind to other substantial reasons why their causes are unpersuasive" (p. 141).

If the author is not named in a signal phrase, place the author's name, the year, and the page number in parentheses after the quotation: (Gitlin, 2001, p. 141). For a long, set-off quotation (more than forty words), place the page reference in parentheses one space after the final quotation.

For quotations from works without page numbers, you may use paragraph numbers, if the source includes them, preceded by the abbreviation *para.*

> Driver (2007) has noticed "an increasing focus on the role of land" in policy debates over the past decade (para. 1).

2. BASIC FORMAT FOR A PARAPHRASE OR SUMMARY

Include the author's last name and the year as in model 1, but omit the page or paragraph number unless the reader will need it to find the material in a long work.

> Gitlin (2001) has argued that critics sometimes overestimate the influence of the media on modern life.

3. TWO AUTHORS

Use both names in all citations. Use *and* in a signal phrase, but use an ampersand (*&*) in a parentheses.

> Babcock and Laschever (2003) have suggested that many women do not negotiate their salaries and pay raises as vigorously as their male counterparts do.

A recent study has suggested that many women do not negotiate their salaries and pay raises as vigorously as their male counterparts do (Babcock & Laschever, 2003).

4. THREE TO FIVE AUTHORS

List all the authors' names for the first reference.

Safer, Voccola, Hurd, and Goodwin (2003) reached somewhat different conclusions by designing a study that was less dependent on subjective judgment than were previous studies.

In subsequent references, use just the first author's name plus *et al.*

Based on the results, Safer et al. (2003) determined that the apes took significant steps toward self-expression.

5. SIX OR MORE AUTHORS

Use only the first author's name and *et al.* in every citation.

As Soleim et al. (2002) demonstrated, advertising holds the potential for manipulating "free-willed" consumers.

6. CORPORATE OR GROUP AUTHOR

If the name of the organization or corporation is long, spell it out the first time you use it, followed by an abbreviation in brackets. In later references, use the abbreviation only.

FIRST CITATION   (Centers for Disease Control and Prevention [CDC], 2006)

LATER CITATIONS   (CDC, 2006)

7. UNKNOWN AUTHOR

Use the title or its first few words in a signal phrase or in parentheses. A book's title is italicized, as in the following example; an article's title is placed in quotation marks.

The employment profiles for this time period substantiated this trend (*Federal Employment,* 2001).

8. TWO OR MORE AUTHORS WITH THE SAME LAST NAME

If your list of references includes works by different authors with the same last name, include the authors' initials in each citation.

S. Bartolomeo (2000) conducted the groundbreaking study on teenage childbearing.

9. TWO OR MORE WORKS BY AN AUTHOR IN A SINGLE YEAR

Assign lowercase letters (*a, b,* and so on) alphabetically by title, and include the letters after the year.

Gordon (2004b) examined this trend in more detail.

10. TWO OR MORE SOURCES IN ONE PARENTHETICAL REFERENCE

List sources by different authors in alphabetical order by authors' last names, separated by semicolons: (*Cardone, 1998; Lai, 2002*). List works by the same author in chronological order, separated by commas: (*Lai, 2000, 2002*).

11. INDIRECT SOURCE

Use the phrase *as cited in* to indicate that you are reporting information from a secondary source. Name the original source in a signal phrase, but list the secondary source in your list of references.

Amartya Sen developed the influential concept that land reform was necessary for "promoting opportunity" among the poor (as cited in Driver, 2007, para. 2).

12. PERSONAL COMMUNICATION

Cite any personal letters, email messages, electronic postings, telephone conversations, or interviews as shown. Do not include personal communications in the reference list.

R. Tobin (personal communication, November 4, 2006) supported his claims about music therapy with new evidence.

13. ELECTRONIC DOCUMENT

Cite a Web or electronic document as you would a print source, using the author's name and date.

Link and Phelan (2005) argued for broader interventions in public health that would be accessible to anyone, regardless of individual wealth.

The APA recommends the following for electronic sources without names, dates, or page numbers:

AUTHOR UNKNOWN

Use a shortened form of the title in a signal phrase or in parentheses (see model 7). If an organization is the author, see model 6.

DATE UNKNOWN

Use the abbreviation *n.d.* (for "no date") in place of the year: (*Hopkins, n.d.*).

NO PAGE NUMBERS

Many works found online or in electronic databases lack stable page numbers. (Use the page numbers for an electronic work in a format, such as PDF, that has stable pagination.) If paragraph numbers are included in such a source, use the abbreviation *para.*: (*Giambetti, 2006, para. 7*). If no paragraph numbers are included but the source includes headings, give the heading and identify the paragraph in the section:

> Jacobs and Johnson (2007) have argued that "the South African media is still highly concentrated and not very diverse in terms of race and class" (South African Media after Apartheid, para. 3).

14. TABLE OR FIGURE REPRODUCED IN THE TEXT

Number figures (graphs, charts, illustrations, and photographs) and tables separately.

For a table, place the label (*Table 1*) and an informative heading (*Hartman's Key Personality Traits*) above the table; below, provide information about its source.

Table 1

Hartman's Key Personality Traits

Trait category	Color			
	Red	Blue	White	Yellow
Motive	Power	Intimacy	Peace	Fun
Strengths	Loyal to tasks	Loyal to people	Tolerant	Positive
Limitations	Arrogant	Self-righteous	Timid	Uncommitted

Note: Adapted from *The Hartman Personality Profile,* by N. Hayden. Retrieved February 24, 2009, from http://students.cs.byu.edu/~nhayden/Code/index.php

For a figure, place the label (*Figure 3*) and a caption indicating the source below the image. If you do not cite the source of the table or figure elsewhere in your text, you do not need to include the source on your list of references.

53c APA style for a list of references

The alphabetical list of the sources cited in your document is called *References.* If your instructor asks that you list everything you have read—not just the sources you cite—call the list *Bibliography.*

A ll the entries in this section of the book use hanging indent format, in which the first line aligns on the left and the subsequent lines indent one-half inch or five spaces. This is the customary APA format.

DIRECTORY TO APA STYLE

APA style for references

Guidelines for author listings
1. One author, *469*
2. Multiple authors, *470*
3. Corporate or group author, *470*
4. Unknown author, *470*
5. Two or more works by the same author, *470*

Print books

6. Basic format for a book, *471*
   SOURCE MAP, *472–73*
7. Editor, *471*
8. Selection in a book with an editor, *471*
9. Translation, *471*
10. Edition other than the first, *474*
11. Multivolume work, *474*
12. Article in a reference work, *474*
13. Republished book, *474*
14. Introduction, preface, foreword, or afterword, *474*
15. Book with a title within the title, *474*

Print periodicals
16. Article in a journal paginated by volume, *475*
17. Article in a journal paginated by issue, *475*
    SOURCE MAP, *476–77*
18. Article in a magazine, *475*
19. Article in a newspaper, *475*
20. Editorial or letter to the editor, *475*
21. Unsigned article, *475*
22. Review, *475*
23. Published interview, *475*

Digital written-word sources
24. Article from an online periodical, *478*
25. Article from a database, *478*
    SOURCE MAP, *480–81*
26. Abstract for an online article, *478*
27. Document from a Web site, *479*
    SOURCE MAP, *482–83*
28. Chapter or section of a Web document, *484*
29. Email message or real-time communication, *484*
30. Online posting, *484*
31. Blog (Web log) post, *484*
32. Wiki entry, *485*

Other sources (including online versions)
33. Computer software, *485*
34. Government publication, *485*
35. Data set, *485*
36. Dissertation, *485*
37. Technical or research report, *486*
38. Conference proceedings, *486*
39. Paper presented at a meeting or symposium, unpublished, *486*
40. Poster session, *486*
41. Film, video, or DVD, *486*
42. Online audio or video file, *486*
43. Television program, single episode, *486*
44. Television series, *487*
45. Audio podcast (downloaded audio file), *487*
46. Recording, *487*

AT A GLANCE

Formatting a List of References

- Start your list on a separate page after the text of your document but before appendices or notes. Continue consecutive page numbers.
- Center the heading *References* one inch from the top of the page.
- Begin each entry flush with the left margin, but indent subsequent lines one-half inch or five spaces. Double-space the entire list.
- List sources alphabetically by authors' (or editors') last names. If no author is given, alphabetize the source by the first word of the title other than *A*, *An*, or *The*. If the list includes two or more works by the same author, list them in chronological order. (For two or more works by the same author published in the same year, see model 5.)
- Italicize titles and subtitles of books and periodicals. Do not italicize titles of articles, and do not enclose them in quotation marks.
- For titles of books and articles, capitalize only the first word of the title and the subtitle and any proper nouns or proper adjectives.
- For titles of periodicals, capitalize all major words.
- Follow the guidelines in 53c for punctuating an entry.

Guidelines for author listings

List authors' last names first, and use only initials for first and middle names. The in-text citations in your text point readers toward particular sources in your list of references (see 53b).

NAME CITED IN SIGNAL PHRASE IN TEXT

Driver (2007) has noted . . .

NAME IN PARENTHETICAL CITATION IN TEXT

. . . (Driver, 2007).

BEGINNING OF ENTRY IN LIST OF REFERENCES

Driver, T. (2007).

Models 1–5 below explain how to arrange author names. The information that follows the name of the author depends on the type of work you are citing—a book (models 6–15), a print periodical (models 16–23), a digital source (models 24–33), or another kind of source (models 34–46).

1. ONE AUTHOR

Give the last name, a comma, the initial(s), and the date in parentheses.

Zimbardo, P. G. (2009).

AT A GLANCE

Combining Parts of Models

What should you do if your source doesn't match the model exactly? Suppose, for instance, that your source is a translation of a republished book with an editor.

- Identify a basic model to follow. If you decide that your source looks most like a republished book, for example, start with a citation that looks like model 13.

- Look for models that show additional elements in your source. For this example, you would need elements of model 9 (for the translation) and model 7 (for the editor).

- Add new elements from other models to your basic model in the order that makes the most sense to you.

- If you still aren't sure how to arrange the pieces to create a combination model, check the *APA Manual* or ask your instructor.

---

2. MULTIPLE AUTHORS

List up to seven authors, last name first, with commas separating authors' names and an ampersand (&) before the last author's name.

> Walsh, M. E., & Murphy, J. A. (2003).

Note: For a work with more than seven authors, list the first six, then an ellipsis (. . .), and then the final author's name.

3. CORPORATE OR GROUP AUTHOR

> Resources for Rehabilitation. (2003).

4. UNKNOWN AUTHOR

Begin with the work's title. Italicize book titles, but do not italicize article titles or enclose them in quotation marks. Capitalize only the first word of the title and subtitle (if any) and proper nouns and proper adjectives.

> *Safe youth, safe schools.* (2009).

5. TWO OR MORE WORKS BY THE SAME AUTHOR

List two or more works by the same author in chronological order. Repeat the author's name in each entry.

> Goodall, J. (1999).

> Goodall, J. (2002).

If the works appeared in the same year, list them alphabetically by title, and assign lowercase letters (*a, b,* etc.) after the dates.

> Shermer, M. (2002a). On estimating the lifetime of civilizations. *Scientific American, 287*(2), 33.

> Shermer, M. (2002b). Readers who question evolution. *Scientific American, 287*(1), 37.

Print books

6. BASIC FORMAT FOR A BOOK

Begin with the author name(s). (See models 1–5.) Then include the publication year, title and subtitle, city of publication, country or state abbreviation, and publisher. The source map on pp. 472–73 shows where to find this information in a typical book.

> Levick, S. E. (2003). *Clone being: Exploring the psychological and social dimensions.* Lanham, MD: Rowman & Littlefield.

7. EDITOR

For a book with an editor but no author, list the source under the editor's name.

> Dickens, J. (Ed.). (1995). *Family outing: A guide for parents of gays, lesbians and bisexuals.* London, England: Peter Owen.

To cite a book with an author and an editor, place the editor's name, with a comma and the abbreviation *Ed.,* in parentheses after the title.

> Austin, J. (1995). *The province of jurisprudence determined.* (W. E. Rumble, Ed.). Cambridge, England: Cambridge University Press.

8. SELECTION IN A BOOK WITH AN EDITOR

> Burke, W. W., & Nourmair, D. A. (2001). The role of personality assessment in organization development. In J. Waclawski & A. H. Church (Eds.), *Organization development: A data-driven approach to organizational change* (pp. 55–77). San Francisco, CA: Jossey-Bass.

9. TRANSLATION

> Al-Farabi, A. N. (1998). *On the perfect state* (R. Walzer, Trans.). Chicago, IL: Kazi.

APA SOURCE MAP: Books

Take information from the book's title page and copyright page (on the reverse side of the title page), not from the book's cover or a library catalog.

1 **Author.** List all authors' last names first, and use only initials for first and middle names. For more about citing authors, see models 1–5.

2 **Publication year.** Enclose the year of publication in parentheses.

3 **Title.** Italicize the title and any subtitle. Capitalize only the first word of the title and the subtitle and any proper nouns or proper adjectives.

4 **City and state of publication.** List the city of publication and the country or state abbreviation followed by a colon.

5 **Publisher.** Give the publisher's name, dropping any *Inc.*, *Co.*, or *Publishers*.

A citation for the book on p. 473 would look like this:

Tsutsui, W. (2004). *Godzilla on my mind: Fifty years of the king of monsters.* New York, NY: Palgrave Macmillan.

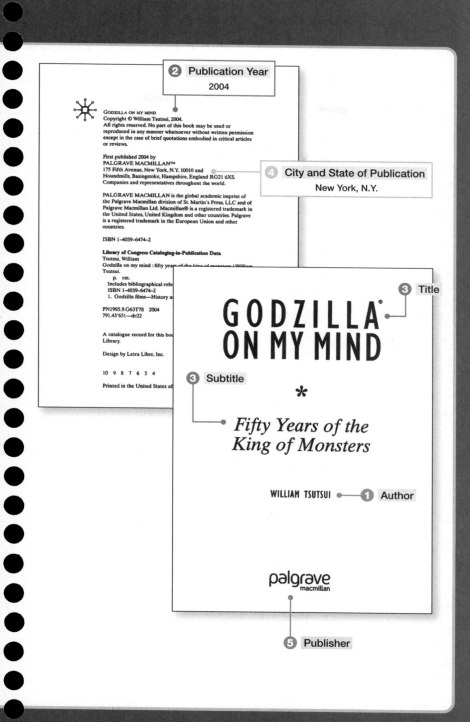

2 Publication Year

2004

GODZILLA ON MY MIND
Copyright © William Tsutsui, 2004.
All rights reserved. No part of this book may be used or
reproduced in any manner whatsoever without written permission
except in the case of brief quotations embodied in critical articles
or reviews.

First published 2004 by
PALGRAVE MACMILLAN™
175 Fifth Avenue, New York, N.Y. 10010 and
Houndmills, Basingstoke, Hampshire, England RG21 6XS.
Companies and representatives throughout the world.

4 City and State of Publication

New York, N.Y.

PALGRAVE MACMILLAN is the global academic imprint of
the Palgrave Macmillan division of St. Martin's Press, LLC and of
Palgrave Macmillan Ltd. Macmillan® is a registered trademark in
the United States, United Kingdom and other countries. Palgrave
is a registered trademark in the European Union and other
countries.

ISBN 1–4039–6474–2

Library of Congress Cataloging-in-Publication Data
Tsutsui, William
Godzilla on my mind : fifty years of the king of monsters / William
Tsutsui.
    p.   cm.
  Includes bibliographical refe
  ISBN 1–4039–6474–2
  1. Godzilla films—History a

PN1995.9.G63T78 2004
791.43'651—dc22

A catalogue record for this boo
Library.

Design by Letra Libre, Inc.

10 9 8 7 6 5 4

Printed in the United States of

3 Title

GODZILLA®
ON MY MIND

3 Subtitle

*

*Fifty Years of the
King of Monsters*

WILLIAM TSUTSUI — **1 Author**

palgrave
macmillan

5 Publisher

473

10. **EDITION OTHER THAN THE FIRST**

> Moore, G. S. (2002). *Living with the earth: Concepts in environmental health science* (2nd ed.). New York, NY: Lewis.

11. **MULTIVOLUME WORK**

> Barnes, J. (Ed.). (1995). *Complete works of Aristotle* (Vols. 1–2). Princeton, NJ: Princeton University Press.

Note: If you cite just one volume of a multivolume work, list that volume, not the complete span of volumes, in parentheses after the title.

12. **ARTICLE IN A REFERENCE WORK**

> Dean, C. (1994). Jaws and teeth. In *The Cambridge encyclopedia of human evolution* (pp. 56–59). Cambridge, England: Cambridge University Press.

If no author is listed, begin with the title.

13. **REPUBLISHED BOOK**

> Piaget, J. (1952). *The language and thought of the child*. London, England: Routledge & Kegan Paul. (Original work published 1932)

14. **INTRODUCTION, PREFACE, FOREWORD, OR AFTERWORD**

> Klosterman, C. (2007). Introduction. In P. Shirley, *Can I keep my jersey?: 11 teams, 5 countries, and 4 years in my life as a basketball vagabond* (pp. v–vii). New York, NY: Villard-Random House.

15. **BOOK WITH A TITLE WITHIN THE TITLE**

Do not italicize or enclose in quotation marks a title within a book title.

> Klarman, M. J. (2007). *Brown v. Board of Education and the civil rights movement*. New York, NY: Oxford University Press.

Print periodicals

Begin with the author name(s). (See models 1–5.) Then include the publication date (year only for journals, and year, month, and day for other periodicals); the article title; the periodical title; the volume number and issue number, if any; and the page numbers. The source map on pp. 476–77 shows where to find this information in a sample periodical.

16. ARTICLE IN A JOURNAL PAGINATED BY VOLUME

O'Connell, D. C., & Kowal, S. (2003). Psycholinguistics: A half century of monologism. *The American Journal of Psychology, 116,* 191–212.

17. ARTICLE IN A JOURNAL PAGINATED BY ISSUE

If each issue begins with page 1, include the issue number (in parentheses and not italicized) after the volume number (italicized).

Hall, R. E. (2000). Marriage as vehicle of racism among women of color. *Psychology: A Journal of Human Behavior, 37*(2), 29–40.

18. ARTICLE IN A MAGAZINE

Ricciardi, S. (2003, August 5). Enabling the mobile work force. *PC Magazine, 22,* 46.

19. ARTICLE IN A NEWSPAPER

Reynolds Lewis, K. (2011, December 22). Why some business owners think now is the time to sell. *The New York Times,* p. B5.

20. EDITORIAL OR LETTER TO THE EDITOR

Zelneck, B. (2003, July 18). Serving the public at public universities [Letter to the editor]. *The Chronicle Review,* p. B18.

21. UNSIGNED ARTICLE

Annual meeting announcement. (2003, March). *Cognitive Psychology, 46,* 227.

22. REVIEW

Ringel, S. (2003). [Review of the book *Multiculturalism and the therapeutic process*]. *Clinical Social Work Journal, 31,* 212–213.

23. PUBLISHED INTERVIEW

Smith, H. (2002, October). [Interview with A. Thompson]. *The Sun,* pp. 4–7.

1 **Author.** List all authors' last names first, and use only initials for first and middle names. For more about citing authors, see models 1–5.

2 **Publication date.** Enclose the date in parentheses. For journals, use only the year. For magazines and newspapers, use the year, a comma, the month (spelled out), and the day, if given.

3 **Article title.** Do not italicize or enclose article titles in quotation marks. Capitalize only the first word of the article title and subtitle and any proper nouns or proper adjectives.

4 **Periodical title.** Italicize the periodical title (and subtitle, if any), and capitalize all major words. Follow the periodical title with a comma.

5 **Volume and issue numbers.** Give the volume number (italicized) and, without a space in between, the issue number (if given) in parentheses. Follow with a comma.

6 **Page numbers.** Give the inclusive page numbers of the article. For newspapers only, include the abbreviation *p.* ("page") or *pp.* ("pages") before the page numbers. End the citation with a period.

A citation for the periodical article on p. 477 would look like this:

Etzioni, A. (2006). Leaving race behind: Our growing Hispanic population creates a golden opportunity. *The American Scholar, 75*(2), 20–30.

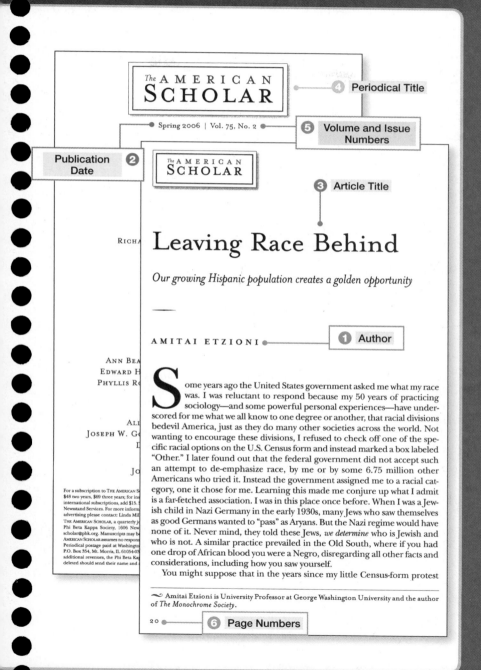

Digital written-word sources

Updated guidelines for citing electronic resources are maintained at the APA's Web site (www.apa.org).

24. ARTICLE FROM AN ONLINE PERIODICAL

Give the author, date, title, and publication information as you would for a print document. Include both the volume and issue numbers for all journal articles. If the article has a digital object identifier (DOI), include it. If there is no DOI, include the URL for the periodical's home page or for the article (if the article is difficult to find from the home page). For newspaper articles accessible from a searchable Web site, give the site URL only.

> Barringer, F. (2008, February 7). In many communities, it's not easy going green. *The New York Times*. Retrieved from http://www.nytimes.com

> Cleary, J. M., & Crafti, N. (2007). Basic need satisfaction, emotional eating, and dietary restraint as risk factors for recurrent overeating in a community sample. *E-Journal of Applied Psychology, 2*(3), 27–39. Retrieved from http://ojs.lib.swin.edu.au/index.php/ejap/article/view/90/116

25. ARTICLE FROM A DATABASE

Give the author, date, title, and publication information as you would for a print document. Include both the volume and issue numbers for all journal articles. If the article has a DOI, include it. If there is no DOI, write *Retrieved from* and the URL of the journal's home page (not the URL of the database). The source map on pp. 480–81 shows where to find this information for a typical article from a database.

> Hazleden, R. (2003, December). Love yourself: The relationship of the self with itself in popular self-help texts. *Journal of Sociology, 39*(4), 413–428. Retrieved from http://jos.sagepub.com

> Morley, N. J., Ball, L. J., & Ormerod, T. C. (2006). How the detection of insurance fraud succeeds and fails. *Psychology, Crime, & Law, 12*(2), 163–180. doi:10.1080/10683160512331316325

26. ABSTRACT FOR AN ONLINE ARTICLE

> Gudjonsson, G. H., & Young, S. (2010). Does confabulation in memory predict suggestibility beyond IQ and memory? [Abstract]. *Personality & Individual Differences, 49*(1), 65–67. doi: 10.1016/j.paid.2010.03.014

AT A GLANCE

Citing Digital Sources

When citing sources accessed online or from an electronic database, include as many of the following elements as you can find:

- **Author.** Give the author's name, if available.
- **Publication date.** Include the date of electronic publication or of the latest update, if available. When no publication date is available, use *n.d.* ("no date").
- **Title.** If the source is not part of a larger whole, italicize the title.
- **Print publication information.** For articles from online journals, magazines, or reference databases, give the publication title and other publishing information as you would for a print periodical (see models 16–23).
- **Retrieval information.** For a work from a database, do the following: if the article has a DOI (digital object identifier), include that number after the publication information; do not include the name of the database. If there is no DOI, write *Retrieved from* followed by the URL for the journal's home page (not the database URL). For a work found on a Web site, write *Retrieved from* and include the URL. If the work seems likely to be updated, include the retrieval date. If the URL is longer than one line, break it only before a punctuation mark; do not break *http://*.

27. DOCUMENT FROM A WEB SITE

Include all of the following information that you can find: the author's name; the publication date (or *n.d.* if no date is available); the title of the document; the title of the site or larger work, if any; volume and issue numbers (if any); page numbers (if any); *Retrieved from* and the URL. Provide your date of access only if an update seems likely. The source map on pp. 482–83 shows where to find this information for an article from a Web site.

Behnke, P. C. (2006, February 22). *The homeless are everyone's problem.* Retrieved from http://www.authorsden.com/visit/viewArticle.asp?id=21017

Hacker, J. S. (2006). The privatization of risk and the growing economic insecurity of Americans. *Items and Issues, 5*(4), 16–23. Retrieved from http://publications.ssrc.org/items/items5.4/Hacker.pdf

What parents should know about treatment of behavioral and emotional disorders in preschool children. (2006). *APA Online.* Retrieved from http://www.apa.org/releases/kidsmed.html

APA SOURCE MAP: Articles from Databases

1 **Author.** Include the author's name as you would for a print source. List all authors' last names first, and use initials for first and middle names. For more about citing authors, see models 1–5.

2 **Publication date.** Enclose the date in parentheses. For journals, use only the year. For magazines and newspapers, use the year, a comma, the month, and the day if given.

3 **Article title.** Capitalize only the first word of the article title and the subtitle and any proper nouns or proper adjectives.

4 **Periodical title.** Italicize the periodical title.

5 **Volume and issue number.** For journals and magazines, give the volume number (italicized) and the issue number (in parentheses).

6 **Page numbers.** For journals only, give inclusive page numbers.

7 **Retrieval information.** If the article has a DOI (digital object identifier), include that number after the publication information; do not include the name of the database. If there is no DOI, write *Retrieved from* followed by the URL of the journal's home page (not the database URL).

A citation for the article on p. 481 would look like this:

Chory-Assad, R. M., & Tamborini, R. (2004). Television sitcom exposure and aggressive communication: A priming perspective. *North American Journal of Psychology, 6*(3), 415–422. Retrieved from http://www.najp.8m.com

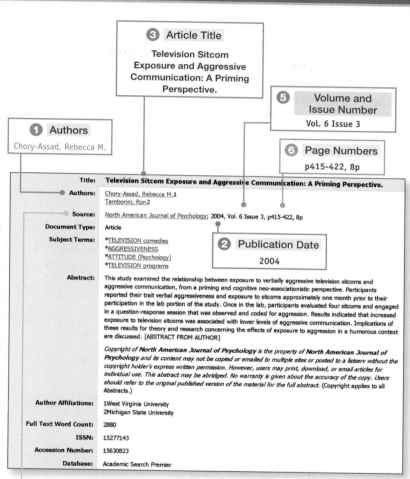

❸ Article Title

Television Sitcom Exposure and Aggressive Communication: A Priming Perspective.

❺ Volume and Issue Number

Vol. 6 Issue 3

❻ Page Numbers

p415-422, 8p

❶ Authors

Chory-Assad, Rebecca M.

Title:	Television Sitcom Exposure and Aggressive Communication: A Priming Perspective.
Authors:	Chory-Assad, Rebecca M.1 Tamborini, Ron2
Source:	North American Journal of Psychology; 2004, Vol. 6 Issue 3, p415-422, 8p
Document Type:	Article
Subject Terms:	*TELEVISION comedies *AGGRESSIVENESS *ATTITUDE (Psychology) *TELEVISION programs

❷ Publication Date

2004

Abstract:

This study examined the relationship between exposure to verbally aggressive television sitcoms and aggressive communication, from a priming and cognitive neo-associationistic perspective. Participants reported their trait verbal aggressiveness and exposure to sitcoms approximately one month prior to their participation in the lab portion of the study. Once in the lab, participants evaluated four sitcoms and engaged in a question-response session that was observed and coded for aggression. Results indicated that increased exposure to television sitcoms was associated with lower levels of aggressive communication. Implications of these results for theory and research concerning the effects of exposure to aggression in a humorous context are discussed. [ABSTRACT FROM AUTHOR]

Author Affiliations:	1West Virginia University 2Michigan State University
Full Text Word Count:	2880
ISSN:	15277143
Accession Number:	15630823
Database:	Academic Search Premier

❹ Periodical Title

North American Journal of Psychology

481

1 Author. If one is given, include the author's name (see models 1–5). List last names first, and use only initials for first names. The site's sponsor may be the author. If no author is identified, begin the citation with the title of the document.

2 Publication date. Enclose the date of publication or latest update in parentheses. Use *n.d.* ("no date") when no publication date is available.

3 Title of work. Capitalize only the first word of the title and subtitle and any proper nouns or proper adjectives.

4 Title of Web site. Italicize the title. Capitalize all major words.

5 Retrieval information. Write *Retrieved from* and include the URL. If the work seems likely to be updated, include the retrieval date.

A citation for the Web document on p. 483 would look like this:

Alexander, M. (2001, August 22). Thirty years later, Stanford Prison Experiment lives on. *Stanford Report*. Retrieved from http://news-service.stanford .edu/news/2001/august22/prison2-822.html

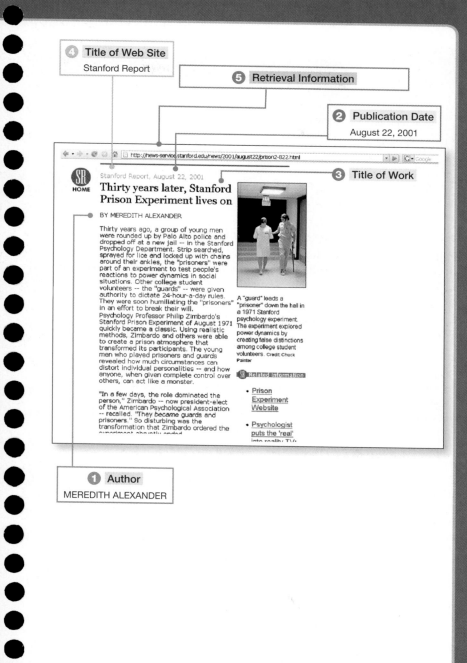

4 Title of Web Site
Stanford Report

5 Retrieval Information

2 Publication Date
August 22, 2001

http://news-service.stanford.edu/news/2001/august22/prison2-822.html

3 Title of Work

Stanford Report, August 22, 2001

HOME

Thirty years later, Stanford Prison Experiment lives on

BY MEREDITH ALEXANDER

Thirty years ago, a group of young men were rounded up by Palo Alto police and dropped off at a new jail -- in the Stanford Psychology Department. Strip searched, sprayed for lice and locked up with chains around their ankles, the "prisoners" were part of an experiment to test people's reactions to power dynamics in social situations. Other college student volunteers -- the "guards" -- were given authority to dictate 24-hour-a-day rules. They were soon humiliating the "prisoners" in an effort to break their will. Psychology Professor Philip Zimbardo's Stanford Prison Experiment of August 1971 quickly became a classic. Using realistic methods, Zimbardo and others were able to create a prison atmosphere that transformed its participants. The young men who played prisoners and guards revealed how much circumstances can distort individual personalities -- and how anyone, when given complete control over others, can act like a monster.

"In a few days, the role dominated the person," Zimbardo -- now president-elect of the American Psychological Association -- recalled. "They became guards and prisoners." So disturbing was the transformation that Zimbardo ordered the experiment abruptly ended

A "guard" leads a "prisoner" down the hall in a 1971 Stanford psychology experiment. The experiment explored power dynamics by creating false distinctions among college student volunteers. Credit Chuck Painter

Related Information

- Prison Experiment Website

- Psychologist puts the 'real' into reality TV:

1 Author
MEREDITH ALEXANDER

483

28. CHAPTER OR SECTION OF A WEB DOCUMENT

Follow model 27. After the chapter or section title, type *In* and give the document title, with identifying information, if any, in parentheses. End with the date of access (if needed) and the URL.

> Salamon, Andrew. (n.d.). War in Europe. In *Childhood in times of war* (chap. 2).
> Retrieved April 11, 2008, from http://remember.org/jean

29. EMAIL MESSAGE OR REAL-TIME COMMUNICATION

Because the APA stresses that any sources cited in your list of references be retrievable by your readers, you should not include entries for email messages, real-time communications (such as IMs), or any other postings that are not archived. Instead, cite these sources in your text as forms of personal communication (see p. 466).

30. ONLINE POSTING

List an online posting in the references list only if you are able to retrieve the message from an archive. Provide the author's name, the date of posting, and the subject line. Include other identifying information in square brackets. End with the retrieval statement and the URL of the archived message.

> Troike, R. C. (2001, June 21). Buttercups and primroses [Electronic mailing list message]. Retrieved from http://listserv.linguistlist.org/archives/ads-l.html

> Wittenberg, E. (2001, July 11). Gender and the Internet [Newsgroup message]. Retrieved from news://comp.edu.composition

31. BLOG (WEB LOG) POST

> Spaulding, P. (2010, April 27). Who believes in a real America? [Web log post]. Retrieved from http://pandagon.net/index.php/site/2010/04

32. WIKI ENTRY

Use the date of posting, if there is one, or *n.d.* for "no date" if there is none. Include the retrieval date because wiki content can change frequently.

> Happiness. (2007, June 14). Retrieved March 24, 2008, from PsychWiki:
>   http://www.psychwiki.com/wiki/Happiness

Other sources (including online versions)

33. COMPUTER SOFTWARE

> PsychMate [Computer software]. (2003). Available from Psychology Software
>   Tools: http://pstnet.com/products/psychmate

34. GOVERNMENT PUBLICATION

> Office of the Federal Register. (2003). *The United States government manual*
>   *2003/2004.* Washington, DC: U.S. Government Printing Office.

Cite an online government document as you would a printed government work, adding the URL. If there is no date, use *n.d.*

> U.S. Public Health Service. (1999). *The surgeon general's call to action to prevent*
>   *suicide.* Retrieved from http://www.mentalhealth.org/suicideprevention
>   /calltoaction.asp

35. DATA SET

> U.S. Department of Education, Institute of Education Sciences. (2009).
>   *NAEP state comparisons* [Data set]. Retrieved from http://nces.ed.gov
>   /nationsreportcard/statecomparisons/

36. DISSERTATION

If you retrieved the dissertation from a database, give the database name and the accession number, if one is assigned.

> Lengel, L. L. (1968). *The righteous cause: Some religious aspects of Kansas*
>   *populism.* Retrieved from ProQuest Digital Dissertations. (6900033)

If you retrieve a dissertation from a Web site, give the type of dissertation, the institution, and year after the title, and provide a retrieval statement.

> Meeks, M. G. (2006). *Between abolition and reform: First-year writing programs,*
>   *e-literacies, and institutional change* (Doctoral dissertation, University of
>   North Carolina). Retrieved from http://dc.lib.unc.edu/etd/

37. TECHNICAL OR RESEARCH REPORT

Give the report number, if available, in parentheses after the title.

McCool, R., Fikes, R., & McGuinness, D. (2003). *Semantic Web tools for enhanced authoring* (Report No. KSL-03-07). Retrieved from www.ksl.stanford.edu /KSL_Abstracts/KSL-03-07.html

38. CONFERENCE PROCEEDINGS

Robertson, S. P., Vatrapu, R. K., & Medina, R. (2009). YouTube and Facebook: Online video "friends" social networking. In *Conference proceedings: YouTube and the 2008 election cycle* (pp. 159–76). Amherst, MA: University of Massachusetts. Retrieved from http://scholarworks.umass.edu/jitpc2009

39. PAPER PRESENTED AT A MEETING OR SYMPOSIUM, UNPUBLISHED

Cite the month of the meeting if it is available.

Jones, J. G. (1999, February). *Mental health intervention in mass casualty disasters.* Paper presented at the Rocky Mountain Region Disaster Mental Health Conference, Laramie, WY.

40. POSTER SESSION

Barnes Young, L. L. (2003, August). *Cognition, aging, and dementia.* Poster session presented at the 2003 Division 40 APA Convention, Toronto, Ontario, Canada.

41. FILM, VIDEO, OR DVD

Nolan, C. (Director). (2010). *Inception* [Motion picture]. United States: Warner Bros.

42. ONLINE AUDIO OR VIDEO FILE

Klusman, P. (2008, February 13). An engineer's guide to cats [Video file]. Retrieved from http://www.youtube.com/watch?v=mHXBL6bzAR4

O'Brien, K. (2008, January 31). Developing countries [Audio file]. *KUSP's life in the fast lane.* Retrieved from http://kusp.org/shows/fast.html

43. TELEVISION PROGRAM, SINGLE EPISODE

Imperioli, M. (Writer), & Buscemi, S. (Director). (2002). Everybody hurts [Television series episode]. In D. Chase (Executive Producer), *The Sopranos.* New York, NY: Home Box Office.

44. TELEVISION SERIES

Abrams, J. J., Lieber, J., & Lindelof, D. (2004). *Lost*. [Television series]. New York, NY: WABC.

45. AUDIO PODCAST (DOWNLOADED AUDIO FILE)

Noguchi, Yugi. (2010, 24 May). BP hard to pin down on oil spill claims. [Audio podcast]. *NPR morning edition*. Retrieved from http://www.npr.org

46. RECORDING

The Avalanches. (2001). Frontier psychiatrist. On *Since I left you* [CD]. Los Angeles, CA: Elektra/Asylum Records.

53d A student research essay, APA style

On the following pages is a paper by Tawnya Redding that conforms to the APA guidelines described in this chapter. Note that this essay has been reproduced in a narrow format to allow for annotation.

Student Writer

Tawnya Redding

 bedfordstmartins.com/everydaywriter
Student Writing

Running Head: MOOD MUSIC   1

Running head
(fifty characters
or fewer)
appears flush
left on first line
of title page

Page number
appears flush
right on first
line of every
page

Title, name,
and affiliation
centered and
double-spaced

Mood Music: Music Preference and the Risk for Depression

and Suicide in Adolescents

Tawnya Redding

Psychology 480

Professor Ede

February 23, 2009

Annotations indicate effective choices or APA-style formatting.

Student Writing
APA

Abstract

There has long been concern for the effects that certain genres of music (such as heavy metal and country) have on youth. While a correlational link between these genres and increased risk for depression and suicide in adolescents has been established, researchers have been unable to pinpoint what is responsible for this link, and a causal relationship has not been determined. This paper will begin by discussing correlational literature concerning music preference and increased risk for depression and suicide, as well as the possible reasons for this link. Finally, studies concerning the effects of music on mood will be discussed. This examination of the literature on music and increased risk for depression and suicide points out the limitations of previous research and suggests the need for new research establishing a causal relationship for this link as well as research into the specific factors that may contribute to an increased risk for depression and suicide in adolescents.

Heading
centered

No indentation

Use of
passive voice
appropriate for
social sciences

Clear,
straightforward
description
of literature
under review

Conclusions
indicated

Double-spaced
text

MOOD MUSIC   3

Full title
centered

Paragraphs
indented

Background
information
about review
supplied

Questions
focus reader's
attention

Boldface
headings
help organize
review

Parenthetical
references
follow APA
style

Mood Music: Music Preference and the Risk for Depression and
Suicide in Adolescents

Music is a significant part of American culture. Since the
explosion of rock and roll in the 1950s, there has been a concern
for the effects that music may have on listeners, and especially
on young people. The genres most likely to come under suspicion
in recent decades have included heavy metal, country, and blues.
These genres have been suspected of having adverse effects on
the mood and behavior of young listeners. But can music really
alter the disposition and create self-destructive behaviors in
listeners? And if so, which genres and aspects of those genres are
responsible? The following review of the literature will establish
the correlation between potentially problematic genres of music
such as heavy metal and country and depression and suicide risk.
First, correlational studies concerning music preference and suicide
risk will be discussed, followed by a discussion of the literature
concerning the possible reasons for this link. Finally, studies
concerning the effects of music on mood will be discussed. Despite
the link between genres such as heavy metal and country and
suicide risk, previous research has been unable to establish the
causal nature of this link.

The Correlation Between Music and Depression and Suicide Risk

Studies over the past two decades have set out to answer
this question by examining the correlation between youth music
preference and risk for depression and suicide. A large portion
of these studies have focused on heavy metal and country music
as the main genre culprits associated with youth suicidality
and depression (Lacourse, Claes, & Villeneuve, 2001; Scheel &
Westefeld, 1999; Stack & Gundlach, 1992). Stack and Gundlach
(1992) examined the radio airtime devoted to country music in 49
metropolitan areas and found that the higher the percentages of

MOOD MUSIC   4

country music airtime, the higher the incidence of suicides among whites. The researchers hypothesized that themes in country music (such as alcohol abuse) promoted audience identification and reinforced a preexisting suicidal mood, and that the themes associated with country music were responsible for elevated suicide rates. Similarly, Scheel and Westefeld (1999) found a correlation between heavy metal music listeners and an increased risk for suicide, as did Lacourse et al. (2001).

Reasons for the Link: Characteristics of Those Who Listen to Problematic Music

Unfortunately, previous studies concerning music preference and suicide risk have been unable to determine a causal relationship and have focused mainly on establishing a correlation between suicide risk and music preference. This leaves the question open as to whether an individual at risk for depression and suicide is attracted to certain genres of music or whether the music helps induce the mood—or both. Some studies have suggested that music preference may simply be a reflection of other underlying problems associated with increased risk for suicide (Lacourse et al., 2001; Scheel & Westefeld, 1999). For example, in research done by Scheel and Westefeld (1999), adolescents who listened to heavy metal were found to have lower scores on the Reason for Living Inventory, a self-report measure designed to assess potential reasons for not committing suicide. These adolescents were also found to have lower scores on several subscales of the Reason for Living Inventory, including responsibility to family along with survival and coping beliefs. Other risk factors associated with suicide and suicidal behaviors include poor family relationships, depression, alienation, anomie, and drug and alcohol abuse (Lacourse et al., 2001). Lacourse et al. (2001) examined 275 adolescents in the Montreal region with a preference for heavy metal and found that this preference was not significantly related to suicide risk when other

Discussion of correlation vs. causation points out limitations of previous studies

Alternative explanations considered

MOOD MUSIC   5

risk factors were controlled for. This was also the conclusion of Scheel
and Westefeld (1999), in which music preference for heavy metal
was thought to be a red flag for suicide vulnerability, suggesting
that the source of the problem may lie more in personal and familial
characteristics.

George, Stickle, Rachid, and Wopnford (2007) further explored
the correlation between suicide risk and music preference by
attempting to identify the personality characteristics of those
with a preference for different genres of music. A sample of 358
individuals was assessed for preference of 30 different styles of
music along with a number of personality characteristics, including
self-esteem, intelligence, spirituality, social skills, locus of
control, openness, conscientiousness, extraversion, agreeableness,
emotional stability, hostility, and depression (George et al.,
2007). The 30 styles of music were then categorized into 8 factors:
rebellious (for example, punk and heavy metal), classical, rhythmic
and intense (including hip-hop, rap, and pop), easy listening,
fringe (for example, techno), contemporary Christian, jazz and
blues, and traditional Christian. The results revealed an almost
comprehensively negative personality profile for those who
preferred to listen to the rebellious and rhythmic and intense
categories, while those who preferred classical music tended to
have a comprehensively positive profile. Like Scheel and Westefeld
(1999) and Lacourse et al. (2001), this study also supports the
theory that youth are drawn to certain genres of music based on
already existing factors, whether they be related to personality or
situational variables.

Reasons for the Link: Characteristics of Problematic Music

Another possible explanation is that the lyrics and themes
of the music have an effect on listeners. In this scenario, music
is thought to exacerbate an already depressed mood and hence

Transition links
paragraphs

contribute to an increased risk for suicide. This was the proposed reasoning behind higher suicide rates in whites in Stack and Gundlach's (1992) study linking country music to suicide risk. In this case, the themes associated with country music were thought to promote audience identification and reinforce preexisting self-destructive behaviors (such as excessive alcohol consumption). Stack (2000) also studied individuals with a musical preference for blues to determine whether the genre's themes could increase the level of suicide acceptability. The results demonstrated that blues fans were no more accepting of suicide than nonfans, but that blues listeners were found to have low religiosity levels, an important factor for suicide acceptability (Stack, 2000). Despite this link between possible suicidal behavior and a preference for blues music, the actual suicide behavior of blues fans has not been explored, and thus no concrete associations can be made.

Need for more research indicated

The Effect of Music on Mood

While studies examining the relationship between music genres such as heavy metal, country, and blues have been able to establish a correlation between music preference and suicide risk, it is still unclear from these studies what effect music has on the mood of the listener. Previous research has suggested that some forms of music can both improve and depress mood (Lai, 1999; Siedliecki & Good, 2006; Smith & Noon, 1998). Lai (1999) found that changes in mood were more likely to be found in an experimental group of depressed women versus a control group. It was also found that both the experimental and control groups showed significant increases in the tranquil mood state, but the amount of change was not significant between the groups (Lai, 1999). This study suggests that music can have a positive effect on depressed individuals when they are allowed to choose the music they are listening to. In a similar study, Siedliecki and

Discussion of previous research

MOOD MUSIC   7

Good (2006) found that music can increase a listener's sense of
power and decrease depression, pain, and disability. Researchers
randomly assigned 60 African American and Caucasian participants
with chronic nonmalignant pain to a standard music group
(offering them a choice of instrumental music types—piano,
jazz, orchestra, harp, and synthesizer), a patterning music group
(asking them to choose music to ease muscle tension, to facilitate
sleep, or to decrease anxiety), or a control group. There were no
statistically significant differences between the two music groups.
However, the music groups had significantly less pain, depression,
and disability than the control group (Siedliecki & Good, 2006).
On the other hand, Martin, Clark, and Pearce (1993) identified a
subgroup of heavy metal fans who reported feeling worse after
listening to their music of choice. Although this subgroup did
exist, there was also evidence that listening to heavy metal
results in more positive affect, and it was hypothesized that those
who experience negative effects after listening to their preferred
genre of heavy metal may be most at risk for suicidal behaviors
(Martin et al., 1993).

Smith and Noon (1998) also determined that music can
have a negative effect on mood. Six songs were selected for the
particular theme they embodied: (1) vigorous, (2) fatigued,
(3) angry, (4) depressed, (5) tense, and (6) all moods. The
results indicated that selections 3–6 had significant effects on
the mood of participants, with selection 6 (all moods) resulting
in the greatest positive change in the mood and selection 5
(tense) resulting in the greatest negative change in mood.
Selection 4 (depressed) was found to sap the vigor and increase
anger / hostility in participants, while selection 5 (tense)
significantly depressed participants and made them more anxious.
Although this study did not specifically comment on the effects

of different genres on mood, the results do indicate that certain themes can indeed depress mood. The participants for this study were undergraduate students who were not depressed, and thus it seems that certain types of music can have a negative effect on the mood of healthy individuals.

Is There Evidence for a Causal Relationship?

Despite the correlation between certain music genres (especially heavy metal) and increased risk for depression and suicidal behaviors in adolescents, it remains unclear whether these types of music can alter the mood of at-risk youth in a negative way. This view of the correlation between music and suicide risk is supported by a meta-analysis done by Baker and Bor (2008), in which the authors assert that most studies reject the notion that music is a causal factor and suggest that music preference is more indicative of emotional vulnerability. However, it is still unknown whether these genres can negatively alter mood at all, and if they can, whether the themes and lyrics associated with the music are responsible. Clearly, more research is needed to further examine this correlation, as a causal link between these genres of music and adolescent suicide risk has yet to be shown. However, even if the theory put forth by Baker and Bon and other researchers is true, it is still important to investigate the effects that music can have on those who may be at risk for suicide and depression. Even if music genres are not the ultimate cause of suicidal behavior, they may act as a catalyst that further pushes adolescents into a state of depression and increased risk for suicidal behavior.

Conclusion indicates need for further research

MOOD MUSIC   9

References

Baker, F., & Bor, W. (2008). Can music preference indicate mental
        health status in young people? *Australasian Psychiatry, 16*(4),
        284–288. Retrieved from http://www3.interscience.wiley.com
        /journal/118565538/home

George, D., Stickle, K., Rachid, F., & Wopnford, A. (2007). The association
        between types of music enjoyed and cognitive, behavioral, and
        personality factors of those who listen. *Psychomusicology, 19*(2),
        32–56.

Lacourse, E., Claes, M., & Villeneuve, M. (2001). Heavy metal music
        and adolescent suicidal risk. *Journal of Youth and Adolescence,
        30*(3), 321–332.

Lai, Y. (1999). Effects of music listening on depressed women in
        Taiwan. *Issues in Mental Health Nursing, 20,* 229–246. doi:
        10.1080/016128499248637

Martin, G., Clark, M., & Pearce, C. (1993). Adolescent suicide: Music
        preference as an indicator of vulnerability. *Journal of the American
        Academy of Child and Adolescent Psychiatry, 32,* 530–535.

Scheel, K., & Westefeld, J. (1999). Heavy metal music and adolescent
        suicidality: An empirical investigation. *Adolescence, 34*(134),
        253–273.

Siedliecki, S., & Good, M. (2006). Effect of music on power, pain,
        depression and disability. *Journal of Advanced Nursing, 54*(5),
        553–562. doi: 10.1111/j.1365-2648.2006.03860.x

Smith, J. L., & Noon, J. (1998). Objective measurement of mood
        change induced by contemporary music. *Journal of Psychiatric
        & Mental Health Nursing, 5,* 403–408.

Stack, S. (2000). Blues fans and suicide acceptability. *Death
        Studies, 24,* 223–231.

Stack, S., & Gundlach, J. (1992). The effect of country music on
        suicide. *Social Forces, 71*(1), 211–218. Retrieved from http://
        socialforces.unc.edu/

Chicago Style 54

The style guide of the University of Chicago Press has long been used in history as well as in other areas of the arts and humanities. The Sixteenth Edition of *The Chicago Manual of Style* (2010) provides a complete guide to *Chicago* style, including two systems for citing sources. This chapter presents the notes and bibliography system. For easy reference, examples of notes and bibliographic entries are shown together in 54b.

 bedfordstmartins.com/everydaywriter
Documenting Sources

54a The basics of *Chicago* style

Why does academic work call for very careful citation practices when writing for the general public may not? The answer is that readers of academic work expect to get certain information from source citations:

- Source citations demonstrate that you've done your homework on your topic or issue and that you are a part of the conversation surrounding it.
- Source citations show that you understand the need to give credit where credit is due when you make use of someone else's intellectual property. (See Chapter 18 for more details.)
- Source citations give explicit directions to guide readers who want to look for themselves at the works you're using.

Guidelines from *The Chicago Manual of Style* will tell you exactly what information you need to include in your citation and how you should format that information.

TYPES OF SOURCES

You will need to be careful to tell your readers whether you read a print version or a digital version of a source that consists mainly of written words. Digital magazine and newspaper articles may include updates or corrections that the print version lacks; digital books may not number pages or screens the same way the print book does. If you are citing a source that has important media elements—such as a film, song, or artwork—consult the "Other Sources" section of the directory (p. 500). And if you can't find a model exactly like the source you've selected, see the box on p. 505.

ARTICLES FROM WEB AND DATABASE SOURCES

You need a subscription to look through most databases, so individual researchers almost always gain access to articles in databases through the computer system of a school or community library that pays to subscribe. The easiest way to tell whether a source comes from a database, then, is that its information is *not* generally available free to anyone with an Internet connection. Many databases are digital collections of articles that originally appeared in edited print periodicals, ensuring that an authority has vouched for the accuracy of the information. Such sources often have more credibility than much of what you find free on the Web.

Connecting parts of citations

Citations in *Chicago* style appear in three places in your text — a note number in the text marks the material from the source, a footnote or an endnote includes information to identify the source (or information about supplemental material), and the bibliography provides the full citation.

Use superscript numbers [1] to mark citations in the text. Place the superscript for each note after the relevant quotation, sentence, clause, or phrase. Type the number after any punctuation mark except the dash, and do not leave space before the superscript. Number citations sequentially throughout the text. When you use signal phrases to introduce quotations or other source material, note that *Chicago* style requires you to use the present tense (*citing Bebout's studies, Meier points out*).

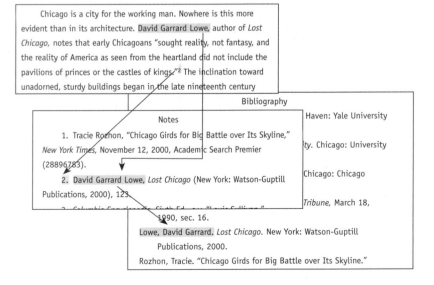

Chicago is a city for the working man. Nowhere is this more evident than in its architecture. David Garrard Lowe, author of *Lost Chicago*, notes that early Chicagoans "sought reality, not fantasy, and the reality of America as seen from the heartland did not include the pavilions of princes or the castles of kings."[2] The inclination toward unadorned, sturdy buildings began in the late nineteenth century

Bibliography

Notes

Haven: Yale University

1. Tracie Rozhon, "Chicago Girds for Big Battle over Its Skyline," *New York Times,* November 12, 2000, Academic Search Premier (28896783).

ty. Chicago: University

2. David Garrard Lowe, *Lost Chicago* (New York: Watson-Guptill Publications, 2000), 123.

Chicago: Chicago

Tribune, March 18, 1990, sec. 16.

Lowe, David Garrard. *Lost Chicago.* New York: Watson-Guptill Publications, 2000.

Rozhon, Tracie. "Chicago Girds for Big Battle over Its Skyline."

Type footnotes at the bottom of the page on which the superscript appears; type endnotes on a separate page at the end under the heading *Notes*. (Check which your instructor prefers.) The first line of each note is indented one-half inch and begins with a number, a period, a space, and the name of the source's author. All remaining lines of the entry are flush with the left margin. Footnotes and endnotes should be single-spaced, with a double space between notes, unless your instructor prefers double-spaced notes.

IN THE TEXT

Sweig argues that Castro and Che Guevara were not the only key players in the Cuban Revolution of the late 1950s.[19]

IN THE FIRST NOTE REFERRING TO THE SOURCE

19. Julia Sweig, *Inside the Cuban Revolution* (Cambridge, MA: Harvard University Press, 2002), 9.

After giving complete information the first time you cite a work, shorten additional references to that work: list only the author's last name, a comma, a short version of the title, a comma, and the page number. If you refer to the same source cited in the previous note, you can use the Latin abbreviation *Ibid.* ("in the same place") instead of the name and title.

IN FIRST AND SUBSEQUENT NOTES

19. Julia Sweig, *Inside the Cuban Revolution* (Cambridge, MA: Harvard University Press, 2002), 9.

20. Ibid., 13.

21. Ferguson, "Comfort of Being Sad," 63.

22. Sweig, *Cuban Revolution*, 21.

The alphabetical list of the sources in your text is usually titled *Bibliography* in *Chicago* style. You may instead use the title *Sources Consulted, Works Cited,* or *Selected Bibliography* if it better describes your list.

In the bibliographic entry, include the same information as in the first note for that source, but omit the page reference. Give the *first* author's last name first, followed by a comma and the first name; separate the main elements of the entry with periods rather than commas; and do not enclose the publication information for books in parentheses.

IN THE BIBLIOGRAPHY

Sweig, Julia. *Inside the Cuban Revolution*. Cambridge, MA: Harvard University Press, 2002.

Start the bibliography on a separate page after the main text and any notes. Continue the consecutive numbering of pages. Center the title *Bibliography*

DIRECTORY TO *CHICAGO* STYLE

Chicago style for notes and bibliographic entries

Print and online books

1. One author, *501*
   SOURCE MAP, *502–3*
2. Multiple authors, *501*
3. Organization as author, *501*
4. Unknown author, *501*
5. Online book, *504*
6. Electronic book (e-book), *504*
7. Edited book with no author, *504*
8. Edited book with author, *504*
9. Selection in an anthology or chapter in a book, with an editor, *504*
10. Introduction, preface, foreword, or afterword, *504*
11. Translation, *505*
12. Edition other than the first, *505*
13. Multivolume work, *505*
14. Reference work, *505*
15. Work with a title within the title, *506*
16. Sacred text, *506*
17. Source quoted in another source, *506*

Print and online periodicals

18. Article in a print journal, *506*
19. Article in an online journal, *507*
20. Journal article from a database, *507*

SOURCE MAP, *508–9*

21. Article in a print magazine, *507*
22. Article in an online magazine, *507*
23. Magazine article from a database, *507*
24. Article in a newspaper, *510*
25. Article in an online newspaper, *510*
26. Newspaper article from a database, *510*
27. Book review, *510*

Online sources

28. Web site, *511*
29. Work from a Web site, *511*
    SOURCE MAP, *512–13*
30. Blog (Web log) post, *511*
31. Email and other personal communications, *511*
32. Podcast, *511*
33. Online audio or video, *514*

Other sources

34. Published or broadcast interview, *514*
35. Video or DVD, *514*
36. Sound recording, *514*
37. Work of art, *515*
38. Pamphlet, report, or brochure, *515*
39. Government document, *515*

(without italics or quotation marks). *The Chicago Manual of Style* recommends single-spacing entries and double-spacing between entries.

54b   *Chicago* style for notes and bibliographic entries

The following examples demonstrate how to format both notes and bibliographic entries according to *Chicago* style. The note, which is numbered, appears first; the bibliographic entry, which is not numbered, appears below the note.

Print and online books

For the basic format for citing a print book, see the source map on pp. 502-3. The note for a book typically includes six elements: author's name, title and subtitle, city of publication, publisher, year, and page number(s) or electronic locator information for the information in the note. The bibliographic entry usually includes all but the page number (and does include a URL or other locator if the book is electronically published), but it is styled differently: commas separate major elements of a note, but a bibliographic entry uses periods.

1. ONE AUTHOR

1. Nell Irvin Painter, *The History of White People* (New York: W. W. Norton, 2010), 119.

Painter, Nell Irvin. *The History of White People*. New York: W. W. Norton, 2010.

2. MULTIPLE AUTHORS

2. Margaret Macmillan and Richard Holbrooke, *Paris 1919: Six Months That Changed the World* (New York: Random House, 2003), 384.

Macmillan, Margaret, and Richard Holbrooke. *Paris 1919: Six Months That Changed the World*. New York: Random House, 2003.

With more than three authors, you may give the first-listed author followed by *et al.* in the note. In the bibliography, list all the authors' names.

2. Stephen J. Blank et al., *Conflict, Culture, and History: Regional Dimensions* (Miami: University Press of the Pacific, 2002), 276.

Blank, Stephen J., Lawrence E. Grinter, Karl P. Magyar, Lewis B. Ware, and Bynum E. Weathers. *Conflict, Culture, and History: Regional Dimensions*. Miami: University Press of the Pacific, 2002.

3. ORGANIZATION AS AUTHOR

3. World Intellectual Property Organization, *Intellectual Property Profile of the Least Developed Countries* (Geneva: World Intellectual Property Organization, 2002), 43.

World Intellectual Property Organization. *Intellectual Property Profile of the Least Developed Countries*. Geneva: World Intellectual Property Organization, 2002.

4. UNKNOWN AUTHOR

4. *Broad Stripes and Bright Stars* (Kansas City, MO: Andrews McMeel, 2002), 10.

Broad Stripes and Bright Stars. Kansas City, MO: Andrews McMeel, 2002.

Take information from the book's title page and copyright page (on the reverse side of the title page), not from the book's cover or a library catalog. Look carefully at the differences in punctuation between the note and the bibliographic entry.

1 **Author.** In a note, list the author(s) first name first. In a bibliographic entry, list the first author last name first. List other authors first name first.

2 **Title.** Italicize the title and subtitle and capitalize all major words.

3 **City of publication.** List the city (and country or state abbreviation for an unfamiliar city) followed by a colon. In a note only, city, publisher, and year appear in parentheses.

4 **Publisher.** Drop *Inc.*, *Co.*, *Publishing*, or *Publishers*. Follow with a comma.

5 **Publication year.** In a bibliographic entry only, end with a period.

6 Page number. In a note only, end with the page number and a period.

Citations for the book on p. 503 would look like this:

ENDNOTE

1. Alex von Tunzelmann, *Red Heat: Conspiracy, Murder, and the Cold War in the Caribbean* (New York: Picador, 2011), 178.

BIBLIOGRAPHIC ENTRY

Von Tunzelmann, Alex. *Red Heat: Conspiracy, Murder, and the Cold War in the Caribbean*. New York: Picador, 2011.

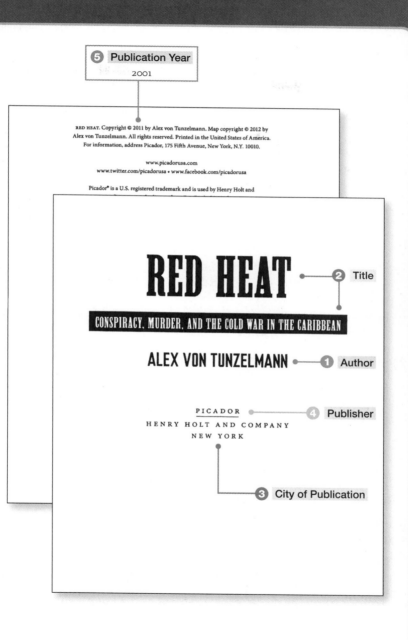

5 Publication Year

2001

RED HEAT. Copyright © 2011 by Alex von Tunzelmann. Map copyright © 2012 by
Alex von Tunzelmann. All rights reserved. Printed in the United States of America.
For information, address Picador, 175 Fifth Avenue, New York, N.Y. 10010.

www.picadorusa.com
www.twitter.com/picadorusa • www.facebook.com/picadorusa

Picador® is a U.S. registered trademark and is used by Henry Holt and

RED HEAT

2 Title

CONSPIRACY, MURDER, AND THE COLD WAR IN THE CARIBBEAN

ALEX VON TUNZELMANN

1 Author

PICADOR

4 Publisher

HENRY HOLT AND COMPANY
NEW YORK

3 City of Publication

5. ONLINE BOOK

5. Dorothy Richardson, *Long Day: The Story of a New York Working Girl, as Told by Herself* (1906; UMDL Texts, 2010),159, http://quod.lib.umich.edu/cgi/t/text/text-idx?c=moa;idno=AFS7156.0001.001.

Richardson, Dorothy. *Long Day: The Story of a New York Working Girl, as Told by Herself*. 1906. UMDL Texts, 2010. http://quod.lib.umich.edu/cgi/t/text/text-idx?c=moa;idno=AFS7156.0001.001.

6. ELECTRONIC BOOK (E-BOOK)

6. Manal M. Omar, *Barefoot in Baghdad* (Naperville, IL: Sourcebooks, 2010), Kindle edition, ch. 4.

Omar, Manal M. *Barefoot in Baghdad*. Naperville, IL: Sourcebooks, 2010. Kindle edition.

7. EDITED BOOK WITH NO AUTHOR

7. James H. Fetzer, ed., *The Great Zapruder Film Hoax: Deceit and Deception in the Death of JFK* (Chicago: Open Court, 2003), 56.

Fetzer, James H., ed. *The Great Zapruder Film Hoax: Deceit and Deception in the Death of JFK*. Chicago: Open Court, 2003.

8. EDITED BOOK WITH AUTHOR

8. Leopold von Ranke, *The Theory and Practice of History*, ed. Georg G. Iggers (New York: Routledge, 2010), 135.

von Ranke, Leopold. *The Theory and Practice of History*. Edited by Georg G. Iggers. New York: Routledge, 2010.

9. SELECTION IN AN ANTHOLOGY OR CHAPTER IN A BOOK, WITH AN EDITOR

9. Denise Little, "Born in Blood," in *Alternate Gettysburgs,* ed. Brian Thomsen and Martin H. Greenberg (New York: Berkley Publishing Group, 2002), 245.

Give the inclusive page numbers of the selection or chapter in the bibliographic entry.

Little, Denise. "Born in Blood." In *Alternate Gettysburgs*. Edited by Brian Thomsen and Martin H. Greenberg, 242–55. New York: Berkley Publishing Group, 2002.

10. INTRODUCTION, PREFACE, FOREWORD, OR AFTERWORD

10. Robert B. Reich, introduction to *Making Work Pay: America after Welfare,* ed. Robert Kuttner (New York: New Press, 2002), xvi.

Reich, Robert B. Introduction to *Making Work Pay: America after Welfare,* vii–xvii. Edited by Robert Kuttner. New York: New Press, 2002.

11. TRANSLATION

11. Suetonius, *The Twelve Caesars,* trans. Robert Graves (London: Penguin Classics, 1989), 202.

Suetonius. *The Twelve Caesars.* Translated by Robert Graves. London: Penguin Classics, 1989.

12. EDITION OTHER THAN THE FIRST

12. Dee Brown, *Bury My Heart at Wounded Knee: An Indian History of the American West,* 4th ed. (New York: Owl Books, 2007), 12.

Brown, Dee. *Bury My Heart at Wounded Knee: An Indian History of the American West,* 4th ed. New York: Owl Books, 2007.

13. MULTIVOLUME WORK

13. John Watson, *Annals of Philadelphia and Pennsylvania in the Olden Time,* vol. 2 (Washington, DC: Ross & Perry, 2003), 514.

Watson, John. *Annals of Philadelphia and Pennsylvania in the Olden Time.* Vol. 2. Washington, DC: Ross & Perry, 2003.

14. REFERENCE WORK

In a note, use *s.v.,* the abbreviation for the Latin *sub verbo* ("under the word") to help your reader find the entry.

14. *Encyclopedia Britannica,* s.v. "carpetbagger."

Do not list reference works such as encyclopedias or dictionaries in your bibliography.

AT A GLANCE

Citing Sources without Models in *Chicago* Style

To cite a source for which you cannot find a model, collect as much information as you can find — about the creator, title, date of creation or update, and location of the source — with the goal of helping your readers find the source for themselves, if possible. Then look at the models in this section to see which one most closely matches the type of source you are using.

In an academic writing project, before citing an electronic source for which you have no model, also be sure to ask your instructor's advice.

15. WORK WITH A TITLE WITHIN THE TITLE

Use quotation marks around any title within a book title.

> 15. John A. Alford, *A Companion to "Piers Plowman"* (Berkeley: University of California Press, 1988), 195.

> Alford, John A. *A Companion to "Piers Plowman."* Berkeley: University of California Press, 1988.

16. SACRED TEXT

> 16. Luke 18:24–25 (New International Version)

> 16. Qur'an 7:40–41

Do not include a sacred text in the bibliography.

17. SOURCE QUOTED IN ANOTHER SOURCE

Identify both the original and the secondary source.

> 17. Frank D. Millet, "The Filipino Leaders," *Harper's Weekly,* March 11, 1899, quoted in Richard Slotkin, *Gunfighter Nation: The Myth of the Frontier in Twentieth-Century America* (New York: HarperCollins, 1992), 110.

> Millet, Frank D. "The Filipino Leaders." *Harper's Weekly,* March 11, 1899. Quoted in Richard Slotkin, *Gunfighter Nation: The Myth of the Frontier in Twentieth-Century America* (New York: HarperCollins, 1992), 110.

Print and online periodicals

The note for an article in a periodical typically includes the author's name, the article title, and the periodical title. The format for other information, including the volume and issue numbers (if any), the date of publication, and the page number(s) to which the note refers, varies according to the type of periodical and whether you consulted it in print, on the Web, or in a database. In a bibliographic entry for a journal or magazine article from a database or a print periodical, also give the inclusive page numbers.

18. ARTICLE IN A PRINT JOURNAL

> 18. Karin Lützen, "The Female World: Viewed from Denmark," *Journal of Women's History* 12, no. 3 (2000): 36.

> Lützen, Karin. "The Female World: Viewed from Denmark." *Journal of Women's History* 12, no. 3 (2000): 34–38.

19. ARTICLE IN AN ONLINE JOURNAL

Give the DOI if there is one. If not, include the article URL. If page numbers are provided, include them as well.

> 19. Jeffrey J. Schott, "America, Europe, and the New Trade Order," *Business and Politics* 11, no. 3 (2009), doi:10.2202/1469-3569.1263.

> Schott, Jeffrey J. "America, Europe, and the New Trade Order." *Business and Politics* 11, no. 3 (2009). doi:10.2202/1469-3569.1263.

20. JOURNAL ARTICLE FROM A DATABASE

For basic information on citing a periodical article from a database in *Chicago* style, see the source map on pp. 508–9.

> 20. W. Trent Foley and Nicholas J. Higham, "Bede on the Britons," *Early Medieval Europe* 17, no. 2 (2009), 157, doi:10.1111/j.1468-0254.2009.00258.x.

> Foley, W. Trent, and Nicholas J. Higham. "Bede on the Britons." *Early Medieval Europe* 17, no. 2 (2009). 154–85. doi:10.1111/j.1468-0254.2009.00258.x.

21. ARTICLE IN A PRINT MAGAZINE

> 21. Terry McDermott, "The Mastermind: Khalid Sheikh Mohammed and the Making of 9/11," *New Yorker,* September 13, 2010, 42.

> McDermott, Terry. "The Mastermind: Khalid Sheikh Mohammed and the Making of 9/11." *New Yorker,* September 13, 2010, 38–51.

22. ARTICLE IN AN ONLINE MAGAZINE

> 22. Tracy Clark-Flory, "Educating Women Saves Kids' Lives," *Salon,* September 17, 2010, http://www.salon.com/life/broadsheet/2010/09/17/education_women/index.html.

> Clark-Flory, Tracy. "Educating Women Saves Kids' Lives." *Salon,* September 17, 2010. http://www.salon.com/life/broadsheet/2010/09/17/education_women/index.html.

23. MAGAZINE ARTICLE FROM A DATABASE

> 23. Sami Yousafzai and Ron Moreau, "Twisting Arms in Afghanistan," *Newsweek,* November 9, 2009, 8, Academic Search Premier (44962900).

> Yousafzai, Sami, and Ron Moreau. "Twisting Arms in Afghanistan." *Newsweek,* November 9, 2009. 8. Academic Search Premier (44962900).

1 **Author.** In a note, list the author(s) first name first. In the bibliographic entry, list the first author last name first, comma, first name; list other authors first name first.

2 **Article title.** Enclose the title and subtitle (if any) in quotation marks, and capitalize major words. In the notes section, put a comma before and after the title. In the bibliography, put a period before and after.

3 **Periodical title.** Italicize the title and subtitle, and capitalize all major words. For a magazine or newspaper, follow with a comma.

4 **Journal volume and issue numbers.** For journals, follow the title with the volume number, a comma, the abbreviation *no.*, and the issue number.

5 **Publication date.** For journals, enclose the publication year in parentheses and follow with a comma (in a note) or with a period (in a bibliography). For other periodicals, give the month and year or month, day, and year, followed by a comma.

6 **Page numbers.** In a note, give the page where the information is found. In the bibliographic entry, give the page range.

7 **Retrieval information.** Provide the article's DOI, if one is given, the name of the database and an accession number, or a "stable or persistent" URL for the article in the database. Because you provide stable retrieval information, you do not need to identify the electronic format of the work (i.e., PDF, as in the example shown here). End with a period.

Citations for the journal article on p. 509 would look like this:

ENDNOTE

1. Howard Schuman, Barry Schwartz, and Hannah D'Arcy, "Elite Revisionists and Popular Beliefs: Christopher Columbus, Hero or Villain?" *Public Opinion Quarterly* 69, no. 1 (2005), 13, doi:10.1093/poq/nfi001.

BIBLIOGRAPHIC ENTRY

Schuman, Howard, Barry Schwartz, and Hannah D'Arcy. "Elite Revisionists and Popular Beliefs: Christopher Columbus, Hero or Villain?" *Public Opinion Quarterly* 69, no. 1 (2005). 2–29. doi:10.1093/poq/nfi001.

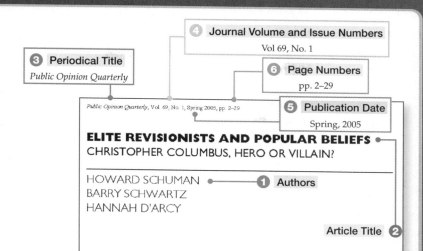

④ Journal Volume and Issue Numbers
Vol 69, No. 1

③ Periodical Title
Public Opinion Quarterly

⑥ Page Numbers
pp. 2–29

⑤ Publication Date
Spring, 2005

Public Opinion Quarterly, Vol. 69, No. 1, Spring 2005, pp. 2–29

ELITE REVISIONISTS AND POPULAR BELIEFS
CHRISTOPHER COLUMBUS, HERO OR VILLAIN?

HOWARD SCHUMAN ● ————— **❶ Authors**
BARRY SCHWARTZ
HANNAH D'ARCY

Article Title ❷

Abstract According to revisionist historians and American Indian activists, Christopher Columbus deserves condemnation for having brought slavery, disease, and death to America's indigenous peoples. We ask whether the general public's beliefs about Columbus show signs of reflecting these critical accounts, which increased markedly as the 1992 Quincentenary approached. Our national surveys, using several different question wordings, indicate that most Americans continue to admire Columbus because, as tradition puts it, "he discovered America," though only a small number of mainly older respondents speak of him in the heroic terms common in earlier years. At the same time, the percentage of Americans who reject traditional beliefs about Columbus is also small and is divided between those who simply acknowledge the priority of Indians as the "First Americans" and those who go further to view Columbus as a villain. The latter group of respondents, we find, show a critical stance toward modal American beliefs much more broadly.

We also analyze American history school textbooks for evidence of influence from revisionist writings, and we consider representations of Columbus in the mass media as well. Revisionist history can be seen as one consequence of the "minority rights revolution" that began after World War II and has achieved considerable success, but the endurance of Columbus's reputation—to a considerable extent even among the

HOWARD SCHUMAN is a research scientist and professor emeritus at the University of Michigan. BARRY SCHWARTZ is a professor emeritus at the University of Georgia. HANNAH D'ARCY is an independent statistical consultant who previously worked for the University of Michigan's Center for Statistical Consultation and Research. We thank Lawrence Bobo and Stanley Presser for stimulating us to do multiple validations, and we are grateful to the editor of *Public Opinion Quarterly* for recommendations that substantially improved our final presentation. In addition, we are much indebted for help during the course of the research to Virginia Hopcroft, Government Documents Librarian at Bowdoin College; Maria Krysan, University of Illinois at Chicago; Alyssa Miller, Evanston, Illinois; and Irina Poznansky, Departmental Librarian, Teachers College, Gottesman Libraries, Columbia University. Support for the research was drawn in part from a National Science Foundation grant (SES-0001844). Address correspondence to Howard Schuman; e-mail: hschuman@umich.edu.

doi:10.1093/poq/nfi001

❼ Retrieval Information
doi:10.1093/poq/nfi001

24. ARTICLE IN A NEWSPAPER

Do not include page numbers for a newspaper article, but you may include the section, if any.

> 24. Caroline E. Mayer, "Wireless Industry to Adopt Voluntary Standards," *Washington Post,* September 9, 2003, sec. E.

> Mayer, Caroline E. "Wireless Industry to Adopt Voluntary Standards." *Washington Post,* September 9, 2003, sec. E.

If you provide complete documentation of a newspaper article in a note, you may not need to include it in the bibliography. Check your instructor's preference.

25. ARTICLE IN AN ONLINE NEWSPAPER

If the URL for the article is very long, use the URL for the newspaper's home page.

> 25. Andrew C. Revkin, "Arctic Melt Unnerves the Experts," *New York Times,* October 2, 2007, http://www.nytimes.com.

> Revkin, Andrew C. "Arctic Melt Unnerves the Experts." *New York Times,* October 2, 2007. http://www.nytimes.com.

26. NEWSPAPER ARTICLE FROM A DATABASE

> 26. Demetria Irwin, "A Hatchet, Not a Scalpel, for NYC Budget Cuts," *New York Amsterdam News,* November 13, 2008, Academic Search Premier (35778153).

> Irwin, Demetria. "A Hatchet, Not a Scalpel, for NYC Budget Cuts." *New York Amsterdam News,* November 13, 2008. Academic Search Premier (35778153).

27. BOOK REVIEW

After the information about the book under review, give publication information for the appropriate kind of source (see models 18–26).

> 27. Arnold Relman, "Health Care: The Disquieting Truth," review of *Tracking Medicine: A Researcher's Quest to Understand Health Care,* by John E. Wennberg, *New York Review of Books* 57, no. 14 (2010), 45.

> Relman, Arnold. "Health Care: The Disquieting Truth." Review of *Tracking Medicine: A Researcher's Quest to Understand Health Care,* by John E. Wennberg. *New York Review of Books* 57, no. 14 (2010), 45–48.

Online sources

In general, include the author (if given); the title of a work from a Web site (in quotation marks); the name of the site (in italics, if the site is an online publication, but otherwise neither italicized nor in quotation marks); the sponsor of the site, if different from the name of the site or name of the author; the date of publication or most recent update; and a URL. If the online source does not indicate when it was published or last modified, or if your instructor requests an access date, place it before the URL.

For basic information on citing works from Web sites in *Chicago* style, see the source map on pp. 512–13.

28. WEB SITE

> 28. Rutgers School of Arts and Sciences, *The Rutgers Oral History Archive,* 2010, http://oralhistory.rutgers.edu/.

> Rutgers School of Arts and Sciences. *The Rutgers Oral History Archive.* 2010. http://oralhistory.rutgers.edu/.

29. WORK FROM A WEB SITE

> 29. Rose Cohen, "My First Job," *The Triangle Factory Fire,* Cornell University School of Industrial and Labor Relations, 2005, http://www.ilr.cornell.edu /trianglefire/texts/.

> Cohen, Rose. "My First Job." *The Triangle Factory Fire.* Cornell University School of Industrial and Labor Relations. 2005. http://www.ilr.cornell.edu /trianglefire/texts/.

30. BLOG (WEB LOG) POST

Treat a blog post as a short work from a Web site (see model 29).

> 30. Jai Arjun Singh, "On the Road in the USSR," *Jabberwock* (blog), November 29, 2007, http://jaiarjun.blogspot.com/2007/11/on-road-in-ussr.html.

Chicago recommends that blog posts appear in the notes section only, not in the bibliography, unless the blog is cited frequently. Check your instructor's preference. A bibliography reference to an entire blog would look like this:

> Singh, Jai Arjun. *Jabberwock* (blog). http://jaiarjun.blogspot.com/.

31. EMAIL AND OTHER PERSONAL COMMUNICATIONS

Cite email messages and other personal communications, such as letters and telephone calls, in the text or in a note only, not in the bibliography. (*Chicago* style recommends hyphenating *e-mail.*)

> 31. Kareem Adas, e-mail message to author, February 11, 2010.

32. PODCAST

Treat a podcast as a short work from a Web site (see model 29) and give as much of the following information as you can find: the author or speaker, the title or a description of the podcast, the title of the site,

CHICAGO SOURCE MAP: Works from Web Sites

1 **Author.** In a note, list the author(s) first name first. In a bibliographic entry, list the first author last name first, comma, first name; list additional authors first name first. Note that the host may serve as the author.

2 **Document title.** Enclose the title in quotation marks, and capitalize all major words. In a note, put a comma before and after the title. In the bibliography, put a period before and after.

3 **Title of Web site.** Capitalize all major words. If the site's title is analogous to a book or periodical title, italicize it. In the notes section, put a comma after the title. In the bibliography, put a period after the title.

4 **Sponsor of site.** If the sponsor is the same as the author or site title, you may omit it. End with a comma (in the note) or a period (in the bibliographic entry).

5 **Date of publication or last modification.** If no date is available, or if your instructor requests it, include your date of access (with the word *accessed*).

6 **Retrieval information.** Give the URL for the Web site. If you are required to include a date of access, put the word *accessed* and the date in parentheses after the URL. End with a period.

Citations for the Web site on p. 513 would look like this:

ENDNOTE

   1. Rebecca Edwards, "The Populist Party," *1896: The Presidential Campaign: Cartoons & Commentary,* Vassar College, 2000, http://projects .vassar.edu/1896/populists.html.

BIBLIOGRAPHIC ENTRY

Edwards, Rebecca. "The Populist Party." *1896: The Presidential Campaign: Cartoons & Commentary. Vassar College.* 2000. http://projects.vassar .edu/1896/populists.html.

projects.**vassar.edu**/1896/populists.html

2 Document Title

The Populist Party

The Rise of Populism

The People's Party (or Populist Party, as it was widely known) was much younger than the Democratic and Republican Parties, which had been founded before the Civil War. Agricultural areas in the West and South had been hit by economic depression years before industrial areas. In the 1880s, as drought hit the wheat-growing areas of the Great Plains and prices for Southern cotton sunk to new lows, many tenant farmers fell into deep debt. This exacerbated long-held grievances against railroads, lenders, grain-elevator owners, and others with whom farmers did business. By the early 1890s, as the depression worsened, some industrial workers shared these farm families' views on labor and the trusts.

In 1890 Populists won control of the Kansas state legislature, and Kansan **William Peffer** became the party's first U.S. Senator. Peffer, with his long white beard, was a humorous figure to many Eastern journalists and politicians, who saw little evidence of Populism in their states and often treated the party as a joke. Nonetheless, Western and Southern Populists gained support rapidly. In 1892 the national party was officially founded through a merger of the Farmers' Alliance and the Knights of Labor. In that year the Populist presidential candidate, James B. Weaver, won over one million votes. Between 1892 and 1896, however, the party failed to make further gains, in part because of fraud, intimidation, and violence by Southern Democrats.

By 1896 the Populist organization was in even more turmoil than that of Democrats. Two main factions had app... orga... "fus...

1896

3 Title of Web Site

Homepage

© 2000, Rebecca Edwards, Vassar College

5 Date of Publication

4 Sponsor of Site

1 Author

the site sponsor (if different from the author or site name), the type of podcast or file format, the date of posting or access, and the URL.

32. Barack Obama, "Weekly Address: A Solar Recovery," *The White House*, podcast video, July 3, 2010, http://www.whitehouse.gov/photos-and-video/video /weekly-address-a-solar-recovery.

Obama, Barack. "Weekly Address: A Solar Recovery." *The White House*. Podcast video. July 3, 2010. http://www.whitehouse.gov/photos-and-video/video /weekly-address-a-solar-recovery.

33. ONLINE AUDIO OR VIDEO

Treat an online audio or video source as a short work from a Web site (see model 29). If the source is downloadable, give the medium or file format before the URL (see model 32).

33. Alyssa Katz, "Did the Mortgage Crisis Kill the American Dream?" YouTube video, 4:32, posted by NYCRadio, June 24, 2009, http://www.youtube.com /watch?v=uivtwjwd_Qw.

Katz, Alyssa. "Did the Mortgage Crisis Kill the American Dream?" YouTube video, 4:32. Posted by NYCRadio. June 24, 2009. http://www.youtube.com /watch?v=uivtwjwd_Qw.

Other sources

34. PUBLISHED OR BROADCAST INTERVIEW

34. Nina Totenberg, interview by Charlie Rose, *The Charlie Rose Show*, PBS, June 29, 2010.

Totenberg, Nina. Interview by Charlie Rose. *The Charlie Rose Show*. PBS, June 29, 2010.

Interviews you conduct are considered personal communications (see model 31).

35. VIDEO OR DVD

35. Edward Norton and Edward Furlong, *American History X,* directed by Tony Kaye (1998; Los Angeles: New Line Studios, 2002), DVD.

Norton, Edward, and Edward Furlong. *American History X.* Directed by Tony Kaye, 1998. Los Angeles: New Line Studios, 2002. DVD.

36. SOUND RECORDING

36. Paul Robeson, *The Collector's Paul Robeson,* recorded 1959, Monitor MCD-61580, 1989, compact disc.

Robeson, Paul. *The Collector's Paul Robeson.* Recorded 1959. Monitor MCD-61580, 1989, compact disc.

37. WORK OF ART

Begin with the artist's name and the title of the work. If you viewed the work in person, give the medium, the date, and the name of the place where you saw it.

> 37. Mary Cassatt, *The Child's Bath,* oil on canvas, 1893, The Art Institute of Chicago, Chicago, IL.

> Cassatt, Mary. *The Child's Bath.* Oil on canvas, 1893. The Art Institute of Chicago, Chicago, IL.

If you refer to a reproduction, give the publication information.

> 37. Mary Cassatt, *The Child's Bath,* oil on canvas, 1893, on *Art Access,* The Art Institute of Chicago, last modified August 2004, http://www.artic.edu/artaccess/AA_Impressionist/pages/IMP_6.shtml#.

> Cassatt, Mary. *The Child's Bath.* Oil on canvas, 1893. On *Art Access,* The Art Institute of Chicago. Last modified August 2004. http://www.artic.edu/artaccess/AA_Impressionist/pages/IMP_6.shtml#.

38. PAMPHLET, REPORT, OR BROCHURE

Information about the author or publisher may not be readily available, but give enough information to identify your source.

> 38. Jamie McCarthy, *Who Is David Irving?* (San Antonio, TX: Holocaust History Project, 1998).

> McCarthy, Jamie. *Who Is David Irving?* San Antonio, TX: Holocaust History Project, 1998.

39. GOVERNMENT DOCUMENT

> 39. U.S. House Committee on Ways and Means, *Report on Trade Mission to Sub-Saharan Africa,* 108th Cong., 1st sess. (Washington, DC: Government Printing Office, 2003), 28.

> U.S. House Committee on Ways and Means. *Report on Trade Mission to Sub-Saharan Africa.* 108th Cong., 1st sess. Washington, DC: Government Printing Office, 2003.

54c An excerpt from a student research essay, *Chicago* style

Student Writer

Amanda Rinder

On the following pages is an essay by Amanda Rinder that conforms to the *Chicago* guidelines described in this chapter. Note that this essay has been reproduced in a narrow format to allow for annotation.

 bedfordstmartins.com/everydaywriter
Student Writing

Title
announces
topic clearly
and succinctly

Title and
writer's name
centered

Course title,
instructor's
name, and
date centered
at bottom of
title page

Sweet Home Chicago: Preserving the Past,

Protecting the Future of the Windy City

Amanda Rinder

Twentieth-Century U.S. History

Professor Goldberg

November 27, 2006

Annotations indicate effective choices or *Chicago*-style formatting.

Rinder 2

Only one city has the "Big Shoulders" described by Carl Sandburg: Chicago (fig. 1). So renowned are its skyscrapers and celebrated building style that an entire school of architecture is named for Chicago. Presently, however, the place that Frank Sinatra called "my kind of town" is beginning to lose sight of exactly what kind of town it is. Many of the buildings that give Chicago its distinctive character are being torn down in order to make room for new growth. Both preserving the classics and encouraging new creation are important; the combination of these elements gives Chicago architecture its unique flavor. Witold Rybczynski, a professor of urbanism, told Tracie Rozhon of the *New York Times,* "Of all the cities we can think of . . . we associate Chicago with new things, with building new. Combining that with preservation is a difficult task, a tricky thing. It's hard to find the middle ground in Chicago."[1] Yet finding a middle ground is essential if the city is to retain the original character that sets it apart from the rest. In order to

Fig. 1. Chicago skyline, circa 1940s. (Postcard courtesy of Minnie Dangburg.)

First page of body text is p. 2

Paper refers to each figure by number

Thesis introduced

Double-spaced text

Source cited using superscript numeral

Figure caption includes number, short title, and source

Opening
paragraph
concludes
with thesis
statement

maintain Chicago's distinctive identity and its delicate balance
between the old and the new, the city government must provide a
comprehensive urban plan that not only directs growth, but calls
for the preservation of landmarks and historic districts as well.

Chicago is a city for the working man. Nowhere is this more
evident than in its architecture. David Garrard Lowe, author of *Lost
Chicago,* notes that early Chicagoans "sought reality, not fantasy, and
the reality of America as seen from the heartland did not include the
pavilions of princes or the castles of kings."[2] The inclination toward
unadorned, sturdy buildings began in the late nineteenth century
with the aptly named Chicago School, a movement led by Louis
Sullivan, John Wellborn Root, and Daniel Burnham and based on

Second
paragraph
provides
background

Sullivan's adage, "Form follows function."[3] The early skyscraper, the
very symbol of the Chicago style, represents the triumph of function
and utility over sentiment, America over Europe, and perhaps, as
Daniel Bluestone argues, even the frontier over the civilization of
the East Coast.[4] These ideals of the original Chicago School were
expanded upon by architects of the Second Chicago School. Frank
Lloyd Wright's legendary organic style and the famed glass and steel
constructions of Mies van der Rohe are often the first images that
spring to mind when one thinks of Chicago.

Clear transition
from previous
paragraph

Yet the architecture that is the city's defining attribute is being
threatened by the increasing tendency toward development. The root
of Chicago's preservation problem lies in the enormous drive toward
economic expansion and the potential in Chicago for such growth. The
highly competitive market for land in the city means that properties
sell for the highest price if the buildings on them can be obliterated

Notes

1. Tracie Rozhon, "Chicago Girds for Big Battle over Its Skyline," *New York Times,* November 12, 2000, Academic Search Premier (28896783).

Newspaper article in database

2. David Garrard Lowe, *Lost Chicago* (New York: Watson-Guptill Publications, 2000), 123.

Book

3. *Columbia Encyclopedia,* Sixth Ed., s.v. "Louis Sullivan."

4. Daniel Bluestone, *Constructing Chicago* (New Haven: Yale University Press, 1991), 105.

5. Alan J. Shannon, "When Will It End?" *Chicago Tribune,* September 11, 1987, quoted in Karen J. Dilibert, *From Landmark to Landfill* (Chicago: Chicago Architectural Foundation, 2000), 11.

Indirect source

6. Steve Kerch, "Landmark Decisions," *Chicago Tribune,* March 18, 1990, sec. 16.

7. John W. Stamper, *Chicago's North Michigan Avenue* (Chicago: University of Chicago Press, 1991), 215.

8. Alf Siewers, "Success Spoiling the Magnificent Mile?" *Chicago Sun-Times,* April 9, 1995, http://www.sun-times.com/.

Newspaper article online

9. Paul Gapp, "McCarthy Building Puts Landmark Law on a Collision Course with Developers," *Chicago Tribune,* April 20, 1986, quoted in Karen J. Dilibert, *From Landmark to Landfill* (Chicago: Chicago Architectural Foundation, 2000), 4.

Reference to previous source

10. Ibid.

11. Rozhon, "Chicago Girds for Big Battle."

Second reference to source

12. Kerch, "Landmark Decisions."

13. Robert Bruegmann, *The Architects and the City* (Chicago: University of Chicago Press, 1997), 443.

Bibliography
starts on new
page

Bibliography

Bluestone, Daniel. *Constructing Chicago*. New Haven: Yale University
    Press, 1991.

Book

Bruegmann, Robert. *The Architects and the City*. Chicago: University
    of Chicago Press, 1997.

Pamphlet

Dilibert, Karen J. *From Landmark to Landfill*. Chicago: Chicago
    Architectural Foundation, 2000.

Newspaper
article

Kerch, Steve. "Landmark Decisions." *Chicago Tribune,* March 18,
    1990, sec. 16.

Lowe, David Garrard. *Lost Chicago*. New York: Watson-Guptill
    Publications, 2000.

Article from
database

Rozhon, Tracie. "Chicago Girds for Big Battle over Its Skyline."
    New York Times, November 12, 2000. Academic Search Premier
    (28896783).

Bibliography
entries use
hanging indent
and are not
numbered

Siewers, Alf. "Success Spoiling the Magnificent Mile?" *Chicago
    Sun-Times,* April 9, 1995. http://www.sun-times.com/.

Stamper, John W. *Chicago's North Michigan Avenue*. Chicago:
    University of Chicago Press, 1991.

CSE Style **55**

Writers in the physical sciences, the life sciences, and mathematics use the documentation and format style of the Council of Science Editors (CSE). Guidelines for citing print and electronic sources can be found in *Scientific Style and Format: The CSE Manual for Authors, Editors, and Publishers,* Seventh Edition (2006).

 bedfordstmartins.com/everydaywriter
Documenting Sources

55a CSE style for in-text citations

In CSE style, citations within an essay follow one of three formats.

- The *citation-sequence format* calls for a superscript number or a number in parentheses after any mention of a source. The sources are numbered in the order they appear. Each number refers to the same source every time it is used. The first source mentioned in the paper is numbered *1,* the second source is numbered *2,* and so on.

- The *citation-name format* also calls for a superscript number or a number in parentheses after any mention of a source. The numbers are added after the list of references is completed and alphabetized, so that the source numbered *1* is alphabetically first in the list of references, *2* is alphabetically second, and so on.

- The *name-year format* calls for the last name of the author and the year of publication in parentheses after any mention of a source. If the last name appears in a signal phrase, the name-year format allows for giving only the year of publication in parentheses.

Before deciding which system to use, check a current journal in the field or ask an instructor about the preferred style in a particular course or discipline.

1. **IN-TEXT CITATION USING CITATION-SEQUENCE OR CITATION-NAME FORMAT**

VonBergen[12] provides the most complete discussion of this phenomenon.

For the citation-sequence and citation-name formats, you would use the same superscript ([12]) for each subsequent citation of this work by VonBergen.

2. **IN-TEXT CITATION USING NAME-YEAR FORMAT**

VonBergen (2003) provides the most complete discussion of this phenomenon.

Hussar's two earlier studies of juvenile obesity (1995, 1999) examined only children with diabetes.

The classic examples of such investigations (Morrow 1968; Bridger et al. 1971; Franklin and Wayson 1972) still shape the assumptions of current studies.

55b CSE style for a list of references

The citations in the text of an essay correspond to items on a list titled *References,* which starts on a new page at the end of the essay. Continue to number the pages consecutively, center the title *References* one inch from the top of the page, and double-space before beginning the first entry.

The order of the entries depends on which format you follow:

- *Citation-sequence format:* number and list the references in the order the references are first cited in the text.
- *Citation-name format:* list and number the references in alphabetical order.
- *Name-year format:* list the references, unnumbered, in alphabetical order.

In the following examples, you will see that the citation-sequence and citation-name formats call for listing the date after the publisher's name in references for books and after the periodical name in references for articles. The name-year format calls for listing the date immediately after the author's name in any kind of reference.

CSE style also specifies the treatment and placement of the following basic elements in the list of references:

- *Author.* List all authors last name first, and use only initials for first and middle names. Do not place a comma after the author's last name, and do not place periods after or spaces between the initials. Use a period after the last initial of the last author listed.
- *Title.* Do not italicize titles and subtitles of books and titles of periodicals. Do not enclose titles of articles in quotation marks. For books and articles, capitalize only the first word of the title and any proper nouns or proper adjectives. Abbreviate and capitalize all major words in a periodical title.

As you refer to these examples, pay attention to how publication information (publishers for books, details about periodicals for articles) and other specific elements are styled and punctuated.

DIRECTORY TO CSE STYLE

CSE style for references

Books

1. One author, *523*
   SOURCE MAP, *524–25*
2. Two or more authors, *523*
3. Organization as author, *526*
4. Book prepared by editor(s), *526*
5. Section of a book with an editor, *526*
6. Chapter of a book, *526*
7. Paper or abstract in conference proceedings, *527*

Periodicals

8. Article in a journal, *527*

9. Article in a weekly journal, *527*
10. Article in a magazine, *528*
11. Article in a newspaper, *528*

Digital sources

12. Material from an online database, *529*
    SOURCE MAP, *530–31*
13. Article in an online journal, *529*
14. Article in an online newspaper, *529*
15. Online book, *532*
16. Web site, *532*
17. Government Web site, *532*

Books

For the basic format for citing a book, see the source map on pp. 524–25.

1. ONE AUTHOR

CITATION-SEQUENCE AND CITATION-NAME

1. Buchanan M. Nexus: small worlds and the groundbreaking theory of networks. New York: Norton; 2003.

NAME-YEAR

Buchanan M. 2003. Nexus: small worlds and the groundbreaking theory of networks. New York: Norton.

2. TWO OR MORE AUTHORS

CITATION-SEQUENCE AND CITATION-NAME

2. Wojciechowski BW, Rice NM. Experimental methods in kinetic studies. 2nd ed. St. Louis (MO): Elsevier Science; 2003.

CSE SOURCE MAP: Books

Note that, depending on whether you are using the citation-sequence or citation-name format or the name-year format, the date placement will vary.

① **Author.** List author(s) last name first, and use initials for first and middle names, with no periods or spaces. Use a period only after the last initial of the last author.

②, ⑥ **Publication year.** In name-year format, put the year of publication immediately after the author name(s). In citation-sequence or citation-name format, put the year of publication after the publisher's name.

③ **Title.** Do not italicize or put quotation marks around titles and subtitles of books. Capitalize only the first word of the title and any proper nouns or proper adjectives.

④ **City of publication.** List the city of publication (and the country or state abbreviation for unfamiliar cities) followed by a colon.

⑤ **Publisher.** Give the publisher's name. In citation-sequence or citation-name format, follow with a semicolon. In name-year format, follow with a period.

A citation for the book on p. 525 would look like this:

CITATION-SEQUENCE OR CITATION-NAME FORMAT

1. Wilson EO. The diversity of life. Cambridge: Belknap Press of Harvard University Press; 1992.

NAME-YEAR FORMAT

Wilson EO. 1992. The diversity of life. Cambridge: Belknap Press of Harvard University Press.

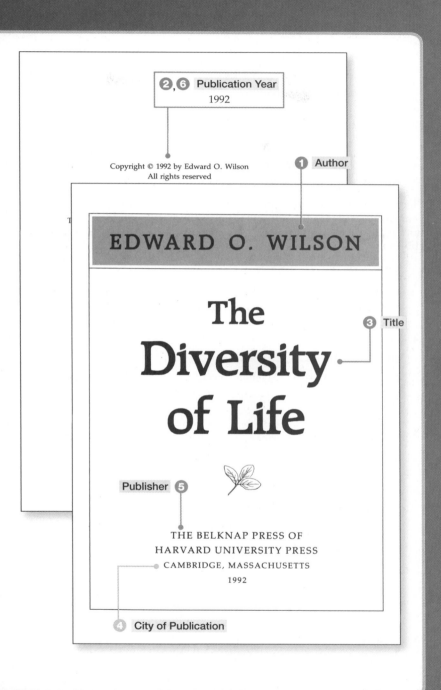

②,⑥ Publication Year
1992

Copyright © 1992 by Edward O. Wilson
All rights reserved

① Author

EDWARD O. WILSON

The

Diversity

of Life

③ Title

Publisher ⑤

THE BELKNAP PRESS OF
HARVARD UNIVERSITY PRESS
CAMBRIDGE, MASSACHUSETTS
1992

④ City of Publication

525

NAME-YEAR

Wojciechowski BW, Rice NM. 2003. Experimental methods in kinetic studies. 2nd ed. St. Louis (MO): Elsevier Science.

3. ORGANIZATION AS AUTHOR

CITATION-SEQUENCE AND CITATION-NAME

3. World Health Organization. The world health report 2002: reducing risks, promoting healthy life. Geneva (Switzerland): The Organization; 2002.

Place the organization's abbreviation at the beginning of the name-year entry, and use the abbreviation in the corresponding in-text citation. Alphabetize the entry by the first word of the full name, not by the abbreviation.

NAME-YEAR

[WHO] World Health Organization. 2002. The world health report 2002: reducing risks, promoting healthy life. Geneva (Switzerland): The Organization.

4. BOOK PREPARED BY EDITOR(S)

CITATION-SEQUENCE AND CITATION-NAME

4. Torrence ME, Isaacson RE, editors. Microbial food safety in animal agriculture: current topics. Ames: Iowa State University Press; 2003.

NAME-YEAR

Torrence ME, Isaacson RE, editors. 2003. Microbial safety in animal agriculture: current topics. Ames: Iowa State University Press.

5. SECTION OF A BOOK WITH AN EDITOR

CITATION-SEQUENCE AND CITATION-NAME

5. Kawamura A. Plankton. In: Perrin MF, Wursig B, Thewissen JGM, editors. Encyclopedia of marine mammals. San Diego: Academic Press; 2002. p. 939–942.

NAME-YEAR

Kawamura A. 2002. Plankton. In: Perrin MF, Wursig B, Thewissen JGM, editors. Encyclopedia of marine mammals. San Diego: Academic Press. p. 939–942.

6. CHAPTER OF A BOOK

CITATION-SEQUENCE AND CITATION-NAME

6. Honigsbaum M. The fever trail: in search of the cure for malaria. New York: Picador; 2003. Chapter 2, The cure; p. 19–38.

NAME-YEAR

Honigsbaum M. 2003. The fever trail: in search of the cure for malaria. New York: Picador. Chapter 2, The cure; p. 19–38.

7. PAPER OR ABSTRACT IN CONFERENCE PROCEEDINGS

CITATION-SEQUENCE AND CITATION-NAME

7. Gutierrez AP. Integrating biological and environmental factors in crop system models [abstract]. In: Integrated Biological Systems Conference; 2003 Apr 14–16; San Antonio, TX. Beaumont (TX): Agroeconomics Research Group; 2003. p. 14–15.

NAME-YEAR

Gutierrez AP. 2003. Integrating biological and environmental factors in crop system models [abstract]. In: Integrated Biological Systems Conference; 2003 Apr 14–16; San Antonio, TX. Beaumont (TX): Agroeconomics Research Group. p. 14–15.

Periodicals

Provide volume and issue numbers for journals. For newspaper and magazine articles, include the section designation and column number, if any, and the date. For all periodicals, give inclusive page numbers. For rules on abbreviating journal titles, consult the CSE manual, or ask an instructor to suggest other examples.

8. ARTICLE IN A JOURNAL

CITATION-SEQUENCE AND CITATION-NAME

8. Mahmud K, Vance ML. Human growth hormone and aging. New Engl J Med. 2003;348(2):2256–2257.

NAME-YEAR

Mahmud K, Vance ML. 2003. Human growth hormone and aging. New Engl J Med. 348(2):2256–2257.

9. ARTICLE IN A WEEKLY JOURNAL

CITATION-SEQUENCE AND CITATION-NAME

9. Holden C. Future brightening for depression treatments. Science. 2003 Oct 31:810–813.

NAME-YEAR

Holden C. 2003. Future brightening for depression treatments. Science. Oct 31:810–813.

10. **ARTICLE IN A MAGAZINE**

CITATION-SEQUENCE AND CITATION-NAME

10. Livio M. Moving right along: the accelerating universe holds secrets to dark energy, the Big Bang, and the ultimate beauty of nature. Astronomy. 2002 Jul:34–39.

NAME-YEAR

Livio M. 2002 Jul. Moving right along: the accelerating universe holds secrets to dark energy, the Big Bang, and the ultimate beauty of nature. Astronomy. 34–39.

11. **ARTICLE IN A NEWSPAPER**

CITATION-SEQUENCE AND CITATION-NAME

11. Kolata G. Bone diagnosis gives new data but no answers. New York Times (National Ed.). 2003 Sep 28;Sect. 1:1 (col. 1).

NAME-YEAR

Kolata G. 2003 Sep 28. Bone diagnosis gives new data but no answers. New York Times (National Ed.). Sect. 1:1 (col. 1).

Digital sources

These examples use the citation-sequence or citation-name system. To adapt them to the name-year system, delete the note number and place the update date immediately after the author's name.

The basic entry for most sources accessed through the Internet should include the following elements:

- *Author.* Give the author's name, if available, last name first, followed by the initial(s) and a period.
- *Title.* For book, journal, and article titles, follow the style for print materials. For all other types of electronic material, reproduce the title that appears on the screen.
- *Medium.* Indicate, in brackets, that the source is not in print format by using designations such as *[Internet]*.
- *Place of publication.* The city usually should be followed by the two-letter abbreviation for the state. No state abbreviation is necessary for well-known cities such as New York, Chicago, Boston, and London or for a publisher whose location is part of its name (for example, University of Oklahoma Press). If the city is implied, put

the city and state in brackets. If the city cannot be inferred, use the words *place unknown* in brackets.

- *Publisher.* For material other than journal articles from Web sites and online databases, include the individual or organization that produces or sponsors the site. If no publisher can be determined, use the words *publisher unknown* in brackets.

- *Dates.* Cite three important dates if possible: the date the publication was placed on the Internet or the copyright date; the latest date of any update or revision; and the date the publication was accessed by you.

- *Page, document, volume, and issue numbers.* When citing a portion of a larger work or site, list the inclusive page numbers or document numbers of the specific item being cited. For journals or journal articles, include volume and issue numbers. If exact page numbers are not available, include in brackets the approximate length in computer screens, paragraphs, or bytes: [2 screens], [10 paragraphs], [332K bytes].

- *Address.* Include the URL or other electronic address; use the phrase *Available from:* to introduce the address. Only URLs that end with a slash are followed by a period.

12. MATERIAL FROM AN ONLINE DATABASE

For the basic format for citing an article from a database, see the source map on pp. 530–31. (Because CSE does not provide guidelines for citing an article from an online database, this model has been adapted from CSE guidelines for citing an online journal article.)

12. Shilts E. Water wanderers. Can Geographic [Internet]. 2002 [cited 2010 Jan 27];122(3):72–77. Academic Search Premier. Ipswich (MA):EBSCO. Available from: http://www.ebscohost.com/ Document No.: 6626534.

13. ARTICLE IN AN ONLINE JOURNAL

13. Perez P, Calonge TM. Yeast protein kinase C. J Biochem [Internet]. 2002 Oct [cited 2008 Nov 3];132(4):513–517. Available from: http://edpex104.bcasj.or .jp/jb-pdf/132-4/jb132-4-513.pdf

14. ARTICLE IN AN ONLINE NEWSPAPER

14. Brody JE. Reasons, and remedies, for morning sickness. New York Times Online [Internet]. 2004 Apr 27 [cited 2009 Apr 30]. Available from: http://www .nytimes.com/2009/04/27/health/27BROD.html

Note that date placement will vary depending on whether you are using the citation-sequence or citation-name format or the name-year format.

1 **Author.** List author(s) last name first, and use only initials for first and middle names.

2, **5** **Publication date.** For name-year format, put publication date after author name(s). In citation-sequence or citation-name format, put it after periodical title. Use year only (for journals) or year month day (for other periodicals).

3 **Article title.** Capitalize first word and proper nouns/adjectives.

4 **Periodical title.** Capitalize major words. Abbreviate journal titles. Follow with *[Internet]* and a period.

6 **Date of access.** In brackets, write *cited* and year, month, and day. End with a semicolon.

7 **Publication information for article.** Give volume number, issue number (in parentheses), a colon, and page numbers. End with a period.

8 **Name of database.** End with a period.

9 **Publication information for database.** Include the city, the state abbreviation in parentheses, a colon, the publisher's name, and a period.

10 **Web address.** Write *Available from* and the brief URL.

11 **Document number.** Write *Document no.* and identifying number.

A citation for the article on p. 531 would look like this:

CITATION-SEQUENCE OR CITATION-NAME FORMAT

1. Miller AL. Epidemiology, etiology, and natural treatment of seasonal affective disorder. Altern Med Rev [Internet]. 2005 [cited 2010 25 May]; 10(1):5–13. Academic Search Premier. Ipswich (MA): EBSCO. Available from http://www.ebscohost.com Document No.: 16514813.

NAME-YEAR FORMAT

Miller AL. 2005. Epidemiology, etiology, and natural treatment of seasonal affective disorder. Altern Med Rev [Internet]. [cited 2010 25 May]; 10(1):5–13. Academic Search Premier. Ipswich (MA): EBSCO. Available from http://www.ebscohost.com Document No.: 16514813.

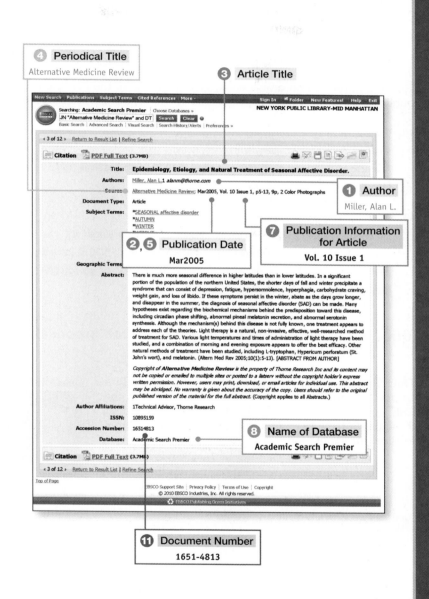

4 Periodical Title

Alternative Medicine Review

3 Article Title

1 Author

Miller, Alan L.

2, 5 Publication Date

Mar2005

7 Publication Information for Article

Vol. 10 Issue 1

8 Name of Database

Academic Search Premier

11 Document Number

1651-4813

15. ONLINE BOOK

15. Patrick TS, Allison JR, Krakow GA. Protected plants of Georgia [Internet].
Social Circle (GA): Georgia Department of Natural Resources; c1995 [cited 2010
Dec 3]. Available from: http://www.georgiawildlife.com/content/displaycontent
.asp?txtDocument=89&txtPage=9

To cite a portion of an online book, give the name of the part after the
publication information: *Chapter 6, Encouraging germination.* See model 6.

16. WEB SITE

16. Geology and public policy [Internet]. Boulder (CO): Geological Society of
America; c2010 [updated 2010 Jun 3; cited 2010 Sep 19]. Available from:
http://www.geosociety.org/geopolicy.htm

17. GOVERNMENT WEB SITE

17. Health disparities: reducing health disparities in cancer [Internet].
Atlanta (GA): Centers for Disease Control and Prevention (US); 2010 [updated
2010 Apr 5; cited 2010 May 1]. Available from: http://www.cdc.gov/cancer/
healthdisparities/basic_info/disparities.htm

55c   An excerpt from a student research proposal, CSE style

The following excerpt from a research proposal by Tara
Gupta conforms to the citation-sequence format in the
CSE guidelines described in this chapter. Note that
these pages have been reproduced in a narrow format
to allow for annotation.

Student Writer

Tara Gupta

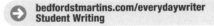

Field Measurements of
Photosynthesis and Transpiration
Rates in Dwarf Snapdragon
(*Chaenorrhinum minus* Lange):
An Investigation of Water Stress
Adaptations

Specific and
informative title

Tara Gupta

Information
centered on
title page

Proposal for a
Summer Research
Fellowship
Colgate University
February 25, 2003

Annotations indicate effective choices or CSE-style formatting.

Water Stress Adaptations 2

Introduction

Dwarf snapdragon (*Chaenorrhinum minus*) is a weedy pioneer plant found growing in central New York during spring and summer. Interestingly, the distribution of this species has been limited almost exclusively to the cinder ballast of railroad tracks[1] and to sterile strips of land along highways[2]. In these harsh environments, characterized by intense sunlight and poor soil water retention, one would expect *C. minus* to exhibit anatomical features similar to those of xeromorphic plants (species adapted to arid habitats).

However, this is not the case. T. Gupta and R. Arnold (unpublished) have found that the leaves and stems of *C. minus* are not covered by a thick, waxy cuticle but rather with a thin cuticle that is less effective in inhibiting water loss through diffusion. The root system is not long and thick, capable of reaching deeper, moister soils; instead, it is thin and diffuse, permeating only the topmost (and driest) soil horizon. Moreover, in contrast to many xeromorphic plants, the stomata (pores regulating gas exchange) are not found in sunken crypts or cavities in the epidermis that retard water loss from transpiration.

Despite a lack of these morphological adaptations to water stress, *C. minus* continues to grow and reproduce when morning dew has been its only source of water for up to 5 weeks (2002 letter from R. Arnold to me). Such growth involves fixation of carbon by photosynthesis and requires that the stomata be open to admit sufficient carbon dioxide. Given the dry, sunny environment, the time required for adequate carbon fixation must also mean a significant loss of water through transpiration as open stomata exchange carbon dioxide with water. How does *C. minus* balance the need for carbon with the need to conserve water?

Headings throughout help organize the proposal

Introduction states scientific issue, gives background information

Documentation follows CSE citation-sequence format

Personal communication cited in parentheses within text but not included in references

Water Stress Adaptations 5

References

1. Wildrlechner MP. Historical and phenological observations of the spread of *Chaenorrhinum minus* across North America. Can J Bot. 1983;61(1):179–187.

2. Dwarf Snapdragon [Internet]. Olympia (WA): Washington State Noxious Weed Control Board; 2001 [updated 2001 Jul 7; cited 2003 Jan 25]. Available from: http://www.wa.gov/agr/weedboard/weed_info/dwarfsnapdragon.html

3. Boyer JS. Plant productivity and environment. Science. 1982 Nov 6:443–448.

4. Manhas JG, Sukumaran NP. Diurnal changes in net photosynthetic rate in potato in two environments. Potato Res. 1988;31:375–378.

5. Doley DG, Unwin GL, Yates DJ. Spatial and temporal distribution of photosynthesis and transpiration by single leaves in a rainforest tree, *Argyrodendron peralatum*. Aust J Plant Physiol. 1988;15(3):317–326.

6. Kallarackal J, Milburn JA, Baker DA. Water relations of the banana. III. Effects of controlled water stress on water potential, transpiration, photosynthesis and leaf growth. Aust J Plant Physiol. 1990;17(1):79–90.

7. Idso SB, Allen SG, Kimball BA, Choudhury BJ. Problems with porometry: measuring net photosynthesis by leaf chamber techniques. Agron J. 1989;81(4):475–479.

Article from government Web site

Article in weekly journal

Article in journal

Includes all published works cited; numbers correspond to order in which sources are first mentioned

For Multilingual Writers

The whole idea of America . . . is imported; we're all imported.

— DEREK WALCOTT

For Multilingual Writers

56 Writing in U.S. Academic Genres *539*
- **a** Meet expectations for U.S. academic writing *539*
- **b** Understand genre conventions *540*
- **c** Adapt structures and phrases from a genre *541*
- **d** Check usage with search engines *541*

57 Clauses and Sentences *542*
- **a** Include explicit subjects and objects *543*
- **b** Follow English word order *543*
- **c** Use noun clauses appropriately *544*
- **d** Choose between infinitives and gerunds *544*
- **e** Use adjective clauses appropriately *546*
- **f** Use conditional sentences appropriately *547*

58 Nouns and Noun Phrases *548*
- **a** Use count and noncount nouns appropriately *548*
- **b** Identify proper nouns *549*
- **c** Use determiners appropriately *549*
- **d** Use articles conventionally *550*
- **e** Arrange modifiers appropriately *553*

59 Verbs and Verb Phrases *554*
- **a** Form verb phrases appropriately *554*
- **b** Use modal auxiliaries (helping verbs) appropriately *557*
- **c** Indicate present and past tenses *558*
- **d** Form perfect and progressive verb phrases *559*
- **e** Use participial adjectives correctly *561*

60 Prepositions and Prepositional Phrases *561*
- **a** Use prepositions idiomatically *561*
- **b** Use two-word verbs idiomatically *562*

For visual analysis Look carefully at the illustration on the front of this tab. What do you think this image suggests about what it means to write in more than one language?

Writing in U.S. Academic Genres **56**

Xiaoming Li, now a college English teacher, says that before she came to the United States as a graduate student, she had been a "good writer" in China—in both English and Chinese. Once in the United States, however, she struggled to grasp what her teachers expected of her college writing. While she could easily use grammar books and dictionaries, her instructors' unstated expectations seemed to call for her to write in a way that was new to her.

Of course, writing for college presents many challenges; such writing differs in many ways from high school writing as well as from personal writing like text messaging or postings to social networking sites. If you grew up speaking and writing in other languages, however, the transition to producing effective college writing can be even more complicated. Not only will you have to learn new information and new ways of thinking and arguing, but you also have to do it in a language that may not come naturally to you—especially in unfamiliar rhetorical situations.

56a Meet expectations for U.S. academic writing.

The expectations for college writing are often taken for granted by instructors. To complicate the matter further, there is no single "correct" style of communication in any country, including the United States. Effective oral styles differ from effective written styles, and what is considered good writing in one field of study is not necessarily appropriate in another. Even the variety of English often referred to as "standard" covers a wide range of styles (see Chapter 22). In spite of this wide variation, several features are often associated with U.S. academic English:

- conventional grammar, spelling, punctuation, and mechanics
- organization that links ideas explicitly
- readable type, conventional margins, and double spacing
- explicitly stated claims supported by evidence (Chapter 14)

- careful documentation of all sources (Chapters 49–55)
- consistent use of an appropriate level of formality (23a)
- conventional use of idioms (Chapter 60)
- conventional academic formats, such as literature reviews, research essays, lab reports, and research proposals

This brief list suggests features of the genre often described as U.S. academic writing. Yet these characteristics can lead to even more questions: What does *conventional* mean? How can a writer determine what is appropriate in any given rhetorical situation?

Most students can benefit from some instruction in how new contexts require the use of different sets of conventions, strategies, and resources. This is especially the case for multilingual writers.

56b Understand genre conventions.

Those who read your college writing—your teachers and peers—will hold some expectations about the features of the texts you produce. Many writers learn these expectations through practice. But if you

---

AT A GLANCE

Features of Genres

Study the features of the kind of text you need to write.

- What does the genre look like? How is the text laid out on the page? How are any visual features incorporated into the main text?
- How long is the whole text, each section, and each paragraph?
- How does the text introduce the topic? Is the main point stated explicitly or implicitly?
- What are the major divisions of the text? Are they marked with transitions or headings?
- How does each section contribute to the main point? How is the main point of each section supported?
- How are the key terms defined? What kind of background information is provided?
- What is the level of formality? Does the text use technical terms or contractions (such as *I'm* and *isn't* instead of *I am* and *is not*)?
- Does the text take a personal stance (*I, we*), address the audience directly (*you*), or talk about the subject without explicitly referring to the writer or the reader?
- How many sources are used in the text? How are they introduced?

have had limited exposure to various types, or *genres*, of academic writing in English, it may be helpful to think about these conventions explicitly.

Genres of texts

At some point in your writing process, you should consider the genre or kind of text the instructor expects you to write. In many cases, the assignment will not be explicit about what the text should look like or accomplish. If you are not sure what kind of text you are supposed to write, ask your instructor for clarification. (Examples may also be available at your school's writing center.) You may want to find multiple examples so that you can develop a sense of how different writers approach the same writing task.

56c Adapt structures and phrases from a genre.

If English is not your strongest language, you may find it useful to borrow and adapt transitional devices and pieces of sentence structure from other people's writing in the genre you are working in. You should not copy the whole sentence or sentence structure, however, or your borrowed sentences may seem plagiarized (Chapter 18). Find sample sentence structures from similar genres but on different topics so that you borrow a typical structure (which does not belong to anyone) rather than the idea or the particular phrasing. Write your own sentences first, and look at other people's sentences only to guide your revision.

The example on p. 542 illustrates effective borrowing. The student writer borrows phrases that are commonly used in academic writing in the social sciences to perform particular functions. Notice how the student also modifies these phrases to suit the needs of the writing situation.

56d Check usage with search engines.

To multilingual writers, search engines such as Google can provide a useful way of checking sentence structure and word usage. For example, if you are not sure whether you should use an infinitive form (*to* + verb) or a gerund (*-ing*) for the verb *confirm* after the main verb *expect* (57d), you can search for both "*expected confirming*" and "*expected to confirm*" in quotation marks to see which search term yields more results. A Google search for "*expected confirming*" yields many entries with a

Original Abstract from a Social Science Paper	Effective Borrowing of Structures from a Genre
Using the interpersonal communications research of J. K. Brilhart and G. J. Galanes, and W. Wilmot and J. Hocker, along with T. Hartman's personality assessment, I observed and analyzed the leadership roles and group dynamics of my project collaborators in a communications course. Based on results of the Hartman personality assessment, I predicted that a single leader would emerge. However, complementary individual strengths and gender differences encouraged a distributed leadership style, in which the group experienced little confrontation and conflict. Conflict, because it was handled positively, was crucial to the group's progress.	Drawing on the research of Deborah Tannen on men's and women's conversational styles, I analyzed the conversational styles of six first-year students at DePaul University. Based on Tannen's research, I expected that the three men I observed would use features typical of male conversational style and the three women would use features typical of female conversational style. In general, these predictions were accurate; however, some exceptions were also apparent.

comma between the two words, indicating that one phrase ends with *expected* and another begins with *confirming*.

On the other hand, a search for *"expected to confirm"* yields many more hits than a search for *"expected confirming."* These results indicate that *expected to confirm* is the more commonly used expression. Be sure to click through a few pages of the search engine's results to make sure that most results come from ordinary sentences rather than from headlines or phrases that may be constructed differently from standard English.

57 Clauses and Sentences

Short phrases, or sound bites, are everywhere — from the Dairy Council's "Got Milk?" to Volkswagen's "Drivers Wanted." These short, simple slogans may be memorable, but they don't say very much. In writing, you usually need more complex sentences to convey meaning. The requirements for forming sentences can differ across languages, and English has its own sets of rules.

57a Include explicit subjects and objects.

English sentences consist of a subject and a predicate. While many languages can omit a sentence subject, English very rarely allows this. Though you might write *Responsible for analyzing data* on a résumé, in most varieties of spoken and written English, you must explicitly state the subject. In fact, with only a few exceptions, all clauses in English must have an explicit subject.

it
► They took the Acela Express to Boston because was fast.
                                               ^

English even requires a kind of "dummy" subject to fill the subject position in certain kinds of sentences.

► **It** is raining.
► **There** is a strong wind.

Transitive verbs (31k) typically require that objects—and sometimes other information—also be explicitly stated. For example, it is not enough to tell someone *Give!* even if it is clear what is to be given to whom. You must say *Give it to me* or *Give her the passport* or some other such sentence. Similarly, saying *Put!* or *Put it!* is not enough when you mean *Put it on the table* or *Put it down!*

Many dictionaries identify whether a verb is transitive (requiring an object) or intransitive (not followed by an object).

57b Follow English word order.

In general, subjects, verbs, and objects (31k) must be placed in specific positions within a sentence.

SUBJECT VERB OBJECT   ADVERB
► **Mario left Venice reluctantly.**

The only word in this sentence that can be moved to different locations is the adverb *reluctantly* (*Mario reluctantly left Venice* or *Reluctantly, Mario left Venice*). The three key elements of subject, verb, and object are moved out of their normal order only to create special effects.

57c Use noun clauses appropriately.

Examine the following sentence:

> In my last year in high school, my adviser urged that I apply to several colleges.

This complex sentence is built out of two sentences, one of them (B) embedded in the other (A):

A. In my last year in high school, my adviser urged B.
B. I (should) apply to several colleges.

When these are combined as in the original sentence, sentence B becomes a noun clause introduced by *that* and becomes the object of the verb *urged* in sentence A. Now look at the following sentence:

> It made a big difference that she wrote a strong letter of recommendation.

Here the two component sentences are C and D:

C. D made a big difference.
D. She wrote a strong letter of recommendation.

In this case, the noun clause formed from sentence D functions as the subject of sentence C so that the combination reads as follows:

> That she wrote a strong letter of recommendation made a big difference.

This sentence is gramatically acceptable but not typical. When a long noun clause is the subject, it is usually moved to the end of the sentence. The result is *It made a big difference that she wrote a strong letter of recommendation*, which inserts the dummy subject *It* as the subject.

57d Choose between infinitives and gerunds.

Infinitives are verbs in the *to* + verb form (*to write, to read, to go*); gerunds are verbs that end in *-ing* and act as subjects or objects within a sentence. In general, infinitives tend to indicate intentions, desires, or expectations, and gerunds tend to state facts. Knowing whether to use a *to* form or an *-ing* form in a particular sentence can be a challenge. Though no simple explanation will make it an easy task, some hints might be helpful (see 56d for another strategy).

▶ **My adviser urged me to apply to several colleges.**
▶ **Applying took a great deal of time.**

In the first sentence, *to apply* conveys the message that the act of applying was something wanted, not yet a fact. In the second sentence, *applying* calls attention to the fact that the application process was actually carried out.

Using infinitives (to forms) to state intentions

▶ Kumar expected **to get** a good job after graduation.

▶ Last year, Fatima decided **to become** a math major.

▶ The strikers have agreed **to go** back to work.

At the moment indicated by the verbs *expect*, *decide*, and *agree* in these sentences, those actions or events were merely intentions. These three verbs, as well as many others that specify intentions (or negative intentions, such as *refuse*), must always be followed by an infinitive, never by a gerund. Many learner dictionaries provide information about verbs that must be followed by an infinitive instead of a gerund.

Using gerunds (-ing forms) to state facts

▶ Jerzy enjoys **going** to the theater.

▶ We resumed **working** after our coffee break.

▶ Kim appreciated **getting** candy from Sean.

In all of these cases, the gerund indicates that the action or event that it expresses has actually occurred. Verbs like *enjoy*, *resume*, and *appreciate* can be followed only by gerunds, not by infinitives. In fact, even when these verbs do not convey clear facts, the verb form that follows must still be a gerund. Again, many dictionaries provide this information.

▶ Kim would appreciate *getting* candy from Sean, but he hardly knows her.

Understanding other rules and guidelines

A few verbs can be followed by either an infinitive or a gerund. With some, such as *begin* and *continue*, the choice makes little difference in meaning. With others, however, the difference in meaning is striking.

▶ Carlos was working as a medical technician, but he **stopped to study** English.

The infinitive *to study* indicates that Carlos intended to study English when he left his job. We don't know whether he actually did study English.

▶ Carlos **stopped studying** English when he left the United States.

The gerund *studying* indicates that Carlos actually did study English but then stopped when he left.

The distinction between fact and intention is not a rule but only a tendency, and it can be outweighed by other rules. For example, use a gerund—never an infinitive—right after a preposition.

eating.
▶ This fruit is safe for ~~to eat.~~
⌃

▶ This fruit is safe ~~for~~ to eat.

us
▶ This fruit is safe for to eat.
⌃

For a full list of verbs that can be followed by an infinitive and verbs that can be followed by a gerund, see *Grammar Troublespots*, Third Edition, by Ann Raimes (Cambridge UP, 2004), or *Cambridge International Dictionary of English* (Cambridge UP, 1999).

57e Use adjective clauses appropriately.

An adjective clause provides more information about a preceding noun.

▶ The company *Yossi's uncle had invested in* went bankrupt.

The subject is a noun phrase in which the noun *company* is modified by the article *the* and the adjective clause *Yossi's uncle invested in*. The sentence as a whole says that a certain company went bankrupt, and the adjective clause identifies the company more specifically by saying that Yossi's uncle had invested in it.

One way of seeing how the adjective clause fits into the sentence is to rewrite it like this: *The company (Yossi's uncle had invested in it) went bankrupt.* This is not a normal English sentence, but it helps demonstrate a process that leads to the sentence we started with. Note the following steps:

1. Change the personal pronoun *it* to the relative pronoun *which*: *The company (Yossi's uncle had invested in which) went bankrupt.*
2. Either move the whole prepositional phrase *in which* to the beginning of the adjective clause, or move just the relative pronoun: *The company in which Yossi's uncle had invested went bankrupt* or *The company which Yossi's uncle had invested in went bankrupt.* While both of these are correct English sentences, the first version is somewhat more formal than the second.
3. If no preposition precedes the relative pronoun, substitute *that* for *which*, or omit the relative pronoun entirely: *The company that Yossi's uncle had invested in went bankrupt* or *The company Yossi's uncle had invested in went bankrupt.* Both of these are correct English sentences. While they are less formal than the forms in step 2, they are still acceptable in much formal writing.

57f Use conditional sentences appropriately.

English distinguishes among many different types of conditional sentences—that is, sentences that focus on questions of truth and that are introduced by *if* or its equivalent. The following examples illustrate a range of different conditional sentences. Each of these sentences makes different assumptions about the likelihood that what is stated in the *if* clause is true.

> ▶ If you *practice* (or *have practiced*) writing frequently, you *know* (or *have learned*) what your chief problems are.

This sentence assumes that what is stated in the *if* clause may be true; as the alternatives in parentheses indicate, any tense that is appropriate in a simple sentence may be used in both the *if* clause and the main clause.

> ▶ If you *practice* writing for the rest of this term, you *will* (or *may*) *understand* the process better.

This sentence makes a prediction about the future and again assumes that what is stated may very well be true. Only the main clause uses the future tense (*will understand*) or some other modal (59a) that can indicate future time (*may understand*). The *if* clause must use the present tense.

> ▶ If you *practiced* (or *were to practice*) writing every single day, it *would* eventually *seem* much easier to you.

This sentence shows doubt that what is stated will happen. In the *if* clause, the verb is either past tense—actually, past subjunctive (32h)—or *were to* + the base form, even though it refers to future time. The main clause contains *would* + the base form of the main verb.

> ▶ If you *practiced* writing on Mars, you *would find* no one to read your work.

This sentence imagines an impossible situation. As with the preceding sentence, the past subjunctive is used in the *if* clause, although past time is not being referred to, and *would* + the base form is used in the main clause.

> ▶ If you *had practiced* writing in ancient Egypt, you *would have used* hieroglyphics.

This sentence shifts the impossibility back to the past; obviously, you aren't going to find yourself in ancient Egypt. But a past impossibility demands a form that is "more past": the past perfect in the *if* clause and *would* + the perfect form of the main verb in the main clause.

bedfordstmartins.com/everydaywriter
Exercise Central > For Multilingual Writers

58 Nouns and Noun Phrases

Although all languages have nouns, English nouns differ from those in some other languages in various ways, such as their division into count and noncount nouns and the use of plural forms, articles, and other modifiers.

58a Use count and noncount nouns appropriately.

Look at the following sentences:

▶ **Research** shows that this chemical can be dangerous.
▶ **Studies** show that this chemical can be dangerous.

Studies is a count noun, and *research* is a noncount noun. Count nouns (also called countable nouns) refer to separate individuals or things that you can count: *a study, a doctor, a book, a tree; studies, doctors,* three *books,* ten *trees.* Noncount nouns (also called mass nouns or uncountable nouns) refer to masses or collections without distinctly separate parts: *research, milk, ice, blood, grass.* You cannot count noncount nouns unless you use a quantifier: *one blade of grass, two glasses of milk, three pints of blood.*

Count and noncount nouns also differ in their use of plural forms. Count nouns generally have singular and plural forms: *study, studies.* Noncount nouns generally have only a singular form: *research.*

COUNT	NONCOUNT
facts	information
suggestions	advice
people (plural of *person*)	humanity
tables, chairs, beds	furniture
letters	mail
pebbles	gravel
beans	rice

Some nouns can be either count or noncount, depending on the meaning.

COUNT   Before there were video games, children played with marbles.
NONCOUNT   The floor of the palace was made of marble.

When you learn a noun in English, it is useful to know whether it is count, noncount, or both. Many dictionaries provide this information.

58b Identify proper nouns.

In addition to count and noncount nouns, English has proper nouns. These nouns include names of people, places, objects, and institutions—for example, *California, Yolanda, IBM,* and *First National Bank.* Proper nouns are always capitalized and generally cannot vary in number, so they are either singular (*John, the* New York Times) or plural (*the Netherlands, the Rocky Mountains*).

58c Use determiners appropriately.

Determiners are words that identify or quantify a noun, such as *this study, all people, his suggestions.*

COMMON DETERMINERS

- the articles *a/an, the*
- *this, these, that, those*
- *my, our, your, his, her, its, their*
- possessive nouns and noun phrases (*Sheila's* paper, *my friend's* book)
- *whose, which, what*
- *all, both, each, every, some, any, either, no, neither, many, much, (a) few, (a) little, several, enough*
- the numerals *one, two,* etc.

Some determiners, such as *a, an, this, that, one,* and *each,* can only be used with singular nouns; others, such as *these, those, all, both, many, several,* and *two,* can only be used with plural nouns. Still other determiners—*my, the,* and *which,* for example—can be used with singular or plural nouns. See the chart on p. 550 for additional examples.

Determiners with singular count nouns

Every singular count noun must be preceded by a determiner. Place any adjectives between the determiner and the noun.

my
▶ sister
  ^

the
▶ growing population
  ^

that
▶ old neighborhood
  ^

Determiners with plural count nouns or with noncount nouns

Noncount and plural count nouns sometimes have determiners and sometimes do not. For example, *This research is important* and *Research is important* are both acceptable but have different meanings.

Remembering which determiners go with which types of noun

The chart below describes which determiners can be used with which types of nouns.

58d Use articles conventionally.

Articles (*a, an,* and *the*) are a type of determiner. In English, choosing which article to use—or whether to use an article at all—can be challenging. Although there are exceptions, the following general guidelines can help.

Using a or an

Use *a* and *an*, indefinite articles, with singular count nouns. Use *a* before a consonant sound (*a car*) and *an* before a vowel sound (*an uncle*).

These determiners . . .	. . . can precede these noun types	Examples
a, an, every, each	singular count nouns some proper nouns	*a* book, *an* American *each* word *every* Buddhist
this, that	singular count nouns noncount nouns	*this* book *that* milk
(*a*) *little, much*	noncount nouns	*a little* milk *much* affection
some, enough	noncount nouns plural count nouns	*some* milk, *enough* trouble *some* books *enough* problems
the	singular count nouns plural count nouns noncount nouns	*the* doctor *the* doctors *the* information
these, those, (*a*) *few, many, both, several*	plural count nouns	*these* books, *those* plans *a few* ideas *many* students *both* hands, *several* trees

Consider sound rather than spelling: *a house, an hour*. Do not use indefinite articles with plural count nouns or with noncount nouns.

A or *an* tells readers they do not have enough information to identify specifically what the noun refers to (in other words, it's an unspecified, or indefinite, noun). The writer may or may not have a particular thing in mind but in either case will use *a* or *an* if the reader lacks the information necessary for identification. Compare these sentences:

▶ I need *a* new coat for the winter.

▶ I saw *a coat* that I liked at Dayton's, but it wasn't heavy enough.

The coat in the first sentence is hypothetical rather than actual. Since it is indefinite to the writer and the reader, it is used with *a*, not *the*. The second sentence refers to a particular coat, but since the writer cannot expect the reader to know which one, it is used with *a* rather than *the*.

If you want to speak of an indefinite quantity rather than just one indefinite thing, use *some* or *any* with a noncount noun or a plural count noun. Note that *any* is used in negative sentences.

▶ This stew needs *some* more *salt*.

▶ I saw *some plates* that I liked at Gump's.

▶ This stew doesn't need *any* more salt.

▶ I didn't see *any* plates that I liked at Gump's.

Using the

The definite article *the* is used with both count and noncount nouns whose identity is already known or is about to be made known to readers. The necessary information for identification can come from the noun phrase itself, from elsewhere in the text, from context, from general knowledge, or from a superlative.

       the
▶ Let's meet at fountain in front of Dwinelle Hall.

> The phrase *in front of Dwinelle Hall* identifies the specific fountain. We know from the use of *the* that there is only one fountain in front of Dwinelle Hall.

▶ Last Saturday, a fire that started in a restaurant spread to a

         The store
nearby clothing store. ~~Store~~ was saved, although it suffered

water damage.

> The word *store* is preceded by *the*, which directs our attention to the information in the previous sentence, where the store is first identified.

the
▶ She asked him to shut door when he left her office.
　　　　　　　　　^

She expects him to understand that she is referring to the door in her office.

The pope
▶ Pope is expected to visit Africa in October.
　^

There is only one living pope, and *the* before *pope* signals that this sentence refers to him. Similar examples include *the president* (*of the United States*), *the earth*, and *the moon*.

the
▶ Bill is now best singer in the choir.
　　　　　　^

The superlative *best* identifies the noun *singer*.

Using the zero article

If a noun appears without *the*, *a* or *an*, or any other determiner (even if it is preceded by other adjectives), it is said to have a zero article. The zero article can be used with plural count nouns (*plans*, *assignments*), noncount nouns (*homework*, *information*), and proper nouns (*Carmen*, *New York*). With plural count nouns and noncount nouns, the zero article is used to make generalizations.

▶ In this world nothing is certain but death and taxes.
　　　　　　　　　　　　　　　　　　　　— BENJAMIN FRANKLIN

The zero article indicates that Franklin refers not to a particular death or specific taxes but to death and taxes in general.

Here English differs from many other languages that would use the definite article to make generalizations. In English, a sentence like *The snakes are dangerous* can refer only to particular, identifiable snakes, not to snakes in general.

It is sometimes possible to make general statements with *the* or *a/an* and singular count nouns.

▶ *First-year college students* are confronted with many new experiences.
▶ *A first-year student* is confronted with many new experiences.
▶ *The first-year student* is confronted with many new experiences.

These sentences all make the same general statement, but the emphasis of each sentence is different. The first sentence refers to first-year college students as a group, the second focuses on a hypothetical student taken at random, and the third sentence, which is characteristic of formal written style, projects the image of a typical student as representative of the whole class.

Modifier Type	Arrangement	Example
determiners	at the beginning of the noun phrase	*these old-fashioned tiles*
all or *both*	before any other determiners	*all these tiles*
numbers	after any other determiners	*these six tiles*
noun modifiers	directly before the noun	*these kitchen tiles*
adjectives	between determiners and noun modifiers	*these old-fashioned kitchen tiles*
phrases or clauses	after the noun	*the tiles on the wall* *the tiles that we bought*

58e Arrange modifiers appropriately.

Modifiers are words that give more information about a noun; that is, they *modify* the meaning of the noun in some way. Some modifiers precede the noun, and others follow it, as indicated in the chart above.

If there are two or more adjectives, their order is variable, but English has strong preferences, described below.

- Subjective adjectives (those that show the writer's opinion) go before objective adjectives (those that merely describe): *these beautiful old-fashioned kitchen tiles.*

- Adjectives of size generally come early: *these beautiful large old-fashioned kitchen tiles.*

- Adjectives of color generally come late: *these beautiful large old-fashioned blue kitchen tiles.*

- Adjectives derived from proper nouns or from nouns that refer to materials generally come after color terms and right before noun modifiers: *these beautiful large old-fashioned blue Portuguese ceramic kitchen tiles.*

- All other objective adjectives go in the middle, and adjectives for which no order is preferred are separated by commas: *these beautiful large decorative, heat-resistant, old-fashioned blue Portuguese ceramic kitchen tiles.*

Of course, the very long noun phrases presented above would be out of place in most kinds of writing. Academic and professional writing tend to avoid long strings of adjectives.

 bedfordstmartins.com/everydaywriter
Exercise Central > For Multilingual Writers

59 Verbs and Verb Phrases

Verbs can be called the heartbeat of every language, but in English the metaphor is especially meaningful. With a few stylistic exceptions, all written English sentences must include a verb. Some of the distinctive features of English verbs include modals, perfect tenses, and progressive forms.

59a Form verb phrases appropriately.

Verb phrases can be built up out of a main verb and one or more helping (auxiliary) verbs (32b).

▶ **Immigration figures rise every year.**
▶ **Immigration figures are rising every year.**
▶ **Immigration figures have risen every year.**
▶ **Immigration figures have been rising every year.**

Verb phrases have strict rules of order. If you try to rearrange the words in any of these sentences, you will find that most alternatives are impossible. You cannot say *Immigration figures rising are every year* or *Immigration figures been have rising every year*. The only permissible change to word order is to form a question, moving the first helping verb to the beginning of the sentence: *Have immigration figures been rising every year?*

Putting helping verbs in order

In the sentence *Immigration figures may have been rising,* the main verb *rising* follows three helping verbs: *may*, *have*, and *been*. Together these helping and main verbs make up a verb phrase.

- *May* is a modal (59b) that indicates possibility; it is followed by the base form of a verb.
- *Have* is an auxiliary verb (32b) that in this case indicates the perfect tense (32e); it must be followed by a past participle (*been*).
- Any form of *be*, when it is followed by a present participle ending in *-ing* (such as *rising*), indicates the progressive tense (32e).
- *Be* followed by a past participle, as in *New immigration policies have been passed in recent years*, indicates the passive voice (32g).

As shown in the chart below, when two or more auxiliaries appear in a verb phrase, they must follow a particular order based on the type of auxiliary: (1) modal, (2) a form of *have* used to indicate a perfect tense, (3) a form of *be* used to indicate a progressive tense, and (4) a form of *be* used to indicate the passive voice. (Very few sentences include all four kinds of auxiliaries.)

Only one modal is permitted in a verb phrase.

be able to
▶ She will ~~can~~ speak Czech much better soon.

Forming helping verbs

Whenever you use a helping verb, check the form of the word that follows. The guidelines that follow describe the appropriate forms.

MODAL + BASE FORM

Use the base form of a verb after *can, could, will, would, shall, should, may, might,* and *must.*

▶ Alice **can** read Latin.
▶ Sanjay **should have** studied for the test.
▶ They **must be** going to a fine school.

	Modal	Perfect *Have*	Progressive *Be*	Passive *Be*	Main Verb	
Sonia	—	has	—	been	invited	to visit a family in Prague.
She	should	—	—	be	finished	with school soon.
The invitation	must	have	—	been	sent	in the spring.
She	—	has	been	—	studying	Czech.
She	may	—	be	—	feeling	nervous.
She	might	have	been	—	expecting	to travel elsewhere.
The trip	will	have	been	being	planned	for a month by the time she leaves.

In many other languages, modals such as *can* and *must* are followed by an infinitive (*to* + base form). In English, only the base form follows a modal.

▶ Alice can ~~to~~ read Latin.

Notice that a modal auxiliary can express tense (for example, *can* or *could*), but it never changes form to agree with the subject.

PERFECT *HAVE* + PAST PARTICIPLE

To form the perfect tenses, use *have*, *has*, or *had* with a past participle.

▶ Everyone has gone home.
▶ They have been working all day.

PROGRESSIVE *BE* + PRESENT PARTICIPLE

A progressive form of a verb is signaled by two elements, a form of the helping verb *be* (*am, is, are, was, were, be,* or *been*) and the *-ing* form of the next word: *The children* are studying.

▶ The children ^are studying in school.

▶ The children are ~~study~~ ^studying in school.

Some verbs are rarely used in progressive forms. These verbs express unchanging conditions or mental states rather than deliberate actions: *believe, belong, hate, know, like, love, need, own, resemble, understand.*

PASSIVE *BE* + PAST PARTICIPLE

Use *am, is, are, was, were, being, be,* or *been* with a past participle to form the passive voice.

▶ Tagalog is spoken in the Philippines.

Notice that with the progressive *be* the following word (the present participle) ends in *-ing*, but with the passive *be* the following word (the past participle) never ends in *-ing*.

▶ Takeo is studying music.
▶ Natasha was taught by a famous violinist.

If the first helping verb in a verb phrase is *be* or *have*, it must show either present or past tense, and it must agree with the subject: *Meredith has played in an orchestra* or *Meredith had played in an orchestra before she joined the band.*

59b Use modal auxiliaries (helping verbs) appropriately.

The nine basic modal auxiliaries (helping verbs) are *can, could, will, would, shall, should, may, might,* and *must.* There are a few others as well, in particular *ought to,* which is close in meaning to *should.* Occasionally *need* can be a modal rather than a main verb.

The nine basic modals fall into the pairs *can/could, will/would, shall/ should, may/might,* and the loner *must.* In earlier English, the second member of each pair was the past tense of the first. The second form still functions occasionally as a past tense, especially in the case of *could.*

▶ Ingrid can ski.
▶ Ingrid could ski when she was five.

But, for the most part, in present-day English, all nine modals typically refer to present or future time. When you want to use a modal to refer to the past, you follow the modal with a perfect form of a helping verb.

▶ If you have a fever, you should see a doctor.
▶ If you had a fever, you should have seen a doctor.

In the case of *must,* refer to the past by using *had to.*

▶ You must renew your visa by the end of this week.
▶ You had to renew your visa by the end of last week.

Using modals to make requests or to give instructions

Modals are often used in requests and instructions. Imagine making the following request of a flight attendant:

▶ Will you bring me a pillow?

This request may appear demanding or rude. Using a modal makes the request more polite by acknowledging that fulfilling the request may not be possible.

▶ Can you bring me a pillow?

Another way of softening the request is to use the past form of *will,* and the most discreet choice is the past form of *can.*

▶ Would you bring me a pillow?
▶ Could you bring me a pillow?

Using the past tense of modals seems more polite than using their present forms because it makes any statement or question less assertive.

Consider the meanings of each of the following instructions:

1. You *can* submit your report electronically.
2. You *may* submit your report electronically.
3. You *should* submit your report electronically.
4. You *must* submit your report electronically.
5. You *will* submit your report electronically.

Instructions 1 and 2 give permission to submit the report electronically but do not require it; 2 is more formal. Instruction 3 makes a strong recommendation; 4 allows no alternative; and 5 implies, "Don't even think of doing otherwise."

Using modals to indicate doubt or certainty

Modals can also indicate how confident the writer is about his or her claims. Look at the following set of examples, which starts with a tentative suggestion and ends with an indication of complete confidence:

▶ The study **might** help explain the findings of previous research.
▶ The study **may** help explain the findings of previous research.
▶ The study **will** help explain the findings of previous research.

59c Indicate present and past tenses.

Every sentence in standard written English must have at least one verb or verb phrase that is not an infinitive (*to write*), a gerund (*writing*), or a participle (*written*) without any auxiliaries. Furthermore, every such verb or verb phrase must have a tense (32e).

In some languages, such as Chinese and Vietnamese, the verb form never changes regardless of when the action takes place. In standard written English, the time of the action must be clearly indicated by the tense form of every verb, even if the time is obvious or it is indicated elsewhere in the sentence.

▶ During the Cultural Revolution, millions of young people ~~cannot~~ go
$\overset{could\ not}{}$

$\overset{were}{}$
to school and ~~are~~ sent to the countryside.

$\overset{called}{}$ $\overset{lives}{}$
▶ Last night I ~~call~~ my aunt who ~~live~~ in Santo Domingo.

Direct and indirect quotations

Changing direct quotations to indirect quotations can sometimes lead to tense shifts.

DIRECT	She said, "My work *is* now complete."
INDIRECT	She *told* me that her work *was* now complete.
INDIRECT	She *tells* me that her work *is* now complete.

In general, the verb introducing the indirect quotation (sometimes called the reporting verb) will agree in tense with the verb in the indirect quotation; there are, however, some exceptions. For example, if the reporting verb is in the past tense but the information that follows holds true in the present, shifting to a present-tense verb is acceptable.

▶ She *told* me that her work *is* as exciting as ever.

In academic writing, reporting verbs are used regularly to refer to ideas from other texts or authors. Depending on the documentation style you use, you will probably use the present tense, the present perfect tense, or the simple past for these verbs.

Lee *claims* that . . .
Lee *writes* . . .
Lee *has argued* that . . .
Lee *found* that . . .

59d Form perfect and progressive verb phrases.

The perfect and progressive auxiliaries combine with the present or past tense, or with modals, to form complex verb phrases with special meanings (32f).

Distinguishing the simple present and the present perfect

▶ My sister drives a bus.

The simple present (*drives*) tells us about the sister's current job. But if you were to add the phrase *for three years*, it would be incorrect to say *My sister drives a bus for three years*. Instead, you need a time frame that goes from the past up to the present. The present perfect or present perfect progressive expresses this time frame.

▶ My sister has driven a bus for three years.
▶ My sister has been driving a bus for three years.

Distinguishing the simple past and the present perfect

▶ Since she started working, she **has bought** a new car and a DVD player.

The clause introduced by *since* sets up a time frame that runs from past to present and requires the present perfect (*has bought*) in the subsequent clause. Furthermore, the sentence does not say exactly when she bought the car or the DVD player, and that indefiniteness also calls for the perfect. It would be less correct to say *Since she started working, she bought a new car and a DVD player.* But if you say when she bought the car, you should use the simple past tense.

▶ She **bought** the car two years ago.

It would be incorrect to say *She has bought the car two years ago* because the perfect cannot be used with definite expressions of time. In this case, use the simple past (*bought*).

Distinguishing the simple present and the present progressive

Use the present progressive tense when an action is in progress right now. In contrast, use the simple present for actions that frequently occur during a period of time that might include the present moment (though the simple present does not necessarily indicate that the action is taking place now).

▶ My sister **drives** a bus, but she **is taking** a vacation now.
▶ My sister **drives** a bus, but she **takes** a vacation every year.

Many languages use the simple present (*drives, takes*) for both types of sentences. In English, however, the first sentence would be incorrect if it said *but she takes a vacation now.*

Distinguishing the simple past and the past progressive

▶ Sally **spent** the summer in Ecuador.

The simple past tense is used in this case because the action occurred in the past and is now finished.

The past progressive tense is used relatively infrequently in English. It is used to focus on duration or continuousness and especially to call attention to past action that went on at the same time as something else.

▶ Sally **was spending** the summer in Ecuador when she *met* her future husband.

59e Use participial adjectives correctly.

Many verbs refer to feelings—for example, *bore, confuse, excite, fascinate, frighten, interest*. The present and past participles of such verbs can be used as ordinary adjectives (see 31l). Use the past participle (which usually ends with *-ed*) to describe a person having the feeling.

▶ The frightened boy started to cry.

Use the present participle (which usually ends with *-ing*) to describe the thing (or person) causing the feeling.

▶ The frightening dinosaur display gave him nightmares.

Be careful not to confuse the two types of adjectives.

> *interested*
▶ I am ~~interesting~~ in African literature.

> *interesting.*
▶ African literature seems ~~interested.~~

> bedfordstmartins.com/everydaywriter
> Exercise Central > For Multilingual Writers

Prepositions and Prepositional Phrases **60**

Words such as *to, from, over,* and *under* show the relations between other words; these words are prepositions, and they are one of the more challenging elements of English writing. You will need to decide which preposition to use for your intended meaning and understand how to use verbs that include prepositions, such as *take off, pick up,* and *put up with.*

60a Use prepositions idiomatically.

Even if you know where to use a preposition, it can be difficult to determine which preposition to use. Each of the most common prepositions has a wide range of applications, and this range never coincides exactly from one language to another. See, for example, how *in* and *on* are used in English.

▶ The peaches are *in* the refrigerator.
▶ The peaches are *on* the table.
▶ Is that a diamond ring *on* your finger?

The Spanish translations of these sentences all use the same preposition (*en*), a fact that might lead you astray in English.

       on
▶ Is that a ruby ring ~~in~~ your finger?

There is no easy solution to the challenge of using English prepositions idiomatically, but the strategies in the box on p. 563 can help.

60b Use two-word verbs idiomatically.

Some words that look like prepositions do not always function as prepositions. Consider the following two sentences:

▶ The balloon rose *off* the ground.
▶ The plane took *off* without difficulty.

In the first sentence, *off* is a preposition that introduces the prepositional phrase *off the ground*. In the second sentence, *off* does not function as a preposition. Instead, it combines with *took* to form a two-word verb with its own meaning. Such a verb is called a phrasal verb, and the word *off*, when used in this way, is called an adverbial particle. Many prepositions can function as particles to form phrasal verbs.

    The verb + particle combination that makes up a phrasal verb is a single entity that usually cannot be torn apart.

       off
▶ The plane took without difficulty. ~~off.~~

The exceptions are the many phrasal verbs that are transitive, meaning that they take a direct object (31k). Some transitive phrasal verbs have particles that may be separated from the verb by the object.

▶ I *picked up my baggage* at the terminal.
▶ I *picked my baggage up* at the terminal.

If a personal pronoun (such as *it*, *her*, or *him*) is used as the direct object, it must separate the verb from its particle.

▶ I *picked it up* at the terminal.

Some idiomatic two-word verbs, however, are not phrasal verbs.

▶ We *ran into* our neighbor on the train.

AT A GLANCE

Using Prepositions Idiomatically

1. Keep in mind typical examples of each preposition.

IN The peaches are *in* the refrigerator.
   There are still some pickles *in* the jar.
   The book you are looking for is *in* the bookcase.

Here the object of the preposition *in* is a container that encloses something.

ON The peaches are *on* the table.
   There are still some pickles *on* the plate.
   The book you are looking for is *on* the top shelf.

Here the object of the preposition *on* is a horizontal surface with which something is in direct contact.

2. Learn other examples that show some similarities and some differences in meaning.

IN You shouldn't drive *in* a snowstorm.

Here there is no container, but like a container, the falling snow surrounds the driver. The preposition *in* is used for other weather-related expressions as well: *in a tornado, in the sun, in the rain*.

ON Is that a diamond ring *on* your finger?

The preposition *on* is used to describe things we wear: *the hat on his head, the shoes on her feet, the tattoo on his back*.

3. Use your imagination to create mental images that can help you remember figurative uses of prepositions.

IN Michael is *in* love.

The preposition *in* is often used to describe a state of being: *in love, in pain, in a panic*. As a way to remember this, you might imagine the person immersed *in* this state of being.

4. Try to learn prepositions not in isolation but as part of a system. For example, in identifying the location of a place or an event, you can use the three prepositions *at, in,* and *on*.

At specifies the exact point in space or time.

AT There will be a meeting tomorrow *at* 9:30 AM *at* 160 Main Street.

Expanses of space or time within which a place is located or an event takes place might be seen as containers and so require *in*.

IN I arrived *in* the United States *in* January.

On must be used in two cases: with the names of streets (but not the exact address) and with days of the week or month.

ON The airline's office is *on* Fifth Avenue.
   I'll be moving to my new apartment *on* September 30.

In such verbs, the second word is a preposition, which cannot be separated from the verb. For example, a native speaker would not say *We ran our neighbor into on the train.* Verbs like *run into* are called prepositional verbs, which are another kind of two-word verb.

In the preceding sample sentence, *ran into* consists of the verb *ran* followed by the preposition *into*, which introduces the prepositional phrase *into our neighbor.* Yet *to run into our neighbor* is different from a normal verb + prepositional phrase, such as *to run into the room.* If you know the typical meanings of *run* and *into*, you can interpret *to run into the room.* Not so with *to run into our neighbor*; the combination *run + into* has a special meaning ("find by chance") that could not be determined from the typical meanings of *run* and *into*.

Prepositional verbs include such idiomatic two-word verbs as *take after*, meaning "resemble" (usually a parent or other older relative); *get over*, meaning "recover from"; and *count on*, meaning "trust." They also include verb + preposition combinations in which the meaning is predictable, but the specific preposition that is required is less predictable and must be learned together with the verb (for example, *depend on*, *look at*, *listen to*, *approve of*). There are also phrasal-prepositional verbs, which are verb + adverbial particle + preposition sequences (for example, *put up with*, *look forward to*, *give up on*, *get away with*).

bedfordstmartins.com/everydaywriter
Exercise Central > For Multilingual Writers

Writing in the Disciplines

Don't underestimate your readers'
intelligence, but don't overestimate their
knowledge of a particular field.

— JULIE ANN MILLER

Writing in the Disciplines

61 Academic Work in Any Discipline *567*
a Reading and writing for every discipline *567*
b Academic assignments and expectations *568*
c Specialized vocabulary *569*
d Disciplinary style *570*
e Use of evidence *571*
f Conventional patterns and formats *571*
g Ethical issues *572*
h Collaboration and communication *572*

62 Writing for the Humanities *573*
a Reading texts in the humanities *573*
b Writing texts in the humanities *573*
c A STUDENT'S CLOSE READING OF POETRY *576*

63 Writing for the Social Sciences *582*
a Reading texts in the social sciences *582*
b Writing texts in the social sciences *583*
c AN EXCERPT FROM A STUDENT RESEARCH ESSAY IN THE SOCIAL SCIENCES *585*

64 Writing for the Natural and Applied Sciences *590*
a Reading texts in the natural and applied sciences *590*
b Writing texts in the natural and applied sciences *591*
c AN EXCERPT FROM A STUDENT CHEMISTRY LAB REPORT *593*

65 Writing for Business *598*
a Reading texts for business *598*
b Writing texts for business *598*
MEMO *600*
LETTER OF APPLICATION *602*
RÉSUMÉ *605*
SCANNABLE RÉSUMÉ *606*

For visual analysis Look carefully at the illustration on the front of this tab. What do you think this image suggests about what it means to write in more than one discipline?

Academic Work in Any Discipline **61**

A recent survey confirmed that good writing plays an important role in almost every profession. One MBA wrote, "Those who advance quickly in my company are those who write and speak well — it's as simple as that." But while writing is always a valuable skill, writing well means different things in different disciplines. As you prepare written assignments for various courses, then, you will need to become familiar with the expectations, vocabularies, styles, methods of proof, and conventional formats used in each field.

61a   Reading and writing for every discipline

Writing is central to learning regardless of the discipline. So whether you are explaining the results of a telephone survey you conducted for a psychology class, preparing a lab report for chemistry, conducting a case study for anthropology, or working on a proposal for material sciences and engineering, writing helps you get the job done.

One good way to learn to write well in a discipline is to read the texts others write. So read a lot, and pay attention to the texts you are reading. To get started, choose an article in an important journal in the field you plan to major in and then answer the following questions:

- How does a journal article in this discipline begin?
- How is the article organized? Does it have specific sections with subheads?
- What sources are cited, and how are they used — as backup support, as counter-examples, or as an argument to refute?
- How does the article conclude?
- What audience does the text seem to address? Is it a narrow technical or disciplinary audience, or is it aimed at a broader reading public? Is it addressed to readers of a specific journal? Is it published in print or online?

Finally, make sure you know whether the articles you are reading are from juried or nonjuried journals (16a). Juried journals use panels of expert readers to analyze proposed articles, so articles in juried journals have been recommended for publication by experts in the field. Nonjuried journals can also offer valuable information, but they may bear the stamp of the editor's biases more strongly than a juried journal would. To find out whether a journal is juried or nonjuried, check the submissions guidelines for information about whether submitted articles are sent to reviewers before publication.

For additional guidelines on reading critically, see Chapter 12.

61b Academic assignments and expectations

When you receive an assignment, your first job is to be sure you understand what that assignment is asking you to do. Some assignments may be as vague as "Write a five-page essay on one aspect of the Civil War" or "Write an analysis of the group dynamics at play in your

---

AT A GLANCE

Analyzing an Assignment

- *What is the purpose of the assignment?* Are you expected to join a discussion, demonstrate your mastery of the topic in writing, or something else?
- *Who is the audience?* The instructor will be one audience, but are there others? If so, who are they?
- *What does the assignment ask of you?* Look for key terms such as *summarize, explain, evaluate, interpret, illustrate,* and *define.*
- *Do you need clarification of any terms?* If so, ask your instructor.
- *What do you need to know or find out to complete the assignment?* You may need to do background reading, develop a procedure for analyzing or categorizing information, or carry out some other kind of preparation.
- *What does the instructor expect in a written response?* How will you use sources? What kinds of sources should you use? How should you organize and develop the assignment? What is the expected format and length?
- *Can you find a model of an effective response to a similar assignment?*
- *What do other students think the assignment requires?* Talking over an assignment with classmates is one good way to test your understanding.

recent collaborative project for this course" (see 63c for one student's response to the latter assignment). Others may be fairly specific: "Collect, summarize, and interpret data drawn from a sample of letters to the editor published in two newspapers, one in a small rural community and one in an urban community, over a period of three months." Whatever the assignment, use the questions in the box on p. 568 (and the information in Chapter 5) to analyze it.

61c Specialized vocabulary

Entering into an academic discipline or a profession is like going to a party where you don't know anyone. At first you feel like an outsider, and you may not understand much of what you hear or see. Before you enter the conversation, you have to listen and observe carefully. Eventually, however, you will be able to join in — and if you stay long enough, participating in the conversation becomes easy and natural.

To learn the routines, practices, and ways of knowing in a new field, you must also make an effort to enter into the conversation. A good way to get started is to study the vocabulary of the field you are most interested in.

Highlight the key terms in your reading or notes to learn how much specialized or technical vocabulary you will be expected to know. If you find only a small amount of specialized vocabulary, try to master the new terms quickly by reading your textbook carefully, looking up key words or phrases, and asking questions. If you find a great deal of specialized vocabulary, however, you may want to familiarize yourself with it methodically. Any of the following procedures may help:

- Keep a log of unfamiliar words used in context. Check definitions in your textbook's glossary or index, or consult a specialized dictionary.

- See if your textbook has a glossary of terms (see Chapter 24) or sets off definitions. Study pertinent sections to master the terms.

- Work with key concepts. Even if they are not yet entirely clear to you, using them will help you understand them. For example, in a statistics class, try to work out (in words) how to do an analysis of *covariance*, step by step, even if you are not sure of the precise definition of the term. Or try to plot the narrative progression in a story even if you are still not entirely sure of the definition of *narrative progression*.

- Take special note of the ways technical language or disciplinary vocabulary is used in online information related to a particular field.

61d Disciplinary style

Another important way to learn about a discipline is to identify its stylistic features. Study pieces of writing in the field with the following in mind:

- *Overall tone.* How would you describe it? (See 5f.)
- *Title.* Are titles generally descriptive ("Findings from a Double-Blind Study of the Effect of Antioxidants"), persuasive ("Antioxidants Proven Effective"), or something else? How does the title shape your expectations?
- *Stance.* To what extent do writers in the field strive for distance and objectivity? What strategies help them to achieve this stance? (See 5d.)
- *Sentence length.* Are sentences long and complex? Simple and direct?
- *Voice.* Are verbs generally active or passive? Why? (See 32g.)
- *Person.* Do writers use the first-person *I* or third-person terms such as *the investigator*? What is the effect of this choice? (See the box below.)
- *Visuals.* Do writers typically use elements such as graphs, tables, maps, or photographs? How are visuals integrated into the text? What role, if any, do headings and other formatting elements play in the writing? (See Chapter 9.)
- *Documentation style.* Do writers use MLA, APA, *Chicago*, or CSE style? (See Chapters 49–55.)

Of course, writings within a single discipline may have different purposes and different styles. A chemist may write a grant proposal, a lab notebook, a literature review, a research report, and a lab report, each with a different purpose and style.

TALKING THE TALK

The First Person

"Is it true that I should never use *I* in college writing?" In much writing in college, using the first-person *I* is perfectly acceptable to most instructors. As always, think about the context — if your own experience is relevant to the topic, you are better off saying *I* than trying too hard not to. But don't overdo it, especially if the writing isn't just autobiographical. And check with your instructor if you aren't sure: in certain academic disciplines, using *I* may be seen as inappropriate.

61e Use of evidence

As you grow familiar with an area of study, you will develop a sense of what it takes to prove a point in that field. You can speed up this process, however, by investigating and questioning. The following questions will help you think about the use of evidence in materials you read:

- How do writers in the field use precedent and authority? What or who counts as an authority in this field? How are the credentials of an authority established? (See 14e.)
- What kinds of quantitative data (countable or measurable items) are used, and for what purposes? How are the data gathered and presented?
- How are qualitative data (systematically observed items) used?
- How are statistics used and presented? Are tables, charts, graphs, or other visuals important, and why?
- How is logical reasoning used? How are definition, cause and effect, analogy, and example used?
- How does the field use primary materials—the firsthand sources of information—and secondary sources that are reported by others? (See 16a.) How is each type of source presented?
- What kinds of textual evidence are cited?
- How are quotations and other references to sources used and integrated into the text? (See Chapter 18.)

61f Conventional patterns and formats

To produce effective writing in a discipline, you need to know the field's generally accepted formats for organizing and presenting evidence. Although these formats can vary widely from discipline to discipline and even from instructor to instructor, common patterns do emerge. A typical laboratory report, for instance, follows a fairly standard organizational framework and usually has a certain look (see 64c for an example). A case study in sociology or education or anthropology likewise follows a typical organizational plan. Ask your instructor to recommend good examples of the kind of writing you will do in the course; then analyze these examples in terms of format, design, and organization. You might also look at major scholarly journals in the field to see what types of formats seem most common and how each is organized.

61g   Ethical issues

Writers in all disciplines face ethical questions. Those who plan and carry out research on living people, for example, must be careful to avoid harming their subjects. Researchers in all fields must be scrupulous in presenting data to make sure that others can replicate research and test claims. And although writers in any discipline should take into consideration their own interests, those of their collaborators, and those of their employers, they must also responsibly safeguard the interests of the general public.

Fortunately, a growing number of disciplines have adopted guidelines for ethics. The American Psychological Association has been a pioneer in this area, and many other professional organizations and companies have their own codes or standards of ethics. These guidelines can help you make decisions about day-to-day writing. Even so, you will no doubt encounter situations where the right or ethical decision is murky at best. In such situations, consult your own conscience first and then talk your choices over with colleagues you respect before coming to a decision on how to proceed.

61h   Collaboration and communication

In contemporary academic and business environments, working with others is a highly valued skill. Such collaboration happens when classmates divide research and writing duties to create a multimedia presentation, when peer reviewers share advice on a draft, or when colleagues in an office offer their views on appropriate revisions for a company-wide document.

Because people all over the world now have the ability to research, study, write, and work together, you must be able to communicate effectively within and across cultures. Conventions for academic writing (or for forms of online communication) can vary from culture to culture, from discipline to discipline, and from one form of English to another. What is considered polite in one culture may seem rude in another, so those who communicate globally must take care to avoid giving offense—or taking it where none was intended. (For more information on writing across cultures, see Chapter 20.)

Writing for the Humanities 62

Disciplines in the humanities are concerned with what it means to be human: historians reconstruct the past; literary critics analyze and interpret texts portraying the human condition; philosophers raise questions about truth, knowledge, beauty, and justice; scholars of languages learn to inhabit other cultures. In these and other ways, those in the humanities strive to explore, interpret, and reconstruct the human experience.

62a Reading texts in the humanities

The interpretation of texts is central to humanities disciplines. A reader in the humanities needs the tools to analyze a text—whether a primary or secondary source, ancient or modern, literary or historical, verbal or visual—and carefully consider the arguments it makes.

To read critically in the humanities (2c and Chapter 12), you will need to pose questions and construct hypotheses as you read. You may ask, for instance, why a writer makes some points or develops some examples but omits others. Rather than finding meaning only in the surface information that texts or artifacts convey, use your own questions and hypotheses to create fuller meanings—to construct the significance of what you read.

To successfully engage texts, you must recognize that you are not a neutral observer, not an empty cup into which meaning is poured. If such were the case, writing would have exactly the same meanings for all of us, and reading would be a fairly boring affair. If you have ever gone to a movie with a friend and each come away with a completely different response, you already understand that a text never has just one meaning. Most humanities courses will expect you to exercise your interpretive powers; the following guidelines will help you build your strengths as a close reader of humanities texts.

62b Writing texts in the humanities

Strong writers in the humanities use the findings from their close examination of a text or artifact to develop an argument or to construct an analysis.

> **AT A GLANCE**
>
> ## Guidelines for Reading Texts in the Humanities
>
> 1. ***Be clear about the purpose of the text.*** The two most common purposes for works in the humanities are to provide information and to argue for a particular interpretation. Pay attention to whether the text presents opinions or facts, to what is included and omitted, and to how facts are presented to the audience. (17c)
>
> 2. ***Get an overall impression.*** What does the work make you think about — and why? What is most remarkable or memorable? What confuses you?
>
> 3. ***Annotate the text.*** Be prepared to "talk back," ask questions, note emerging patterns or themes, and point out anything out of place or ineffective. (See Chapter 12.)
>
> 4. ***Look at the context.*** Consider the time and place represented in the work as well as when and where the writer lived. You may also consider social, political, or personal forces that may have affected the writer.
>
> 5. ***Think about the audience.*** Who are the readers or viewers the writer seems to address? Do they include you?
>
> 6. ***Pay attention to genre.*** What category does the work fall into (graphic novel, diary, political cartoon, sermon, argumentative essay, Hollywood western)? What is noteworthy about the form? How does it conform to or subvert your expectations about the genre? (5f)
>
> 7. ***Note the point of view.*** Whose point of view is represented? How does it affect your response?
>
> 8. ***Notice the major themes.*** Are specific claims being advanced? How are these claims supported?
>
> 9. ***Understand the difference between primary and secondary sources.*** Primary sources provide firsthand knowledge, while secondary sources report on or analyze the research of others. (16a)

Assignments

Common assignments that make use of these skills of close reading, analysis, and argument include summaries, response pieces, position papers, critical analyses of primary and secondary sources, and research-based projects. A philosophy student, for example, might need to summarize an argument, critique a text's logic and effectiveness, or discuss a moral issue from a particular philosophical perspective. A literature assignment may ask a reader to look very closely at a particular text ("Examine the role of chocolate in Toni Morrison's *Tar Baby*") or to go well beyond a primary text ("Discuss the impact of agribusiness on modernist novels"). History students often write books or articles ("Write a critical review of Jane Addams's *Twenty Years at Hull-House*, paying special attention to the writer's purpose and goals and relating these to the larger settlement house movement in America") along with primary source analyses or research papers.

For papers in literature, modern languages, and philosophy, writers often use the documentation style of the Modern Language Association; see Chapters 49–52 for advice on using MLA style. For papers in history and other areas of the humanities, writers often use the documentation style of the University of Chicago Press; see Chapter 54 for advice on using *Chicago* style.

Analysis and critical stance

To analyze a text, you need to develop a critical stance—the approach you will take to the work—that can help you develop a thesis or major claim (see 5d and 7b). To evaluate the text and present a critical response to it, you should look closely at the text itself, including its style; at the context in which it was produced; and at the audience the text aims to reach, which may or may not include yourself.

A close look at the text itself includes considering its genre, form, point of view, and themes, and looking at the stylistic features, such as word choice, use of imagery, visuals, and design. Considering context means asking why the text was created—thinking about the original (and current) context and about how attitudes and ideas of its era may have influenced it. Considering audience means thinking about who the intended audience might be, and about how people outside this intended group might respond. Think about your personal response to the text as well. (See also Chapters 5, 12, and 13.)

Carrying out these steps should provide you with plenty of material to work with as you begin to shape a critical thesis and write your analysis. You can begin by grounding your analysis in one or more important questions you have about the work.

Writing a literary analysis

When you analyze or interpret a literary work, think of your thesis as answering a question about some aspect of the work. The guiding question you bring to the literary work will help you decide on a critical stance toward the work. For example, a student writing about Shakespeare's *Macbeth* might find her curiosity piqued by the many comic moments that appear in this tragedy. She could build on her curiosity by turning the question of why Shakespeare uses so much comedy in *Macbeth* into the following thesis statement, which proposes an answer to the question: "The many unexpected comic moments in *Macbeth* emphasize how disordered the world becomes for murderers like Macbeth and his wife."

 bedfordstmartins.com/everydaywriter
Writing about Literature

62c   A student's close reading of poetry

The following paper, a close reading of two poems by E. E. Cummings, was written by Bonnie Sillay, a student at the University of Georgia. This essay follows MLA style (see Chapters 49–52). Bonnie is creating her own interpretation, so the only works she cites are the poems she analyzes. Note that this essay has been reproduced in a narrow format to allow for annotation. (For sample research papers in MLA style, see 14k and Chapter 52.)

Student Writer

Bonnie Sillay

 bedfordstmartins.com/everydaywriter
Student Writing

1"

Bonnie Sillay

Instructor Angela Mitchell

English 1102

December 4, 2011

Name,
instructor,
course
number,
and date on
left margin,
double-spaced

"Life's Not a Paragraph"

Title centered

Throughout his poetry, E. E. Cummings leads readers deep
into a thicket of scrambled words, missing punctuation, and
unconventional structure. Within Cummings's poetic bramble,
ambiguity leads the reader through what seems at first a confusing
and winding maze. However, this confusion actually transforms
into a path that leads the reader to the center of the thicket where
Cummings's message lies: readers should not allow their experience
to be limited by reason and rationality. In order to communicate
his belief that emotional experience should triumph over reason,
Cummings employs odd juxtapositions, outlandish metaphors,
and inversions of traditional grammatical structures that reveal
the illogic of reason. Indeed, by breaking down such formal
boundaries, Cummings's poems "since feeling is first" and "as
freedom is a breakfastfood" suggest that emotion, which provides
the compositional fabric for our experience of life, should never be
defined or controlled.

Present
tense used to
discuss poetry

Foreshadows
discussion of
work to come

Introductory
paragraph
ends with
thesis
statement

In "since feeling is first," Cummings urges his reader to
reject attempts to control emotion, using English grammar as one
example of the restrictive conventions present in society. Stating
that "since feeling is first / who pays any attention / to the syntax
of things" (lines 1-3), Cummings suggests that emotion should
not be forced to fit into some preconceived framework or mold. He
carries this message throughout the poem by juxtaposing images
of the abstract and the concrete—images of emotion and of English
grammar. Cummings's word choice enhances his intentionally

Quotation cited
parenthetically

Annotations indicate effective choices or MLA-style formatting.

Student Writing

Paper header
on each page
includes last
name and page
number

Transition
sentence
connects the
previous
paragraph to
this one

Quotation
introduced
effectively

Writer uses a
metaphor that
captures the
spirit of
Cummings's
point

Quotation
integrated
into writer's
sentence

strange juxtapositions, with the poet using grammatical terms that suggest regulation or confinement. For example, in the line "And death i think is no parenthesis" (16), Cummings uses the idea that parentheses confine the words they surround in order to warn the reader not to let death confine life or emotions.

The structure of the poem also rejects traditional conventions. Instead of the final stanzas making the main point, Cummings opens his poem with his primary message, that "feeling is first" (1). Again, Cummings shows that emotion rejects order and structure. How can emotion be bottled in sentences and interrupted by commas, colons, and spaces? To Cummings, emotion is a never-ending run-on sentence that should not be diagramed or dissected.

In the third stanza of "since feeling is first," Cummings states his point outright, noting "my blood approves, / and kisses are a better fate / than wisdom" (7-9). Here, Cummings argues for reveling in the feeling during a fleeting moment such as a kiss. He continues, "the best gesture of my brain is less than / your eyelids' flutter" (11-12). Cummings wants the reader to focus on a pure emotive response (the flutter of an eyelash)—on the emotional, not the logical—on the meanings of words instead of punctuation and grammar.

Cummings's use of words such as *kisses* and *blood* (8, 7) adds to the focus on the emotional. The ideas behind these words are difficult to confine or restrict to a single definition: kisses mean different things to different people, blood flows through the body freely and continually. The words are not expansive or free enough to encompass all that they suggest. Cummings ultimately paints language as more restrictive than the flowing, powerful force of emotion.

Student Writing

The poet's use of two grammatical terms in the last lines, "for life's not a paragraph / And death i think is no parenthesis," warns against attempts to format lives and feelings into conventional and rule-bound segments (15-16). Attempts to control, rather than feel, are rejected throughout "since feeling is first." Emotion should be limitless, free from any restrictions or rules.

While "since feeling is first" argues that emotions should not be controlled, ordered, or analyzed, "as freedom is a breakfastfood" suggests the difficulty of defining emotion. In this poem, Cummings uses deliberately far-fetched metaphors such as "freedom is a breakfastfood" and "time is a tree" (1, 26). These metaphors seem arbitrary: Cummings is not attempting to make profound statements on time or freedom. Instead, he suggests that freedom and time are subjective, and attempts at narrow definition are ridiculous. Inversions of nature, such as "robins never welcome spring" and "water most encourage flame" (16, 7), underscore emotion's ability to defy reason. These inversions suggest the arbitrariness of what "since feeling is first" calls "the syntax of things" (3).

Although most of "as freedom is a breakfastfood" defies logic, Cummings shifts the tone at the end to deliver one last metaphor: "but love is the sky" (27). The word *but* separates this definition from the rest of the poem and subtly implies that, unlike the metaphors that have come before it, "love is the sky" is an accurate comparison. In order to reach this final conclusion, however, Cummings has taken his readers on a long and often ambiguous journey.

Nevertheless, the confusion has been deliberate. Cummings wants his readers to follow him through the winding path through

Paragraph reiterates Cummings's claim and sums up his argument

Clear and explicit transition from discussion of first poem

Sillay 4

the thicket because he believes the path of the straight and narrow limits the possibilities of experience. Through the unconventionality of his poetic structures, Cummings urges his readers to question order and tradition. He wants his readers to realize that reason and rationality are always secondary to emotion and that emotional experience is a free-flowing force that should not be constrained. Cummings's poetry suggests that in order to get at the true essence of something, one must look past the commonsensical definition and not be limited by "the syntax of things."

Writer returns to the image of the thicket from the introduction to create a closing that resonates with the opening

Sillay 5

Student Writing

Works Cited

Cummings, E. E. "as freedom is a breakfastfood." *E. E. Cummings: Complete Poems 1904-1962*. Ed. George J. Firmage. New York: Liveright, 1991. 511. Print.

---. "since feeling is first." *E. E. Cummings: Complete Poems 1904-1962*. Ed. George J. Firmage. New York: Liveright, 1991. 291. Print.

Second work by same author uses three hyphens in place of name

63   Writing for the Social Sciences

W hen do most workers begin to save toward retirement? What role do television ads play in a voter's decision-making process? How do children learn to read? The social sciences—psychology, anthropology, political science, speech, communication, sociology, economics, and education—try to answer such questions. The social sciences share with the humanities an interest in what it means to be human, and they share with the natural and applied sciences the goal of engaging in systematic, observable study. All the social sciences aim to identify, understand, and explain patterns of human behavior.

63a   Reading texts in the social sciences

Strong readers in the social sciences—as in any subject—ask questions, analyze, and interpret as they read, whether they are reading an academic paper that sets forth a theoretical premise or overall theory and defends it, a case study that describes a particular case and draws out inferences and implications from it, or a research report that presents the results of an investigation into an important question in the field. Most of what students read in the social sciences is trying to prove a point, and readers need to evaluate whether that point is supported.

The social sciences, like other disciplines, often use specialized vocabulary as shorthand for complex ideas that otherwise would take paragraphs to explain.

Qualitative and quantitative studies

Different texts in the social and natural sciences may call for different methods and strategies. Texts that report the results of *quantitative* studies collect data represented with numerical measurements drawn from surveys, polls, experiments, and tests. For example, a study of voting patterns in southern states might rely on quantitative data such as statistics. Texts that report the results of *qualitative* studies rely on nonnumerical methods such as interviews and observations to reveal social patterns. A study of the way children in one kindergarten class develop rules of play, for instance, would draw on qualitative data—observations of social interaction, interviews with students and teachers, and so on. Of course, some work in the social and behavioral sciences combines quantitative and qualitative data and methods: an educational report might begin with statistical data related to a problem and then move to a qualitative case study to exemplify what the statistics reveal.

In the social sciences, both quantitative and qualitative researchers must determine what they are examining and measuring in order to get answers to research questions. A researcher who studies childhood aggression must first define and measure *aggression*. If the research is qualitative, a researcher may describe types of behavior that indicate aggression and then discuss observations of children and interviews with teachers and peers about those behaviors. A quantitative researcher, on the other hand, might design an experiment that notes how often children hit a punching bag or that asks children to rate their peers' aggression on a scale of one to ten.

It's important to recognize that both quantitative and qualitative studies have points of view, and that researchers' opinions influence everything from the hypothesis and the design of the research study to the interpretation of findings. Readers must consider whether the researchers' views are sensible and solidly supported by evidence, and they must pay close attention to the kind of data the writer is using and what those data can—and cannot—prove. For example, if researchers of childhood aggression define *aggression* in a way that readers find unpersuasive, or if they observe behaviors that readers consider playful rather than aggressive, then the readers will likely not accept their interpretation of the findings.

Conventional formats

Make use of conventional disciplinary formats to help guide your reading in the social sciences. Many such texts conform to the format and documentation style of the American Psychological Association (APA). In addition, articles often include standard features—an abstract that gives an overview of the findings, followed by the introduction, review of literature, methods, results, discussion, and references. Readers who become familiar with such a format can easily find the information they need. (For more on APA style, see Chapter 53.)

63b Writing texts in the social sciences

Perhaps because the social sciences share concerns with both the humanities and the sciences, the forms of writing within the social sciences are particularly varied, including summaries, abstracts, literature reviews, reaction pieces, position papers, radio scripts, briefing notes, book reviews, briefs, research proposals, research papers, quantitative research reports, case studies, ethnographic analyses, and meta-analyses. Such an array of writing assignments could seem overwhelming, but in fact these assignments can be organized under five main categories:

- *Writing that encourages student learning*—reaction pieces, position papers
- *Writing that demonstrates student learning*—summaries, abstracts, research papers
- *Writing that reflects common on-the-job communication tasks undertaken by members of a discipline*—radio scripts, briefing notes, informational reports
- *Writing that requires students to analyze and evaluate the writings of others*—literature reviews, book reviews, briefs
- *Writing that asks students to replicate the work of others or to engage in original research*—quantitative research reports, case studies, ethnographic analyses

Many forms of writing in the social sciences call either explicitly or implicitly for argument (see Chapter 13). If you write an essay reporting on the results of a survey you developed about attitudes toward physician-assisted suicide among students on your campus, you will make an explicit argument about the significance of your data. But even in other forms of writing, such as summaries and book reports, you will implicitly argue that your description and analysis provide a clear, thorough overview of the text(s) you have read.

The literature review

Students of the social sciences carry out literature reviews to find out the most current thinking about a topic, to learn what research has already been carried out on that topic, to evaluate the work that has been done, and to set any research they will do in context. The following guidelines are designed to help you explore and question sources, looking for flaws or gaps. Such a critical review could then lead to a discussion of how your own research will avoid such flaws and advance knowledge.

- What is your topic of interest? What is the dependent variable (the item or characteristic being studied)?
- What is already known about this topic? What characteristics does the topic or dependent variable have? How have other researchers measured the item or characteristic being studied? What other factors are involved, and how are they related to each other and to your topic or variable? What theories are used to explain the way things are now?
- How has research been done so far? Who or what has been studied? How have measurements been taken?

- Has there been change over time? What has caused any changes?
- What problems do you identify in the current research? What questions have not been answered yet? What conclusions have researchers drawn that might not be warranted?
- What gaps will your research fill? What new information or ideas does it contribute? What problems do you want to correct?

63c An excerpt from a student research essay in the social sciences

An excerpt from an essay by Merlla McLaughlin appears on the following pages. It conforms to the APA guidelines described in Chapter 53. Note that this essay has been reproduced in a narrow format to allow for annotation.

Student Writer

Merlla McLaughlin

bedfordstmartins.com/everydaywriter
Student Writing

Running head: LEADERSHIP ROLES   1

Running head
with shortened
title appears
flush left at
the top of
each page;
page number
appears flush
right

Title, name,
and affiliation
centered and
double-spaced

          Leadership Roles in a Small-Group Project

                   Merlla McLaughlin

                    Psychology 101

                     Dr. Suarez

                 18 March 2009

Annotations indicate effective choices or APA-style formatting.

LEADERSHIP ROLES   2

Abstract

Using the interpersonal communications research of J. K. Brilhart and G. J. Galanes as well as that of W. Wilmot and J. Hocker, along with T. Hartman's Personality Assessment, I observed and analyzed the leadership roles and group dynamics of my project collaborators in a communications course. Based on results of the Hartman Personality Assessment, I predicted that a single leader would emerge. However, complementary individual strengths and gender differences encouraged a distributed leadership style, in which the group experienced little confrontation. Conflict, because it was handled positively, was crucial to the group's progress.

Student Writing

Heading centered

No indentation

Study described

Key points of report discussed

Double-spaced text

Student Writing

Full title, centered

Paragraphs indented

Questions indicate the focus of the essay

Headings help organize the report

APA-style parenthetical reference

Background information about team members' personality types

Chart displays information concisely

Chart referred to in preceding text

Source of table listed

Leadership Roles in a Small-Group Project

Although classroom lectures provide students with volumes of information, many experiences can be understood only by living them. So it is with the workings of a small, task-focused group. What observations can I make after working with a group of peers on a class project? And what have I learned as a result?

Leadership Expectations and Emergence

The six members of this group were selected by the instructor; half were male and half were female. By performing the Hartman Personality Assessment (Hartman, 1998) in class, we learned that Hartman has associated key personality traits with the colors red, blue, white, and yellow (see Table 1). The assessment identified most of us as "Blues," concerned with intimacy and caring. Because of the bold qualities associated with "Reds," I expected that Nate, our only "Red" member, might become our leader. (Kaari, the only "White," seemed poised to become the peacekeeper.) However, after Nate missed the first two meetings, it seemed that Pat, who contributed often during our first three meetings, might emerge as leader. Pat has strong communications skills, a commanding presence, and displays sensitivity to others. I was surprised, then,

Table 1

Hartman's Key Personality Traits

Trait category	Color			
	Red	Blue	White	Yellow
Motive	Power	Intimacy	Peace	Fun
Strengths	Loyal to tasks	Loyal to people	Tolerant	Positive
Limitations	Arrogant	Self-righteous	Timid	Uncommitted

Note. Table is adapted from information found at The Hartman Personality Profile, by N. Hayden. Retrieved February 15, 2004, from http://students.cs.byu.edu/~nhayden/Code/index.php

LEADERSHIP ROLES   7

References

Brilhart, J. K., & Galanes, G. J. (1998). *Effective group discussion* (9th ed.). Boston: McGraw-Hill.

Hartman, T. (1998). *The color code: A new way to see yourself, your relationships, and your life*. New York: Scribner.

Hayden, N. (n.d.). *The Hartman Personality Profile*. Retrieved February 15, 2009, from http://students.cs.byu.edu/ ~nhayden/Code/index.php

Wilmot, W., & Hocker, J. (1998). *Interpersonal conflict* (5th ed.). Boston: McGraw-Hill.

Student Writing

List starts on new page

Book

Web site

Entries alphabetized

First line of entry flush left; subsequent lines indent

64 Writing for the Natural and Applied Sciences

W hether they are studying geological faults or developing a stronger support structure for suspension bridges, scientists and engineers in the natural and applied sciences want to understand how the physical and natural worlds work. Natural sciences such as biology, chemistry, and physics study the natural world and its phenomena; applied sciences such as nanotechnology and mechanical engineering apply knowledge from the natural sciences to practical problems. More than many other scholars, scientists and engineers are likely to leave the privacy of their office or lab to engage in fieldwork and experimentation. Whether done in the lab or the field, however, writing—from the first grant proposal to the final report or scientific paper—plays a key role in the natural and applied sciences.

64a Reading texts in the natural and applied sciences

Scientists and engineers work with evidence that can be observed, verified, and controlled. Though they cannot avoid interpretation, they strive for objectivity by using the scientific method—observing or studying phenomena, formulating a hypothesis about the phenomena, and testing that hypothesis through controlled experiments and observations. Scientists and engineers aim to generate precise, replicable data; they develop experiments to account for extraneous factors. In this careful, precise way, scientists and engineers identify, test, and write persuasively about theoretical and real-world problems.

Identifying argument

As you read in the sciences, try to become familiar with disciplinary terms, concepts, and formats as soon as possible, and practice reading—and listening—for detail. If you are reading a first-year biology textbook, you can draw upon general critical-reading strategies. In addition, charts, graphs, illustrations, models, and other visuals often play an important role in scientific writing, so your ability to read and comprehend these visual displays of knowledge is particularly important. (See Chapter 12.)

When you read a science or engineering textbook, you can assume that the information presented there is authoritative and as objective as possible. When you read specialized materials, however, recognize that although scholarly reports undergo significant peer review, they nevertheless represent arguments (see Chapter 13). The connection between facts and claims in the sciences, as in all subject areas, is created by the author rather than simply revealed by the data. So read both facts and claims with a questioning eye: Did the scientist choose the best method to test the hypothesis? Are there other reasonable interpretations of the experiment's results? Do other studies contradict the conclusions of this experiment? When you read specialized texts in the sciences with questions like these in mind, you are reading—and thinking—like a scientist. (For additional information on assessing a source's credibility, see 17c.)

Conventional formats

As you advance in your course work, you will need to develop reading strategies for increasingly specialized texts. Many scientific texts conform to the format and documentation style of the Council of Science Editors (CSE); for more on CSE style, see Chapter 55. (However, you should be prepared to follow an instructor's guidelines for citation and references if another style is used in your discipline or in a particular course.) In addition, articles often include standard features—an abstract that gives an overview of the findings, followed by an introduction, literature review, materials and methods, results, discussion, and references.

You might expect to read a journal article for a science or engineering course from start to finish, giving equal weight to each section. However, an experienced reader in sciences and engineering might skim an abstract to see if an article warrants further reading. If it does—and this judgment is based on the reader's own research interest—he or she might then read the introduction to understand the rationale for the experiment and then skip to the results. A reader with a specific interest in the methods will read that section with particular care.

64b Writing texts in the natural and applied sciences

Students in the sciences and engineering must be able to respond to a diverse range of writing and speaking tasks. Often, they must maintain lab or engineering notebooks that include careful records of experiments. They also write memos, papers, project proposals and reports, literature reviews, and progress reports; in addition, they may develop print and Web-based presentations for both technical and lay audiences (see 3c). Particularly common writing assignments in the sciences are the literature review, research proposal, and research report.

For a student literature review, see 53d.

Scientists undertake *literature reviews* to keep up with and evaluate developments in their field. Literature reviews are an essential first step in any research effort, for they enable scientists to discover what research has already been completed and how they might build on earlier efforts. Successful literature reviews demonstrate a student's ability to identify relevant research on a topic and to summarize and in some instances evaluate that research.

Most scientists spend a great deal of time writing research or *grant proposals* aimed at securing funds to support their research. Undergraduate writers often have an opportunity to make similar proposals—to an office of undergraduate research or to a science-based firm that supports student research, for instance. Funding agencies often have guidelines for preparing a proposal. Proposals for research funding generally include the following sections: title page, introduction, purpose(s) and significance of the study, methods, timeline, budget, and references. You may also need to submit an abstract.

For a student research proposal, see 55c.

Research reports, another common writing form in the sciences, may include both literature reviews and discussions of primary research, most often experiments. Like journal articles, research reports generally follow this form: title, author(s), abstract, introduction, literature review, materials and methods, results, discussion, and references. Many instructors ask students to write lab reports (64c), which are briefer versions of research reports and may not include a literature review.

Today, a great deal of scientific writing is collaborative. As students move from introductory to advanced courses and then to the workplace, they increasingly find themselves working as part of teams or groups. Indeed, in such areas as engineering, collaborative projects (6g) are often the norm.

Style in the natural and applied sciences

In general, use the present tense for most writing you do in the natural and applied sciences. Use the past tense, however, when you are describing research already carried out (by you or others) or published in the past (32e).

Writers in the sciences need to produce complex figures, tables, images, and models and use software designed to analyze data or run computer simulations. In addition, they need to present data carefully. If you create a graph, you should provide headings for columns, label axes with numbers or units, and identify data points. Caption figures and tables with a number and descriptive title. And avoid orphan data—data that you present in a figure or table but don't comment on in your text.

Finally, make sure that any writing you do is as clear, concise, and grammatically correct as possible to ensure that readers see you as capable and credible.

64c An excerpt from a student chemistry lab report

The following piece of student writing is excerpted from a lab report on a chemistry experiment by Allyson Goldberg, a student at Yale University. Note that these sample pages have been reproduced in a narrow format to allow for annotation.

Student Writer

Allyson Goldberg

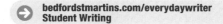

bedfordstmartins.com/everydaywriter
Student Writing

Title page includes relevant information about lab

Chemistry 119L Laboratory Report
Evaluation of the Value of the Gas Constant R

Allyson Goldberg

Date of Experiment: Monday, September 27, 2010

Goldberg 2

Introduction

The purpose of this investigation was to experimentally determine the value of the universal gas constant, R. To accomplish this goal, a measured sample of magnesium (Mg) was allowed to react with an excess of hydrochloric acid (HCl) at room temperature and pressure so that the precise amount and volume of the product hydrogen gas (H_2) could be determined and the value of R could be calculated using the ideal gas equation, $PV=nRT$.

Introduction explains purpose of lab and gives overview of results

Materials & Methods

Two samples of room temperature water, one about 250mL and the other about 400mL, were measured into a smaller and larger beaker respectively. 15.0mL of HCl was then transferred into a side arm flask that was connected to the top of a buret (clamped to a ringstand) through a 5/16" diameter flexible tube. (This "gas buret" was connected to an adjacent "open buret," clamped to the other side of the ringstand and left open to the atmosphere of the laboratory at its wide end, by a 1/4" diameter flexible tube. These two burets were adjusted on the ringstand so that they were vertically parallel and close together.) The HCl sample was transferred to the flask such that none came in contact with the inner surface of the neck of the flask. The flask was then allowed to rest, in an almost horizontal position, in the smaller beaker.

Materials and methods section explains lab setup and procedure

The open buret was adjusted on the ringstand such that its 20mL mark was horizontally aligned with the 35mL mark on the gas buret. Room temperature water was added to the open buret until the water level of the gas buret was at about 34.00mL.

Passive voice throughout typical of writing in natural sciences

A piece of magnesium ribbon was obtained, weighed on an analytical balance, and placed in the neck of the horizontal side arm flask. Next, a screw cap was used to cap the flask and form an airtight seal. This setup was then allowed to sit for 5 minutes in order to reach thermal equilibrium.

After 5 minutes, the open buret was adjusted so that the menisci on both burets were level with each other; the side arm flask was then tilted vertically to let the magnesium ribbon react with the HCl. After the brisk reaction, the flask was placed into the larger beaker and allowed to sit for another 5 minutes.

Next, the flask was placed back into the smaller beaker, and the open buret was adjusted on the ringstand such that its meniscus was level with that of the gas buret. After the system sat for an additional 30 minutes, the open buret was again adjusted so that the menisci on both burets were level.

This procedure was repeated two more times, with the exception that HCl was not again added to the side arm flask, as it was already present in enough excess for all reactions from the first trial.

Results and calculations show measurements and calculations of final value of R

Results and Calculations

Trial #	Lab Temp. (°C)	Lab Pressure (mbar)	Mass of Mg Ribbon Used (g)	Initial Buret Reading (mL)	Final Buret Reading (mL)
1	24.4	1013	0.0147	32.66	19.60
2	24.3	1013	0.0155	33.59	N/A*
3	25.0	1013	0.0153	34.35	19.80

*See note in Discussion section.

Goldberg 8 Student Writing

References

Ganapathi N. Chemistry 119L laboratory manual. New Haven (CT):
   Yale University Press; 2004.

Oxtoby DW, Gillis HP, Nachtrieb NH. Principles of modern chemistry.
   5th ed. Farmington Hills (MI): Thompson Learning; 2002.

65 Writing for Business

Written communication is essential in identifying and solving the complex problems of today's companies. To succeed in business, you need to know how to manage many kinds of writing—from negotiating an ever-increasing number of email messages to communicating effectively with readers from Manhattan, Montgomery, Mexico City, and Mumbai.

65a Reading texts for business

Readers in business face a dizzying array of demands. A team of businesspeople today has almost unlimited access to information and to people, such as economists and scientists, whose expertise can be of use in the business world. Somehow, the members of this team need to negotiate a huge stream of information and to evaluate that information.

To meet these demands, you can draw on general strategies for effective reading (see Chapter 12). One such strategy—keeping a clear purpose in mind when you read—is particularly important when you are engaged in work-related reading. Are you reading to solve a problem? to gather and synthesize information? to make a recommendation? Knowing why you are reading will increase your productivity. Time constraints and deadline pressures will also affect your decisions about what and how to read; the ability to identify important information quickly is a skill you will cultivate as a business reader.

65b Writing texts for business

Writing assignments in business classes serve two related functions. While their immediate goal is to help you master the theory and practice of business, these assignments also prepare you for the kinds of writing you will face in the world of work. For this reason, students in *every* discipline need to know how to write effective business memos, emails, letters, résumés, and reports.

Memo

Memos are a common form of print or electronic correspondence sent within and between organizations. Memos tend to be brief, internal documents, often dealing with only one subject.

AT A GLANCE

Guidelines for Writing Effective Memos

- Write the name of the recipient, your name, the subject, and the date on separate lines at the top.
- Begin with the most important information: depending on the memo's purpose, you may have to provide background information, define the task or problem, or clarify the memo's goal.
- Use your opening paragraph to focus on how the information you convey affects your readers.
- Focus each subsequent paragraph on one idea pertaining to the subject.
- Present information concisely and from the readers' perspective.
- Emphasize exactly what you want readers to do and when.
- Use attachments for detailed supporting information.
- For print memos, initial your memo next to your name.
- Adjust your style and tone to fit your audience.
- Attempt to build goodwill in your conclusion.

Following is a memo, written by two student writers, Michelle Abbott and Carina Abernathy, that presents an analysis and recommendation to help an employer make a decision.

Student Writer

Michelle Abbott

Student Writer

Carina Abernathy

bedfordstmartins.com/everydaywriter
Student Writing

MEMO

❖ *Jenco* ❖

INTEROFFICE MEMORANDUM

TO: ROSA DONAHUE, SALES MANAGER

FROM: MICHELLE ABBOTT & CARINA ABERNATHY

SUBJECT: TAYLOR NURSERY BID

DATE: 1/30/2012

CC:

Paragraphs not indented

Opening paragraph provides background and states purpose

As you know, Taylor Nursery has requested bids on a 25,000-pound order of private-label fertilizer. Taylor Nursery is one of the largest distributors of our Fertikil product. The following is our analysis of Jenco's costs to fill this special order and a recommendation for the bidding price.

Most important information emphasized

The total cost for manufacturing 25,000 pounds of the private-label brand for Taylor Nursery is $44,075. This cost includes direct material, direct labor, and variable manufacturing overhead. Although our current equipment and facilities provide adequate capacity for processing this special order, the job will involve an excess in labor hours. The overtime labor rate has been factored into our costs.

Double-spaced between paragraphs

Options presented

The absolute minimum price that Jenco could bid for this product without losing money is $44,075 (our cost). Applying our standard markup of 40% results in a price of $61,705. Thus, you could reasonably establish a price anywhere within that range.

Relevant factors explained

In making the final assessment, we advise you to consider factors relevant to this decision. Taylor Nursery has stated that this is a one-time order. Therefore, the effort to free this special order will not bring long-term benefits.

Final recommendation

Finally, Taylor Nursery has requested bids from several competitors. One rival, Eclipse Fertilizers, is submitting a bid of $60,000 on this order. Therefore, our recommendation is to slightly underbid Eclipse with a price of $58,000, representing a markup of approximately 32%.

Closing builds goodwill by offering further help

Please let us know if we can be of further assistance in your decision on the Taylor Nursery bid.

Email

Business email can be formatted much like a print memo but is easier to create and store and faster to distribute. Remember, however, that email is essentially public and that employers have easy access to email written by employees. As always, it's best to use discretion and caution in email, especially on the job.

Letter

Despite the popularity of email, letter-writing remains an important skill. When you send a business or professional letter, you are writing either as an individual or as a representative of an organization. In either case, and regardless of your purpose, a business letter should follow certain conventions.

The letter of application or cover letter (p. 602) often accompanies a résumé. The purpose of a letter of application is to demonstrate how the experiences and skills you outline in your résumé have prepared you for a particular job; it is important to focus on how you can benefit the company, not how the company can help you. If you are responding to a particular advertisement, mention it in the opening paragraph. Finally, be sure to indicate how you can be reached for an interview.

The following application letter for a summer internship was written by Nastassia Lopez, a student at Stanford University. Note that the letter has been reproduced in a narrow format to allow for annotation.

Student Writer

Nastassia Lopez

bedfordstmartins.com/everydaywriter
Student Writing

LETTER OF APPLICATION

Letterhead provides contact information

1″

Nastassia Rose Lopez

523 Brown Avenue

Stanford, CA 94305

650-326-6790 / nrl87@gmail.com

February 1, 2010

Inside address with full name, title, and address

Mr. Price Hicks
Director of Educational Programs and Services
Academy of Arts and Sciences
5220 Lankersheim Blvd.
North Hollywood, CA 91601

Salutation addresses a specific person

Dear Mr. Hicks:

Opening provides information and lists major goals

I am an enthusiastic Stanford student who believes that a Development Internship at the Academy of Arts and Sciences would greatly benefit both the Academy and me. A Los Angeles native in my first year at Stanford, I'm a serious student who is a hard worker. My current goal is to comprehend the full scope of the entertainment industry and to learn the ropes of the craft.

Background information illustrates skills and strength of interest

As an experienced writer, I am attracted to the Development Department because I am curious to learn the process of television production from paper to screen. In high school, I was enrolled in Advanced Placement Writing, and I voluntarily took a creative writing class. At Stanford, I received High Honors for maintaining an excellent grade-point average across all my classes, including several writing-intensive courses.

My passion for writing, producing, directing, and learning is real. If my application is accepted, I will bring my strong work ethic, proficiency, and creativity to the Academy.

Thank you very much for your time and consideration. My résumé is enclosed, and I look forward to hearing from you.

Sincerely yours,

Four line spaces for signature

Nastassia Rose Lopez

Nastassia Rose Lopez

AT A GLANCE

Guidelines for Writing Effective Letters

- Use a conventional format. (See p. 602.)
- Whenever possible, write to a specific person (*Dear Tom Robinson* or *Dear Ms. Otuteye*) rather than to a general *Dear Sir or Madam*.
- Open cordially and be polite — even if you have a complaint.
- State the reason for your letter clearly. Include whatever details will help your reader see your point and respond.
- If appropriate, make clear what you hope your reader will do.
- Express appreciation for your reader's attention.
- Make it easy for your reader to respond by including contact information and, if appropriate, a self-addressed, stamped envelope.

Résumé

While a letter of application usually emphasizes specific parts of the résumé, telling how your background is suited to a particular job, a résumé summarizes your experience and qualifications and provides support for your letter. An effective résumé is brief, usually one or two pages.

Research shows that employers generally spend less than a minute reading a résumé. Remember that they are interested not in what they can do for you but what you can do for them. They expect a résumé to be formatted neatly, and your aim is to use clear headings and adequate spacing that will make it easy to read. Although you may be tempted to use colored paper or unusual type styles, avoid such temptations. A well-written résumé with a standard format and typeface is the best way to distinguish yourself.

Your résumé may be arranged chronologically (from most to least recent) or functionally (based on skills or expertise). Include the following information:

1. *Name, address, phone numbers, and email address.*
2. *Career objective(s).* List immediate or short-term goals and specific jobs for which you realistically qualify.
3. *Educational background.* Include degrees, diplomas, majors, and special programs or courses that pertain to your field of interest. List honors and scholarships and your grade-point average if it is high.
4. *Work experience.* Identify each job—whether a paying job, an internship, or military experience—with dates and names of organizations. Describe your duties by carefully selecting strong action verbs.
5. *Skills, personal interests, activities, awards, and honors.*

6. *References.* List two or three people who know your work well, first asking their permission. Give their titles, addresses, and phone or fax numbers. Or simply say that your references are available on request.
7. *Keywords* (for a scannable résumé). In general, nouns function as keywords for résumés that are scanned by search engines. Look for places where you can convert verbs (*performed laboratory tests*) to nouns (*laboratory technologist*). Place the most important keywords toward the beginning of the résumé.

Increasingly, job seekers are composing online résumés as hypertext screen documents, which make keywords more visible to search engines and thus tend to produce more hits. In addition, some businesses ask applicants to fill out résumé forms on company Web sites. In such cases, take special care to make sure that you have caught any error or typo before submitting the form.

The following pages show student Dennis Tyler's résumé in two formats, one in conventional print style, the other formatted for scanning.

Student Writer

Dennis Tyler Jr.

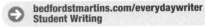

bedfordstmartins.com/everydaywriter
Student Writing

RÉSUMÉ

DENNIS TYLER JR.

CURRENT ADDRESS
P.O. Box 12345
Stanford, CA 94309
Phone: (650) 498-4731
Email: dtyler@yahoo.com

PERMANENT ADDRESS
506 Chanelle Court
Baton Rouge, LA 70128
Phone: (504) 246-9847

Name in
boldface and
larger type size

CAREER OBJECTIVE Position on editorial staff of a major newspaper

EDUCATION

Position being
sought

9/00–6/04	**Stanford University,** Stanford, CA
	BA, ENGLISH AND AMERICAN STUDIES, June 2004
9/02–12/02	**Morehouse College,** Atlanta, GA
	STANFORD STUDY EXCHANGE PROGRAM

Educational
background

EXPERIENCE

6/03–9/03	**Business Scholar Intern,** Finance, AOL Time Warner, New York, NY
	Responsible for analyzing data for strategic marketing plans. Researched the mergers and acquisitions of companies to which Time Inc. sells advertising space.
1/02–6/03	**Editor-in-Chief,** *Enigma* (a literary journal), Stanford University, CA
	Oversaw the entire process of *Enigma*. Edited numerous creative works: short stories, poems, essays, and interviews. Selected appropriate material for the journal. Responsible for designing cover and for publicity to the greater community.
8/02–12/02	**Community Development Intern,** University Center Development Corporation (UCDC), Atlanta, GA
	Facilitated workshops and meetings on the importance of home buying and neighborhood preservation. Created UCDC brochure and assisted in the publication of the center's newsletter.
6/02–8/02	**News Editor,** *Stanford Daily,* Stanford University, CA
	Responsible for editing stories and creating story ideas for the newspaper. Assisted with the layout for the newspaper and designs for the cover.

Work
experience
relevant to
position being
sought

SKILLS AND HONORS

- Computer Skills: MS Word, Excel, PageMaker, Microsoft Publisher; Internet research
- Language: Proficient in Spanish
- Trained in making presentations, conducting research, acting, and singing
- Mellon Fellow, Gates Millennium Scholar, Public Service Scholar, National Collegiate Scholar
- Black Community Service Arts Award, 2003–2004

Talents and
honors not
listed above

REFERENCES   Available upon request

SCANNABLE RÉSUMÉ

Student Writing

Dennis Tyler Jr.

Each phone number or email address on a separate line

Current Address
P.O. Box 12345
Stanford, CA 94309
Phone: (650) 498-4731
Email: dtyler@yahoo.com

Standard typeface (Times Roman) and type size

Permanent Address
506 Chanelle Court
Baton Rouge, LA 70128
Phone: (504) 246-9847

Keywords to aid in computer searches

Keywords: journalist; journal editor; literary publishing; finance; community development; design; leadership; newspaper writer; PageMaker; Spanish; editor-in-chief

Education
BA in English and American Studies, June 2004, Stanford University, Stanford, CA
Morehouse College Study Exchange, fall 2002, Atlanta, GA

White space separates sections

Experience
Business Scholar Intern, fall 2003
Finance, AOL Time Warner, New York, NY
Data analyst for strategic marketing plans. Researcher for the mergers and acquisitions of companies to which Time Inc. sells advertising.

No underlining, italics, boxes, borders, or columns

Editor-in-Chief, 2002–2003, Enigma (a literary journal), Stanford University, CA
Oversaw the entire process of Enigma. Editor for numerous works: short stories, poems, essays, and interviews. Content selection for the journal. Cover design and publicity to the greater community.

Community Development Intern, fall 2002
University Center Development Corporation (UCDC), Atlanta, GA

Verbs converted to nouns wherever possible

Workshops on the importance of home buying and neighborhood preservation. Publication responsibility for UCDC brochure and the center's newsletter.

News Editor, summer 2002, Stanford Daily, Stanford University, CA
Story editor for the newspaper. Layout and cover design for the newspaper.

Skills and Honors
Computer skills: MS Word, Excel, PageMaker, Microsoft Publisher; Internet research

Keywords used in body of résumé wherever possible

Language: Proficient in Spanish
Trained presenter, researcher, actor, singer
Mellon Fellow, Gates Millennium Scholar, Public Service Scholar, National Collegiate Scholar
Black Community Service Arts Award, 2003–2004

References
Available upon request

Acknowledgments

Text credits: p. 127, Cord Jefferson, "Is the Internet Warping Our Brains?" from Good, July 18, 2011, http://www.good.is/post/is-the-internet-warping-our-brains/. Copyright © 2011 by Good Worldwide, LLC. Reprinted by permission of Good Worldwide, LLC.

Art credits: p. 21, Mike Enright/www.menright.com; **p. 28,** Photograph by Shuqiao Song; **p. 41,** Courtesy of Joelle Hann; **p. 42,** Brian Swirsky; **p. 43,** © Seeds of Solidarity Education Center; **p. 68,** Mike Enright/www.menright.com; **p. 69,** Animal Locomotion/Bridgeman Art; **p. 69,** © 2010 Wolters Kluwer Health, Lippincott Williams and Wilkins; **p. 70,** Mike Enright/www.menright.com; **p. 78,** Mike Enright/www.menright.com; **p. 79,** Royalty Free/Getty Images; **p. 80,** Mike Enright/www.menright.com; **p. 82,** Bettmann/Corbis; **p. 83,** Mike Enright/www.menright.com; **p. 91,** Louis Mazatanta/National Geographic Stock; **p. 97,** Courtesy of www.airconditioning and refrigeration guide.com; **p. 98,** Doug Fowler; **p. 98,** Mike Enright/www.menright.com; **p. 99,** Mike Enright/www.menright .com; **p. 131,** Craig F. Walker/The Denver Post; **p. 135,** From *Fun Home: A Family Tragicomic* by Alison Bechdel. Reprinted by Permission of Houghton Mifflin Harcourt Publishing Company. All rights reserved; **p. 139,** Photograph by Wendy Annibell; **p. 140,** Spur Design; **p. 143,** Adbusters Media Foundation; **p. 147** (both images), David King Collection; **p. 156,** Sustainable Foods; **p. 157,** Jan Weber/As We Sow; **p. 161,** Emanuel Saez/University of California Berkley; **p. 162,** Tom Tomorrow; **p. 163,** Getty Images; **p. 181** (upper left), *Michigan Quarterly Review;* (lower left) Courtesy of Ecology and Sociology; (upper right) *Scientific American;* (lower right) Salon.com; **p. 186,** University of North Carolina; **p. 188** (upper and lower), EBSCOhost; **p. 199,** Harvard University/Nieman Reports; **p. 201,** Ungar, Mark. "Prisons and Politics in Contemporary Latin America," *Human Rights Quarterly* 25:4 (2003): 909–10. © 2003 The Johns Hopkins University Press. Reprinted with permission of The Johns Hopkins University Press; **p. 223,** courtesy of Shuqiao Song; **p. 243,** From "Today's Demon: Lost Worlds," *One! Hundred! Demons!* by Lynda Barry, Copyright © 2002 by Lynda Barry, published by Sasquatch Books; **p. 405,** EBSCOhost; **p. 406,** www.sutjhally.com; **p. 416,** *The Value of Nothing* by Raj Patel. Reprinted with permission of Picador Press; **p. 416,** courtesy of Alisa Quart, *Columbia Journalism Review;* **p. 417,** Nobelprize.org; **p. 417,** Mike Enright/www.menright.com; **p. 423,** *The Value of Nothing* by Raj Patel. Reprinted with permission of Picador Press; **p. 429,** courtesy of Alisa Quart, *Columbia Journalism Review;* **p. 433,** EBSCOhost; **p. 437,** Nobelprize.org; **p. 468,** Alexander, Meredith. "Thirty Years Later, Stanford Prison Experiment Lives On," Stanford Report (online), August 22, 2001, http://news.stanford.education/2001 /prison2--822.html. Photo: Chuck Painter/Stanford News Service; Palgrave Macmillan; Everett Collection; *The American Scholar;* **p. 473,** Palgrave Macmillan; **p. 477,** *The American Scholar;* **p. 481,** EBSCOhost; **p. 483,** Alexander, Meredith. "Thirty Years Later, Stanford Prison Experiment Lives On," Stanford Report (online), August 22, 2001, http://news .stanford.education/2001/prison2--822.html. Photo: Chuck Painter/Stanford News Service; **p. 500,** *Red Heat: Conspiracy, Murder, and the Cold War in the Caribbean* by Alex Von Tunzelmann. Reprinted with permission of Picador Press; **p. 503,** *Red Heat: Conspiracy, Murder, and the Cold War in the Caribbean* by Alex Von Tunzelmann. Reprinted with permission of Picador Press; **p. 509,** EBSCOhost; **p. 523** (upper), Reprinted by permission of the publisher from *The Diversity of Life* by Edward O. Wilson, Cambridge, Mass.: The Belknap Press of Harvard University Press, Copyright © 1992 by Edward O. Wilson; (lower) EBSCOhost; **p. 525,** Reprinted by permission of the publisher from *The Diversity of Life* by Edward O. Wilson, Cambridge, Mass.: The Belknap Press of Harvard University Press, Copyright © 1992 by Edward O. Wilson; **p. 531,** EBSCOhost.

Index

A

a, an (articles), 550–51
  deciding when to use, 299
  usage, 256
abbreviations, 390–94
  in different fields (Talking about
    Style), 393
  editing for (At a Glance), 390
  periods with, 371
  texting (Talking the Talk), 246
absolute concepts, 343
absolute phrases, 307
abstract and concrete words, 250
abstracts
  APA style, 489
  CSE style, 527
  dissertation, citing in MLA style, 446
  for periodical articles, 187
  purpose of, 202
academic courses, citing Web sites
    (MLA style), 438
academic institutions, citing Web sites
    (MLA style), 438
academic reading. *See* critical reading
academic writing
  arguments, 136–72
  authority, establishing, 15
  for business courses, 598–606
  collaboration, 572
  compared to informal writing, 14
  cultural contexts. *See* multilingual
    writers
  directness, 15–16
  disciplinary language, 569
  disciplinary style, 570
  ethical guidelines, 572
  and evidence, 571
  first person in, 570
  formats, 571
  formatting. *See* designing texts
  genres, 540–41
  in humanities, 573–81
  instructor expectations, 12, 17, 539–40
  multimodal presentations, 20–36
  in natural and applied sciences,
    590–97
  purpose, understanding, 50–51
  research, planning, 17
  research project, 175–227
  in social sciences, 582–89
  stance, rhetorical, 51–52
  U.S. academic style, features of, 16,
    539–40
  visuals in. *See* visuals
accept, except, 256
active reading, strategies for, 16–17
active voice The form of a **verb** when
the **subject** performs the action: *Lata
sang the chorus.*
  advantages of, 115, 287, 321
  shifts between passive voice and, 282
addresses
  commas with, 364
  numbers in, 394
ad hominem fallacy, 144
adjective, 298–99, 339–42 A word that
modifies, quantifies, identifies, or describes
a **noun** or words acting as a noun.
  adjective-adverb confusion, 340–41
  commas with, 363
  comparatives, superlatives, 298,
    341–42
  editing (At a Glance), 339
  ending in *–ing* and *–ed*, 561
  and linking verbs, 339–40
  phrases, 306–7
adjective clauses, 309, 361–62
  for multilingual writers, 546
adverb, 299, 339–42 A word that quali-
fies, modifies, limits, or defines a **verb**, an
adjective, another adverb, or a **clause**,
frequently answering the question *where?
when? how? why? to what extent?* or
under what conditions?
  adjective-adverb confusion, 340–41
  comparatives, superlatives, 299,
    341–42
  conjunctive adverbs, 299
  editing (At a Glance), 339
  phrases, 306
adverb clauses, 309, 361–62
advertisements, citing (MLA style), 445
advice, advise, 256
affect, effect, 256
afterwords, citing
  in *Chicago* style, 504
  in MLA style, 425

age, assumptions about, 238–39

aggravate, 256

agreement The correspondence
between a **pronoun** and its **antecedent**
in **person**, number, and gender (*Mr. Fox
and his sister*) or between a **verb** and its
subject in person and number (*She and
Moe are friends*).

   pronoun-antecedent agreement, 10,
      335–38
   subject-verb agreement, 323–29
alignment, in design, 91
all ready, already, 256
all right, alright, 256
all together, altogether, 256
allude, elude, 256
allusion, illusion, 256
almanacs, 184
almost, 345
along with, 325
a lot, 256
America, American, 240
American Psychological Association
      (APA). *See also* APA style
   ethical code, 572
   guide to electronic references, 478–85
among, between, 257
amount, number, 257
ampersand (&), in in-text citations
      (APA style), 464–65
an, a (articles), 299, 550–51
analogy, 251
   developing paragraphs with, 82–83
   in emotional appeals, 162
analysis. *See also* academic writing;
      writing process
   literary analysis, 575–76
   rhetorical, student model, 148–51
AND, in electronic searches, 185
and/or, 257
annotated bibliography, 195
annotation
   for critical reading, 125–28
   of research sources, 211

antecedent, 296–97, 335–38 The **noun**
or noun **phrase** that a **pronoun** replaces.

anthologies, citing
   in *Chicago* style, 504
   in MLA style, 413, 420–21,

anticlimax, and humor, 275
any body, anybody, 257
anybody, gender-neutral approach, 337
any one, anyone, 257
anyplace, 257
anyway, anyways, 257

APA style, 461–96 The citation style
guidelines issued by the American
Psychological Association.

   content notes in, 462–63
   directory to in-text citation models, 463
   directory to model references, 468
   in-text citations in, 463–67
   formatting paraphrases and quota-
      tions in, 464
   formatting reference list in, 469
   quotations, integrating, 213
   references list, 467–87
      author listings, 469–71
      books, 471–74
      electronic sources, 478–85
      formatting (At a Glance), 469
      miscellaneous sources, 485–87
      print periodicals, 474–77
   student research essay in, 487–96
   verb tense guidelines, 318, 464
apostrophes, 373–75
   in contractions, 374
   editing for (At a Glance), 373
   errors (Top Twenty), 9
   in plurals, , 375
   in possessive forms, 373–74
appeals, 138–41
   credibility, creating, 154–63
   emotional, 138–39, 161–63
   ethical, 139, 155–56
   logical, 139–40, 156–61
   in visual arguments, 140–41
applied sciences. *See* natural and
      applied sciences

appositive, 362 A **noun** or noun **phrase**
that adds identifying information to a preceding noun or noun phrase: *Zimbardo,
an innovative researcher, designed the
experiment.*

appositive phrases, 307
apt, liable, likely, 257
Arab, usage, 240
arguable statements, 153

argument, 136–72 A text that makes and
supports a **claim**.
   analyzing, 136–51
   appeals, identifying, 138–41
   arguable statements, criteria for,
     153
   audience analysis, 154
   claims in, 141–43, 153, 165
   classical structure, 164
   counterarguments, 155–56, 165
   credibility, creating, 154–63
   cultural contexts, 138
   designing, 166
   as exploration of ideas (Talking the
     Talk), 152
   fallacies, 144–47
   purposes of, 151–52
   reviewing (At a Glance), 152
   rhetorical analysis, student model,
     148–51
   sources, consulting, 163
   student model, 167–72
   Toulmin, 141–43, 165
   visual arguments, 140–41,
     143
   working thesis for, 153
Aristotle, 138, 160
articles (*a, an, the*), 299, 550–52
articles in periodicals
   citing in APA style, 474–77
   citing in *Chicago* style, 506–9
   citing in CSE style, 527–28
   citing in MLA style, 426–30
   evaluating, 196–97, 200–201
   locating, 188–89
art works, citing
   in *Chicago* style, 515
   in MLA style, 443–44
as, 257
as if, like, 257
assignments. *See* common assignments;
   writing assignments
associational organization, 70
assumptions
   in arguments, 141–42, 154, 160,
     165
   unstated, avoiding, 237–41
assure, ensure, insure, 257
as to, 257

At a Glance boxes
   abbreviations and numbers, editing,
     390
   adjectives and adverbs, editing, 339
   APA references list, formatting, 469
   apostrophes, editing for, 373
   appropriate language and spelling,
     editing for, 245
   arguments, analyzing, 137
   arguments, reviewing, 152
   assignments, analyzing, 568
   business letters, guidelines for
     writing, 603
   capitalization, editing for, 386
   commas, editing for, 359
   comma splices and fused sentences,
     editing, 348
   common ground, building with
     language, 236
   conciseness, editing for, 285
   consistency and completeness,
     editing for, 277
   coordination, subordination, and
     emphasis, editing for, 269–70
   cultures, communicating across, 232
   electronic sources, citing, 479
   end punctuation, editing for, 370
   genres, features of, 540
   hyphens, editing for, 397
   interviews, conducting, 191
   italics, editing for, 395
   language variety, 242
   memo, guidelines for writing, 599
   misplaced or dangling modifiers,
     editing, 344
   MLA citation for visuals, 444
   MLA digital sources, citing, 430
   MLA list of works cited, formatting,
     418
   MLA print periodical entries, format-
     ting, 427
   models, combining parts of, 424,
     470
   models, sources without, APA
     citation, 484
   note-taking guidelines, 207
   observations, conducting, 192
   online text, creating, 20
   oral presentations, preparing, 25

parallelism, editing for, 279–80
paraphrasing guidelines, 209
plagiarism, avoiding, 219
potential sources, examining, 202
prepositions, idiomatic use, 563
pronouns, editing, 330
punctuation, effective use, editing for, 381
quotation marks, editing for, 376
quoting, paraphrasing, summarizing, 212
semicolons, editing for, 368
sentence fragments, editing, 352
sentence patterns, basic, 302–3
sentence variety, editing for, 288
sexist pronouns, editing, 337
shifts, confusing, 283
sources without models, citing, 440, 505
subject-verb agreement, editing for, 324
summarizing guidelines, 210
survey questionnaire, designing, 192
Top Twenty (common errors), 4
U.S. academic style, 16
verbs, editing in own writing, 311
verb tense, editing, 320
visuals, attitude and point of view in, 56
visuals, effective use, 100
writing inventory, taking, 11
writing to make something happen, 37
atlases, 184
audiences, 52–54
for arguments, 154
formality of language and, 246–48
for online texts, 21–22
for oral presentations, 26
for public writing, 37–38
recognizing (Talking the Talk), 176
for research projects, 176
reviewing draft for, 101–2
in rhetorical situation, 49, 52–54
sources, evaluating for, 195
and tone, 55
world audiences. *See* cultural contexts

audio content
    incorporating, 215–16
    reviewing draft for, 102
    revising, 111
    tone of, 55
    types of, 22
audio sources, citing,
    in APA style, 486–87
    in *Chicago* style, 514
    in MLA style, 441–42
authority
    cultural contexts, 233
    establishing your, 15
    as evidence for argument, 158
authors
    APA style, citing
        in references list, 469–71
        in text, 463–67
    Chicago style, citing, 501–6
    credibility of, evaluating, 196
    CSE style, citing, 522–27
    MLA style, citing
        in text, 410–14
        on works cited list, 417–20
a while, awhile, 257

B

bad, badly, 257, 340–41
bandwagon appeal fallacy, 144
bare, bear, 257
bar graphs, 97
base form, 312–16 The form of a **verb** listed in a dictionary (*go*).
be, forms of, 304, 312–13
    as helping verbs, 296, 313, 554–55
    everyday use of (Talking about Style), 312
    nonstandard use, 312
    progressive tenses, 556
    and wordiness, 287
because of, due to, 257
begging the question fallacy, 145
being as, being that, 258
believing and doubting game, 137
beside, besides, 258
between, among, 257

bibliogaphies
  in APA style, 467
  in *Chicago* style, 499–500
  as library resources, 189
  working bibliographies, 194–95
biographical resources, 183
block quotations, 376–77
blogs (Web logs)
  citing in APA style, 484
  citing in *Chicago* style, 511
  citing in MLA style, 438
  features of, 22
  for research project, 179
bookmarking Web sites, 190
books
  citing in APA style, 471–74
  citing in *Chicago* style, 501–6
  citing in CSE style, 522–27
  citing in MLA style, 420–26, 434
  indexes, as research source, 187
  library search, 186–87
  titles of, italics for, 395
  in working bibliographies, 194
Boolean operators (AND, NOT, OR) for
  electronic searches, 185
brackets
  in direct quotations, 214
  usage, 382
brainstorming, 58
brake, break, 258
breath, breathe, 258
bring, take, 258
British, English, usage, 240
business writing, 598–606
  cultural contexts, 235
  email messages, 601
  letters, 601–3
  memos, 598–600
  résumés, 603–6
but, yet, 258
but that, but what, 258

C

can (modal auxiliary verb), 258,
  557
can, may, 258
can't hardly, 258
can't help but, 258

capitalization, 386–90
  editing for (At a Glance), 386
  headings, 96
  lines of poetry, 387
  proper adjectives and proper nouns,
    299, 387
  titles of persons, 388–89
  titles of works, 389
  in Top Twenty (common errors), 7
  unnecessary, 389–90
cartoons
  citing in MLA style, 414, 444–45
  as visuals, 98
case, 329–35 The form of a **noun** or
  pronoun that reflects its grammatical
  role: *He ate* (subjective). *His food was*
  cold (possessive). *I saw him* (objective).

  in compound structures, 334
  in dependent clauses, 333–34
  in elliptical constructions, 334–35
  objective case, 331
  possessive case, 332
  subjective case, 330–31
  we and *us* before nouns, 335
  who, whom, whoever, whomever,
    333–34
catalogs, library, 183
cause and effect
  developing paragraphs with, 83
  supporting an argument with,
    159
  transitions to signal, 87
CDs, citing,
  in *Chicago* style, 514
  in MLA style, 441–42
censor, censure, 258
certainty, modals to indicate, 558
charts
  misleading, 147–48
  MLA style, citing, 414–15, 444
  symbols in, abbreviating, 392–93
  as visuals, 96–97
Chicago style, 497–520 Citation
  guidelines based on *The Chicago Manual*
  of Style.

  directory, 500
  formatting guidelines, 499–500
  in-text citations, 498

notes and bibliographic entries, 500–515
  books, 501–6
  electronic sources, 507–14
  miscellaneous sources, 514–15
  periodicals, 506–9
  quotations, integrating, 213
  student research essay, 515–20
chronological organization
  of information, 68–69
  of narratives, 79
  of process descriptions, 83
  résumés, 603
citation-name format (CSE style), 521–22
citation-sequence format (CSE style), 521–22

claim, 141–43, 153, 160 An arguable statement.

class discussions, guidelines, 24
classical format for arguments, 164
classification, developing paragraphs with, 81

clause, 308–9 A group of words containing a **subject** and a **predicate**. An **independent clause** can stand alone as a sentence, while a **dependent clause** must be attached to an independent clause.

  and comma splices, 347–51
  conjunctive adverbs with, 299
  in fused (run-on) sentences, 347–51
clichés, 251
climactic order, position of ideas in sentences, 274–75
close reading. *See* literary analysis
clustering, 60–61

coherence, 85–88, 102 Also called "flow," the quality that makes a **text** seem unified.

collaboration, 62–63, 572
collective nouns, 296
  pronoun-antecedent agreement with, 336
  subject-verb agreement with, 10, 326–27
college writing. *See* academic writing
colloquial language, 246–47
colons, 383–84
  with quotation marks, 379
color, in text design, 93
comics, citing (MLA style), 444–45
commands (imperative mood), 322
commas, 358–67
  with absolute phrases, 307
  with addresses, 364
  with appositives, 362
  for clarity, 366
  in compound sentences, 9, 310, 359–60
  with contrasting elements, 364
  with coordinating conjunctions, 7, 9, 349, 359–60
  with dates, 364
  with direct address, 364
  editing for (At a Glance), 359
  with independent clauses, 308, 349
  with interjections, 364
  with introductory elements, 6, 358
  with items in series, 362–63
  with nonrestrictive elements, 8, 360–62
  with numbers, 365
  with parentheses, 381–82
  with parenthetical expressions, 363
  with quotation marks, 6–7, 365, 379–80
  with tag questions, 364
  with transitional expressions, 363
  unnecessary, 7, 334, 359

comma splice, 347–52 An error in formal writing resulting from joining two **independent clauses** with only a comma.

  in context (Talking about Style), 351
  editing (At a Glance), 348
  in literary writing, 351
  in Top Twenty, 9–10
commenting on a draft, 104–5
comments, instructor, 106–8
common assignments. *See also* writing assignments
  in business classes, 598–604
  in humanities, 574–75
  in natural and applied sciences, 591–92
  in social sciences, 583–85

common errors. *See* Top Twenty

common ground, language that builds, 236–41
    establishing credibility with, 155
    using (At a Glance), 236

common knowledge, 217

communicator, in rhetorical situation, 49

company names
    abbreviations in, 392
    capitalizing, 388

comparative, 341–43 The *-er* or *more* form of an **adjective** or **adverb** used to compare two things (*happier, more quickly*).

compare to, compare with, 258

comparison and contrast, developing paragraphs with, 81–82

comparisons
    complete, editing for, 278
    as evidence in argument, 162
    transitions to signal, 87

compass directions, capitalizing, 389

complement, compliment, 258

complete sentence. *See* sentence

complex sentences, 310

compose, comprise, 258

compound adjectives, hyphens with, 11, 397–98

compound antecedents, pronoun-antecedent agreement, 335–36

compound-complex sentences, 310

compound constructions and commas, 367

compound nouns
    hyphens in, 397
    possessive forms of, 374

compound numbers, hyphens with, 398

compound predicates, 304
    as sentence fragments, 354

compound sentences, 310
    commas in, 9, 359–60
    missing commas in (Top Twenty), 9
    pronoun case in, 334

compound subjects, 303
    subject-verb agreement, 325–26

compound words
    and hyphens, 397–98
    spell-checker errors, 252

comprise, compose, 258

concession, transitions to signal, 88

conciseness, 285–87 Using the fewest possible words to make a point effectively.
    editing for (At a Glance), 285
    in headings, 96

conclusions, 89, 224–25
    of oral presentations, 26–27
    revising, 111
    of sentences, dash for emphasis, 383
    of sentences, emphasis in, 274
    in syllogisms, 159–60
    transitions to signal, 88

concrete words, 250

conditional sentences, 547

conference proceedings, citing
    in APA style, 486
    in *Chicago* style, 527
    in MLA style, 446

conjunction, 300–302 A word or words joining **words**, **phrases**, or **clauses**.
    and emphasis, 269
    parallelism with, 280–81

conjunctive adverbs, 299, 301–2
    commas with, 363
    linking clauses with semicolons and, 368

connotation, 249

conscience, conscious, 258

consensus of opinion, 258

consequently, subsequently, 258

consistency, editing for (At a Glance), 276–77

context for writing, 49–50

continual, continuous, 259

contractions, 374

contrast
    developing paragraphs with, 81–82
    in visual design, 91

contrasting elements
    commas with, 364
    transitions to signal, 87

conventions (Talking the Talk), 14

coordinate adjectives, commas to separate, 363

coordinating conjunctions, 300–301
The words *and, but, for, nor, or, so,* and
yet, which give the same emphasis to
both the elements they join: *Restaurants
are expensive, so I cook.*

 commas with, 7, 9, 349, 359–60
 with compound predicates, 304
 in compound sentences, 310
 with compound subjects, 303
 linking clauses with, 349, 368
 parallelism with, 280–81
coordination, 269–71
corporate authors. *See* organizations as
 authors, citing
correlative conjunctions, 301 Paired
conjunctions (*both . . . and, either . . . or,
neither . . . nor, not only . . . but also*) used
to connect equivalent elements.

 with compound subjects, 303
 parallelism with, 281
could, as modal, 296, 313, 557
could of, 259
Council of Science Editors (CSE) style.
 See CSE style
counterarguments, 155–56, 204
count and noncount nouns, 296,
 548–52
cover letters, 601–3
credibility
 in arguments, establishing, 154–63
 in sources, evaluating, 196–201
 of statistics, 148
 and variety of English used, 244
criteria, criterion, 259
critical reading, 123–36
 as active reading, 16–17
 analyzing text, 130–32
 annotating text, 126–28
 business texts, 598
 in humanities (At a Glance),
  574
 in natural and applied sciences,
  590–91
 previewing text, 123–25
 in social sciences, 582
 of sources, 197–203
 student writing model, 134–36
 summarizing text, 129
critical stance, 575

critical thinking
 arguments, analyzing, 136–51
 critical reading, 123–36
CSE style, 521–35 The citation style
guidelines issued by the Council of
Science Editors.

 directory, 523
 in-text citations, 521–22
  citation-name format, 521–22
  citation-sequence format,
   521–22
  name-year format, 521–22
 references list, 523–32
  author listings, 523–27
  books, 523–27
  electronic sources, 528–32
  periodicals, 527–28
 student research proposal, 532–35
cultural contexts, 233–36. *See also*
 multilingual writers
 of arguments, 138
 and authority of writer, 233
 and business writing, 235
 communicating across cultures (At a
  Glance), 232
 evidence, nature of, 234
 and formality, 235–36
 meaning, clarifying, 232–33
 norms and culture, 231–32
 and organizing writing, 234–35
 and writing style, 235–36

D
dangling modifiers, 346
 editing (At a Glance), 344
dashes, 382–83
 linking clauses with, 351
 with quotation marks, 379
data, 259
data analysis, research data, 193
databases, 183–85
 abstracts in, 187
 in APA style, citing, 478–79
 in *Chicago* style, citing, 507–9
 in CSE style, citing, 529–31
 and digital object identifier (DOI),
  478–79
 full-text, 187

databases *(continued)*
in MLA style, citing, 413–14,
431–33
periodical indexes, 187–89
search options, 184–85
for social sciences. *See also* articles in
periodicals
dates
commas with, 364
numbers in, 394
declarative sentences, 311
deductive reasoning, 159–60
definitions
cultural contexts and, 232–33
developing paragraphs with, 80
quotation marks for, 378
demonstrative pronouns, 297
denotation, 249
dependent clause, 271–74, 310 Sometimes called a "subordinate clause," a
word group that contains a **subject** and
a **predicate** but can't stand alone as a
sentence because it begins with either a
subordinating conjunction (*because*,
although) or a **relative pronoun** (*that*,
which).
relative pronouns in, 298
as sentence fragments, 354
sentence variety, 290
who, whom, whoever, whomever in,
333–34
depend on, 564
descriptions, development, 80
designing texts, 90–100
for arguments, 166
design principles, 90–92
editing, 115
for portfolio, 118–19
print vs. electronic delivery, 90
research project, 222
revising, 111
details
concrete, 161
in description, 80
developing paragraphs with,
77
and emotional appeals, 161
and subordination, 271
of visuals, 78

determiners, 298, 549–50
diagrams, 97
diction. *See* word choice
dictionary entry, citing (MLA), 413
different from, different than, 259
digital sources
citing in APA style, 478–85
citing in *Chicago* style, 507–14
citing in CSE style, 528–32
citing in MLA style, 430–39
guidelines (At a Glance), 430 (MLA),
479 (APA)
direct address, 364
direct discourse, shifts in, 283
directness, in writing, 15–16
direct objects, 305
explicit, 543
infinitives as, 544–45
noun clauses as, 308
noun phrases as, 306
pronoun case in, 331
direct quotations
changing to indirect, 558
and quotation marks, 375–76
disabilities, considering
audience analysis, 54
color perception, 93
freespeaking, 59
knowing your readers, 241
oral presentation accessibility, 27
references to, 240
and spelling, 255
Web texts accessibility, 23
disciplinary language, 569
disciplinary style, 570
discourse, shifts in, 283
discreet, discrete, 259
disinterested, uninterested, 259
disruptive modifiers, 345–46
dissertations, citing
in APA style, 485
in MLA style, 446
distinct, distinctive, 259
division, developing with, 81
do, forms of, as helping verbs, 313
documentation. *See also* APA style;
Chicago style; CSE style; MLA style
missing or incomplete (Top Twenty),
5–6

need for, 217–18
of visuals, 99
document design. *See* designing texts
doesn't, don't, 259
DOI (digital object identifier), 478–79
dots. *See* ellipses
doublespeak, 248
doubt, modals to indicate, 558
doubting game, 137
drafting. *See also* writing process
  guidelines for planning and, 67–74
  research project, 224–27
  reviewing draft, 100–106
  working thesis, 64–67
due to, because of, 257
DVDs, citing
  in APA style, 486
  in *Chicago* style, 514
  in MLA style, 440

E

each
  pronoun-antecedent agreement with, 336–37
  subject-verb agreement with, 325
each other, one another, 259
e-books, citing (*Chicago*), 504
-ed, -d endings
  for adjectives, 561
  for past forms of regular verbs, 313
editing, 112–17. *See also* At a Glance
  adjectives, 340
  adverbs, 340
  colons, 384
  comma splices, 348–51
  for coordination and subordination, 273–74
  design, 115
  for emphasis, 269–70
  fused (run-on) sentences, 348–51
  misplaced or dangling modifiers, 312
  for misspelling, 115
  paragraphs, 75
  for parallelism, 279–81
  research project, 226

sentence length, 112–13, 288–89
  for sentence variety, 288–89
  word choice, 114
editions of books, citing
  in APA style, 474
  in *Chicago* style, 505
  in MLA style, 425
editorials, citing
  in APA style, 475
  in MLA style, 427, 434
editors, citing
  in APA style, 471
  in *Chicago* style, 504
  in CSE style, 526
  in MLA style, 420–21
effect, affect, 256
either-or fallacy, 146
electronic communication, 17–19
electronic sources. *See* digital sources
elicit, illicit, 259
ellipses, for omitted words, 214, 385–86
elliptical structures, 277–78, 334–35
elude, allude, 256
email
  APA style, citing, 466, 484
  business use of, 601
  capital letters in, 389–90
  Chicago style, citing, 511
  MLA style, citing, 439
  writing, guidelines for, 18
emigrate from, immigrate to, 259
emotional appeals, 138–41, 161–63
emphasis, 269–70
  dashes for, 382–83
  italics for, 395
  order for, 274–75
encyclopedias, 183
endnotes, *Chicago* style, 500–515
end punctuation, editing for (At a Glance), 370
English, British, usage, 240
English, varieties of, 242–44
ensure, assure, insure, 257
enthused, enthusiastic, 259
enthymeme, 142
equal ideas, relating with coordination, 270–71
equally as good, 259

-er, -est. *See* comparative; superlative
errors, common. *See* Top Twenty
-es, -s endings
  plural nouns, 255, 296
  verbs, 312, 324
essays. *See* academic writing; writing
    assignments; writing process
ethical appeals, 139, 140–41, 154–56
ethical guidelines, 572
ethnic groups
  assumptions about, 238–39
  capitalizing names of, 387
  and language variety, 244
ethos, 138
euphemisms, 247–48
every day, everyday, 259
every one, everyone, 260
everyone, gender-neutral approach,
    337
evaluating sources, 193–203
evidence, 141–42 Support for an argument's **claim**.
  in cultural contexts, 234
  evaluating, 202–3, 571
examples
  colons with, 383
  developing paragraphs with,
    80–81
  establishing credibility with,
    156–57
  transitions to signal, 87
except, accept, 256
exclamation points, 365, 372
  with quotation marks, 379
exclamatory sentences, 311
experts, using as sources, 191
explanatory notes, MLA style,
    408–9
expletive constructions, 287
explicit, implicit, 260
exploring ideas, 58–62
  brainstorming, 58
  clustering, 60–61
  collaboration for, 62–63
  freespeaking, 59
  freewriting (looping), 58–59
  imagery for, 59–60
  narrowing topic, 64

questions for, 61–62
research project, 175–76
sources, using for, 62

F
Facebook, 12–14
  event invitation, 42
  posting, citing (MLA), 439
fairness, and credibility, 155–56
fallacies, 144–48
  ad hominem, 144
  bandwagon appeal, 144
  begging the question, 145
  charts and graphs, misleading, 147–48
  in-crowd appeal, 145
  either-or, 146
  false analogy, 145
  false authority, 144
  flattery, 144–45
  guilt by association, 144
  hasty generalization, 146
  non sequitur, 145
  oversimplification, 146
  photographs, misleading, 146–47
  post hoc, 145
  straw man, 146
  veiled threat, 145
false analogy, 145
false authority, 144
family relationship words, capitalizing,
    7, 389
farther, further, 260
faulty predication, 276–77
faulty sentence structure, 276–77 A
common writing problem in which a
sentence begins with one grammatical
pattern and switches to another (also
called "mixed structure").
fewer, less, 260
field research, 191–93
figurative language 161, 250–51
  for topic selection, 59–60
figures, citing, 414, 444
films, citing
  in APA style, 486
  in MLA style 440
finalize, 260

firstly, secondly, 260
first person (*I*) in academic writing, 570
flattery, 144–45
flaunt, flout, 260
flow. *See* coherence
flyer, student model, 40
fonts. *See* typefaces
footnote numbers with quotation
marks, 379
footnotes, citing,
in *Chicago* style, 500–515
in MLA style, 462–63
foreign languages, using words from,
54, 244–45, 396
forewords, citing
in *Chicago* style, 504
in MLA style, 425
formality, appropriate, 246–48
cultural contexts, 235–36
formal outlines, 71–72
formal rhetorical situations, 49
formal writing, 18–19, 49. *See also*
academic writing
correctness or stuffiness (Talking the
Talk), 333
formal audiences, 53
formatting. *See also* designing texts
APA references list (At a Glance), 469
APA style, 469
Chicago style, 499–500
MLA list of works cited (At a
Glance), 418
online texts, 23
former, latter, 260
forums, online, guidelines for, 18–19
fractions
hyphens in, 398
numbers in, 394
slashes in, 385
subject-verb agreement with, 326
fragment, 12, 352–54 A group of words
that is not a complete sentence but is
punctuated as one. Usually a fragment
lacks a **subject**, a **verb**, or both, or it is a
dependent clause.
freespeaking, 59
freewriting (looping), 58–59
further, farther, 228

fused sentence, 9, 347–52 Sometimes
called a "run-on," a sentence in which
two **independent clauses** are run
together without a **conjunction** or
punctuation between them (*My dog
barked he woke me up*).

future tenses, 319–20
future perfect, 320
future perfect progressive, 320
future progressive, 320
simple future, 319

G

games, computer, citing (MLA), 442
gender-neutral language, 237–38, 337
general and specific words, 249–50
general indexes, 187
generalizations
inductive, 159–60
with zero article, 552
genre, 55, 540–41 A form of communication used for a particular purpose
and incorporating certain conventional
features. Some common examples
include lab reports, researched essays,
brochures, invitations, etc.

for public writing, 38
reviewing draft for, 101–2
geographical area, assumptions about, 240
geographical names, capitalizing, 388
gerund, 307 A verbal form that ends in
-ing and functions as a **noun**: *Sleeping
is a bore.*

and possessive-case pronouns, 332
to state facts, 545
glossary of usage, 256–65
good, well, 260, 340–41
good and, 260
Google, 190, 541
Google Scholar, 190
government institutions
abbreviations in, 391–92
capitalizing names, 388
government sources, 189–90
citing in APA style, 485
citing in *Chicago* style, 515

government sources *(continued)*
  citing in CSE style, 532
  citing in MLA style 413, 445–46
grammar, 294–354. *See also* parts of
  speech
grammatical terms (Talking the Talk),
  295
graphic narratives, citing (MLA), 424
graphs
  bar graphs, 97
  citing, 414–15, 444
  misleading data in, 147–48
  symbols in, abbreviating, 392–93
group authors. *See* organizations as
  authors
guilt by association fallacy, 144

H
hanged, hung, 260
hasty generalizations, 146
have, forms of
  as helping verbs, 296, 313, 554–55
  perfect tenses, 556
  third-person singular, 324
having, present-perfect participle,
  320–21
he, she (personal pronouns), 260
headings
  and document design, 91, 95–96
  in formal outlines, 71–72
  of notes, 205
  typefaces, 95–96
  wording of, 96

helping verb, 296, 313, 554–58 A **verb**
such as a form of *be*, *do*, or *have* or a
modal combined with a main verb.

her, his (possessive pronouns), 260,
  297
here, opening sentences with, 304
herself, himself, myself, yourself (reflexive
  pronouns), 260, 297
hierarchical organization, 73
his, her (possessive pronouns), 260,
  297
hisself, 260
historical sources, evaluating, 182
homonyms, errors with, 6, 251–52
hopefully, 260
however. *See* conjunctive adverbs

humanities, writing for, 573–81
  assignments, types of, 574–75
  critical reading (At a Glance),
    574
  critical stance of writer, 575
  literary analysis, 575–76
humor, and anticlimax (Talking about
  Style), 275
hundred, 395
hung, hanged, 260
hyphens, 11, 397–99
  editing for (At a Glance), 397
  unnecessary, 398–99
  unnecessary or missing (Top
    Twenty), 11
hypothesis to working thesis, 178–80

I
ibid. (in the same place), 499
ideas
  equal, linking with coordination,
    270
  paired, 280–81
  for writing, exploring, 58–62
idioms, learning, 251
i.e. (that is), 392
if, 322, 547
illusion, allusion, 256
illustrations, as visuals, 98
IM (instant messaging). *See* text
  messages
imagery, 59–60
immigrate to, emigrate from, 259
impact, 261
imperative mood (commands), 282,
  322
imperative sentences, 311
  you as implied subject of, 303
implicit, explicit, 260
implicit thesis statements, 65
imply, infer, 261
in-crowd appeal fallacy, 145

indefinite pronoun, 327 A word such as
each, *everyone*, or *nobody* that does not
refer to a specific person or thing.

  apostrophes, 373
  pronoun-antecedent agreement, 10,
    336
  sexist pronouns, 337

independent clause, 308–10 A word group containing a **subject** and a **predicate** that can stand alone as a **sentence**.

indexes, for research, 187–89

indicative mood, 282, 322

indirect discourse, shifts in, 283

indirect objects, 305

    pronoun case with, 331

indirect questions, 370

indirect quotations, 365, 379, 559

indirect sources, citing

    in APA style, 464

    in MLA style, 412

inductive reasoning, 159–60

infer, imply, 261

infinitive, 307, 320 *To* plus the **base form** of a verb (*to go, to run, to hit*), which can serve as a noun, an adverb, or an adjective: *One option is to leave* (noun). *We stopped to rest* (adverb). *He needs time to adjust* (adjective).

    disruptive modifiers in, 345–46

    and gerunds (multilingual writers), 544–46

    subjects of, pronoun case in, 331

infinitive phrases, 307

informal rhetorical situations, 49

informal writing, 12–14, 19

    audiences for, 53

    compared to academic writing, 14

-ing words

    as adjectives, 306–7, 561

    as nouns (gerunds), 307, 545

    as present participles of verbs, 312

    in progressive tenses, 317–20, 559–60

inside of, outside of, 261

instant messaging. *See* text messages

instructor comments, 106–8

instructor expectations, 12, 17, 539–40

insure, ensure, assure, 257

integrating sources, 211–16

intensive pronouns, 297

intentions, infinitives for, 545

interact, interface, 261

interjection, 302, 364 An exclamation of surprise or other strong emotion: *Ouch!*

interlibrary loans, 189

Internet searches, 189–90

    to check usage, 541–42

Internet sources

    annotating, 211

    authoritative sources online, 190

    citing. *See* digital sources

    evaluating, 198–99

    wikis (Talking theTalk), 183

    in working bibliographies, 194

interrogative pronouns, 298

interrogative sentences, 311

interviews

    APA style, citing, 466, 475

    conducting (At a Glance), 191

    MLA style, citing, 441, 446

in-text citations

    APA style, 463–67

    CSE style, 521–22

    MLA style, 409–15

intransitive verbs, 305, 317, 543

introductions

    citing in *Chicago* style, 504

    citing in MLA style, 425

    developing, 88–89, 224

    oral presentations, 26–27

    research projects, 224

    reviewing draft for, 102

    revising, 111

introductory elements, commas with, 5. 358

irony, quotation marks with, 378

irregardless, regardless, 261

irregular forms

    comparatives and superlatives, 342

    plural nouns, 296, 328

    verbs, 314–16

irregular verb, 314–16 A **verb** that does not form the past tense and past participle by adding *-ed* or *-d* to the **base form**.

issues, exploring, 152

is when, is where, 261, 277

it

    opening sentences with, 114, 287

    vague use of, 338

italics, 395–96

items in series

    colons with, 384

    commas with, 362–63, 367

    parallelism, 279–80

    semicolons with, 369

it is, avoiding, 287

its, it's, 261, 297, 374

J

jargon, 247
journal articles.
  in APA style, 475–78
  in *Chicago* style, 506–9
  in CSE style, 527, 530–31
  in MLA style, 426, 431
journalist's questions, 62
just as, so, 301

K

key words
  in oral presentations, 27
  in paragraphs, 85–86
  and purpose for writing, 176
  in scanable résumés, 604
keyword searches, 184–85, 190
kind, sort, type, 261
kind of, sort of, 261
know, no, 261
knowledge, credibility established
  with, 154–55

L

lab reports, 593–97
language. *See also* word choice
  appropriate, editing for (At a
    Glance), 245
  assumptions, avoiding, 237–41
  bringing in another, 54, 244–45
  colloquial, 246–47
  and common ground, 236–41
  doublespeak and euphemisms,
    247–48
  figurative, 250–51
  gender-neutral, 237–38
  glossary of usage, 256–65
  jargon, 247
  pompous, 247–48
  and rhetorical situation, 53–54
  slang, 246–47
  stereotypes, avoiding, 237
  use and cultural contexts, 235–36
  varieties of (At a Glance), 242
  for world audience. *See* cultural
    contexts
language names, capitalizing, 387

language that builds common ground,
  236–41
language variety, 242–45
later, latter, 261
latter, former, 260
lay, lie, 261, 316–17
leave, let, 261
lectures and speeches, citing (MLA),
  442–43
legal sources, citing, 447
lend, loan, 261
less, fewer, 260
less, least, 298
let, leave, 261
letters (texts), 601–3
  APA style, citing, 466
  Chicago style, citing, 511
  guidelines for writing (At a Glance),
    603
  letter of application, student sample,
    602
  MLA style, citing, 446
  reflective statements, 119–20
letters of the alphabet
  italics for, 396
  plurals, 375
letters to the editor
  APA style, citing, 475
  MLA style, citing, 427, 434
Library of Congress, online, 190
*Library of Congress Subject Headings
  (LCSH)*, 184
library research, 182–89
  catalogs, 183, 186
  databases, 183–85
  indexes, 187–89
  reference librarians, 182
  search options, 184–85
lie, lay, 261, 316–17
like, as if, as, 257
"like" buttons, 23
limiting modifiers, 345
linear organization, 73

linking verb, 304 A verb that suggests a
state of being, not an action.

  and adjectives, 298, 339–40
  and subject-verb agreement, 328
links, in online texts, 23
listen to, 564

list of works cited. *See* MLA style
lists
  colon in, 384
  numbers in, 381
literally, 262
literary analysis, 575–81
literary works, citing (MLA), 412
literature review
  in natural and applied sciences, 592
  in social sciences, 583–89
live performances, citing (MLA), 443
loan, lend, 261
logical appeals, 139–40, 156–61
logical organization, 69
logos, 138, 156
logs, research, 179
looping, 58–59
loose, lose, 262
lots, lots of, 262
-*ly* words (adverbs), 299, 340

M

magazine articles, citing. *See also*
    articles in periodicals
  APA style, 475
  Chicago style, 507
  CSE style, 528
  MLA style, 426
magazines
  online, 190
  as research source, 181–82
  titles, italics for, 378, 396
main clause. *See* independent clause
main idea
  developing in paragraphs, 75–77
  distinguishing with subordination,
    271–74
  topics. *See* exploring ideas; topic
    selection
main verbs. *See* verbs
major premise of syllogism, 159–60
man, mankind, 262
manuscripts, MLA style, 447
maps
  MLA style, citing, 414–15, 444
  as visuals, 97
margins, white space and, 92–93
may, as modal, 258, 554–55, 557

may be, maybe, 262
meaning
  clarifying for other cultures,
    232–33
  reviewing draft for, 100
meanwhile, 302
media, 262
memos, 598–600
  guidelines for writing (At a Glance),
    599
messaging. *See* text messages
metaphors, 250
  and emotional appeals, 161
might, as modal auxiliary, 313, 557
mine, my, 297
minor premises, of syllogisms, 159–60
misplaced modifiers, 344–45
mixed metaphors, 250
mixed structures in sentences, 276–77

MLA style, 403–57 The citation style
guidelines issued by the Modern
Language Association.

  block quotations, lines of prose or
    poetry, 377
  directory to in-text citations,
    409–10
  directory to works-cited models,
    416–17
  explanatory and bibliographic notes,
    408–9
  in-text citations, 409–15
  list of works cited, 416–47
    author listings, 417–20
    books, 420–26
    digital sources, 430–39
    formatting guidelines (At a
      Glance), 418
    government publications, 445–46
    multimedia sources, 440–45
    print periodicals, 426–30
  quotations, integrating, 213
  student research essay, 447–547
  visuals, 215–16, 414–15

modal, 313, 557–58 A kind of **helping
verb** that has only one form and shows
possibility, necessity, or obligation: *can,
could, may, might, must, shall, should,
will, would, ought to.*

modifier, 339–46 A word, phrase, or **clause** that acts as an **adjective** or an **adverb**, qualifying the meaning of another word, phrase, or clause.

    adjectives and adverbs, 339–43

    placement, 343–46

    order in sentences, 553

mood, 282, 322–23 The form of a **verb** that indicates the writer's attitude toward the idea expressed. The indicative mood states fact or opinion (*I am happy*); the imperative gives commands (*Keep calm*); and the subjunctive refers to a condition that does not exist (*If I were rich . . .*).

moral, morale, 262

more, most, 298

multilingual writers, 539–64

    adjective clauses, 546

    adjective sequence, 341

    adjectives with plural nouns, 340

    American spellings, recognizing, 253

    articles, 299, 550–52

    British English, 243

    capitalization, 390

    class participation, 25

    conditional sentences, 547

    count and noncount nouns, 296, 548

    determiners, 549–50

    English, global varieties of, 243

    explicit points, 76

    fancy words, avoiding, 248

    genres, understanding, 540–41

    genre structures and phrases, adapting, 541

    gerunds, 545–46

    helping verbs, 555–56

    hundred, use of term, 395

    idioms, learning, 251

    infinitives, 544–46

    modal auxiliaries (helping verbs), 313, 555–56

    modifiers, 553

    noun clauses, 544

    participial adjectives, 561

    past tense, 558–59

    peer review, 103

    perfect and progressive tenses, 559–60

    personal experience, 155

plagiarism as a cultural concept, 218

prepositions, idiomatic, 561–64

present tense, 558–59

proper nouns, 549

quotation marks, 380

quotations, tense shifts, 559

reading patterns, 94

reported speech, shifting tenses in, 284

reviewing drafts, 101

reviewing thesis, 221

sentence length, 350

sources, identifying, 211

subjects and objects of sentences, 543

subjunctive mood, 323

thesis, stating explicitly, 67

topic, choosing, 60

U.S. academic style, 539–40

usage, checking online, 541–42

verb phrases, 554–56

word order, 543

multimedia, library resources, 189

multimodal text, 20–36 A **text** that may include oral, visual, or audio elements in addition to (or instead of) words on a page.

multiple negatives, 343

musical works

    MLA style, citing, 442

    titles, italics for, 396

Muslim, Moslem, usage, 240

must, as modal auxiliary, 296, 313, 557

my, mine, 297

myself, himself, herself, yourself (reflexive pronouns), 260, 297

N

name-year format (CSE), 521–22

narratives

    developing paragraphs with, 79

    establishing credibility with, 157–58

narrowing topics, 64

natural and applied sciences, 590–97

    assignments, types of, 591–92

    critical reading for, 590–91

    formats for writing, 591

lab report, student model, 593–97
  style in, 592–93
n.d. (no date), 466, 485
negatives, multiple (Talking about
    Style), 343
newsletters, 41–42
newspaper articles, citing
  APA style, 475
  Chicago style, 510
  CSE style, 528–29
  MLA style, 427, 431
no, know, 261
noncount nouns, 296, 548, 550–52
none, 297

nonrestrictive element, 8, 360–61 A
word, **phrase**, or **clause** that provides
more information about, but does not
change, the essential meaning of a
sentence. Nonrestrictive elements are
set off from the rest of the sentence with
commas: *My instructor, who is perceptive, liked my introduction.*

NOT, in electronic searches, 185
note cards, for oral presentations, 30
notes. *See also* endnotes; footnotes
  APA style, 462–63
  Chicago style, 498
  ibid. (in the same place), 499
  MLA style, 408–9
note-taking, 205–11
  guidelines (At a Glance), 207
  paraphrasing, 207–9
  quoting, 206–7
  summarizing, 209–10

noun, 296, 548–53 A word that names a
person, place, thing, or idea.

noun clauses, 308, 544
noun phrases, 306
number, amount, 257
number, shifts in, 282–83
numbers, 394–95
  commas with, 365
  in different fields (Talking about
      Style), 393
  editing (At a Glance), 390
  hyphens with, 398
  plurals, 375
  used as terms, italics for, 396

object A **noun** or **pronoun** receiving
the action of a **verb** (*We mixed paints*)
or following a **preposition** (*on the road*).
See direct objects; indirect objects.

object complements, 303, 305
objective case, 331
  in compound structures, 334
observations, 191–92
  conducting (At a Glance), 192
off, of, 262
OK, O.K., okay, 262
omissions, ellipses for, 385–86
on account of, 262
one another, each other, 259
online sources, citing. *See* digital
      sources, citing
online texts, 20–24. *See also* informal
      writing
  accessible, 23
  creating (At a Glance), 20
  features of, 22–23
  structure, designing, 24
or (coordinating conjunction),
      359–60
  in compound antecedent, 310
  subject-verb agreement and,
      326
OR, in electronic searches, 185
oral presentations, 25–36
organization of writing, 67–70
  and cultural contexts, 234–35
  instructor comments on, 107
  for online texts, 24
  reviewing draft for, 101–2
  revising, 111
  by subject, 222–23
  visuals, 70
organizations as authors, citing,
  in APA style, 470
  in *Chicago* style, 502
  in CSE style, 526
  in MLA style, 411, 419
ought to, as modal auxiliary, 313
our, ours, 297
ourselves, 297
outlines, 71–72, 223
oversimplification fallacy, 146
owing to the fact that, 262

P

page numbers
  in APA in-text citations, 464
  in MLA in-text citations, 409–14
  pagination, formats for, 94
  sources without, 413–14 (MLA), 467
    (APA)
paper, quality of, for print texts, 93–94
papers
  presented at conference, citing (CSE),
    527
  presented at symposium, citing
    (APA), 486
  writing. *See* academic writing; writ-
    ing assignments; writing process
paragraphs, 75–88
  coherence (flow), 85–88
  conclusions, 89
  details in, 77
  development of, 79–84
  introductions, 87–89
  length, 76, 85
  topic sentences, 76–77
parallelism, 279–81
  for paragraph coherence, 86
paraphrases, 207–9, 214–15
  in APA style, 464
  avoiding plagiarism in, 207–9
  guidelines for (At a Glance), 209
  as indirect discourse, 283
  present tense in, 318
  signal verbs with, 214–15
  sources of, acknowledging, 217–18
  when to use (At a Glance), 212
parentheses, 380–82
  with other punctuation, 381–82
  question marks in, 371
  searches using, 185
parenthetical expressions, commas to
  set off, 363
participial adjectives, 561
participial phrases, 307–8, 320–21
  restrictive and nonrestrictive,
    362

participle, 312–16, 556 A word formed
from the **base form** of a **verb**. The
present participle always ends in *-ing*
(*going*). The past participle ends in *-ed*
(*ruined*) unless the verb is **irregular**. A
participle can function as an **adjective**
(*the singing frog*, *a ruined shirt*) or form
part of a **verb phrase** (*You have ruined
my shirt*).

parts of speech, 295–302 The eight
grammatical categories describing how
words function in a sentence (**adjectives,
adverbs, conjunctions, interjections,
nouns, prepositions, pronouns,
verbs**).

passed, past, 262

passive voice, 282, 321 The form of a
verb when the **subject** is being acted
on, not acting: *The batter was hit by a
pitch.*
  constructing, 555–56
past, passed, 262
past participles, 312
  -ed, -d endings, 313
  of irregular verbs, 314–16
past perfect progressive tense, 319
past perfect tense, 319
past progressive tense, 319, 560
past subjunctive, 322
past tense forms, 312, 319
  of *be*, 313
  -ed, -d endings, 313
  of irregular verbs, 314–16
  for multilingual writers, 559
pathos, 138
PDF files, citing
  in APA style, 466
  in MLA style, 414
peer review, 102–6
per, 262
percent, percentage, 262

perfect progressive tense, 317–20 The
tense of a **verb** showing an ongoing
action completed at some point in the
past, present, or future: *The workers
had been striking for a month before the
settlement. He has been complaining for
days. The construction will have been
continuing for a year in May.*

perfect tense, 317–20 The **tense** of a
verb showing a completed action in the
past, present, or future: *They had hoped
to see the parade but got stuck in traffic.*

I have never understood this equation. By then, the governor will have vetoed the bill.

  for multilingual writers, 559–60
periodicals. *See also* articles in
    periodicals
  APA style, citing, 474–77
  articles in, locating, 188–89
  Chicago style, citing, 506–9
  CSE style, citing, 527–28
  evaluating articles in, 196–97, 200–201
  indexes, 187–89
  MLA style, citing, 426–30
  scholarly and popular sources,
    181–82
  in working bibliographies, 194
periods, 370–71
  with parentheses, 381
  with quotation marks, 378

person, 282–83 The point of view of a
subject. The first person refers to itself
(*I*); the second person addresses *you*; the
third person refers to someone else (*they*).

  in academic writing, 570
  and verb forms, 295
personal communication, citing
  in *Chicago* style, 511
  in MLA style, 466
personal pronouns, 297
persuasive writing. *See* argument; writing assignments; writing process
photographs, 99
  citing in MLA style, 414–15, 443–44
  misleading, 146–47
phrasal verbs, 296, 562–64

phrase, 306–7 A group of words that
lacks a **subject**, a **verb**, or both.

  restrictive and nonrestrictive, 362
  verb, 296, 306, 554–55
phrase fragments, 353
pie charts, 97
place, transitions to signal, 87
plagiarism, avoiding, 207–9, 218–20
plenty, 263
plurals
  count and noncount nouns, 296, 548
  first, second, and third person, 312
  irregular forms, 296
  possessive nouns, 296, 373–74

  spelling rules for, 255, 296
  subject-verb agreement and, 323–29
plus, 263
podcasts
  citing in APA style, 487
  citing in *Chicago* style, 511, 514
  citing in MLA style, 443
  features of, 22
poetry
  capitalization, 387
  literary analysis, student model,
    576–81
  MLA style
    block quotations, 377
    in-text citations, 377, 396, 412
  slashes between lines, 385
  titles, 377, 396
pompous language, 247–48
popular sources, 181–82
portfolios, preparing, tips for, 118–19

possessive form, 9, 296, 373–74 The
form of a **noun** or **pronoun** that shows
possession. Personal pronouns in the possessive case don't use apostrophes (*ours,
hers*), but possessive nouns and indefinite
pronouns do (*Harold's, everyone's*).

possessive pronouns, 297, 332
  as antecedents, 338
posters
  in oral presentations, 30
  student model, 39
post hoc fallacy, 145
PowerPoint. *See* presentations
precede, proceed, 263
precedents, 157

predicate, 294–95, 304–5 The **verb** and
related words in a **clause** or sentence.
The predicate expresses what the subject
does, experiences, or is. The simple
predicate is the verb or **verb phrase**: *We
have been living in the Atlanta area.* The
complete predicate includes the simple
predicate and its **modifiers**, **objects**,
and complements: *We have been living in
the Atlanta area.*

prefaces, citing
  in *Chicago* style, 504
  in MLA style, 425

prefixes, hyphens with, 398
premises, in syllogisms, 159–60
prepositional phrases, 306
    commas with, 362
preposition, 299–300, 561–64 A word or
word group that indicates the relationship
of a **noun** or **pronoun** to another part of
the sentence: *From the top of the ladder
we looked over the rooftops.*
presentations, 25–36
    audience analysis, 26
    guidelines for, 35–36
    introductions and conclusions,
        26–27
    notes, speaking from, 30
    organization, 27
    preparing for (At a Glance), 25
    purposes for speaking, 26
    scripts, 28–30
    signpost language in, 27, 30
    student model script and slides, 29
    transitions in, 27
    visuals, integrating, 30–35
present participles, 312, 556
present perfect participles, 321
present perfect progressive tense,
    319
present perfect tense, 319, 559–60
present progressive tense, 286, 559–60
present subjunctive, 322
present tense, 318–19, 559–60
    be, forms of, 313
pretty, 263
Prezi. *See* presentations
primary source, 180–81 A research
source that offers firsthand knowledge of
its subject.
principal, principle, 263
problem and solution, developing
    paragraphs with, 84
proceed, precede, 263
process, developing paragraphs with,
    83
progressive tense, 317–20, 559–60
The **tense** of a **verb** showing a continuing action in the past, present, or future:
He was snoring during the lecture. The
economy is improving. Business schools
will be competing for this student.

pronoun, 296–98, 329–38 A word used
in place of a **noun**.

    gender-neutral, 238, 337
    as subject complements, 304
pronoun-antecedent agreement, 10,
    335–38
    in Top Twenty, 10
pronoun reference, vague (Top
    Twenty), 6, 337–38
proofreading, 115–16, 227
    for spelling, 252–53
proper adjectives
    capitalization, 7, 299, 387
    order in sentences, 508, 553
proper nouns, 296
    capitalization, 7, 387, 549
    for multilingual writers, 549,
        552
    spell-checker errors, 252
    zero article with, 552
proximity, in document design, 91
public speaking. *See* presentations
public writing, 36–44
    writing to make something happen
        (At a Glance), 37
publisher's imprint, citing (MLA), 426
punctuation, 358–99
    apostrophes, 373–75
    brackets, 382
    colons, 383–84
    commas, 358–67
    dashes, 382–83
    effective use, editing for (At a
        Glance), 381
    ellipses, 385–86
    exclamation points, 372
    hyphens, 397–99
    parentheses, 380–82
    periods, 370–71
    question marks, 371
    quotation marks, 375–80
    semicolons, 367–69
    slashes, 385
purposes
    arguments, 151–52
    and choosing visuals, 56
    key words for, 176
    for online texts, 21
    for oral and multimedia presenta-
        tions, 26

for public writing, 37
reviewing draft for, 101–2
understanding assignments, 50–51

Q

qualifiers in arguments, 141–43
qualitative studies, 582–83
quantitative studies, 582–83
question marks, 371
  with quotation marks, 334, 371, 379
questionnaires, designing, 192
questions
  to explore a topic, 61–62
  in indicative mood, 322
  indirect, 370
  interrogative pronouns, 298, 332–33
  interrogative sentences, 311
  for questionnaires, 192
  research, 178, 197
  subject of sentence in, 303
  tag, 364
quotation, quote, 263
quotation marks, 375–80
  commas with, 6, 365
  for definitions, 378
  editing for (At a Glance), 376
  in electronic searches, 185
  with end punctuation, 334, 371, 377–79
  for irony and invented terms, 378
  with lines of poetry, 377
  misused, 379
  single, 376
  for titles of works, 377–78
quotations
  in APA style, 213
  block quotations, 377
  brackets for changed words, 214
  brief versus long, incorporating, 213
  colons with, 384
  as direct discourse, 283
  direct quotations, 375–76
  ellipses for deleted words in, 214
  indirect quotations, 334, 379
  integrating into writing, 212–15
  mechanical errors with (Top
    Twenty), 6–7
  in MLA style, 213
  note-taking with, 206–7
  note-taking guidelines (At a Glance),
    207
  poorly integrated (Top Twenty), 10
  within quotations, 376
  signal words for, 214–15
  sources of, acknowledging, 217–18
  tenses with, 318
  when to use (At a Glance), 212

R

race, assumptions about, 238–39
raise, rise, 263, 316–17
rarely ever, 263
ratios, colons in, 384
reading, 123–36. *See also* critical reading
real, really, 263
real-time communication, citing (APA),
  484
reasoning, critical, 159–60
  Toulmin's system, 160
reason . . . is because constructions, 277
reasons, in arguments, 141–42, 160
reason why, 263
reciprocal pronouns, 298
reference librarians, 182
references list
  in APA style, 467–87
  in CSE style, 523–32
  formatting for APA (At a Glance), 469
reference works, citing
  in APA style, 474
  in *Chicago* style, 505
  in MLA style, 425, 435
reflecting on writing, 117–20
  for portfolios, 118–19
  questions to ask, 117–18
reflective writing, student sample,
  119–20
reflexive pronouns, 297
regardless, irregardless, 261
regional varieties of language,
  242–44
regular verb, 313 A **verb** that forms
the **past tense** and **past participle** by
adding *-d* or *-ed* to the **base form** (*care,
cared, cared; look, looked, looked*).
reiteration, developing paragraphs
  with, 84
relative pronouns, 272, 298, 308
  and subject-verb agreement,
    327–28

religion, assumptions about, 240–41
repetition
  in document design, 91
  transitions, to signal, 88
reports. *See also* academic writing; writing assignments
  APA style, citing, 486
  Chicago style, citing, 515
  lab, student model, 593–97
  MLA style, citing, 445
  online, sample, 43–44
  psychology, student research essay, 585–89
requests, modals to signal, 558
research (research project), 175–227
  audience analysis, 176
  conclusions, 224–25
  design, 222
  drafting, 224–27
  field research, 191–93
  hypotheses in, 178
  introductory paragraphs, 224
  for natural and applied sciences, 592
  with open mind (Talking the Talk), 195
  organizing, 222–23
  planning, 17, 177–79
  prewriting choices, refining, 220–21
  research logs, 179
  research question, 178, 197
  reviewing drafts, 225
  revising, 109–11
  revising and editing, 226–27
  rhetorical stance, 176
  for social sciences, 582–83
  sources, 180–220
  supporting information for, 67
  thesis statements, 178, 221–22
  titles, 224
  topics, exploring, 175–76
  working thesis, 64–67, 179–80
research questions
  evaluating, 197
  formulating, 178
respectively, respectfully, 263

restrictive element, 360–61 A word, **phrase**, or **clause** that changes the essential meaning of a sentence. A restrictive element is not set off from the rest of the sentence with commas or other punctuation: *The tree that I hit was an oak.*

  commas, unnecessary, 7, 360, 366
résumés, 603–6
review indexes, 187
reviewing drafts, 100–106
  of arguments, 152
  elements to review, 100–102
  by instructors, 106–8
  peer review, 102–6
  of research project, 225
reviews, citing,
  in *Chicago* style, 510
  in MLA style, 427, 434
revision, 109–11
  of research project, 226–27
  scope of (Talking the Talk), 111
  student sample, 116–17
rhetorical analysis. *See also* argument
  student sample, 148–51
rhetorical situation, 48–56 The whole context for a piece of writing, including the person communicating, the topic and the person's attitude toward it, and the intended audience.

  audience analysis, 52–54
  context in, 54–56
  formal and informal, 49
  of online texts, 21–22
  purpose, 50–51
  stance, 51–52
  student sample situation, 56–57
  time/length factors, 54–55
  visuals, choosing, 56
rhetorical stance, 51–52
  for research project, 176
  reviewing draft for, 101–2
  of sources, evaluating, 197, 202
  synthesis from sources, 204
rise, raise, 263, 316–17
run-on sentences. *See* fused sentence

S

-s, -es endings
plural nouns, 255, 296
verbs, 312, 324
sans serif fonts, 94
scholarly sources, 181–82
online, locating, 190
sciences, forms of writing in, 583
science terms, abbreviations in, 391–92
scores, numbers in, 394
scripts for oral presentations, 28–30
search engines, usage, for multilingual
writers, 541–42
searching
keyword. *See* keyword searches
library sources, 184–85

secondary source, 180–81 A research
source that reports information from
research done by others.

secondly, firstly, 260
second person, 282, 312
semicolons, 367–69
clauses, linking with, 301, 349, 360,
368
in compound sentences, 310
editing for (At a Glance), 368
equal ideas, relating with, 270–71
misused, 369
with quotation marks, 379

sentence, 294–95, 302–5, 308–10 A
group of words containing a **subject** and
a **predicate** and expressing a complete
thought.

length of, 112–13, 288–89, 350
for multilingual writers, 543–44
patterns, basic (At a Glance), 302–3

sentence fragment, 12, 352–54 A group
of words that is not a grammatically
complete sentence but is punctuated as
one. Usually a fragment lacks a **subject**, a
verb, or both, or it is a **dependent clause**.

sentence variety, 288–90
editing for (At a Glance), 288
sequence, transitions to signal, 87
series. *See* items in series
serif fonts, 94
set, sit, 263, 316–17

sexist language, 237–38, 337
pronouns, editing (At a Glance), 337
sexual orientation, assumptions about,
241
shall, as modal, 296, 313, 557
she, he, 260
shifts, 281–84
confusing (At a Glance), 283
between direct and indirect
discourse, 283
in mood, 282
in person/number, 282–83
in tone, 283–84
in verb tense, 8, 282
in voice, 282
in word choice, 283–84
should, as modal auxiliary, 296, 313, 557
sic (so), 382
signal phrases, 214–15
signal words
for APA in-text citations, 464–65
for MLA in-text citations, 409–10
for quotations, 214
signpost language, in oral presentations, 27, 30
similes, 250
and emotional appeals, 161
simple predicates, 304
simple sentences, 310
simple subjects, 303

simple tenses, 318–19, 559–60 Past (*It
happened*), present (*Things fall apart*), or
future (*You will succeed*) forms of verbs.

since, 263
sit, set, 263, 316–17
situations for writing. *See* rhetorical
situations
slang, 246–47
slashes, 385
slides, PowerPoint, 30–35
so (coordinating conjunction), 263,
359–60
social bookmarking sites, 190
social classes, assumptions about, 240
social media. *See also* Facebook;
informal writing
and informal writing, 12–14
sites, MLA style, citing, 439

social sciences, writing for, 582–89
    critical reading, 582
    student model, 585–89
someplace, 264
some time, sometime, sometimes, 264
sort, kind, type, 261
sort of, kind of, 261
sound recordings. *See* audio sources,
    citing
sources, 180–220
    for arguments, 163
    articles, evaluating, 197–203
    citations, abbreviations in, 392
    data interpretation, 193
    digital. *See* digital sources, citing
    documenting. *See* documentation
    evaluating credibility, 196–201
    excessive use, avoiding, 216
    historical, 182
    importance of, 193
    integration in writing, 211–16, 227
    interviews, 191
    library. *See* library research
    list of, preparing, 227
    note-taking, 205–11
    observations, 191–92
    online texts, giving credit, 23
    plagiarism, avoiding, 219–20
    popular sources, 181–82
    potential, examining (At a Glance), 202
    primary sources, 180–81
    for research project, 178
    scholarly sources, 181–82
    secondary sources, 180–81
    surveys, 192
    synthesizing, 203–5
    working bibliography, 194–95
spatial organization, 68
specialized indexes, 187
spell checkers, 251–52
    limitations of, 115
    and spelling errors (Top Twenty), 6
    and wrong-word errors (Talking the
        Talk), 252
    and wrong-word errors (Top
        Twenty), 5
spelling, 254–55
    editing for (At a Glance), 245
    errors, in Top Twenty, 6
    homonym errors, 6, 253

spoke-and-hub organization, 73
squinting modifiers, 345
stance, rhetorical, 51–52
standard English, 242
states abbreviations, 393
stationary, stationery, 264
statistics, 147–48
    numbers in, 394
stereotypes, avoiding, 237
storyboards, to organize information,
    72–74
straw man fallacy, 146
streaming media, 22
styles, disciplinary, 570
subheadings, purpose of, 202

subject, 294–95, 303–4 The **noun** or
pronoun and related words that indicate
who or what a sentence is about. The
simple subject is the noun or pronoun: *The
timid gray mouse ran away.* The complete
subject is the simple subject and its modifiers: *The timid gray mouse ran away.*

    explicit, 543
subject complements
    as adjectives, 302
    hyphens, unnecessary, 399
    and linking verbs, 304, 339–40
    noun clauses as, 308
    pronoun case, 331
subjective case, 330–31
    in compound structures, 334
subject-verb agreement, 323–29
    and ambiguous antecedents, 337–38
    editing for (At a Glance), 324
    and possessive antecedents, 338
    and third-person singular subjects, 324
subject word searching, 184

subjunctive mood, 282, 322 The form
of a **verb** used to express a wish, a
suggestion, a request or requirement, or
a condition that does not exist: *If I were
president, I would change things.*

subordinate clause. *See* dependent clause

subordinating conjunction, 269–70,
272, 301, 308 A word or **phrase** such as
although, because, or *even though* that
introduces a **dependent clause**: *Think
carefully before you answer.*

subordination, 271–74
  editing for (At a Glance), 269–70
  excessive, avoiding, 273–74
  main ideas, distinguishing with, 271–74
  power of (Talking about Style), 273
suffixes
  hyphens with, 398
  and spelling rules, 254
summary A brief retelling of the main points of a **text**.
  guidelines for (At a Glance), 210
  incorporating in writing, 214–15
  for notes, 209–10
  sources, acknowledging, 217–18
  when to use (At a Glance), 212
superlative The *-est* or *most* form of an **adjective** or **adverb** used to compare three or more items (*happiest, most quickly*).
superscript numbers
  APA style, content notes, 462–63
  Chicago style citations, 498–99
  CSE style citations, 521
  MLA style, explanatory/ bibliographic notes, 408–9
supporting evidence. *See also* sources
  reviewing draft for, 102
  revising, 110
  and working thesis, 67
supposed to, used to, 264
sure, surely, 264
surface errors, 3
surveys, 192
syllogisms, elements of, 159–60
syntax The arrangement of words in a sentence.
synthesis, 193, 203–5 Grouping ideas and information together in such a way that the relationship among them is clear.

T
tables
  in MLA style, 414–15
  as visuals, 97
tag questions, commas with, 364
take, bring, 258

Talking about Style boxes
  abbreviations and numbers in different fields, 393
  anticlimax and humor, 275
  be, everyday use of, 312
  comma splices in context, 351
  multiple negation, 343
  subordination, 273
  technical and scientific writing, voice for, 322
  technical writing, 289
Talking the Talk boxes
  arguments, 152
  assignments, 53
  audience, recognizing, 176
  conventions, 14
  first person (*I*) in academic writing, 570
  formality, correctness, or stuffiness, 333
  grammatical terms, 295
  research with an open mind, 195
  revision, 111
  spell checkers and wrong-word errors, 252
  texting abbreviations, 246
  visual texts, 131
  writing something new, 216
technical writing
  disciplinary style, 570
  disciplinary vocabulary, 569
  passive voice, use of, 323
  sentence length (Talking about Style), 289
television shows, citing,
  in APA style, 486–87
  in MLA style, 440–41
tense, 317–21 The form of a **verb** that indicates the time when an action takes place — past, present, or future. Each tense has **simple** (*I enjoy*), **perfect** (*I have enjoyed*), **progressive** (*I am enjoying*), and **perfect progressive** (*I have been enjoying*) forms.
testimony, as evidence, 158
text Traditionally, words on paper, but now anything that conveys a message.
  online, 20–24
  in rhetorical situation, 49
  visual (Talking the Talk), 131

texting, 19, 246
than, then, 264
that
 introducing quotation with, 334
 as relative pronoun, 298
 vague use of, 338
that, which, 264
the (article), 299, 551–52
their, theirs, 297
theirselves, 264
themselves, 297
then, 302
there, opening sentences with, 114, 287,
 304
therefore, 299, 302
there is, there are, 329
there was, there were, 329
thesis statements, 64–67, 221–22
 research project, 178
 revising, 110
they, indefinite use of, 338
thinking, critical. *See* critical thinking
third person, 282
 singular and plural, 312, 324
this, vague use of, 338
thorough, threw, through, 264
time
 numbers in, 394
 subordinating conjunctions, 301
 transitions to signal, 87
time management, 24, 177
titles
 capitalizing, 389
 colons in, 384
 italics for, 378, 395–96
 quotation marks for, 377–78
 for research projects, 224
 reviewing draft for, 102
 revising, 111
 and subject-verb agreement, 329
 within titles, citing, 426, 474, 506
 of visuals, 98
titles of persons
 abbreviating, 391
 capitalizing, 389
 commas with, 365
to, too, two, 264
to forms (infinitives), 307, 320, 545. *See
 also* infinitive

tone
 considering for assignment, 55
 shifts in, 283–84
 of source, evaluating, 202
tone of voice, oral presentations, 35
topic selection, 49–50. *See also* exploring
 ideas
topic sentences, 76–77
Top Twenty (common errors), 4–12
 apostrophe, unnecessary or missing,
 9
 capitalization, unnecessary or
 missing, 7
 commas, missing after introductory
 element, 5
 commas, missing in compound
 sentences, 9
 commas, missing with nonrestrictive
 element, 8
 commas, unnecessary, 7
 comma splice, 9–10
 documentation, incomplete or
 missing, 5–6
 fused (run-on) sentences, 9
 hyphens, unnecessary or missing, 11
 list of (At a Glance), 4
 pronoun-antecedent agreement
 errors, 10
 pronoun reference, vague, 6
 quotations, mechanical errors, 6–7
 quotations, poorly integrated, 10
 sentence fragments, 12
 sentence structure, faulty, 8
 spelling errors, 6
 verb tense shifts, 8
 words, missing, 7–8, 277–78
 wrong-word errors, 3–5
Toulmin arguments, 141–43
 organization of, 165
 reasoning system of, 160

transition, 86-88 A word or **phrase** that
signals a progression from one sentence
or part of a sentence to another.

 sentence variety with, 289
 signpost language, 27

transitive verb, 305, 543 A **verb** that
acts on an **object**: *I posted my review
online.*

translations, citing
    in APA style, 471
    in *Chicago* style, 505
    in MLA style, 421, 424
Twitter, 13, 284. *See also* informal writing
two, too, to, 264
type, sort, kind, 261
typefaces, 94–95
typos, 252

U

uninterested, disinterested, 259
unique, 264
units of measurement, 392–93
unknown authors, citing
    in APA style, 470
    in *Chicago* style, 504
    in MLA style, 411, 419, 424
unpublished works, citing, 447
unsigned articles, citing, 475
URLs, slashes in, 385
U.S. academic style
    features of (At a Glance), 16
    and multilingual writers, 539–40
U.S. Government Printing Office (GPO
        Access), 189
us or *we* before nouns, 335

V

veiled threat fallacy, 145
verbals, 306–7

verb, 295–96, 304–5, 311–23 A word
or **phrase**, essential to a sentence, that
expresses the action of a sentence or
clause. Verbs change form to show
tense, number, **voice**, and **mood**.

    base forms, 312
    be, forms of, 304
    editing (At a Glance), 312
    helping, 296, 313
    intransitive, 305
    irregular forms, 314–16
    linking, 304
    mood, 282, 322–23
    for multilingual writers, 562–64
    predicates, 304–5
    regular forms, 313

    revising, 115
    strong, 287
    tense, 317–21
    transitive, 305
    voice, 321–22

verb phrase, 296, 554–55 A **main verb**
and one or more **helping verbs**, acting
as a single verb.

verb tense. *See* tenses
very, 264
video content
    reviewing draft for, 102
    revising, 111
    types of, 22
videos, citing
    in APA style, 486
    in *Chicago* style, 514
    in MLA style, 440
visual argument, 139–41, 156, 162–63
visual rhetoric, 90
visuals, 95–100
    attitude and point of view in, 56
    documentation of, 99
    effective use of (At a Glance), 100
    incorporating, 215–16
    misleading, 146–48
    MLA style
        in-text citations, 215–16, 414–15
        in list of works cited, 443–45
    numbers and titles for, 98, 100
    online texts, formatting, 23
    for oral presentations, 30–35
    organizing, 70
    point of view in, 56
    to provide details, 78
    reviewing draft for, 102
    tone of, 55
    visual texts (Talking the Talk),
        131
visual structure, in design, 90–91

voice, 295, 321–22 The form of a **verb**
that indicates whether the subject is acting or being acted on. In the active voice,
the subject performs the action: *Parker
played* the saxophone. In the **passive
voice**, the subject receives the action:
The saxophone was played by Parker.

W

warrant, 142 An assumption, sometimes
unstated, that connects an argument's
claim to the reasons for making the claim.
way, ways, 297
Webcasts. *See* podcasts
Web logs. *See* blogs (Web logs)
Web sites
   citing in APA style, 479–84
   citing in *Chicago* style, 512–13
   citing in CSE style, 532
   citing in MLA style, 435–37
   features of, 22
well, good, 260, 340–41
we or *us* before nouns, 335
where, 265
which
   adjective clause with, 361
   as determiner, 549
   as interrogative pronoun, 298
   subject-verb agreement, 327
   vague use of, 338
which, that, 264
whichever, 298
white space, and design, 92–93
who
   as interrogative pronoun, 298
   subject-verb agreement, 327–28
who, whom, 265
   in dependent clauses, 333
   in questions, 332–33
whoever, 298
whoever, whomever, in dependent clauses,
      334
whose, as determiner, 549
who's/whose, 265
wikis
   citing in APA style, 485
   citing in MLA style, 438–39
   features of, 22
   as research source (Talking the Talk),
      183
wildcards, in searches, 185
will, as modal, 296, 313, 557
winning, and arguments, 151
word choice, 246–51
   disciplinary language, 569
   editing, 114

instructor comments on, 108
   oral presentations, 27–28
   shifts in, 283–84
   unnecessary, redundant, and empty
      words, 285–86
word errors (Top Twenty)
   missing word, 7–8, 277–78
   wrong word, 3–5, 252
words as words, subject-verb agree-
      ment in, 329
working bibliography, 194–95
working thesis, 64–67
   of arguments, 153
   for research project, 179–80
   testing, 222
works cited. *See* MLA style
world audiences. *See* cultural contexts
would, modal, 296, 313, 547, 557
writing assignments. *See also* academic
      writing
   analyzing (At a Glance), 568
   argument, 136–72
   business writing, 598–606
   changes in (Talking the Talk), 53
   in humanities, 574–75
   narratives, 79
   in natural and applied sciences,
      591–92
   reflective statement, 119–20
   in social sciences, 583–85
writing inventory, taking (At a Glance),
      11
writing process, 45–120
   designing texts, 90–100
   drafting, 74
   editing, 112–17
   ideas for writing, exploring, 58–62
   narrowing topic, 64
   paragraph development, 75–88
   reflecting on writing, 117–20
   reviewing drafts, 100–106
   revising, 109–11
   thesis, working, 64–67
   writing situations, 48–56
writing to make something happen in
      the world, 36–44
wrong word (Top Twenty), 3–5
   and spell checkers, 252

Y

yet, but, 258
you (second person)
    as implied subject, 303
    indefinite use of, 338
your, you're, 265
your, yours, 297
yourself, myself, himself, herself (reflexive
    pronouns), 260, 297

yourselves, 297
YouTube, 23
    podcasts, citing (MLA), 443

Z

zero article, 552

Directories

Directory of Storyboard Art

Rhetorical Situations: Choose Your Topic   50
Rhetorical Situations: Consider Your Purpose and Stance   51
Rhetorical Situations: Imagine Your Audience   53
Working Thesis: Plan Your Approach   64
Working Thesis: Refine Your Topic   65
Working Thesis: Craft Your Message   66
Peer Review: Work with a Writer   104
Peer Review: Work with Reviewers   106
Revision: Read All Comments Carefully   109
Revision: Plan Your Next Draft   110
Editing: Polish Your Draft   112
Critical Reading: Preview   124
Critical Reading: Read Carefully   126
Critical Reading: Summarize   129
Critical Reading: Analyze   130
Synthesis: Finding Patterns   203
Synthesis: Combining Ideas   204

Directory of Student Writing

In the Book

Twitter posts: Parker   13
Facebook post: Michalski   13
Oral presentation excerpts: Song,"Residents of a Dys*FUN*ctional
   HOME"   26–35
Poster: Rao   39
Flyer: Mumford   40
Event promotion: Swirsky   42
Final draft: Lesk, "Red, White, and Everywhere"   57
Portfolio cover letter: Kung   119
Critical reading: Song, "Residents of a Dys*FUN*ctional *HOME*"   133
Rhetorical analysis: Ateyea, "A Curse and a Blessing"   148
Argument essay: Pfeifer, "Devastating Beauty"   167
MLA-style research essay: Craig, "Texting and Messaging: The Language
   of Youth Literacy"   447
APA-style literature review: Redding, "Mood Music: Music Preference and
   the Risk for Depression and Suicide in Adolescents"   487
Chicago-style research essay: Rinder,"Sweet Home Chicago: Preserving the
   Past, Protecting the Future of the Windy City"   515

CSE-style research essay: Gupta, "Field Measurements of Photosynthesis and Transpiration Rates in Dwarf Snapdragon" *532*

Close reading of poetry: Sillay, "Life's Not a Paragraph" *576*

Psychology research essay: McLaughlin, "Leadership Roles in a Small-Group Project" *585*

Chemistry lab report: Goldberg *593*

Memo: Abbott and Abernathy *599*

Letter of application: Lopez *601*

Print résumé: Tyler *605*

Scannable résumé: Tyler *606*

On the Web Site

Go to **bedfordstmartins.com/everydaywriter** > **Student Writing** for model essays, drafts, research projects, annotated bibliographies, presentations, and work created for disciplines other than English.

For Multilingual Writers

CHAPTERS OF ADVICE

Chapter 56: Writing in U.S. Academic Genres *539*

Chapter 57: Clauses and Sentences *542*

Chapter 58: Nouns and Noun Phrases *548*

Chapter 59: Verbs and Verb Phrases *554*

Chapter 60: Prepositions and Prepositional Phrases *561*

BOXED TIPS

Speaking Up in Class *25*

Bringing in Other Languages *54*

Using Your Native Language to Explore Ideas *60*

Stating a Thesis Explicitly *67*

Being Explicit *76*

Reading Patterns *94*

Asking an Experienced Writer to Review Your Draft *101*

Understanding Peer Review *103*

Counting Your Own Experience *155*

Identifying Sources *211*

Plagiarism as a Cultural Concept *218*

Asking Experienced Writers to Review a Thesis *221*

Global Varieties of English *243*

Avoiding Fancy Language *248*

Learning Idioms *251*
Recognizing American Spellings *253*
Shifting Tenses in Reported Speech *284*
Using Count and Noncount Nouns *296*
Deciding When Articles Are Necessary *299*
Using Modal Auxiliaries *313*
Using the Subjunctive *323*
Using Adjectives with Plural Nouns *340*
Determining Adjective Sequence *341*
Judging Sentence Length *350*
Quoting in American English *380*
Learning English Capitalization *390*
Using the Term *Hundred* *395*

IF YOU SPEAK . . .

Arabic *240, 390*
British English *240, 253, 380*
Chinese *234, 390, 558*
Dutch *390*
French *380*
German *380, 390*
Hebrew *390*

Hindi *390*
Indian English *244, 253*
Japanese *233*
Russian *340*
Spanish *239, 244, 340, 562*
Tagalog *232*
Vietnamese *558*

Considering Disabilities

Accessible Web Texts *23*
Accessible Presentations *27*
Your Whole Audience *54*
Freespeaking *59*

Color for Contrast *93*
Know Your Readers *241*
Spelling *255*

Talking the Talk

Conventions *14*
Assignments *52*
Paragraph Length *76*
Revision *111*
Critical Thinking *125*
Visual Texts *131*
Arguments *152*
Reaching an Audience *176*
Wikis as Sources *183*

Research with an Open Mind *195*
Saying Something New *216*
Texting Abbreviations *246*
Spell Checkers and Wrong-Word Errors *252*
Grammatical Terms *295*
Correctness or Stuffiness? *333*
The First Person *570*

MM

Understanding and Composing Multimodal Projects

MM Understanding and Composing Multimodal Projects

MM1 Introduction, MM-5

MM2 Analyzing written words, MM-14

MM3 Analyzing sound, MM-21

MM4 Analyzing static images, MM-27

MM5 Analyzing moving images, MM-36

MM6 Analyzing multimodal texts, MM-43

MM7 Starting your own multimodal project, MM-51

MM8 Considering your purpose and audience, MM-54

MM9 Planning your project, MM-60

MM10 Managing your project, MM-71

MM11 Outlining and drafting your project, MM-76

MM12 Emphasizing important information, MM-82

MM13 Revising and editing your multimodal project, MM-87

MM14 Integrating and documenting sources, MM-94

MM15 Presenting or publishing your project, MM-100

Index, MM-107

MM

Understanding and Composing Multimodal Projects

A Hacker Handbooks Supplement

Dànielle Nicole DeVoss
Michigan State University

BEDFORD / ST. MARTIN'S   BOSTON ◆ NEW YORK

Manufactured in the United States of America.

7   6   5   4   3   2
f   e   d   c   b   a

For information, write: Bedford/St. Martin's, 75 Arlington Street, Boston, MA 02116   (617-399-4000)

ISBN 978-1-4576-1779-9

ACKNOWLEDGMENTS

Acknowledgments and copyrights can be found at the back of the book on pages MM-105 to MM-106, which constitute an extension of the copyright page. It is a violation of the law to reproduce these selections by any means whatsoever without the written permission of the copyright holder.

MM

Understanding and Composing Multimodal Projects

MM Understanding and Composing Multimodal Projects

MM1 Introduction, MM-5

MM2 Analyzing written words, MM-14

  a Genre: In what kind of document do the written words appear? MM-15

  b Features: What do the words look like? MM-15

  c Purpose and audience: What is the purpose of the written words? Who is the intended reader? MM-17

  d Meaning: What effect do the words have on the reader? MM-20

MM3 Analyzing sound, MM-21

  a Genre: What kind of sound is it? MM-21

  b Features: Examine the pitch, pace, and volume of the sound, MM-24

  c Purpose and audience: What is sound being used for? Who is the intended listener? MM-25

  d Meaning: What effect does sound have on the listener? MM-25

MM4 Analyzing static images, MM-27

  a Genre: What kind of image is it? MM-27

  b Features: Examine the context, perspective, and elements of the image, MM-30

  c Purpose and audience: What is the image meant to convey? Who is the intended viewer? MM-33

  d Meaning: What effect does the image have on the viewer? MM-33

MM5 Analyzing moving images, MM-36

  a Genre: What kind of moving image is it? MM-37

  b Features: Perspective, composition, and editing, MM-39

  c Purpose and audience: What are the moving images being used for? Who is the intended viewer? MM-40

  d Meaning: What effect do the moving images have on the viewer? MM-41

MM6 Analyzing multimodal texts, MM-43

  a Genre: What kind of multimodal text is it? MM-44

  b Features: Which modes are represented? How do they work on their own and with each other? MM-46

  c Purpose and audience: What is the composition doing? Whom is it intended to reach? MM-48

  d Meaning: What effect does the multimodal composition have on the viewer? MM-49

MM7 Starting your own multimodal project, MM-51

a Getting direction from the assignment, MM-51
b Considering the "So what?" question, MM-52
c Understanding expectations, managing your time, MM-53

MM8 Considering your purpose and audience, MM-54

a Prewriting with your purpose in mind, MM-55
b Identifying your audience's needs and perspectives, MM-56
c Connecting with your audience, MM-58
d Recognizing an unintended audience, MM-59

MM9 Planning your project, MM-60

a Understanding your own composing process, MM-61
b Collaborating effectively with others, MM-63
c Deciding on a main idea, MM-65
d Planning support, MM-67
e Choosing a genre and delivery method, MM-68

MM10 Managing your project, MM-71

a Saving all your files in one place, MM-71
b Keeping track of files, MM-73
c Using clear file names, MM-75
d Keeping track of versions when sharing files, MM-75

MM11 Outlining and drafting your project, MM-76

a Choosing the right organizing tool, MM-76
b Drafting to support your main idea, MM-80

MM12 Emphasizing important information, MM-82

a Determining what needs emphasis, MM-83
b Choosing a strategy for creating emphasis, MM-84

MM13 Revising and editing your multimodal project, MM-87

a Seeking and using feedback, MM-88
b Revising and remixing, MM-90
c Editing, MM-92

MM14 Integrating and documenting sources, MM-94

a Documenting sources, MM-94
b Knowing when a citation is needed, MM-95
c Determining how to integrate sources, MM-95
d Figuring out how to document sources, MM-96

MM15 Presenting or publishing your project, MM-100

a Knowing your options, MM-100
b Spaces for presenting and publishing, MM-101
c Making your project accessible and usable, MM-103

Index, MM-107

MM1 Introduction

In many of your college courses, you will be asked to read, analyze, and compose texts. The way you interact with texts can determine your success in college. The good news is that you have been reading, analyzing, and composing for years. Think of a magazine you read often, a job ad you once replied to, a Web site you've frequently visited, a book you discussed with friends, or a Facebook comment you recently made. Your college courses may give you the opportunity to analyze and compose *multimodal* texts as well, texts that rely on a combination of modes, such as images, words, and sounds, to communicate an idea. A common example is a print advertisement, a text that communicates meaning with both words and an image.

Understanding and Composing Multimodal Projects will help you take a broader look at yourself as a reader and as a writer.

MM1-a What does it mean to "read" a text?

This book asks you to take a new look at the act of reading. You know that a person can read an article, but can he "read" a painting? Someone can read a book, of course, but can she "read" a podcast? Your immediate answer might be "No, of course not!" but if you can rethink what it means to read—and consider that reading can mean taking a closer look or listening critically—your answer might be "Well, maybe!" This book also asks you to reconsider what is meant by the word text. Most people would call an essay or a poem a text. Can a movie soundtrack or a cartoon be called a text?

To dig into these terms, compare John Keats's drawing in Figure 1–1 (p. MM-6), an ancient urn, with his 1819 poem "Ode on a Grecian Urn." What are the characteristics that might lead us to call the drawing a text? What are the characteristics that might lead us to call the poem a text? How would we "read" the image of the urn? How do we "read" the poem?

Here is an excerpt from Keats's "Ode on a Grecian Urn":

O Attic shape! Fair attitude! with brede
Of marble men and maidens overwrought,
With forest branches and the trodden weed;
Thou, silent form, dost tease us out of thought
As doth eternity: Cold Pastoral!
When old age shall this generation waste,
Thou shalt remain, in midst of other woe
Than ours, a friend to man, to whom thou say'st,
"Beauty is truth, truth beauty,"—that is all
Ye know on earth, and all ye need to know.

If reading means discovering what a text is saying, it's helpful to consider how the text is presenting its meaning. In the poem, meaning is presented through written words. The drawing shows details from the actual urn, including images that communicate meaning. Both "texts" tell a story for a purpose and to an audience.

Reading may also require careful attention to the historical and cultural context in which a text is created. A text always emerges out of a time and a place and a social situation. To read Keats's poem effectively may require knowing something about the English Romantic literary movement. To read the image of the urn effectively may require a familiarity with the uses of urns and other pottery in ancient Greece.

FIGURE 1–1 JOHN KEATS'S DRAWING OF AN ANCIENT URN.

Almost anything can be read—that is, carefully approached and analyzed for *what* it does and *how* it does what it does. Almost anything can be a text—that is, something that conveys meaning. Reading carefully and critically often means asking questions about a text. When and by whom was the text created? What purpose was it intended to serve? What assumptions does the creator or composer make about the audience? Reading for a college course requires active, thoughtful investigation.

MM1-b What is multimodal composing?

This book refers to texts that include more than one way of presenting an idea as *multimodal*. Multimodal texts are those that draw on multiple (multi) modes of conveying information, including words, numbers, images, graphics, animations, transitions, sounds (voice and music), and more.

WORDS   = MONOMODAL TEXT

WORDS + [____] = MULTIMODAL TEXT

When ancient orators, or public speakers, tried to persuade audiences, they did so orally with the words they spoke and their tone of voice—but they also did so with another mode, their physical gestures.

Speakers throughout history have communicated their meaning by combining modes, or ways of presenting their message. The best, most convincing speakers know that a gesture combined with a word can be powerful—and when the word is spoken in a particular tone, it can be even more so. Clasped, raised hands can convey pleading or imploring, for instance, while a clenched fist often conveys might and strength.

SPEECH + GESTURES = MULTIMODAL TEXT

This is multimodal composing.

Think back to a high school earth science class, where you may have been studying earthquakes and plate tectonics. You may have had to compose a project that called for diagrams to represent the different types of plate movements within the earth's crust; a report on the specific physical features of a recent earthquake—Indonesia (2007), Chile (2010), Haiti (2010), or Japan (2011); and a brief slide show presentation of cause-and-effect findings to the class.

WORDS + IMAGES + SPEECH = MULTIMODAL TEXT

This is multimodal composing.

Using multiple modes causes us to rethink terminology. You may be accustomed to referring to those who compose texts as *authors* or *writers*. You may also use the term *writing* to describe most acts of communicating ideas. This book will describe communicating ideas as *composing*, which literally means "to produce something by putting together." And this book will refer to those who compose multimodal texts as *composers*.

Composers of texts may combine modes, and in some ways this makes their work more complicated. Composers have more options for sending a message, sharing an idea, posing an argument, teaching other people how to do something, and so forth. In other ways, combining modes makes composers' work more exciting and effective. They can send, share, teach, and explain in ways that include words *and* other elements.

MM1-c Composing *hasn't* changed

In some ways, composing has not changed all that much. It has always been crucial to how meaning is made and shared—how we communicate ideas from person to person, community to community, and generation to generation. Composing has always served to capture, save, and deliver ideas, messages, and meanings. Ancient cultures, for example, composed petroglyphs, rock carvings on cave walls and the sides of mountains, to share their ideas in a lasting way (Figure 1–2).

FIGURE 1–2 ANCIENT PETROGLYPHS ON CAVE WALLS.

(*Source:* US National Park Service; Pgiam)

FIGURE 1–3 MEDIEVAL ILLUMINATED MANUSCRIPT.

(*Source:* Duncan Walker)

Further, composing has often, to some extent, been multimodal. As far back as the fifth century CE, for example, monks created illuminated manuscripts—richly decorated books that combined illustrations and words. (Figure 1–3).

Though today's printed brochures aren't handwritten or decorated with gold leaf, they are a similarly effective combination of modes (words and images). Think about a catalog that includes full-color, glossy pages and perhaps a QR (quick response) code you can scan with your cell phone for more information (Figure 1–4). Or think about an e-book, which might include the typical contents of a printed book—a table of contents, numbered pages, lots of text, and so on—but which can also contain embedded video clips and animations.

FIGURE 1–4 QR (QUICK RESPONSE) CODE. (*Source:* Denso Wave Incorporated)

MM1-d Composing *has* changed

Composing has, in some ways, changed significantly in recent years. Today's composers blog, podcast, craft digital stories, prepare slide show presentations, design Web pages, write short blurbs to post as status updates and news, and much more. The ways in which composing has changed result primarily from a few recent technological innovations:

- The speed with which we can share and distribute documents. No longer do we have to take the time to print a document and mail it to others; instead, we can zip it along to others via e-mail or social media spaces.

- The ease with which we can draw on multiple media in one document. Word processing applications, for instance, allow writers to incorporate images. Web page creation spaces encourage composers to embed links to video-sharing sites like YouTube.

- Access to a range of media and materials. When writers wanted to compose a multimodal document before computer software made it easy to do so, they would have to physically cut and paste—with scissors and glue—to embed images in a textual document. Today, electronic copy-and-paste functions allow writers to almost seamlessly pull media from different online spaces and move those media across applications.

Together, these changes provide a broader context for composing *and* for sharing texts. Both the composers of centuries-old manuscripts and the composers of days-old YouTube videos thought about their purposes for communicating, the audiences they were trying to reach, the technology available to them at the time, and which modes were most useful in communicating their ideas.

MM1-e Composing in college

Most academic work involves producing traditional written pages that demonstrate certain elements of good writing: attention to your purpose and your audience; clear thesis statements; strong, well-formed paragraphs; evidence that might include citations and examples; bibliographies or works cited pages; and so on. Across academic disciplines, you'll be expected to approach, understand, and analyze different types of multimodal texts as well.

1. $-5y + 3 = 2 (4y + 12)$

2. $\frac{4}{x^2 - 2x} - \frac{2}{x - 2} = -\frac{1}{2}$

3. $x\sqrt{x} = -x$

4. $|x - a| = a^2 - x^2$

5. $4x^2 + 1 - 2x^2 + 2 = 8$

6. $\log_2 (2x - 1) + x = \log_4 (144)$

7. $\begin{cases} x^2 + y^2 = 17 + 2x \\ (x - 1)^2 + (y - 8)^2 = 34 \end{cases}$

FIGURE 1–5 A MULTI-MODAL TEXT FROM A MATH COURSE.
(*Source:* umsolver.com)

For instance, in math courses, you will encounter equations that include not only numbers but also a range of shapes and figures with particular meaning (Figure 1–5). In a geology or physics course, you might study images that show various movements of the earth's crust (Figure 1–6). In an art history course, you might encounter collages by famous artists and be expected to interrogate them, analyze their meaning, and talk about your response to them (Figure 1–7).

In a variety of college courses, you'll also be expected to plan, outline, and create different types of multimodal texts.

FIGURE 1–6 A MULTIMODAL TEXT FROM A GEOLOGY COURSE. (*Source:* US Geological Survey)

FIGURE 1–7 A MULTIMODAL TEXT FROM AN ART HISTORY COURSE. (*Source:* Gilbert Mayer)

In an introduction to economics course, you might be asked to work in a group to prepare and present a slide show analyzing financial trends.

For an English class, you might be asked to write weekly blog posts in response to assigned readings.

In a biology class, you might be assigned to photograph a particular area over time to construct a visual record of the changes in foliage.

Constructing each of these multimodal texts—a slide show, a blog, a visual record—will require you to think critically and carefully about the different elements you might include (sound, video, charts, photographs, data, words) and how to compose with audience, purpose, organization, clarity, and responsibility in mind.

MM1-f Composing beyond college

College isn't the only place where you might have to analyze and produce multimodal texts. You may, for example, encounter public service ads like the one in Figure 1–8, which combines words and an image

FIGURE 1–8 A MULTIMODAL PUBLIC SERVICE AD. (*Source:* Sonda Dawes)

to prompt you to think about making an emergency plan for yourself and your family. Or you may be part of a community group hosting a fundraising event, for which you'll have to create eye-catching, compelling flyers to attract both sponsors and participants.

Knowing how to produce multimodal texts will be an asset as you start to look for a job. In a 2009 document called "Workplace Writing Skills," educator Christine Polk pointed out that although businesses and organizations rely on efficient and effective communication to profit and thrive, many people struggle to write effectively in the workplace. Job ads — seeking everything from engineering architects to park rangers to grocery store managers — often emphasize the ways in which companies and organizations value candidates who can effectively communicate in multimodal ways. Job candidates today may be expected to produce projects like these:

technical reports that include data or diagrams

planning documents that communicate the rationale for and placement of products in a retail environment

announcements to the public that include text and maps or illustrations

training videos for customers or new employees

Web site content to draw in clients or customers

Analyzing and composing multimodal texts in college can give you the practice you need to communicate effectively in civic, personal, or professional situations in the future.

MM1-g What this book offers

This book is anchored by the concepts discussed in the previous sections: that is, how composing has and hasn't changed, an expanded notion of what composing is, and the importance of composing in and outside of the classroom.

This book offers the following:

a process for analyzing multimodal texts

a vocabulary for analyzing multimodal texts

a process for producing multimodal texts

a close look at two students' multimodal composing processes

a way of thinking about the relation between analyzing and producing multimodal texts

Sections MM1 through MM6 will help you hone your skills of analysis as you explore different types of modes and texts. Sections MM7 through MM15 will help you think about the best processes, practices, and tools for conveying your own ideas in a multimodal composition.

Keep in mind that effective compositions transcend specific software programs and digital spaces. If you can adopt the habits of carefully analyzing and crafting different types of texts, you will become a flexible, smart communicator who knows how to select the best tool for the job and the best techniques for the composing task at hand.

MM1-h A toolkit for analyzing and composing multimodal texts

As a first step in looking at multimodal texts, you need to learn to identify the different modes a composer is using and to examine them separately. Sections MM2 through MM6 ask you to read and analyze written words, sounds, static images, moving images, and multimodal texts. The book includes a toolkit that helps you evaluate individual modes and multimodal compositions. You will learn to think in terms of What? How? Who? and Why? as you answer questions like these in sections MM2 through MM6:

Genre. What kind of text is it? A slide show? An audio essay? An advertisement?

Features. How would you describe the elements of the text? What styles and treatments has the composer used to create emphasis, maintain clarity, or inspire feeling?

Purpose and audience. What is the text doing? For what reason was the text created? Who is the intended reader/viewer/listener?

Meaning. What is your interpretation of the text? (Keep in mind that your interpretation—your take on the meaning—may differ from the composer's intended message.)

Sections MM2 through MM6 include specific advice about how to apply these tools to different types of texts—those composed of written words, sounds, static (or still) images, or moving images—and to compositions that combine these modes.

≡ MM2 Analyzing written words

When written words appear alone in a document, it's clear that they have a message to convey. In much academic writing, the design of the document seems "invisible," whether the message is simple or complex. In other words, academic writers often avoid decorative or unusual fonts (such as Comic Sans) or font treatments (such as color)

Analyzing written words

Genre

In what kind of document do the words appear? A brochure? A letter? An essay?

Features

Is the text in a single font or a variety of fonts? How would you describe the font(s)? Are there different colors and sizes? Do you notice bold, italic, or highlighted words? Are any words animated—do they move or change in shape, color, or size?

Purpose and audience

What is the purpose of the text? Is it meant to teach, guide, warn, entertain, or provoke the reader?

Who is the intended audience for the written words? Readers who will take time to read them? Or readers who will need to grasp the message quickly? Are they consumers, children, workers, fans, protesters, commuters, or a mixed group?

Meaning

How do genre, features, purpose, and audience work together to convey a message? How do you interpret the use of the written words? (Keep in mind that your interpretation—your take on the meaning—may differ from the composer's intended message.)

that might distract readers or discourage them from taking the message seriously.

When used thoughtfully, however, different fonts and features can add meaning to written words and can be especially appropriate in multimodal compositions. Whether created for academic, professional, or creative purposes, multimodal compositions may use a variety of treatments and even animations to boost or otherwise alter the meaning of written words. When you're analyzing how written words function in a composition, consider the questions in the chart on page MM-14.

MM2-a Genre: In what kind of document do the written words appear?

Often you'll form ideas about the content of a document as soon as you look at it, before you read a single word. Determining what type of document you're dealing with is a key step in analyzing the words within the document.

Take a look at the document thumbnails in Figure 2–1. Although you can't read all of the words, thinking about where the words appear and how the overall document is formatted will give you a sense of what kind of information the words might convey.

Look closely at image (a) on page MM-16. How much space appears between the lines of text? What do you think is the function of the words in the upper left corner? What likely appears centered after those words? Answers to these questions tell us that these words are probably part of a traditional essay, with space devoted to the author's name, course, and date in the top left and the title centered on the line below.

Now consider image (d). How are the words arranged? The way the words are chunked together and placed in columns reveals at a glance that they are words in a menu. The arrangement of words in the document tells us what kind of information to expect—a list of foods organized by course: appetizers, entrees, and desserts. Imagine trying to read a menu without categories or labels, in which all the content is lumped together without being organized or easily identifiable.

MM2-b Features: What do the words look like?

We're so used to gathering meaning from written words simply by reading them that it may seem strange at first to analyze what the words look like. Words can, however, appear in a variety of sizes, shapes, colors, styles, and static or animated configurations. One of the first things

(a)

(b)   (*Source:* FEMA)

(c)   (d)

FIGURE 2–1 EVERYDAY TEXTS.

to note is the font (or *typeface*) in which the words appear. Graphic designers often talk about fonts as the "voice" of the page.

When considering the effect that font choice has on a text, think about what adjectives you might associate with a particular font. For instance, you might describe Comic Sans as *fun*, *childish*, and *handwritten*. Even if you have never seen Comic Sans before, the scrawled feeling of the irregular shapes and angles of the letters will call such adjectives to mind. Understanding the visual aspects of written texts requires that we pay attention to the shape and the feel of the typeface itself.

What adjectives would you associate with the following typefaces?

Bauhaus 93

Broadway

COPPERPLATE GOTHIC

Kunstler Script

Forte

Times New Roman

As you consider the font, think about any treatment or formatting applied to it. For example, how has capitalization been applied? Are the words in *sentence case* (standard capitalization for a sentence) or some other case?

> Sentence case appears with an initial capital letter and a period at the end.
>
> all lowercase is written in all lowercase letters.
>
> ALL CAPS IS WRITTEN IN ALL CAPITAL LETTERS.
>
> mIxED cAsE iS a mIxTuRe oF cApItAL aNd LoweRCaSe leTterS.

What do you associate with each of these capitalization styles? In academic writing, sentences are usually presented in sentence case, and all caps is usually used only for headings or subheadings. In informal, creative, or multimodal texts, all caps might be used for emphasis or to signify "yelling" or some other strong emotion.

When considering the features of words, check for typographic elements, such as text set in bold, italics, quotation marks, color, or different sizes or text set with strikethrough or highlighting. Each of these elements shapes the way readers interact with the text. Words that convey a warning, for example, might be set in red, a color associated with fire and stop signs. If different font sizes are used in a text, readers will assume that larger words are more important than smaller ones.

MM2-c Purpose and audience: What is the purpose of the written words? Who is the intended reader?

Take a look at the text on the next page, a letter by Gerald Gainley, the CEO of Canyon Cove Chemicals. The company wants to expand its facilities; however, the local government has blocked that expansion because of concern over environmental damage and unchecked

LETTER WRITTEN TO A SPECIFIC AUDIENCE

Dear Springfield and All of the Supporters of Canyon Cove Chemicals:

I write to you to convey my dismay and disappointment with the city council, our elected governing body.

Earlier today, as you may know, the city council, under the leadership of Stanley Burris, decided to block the development of a new Canyon Cove Chemicals refining facility on Oak Wood Road, just ten miles north of our city center and north of the city offices in which this decision was made.

This decision was prefaced by a self-serving, self-promotional, unnecessarily accusatory statement made by Council Chair Burris, who attacked Canyon Cove Chemicals.

Canyon Cove Chemicals has been devoted to and supportive of our local community for more than seventy-five years. We have sponsored the little league teams on which our children have played. We have donated funds to build the playgrounds and skate park at which our youngsters enjoy outdoor activities. We have allocated a part of our annual revenue to supporting our high schoolers in continuing their education at our two area community colleges.

For Council Chair Burris to accuse the company of greed and overdevelopment is not only a travesty but also a threat to our fine community.

Better facilities for Canyon Cove Chemicals will mean more revenue and will provide our company with the ability to participate even more in supporting our community.

"I PERSONALLY GUARANTEE THAT CANYON COVE CHEMICALS, IF OUR FACILITIES EXPANSION MOVES FORWARD, WILL DONATE TWICE AS MUCH IN THE COMING YEAR AS WE DONATED LAST YEAR."

I will stake my reputation and the reputation of the company I so proudly run on this claim.

Gerald Gainley
CEO, Canyon Cove Chemicals

industrial growth in the area. In response, Gainley distributed this letter to the local media and posted it on the company's Web site.

Why do you think Gainley wrote this letter? What was his purpose in writing it? The CEO addresses the letter to the entire city ("Dear Springfield") and "All of the Supporters of Canyon Cove Chemicals," indicating that he hopes to maintain support for the company despite the fact that it suffered a bad outcome in a city council vote. To be successful, his message needs to appeal to the general public and especially to readers who work for the company, support the company, or are active in local government (as representatives and voters, for example). The letter has to ease their concerns and draw attention to the benefits the company brings to the city. Think about the choices Gainley makes as he tries to accomplish those goals. Consider his words as well as their typographical treatment.

In the letter, Gainley uses two different fonts. Comic Sans looks handwritten and is rarely used in professional communication. Times New Roman is a more standard font, often used in newspapers, books, and other publications. What message does each font convey to the reader? Comic Sans might not be an effective choice for someone who wants to be taken seriously, but a handwritten font does underscore the personal feel of Gainley's communication—he is speaking on behalf of the company, but he's also speaking as someone who has a personal stake in the company and the community. Think about how the effect of the text would be different if all of the words were set in Times New Roman.

Note Gainley's capitalization choices as well. Some statements are in sentence case, and others are in all caps (see p. MM-17). How do you think the CEO wants readers to feel about the all caps statement in quotation marks near the end of his letter? Formatting the statement in all caps adds emphasis and might be intended to convey Gainley's commitment to the words. Perhaps the quotation marks are meant to show that his promise is a quotable statement—one he expects community members to hold him to.

Consider also what the letter is *not*. It's not a television or radio spot. Why do you think Gainley chose a letter to the city to convey his message? Why do you think he sent the letter to local television and radio stations and posted the letter on the company Web site? Gainley could have paid to run television and radio ads to convey this message. Perhaps he felt that a written statement would have a more personal, sincere feel; the letter format allows him to address all residents of Springfield and the surrounding area directly—including those who work for the company or have family members who have benefited from the company's local donations and support. Why do you think he chose not to include any images? He may have felt that a picture would draw attention away from his words or that a picture of himself or the proposed new facility might make it harder for readers to think of him as their peer. His repeated use of the phrase *our community* makes it clear that he counts himself a citizen, not just the head of a company.

MM2-d Meaning: What effect do the words have on the reader?

Given what you know about Gainley's written statement regarding the city council's vote against Canyon Cove Chemicals' plan for expansion, what do you think of Gainley's chosen mode of expression—written words—and his decisions about how to present those words? Do you think his letter had the desired effect?

In an essay for his communications class, student—and Springfield resident—John Nikolakakis wrote the following analysis of Gainley's letter:

> In his letter to the city of Springfield, Gerald Gainley, the CEO of Canyon Cove Chemicals, expresses his "dismay" and, at times, disgust at a recent city council decision, in which the members voted against allowing the company to expand its facilities in north Springfield. He characterizes the city council members as shortsighted and essentially accuses them of putting the city in peril; that is, he doesn't say it directly, but he does imply that the company could move to another city, and then Springfield would lose the support and economic donations of the company. Gainley also makes an interesting promise to the city of Springfield.
>
> Gainley makes two textual choices that are worth attention: his use of fonts and his use of all capital letters (ALL CAPS). Gainley has formatted his letter almost entirely in Comic Sans. The font looks handwritten and may be perceived as bubbly and childish. Some of Gainley's critics have charged that the use of Comic Sans in this situation is inappropriate. If he were writing more formally, that criticism would be totally on the mark, but he wants the letter to be personal and to make him seem like a friend to its readers. The average Springfield citizen, Gainley's audience, will likely feel that the font is approachable and appropriate for a personal appeal.
>
> Interestingly, one sentence in the letter is not in Comic Sans. When Gainley pledges that Canyon Cove Chemicals "WILL DONATE TWICE AS MUCH IN THE COMING YEAR AS WE DONATED LAST YEAR" if the company is allowed to expand its facilities, the promise is set in Times New Roman and ALL CAPS. Both of these formatting choices show that Gainley wants the statement to stand out from the

rest of his letter and carry an official weight; he regards these words as a solemn oath to his readers.

When you analyze written words, it's important to consider the composer's choices of document type, font, and formatting. These choices may enhance or work against the composer's intended message. As you develop your own interpretation of the overall meaning of the text, think about how genre, features, purpose, and intended audience affect the reader's experience.

ACTIVITY MM2–1: Your understanding

Find a campaign banner or bumper sticker from a campus, local, or national election. Write a paragraph in which you analyze the features of the text you've selected. What font is used? What meaning does the font convey? What methods of emphasis are used with the text (for example, boldface or underline)? Think about the intended purpose and audience for the campaign piece and determine what message the text and the piece as a whole convey about the political candidate.

MM3 Analyzing sound

Sound is everywhere. Birds chirp, cars honk, music plays. Sometimes it's just in the background, but sometimes it's used for deliberate effect. Think about how sound functions in gambling casinos. Until recently, slot machines dispensed coins to winners. The noise of coins dropping from the winning machine was deliberately magnified so that other gamblers would notice and be encouraged to continue gambling. Most casinos have shifted to a receipt-based system—the machine generates a receipt that a gambler can turn in for cash. Because the sound of coins dropping out of a machine is so effective, however, machines still make that sound, even though no coins are involved. Sound can convey meaning on its own or enhance meaning when combined with other modes. When analyzing sound, consider the questions in the chart on page MM-22.

MM3-a Genre: What kind of sound is it?

Although we're surrounded by sound, we don't give it much thought most of the time. Even the music we listen to is often just background for other activities, unless we're studying music. But sound influences those who can hear it, even if they're not fully aware of the effect.

Analyzing sound

Genre

What kind of sound is it? Is it speech, music, or a noise associated with a particular object, for example?

Features

How would you describe the sound? Is it loud or quiet? Does it have a high or a low pitch? Is its pacing fast or slow? Is it in the background or in the foreground? Are certain sounds louder or quieter than others?

Purpose and audience

What is the purpose of the sound? Does it provide atmosphere? Is it accompanying something else, such as an image? Or is it the main or only mode of communication?

Who is the intended audience for the sound? A single listener with headphones? A room full of people? Children or adults? Experts or nonexperts? Sympathizers or opponents?

Meaning

How do genre, features, purpose, and audience work together to convey a message? How do you interpret the use of sound? (Keep in mind that your interpretation—your take on the meaning—may differ from the composer's intended message.)

Consider the music in a movie, which usually consists of the score (original music composed for the movie) and licensed music (clips from songs or orchestral works, for example). After you watch a movie, a few catchy tunes or notes might stick in your head, but for the most part you won't be able to describe what the music was like throughout the movie. And yet successful music will affect the way you perceive the entire film. A trumpet solo might make a scene or character seem more heroic, for example. Soft music might encourage viewers to feel thoughtful in a somber moment. Loud, fast-paced music might accompany a chase scene to enhance the sense of speed or urgency.

Music is just one type of sound that can be part of a movie soundtrack. To think about how sound as a whole functions in a composition such as a movie, you first need to identify what kinds of sounds are involved. A soundtrack can include dialogue—one or more people talking. It can also include sound effects—sounds associated with particular animals or objects, such as birdsong to signal morning or cars honking to provide a busy urban atmosphere. And the music might be a scene-setting background melody or part of a performance happening on the screen. You can use these categories to identify types of sounds in audio-only or multimodal compositions and to examine what purposes individual sound elements serve in a larger composition.

In movies, sound often provides a supporting role. Unless it's dialogue, sound is usually in the background, enhancing the action on-screen. What about sound in compositions that are strictly audio? A podcast, for example, can be an audio-only file designed to be downloaded from the Internet and listened to on a computer or portable music player.

In one composition class, students were asked to create a podcast on a compelling local issue. Before they wrote or recorded anything of their own, they analyzed podcasts created by other students. First-year student Talia Souza chose to analyze a podcast titled "Hustlers, Street Vendors, and Farmers," in which the author, King Anyi Howell, visited a Los Angeles farmers' market geared toward black customers. Souza knew she wanted to do something related to food and farming, and she was interested in Howell's focus on selling food in one community. Howell's podcast offered a rich mix of spoken text and background sounds for Souza to analyze.

Souza listened several times, first for content, then a second time to take careful notes on the content. The third time through, she listened for the various background sounds and made some notes on the podcast as a whole:

Narration by Molly Adams (welcome and intro)

Then upbeat, jazzy music (horns and drums?) plays under Molly's voice

Music fades out as Molly introduces the piece

King Anyi Howell's piece starts with the sound of two men talking, outside—can hear what sounds like car traffic and people walking by; can hear the rustling of one of the men putting something in a bag; can hear the men talking about the cost of what's being bagged

Howell's voice comes in over the two men talking, explaining that he's at a farmers' market

Howell describes the busy intersection (can hear street sounds in the background)

Howell introduces a young woman, a shopper who describes the market

ONLINE hackerhandbooks.com/multimodal
> Multimodal resources > Podcast
> King Anyi Howell, "Hustlers, Street
Vendors, and Farmers"

Howell describes a group of vendors, with men talking in the background

Sounds in piece: narration (by writers); clips of people talking; music; street noises

Whether you're analyzing sound in conjunction with other modes (when it's used in a movie, for example) or on its own (as in an audio podcast), it's a good idea to listen to the soundtrack or audio track several times. So that you can focus on the sound, do not take notes until the second or third time you listen. If there are layers of sound (talking in the foreground and street noise in the background, for example), first examine those elements separately and then think about how they work together.

MM3-b Features: Examine the pitch, pace, and volume of the sound

When analyzing sound, you'll also want to consider qualities like pitch, pace, and volume. *Pitch* is a measure of the highness or lowness of sound. A child's voice, for example, is often high-pitched, whereas a lion's roar is low-pitched. In speech, pitch provides inflection, which affects how listeners interpret the words being spoken. A statement that pitches upward at the end usually sounds like a question. If you've seen the movie *Ferris Bueller's Day Off*, you probably remember the scene in which a teacher (played by Ben Stein) takes attendance. The teacher's monotonous delivery of the students' names reflects his overall persona in the classroom: flat and boring. The camera pans to show his students falling asleep before class has even begun. This serves as a humorous justification for Ferris's skipping class.

Pitch can offer valuable clues about what's happening in a segment or piece. When people become frightened or stressed, the pitch of their voice tends to go higher. Higher pitch in movie music can emphasize anxiety and fright on-screen and inspire those feelings in the audience.

In addition to pitch, think about pace and volume when analyzing sound. Does the sound seem to be fast or slow (*pace*)? Is one sound louder or softer than another (*volume*)? Does the pace or volume of a particular sound change? What is the effect of any changes on the listener? In the movie *Jaws*, pace and volume work together to create suspense. A simple set of tones plays when the shark is near. These tones get faster and louder as the shark gets closer to an unsuspecting swimmer, encouraging a sense of panic in the audience.

MM3-c Purpose and audience: What is sound being used for? Who is the intended listener?

When people use sound to convey a message, they usually make deliberate choices based on their intended message and the listeners they're trying to reach. When you analyze sound, it's important to think about the composer's choices. Consider King Anyi Howell's podcast, described on page MM-23. Why did Howell choose to create a podcast rather than make a movie to be watched or write a story to be read? Perhaps Howell imagined that a single listener, surrounded by the sounds of the podcast, would be more absorbed in the story than a viewer distracted by images on-screen or a reader with only words on paper to consider. A listener has to imagine the images; the background sounds Howell provides along with the spoken story makes those images vivid and absorbing.

MM3-d Meaning: What effect does sound have on the listener?

When you analyze sound, it's important to consider the composer's choice of sounds and the pitch, pace, and volume of those sounds. These choices may enhance or work against the composer's intended message. The following is an excerpt from Talia Souza's analysis of sound in King Anyi Howell's podcast, which Souza wrote in preparation for creating her own podcast.

> This podcast is hosted by Molly Adams, who provides a brief introduction with upbeat, jazzy music playing in the background. When the introduction is over, the main podcast begins. In it, King Anyi Howell uses three types of sounds. The first is human voice. Howell narrates the podcast, explaining the scene to listeners and interacting with the people he recorded for the podcast. He also includes segments of people talking, interacting with each other, and responding to his questions.
>
> The second type of sound is background noises, which include street sounds that help set the scene: car engine revving, cars whooshing by, plastic grocery bags crinkling, and change jingling. The third type of sound is music playing. Rather than using recorded studio music, Howell includes the sounds of live music being played at the farmers' market, so listeners can hear not only the music but also other noise, such as people talking. This makes the music feel more authentic and shows how the music is part of the market scene. At the end of the podcast,

Adams provides a conclusion, and the lively, jazzy music plays underneath her voice again.

What I took from this podcast that I want to apply in my podcast is to interview people and include other people's voices. It's one thing for me to say that people believe a particular thing or hold a certain opinion, but it's more compelling to include other people's voices saying what they believe. This worked really well in Howell's podcast. Also, music and sounds can enhance a podcast and help listeners better imagine a place. Right now, my plan is to do a podcast about the dining options in the student union and how healthy they are (or aren't). If I record in the student union and interview people there, it will help my listeners imagine the space. Another aspect I liked was that Howell included a clear introduction and conclusion. I don't want someone else to do my intro and conclusion, as Adams did in Howell's podcast, but I like the idea of setting up the main part of the podcast and then concluding it at the end.

Although a composer's choices about the type of sound and its qualities are usually deliberate, they don't necessarily convey the same meaning to all listeners in all contexts. They may not work the way the composer intended, or they may carry additional meanings the composer didn't anticipate. As you develop an interpretation about the meaning of sound on its own or as part of a multimodal piece, be sure to consider genre, features, purpose, and audience together.

ACTIVITY MM3–1: Your understanding

Online movie trailers, used to advertise and preview movies, are approximately three to four minutes long. Television ads for movies are typically much shorter and limited in terms of how they grab viewers' attention and condense the story line. In your Web browser, conduct a search for "movie trailer." Scan the results and select a movie trailer to watch. Choose a full-length trailer so that you'll have more audio material to work with for this activity.

Close your eyes and listen to the trailer; do not watch it. Closing your eyes will allow you to focus on just the sounds. As you listen, identify the different sounds you're hearing and think about what function they serve, what feelings they evoke in you, how they are sequenced together, and so on. Then watch the trailer. You'll hear the sounds, see the sequences of images, and perhaps begin to note how they fit together. As you play the trailer a third time, create a list—somewhat like Souza's list on page MM-23—of the different sounds you hear. Once you have a list, identify each sound by genre and think about how the sound helps convey meaning in the trailer. Create a chart like the one on page MM-27 to record your notes. Consider adapting the chart and using it to document sounds in the different types of texts you study.

STUDENT NOTES ON A *SHREK* MOVIE TRAILER

Time	Sound	Purpose
:02-:10	man singing with symphony-like music	establishes context; creates opening for trailer
:11-:20	prince talking to big mirror hanging on the wall, mirror talking back; crowd of knights gasp	helps to set plot; prince's voice is kind of pompous-sounding; sound of gasps creates sense of disbelief
:21-:22	knight smashes small mirror	shows that prince is malicious! sound of mirror shattering contrasts with the opening singing/music
:23-:24	knight turns back to talk to big mirror	establishes a threat!
:25-:33	different symphony-like music with voice-over explaining plot of movie	continues to explain plot of movie; narrator's voice-over rhymes and feels storytelling-like

☰ MM4 Analyzing static images

On any given day, you'll encounter images on billboards, road signs, maps, posters, flyers, brochures, product packaging, logos, advertisements, and so on. Images are all around us. Whether they're selling a product, conveying a message, sending a warning, or informing us about a law, they all have something to say. Although often we don't consider them carefully or critically, most images are designed to plant ideas or influence our decisions. When you want to analyze an image—to pick apart its message and how it works—think about the questions in the chart on page MM-30.

MM4-a Genre: What kind of image is it?

One of the first things you'll want to do when analyzing a static (or still) image is to determine what kind of image it is. Certain types of images do certain work and should be used for specific purposes. Consider the images in the chart on pages MM-28 and MM-29. The genre of each example is given along with a common use for each type of image.

Think about an image you see every day—perhaps a billboard or subway map you see on your way to work or class. What type of image is it? What does it mean to you? How might it work differently—or not work at all—if it were a different type of image?

Genre: What kind of image is it?

Photograph

Photographs can be used to represent specific places, people, or things.

Sketch

Sketches provide an artistic rendering of places, people, or things.

Map

Maps show specific locations or routes to locations.

Clip art

Clip art can provide generic representations of a places, people, or things.

Sources (top to bottom): Straga; Danussa; Jami Garrison; Sapik.

Chart

Charts provide data in a format that is easy to read at a glance.

Diagram

Diagrams can be used to represent parts or functions of an object or process that are not usually visible.

Source (for both images): US Geological Survey.

Take a look at Figure 4–1, an image included in a set of instructions for applying women's hair dye. The image is a sketch, meant to represent any woman who might use the hair dye. If a photograph of a particular woman were used instead, viewers who look nothing like her might not be able to relate to her. But by using a sketch with generic features, the manufacturers are inviting all prospective users to imagine themselves following the instructions and using the hair dye carefully.

FIGURE 4–1 IMAGE ACCOMPANYING A SET OF INSTRUCTIONS. *(Source:* RetroClipArt)

Analyzing static images

Genre

What kind of image is it? Is it a photograph, cartoon, painting, map, chart, or diagram, for example?

Features

Is the image in color or black and white? In what context does the image appear? For example, is it large format (perhaps a poster) or small format (such as food packaging)? If the image has depth, what elements are in the foreground and the background? What is the perspective of the image (is it a close-up or an aerial view, for example)?

Purpose and audience

What is the purpose of the image? Is it accompanied by other modes, such as sound or written words? Or does it convey meaning on its own? Is it meant to teach, guide, warn, entertain, or provoke the viewer?

Who is the intended audience for the image? Someone zooming by in a car with only seconds to process the message? Someone who will spend time examining the image? Children or adults? Experts or nonexperts?

Meaning

How do genre, features, purpose, and audience work together to convey a message? How do you interpret the use of the image? (Keep in mind that your interpretation—your take on the meaning—may differ from the composer's intended message.)

MM4-b Features: Examine the context, perspective, and elements of the image

As you analyze an image, think about the context in which it appears. In other words, what surrounds the image? Is it an illustration in a book, a photo in a magazine, a warning in a building or vehicle, a painting in a gallery? How is the image presented? Do you have time to look at it, or do you need to absorb its meaning quickly? Does it need to be interesting, or straightforward? Should it make you want to buy something, find out more about something, or avoid something?

Think about images in product instructions. Because consumers usually want the assembly or use of a product to be as simple as possible, instructions typically use basic or generic images to illustrate steps, tips, or cautions. It can be difficult, however, to convey a clear message with a simple illustration.

In a technical writing course, students were asked to select a set of product instructions and choose one image from the instructions to analyze. Working with a one-page instruction sheet that came with an electric blanket he had recently purchased, Arman Chavva focused on the image of a dog's head with a circle and slash drawn over it.

The image I chose to analyze in this set of instructions appeared in a list titled "Instructions for Use." The image was next to item #17, "Do not use with pets."

I chose this image because it is ineffective. The image shows a specific breed of dog, so a literal translation might be "no German shepherds." "No German shepherds" does not mean the same thing as "Do not use with pets."

Source: Boffi.

The technical writer who created the instructions was right in using the circle and slash, which in most cultures means "NO" or "DO NOT." However, the writer should probably have used a more general image to send the message of "pets." A photograph of a specific breed of dog doesn't send a general message. Instead, the author could have used simple shapes or clip art of a bird, a cat, and a dog, with the circle and slash over the shapes. The simple shapes would make users think of animals in general rather than one particular animal or one particular breed of animal.

In addition to thinking about the context of an image, you'll want to consider its perspective. All images present a point of view.

The extreme low-angle shot of a dandelion in Figure 4–2 challenges our notions of this summertime weed. The photographer has shot the dandelion from underneath—from the point of view of the grass or the earth—and has made it look majestic rather than mundane.

It's often helpful to think about perspective and elements of an image together. These are often referred to collectively as the *composition* of the

FIGURE 4–2 PHOTOGRAPH SHOWING AN UNUSUAL PERSPECTIVE. (*Source:* Dleonis)

image. If the image you're analyzing is a photograph of a man, you should ask yourself whether the man appears close up or far away. Is his whole body in view, or is only part of him visible? Are you viewing him head-on, from the side, from above, or from below? What about other elements in the photo? Is the man in front of, behind, or surrounded by anything? How do the perspective and the elements affect your impression of the man in the picture? For example, if the perspective makes it seem as though you're viewing him from above and perhaps through a door frame, he may appear powerless or even trapped.

Consider, for example, the well-known photograph *Migrant Mother*, taken by Dorothea Lange in 1936 (Figure 4–3). The woman looks slightly to the side of the camera; her eyes don't meet the viewer's gaze. Her expression might be troubled, but she doesn't look to the viewer (or the photographer) for help. She is surrounded by her children, whose faces are turned from the camera and buried in her arms. It is also worth noting what's *not* in the photo. We don't see a father or any other adults. These absences lead us to believe that this woman cares for these children alone.

FIGURE 4–3
MIGRANT MOTHER **BY DOROTHEA LANGE, 1936.** (*Source:* Library of Congress/Farm Security Administration)

MM4-c Purpose and audience: What is the image meant to convey? Who is the intended viewer?

Think about the perspective and the elements of the *Migrant Mother* photograph. Why do you think the photographer took this photo? What is the photographer's purpose? What is your overall impression of the scene? Many viewers will conclude that the woman in the photograph represents strength in the face of hardship and despair.

Part of analyzing an image involves asking *Why did the artist create this image?* Sometimes responses to this question are left to interpretation; at other times, however, determining purpose can mean doing research. A bit of research would reveal that Lange was one of a number of photographers commissioned by the US government to travel throughout the United States and document the lives of Americans during the Dust Bowl in the 1930s. Her photographs, which captured the poverty and despair of people uprooted from their homes, were intended to inspire and educate. But inspire and educate whom? It could be said that her audience, or intended viewers, were both contemporary Americans not directly affected by the ecological disaster and future generations. Asking *why* and *for whom* can be helpful in determining the message and the meaning of an image.

MM4-d Meaning: What effect does the image have on the viewer?

As you develop an interpretation about the meaning of an image on its own or as part of a multimodal piece, be sure to consider genre, features, purpose, and audience together. Although a composer's choices about the type of image and its features are usually deliberate, they don't necessarily convey the same meaning to all viewers in all contexts. They may not work the way the composer intended, or they may carry additional meanings the composer didn't anticipate.

Consider student writer Ian Washburn's analysis of two news photos showing the toppling of a Saddam Hussein statue in 2003, during the United States' war with Iraq.

> The two photos tell two different stories about what happened in Firdos Square in Baghdad in April 2003. At the time the event occurred, I was stationed nearby in Baghdad. Major media outlets, including BBC, CNN, Fox News, and others, ran photos like the top image in fig.1 [see next page]—showing a cheering, chanting, supportive crowd. The US government itself shared some photos from a similar perspective.
>
> Later, however, other photos from the day emerged on the Web, like the bottom image in fig. 1, which some bloggers and commentators used as proof in claiming that

Fig. 1. Two views of the toppling of a Saddam Hussein statue, Baghdad, 2003 (UPI/Newscom; Nickelsberg).

the toppling of the statue was a staged "media event." What is clear in these pictures is that US tanks were stationed at each exit into and out of the area and that the crowd was pushed close to the statue and photos were shot primarily from behind the crowd, to create an illusion of a very big gathering (estimates indicate that about a hundred Iraqi citizens were there for the toppling of the statue).

The event did happen, and the event was important in the war against terror. However, the ways that the photographs were taken and presented tell a different story about *how* the events happened that day.

In his analysis, Washburn interprets the differences in the images by studying both the perspective and the point of view of each. He also hints at the purpose of the image in his discussion of the initially released photo. Examining static images in this way helps the viewer think carefully about a composer's message and consider possible meanings.

ACTIVITY MM4–1: Your understanding

This image of Barack Obama originally appeared on posters during the 2008 presidential campaign. Consider the context of the image. How was this image used? How was it distributed? In what larger cultural and historical context was it important? Who was the intended audience?

Next think about how the image was transformed by various artists in other contexts. Consider the following examples. (You may find additional examples online by conducting an image search with terms like *obama* and *hope* and *poster* and *remix*.)

What effect does each image have on the viewer? Who do you think is the intended audience for each image? Why do you think the artists chose to invoke the Obama campaign poster when creating each of these images? What can you find out about the cultural and historical context in which these images were created?

Source: Shepard Fairey

Sources (left to right): Michael Ian Weinfeld; Timothy P. Doyle; Mike Rosulek

MM5 Analyzing moving images

Today almost anyone can make a video and post it to YouTube. The opportunity is fairly new, however; before the Web and digital cameras, much of the video seen in an everyday context was "professional grade"—television shows, television ads, and movies, for instance. Today's composing tools allow users to craft moving images that can range from animated GIFs to moving type to digital video; the technology for making video has changed, and the term *moviemaker* is broader than it used to be.

The images in Figure 5–1 were created in 1887 by Eadweard Muybridge. To create the sequence of images, Muybridge placed a series of cameras in a row, with strings attached to the shutters. As the horse's legs hit the strings, a photo was snapped. In sequence, the photos show the physical movement of a galloping horse. This example is not necessarily a "moving image" as we think of it today, but it is the first photographic representation of a sequence of movement. What started out as a bet between friends—*Does a galloping horse ever have all four hooves off the ground at the same time?*—led to the birth of a new technology.

FIGURE 5–1 A SEQUENCE OF STILL IMAGES THAT REPRESENTS MOVEMENT. (*Source:* Library of Congress Prints and Photographs Division)

Analyzing moving images

Genre

What kind of moving image is it? Is it a feature-length film, a brief home-shot video clip, an animated sequence in a video game?

Features

What is the viewer's perspective? How are the elements of the images arranged? Do the images change quickly or slowly? Are any special effects used? How are the moving images combined with sound or words?

Purpose and audience

What is the purpose of the moving image? What did the composer hope to achieve with it?

Who is the intended audience? A viewer watching alone on a computer monitor? A large audience in a theater? Consumers? Students?

Meaning

How do genre, features, purpose, and audience work together to convey a message? How do you interpret the use of elements in the moving image? (Keep in mind that your interpretation—your take on the meaning—may differ from the composer's intended message.)

Today moving images entertain us, inform us, teach us, and encourage us to spend money. When you start to look critically at moving images, consider the questions in the chart above.

MM5-a Genre: What kind of moving image is it?

When it comes to moving images, the term *genre* can be used to describe thematic differences among feature films, such as "adventure" or "romantic comedy" or "documentary." Using terminology like this provides a convenient way to classify movies.

Because your examination of moving images may go beyond feature films, however, this section uses the term *genre* to discuss format rather than theme. Moving images can range from simple animated sequences to complex full-length movies. The chart on page MM-38 defines common genres.

Common genres (types) of moving images

GENRE	DESCRIPTION
Flip book	A physical animation created by drawing the same figure with slight changes on multiple pages and then flipping the pages to create an illusion of motion.
Simple animation	A computer-based animation using a series of still images and applying software techniques to make the images appear to be moving.
Stop-motion animation	An animated video effect created by moving an object a small amount at a time, photographing it each time, and then sequencing the images together to create a sense of movement.
Photo-realistic animation	Animation created through complex drawing, drafting, and computer rendering. The movies *Toy Story* and *Shrek* are examples of this kind of animation.
Playable animation	Animation sequences created by software designers and programmers for the specific purpose of interaction by viewers or players. These can be as simple as banner ads that change when viewers hover a cursor over the ad or sequences in longer video games.
Video clip	A short video that is typically created with a cell phone camera or a digital camera and posted, often unedited, to a site such as YouTube. Some video clips are edited before posting, especially those used for instructional or news purposes.
Film	Usually a feature-length motion picture, or movie. Perhaps the most common genre of moving image, film is used to bring fiction and nonfiction to life for entertainment and education.

MM5-b Features: Perspective, composition, and editing

As you analyze moving images, think about features such as perspective, composition, and editing. As a viewer of the moving image, you occupy a certain perspective. When viewing an instructional video, you are often the novice or student watching a teacher or trainer who walks viewers through a series of steps or a process for doing something. When you play a video game, you are often one of the characters in the game. Typically when you watch a movie, you are an observer, completely outside the action of the moving images. Perspective influences how viewers perceive what's happening on-screen.

For an assignment that required students to choose a movie and analyze one production aspect or element, Ellen Yin chose *Cloverfield*, a moving image that offers viewers an unusual perspective. The following is an excerpt from her essay.

> For most movies, the audience is supposed to be unaware of the camera. Viewers are supposed to have an experience of watching the movie and forgetting the existence of a camera filming and a stage, set, crew, and director. When we watch the Harry Potter movies, it's as if we're there observing the changes in the characters. When we watch *Transformers: Dark of the Moon*, it's as if we're there witnessing the battles between the Autobots and the Decepticons. The 2008 movie *Cloverfield*, however, was shot in a way that differs from most major movies; *Cloverfield* was shot primarily from a first-person perspective. The premise of the movie is that viewers are watching footage captured on a digital video camera found abandoned in New York City after the recorded action. This choice has a huge impact on viewers. Rather than being something we can overlook, the camera becomes a key element in the experience of watching the movie. The viewer feels as if she or he is holding the camera. By offering this first-person, handheld, low-quality perspective, *Cloverfield* forces viewers to join the main characters in their fight for survival.

Cloverfield is an example of a movie shot from a first-person perspective—making viewers feel as if they are there, experiencing the action themselves; the camera functions as the viewers' eyes (see Figure 5–2). This technique is sometimes called a *point of view perspective* or *subjective viewpoint*.

Another type of perspective is called *third-person view*. Video games often use this perspective: The "camera" is above and behind the player character, providing a bird's-eye view rather than the character's point of view.

Another quality of moving images to consider is the composition, or the artist's arrangement of the elements of the image—the

FIGURE 5–2 POINT-OF-VIEW PERSPECTIVE FROM THE MOVIE *CLOVERFIELD*.
(*Source:* Moviestore Collection)

people, props, products, and landscape. As a viewer, you might think critically about whether the people in the video seem close to or far away from the camera or close to or far away from other people. Or perhaps there are no people at all. Besides the frame of the movie, TV, or computer screen, can you find other "frames" as well — a window, perhaps, or an archway? Which on-screen elements seem to be emphasized in some way? Also consider what's *not* on-screen. Thinking carefully about what the composer may have left out of a scene could prompt an interesting analysis.

Professional film and TV producers use editing — choosing and sequencing shots — to craft a story and elicit a certain response from viewers. Some amateur video is edited (video-editing software can be inexpensive and easy to learn), and some isn't — usually depending on the composer's purpose and access to technology. When analyzing moving images, consider how editing affects the pace of the action and the narrative. Does the action proceed quickly from one shot to the next, as in a chase scene in an adventure movie? Or is the action more continuous? Does it proceed more slowly, as in a scene in which a character is shown deep in thought and gazing out a train window?

MM5-c Purpose and audience: What are the moving images being used for? Who is the intended viewer?

Creators of moving images make deliberate choices based on their purpose, or reason for creating the work, and on the viewers they're trying to reach. Thinking carefully about a composer's choices can help you understand the work and also help you prepare for making your own choices as a composer of similar works. It's important to ask both *why* the composer decided to convey a message with a moving image and *what* message a composer is trying to convey.

Think about a national news broadcast, for example, which usually involves some combination of desk reporting, field reporting, and presentation of feature reports that were filmed and edited before the broadcast. Why are the various stories handled differently? Why do the producers decide to use moving images to present certain topics? Perhaps previously filmed material is needed because reporters can't get access to the subject at the time of the live broadcast. Maybe the story requires clips from a variety of sources for support, and those can't be pieced together on the spot. Or showing action is more likely to elicit an emotional response than showing a still image while a reporter narrates an event.

Filming and editing ahead of time also allows composers to shape the story for their target audience. Anything that might bore or offend the audience can be removed, and anything that's particularly effective can be emphasized. Next time you watch an edited news feature, think about who the intended audience is and how the feature has been shaped to reach that audience. Take a filmed, edited story about rising gas prices, for example. Many such features include at-the-pump interviews. What do you see in the moving image? How would you describe the people being interviewed—their gender, race, clothing, age? What kinds of cars are they driving: sports cars, minivans, cars in good or poor repair? Do they appear to be driving to work or taking a road-trip vacation? Are they smiling or frowning? Are they holding anything in their hands? Try to describe the feature's target audience—viewers most likely to identify with the people being interviewed. Would the audience identify as closely if only still images of drivers and gas pumps were used to support the story? Asking *why* and *for whom* a moving image has been created can be helpful in determining its message and meaning.

MM5-d Meaning: What effect do the moving images have on the viewer?

Although a composer's choices about the type of moving image and its features are usually deliberate, they don't necessarily convey the same meaning to all viewers in all contexts. They may not work the way the composer intended, or they may carry additional meanings the composer didn't anticipate.

Read an excerpt from student writer LeShawn Carter's analysis of a theme in *American Beauty*, a full-length film he viewed in an introduction to film study course. Carter is careful to consider the director's technical choices and composition in his analysis of the scene.

> Sam Mendes's *American Beauty* has no shortage of scenes in which the camera work and mise-en-scène suggest that the characters are trapped. Lenny Burnham is shown, for example, encased in window and door frames and is tightly framed by the camera. One scene in which the eye seems to get a break is the plastic bag scene, which we're supposed to see as beauty and perhaps freedom as we watch a plastic bag dance around in the breeze. The bag seems to move freely, but in fact the bag is not free at all. Mendes shoots the scene so that the bag is still constrained by the wind and the wall. It tries to escape but is pulled back into the shot again and again—reinforcing the theme.

As you develop an interpretation about the meaning of a video, an animation, or a film, be sure to ask questions about the genre or type of moving image, its features, and the purpose and audience for which the text was composed.

ACTIVITY MM5–1: Your understanding

Public service announcements (PSAs) are advertisements meant not to sell a product but to encourage or discourage particular behaviors or to call an audience to action (to contribute to a political campaign or to recycle, for example).

Search online for the original 1980s "brain on drugs" PSA, sometimes called the "fried egg" PSA. This PSA was shot from a first-person perspective. In the PSA, we are looking down as an egg is broken into a pan and begins to fry, while a voiceover says, "This is your brain on drugs."

Next search for an updated version of the PSA released in the 1990s, starring then-popular actor Rachel Leigh Cook. In this ad, Cook is the narrator. Rather than a first-person perspective, this version is shot more typically—viewers watch Cook smash the egg and then destroy the kitchen in which she appears.

Source: Partnership for a Drug-Free America

Why do you think each of these techniques was chosen? Which do you think works better? Would the impact or effect of the older PSA be different if it had been shot with an actor and as a scene? How so? Would the impact or effect of the newer PSA be different if it had been shot from a first-person perspective, as if the viewer were the person smashing the egg and destroying the kitchen?

What other advertisements—either public service advertisements or ads for products—have you seen shot from a first-person perspective? Were they effective? Why or why not?

ACTIVITY MM5–2: Your understanding

Most moving images we see are not interactive. That is, we watch them or somewhat passively receive the content. Some artists and advertisements, however, have thought a bit more creatively and innovatively about inspiring interaction with moving images.

The following still images are from a Skittles online ad campaign. In each of the ads, the viewer is invited to place his or her finger on the screen, at the spot indicated by the candy. The moving image that then plays is interactive with the viewer's finger. Do a Web search to find other ads from this campaign. What difference does the interactivity make? How does the ad feel different, or how do you respond differently to it, because of its interactive nature?

Source: BBDO Toronto; Wm. Wrigley Jr. Company

≡ MM6 Analyzing multimodal texts

Though the discussions in sections MM2 through MM5 each focused on a single mode, many of the examples in those sections were actually multimodal texts—texts that communicate with some combination of written words, static images, moving images, and sound. Look back at the brochure (image b) on page MM-16. The discussion in the text focuses on how words are arranged in different types of documents, but the brochure includes images as well. This section addresses analyzing different modes *together* in a multimodal composition, a task that is not as daunting as it may seem. On some level, you think about multimodal texts every day, simply because most texts *are* multimodal. Recipes and food packaging often include words

Analyzing multimodal texts

Genre

What kind of multimodal composition is it? An article with words and images, for example? A short film with sound and moving images?

Features

What modes (written words, sound, static images, moving images) are present in the composition? How does each mode work individually? How do the modes work together?

Purpose and audience

What is the purpose of the multimodal composition? Is it intended to provide information or argue a case, for example?

Who is the intended audience? The general public? Teenagers? Retirees? Professionals in a particular field?

Meaning

How do genre, features, purpose, and audience work together to convey a message in the multimodal composition? How do you interpret the combined effect of the modes used in the composition? (Keep in mind that your interpretation—your take on the meaning—may differ from the composer's intended message.)

and images. Television commercials usually include words, sound, and moving images. Even children's books, with words and illustrations, are multimodal.

When you start to look critically at multimodal texts, consider the questions in the chart at the top of the page.

MM6-a Genre: What kind of multimodal text is it?

Not only do people encounter multimodal texts every day, but they also create them every day. Personal photo albums with captions, slide shows with images and audio voice-over, social media posts with images and words—these are just a few common genres of multimodal composition. Different genres afford a composer different opportunities for sharing and shaping a message. For example, someone who wants to provide categories and subcategories of information might build an informational Web site, especially if the

Common genres of multimodal compositions

GENRE	DESCRIPTION
Informative Web site	Informative Web sites usually present statistics, research data, definitions, or other factual information. The Web site format allows composers to provide a large amount of information in manageable categories. A public transit Web site might, for example, have separate pages for timetables, maps, and policies.
Artistic video	Composers use artistic videos to present ideas on personal, political, environmental, and other themes. The video format allows composers to control the sequence of ideas.
Instructional video	Instructional videos often demonstrate steps for learning, creating, or installing something. A furniture manufacturer may, for example, provide an informational video to demonstrate the step-by-step assembly of a chair.
Slide presentation	Composers typically use slide presentations to present ideas and information in small chunks and in a particular sequence. A presenter might use slides to show how a proposed business plan could lead to corporate growth, for example.
Print advertisement	Print advertisements often occupy all or part of a page in a magazine, journal, or newspaper and can be used to promote products, services, or events. Because their space is limited and most readers won't spend more than a few seconds looking at them, print advertisements need to present key information at a glance.
Television commercial	In general, television commercials promote products, services, or events. Usually less than a minute long, commercials often rely on jingles and slogans to engage the viewer and convey their message in a quick, memorable way.

material doesn't need to be viewed in a particular sequence. If the order of information is essential, the composer might choose instead to create an informational video, to ensure that no one views the material out of order. When you're analyzing multimodal compositions, identify the genre and ask yourself why the composer chose that genre. The chart on page MM-45 shows common genres of multimodal compositions.

MM6-b Features: Which modes are represented? How do they work on their own and with each other?

When you analyze a multimodal composition, thinking about each mode on its own can be a helpful first step to interpreting the composition as a whole. Ask yourself what modes are present. Written words and static images? Audio and moving images? Then consider the role of each mode within the composition. What work does each mode do? For example, do written words convey information or make a plea? Does audio evoke an emotional response? Do moving or static images illustrate a concept or provide background?

Remember to consider the features of each mode as well. Are written words large or small? Bold or fine? Where do they appear? What size are the images, and how are they arranged? How are moving images sequenced? How loud or quiet is the audio? If you consider the modes separately, you'll be better equipped to think about how they work together.

Take a look at Figure 6–1, a public service message commissioned by the World Wildlife Fund, a group devoted to protecting nature. The composition uses two modes: written words and a static image. Which mode grabs your attention first? For most viewers, the cheetahs immediately draw the eye. But why? Think about the surrounding space. The background focus is so soft that no other distinct objects appear, only a dark blur. The cheetahs, however, are in sharp focus in the foreground. Their striking spots stand out against the muted background. It would be easy for a viewer to glance quickly at the public service message and see nothing but an adorable photo of cheetahs, except for one thing: the tags on their backs. Marked with "S" and "XL," these are unmistakably clothing tags. What at first appears to be a touching scene of mother and cub becomes more sinister with the recognition of these tags. These animals are going to be used for clothing.

Fashion claims more victims than you think.
WWF

FIGURE 6–1 A PUBLIC SERVICE MESSAGE. (*Source:* World Wildlife Fund)

Student writer Wayne Anderson made the following argument about the ad:

The makers of the ad could have inspired outrage by showing a violent image of cheetahs that had been killed for their furs. They probably recognized, however, that many viewers would instinctively look away and try to forget the image rather than absorb the message. By emphasizing the image of the two cheetahs, the mother guiding her cub in their natural habitat, the ad designers draw in their audience and elicit a sentimental response. Some viewers will feel sympathy and want the cheetahs to survive.

The image alone, however, does not convey the whole message. It delivers a troubling truth and makes viewers feel sympathetic and sad, but it might not have a lasting influence. The text in the upper right corner adds a subtle punch: "Fashion claims more victims than you think." The statement plays on the familiar concept of fashion victims, people whose clothing choices make them look ridiculous. Here the term *victim* is being applied to the cheetahs that may be killed to gratify someone's fashion sense. If the image showed two adult cheetahs or an entire group, the image probably would not be as effective. It's easier for most people to think of cubs especially as needing protection from harm. Maybe the term *victim* is supposed to make viewers feel protective and not just sympathetic. Playing on this familiar phrase also helps make the message memorable.

MM6-c Purpose and audience: What is the composition doing? Whom is it intended to reach?

When you think about the purpose of a multimodal composition, you might ask, *What is this composition meant to accomplish? Convey information? Inspire action or feeling? Make an argument?*

Thinking about audience, you might ask, *Whom is this meant to appeal to? Whom is this designed or written for? What assumptions is the composer making about the audience's beliefs and values?*

Consider again the two cheetahs. Why do you think the composers of that message decided to use the pronoun *you* in "Fashion claims more victims than you think"? Most public service messages aim to encourage or discourage specific behaviors. If the statement read "Fashion claims more victims than people think," it might be easier for the audience to dismiss the issue as someone else's fault or problem. Perhaps the composers hoped that addressing the statement to "you" would empower their audience to act—to refuse to buy furs or to spread the message. If the words are essential for reaching the audience, why do you think they're so small? Would the effect be different if they spanned the top or bottom of the image? Perhaps some viewers would feel alienated if they encountered the direct address (*you*) and the word *victim* before developing a sympathetic feeling toward the cheetah mother and cub.

Or take the example of restaurant menus. What is the purpose of a menu? The straightforward answer might be "to provide food options." But a menu might have other purposes as well: to differentiate a particular restaurant from its competitors, to show that the restaurant specializes in a particular type of food (for example, using the colors of the Italian flag or photos of pasta to show that the food is Italian), or to explicitly call attention to healthier menu options or options for people who have food allergies.

Who is the audience for a menu? The simple answer might be "hungry customers." But imagining how customers might encounter the menu reveals more about the intended audience. Although some customers viewing the menu might already be seated in the restaurant, others might be considering the menu online, trying to decide where to eat dinner. In making their decision, they might be comparing the menu side-by-side with another restaurant's menu. They might be considering different factors related to their dining decision, such as how much money they want to spend on their dinner. Higher prices might indicate that the restaurant aims to attract an older crowd. Unusual font choices might mean that the restaurant seeks an eclectic audience.

For multimodal compositions, the actual audience might be much broader than the intended audience, so it's important to consider how and where the composition has been published. Student composer Marisa Williamson created a video essay, "To the Children of America," for a class. Though her intended audience was fairly limited—her instructor and her peers—her actual audience grew when she published her school project on a video-sharing Web site. Williamson's project is featured in sections MM7 through MM15 of this book.

MM6-d Meaning: What effect does the multimodal composition have on the viewer?

Although a composer's choices about the modes integrated into a multimodal composition are usually deliberate, they don't necessarily convey the same meaning to all viewers in all contexts. They may not work the way the composer intended, or they may carry additional meanings the composer didn't anticipate.

In the following excerpt, student writer Marley Cole analyzes item collecting in role-playing video games. Her attention to sound, images, and other features of the games leads her to disagree with one of her sources. In her essay, she includes both text and screen captures from in-game play to support her points.

> *Gamasutra* writer Kris Graft suggests that the desire to collect items in a game world is similar to compulsive hoarding in the real world. The consequences of gathering items may not be as negative for the gamer, but gamers and hoarders, according to Graft, experience similar degrees of emotional investment and gratification when they acquire objects. Graft, however, does not account for the limits placed on acquisition in many game worlds and the penalties incurred when the gamer ignores those limits. Usually, a character cannot carry more than a certain amount. Sometimes that amount increases when the character gets stronger, but there is always a limit. When the character's pack is full, that

character can't pick up new items (see the image on right for an in-game inventory example). The character is forced to discard or sell old items to make room for new ones.

In some games, overburdened characters can't even move until they discard items. Rather than facilitating virtual hoarding, video games actually force

Source: Electronic Arts.

gamers to be strategic about what they keep with them. In addition, the experience of parting with items is often positively reinforced. Selling an item can be accompanied by the sound of coins dropping into a pouch or the sight of a money count going up. A character who has lightened his pack might even be able to move faster.

Cole determines meaning by analyzing sounds and images in a multimodal text, a video game. As you develop an interpretation about the meaning of a multimodal piece, be sure to consider genre, features, purpose, and audience. Pulling together your individual impressions of the text's elements can help you look critically at the text as a whole.

ACTIVITY MM6–1: Your understanding

Many public service announcements (PSAs) are advertisements meant to encourage or discourage particular behaviors (such as voting or littering) or to call an audience to action (for example, contributing to a charitable organization).

Choose a nonprofit or community action or awareness organization. Find a campaign that the group has run or is running, and identify at least three different campaign components (such as a poster, a radio spot, a television PSA, a Web-based PSA, an interactive game). Analyze each of the three pieces, describing which modes are used, how the modes are layered together (or not), and how well you think each piece serves its purpose.

Some historical and contemporary campaigns you might look at include Rosie the Riveter, wildfire prevention, ready.gov, Make a Wish Foundation, and the Humane Society. You might also focus on the World Wildlife Fund campaign mentioned in MM6-b.

MM7 Starting your own multimodal project

Sections MM2 through MM6 focused on analyzing individual and multiple modes in the works of others. Sections MM7 through MM15 will help you think about your own multimodal composing. As you develop your own project, you'll want to keep genre, features, purpose, audience, and meaning in mind, just as you do when you analyze. Think about questions like these as you plan and compose:

Genre: What kind of composition do you plan to create? A video? A Web site? A poster with images and written words? (Depending on the genre, you may need to budget more time for the assignment, brush up on technical skills, or collaborate with others.)

Features: What kinds of images, colors, design elements, fonts, and type treatments are appropriate for your composition? What would make your composition most effective? Adding voiceover narration or including information in callout boxes, for example?

Purpose and audience: What does your composition need to do? Does it need to inform, instruct, argue, entertain, or persuade? Whom does it need to reach? Novices who need basic information? Experts who need to see detailed support? Children who would respond well to a colorful presentation? People who agree or disagree with you?

Meaning: What message do you want to convey? What is the goal of your project? How do your chosen genre and features help you achieve your purpose and reach your audience?

Keep in mind that you may not be able to answer all of these questions before you begin gathering information and drafting. The answers you come up with early on may change as you investigate your topic and begin to build your project. It's a good idea to revisit these questions throughout your composing process.

MM7-a Getting direction from the assignment

The composing process often begins with an assignment, which may provide answers to some of your questions about genre, features, purpose, audience, and meaning. Take a look at this assignment about binge drinking, for example:

> Design a six-panel brochure that persuades college students not to binge drink. Your headings and body text—along with any graphs, diagrams, or photos—should work together to define the term and discuss the dangers of binge drinking.

The assignment provides the topic—binge drinking—and requires a specific multimodal genre—a brochure with images and written words. It also provides a general purpose—to persuade—and a target audience—college students. It's up to the student to determine the specific message. For example, *Binge drinking can lead to health problems that plague drinkers long after college* or *One night of binge drinking can be fatal and isn't worth the risk.* The student will need to think about what features will help make that message persuasive. What colors, typefaces, and images, for example, will be appropriate for the message?

MM7-b Considering the "So what?" question

If the assignment does not specify a topic, choose one that allows you to explore a genuine interest or address a real concern your audience may have.

Effective composers take stock of their own goals and the needs of their readers, asking *What, aside from a good grade, motivates me to compose?* Make sure you have a reason for composing—a reason that addresses the "So what?" question. A project that stems from genuine motivation will be more engaging to your audience. One student writer made a chart to help her decide how to respond to this prompt: *Persuade fellow students to take your side in a campus debate.*

SAMPLE STUDENT NOTES: DECIDING ON A TOPIC

Possible topic: Should the college convert two acres of campus green space to additional parking spaces for commuter students?	So what?	Hm. I'm not a commuter, so it's not that critical to me.
Possible topic: Should the college publish the school newspaper in an online format only and abandon a paper publication?	So what?	Seems like a no-brainer to me. We're all on our devices 24/7 anyway. And going online only is greener, right?
Possible topic: Should the college add a general education requirement that each full-time student must complete a minimum of 12 hours of community service by the end of the second year?	So what?	Volunteerism should absolutely NOT be required. I can convince fellow students that a requirement goes against the concept of volunteering—of giving back out of a sense of goodness. Plus, being a college student means making your OWN decisions.

The student chose this topic because she cared about it, felt her readers would care about it, and felt she could make compelling points to support her views.

You need to consider the "So what?" question even if your purpose is not to persuade or argue. If the assignment is to demonstrate a process for instruction purposes, think about what you can bring to that project that will make it especially clear or helpful. Your audience will see value in your work if you are invested in it.

MM7-c Understanding expectations and managing your time

Even if the assignment is detailed and clear, you'll probably have questions for your instructor as you get started. You'll want to consider questions like these, which are typical of almost any writing assignment:

- Do you need to run ideas by your instructor before you get started?
- Will you have time in class to work on the assignment?
- How can you break your project down into manageable steps?
- What sorts of research should you do? Should you conduct field research, such as interviews? Or should you focus on library sources, like books and journal articles?
- Are you working on your project alone? With a partner? Or with a group?
- How will the project be evaluated?

You'll also want to consider additional questions, however, that relate more to the multimodal aspects of the project, such as the following:

- Can you include images, videos, or sound clips in your composition?
- If you want to include links in your essay, how should you present those links?
- Where can you go for help if you've never created a multimodal composition before?
- What options do you have for sharing drafts and getting feedback if your project is a large file or in several pieces?
- If your final project is a large file, how should you submit it?
- How should you present a list of works cited for something like a video or a podcast?

Getting answers to questions like these before you begin your project can help clarify some of the details of your project and ensure that the project starts smoothly.

ACTIVITY MM7–1: Your understanding

Before moving further, take some time to view the two student projects discussed in sections MM7 through MM15. (Visit the URL at the bottom of this page.) One, an informative Web site, offers an overview of loose leaf tea. The other, a video essay, explores how YouTube helps young people experience events of the past. How are these compositions multimodal? Identify some of the successful features of each.

ACTIVITY MM7–2: Your project

Review a monomodal writing assignment you recently completed or a piece of writing you composed on your own (a traditional five-page academic essay, perhaps). Imagine if you had been asked to produce the composition as a multimodal piece instead. What genre would have been effective for your purpose, audience, and message? A slide show? A movie? A Web page? A collage? Consider some of the materials you might have drawn on to craft the piece as a multimodal composition: audio, video, animation or movement, still images, and so on. Write briefly about what you might have done and why.

MM8 Considering your purpose and audience

Purpose is the goal of your work—your aim or objective. Your purpose will inform many of the decisions you make as a composer. Your audience is made up of the people who will read, view, or listen to your work. When you're composing in college, it's easy to think that your audience is limited to "the teacher." Yes, your instructor is part of your audience, but usually your instructor is not your primary audience or the only audience you are writing to.

Often, the assignment will suggest or require both a purpose and an audience. In a composition course, for example, an instructor might ask each student to use photos and written words to argue a position in a current campus debate. In a marketing course, the assignment might call for a slide show presentation that analyzes consumer trends over time. In a natural sciences class, the assignment might ask students to write and direct a public service announcement that informs viewers about hurricane preparedness. These are all examples of academic projects, but the purposes are different for each. In these examples, the composition student's purpose is to *argue*, the marketing student's purpose is to *analyze*,

ONLINE **hackerhandbooks.com/multimodal**
> Multimodal resources > Student multimodal projects
> D'Amato, "Loose Leaf Teas"
> Williamson, "To the Children of America"

and the natural sciences student's purpose is to *inform*. If, for example, the natural sciences student produced a short digital movie in which he made an argument that state agencies need more funding for hurricane preparedness, he would probably not be satisfying the assignment.

Audience considerations also influence the content and presentation of your project. Sometimes your instructor will give you guidance about who your audience is—other students on your campus, for example, or state legislators. Sometimes the assignment will direct you to address a particular audience, such as student athletes or readers of your campus newspaper. If your purpose is to persuade, your main audience will probably be those who disagree with you or are undecided. If your purpose is to instruct, your audience will probably be nonexperts, those who need basic or step-by-step information.

MM8-a Prewriting with your purpose in mind

Student composer Alyson D'Amato was assigned to create an informative text—that is, a text that teaches readers about a topic. D'Amato began thinking about what she needed to do by reviewing the assignment for the project.

ASSIGNMENT FOR AN INFORMATIVE PROJECT

Think about the ways in which information is provided in our culture. Your assignment is to take a subject that's familiar to you and to compose a multimodal project that informs or instructs your audience or explains something to them. You can create a slide show presentation, a Web site, a brief video, or something else. Engage your audience, make your purpose clear, deliver your information, and provide enough examples so that your audience comes away with a good grasp of the topic.

From the assignment, D'Amato knew she needed to create an informative, explanatory piece. She knew that she was expected to produce a multimodal project. Her instructor invited students to choose a topic they were interested in.

When D'Amato received the assignment, she analyzed her purpose. Her initial notes looked something like this:

- explain something, provide information
- include pictures and words
- teach people about something new or unknown
- start with what I know and care about

D'Amato's instructor provided the initial, formal purpose for the project: to create an informative piece. D'Amato decided that she had to do some additional prewriting to help her determine why the topic mattered to her.

> My purpose: Create something about brewing your own tea and teaching people how to do so. I love tea and make my own teas—I want to teach other people that making tea means more than dunking a tea bag in a mug!
>
> - explain something, provide information
>   - — capture audience's attention
>   - — teach them to do something that might be new to them
> - include pictures and words
>   - — explain using text and use photos to illustrate the text
>   - — use pictures to keep people's attention
>   - — use pictures people can relate to (not too artistic or unrecognizable or anything)
> - teach people about something new or unknown
>   - — use language people will understand—like the newspaper
>   - — explain terms that might be unfamiliar
> - start with what *I know* and *care* about
>   - — explain why it's important to me
>   - — explain why it might be important to others—answer the "So what?" question!

It's fine to start out fairly broad, but before you begin drafting and creating, you'll want to have a strong sense of what you want and need to accomplish with your multimodal composition. D'Amato's notes provide a good model for how you might start thinking about your purpose.

MM8-b Identifying your audience's needs and perspectives

In the previous example, student composer Alyson D'Amato was asked in her assignment to "engage" her audience. To determine what the audience will find engaging, composers first need to *identify* an audience. Here are some questions you might ask as you think about who your audience is:

- Does the assignment provide any direction about who the audience is? What clues about audience has your instructor provided?

- Is there a particular audience you want to reach?
- Could you have more than one audience?
- What do you know about your audience's life experiences? Interests? Demographics (age, race, socioeconomic status, level of education, location)?
- What are the most effective ways to engage your audience members—attract their attention, get them interested, help them learn, and so forth?

Finding answers to these questions will allow you to see your topic from your audience's perspective.

Sometimes professionals in marketing or product development will create "profiles" of different types of people who make up their intended audience. These profiles help them to imagine specific details behind a general idea like "audience." For a project in a technical writing class, students were asked to write a proposal for a new, Web-based application to be used by their peers at the university on the school's Web site. To get a sense of the possible audience for their Web-based app, a group of students worked together to create user profiles. They interviewed other students and came up with two user profiles.

Group 1   One potential user group is made up of residential students who are online at least 7 hours a day and who primarily use Facebook to stay connected with friends. These users visit Web sites only to seek information not available through Facebook. They use the college Web site to look up their class schedules and check grades and sometimes to look for news about what's going on around campus. One student told us: "If there was a way to sync up the college Web site with Facebook, that'd be great!"

Group 2   Another potential user group is made up of commuter students, many of whom have transferred from a community college. They live off-campus and are not online as often as those in the first user group. Most work at least part-time and use the Internet primarily for work-related e-mail and projects. This group typically uses the college Web site only when enrolling for classes. One student told us: "I guess I'd need a reason to use the school site more."

You might create a similar profile for your audience. Or you might just do some brainstorming in answer to questions like these:

- Where are your readers/viewers/listeners from?
- When were they born?

- What groups or causes are they involved with?
- What experiences have they had with your topic?
- What are the best ways to reach them?
- How are they likely to receive your message?

NOTE: When creating profiles of your potential audience members, keep in mind that people are diverse. Creating audience profiles is helpful when it gives you a sense of the people you are trying to reach and what they are interested in and value. Your profiles should not turn into stereotypes that lead you to make faulty assumptions that homogenize or alienate your audience.

MM8-c Connecting with your audience

With your purpose in mind and your audience profile under way, you are ready to think about the best way to connect with your audience. The benefit of composing multimodally is that you have options for communicating your message. Consider the following scenarios and think about what decisions you would have to make to best connect to these audiences (highlighted).

- You are composing for a group of local second graders to teach them about air quality.
- You are composing for other college students to share advice on making sound financial decisions.
- You are composing for your school's administration to propose building a war memorial on campus.

How can you appeal to these audiences in these situations? The second graders, for instance, might need pictures to help explain the concept of air quality. The college students might be interested in hearing audio clips from other students who have faced specific financial challenges. You might reach the school administrators by knowing the school's mission statement and core values and presenting slides that connect those values to your proposal.

When student composer Marisa Williamson began working on her composition, she did some talking, reading, and exploring. Her assignment was to present an argument creatively on a topic of her choice and for an audience of her choice. She was familiar with writing argument essays; for this project, however, she decided to compose a video argument. Williamson wanted to explore historic events that had national attention in the United States and somehow tie them together. She wanted to connect to people her own age, so she began by thinking about events from her own childhood that made a lasting impression on her and had national significance. The event that stood out most clearly was the September 11, 2001, terrorist attack that destroyed the twin towers of the World Trade Center in New York City.

Williamson realized that what she was thinking about wasn't an argument yet. She started to think about other national events that were captured on film or video, what they have in common, and what it means to her generation to experience historic moving images recorded before their birth. To brainstorm ways of effectively reaching her audience, she also thought about arguments that she had encountered that had affected her thoughts or feelings on a subject. This process helped Williamson start shaping her argument and planning her project.

MM8-d Recognizing an unintended audience

Keep in mind that your composition will sometimes have a broader audience than your purpose or your assignment suggests or than you intended to reach. Because multimodal compositions often live online or in some portable electronic format, they typically can be publicly viewed or shared. Someone who runs a Web search on your name, for example, may find your project. Your project may also have a longer life span than you intend. If you take down a Web site you've created, pieces of it may have been downloaded and shared elsewhere by others. Even if you're creating your project for a specific group of people, make sure your work is something you'd be comfortable sharing with a broader audience that may include friends, family members, or future employers, for example.

ACTIVITY MM8–1: Your understanding

Look around campus for a poster that catches your eye. It could be hanging in the financial aid office, in the writing center, on an instructor's office door, or even in the kitchen of the dining hall. Take a picture of the poster or sketch it out on a notepad to refer to later. Identify the purpose or purposes of the poster. What clues help you identify the purpose?

ACTIVITY MM8–2: Your understanding

Take a look at just the home page of the following sites:

- the main Web site for your school
- the Web site of a professor at your school

- the Web site of a fast-food restaurant in your area
- the Web site of a small, locally owned restaurant in your area
- the Web site of the company that made the car you drive or that makes the car you'd like to drive
- the Web site for a branch or an agency of the US government (for example, the White House, the IRS, the FBI)
- the Web site for an individual who serves in the US government (such as a member of Congress)

As you look at each home page, generate a list of notes about who you think the primary audience is for each Web site. How do you know that this is the audience? What information—textual or visual—provides clues about who the audience is?

ACTIVITY MM8–3: Your project

With a current project in mind—in any class—consider your audience for composing. Take notes on the following questions.

- What sort of information do you need to gather about your audience? How will you go about gathering that information?
- Your audience members might have specific questions that are pertinent to their needs. Can you anticipate what those questions might be?
- Some members of your audience might be resistant to or skeptical about your topic; you might need to appeal to them using different types of evidence. What kinds of evidence might work best?

≡ MM9 Planning your project

Composing a multimodal project requires planning, and planning takes time. You'll have to settle on a process that works for you or, if you're collaborating with one or more classmates, that works for all of you. You'll also have to identify a main idea and the best genre (an inspirational video or an informative Web site, for example) for expressing that main idea. If the genre is not your choice but has been assigned, it will take planning to figure out how to best communicate the main idea in a particular type of composition. Planning is hard work, but it's also full of opportunities to think and rethink, shape and reshape your project.

Sometimes you will start a project in one direction—perhaps thinking something like *I'll create a Web page that teaches people how*

choosing a genre • developing a process •
stages of the project • a flexible composing process
MM9-a   MM-61

to tie fly-fishing lures—and find, as you do research and think about your audience and purpose, that a video might be a better way to instruct your audience. The good news is that you don't have to have everything planned before you start to compose.

MM9-a Understanding your own composing process

Have you ever put together, or watched someone else put together, a thousand-piece puzzle? Approaches for completing a puzzle vary. Some people start methodically with the border. Others start with a key image in the center of the puzzle and work outward. Still others work randomly, fitting together islands of puzzle pieces here and there and eventually joining them. There's no right way; it's just a matter of figuring out what method works for each puzzle and for the person putting it together.

Composers, too, have their own preferred ways of working, so it's important to think flexibly about the composing process. Sometimes you'll see the composing process presented in a fairly linear way, like this:

1. Brainstorm
2. Plan
3. Research
4. Compose
5. Revise

Those basic steps find their way into most projects, and the process usually begins with brainstorming and ends with revision, but composers usually take each step more than once and at several times throughout the process. Consider student composer Marisa Williamson's project: a video essay.

In talking with other people in her class and with friends, Williamson found that all of them had seen iconic footage and pictures from events in recent history, but few could remember key words spoken about the events or by those involved in the events. Based on what she knew about her audience, Williamson decided—with rough ideas about her purpose and how to proceed—to knit video clips, still images, audio files, and her own narration together to make an argument that would appeal to her peers. She used a video-editing application that allowed her to combine, sequence, and edit all the materials she had gathered and also to layer in text and titles.

A linear rendering of Williamson's composing process might look something like this:

1. Brainstorm about purpose and audience
2. Gather images and video
3. Choose songs
4. Write and record narration
5. Input images, audio, video, and narration
6. Add text
7. Produce video

Represented visually, Williamson's composing process might look something like Figure 9–1.

FIGURE 9–1 VISUALIZATION OF A LINEAR APPROACH TO THE COMPOSING PROCESS FOR A MULTIMODAL PROJECT.

This is a fairly neat and orderly way of visualizing the elements that are part of a composing process, and certainly these are important steps in the process. The way Williamson compiled, wrote, and thought through the different elements of her composition, however, might actually be better and more accurately represented visually as in Figure 9–2.

The student's composing process was not so much a linear path as it was a series of loops in which she revisited stages and elements of her composition. She began by gathering and watching different videos. She then selected some still images, collected some songs, and scripted her narration. Each of these pieces affected her thoughts about and presentation of the others. She went back to the video to edit it and to trim pieces, add to other pieces, and sequence

FIGURE 9–2 VISUALIZATION OF A REALISTIC APPROACH TO THE COMPOSING PROCESS FOR A MULTIMODAL PROJECT.

clips together. She worked with the music, trimming and editing and deciding how to layer it under her narration and on top of the video and images. She found different audio clips and replaced or changed the audio in the project. She did this over and over again, while she also continued to write and edit her script to reflect changes in the sequence of video pieces and images. What was essential for Williamson was budgeting enough time for the shaping and thinking and *re*shaping and *re*thinking.

MM9-b Collaborating effectively with others

Working in a pair or in a group can change your composing process—how you go about brainstorming, drafting, researching, and revising. The old saying is that "two heads are better than one," and composing with a group can be enriching. Collaborative work gives you an opportunity to explore ideas and practices that your peers bring to the project. It's also valuable practice for work you will do outside of school. Many professional projects are done in teams.

Collaborating effectively takes practice. It helps to pay attention to how you best work and how you best work with others. Here are a few important tips for working with a partner or a group:

Do the work together, and learn from each other. Sometimes students look at collaborative work as just a matter of divvying up tasks (for instance, one person does the research, another does the writing, and another does the designing and production). Managing a project in this way can result in a piece of work that looks somewhat like Frankenstein's monster—lots of pieces stitched together into a messy whole. Stronger, more coherent work is the result of people truly collaborating and working together on *every* aspect of a project. The process of doing so allows group members to learn from one another's strengths, and, in turn, everyone in the group becomes a stronger, more capable composer.

Organize yourselves, and stay on task. Functioning well as a group means checking in often and planning together. Three

Assessing your strengths as a collaborator

I am good at being a **team leader**.	yes	no	kind of
I am good at being a **team member**.	yes	no	kind of
I am good at **communication** (asking good questions and facilitating discussions).	yes	no	kind of
I am good at thinking about the **big picture** (staying focused on the main idea or goal of the project).	yes	no	kind of
I am good at thinking about **small details** (completing individual tasks and keeping track of smaller parts of the project).	yes	no	kind of
I am good at doing **research** (performing Web searches, gathering information from library databases, and conducting surveys or interviews with people).	yes	no	kind of
I am good at **design** work (working with or creating images, or thinking about layouts and color schemes).	yes	no	kind of
I am good at **writing** (brainstorming, drafting, and editing written materials).	yes	no	kind of
I have good **technology** skills (creating basic Web pages, making slide show presentations, and doing some work with digital video).	yes	no	kind of

ways to keep your group focused and make progress are to set up specific meeting times, to have someone take notes when you meet as a group, and to make sure everyone knows who's doing what for the project.

Know your own strengths, and be ready to admit your weaknesses. One way to start, especially if you're working with classmates you don't know, is to think about how you typically like to function in a team or a group. What do you do well? Individual members can assess their strengths by using a questionnaire (see the checklist on p. MM-64). The responses on the questionnaire can help you get to know each other and start a conversation about how to move forward.

MM9-c Deciding on a main idea

Just as well-planned essays begin with a working thesis statement, your multimodal project should have a main idea around which the entire composition is focused. And be sure that your main idea addresses the "So what?" question (see section MM7-b)—your main idea should be compelling and interesting and address a question or concern of interest to others. Having a main idea will help you select the best images, audio, and other elements to support that main idea. You may have to whittle away at a big, general idea to settle on a manageable main idea.

As you get started on a project, you'll likely have lots of ideas to explore. Sometimes it's tempting to stick with a broad subject. Most writers find, however, that doing so can actually be a problem, as there's too much material to cover and it's tricky to figure out how to approach the subject. "The World Wide Web," for instance, is a gigantic subject, but certainly a lot of academic writers get a lot of mileage out of projects about the Web. The trick is to ask questions about the subject in an attempt to narrow it to a topic and to find your particular angle, one that matters to you.

BROAD SUBJECT	The World Wide Web
QUESTION	*Great for shopping and communication, but what good is it doing in the world?*
NARROWER TOPIC	Using the Web during and after a disaster
QUESTION	*Where have we seen this? What has been the effect? Why is it important?*
MAIN IDEA	How Japanese citizens are using the Web as a tool for activism in the aftermath of the 2011 nuclear disaster and slow government response

Brainstorming ideas and then focusing and whittling down those ideas is a great way to get started. When student composer Alyson D'Amato started thinking about creating a project focused on tea (a broad subject), she came up with a list of possible angles:

organic tea	tea growing	history of tea
store-bought tea	tea brands or	tea flavors
black teas	companies	uses of tea
green teas	fair trade teas	bottled tea vs. brewed
tea and health	tea plants	tea
tea in different	tea popularity	serving tea (different
cultures	brewing tea yourself	rituals)

D'Amato knew that she couldn't address all of these possibilities in one project. Some of the issues—tea in different cultures, for example—seemed too complex for the scope of the assignment. Other ideas—store-bought tea, for example—seemed as though they might not be interesting for her or her audience.

She identified three possibilities from the big list she generated, and then she brainstormed what she might cover for each of those possibilities:

- black teas vs. green teas
  - — focus on compare and contrast?
  - — the differences in the plants
  - — the differences in the flavors
  - — the growing popularity of green tea
- serving tea
  - — historical tools, like really old tea-serving pitchers
  - — different cultural rituals (like "high tea" in England)
  - — different types of ceremonies involving tea
  - — from rituals and ceremonies to tea bags in a box bought at the grocery store
- brewing tea yourself
  - — why do it when tea bags are so easy?
  - — differences between tea bags and loose leaf tea
  - — health benefits of tea
  - — loose leaf tea recipes

Because she was so personally interested and invested in tea brewing herself, D'Amato decided to choose the third option, to compose a project that would teach people about brewing tea. She knew she would further develop and refine her main idea as she researched her topic, but now she had a focused starting point. (See your handbook for more on narrowing a subject to a topic and more on developing thesis statements.)

MM9-d Planning support for your main idea

A multimodal project often gives you new opportunities for presenting evidence in support of a main idea. You may think of evidence only as quotations from sources or perhaps as data from experiments. Multimodal projects allow you to think more broadly. You can support your idea with quoted written words — but also with quotations in the form of podcasts and other audio files. You can include data in the form of graphs and tables — but you can also present data in animations. Support in a multimodal composition can take the form of words, images, audio/sound, video, and so on.

Think about the visual rendering of student composer Marisa Williamson's writing process in Figure 9–1 (p. MM-62). As the visual shows, she chose to mix images, video, and audio (speech clips, music clips, and her own narration) in her video essay. Since she was planning to argue the thesis that online video-sharing sites such as YouTube bring together people of different generations by letting viewers experience events of the past, she knew that her best evidence was going to be YouTube videos. She made a list of possible events to include.

John F. Kennedy's inaugural address	Iranian hostage crisis
Martin Luther King Jr.'s "Dream" speech	Geraldine Ferraro's candidacy
Assassination of John F. Kennedy	Assassination attempt: Ronald Reagan
Assassination of Martin Luther King Jr.	Birth of MTV
Assassination of Robert F. Kennedy	Space shuttle *Challenger*
Landing on the moon	Million Man March
Woodstock	September 11
Apollo 13 crisis	Hurricane Katrina
1976 Bicentennial	

Marisa's list included patriotic events, political events, cultural events, tragic events, and natural disasters. When she reviewed her list, she decided that she wanted to focus on just one of these categories of events. The event that resonated most strongly for her was the September 11 attacks. She remembered the strong sense of unity that followed throughout the country. So she decided to focus specifically on tragedies that have brought people together in the past and connect generations now through YouTube footage. Even after making that decision, she felt she needed to whittle the list down to one or two tragedies for each generation, so that her audience could easily connect with what other generations had felt.

Since Williamson wanted her audience to be able to experience what each generation saw and heard as these tragedies occurred, she chose to include as evidence excerpts from iconic speeches (of John F. Kennedy, Martin Luther King Jr., Ronald Reagan) to layer over the images and videos. She could have chosen to support her argument — that YouTube provides much more than a casual distraction — with clips of people talking about how video-sharing sites have revolutionized the way we experience and *re*experience events. But she thought primary sounds would be more powerful, more convincing support.

As you mine for and select evidence for your project, keep your purpose in mind. What are you trying to achieve — and why? What types of evidence will help you do so convincingly? Also keep your audience members in mind — their age, experiences, biases, and needs. What kind of evidence will be most effective?

Be sure to evaluate any potential evidence for relevance (to your purpose and audience), authority, currency, and accuracy. You'll need to question whether a photo, a podcast, a video, or anything else you choose will be compelling and credible to your audience. See your handbook's section on evaluating sources.

MM9-e Choosing a genre; deciding on a delivery method

Deciding how to deliver your ideas is an important part in planning your project. First, you'll need to think about your audience and purpose: Whom are you composing for — and why? When you're mulling over how to deliver your ideas, you'll also have to think about the support you plan to include in your composition.

When Alyson D'Amato began to plan her project, she thought about the ways in which people would want to learn about her topic. She felt that a slide show presentation about brewing tea wouldn't be too interesting and wouldn't really fit her purpose, especially since most slide show presentations are designed to be delivered by a speaker. She knew she wanted people to be able to easily access and use her information, and she knew they'd probably need to go through the information on their own.

She considered creating a video and was excited about the idea of actually recording herself talking about tea and making tea, but she wasn't sure how to include the recipes she wanted to share with her audience. To help organize herself as she considered different ways to convey the information, D'Amato created a table listing the pros and cons of different delivery methods (see p. MM-70).

D'Amato decided that a Web site would be the best way to share her ideas. With a Web site, she knew she could include written words and images, maybe embed video, and create an overall organization that would allow viewers to experience her site at their own pace.

Considering different formats, as D'Amato did, is an important part of your planning. For more on the technical aspects of delivering your project, see section MM15.

ACTIVITY MM9–1: Your understanding

Review a writing assignment you recently completed or a piece of writing you composed on your own. Imagine that it had been a collaborative, group project. How do you think your composing processes would have been different? What would you have learned or gained by collaborating? How might the project have turned out differently? What difficulties or opportunities might you have encountered if the project had been collaborative?

ACTIVITY MM9–2: Your understanding

Consider the broad subjects in the following list. Narrow each one by asking questions. Propose a manageable topic for a multimodal composition for at least two of the four subjects.

- The most recent presidential election
- Video games
- Social networking sites
- Environmental issues

ACTIVITY MM9–3: Your project

For a project you are currently planning, take some time to consider your own main idea. Is it narrow enough? Do you have a specific angle on the subject? Pair up with a classmate and share your idea. Pitch your plan for gathering support and seek feedback from your classmate. Are you planning the most convincing support for your main idea? Take notes from your conversation.

SAMPLE STUDENT NOTES: DECIDING ON A DELIVERY METHOD

Delivery method	Pros (+) and cons (-)
Slide show	+ Viewers can watch slides at their own pace and navigate back or skip ahead. + I can use images, written words, and links. + I can include any recipes I want to share. + I can use text animations to spice things up. - Slide show presentations often seem dry and not engaging. - The final file might be really large, and my audience would probably have to download it to view it. - To view my project, my audience might need to have the same slide show software I have.
Video	+ Video would seem cooler than a slide show. I could include a soundtrack with music and voiceover. + Actually watching someone make tea in a video might be more helpful than written instructions. + Video would allow me to control the sequence of information, but that's not really important to me for this project. - I'm not sure how I would include my recipes so that they could be saved and used. Maybe a download link at the end of my video? - I'd have to keep it short or risk boring my audience. - Video can be hard to edit. If I change any visuals, I might have to adjust the soundtrack.
Web site	+ A Web site would be easy to share. All I'd have to do is provide a URL. + Viewers would be able to control the order in which they see information and easily revisit things they find interesting. + I could include my recipes on the pages or as downloadable files. + I could include any image, audio, or video files I wanted to. + There are plenty of free Web site builders online that I can use.

≡ **MM10** Managing your project

A huge part of imagining, drafting, creating, revising, and publishing a multimodal project is managing the pieces of the project. When you write a typical academic essay, you often work with only one piece: your document filled with written words. When working on a multimodal project, you might be managing two, three, four, or dozens of pieces, most if not all of which are electronic files. Each of these files likely has a different name and is of a different type. It's easy to feel overwhelmed when negotiating .wmv, .mov, .bmp, .m4v, .pdf, .jpg, and other files.

This section offers a few good practices for managing files across a multimodal project:

- Saving all your files in one place
- Keeping track of where your sources came from
- Using clear, descriptive names when saving your files
- Keeping track of versions when sharing your files with others

MM10-a Saving all your files in one place

Before you really dig into a project, decide where you're going to work on it. If your project is digital and will include images, audio segments, or movie clips, for example, that workspace is probably a folder on your computer. With multimodal projects, often the different components need to sync with or "talk to" one another. If one file is saved on your computer's desktop and another file is saved in a "My Documents" folder, the applications you use to compile your project might not be able to find all the files. And you might not be able to find all the files either!

When Williamson began gathering clips and working on her video project, she created a "Writing Class Project" folder on her USB drive. This was a useful initial storage space for all her files. You can see in Figure 10–1 that she has sound files, video clips, and some word processing documents stored in the folder.

Fairly quickly, however, Williamson realized that she needed to be more organized—by the time she had twenty files in her "Writing Class Project" folder, she found it was getting harder and harder to sort through all the files and find specific pieces.

She created three separate folders within her "Writing Class Project" main folder—one for music, one for video clips, and another for audio clips (Figures 10–2 and 10–3). She left her word processing documents in the main folder because they dealt with the overall project, whereas the files in the subfolders were pieces of the larger project.

Williamson's file-saving strategy isn't the only way to save files for a major project, but she found that it worked well for her, and it's a good example of how you can create a file management system for a multimodal composing project.

FIGURE 10–1 FOLDER FOR STORAGE OF MULTIMODAL FILES.

FIGURE 10–2 FOLDER FOR A MULTIMODAL PROJECT ORGANIZED WITH SUBFOLDERS FOR MUSIC, VIDEO CLIPS, AND AUDIO CLIPS.

FIGURE 10–3 SUBFOLDER CONTAINING ALL THE VIDEO CLIPS FOR A MULTIMODAL PROJECT.

MM10-b Keeping track of all your files

As you brainstorm and research your project, gathering and selecting examples, resources, and other materials, you might think, "Oh, I'll remember where I found this!" But as you collect pieces from a variety of sources over a span of time, you will probably lose track of where you found at least a few things, and that can cause you problems further down the road. For example, if you use an audio quote in a draft of your project and later decide you'd like to include a few seconds more of what the speaker said, you'll have to find not only the original sound file but also the exact moment when the words you've quoted are spoken. Your job will be much easier if you've got the whole sound file in your project folder along with some notes about the speaker, where the file came from, when you downloaded the file, and the time stamp for the words you're interested in using. You may want to keep your notes in a list that provides key information about each of the files you're collecting.

Figure 10–4 shows part of a list Williamson kept in her "notes and storyboard" word processing document in her "Writing Class Project" folder.

📄 Video assignment-sources.docx

File   Edit   View   Insert   Format   Tools   Table   Window

VIDEO SOURCES

John F. Kennedy. "Inaugural Speech."

http://www.youtube.com/watch?v=P1PbQlVMp98&feature=player_embedded

- found and viewed for the first time on January 27
- 4:32 long; recorded on Friday, January 20, 1961; posted to YouTube by evgondemand.com (site that offers pay-per-view access to famous speeches)
- visual focus is on Kennedy speaking at podium; audio is entirely Kennedy
- Kennedy's addressing people in attendance (vice pres, reps, citizens)
- good audio clips — maybe use in project?
  - :53-:54 "the world is very different now" (talking about how we can abolish poverty, but that it's hard because there are still issues around the world)
  - 1:36-2:21 "let the word go forth . . . we are committed today at home and around the world" (talking about defending human rights)

"Footage of JFK motorcade is discovered"

http://www.youtube.com/watch?v=d300ziN3wKA

- found and viewed for the first time on January 29
- 40 seconds long; posted to YouTube and tagged: "The silent, 8 mm color film is 'the clearest, best film of Jackie in the motorcade,' said Gary Mack, curator of the Sixth Floor Museum, which focuses on Kennedy's life and assassination."
- video sequence: people waving at the camera; broader street scene with motorcade coming down the street; motorcade passes by; shot of crowd again and then Texas School Book Depository; quick crowd shot (no audio)
- not sure how I might use this in my project; there are some pretty clear shots of Kennedy and Jackie in the car

"JFK Assassination Motorcade from Love Field to Dealey Plaza on to Parkland Hospital 22 Nov 1963"

http://www.youtube.com/watch?v=WnlL-pucCj0

- found and viewed for the first time on January 29
- 15 minutes long; posted to YouTube and tagged: "A chronological collection of original film footage, news reports and still photos, as John F Kennedy travels from Love Field in Dallas Texas through Dealey Plaza, and onto Parkland Hospital."
- voiceover: "the weather couldn't be better . . ." (a newscaster?); music in the background (part of the original video, or added by whoever compiled this?)
- voiceover describes what Kennedy and Jackie are doing — at the airport, shaking hands, heading to the limo to go downtown, limo pulling away; cut to clip showing motorcade
- 2:16 — audio changes to a different voice describing the motorcade and where it's going (recording doesn't sound as old); music is more ominous and heavy
- 3:46 — cool shot of the motorcade from behind (maybe use in project?)
- 5:08 — footage gets slower and choppy (effect created by whoever shot the video?)

FIGURE 10–4 SOURCES AND NOTES FOR A VIDEO ASSIGNMENT.

MM10-c Using clear, descriptive names when saving files

File names like "audio piece" or "draft 2" don't mean much when you're working with and compiling lots of files. One way to manage your files is to use a descriptive and consistent naming system. For instance, you might decide to include the word *audio* in the file name of all your audio clips: "audio_opening_music" and "audio_jayne_talking."

You might also consider date stamping your files when you save them. Your computer does this automatically, but it helps sometimes to see the date in the file name ("writing project May 5" or "writing project 05_08_12," for example). Doing so will help you make sure that when you resume working on your project, you're working with your most recent draft. Date stamping can also help you avoid writing over earlier drafts, which you might need later.

MM10-d Keeping track of versions when sharing files with others

Part of managing files, especially when you work collaboratively, is developing a system for sharing files. It's easy, and frustrating, to end up with multiple versions of a file that have to be merged. Say, for instance, that you are working on a project with two other students, John and Chelsea. You each have a copy of your project. John is making changes to it, and Chelsea is making changes to it. Suddenly, you have three different versions of your project: yours, John's, and Chelsea's. Figuring out who made what changes and getting all of those changes into a single draft is difficult and time-consuming.

Passing around one file and working on that one file individually is a good approach. If you're passing around a file, make sure that only one member of your group works on that file at a time. Or try uploading the file to a collaborative workspace, so that all members of your group make changes to a single version. Whatever strategy you adopt, maintaining good communication with your group members is essential.

ACTIVITY MM10–1: Your understanding

Online tools that help you create, manage, and save files can be especially helpful when you're working with files you need to share with others. Look online for three such tools (GoogleDocs, for example) and generate a list of pros and cons for each. As you create your list, think about what criteria are important to you. Here are a few questions to help you get started:

- Does the tool let you save multiple files in one place?
- How large can the files be?

- What types of files are allowed? Documents? Audio files? Image or movie files?
- Do files remain posted until you take them down? Or do they expire after a set time?
- Does the tool allow multiple people to edit a file at the same time?
- Does the tool record information about who makes saved changes?
- Can you easily download the file after all changes have been made and saved?

ACTIVITY MM10–2: Your project

Come up with a file-saving strategy for a project you're about to begin. If you're already working on something, describe your current file-saving strategy and think about what's working well and what you might improve. Think about how you want to handle different types of files, for example, and how you want to manage your series of drafts.

MM11 Outlining and drafting your project

In section MM9, on planning your project, you saw a visualization of Marisa Williamson's writing process—a visualization that was not neat and orderly (see Figure 9–2, p. MM-63). In the process of working on her project, Williamson moved back and forth across the pieces she was developing and working with, selecting an image here, identifying a video piece to use there, revising her narration before recording it. Although Williamson's *process* might have seemed a bit haphazard, her final *product* is sequenced, polished, and very well organized.

Your ideas might be expressed in written words, in audio, in moving images, in still images, or in some combination. Regardless of the media you're working with, organizing your ideas before and as you draft will help you meet your goals as a composer and will help you meet your audience's needs.

MM11-a Choosing the right organizing tool for your multimodal project

How you organize the information you're presenting depends on the type of document you will produce and what different modes you might use. A slide show presentation, for instance, is typically linear.

Most slide shows have a title slide, an introduction slide or two, body slides, a conclusion slide, and so forth (see Figure 11–1). If you're giving background information or presenting a problem that needs solving, you will want to do so early in your slide presentation. If

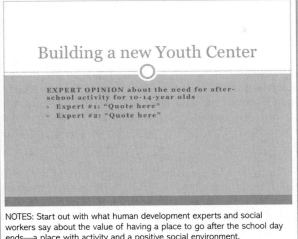

Template design allows the composer to focus on developing ideas instead of appearances.

The composer uses notes to plan evidence.

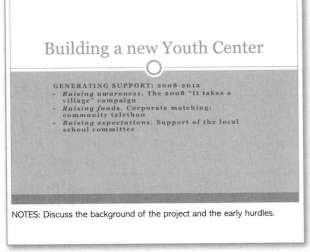

Notes help the composer create distinct goals for each slide.

FIGURE 11–1 DRAFTING A SLIDE SHOW PRESENTATION WITH NOTES.

you are giving reasons for support, think about how to arrange those reasons: Strongest first? Strongest last? The notes feature in Power-Point and other presentation software can help you as you play with arrangement and build your script. What also helps is that you can move slides around fairly easily. Slide show templates can help you figure out what information should be placed where.

Unlike a slide presentation, Web sites don't function in a linear way. They can be arranged with hyperlinks across pages, so you may not want to create a specific path for readers; instead, you can give them different options for experiencing your ideas. What is most important in organizing Web site content is making sure your categories of information are clear.

After Alyson D'Amato had considered her purpose and audience, determined her genre (an informative site), and started planning her content (brewing tea), she considered the different ways she could present information on a Web site. Having one long page readers would scroll down to read didn't seem ideal—nor did it seem to her like a good way to effectively create a Web page.

D'Amato decided to create a wireframe, or mock-up, of her project before starting to build her Web site. At first, D'Amato was going to have only three main links: to her tea story, to brewing tea, and to tea types. "Making blends" was going to be a link within the brewing tea page, and black, green, and white tea information was going to be linked from the tea types page.

She decided, however, that she didn't want to bury all of that information and make users click to a page and then link deeper to get to information she thought was important, so she planned for six main links, shown in Figure 11–2.

How you organize the information you're presenting also depends on your purpose. If you are teaching your readers to do something new, you will probably need to provide straightforward, step-by-step,

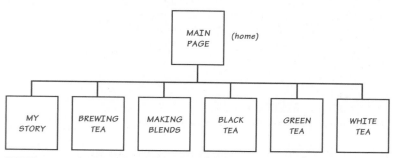

FIGURE 11–2 REVISED WIREFRAME FOR A WEB SITE.

numbered instructions. If you are composing a video essay that inspires people to reflect or to take action, you may have more flexibility in arranging your information for impact.

Once you have a strong sense of your topic and main idea and you've begun to assemble support, you'll want to think about organizing your ideas. Often for traditional essays, instructors focus on creating outlines, where you begin with a thesis statement and then develop the key ideas you will express in the body of your paper. Creating an outline is also an effective way to get started on a multimodal piece, because regardless of what you choose to include and how you choose to share information, it's crucial to have some guiding organization—a skeleton that you can flesh out in a draft.

Other tools can be useful for organizing your ideas. For instance, moviemakers often use a storyboard to think about how they will express ideas. A storyboard provides a space for a composer to describe the scene being set, any text that will appear on the screen, and the music or other sounds that will be in the scene. There's also room for the composer to add specific notes and a place for describing a transition (see Figure 11–3).

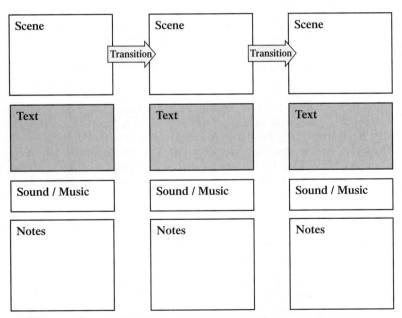

FIGURE 11–3 STORYBOARD FOR A MULTIMODAL PROJECT, WITH SPACE FOR THE SCENE, TEXT, SOUND OR MUSIC, AND NOTES.

MM11-b Drafting to support your main idea

Once you've settled on a main idea and sketched some sort of outline (or wireframe or storyboard), you'll need to gather and select the content that will best support that main idea. This is a good time to take another look at the assignment. Reread the requirements and the prompt(s) to which you're responding.

There's nothing magical about drafting. It takes time, of course, and it helps to have notes about your main idea, your evidence, and your organization close by. Successful drafters ask, anticipate, and respond to questions as they work through a draft, whether they realize it or not. A writer who is composing an instructional booklet may ask, for example, *How do people learn something new?* or *How did I learn to do what I'm trying to describe?*

Think about creating a multimodal document that teaches people how to plant trees. Your main idea might be "A healthy tree starts with a proper planting." You know your audience will want to know what constitutes "a proper planting." You decide there are steps, but how many steps? What's the first step? Once you start fleshing out the steps—considering the climate, assessing how the roots are contained, digging the hole—you need to anticipate and respond to questions at each step: How big should the hole be? How deep? Why? How is the root ball set in? During your drafting, you might even ask which of the steps need illustrations or photos to complete the teaching or, in other words, to fulfill your purpose for your audience.

When you're composing a text that is less concrete—an interpretation or analysis, perhaps—you might find that questioning helps you get from a rough outline to full paragraphs. One student was assigned to write an interpretation of song lyrics or a poem of his choice. The assignment also included a requirement that students illustrate some part of the song or poem. The student chose the song "Pumped Up Kicks" by Foster the People, listened to the song and read through the lyrics numerous times, brainstormed some ideas that focused on the song's main character, and wrote a rough outline.

ROUGH OUTLINE

Interpretation of "Pumped Up Kicks"

Main idea: If the song is Robert's "story," is there any way he, who shoots and murders peers, can be seen as a sympathetic character? Close, but no.

- Robert is alone and lonely, and that's something the audience can understand and maybe relate to.
- Robert has a negative relationship with the "other" kids, and the audience can understand that fact as a powerful motivator.

- Robert makes devastating choices, so extreme that it's hard for the audience to relate.

The student was comfortable enough with his main idea and proceeded to draft an introduction focusing on what makes a character sympathetic. The following shows how he went about developing a paragraph from the first point in his rough outline.

Point in the rough outline	The composer's questions	Draft paragraph
Robert is alone and lonely, and that's something the audience can understand and maybe relate to.	*How can I tell Robert is alone? Where do I see this in the lyrics? Does alone = lonely?*	The lyrics show us a boy, a "kid," whose "Daddy works a long day" and who spends the day unsupervised. Robert is alone in his house and alone in his thoughts as he spends idle time digging in "his dad's closet" and trying his father's cigarettes. There's not really a hint of any kind of relationship (at least a positive relationship) in the story.
	Do I care? Does his loneliness make him sympathetic?	The father comes "home late," probably repeatedly, and Robert is left waiting "for a long time." There doesn't seem to be a mother figure or siblings. Even if we can't relate to Robert, maybe we can understand his actions as being the result of an unloving home environment. His being alone and lonely generates sympathy.

As the student moves from outline to draft, he successfully identifies evidence from the lyrics to support his point. He still needs to consider images that might help him communicate his analysis of the lyrics. After all, his assignment asks him to illustrate a part of the poem or lyrics. He's off to a good start, however.

When you proceed from your ideas and notes to full sentences and strings of ideas, keep in mind that a *draft* is flexible. The goal is to get something down on paper that makes some sense and can be played with and questioned later by you, a peer, or another reader. It helps to ask, anticipate, and respond to questions you have or your reader might have. And of course it helps to keep your purpose for writing and your audience in mind as you draft.

ACTIVITY MM11–1: Your understanding

To experiment with one type of organizing tool for a multimodal composition, try "reverse engineering" a brief video or a fairly simple Web site. Identify a video or Web site and strip it down to either an outline, a wireframe, or a storyboard.

ACTIVITY MM11–2: Your project

Take a current assignment and, as you work your way through your ideas for the assignment, try out at least one of the organizing tools discussed in this section. Write a brief reflective paragraph about whether the strategy was or was not helpful to you as you moved on to the drafting stage.

MM12 Emphasizing important information

When you look at a document, you'll notice that some information is emphasized, or treated more prominently, to catch the reader's attention or communicate a main idea. In print documents, emphasis is usually achieved by the placement of information on the page. Take a look at the sample documents, a résumé and a brochure, in Figures 12–1 and 12–2. What information jumps out at you? What information do you think is the most important in each one?

When you examine the résumé, think about the context and purpose of a résumé. The "work" a résumé does is to "sell" the author—to best portray his or her abilities, skills, and experiences. The author emphasizes his name with boldface type and centered placement. He presents categories that will be of interest to his reader in a consistent way. The second document, a brochure, would appear folded, with the panel on the right as the "cover." The emphasis is on a photograph of a puppy and a child. Why? The composer made choices to inspire the reader to act on behalf of the family pet.

Composers use different methods of emphasizing important information, depending on the type of composition they're producing. If you have written traditional essays, you may be used to creating emphasis with your words and sentence structure—using

FIGURE 12–1 A RÉSUMÉ.

FIGURE 12–2 A BROCHURE. (*Source:* FEMA)

phrases like "and most important" or "the strongest evidence yet." In traditional essays, information is expressed in written words, and it's up to your readers to be able to discern what information is critical without the aid of visual cues. When you compose multimodal essays, you'll have to first determine what information is most important to emphasize, given your purpose and audience, and then how you can best emphasize that information, given your genre and modes.

MM12-a Determining what needs emphasis

Before you can make decisions about how to emphasize certain information, you need to decide what information is most crucial to convey. This decision depends on your audience and your purpose.

If your purpose is to inform and your audience is peers (other college students) who are new to the topic, you'll want to think about overarching categories of information and what might motivate your audience to engage with the information. If your purpose is to persuade your audience to embrace your position in a debate, the most important information to emphasize might be the evidence you provide to support your key points.

Student composer Alyson D'Amato, who created an informative Web site about brewing tea, wanted to emphasize the benefits of brewing loose leaf tea and the pleasures of creating custom blends. She didn't want these ideas to get buried under other basic information such as different kinds of tea leaves. To start identifying information that needs emphasis in your own composition, think about the following questions:

- What is your reason for composing? What are you trying to accomplish, and why?
- Who are your audience members? What information is going to be most appealing to them? Most convincing?
- What's the main thing you want your readers to remember after they've experienced your composition?

MM12-b Choosing a strategy for creating emphasis

In a text-only document with minimal design, the words themselves carry importance; that is, how you format words and sentences and where you place them help provide emphasis. You would probably express an important idea in a topic sentence at the start of a paragraph, for example, rather than bury it in the middle of a long paragraph. In a text-only document with design features, important ideas can be emphasized with font choice and by styling words with boldface, underline, italics, and type size. Look at the documents in Figure 12–3. From a glance, what would you assume to be the most important information in each one?

The large boldface text in the first and third examples is likely the most important information. The first example also includes a "pull quote," which draws readers' eyes to the right side of the page. The second example includes some boldface text and a bulleted list, which help key information stand out from the rest of the text. In the third example, readers might assume that the text block at the bottom of the page is less important than the spaced-out, right-aligned text at the top of the page.

Consider the front page of Alyson D'Amato's Web site (Figure 12–4). Perhaps the most important information on the front page is the list of links at the top of the page, which allows readers to see the different topics addressed on the Web site and to go to the different pages of the site. This navigation bar stays at the top of each page, so readers can easily move around on the site from whichever page they land on. D'Amato has also emphasized the photo of tea leaves—with her audience (tea novices) in mind.

FIGURE 12-3 DOCUMENTS, SHOWING DIFFERENT WAYS TO CREATE EMPHASIS.

On the Web site home page, the body text appears in somewhat standard-size text, organized into paragraphs. The front page text is important, but perhaps not as important as the navigation bar.

If you listen to student composer Marisa Williamson's video, which argues that tragedies—even those experienced only on You-Tube—knit us together, you'll notice that she repeats some audio clips throughout the video. This repetition of information makes it stand out as particularly important.

She repeats three key audio clips across her work:

- "The world is very different now." (John F. Kennedy)
- "Now is the time." (Martin Luther King Jr.)
- "We cannot turn back." (Martin Luther King Jr.)

FIGURE 12–4 FIRST PAGE OF A WEB SITE, SHOWING LINKS, AN IMAGE, AND TEXT.

These clips contribute to her main idea that online video is now one of the primary ways that we experience formative events. She deliberately chose *not* to repeat a phrase that John F. Kennedy is perhaps most famous for: "Ask not what your country can do for you—ask what you can do for your country." Because this famous line is heard only once in Williamson's composition, it stands out as being particularly meaningful.

Another way that the student creates dramatic emphasis is by beginning and ending with audio clips of Ronald Reagan, US president in 1986 when the space shuttle *Challenger* disaster occurred.

You have a number of strategies for emphasizing important information at your disposal as you craft a multimodal piece. In a PowerPoint slide, you might style headings so that they communicate your key ideas prominently, and you might use bullet points to emphasize steps or points in your presentation. In an advertisement, you might add white space around a product shot to call attention to it. In a podcast, you might pause and use silence for emphasis. In a video, you might use subtitles to reinforce a message. Considering your purpose for composing, determining your audience, and understanding the genre in which you are composing are important steps in figuring out how to make an impact.

ACTIVITY MM12–1: Your understanding

In section MM8, you looked at the home pages of a few Web sites to identify the primary audience of each (see p. MM-59). Take a look again at the following sites, with emphasis in mind:

- the main Web site of your school
- the Web site of a professor at your school
- the Web site of a fast-food restaurant in your area
- the Web site of a small, locally owned restaurant in your area
- the Web site of the company that made the car you drive or that makes the car you'd like to drive
- the Web site for a branch or an agency of the US government (for example, the White House, the IRS, the FBI)
- the Web site for an individual who serves in the US government (such as a member of Congress)

As you look at each multimodal text, identify what information the composer seems to be emphasizing. How do you know it's important? What are some of the techniques used to highlight the most important information? Write brief notes for each piece, and be prepared to discuss them in class.

ACTIVITY MM12–2: Your project

For a project you are currently working on, make notes about the information you want to emphasize and some strategies you can use to do so. Take into consideration your purpose, your audience, and the genre you are working in. What textual formatting options might you use to draw attention to your key points? What visuals might you embed to support those points? Are there audio clips (dialogue, music, sound effects) or video clips that might help articulate the main points in your project?

☰ MM13 Revising and editing your multimodal project

Very few writers sit down, write a first draft of a paper, and submit it for a successful grade. More typically, writers work on a draft in chunks, circling back occasionally to reread and rewrite. You may find that your instructors build time into an assignment for feedback, revising, and editing. Even if they don't, it's useful to set aside some time so that you can move comfortably from a first or second draft to a final piece. Revising and editing a multimodal composition may take substantially more time than revising and editing a traditional essay.

Your handbook includes advice about revising and editing. For the purposes of this brief discussion, keep in mind the following distinctions:

In general, **revising** involves

- rethinking your point or purpose
- reshaping your approach to fit your audience's needs
- reorganizing or strengthening evidence to help you achieve your purpose
- rearranging whole parts of your composition
- revisiting your message

In general, **editing** involves

- checking to see if sentences and paragraphs progress logically
- adding transitions where necessary to improve coherence
- changing wordy phrases
- deleting sentences that are off-topic
- making sure that word choice is precise and tailored to the purpose and audience

When revising and editing a traditional, words-only document, a writer might move around, add, or delete whole passages or sentences in a word processing program. The writer might print out a draft to mark corrections, changes, or points that need more clarification. The processes of revising a multimodal project, however, might be quite different, depending on the modes used. The overall point of revising and editing, whether your composition is multimodal or monomodal, is to make your work stronger, clearer, better organized, and on target for your purpose and audience.

MM13-a Seeking and using feedback

Before you revise and edit, it may help to seek feedback from classmates, your instructor, a tutor, or a friend. Tell each reviewer whether you want feedback about larger, more global issues (organization, main point, use of audio/visual/textual evidence, overall message) or surface-level issues (clear sentences, precise words, sentence logic). In other words, tell reviewers whether you are approaching a revising stage or an editing stage. Before you share a draft with a reviewer, think about three key questions you might want your reviewer to answer, and share those questions with him or her.

After student composer Alyson D'Amato had made initial decisions based on her purpose, audience, and content and after she had outlined and drafted her project, an informative Web site about tea, she met with a tutor at her school's writing center to get feedback on her site. Figure 13–1 shows a page from her draft site. She asked the tutor the following questions:

1. The assignment says that we have to have a good navigation, or a clear introduction and way for the reader/viewer to move through the composition. Is the navigation clear? How can I improve it?

2. I'm not sure about the pictures I've included, but I don't know what I would replace them with. Can you comment on the visuals?

3. Do you think that the text is well written and flows well? Can you point out areas that could be stronger?

D'Amato and her tutor spent some time looking at her site, and the tutor had D'Amato read parts of it out loud. They also looked at

FIGURE 13–1 DRAFT STUDENT PROJECT: AN INFORMATIVE WEB SITE.

a few other informative Web sites for ideas and inspiration. D'Amato left with a set of priorities for revising her work. The following are her revision goals.

ALYSON D'AMATO'S REVISION GOALS

- There's too much to read on each page. Streamline. We looked at another Web site with similar navigation but more manageable content. We came up with a way to break up the text.
- The tea photos are cool, but they don't really make sense, especially since one has a tea bag in it and my site is about brewing loose leaf teas. Maybe replace with images of loose leaf tea.
- The tutor also asked why I chose the font for "LOOSE LEAF TEA," and I just thought it looked cool. We looked at some other tea sites, and they all used a more elegant type of font that might be easier to read and more appealing to people interested in tea. Choose new font.
- The site will need more of an introduction—the tutor said I just jumped right into it here. There are also chunks of info that don't really fit or flow well. I marked those and need to revise them. NOTE TO SELF!!! Do this before reworking the text on different pages!
- The tutor also asked why I took up so much room on the left side with my name and class info. He suggested that because my audience is potential tea fans generally, I might want to cut the class-specific info, because it really makes this look like a student project, which some people might not take seriously.

Creating a list of goals is a good way to make the transition between feedback and revising. Keep in mind that you don't have to make every change a reviewer suggests. Look at the reviewer's suggestions through the lens of your own purpose, audience, and assignment. Not every suggestion is going to be right for your project. If you seek feedback from three reviewers, however, and all three say that your project seems a little hard to follow, you know that organization is going to be one area in which you'll want to focus your revision efforts.

MM13-b Revising and remixing a multimodal composition

Writers typically revise a draft by moving sentences or paragraphs around their paper. Word processing software makes it easy for writers to cut and paste chunks of text in a words-only draft. When a writer, for example, reads the final paragraph in a draft and realizes—either on his or her own or with a reader's help—that the main point is buried in the concluding paragraph, it's easy enough to move a sentence or group of sentences from one place to another and rewrite as needed.

When revising a multimodal piece, you might have to ask different kinds of revision questions depending on the mode(s) you've chosen to communicate your main idea.

- In revising a speech, you might ask, *Where is it important to pause and perhaps seek audience interaction? How can my speech be stronger with the use of props or visual aids?*

- In revising a slide show presentation, you might ask, *Is the balance of text and visuals right? Do I need this whole table as evidence, or can I use just a detail from it? Are the slides progressing at the right pace for my audience, mainly senior citizens?*

- In revising a video, you might ask, *Would narration help to provide "glue" between the testimony of my interviewees? Is the background music too distracting?*

Thinking about revision as *remix* can be helpful in approaching a multimodal project. *Remix* is a term typically used to describe the process of taking an original audio track and adding other elements. Perhaps one of the most infamous remixes in recent times was Danger Mouse's 2004 release of *The Grey Album*. To produce the album, Danger Mouse took Jay-Z's *Black Album* (2003) and remixed it with the Beatles' *White Album* (1968). Together, the lyrics and music from both albums—mixed and merged together—took on an entirely different tone and meaning.

A useful way to think about revision with a multimodal composition is that you are "remixing" your own work—taking an original piece or set of pieces and rearranging them, resequencing them, and perhaps adding elements. This remixing might result in a composition with more impact, better focus, or more awareness of the audience.

Student composer Marisa Williamson found that to revise her video essay, she had to keep circling back and remixing the elements of her draft. She had a lot of what she needed in her first draft; for her, revising meant rearranging in response to feedback from her classmates.

For example, when Williamson initially drafted her video piece, she sequenced the images and video chronologically—she included the images and video of John F. Kennedy's assassination first (1963), followed by footage related to Martin Luther King Jr.'s assassination (1968) and the space shuttle *Challenger* disaster (1986), and ended with video of the September 11 terrorist attacks in New York City (2001).

Fellow students who saw the draft suggested that she didn't need to tell the story chronologically to make her point. She resequenced the clips and even tried looping, or repeating, some of the clips for emphasis. Also, Williamson wasn't sure how she wanted to include her own words in her video. In her first draft, she included her words by scrolling them along the bottom of the movie. Her classmates, however, suggested that this was distracting and that it might be interesting to record and layer her own voice over the music. She tried that at the revising stage.

MM13-c Editing a multimodal composition

Editing is a stage in which a composer takes a closer look at the composition and asks, *Is it clear? Does it make sense?* Editing a words-only composition means looking at words and sentences and the transitions between sentences and paragraphs. Editing a multimodal composition can be a bit more complicated, in part because multimodal projects require composers to work across different modes and sometimes across different software. As you edit your project, you might find the questions in the following chart helpful.

Editing multimodal compositions

Editing words

- Have you chosen the clearest, most appropriate words for your purpose and audience?
- Are your sentences and paragraphs in logical order?
- Have you included transitions between sentences and paragraphs to improve the flow of your ideas?
- Could your ideas be expressed in more concise language?
- Do grammar or spelling errors distract from your message?

Editing sounds

- Is the volume appropriate? Do any sounds drown out other elements?
- Is the pace of the narration right? Not too slow or too fast?
- Do you need more sound or more silence?
- Is your sound synched properly to any static or moving images that go with it?

Editing static images

- Have you chosen the clearest, most appropriate images for your purpose and audience?
- Do you need more visual evidence? Do you have the right kind of visuals? Would a graph, for example, be better than a photograph for your composition?
- Have you used captions as needed for the images? Some visuals can't speak for themselves.
- Are the images you've chosen presented at an appropriate size?

Editing moving images

- If you're using video clips, is the length appropriate?
- Is the purpose of the moving images clear in your composition?
- Are the moving images emphasizing the right content?

Editing for consistency and clarity

- If you've made changes in one mode (edited words in the narration, for instance), do you need to make changes in another (edit words that appear on-screen)?
- If you've produced slides, do they have a consistent design?
- Are you using colors, font sizes, and headings purposefully and consistently?
- If you have navigation elements in your project, is it clear to your users/viewers how to get from one place to another?

Crediting and citing

- Have you cited the works you're quoting from, paraphrasing, or summarizing?
- Have you credited the artists whose music you've used?
- Have you credited the creators or photographers of the images you've used?
- Have you credited the composers of the video clips you've used?

ACTIVITY MM13–1: Your understanding

Popular examples of remixes are multimodal compositions in which composers rearrange the events in movie trailers to create a different, alternative tone or meaning. If you search the Web for "remixed" or "recut" movie trailers, you may find one that positions *The Hunger Games* as a comedy and *Twilight* as a creepy stalker film. Find two or three different remixed movie trailers. Identify what elements are probably "original" to the trailer, and then identify what elements have been remixed, added, or changed. What effect does the remix have? Why?

ACTIVITY MM13–2: Your project

Think about a project you're currently working on. Make a plan to seek feedback from a teacher, tutor, classmate, or friend. Make a list of three or four questions you want to ask this person. What sort of advice or feedback do you hope to get? After you meet with this person, compose a brief list of revision goals.

MM14 Integrating and documenting sources

Most composers at some point depend on source material—words, data, audio, or images that come from elsewhere. Writers in medicine depend on clinical studies; caseworkers in the social sciences depend on interviews; filmmakers depend on scripts. Responsible composers integrate and document their sources according to the conventions of their field. These conventions don't always translate well from field to field. Imagine watching a movie and having citations to reference material appear on the screen throughout the movie. Likewise, imagine reading an academic article that makes claims but offers no support and no citations. When you are composing, you will want to pay attention to the expectations for crediting your sources in the type of composition you are creating.

MM14-a Understanding why documenting sources is important

Giving formal credit to sources is necessary for a few key reasons. Documenting sources allows you to

- make evident to an audience that you have done your homework, researched the topic thoroughly, and are aware of larger conversations, discussions, and research related to the topic
- direct an audience to the original material that you gathered and used to conduct research and write up your findings
- give credit where credit is due, acknowledging your use of someone else's ideas—whether they're expressed in written words, static or moving images, sound, or multiple modes.

You may be familiar with instructors' expectations about different documentation styles (MLA, APA, *Chicago*, CSE). Your handbook covers how to cite sources in your written work using one of these styles.

MM14-b Knowing when a citation is needed

Sources don't always have to be formal academic articles or books. One of the trickiest aspects of citing your sources and documenting your work is recognizing what should be cited, regardless of the type of composition you are crafting.

You should generally cite a source in these cases:

- when you use or refer to somebody else's words or ideas from a magazine, book, newspaper, song, TV program, movie, Web page, computer program, letter, advertisement, or any other medium
- when you use information obtained through interviewing another person
- when you use data from experiments that you did not conduct
- when you use diagrams, illustrations, charts, or photos that you did not create
- when you use audio or video clips that you did not create

Typically, you do not need to document a source in these cases:

- when you are writing from your own experiences, your own observations, your own insights, your own thoughts, or your own conclusions about a subject
- when you are using "common knowledge"—folklore, common-sense observations, or shared information within your field of study or cultural group
- when you are compiling generally accepted facts
- when you are writing up your own experimental result

MM14-c Determining how to integrate sources in a multimodal composition

The Internet makes it easy to find images, photographs, articles, songs, sounds, and other material with a few clicks. With a fast Internet connection, downloading such materials is convenient. Most computer programs, from spreadsheet applications to presentation software to word processing tools, allow users to include images, sounds, and the like in their documents. Video production applications allow composers to include audio tracks and text on-screen.

Much of what you find on the Web, however, is owned by others—in other words, it is the copyright-protected property of other individuals. This doesn't mean that students can't use the materials for class projects, but being a college writer means knowing how to integrate and acknowledge sources responsibly and correctly.

When you integrate words (a quotation from, a paraphrase of, or a summary of source material) into a words-only document, you will typically do so with a signal phrase and a parenthetical reference.

The student's point.

> Many parents worry that youth and teens are meeting strangers online and that these relationships pose dangers. According to research funded by the MacArthur Foundation, however, youth and teens use digital media mainly to "extend" relationships they already have (Ito et al.). The danger comes when these existing relationships turn bad.

The student's signal phrase.

Material from the source, followed by a parenthetical citation.

The student's comment on the source.

In multimodal projects, however, using a signal phrase and a parenthetical reference may be disruptive. Slide show composers who include images on slides usually do so with design in mind, placing images near key words or ideas for emphasis. During a talk, the presenter might refer to a particular image: *As you can see from this table, the number of people in America who identify themselves as biracial has tripled in the past fifteen years*. The speaker may give the source of the information in the talk, include a source line in smaller type under the image, or include a bibliography in a final slide.

You may have a great deal of flexibility when *integrating* sources in a multimodal project. College instructors will expect you to *document* your sources; in doing so, you will have a little less flexibility. Be sure to ask your instructor for guidelines.

MM14-d Figuring out how to document sources in a multimodal composition

Composers can cite sources in different ways, for different modes. Student Marisa Williamson provides a separate works cited page for her video essay "To the Children of America," because that is what the assignment requires. She credits the owners of the music she used, the audio clips she used, and the images and video she used. Her works cited list provides enough information for her audience to find the complete, original files that she edited for her project. If she creates a video essay for another course, she might follow a convention typical of movies and include a credits section at the end of her video.

Another example of how sources are cited differently in different types of compositions is shown on the works cited page of Alyson D'Amato's Web site. D'Amato was, for much of the content, the expert. That is, she didn't need to do a lot of research because she knew a great deal about selecting and brewing tea. She was interested in learning more about tea rituals and tea history, so she cited the works she consulted as she worked on her site, and she also created a list of links to Web sites she mentioned on her own site (see Figure 14–1).

Identifying what citation conventions are typical of the delivery mode you plan to use and following those conventions is part of multimodal composing. See the chart on pages MM-98 and MM-99.

The list of genres in the chart is not exhaustive, but it gives some sense of the ways in which composers of multimodal works can document the use of materials and information they did not create. Depending on the course for which you are composing, you may be asked to consult a particular academic citation style, such as MLA, APA, or *Chicago*. See your handbook for more on documenting sources in these styles.

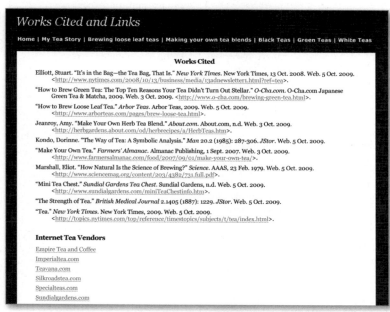

FIGURE 14–1 WEB PAGE SHOWING WORKS CITED, INCLUDING LINKS TO RELATED WEB SITES.

Documentation conventions for different genres

Genre	Documentation convention	Reason
Essay, article, or scientific report	Typically in a works cited or reference list at the end of the essay	For an author to show that she or he has done research and thoroughly explored the topic For others to access this original work that the author consulted
Slide show presentation	At the very end, embedded in a separate slide typically called "sources" or "works cited"	For an author to show that she or he has done research and thoroughly explored the topic For others to access this original work that the author consulted To give credit and provide information for video clips, music, and other material produced by someone other than the presentation's composer
Song lyrics	Usually in the liner notes, where the artist gives formal credit or points toward permission to use copyrighted lyrics	To give credit to the original author of the lyrics or text being set to music
Music	Usually in the liner notes, where the artist gives formal credit or points toward permission to use copyrighted music	To give credit to the original artist or composer

Genre	Documentation convention	Reason
Full-length movie	At the very end, embedded within what are typically called the "closing credits"	To list cast and crew

To provide location information and acknowledge the help of a community

To include complete names and artists for songs used in the movie

For major motion pictures, there are strict standards regarding who gets credited and in what order. |
| **Short video** | At the very end, embedded within what are typically called the "credits" | For an author to show that she or he has done research and thoroughly explored the topic

For others to access this original work that the author consulted

To give credit and provide information for video clips, music, and other material produced by someone other than the video's composer |
| **News broadcast** | Usually mentioned by the reporter orally within the story itself

Can be a mention of a story from another news source

Can be credit given to an ordinary citizen | For the station or reporter to give credit to the original person who broke the story or provided the information

To include more perspectives and viewpoints in a story |

ACTIVITY MM14–1: Your understanding

Review a writing assignment you recently completed that required you to produce an essay or some other traditional document. How did you integrate and document your sources for the assignment? Imagine re-creating the composition in another format—perhaps as a video or a slide show presentation. How would your handling of the sources change?

ACTIVITY MM14–2: Your project

It's important to keep a working bibliography whenever you work with sources. Consult your handbook's guidelines for compiling and maintaining a working bibliography, and create a working bibliography for your current project.

MM15 Presenting or publishing your project

When you produce a typical essay, you usually turn in a printed, paper copy of that essay to your instructor, or perhaps you turn it in by uploading the word-processed document to a course management system like Blackboard or CompClass. Submitting the work is easy because most students have access to printers and because most essays—even those with a few images—are small electronic files.

Files that include multimodal projects, however, can be extremely large. Or you may have produced a multi*file* project. Submitting and sharing the project sometimes cannot be done by e-mail or on paper.

It's important to consider where and how you will publish your multimodal project. Will you post a video on a video-sharing site like YouTube? Will you create a Web site that your school can host? Will you upload a slide show to your course page? Your instructor may give guidelines about sharing your work with your intended audience. This section includes some tips for thinking through this final stage of the project.

MM15-a Knowing your options for presenting and publishing multimodal works

The first step in deciding how to present or publish your project is knowing the different spaces available to you.

Your instructor may recommend specific presentation or publication spaces for your project. For instance, some schools have their own intranet where students can store projects. Your instructor may prefer that you upload your work to a course management site or system.

There are many other options to consider. You may need to poke around online or consult with peers about the following:

Video-hosting sites: Web sites that allow you to upload video and that will generate a stable URL for your video. (One example: YouTube)

Web-creation sites: Web sites where you can compile and create your own Web site. These often allow you to copy and paste text, add images, and create links. (One example: Weebly)

Web-hosting sites: Web sites where you can upload your Web files and create your own Web site with a unique URL. These sites often have built-in Web-creation options, too. (One example: GoDaddy)

Slide show creation and hosting sites: Web sites that allow you to build a slide show presentation and store it for others to view. (One example: Prezi)

MM15-b Considering the pros and cons of the spaces available for presenting and publishing multimodal work

If you have a choice about how and where to share your work, you may want to consider the pros and cons of different spaces. See the chart on pages MM-102 and MM-103.

Once you've chosen a specific type of space for creating or hosting your project and then chosen a specific site, you'll need to familiarize yourself with the options that site provides. Your instructor may be able to help. You will probably need answers to at least a few of the following questions:

- Do you need an account to work in the space? If so, do you have to pay for the account?
- Will your readers/viewers need a password to access your work?
- Will your readers/viewers have to set up an account to access your work?
- Will your readers/viewers have to download or install any special software to view your work?
- How long will your work be available on the site?
- Will ads appear in or near your work when it is on the site?

Presentation spaces for multimodal projects

Presentation space	Pros	Cons
Your campus course management space	Password-protected, so only your instructor and perhaps other students in your class can access your work	Typically does not offer building and creation tools—just offers storage space Usually limited in terms of file size for student projects (so a 10 MB slide show might be fine, but a 100 MB video project might be too big)
Video-hosting sites	Allow you to upload and store big files Allow you to create videos that aren't software dependent (i.e., users/viewers don't have to have a specific type of software to see the video) Usually allow users to post comments and share feedback	Are often advertisement-based, so ads may appear around or even on top of your video Sometimes generate long and hard-to-remember URLs
Web-creation sites	Can make Web site creation and design easy	Are sometimes subscription- or fee-based (you have to pay to use them) Some are less intuitive than others
Web-hosting sites	Allow you to purchase your own URL Usually provide storage space for many different file types and sizes	Are sometimes subscription- or fee-based (you have to pay to use them) Can have complicated interfaces, making uploading your content difficult

Presentation space	Pros	Cons
Slide show creation and hosting sites	Allow you to create slide show presentations that aren't software dependent (i.e., users/viewers don't have to have a specific type of software to see the presentation) Can make slide show creation and design easy	Are sometimes subscription- or fee-based (you have to pay to use them) Some are less intuitive than others

MM15-c Making your project accessible and usable

In earlier sections, you read about taking into consideration the needs of your audience. Often you need to think about whether your project will be accessible and usable to your audience. If it's not, you won't be able to communicate your message. *Accessibility* typically refers to someone's physical ability to access something. For instance, a building that has only steps at its entry is not physically accessible for people using wheelchairs. In terms of multimodal projects, accessibility refers to someone's ability to hear, see, or generally put to use a text. Multimodal texts that are not accessible have a more limited audience. For example, a person with hearing deficits might be unable to use a video lecture online because she can't hear the speaker and no transcript is provided.

Usability typically refers to ease of use—how easy it is to navigate a Web site or learn to use a product, for example. In terms of multimodal projects, usability has to do with how easy or difficult it is for the audience to find, experience, and understand the composer's ideas. For example, if a multimodal text needs to be downloaded for viewing, the composer can improve usability by reducing the file size to accommodate slower Internet connections.

Not everyone has a fast Internet connection or access to a computer. Not all of the audience for your multimodal work can see or hear, or can see or hear well. You can't plan for every possible audience need, but you can compose multimodal pieces that allow you to reach the widest possible audience. Here are some guidelines to keep in mind.

Consider what format works best for your audience. For many projects, your instructor is your main audience. If your instructor doesn't tell you the format in which you should submit your project, ask. It's better to know up front than to wrestle later with converting a complete project from one interface or delivery system to another. For other projects, you might have different audiences—the campus community, for instance, or YouTube users in general. To best create for your audience, you have to know their technical expectations and also the technical specifications of your delivery choice. For instance, if your instructor has asked you to upload your project to your course management system, that system might have a maximum upload file size, so you'll have to compress your file in order to share it. YouTube and other video-sharing spaces often have time restrictions; YouTube restricts general users to ten-minute clips.

Build in accessibility features. If, for instance, you suspect that your audience might include people who don't hear well or at all, you might add captions to your project. The captions might describe the sounds in your video ([MUSIC] or [LOUD FOOTSTEPS]) and might also offer written text for what's being heard or said in your piece. If you suspect that your audience might include people with vision difficulties, you might provide a text-only transcript of your piece. Most people with visual impairment use a program called a "screen reader," a kind of software that reads text to them. Screen readers, however, cannot easily translate text saved in a slide show presentation or in a movie. Including a transcript of your piece for a screen reader helps make your work accessible to those with vision problems. Providing captions and transcripts can also help reach members of your audience who experience technical difficulties and cannot get clear audio or a clear visual display.

ACTIVITY MM15–1: Your understanding

Find one additional example site for each of the types included in the list in MM15-a. Once you've chosen your example sites, read through their "about" pages and also look through the help areas of their sites. Think about your own degree of technical expertise and your experience with each kind of site. How easily could you become proficient in using each site?

ACTIVITY MM15–2: Your project

For a project you're currently planning or drafting, write a brief page of notes about what you may need to consider so that your audience will find your composition usable and accessible.

Acknowledgments

Figure 1–1: Grecian urn. Illustration by John Keats from Public Domain.

Figure 1–2: Geoglyph photograph. Courtesy of the U.S. National Park Service/U.S. Department of the Interior. Petroglyph photograph. Copyright © Pgiam/istockphoto.com.

Figure 1–3: Illuminated manuscript. Copyright © Duncan Walker/ istockphoto.com.

Figure 1–4: Quick Response Code. QR Code is a registered trademark of DENSO WAVE Incorporated. http://www.qrcode.com/faqpatent-e.html.

Figure 1–5: Numbered math equations. Courtesy of http://umsolver.com. "UMS software's free Algebraic Equation Solver will solve and explain any algebraic equation or system of equations."

Figure 1–6: Tectonic plates. Illustration courtesy of the U.S. Geological Survey. Simkin and others, 2006.

Figure 1–7: Music collage. Copyright © Gilbert Mayer/Superstock.

Figure 1–8: "Where is your family?" billlboard image. Copyright © Sonda Dawes/The Image Works.

Figure 2–1c: Pets brochure. Courtesy of FEMA/www.ready.gov.

Page MM-28: River photograph. Copyright © straga/shutterstock.com.

Page MM-28: Sketch of bridge. Copyright © Danussa/shutterstock.com.

Page MM-28: Map of Michigan. Copyright © Jami Garrison/istockphoto.com.

Page MM-28: River clip art. Copyright © Sapik/shutterstock.com.

Page MM-29: Flood tracking bar graph. Illustration courtesy of the U.S. Geological Survey.

Page MM-29: Elwha River diagram. Illustration courtesy of the U.S. Geological Survey. Duda, J. J., Warrick, J. A., and Magirl, C. S., 2011, Elwha River dam removal—Rebirth of a river: U.S. Geological Survey Fact Sheet 2011-3097, 4 p. Illustrator: Jonathan A. Warrick.

Figure 4–1: Woman washing hair illustration. Copyright © RetroClipArt/ shutterstock.com.

Page MM-31: German shepherd photograph. Copyright © gualtiero boffi/ shutterstock.com.

Figure 4–2: Dandelion photograph. Copyright © Dleonis/Dreamstime.com.

Figure 4–3: Migrant Mother by Dorothea Lange, 1936. Library of Congress/ Farm Security Administration, Office of War Information Photograph.

Page MM-34: CNN frame grab of Saddam Hussein statue falling. Uniphotos/ Newscom. Saddam Hussein statue toppling photograph. Copyright © Robert Nickelsberg/Getty Images.

Page MM-35: Obama HOPE poster. Courtesy of SHEPARD FAIREY/ OBEYGIANT.COM.

Page MM-35: POPE illustration. Courtesy of © Michael Ian Weinfeld.

Page MM-35: CHANGE INTO A TRUCK poster. Copyright © Timothy P. Doyle, 2009, www.mrdoyle.com.

Page MM-35: VERY GRADUAL CHANGE poster. Copyright © Mike Rosulek, 2009.

Figure 5–1: Illustration with photographs, by Eadweard Muybridge, 1878, Courtesy of the Library of Congress Prints and Photographs Division Washington, D.C. 20540 USA.

Figure 5–2: Flip still from *Cloverfield*. Moviestore Collection Ltd./Alamy.

Page MM-42: "Fried egg"/"brain on drugs" PSA image. The Partnership for a Drug-Free America, Inc.

Page MM-43: "Touch the Rainbow" Skittles advertisement. Images used with permission from Wm. Wrigley Jr. Company. Copyright © 2011. All rights reserved. SKITTLES, the S Device, and all affiliated designs are trademarks of Wm. Wrigley Jr. Company or its affiliates. Title: Touch Skittles on YouTube; Client: Wrigley Canada; Product/Service: Skittles; Agency: BBDO Toronto; Writer: Chris Joakim; Art Director: Mike Donaghey; Creative Directors: Carlos Moreno, Peter Ignazi; Account Management: Chitty Krishnappa, Bhreagh Rathbun; Producer: Ann Caverly; Planner: Zach Klein; Marketing Management: Dan Alvo, Laura Amantea, Thomas Tse; Directors: Woods & Low; Production house: OPC/FamilyStyle; Executive Producers: Harland Weiss, Donovan Boden; Producer: Dwight Phipps; Director of Photography: Vinit Borrison; Editorial: Griff Henderson, Posterboy Edit; Visual FX: AXYZ; Color Transfer: Notch; Audio: Eggplant; Online producer: Amy Miranda—Lunch; Online programming/FX: Pixel Pushers; Media: OMD; Seeding: Denizen.

Page MM-43: Man eating Skittles advertisement. Images used with permission from Wm. Wrigley Jr. Company. Copyright © 2011. All rights reserved. SKITTLES, the S Device, and all affiliated designs are trademarks of Wm. Wrigley Jr. Company or its affiliates. Title: Touch Skittles on YouTube; Client: Wrigley Canada; Product/Service: Skittles; Agency: BBDO Toronto; Writer: Chris Joakim; Art Director: Mike Donaghey; Creative Directors: Carlos Moreno, Peter Ignazi; Account Management: Chitty Krishnappa, Bhreagh Rathbun; Producer: Ann Caverly; Planner: Zach Klein; Marketing Management: Dan Alvo, Laura Amantea, Thomas Tse; Directors: Woods & Low; Production house: OPC/FamilyStyle; Executive Producers: Harland Weiss, Donovan Boden; Producer: Dwight Phipps; Director of Photography: Vinit Borrison; Editorial: Griff Henderson, Posterboy Edit; Visual FX: AXYZ; Color Transfer: Notch; Audio: Eggplant; Online producer: Amy Miranda—Lunch; Online programming/FX: Pixel Pushers; Media: OMD; Seeding: Denizen.

Figure 6–1: Cheetah PSA advertisement. Used with permission © World Wildlife Fund/wwf.org.

Page MM-50: Dragon Age II video game inventory screen. Dragon Age II image used with permission of Electronic Arts Inc.

Alyson D'Amato, "Loose Leaf Teas" Web site. Used with permission.

King Anyi Howell podcast. This story was produced by Youth Radio, a Peabody Award–winning media production company.

Marisa Williamson, "To the Children of America" video essay. Used with permission.

Index

Accessibility, of multimodal projects,
  MM: 103–04
Activities
  for creating a working
    bibliography, **MM**: 100
  for emphasizing information in
    multimodal projects, **MM**: 87
  for integrating and documenting
    sources, **MM**: 100
  for managing your own project
    files, **MM**: 76
  for narrowing topics for
    multimodal projects, **MM**: 69
  for organizing a multimodal
    project, **MM**: 82
  for revising multimodal projects,
    MM: 93–94
  for transforming a monomodal
    project to a multimodal project,
    MM: 54
  for understanding accessibility and
    usability, **MM**: 104
  for understanding audience,
    MM: 59–60
  for understanding collaborative
    projects, **MM**: 69
  for understanding emphasis,
    MM: 87
  for understanding moving images,
    MM: 42–43
  for understanding multimodal
    composing, **MM**: 54
  for understanding multimodal
    texts, **MM**: 50
  for understanding purpose, **MM**: 59
  for understanding sound, **MM**: 26–27
  for understanding static images,
    MM: 35
  for understanding tools for
    managing files, **MM**: 75–76
  for understanding written words,
    MM: 21
Advertisement, print, **MM**: 45
American Beauty, analysis of,
  MM: 42
Analysis
  of moving image (student samples),
    MM: 39, 42

of multimodal text (student
  sample), **MM**: 47–48
of sound (student sample),
  MM: 25–26
of static image (student samples),
  MM: 31, 33–34
of video game (student sample),
  MM: 49–50
of written words (student sample),
  MM: 20–21
Animation, as moving image,
  MM: 37, 38
Art history, multimodal images for,
  MM: 10–11
Assignments
  asking questions about,
    MM: 53
  understanding for multimodal
    projects, **MM**: 51–52
Audience
  identifying for multimodal projects,
    MM: 56–58
  for moving images, **MM**: 37, 40–41
  for multimodal texts,
    MM: 44, 48–49
  profile of, **MM**: 57–58
  questions about
    for analyzing multimodal
      texts, **MM**: 14
    for composing multimodal
      projects, **MM**: 51, 54–55,
      56–58
  for sample video project,
    MM: 58–59
  for sound, **MM**: 22, 25–26
  for static images, **MM**: 27, 33
  unintended, **MM**: 59
  for written words,
    MM: 14, 17–21

Biology, multimodal assignments in,
  MM: 11
Brain on drugs PSA, **MM**: 42–43
Brainstorming, for thesis of
  multimodal project,
  MM: 65–66, 67–68
Brochure, emphasizing information
  in, **MM**: 82–83

Capitalization (caps, lowercase, mixed case), **MM**: 17
  appropriate uses of, **MM**: 19
Case. *See* Capitalization
Cave paintings, **MM**: 7–8
Chart, as type of image, **MM**: 29
Clip art, as type of image, **MM**: 28
Cloverfield (movie), analysis of, **MM**: 39
Collaboration, and multimodal projects, **MM**: 63–65
Comic Sans font, **MM**: 17, 18–19
Commercial, TV, **MM**: 45
Composers, of multimodal works, **MM**: 7
Composing
  changes in, **MM**: 7–10
  in college, **MM**: 10–11
  multimodal, historical, **MM**: 7–9
  process for multimodal project, **MM**: 61–63
  visual representations of process, **MM**: 62, 63
Composition, in moving images, **MM**: 39–40
Context, for images, **MM**: 30–31
Copy-and-paste functions, and multimodal composing, **MM**: 9

Delivery method, **MM**: 68–69, 70
Diagram, **MM**: 29
Dialogue, in movie, **MM**: 22–23
Documenting sources
  conventions for, in different genres, **MM**: 98–99
  in multimodal projects, **MM**: 94–100
Drafting multimodal projects, **MM**: 80–82

Economics, multimodal assignments in, **MM**: 11
Editing
  of moving images, **MM**: 40
  of multimodal project, **MM**: 88, 92–93
Electronic files. *See* Files, electronic
Elements, of static images, **MM**: 30–31
Emphasizing information, **MM**: 82–87
  in Web site, **MM**: 84
English, multimodal assignments in, **MM**: 11

Features
  of moving images, **MM**: 37, 39–40
  of multimodal texts, **MM**: 44, 46–48

questions about
  for analyzing multimodal texts, **MM**: 13
  for composing multimodal projects, **MM**: 51
of sound, **MM**: 22, 24
of static images, **MM**: 27, 30–32
of written words, **MM**: 14, 15–17
Feedback
  for draft of Web site project, **MM**: 88–90
  for revising multimodal projects, **MM**: 90
Files, electronic
  managing for multimodal project, **MM**: 71–76
  online tools for managing, **MM**: 75–76
  saving, **MM**: 71–72, 75
  sharing, **MM**: 75
Film
  analysis of, **MM**: 42
  as moving image, **MM**: 38
Flip book, as moving image, **MM**: 38
Fonts, analyzing, **MM**: 15–17, 19, 20–21
Formatting written words (bold, italics, and so on), **MM**: 14

Genre
  choosing for multimodal project, **MM**: 68–69
  of moving images, **MM**: 37–38
  of multimodal texts, **MM**: 44, 45
  questions about
    for analyzing multimodal texts, **MM**: 13
    for composing multimodal texts, **MM**: 51
  of sound, **MM**: 22–24
  of static images, **MM**: 27–29, 30
  of written words, **MM**: 14, 15
Geology, multimodal images for, **MM**: 11

Howell, King Anyi, and composing a podcast, **MM**: 23–24

Images
  moving, **MM**: 36–43
  static, **MM**: 27–35
Images, in documents, **MM**: 9–10
Instructions, static images in, **MM**: 29, 30–31
Integrating sources, in multimodal projects, **MM**: 94, 95–96
  conventions for, in different genres, **MM**: 98–99

Keats, John, **MM**: 5–6

Letter, as written text
  meaning of, **MM**: 20–21
  purpose of and audience for,
    MM: 17–20

Main idea. *See* Thesis
Managing multimodal projects,
  MM: 71–76
Manuscripts, illuminated, **MM**: 8, 9
Map, **MM**: 28
Math equations, as multimodal
  compositions, **MM**: 10
Meaning
  of moving images, **MM**: 37, 41–43
  of multimodal texts, **MM**: 44,
    49–50
  questions about
    for analyzing multimodal
      texts, **MM**: 14
    for composing multimodal
      projects, **MM**: 51
  of sound, **MM**: 22, 25–27
  of static images, **MM**: 27, 33–35
  of written words, **MM**: 14, 20–21
Migrant Mother (photograph,
  Dorothea Lange), **MM**: 32
Modes, in multimodal texts,
  MM: 46
Multimodal, meaning of, **MM**: 6–7
Multimodal assignments, in various
  disciplines, **MM**: 10–11
Multimodal projects, examples of. *See*
  Sample student projects
Multimodal texts, **MM**: 43–50
  analyzing modes separately,
    MM: 46
Music, in movies, **MM**: 21–23
Muybridge, Eadweard, and moving
  image of horse, **MM**: 36

News broadcasts, purpose of and
  audience for, **MM**: 41
Note taking, about podcast,
  MM: 23–24

Obama, Barack, poster, **MM**: 35
  transformed by other artists,
    MM: 35
"Ode on a Grecian Urn" (John Keats),
  MM: 5
Organizing multimodal projects,
  MM: 76–82
  tools for, **MM**: 76–78
Outlines, for multimodal projects,
  MM: 79, 80–82

Pace, of sound, **MM**: 24
Perspective
  first-person, of moving image,
    MM: 39–40
  of moving images, **MM**: 39–40
  of static images, **MM**: 30–32
  third-person, of moving images,
    MM: 39
  in video games, **MM**: 39
Photograph, **MM**: 28
Pitch, of sound, **MM**: 24
Planning, for multimodal project,
  MM: 60–70
Podcast, composing, **MM**: 23–24
  notes on, **MM**: 23–24
Presenting a multimodal project.
  See Publishing a multimodal
  project
Prewriting, for multimodal project,
  MM: 55–56
Professional. *See* Workplace,
  multimodal projects in
Profile, of audience, for multimodal
  project, **MM**: 57–58
Public service announcements (PSAs),
  MM: 11–12, 42–43, 50
  brain on drugs, **MM**: 42–43
  World Wildlife Fund, **MM**: 46–48
Publishing a multimodal project,
  MM: 100–04
  online resources for, **MM**: 100–01
  spaces for, **MM**: 101–03
Purpose
  of moving images, **MM**: 40–41
  of multimodal texts, **MM**: 48–49
  questions about
    for analyzing multimodal
      texts, **MM**: 14
    for composing multimodal
      projects, **MM**: 51
  of sound, **MM**: 22, 25
  of static images, **MM**: 30, 33
  of written words, **MM**: 14, 17–20

Quick response (QR) code, **MM**: 9

Reading a text, definitions of, **MM**: 5–6
Remixing a multimodal project,
  MM: 90–92. *See also* Revising
Résumé, emphasizing information in,
  MM: 82–83
Revising
  of multimodal projects,
    MM: 87–90
  remixing as strategy for,
    MM: 90–92
  of Web site project, **MM**: 89–90

Saddam Hussein statue, photographs
of, **MM**: 33–34
Sample student projects (composing)
informative Web site, **MM**: 55–56,
66–67, 68–70, 78, 84, 89–90, 97
video essay, **MM**: 54, 58–59, 61–63,
67–68, 71–74, 76, 85–86, 91–92, 96
Sample student writing (analysis)
of moving image, **MM**: 39, 42
of multimodal text, **MM**: 47–48
of public letter, **MM**: 20–21
of sound, **MM**: 25–26
of static image, **MM**: 31, 33–34
of video game, **MM**: 49–50
Score, for movie, **MM**: 22
Sketch, **MM**: 28
with generic features, **MM**: 29
Skittles, ad campaign, **MM**: 43
Slide presentation, **MM**: 45, 76–78
Slide shows
creation and hosting sites,
MM: 101
as multimodal compositions,
MM: 7
Software, for video editing, **MM**: 40
Sound
as background, **MM**: 22–23
in multimodal texts, **MM**: 46
Sound, analyzing, **MM**: 21–27
Sound, effect on listener, **MM**: 25–26
Soundtrack, for movie, **MM**: 22–23
Speakers, and multimodal delivery,
MM: 6–7
Storyboard, for organizing video
projects, **MM**: 79
Support, for thesis for multimodal
project, **MM**: 67–68

Text
definitions of, **MM**: 5
meaning of, **MM**: 5–6
Thesis
for multimodal projects,
MM: 65–66
support for, **MM**: 67–68
Times New Roman, appropriate uses
of, **MM**: 19
Toolkit, for analyzing and composing
multimodal texts, **MM**: 13–14

Trailers, movie, **MM**: 26–27
Typeface. *See* Fonts
Typography. *See* Formatting written
words

Usability, of multimodal projects,
MM: 103–04

Video
artistic, **MM**: 45
emphasizing information in,
MM: 85–86
instructional, **MM**: 45
revision of, **MM**: 91–92
sample student project, **MM**: 54,
58–59, 61–63, 67–68, 71–74, 76,
85–86, 91–92, 96
Video clip, as moving image,
MM: 38
Video games, as multimodal texts,
MM: 49–50
Video-hosting Web sites,
MM: 101
Volume, of sound, **MM**: 24

Web-creation sites, **MM**: 101
Web-hosting sites, **MM**: 101
Web site
emphasizing information in,
MM: 84
informational, **MM**: 45
planning, **MM**: 78
revision of, **MM**: 89–90
sample student project,
MM: 55–56, 66–67, 68–70, 78,
84, 89–90, 97
Wireframe, for Web site project,
MM: 78
Workplace, multimodal projects in,
MM: 7–8
World Wildlife Fund
audience for, **MM**: 48
multimodal public service ad,
MM: 46–48
Written words, analyzing,
MM: 14–21
Written words, formatting of, in
various documents,
MM: 15–17

Portfolio Keeping

A Guide for Students

Second Edition

Nedra Reynolds
Rich Rice

Portfolio
Keeping

A Guide for Students

Second Edition

Nedra Reynolds
Rich Rice

PORTFOLIO KEEPING

A Guide for Students

Second Edition

PORTFOLIO KEEPING

A Guide for Students

Second Edition

Nedra Reynolds
University of Rhode Island

Rich Rice
Texas Tech University

Bedford/St. Martin's   BOSTON ◆ NEW YORK

FOR BEDFORD/ST. MARTIN'S

Senior Production Editor: Bridget Leahy
Production Editor: Kerri Cardone
Production Supervisor: Matthew Hayes
Marketing Manager: Karita dos Santos
Copyeditor: Barbara Bell
Cover Design: Kim Cevoli
Composition: Jan Ewing, Ewing Systems
Printing and Binding: Malloy Lithographing, Inc.

President: Joan E. Feinberg
Editorial Director: Denise B. Wydra
Editor in Chief: Karen S. Henry
Director of Editing, Design, and Production: Marcia Cohen
Managing Editor: Elizabeth M. Schaaf

Library of Congress Catalog Card Number: 2005932491

Manufactured in the United States of America.

1 0 9 8 7
f e d c b a

For information, write: Bedford/St. Martin's, 75 Arlington Street, Boston, MA 02116 (617-399-4000)

ISBN: 0–312–41909–0
EAN: 978–0–312–41909–7

Preface for Instructors

Portfolio Keeping: A Guide for Students is a supplemental text for college composition courses that guides students through the decisions involved in creating a common-tools writing portfolio — that is, tools that are available and familiar to most writers and most audiences. With an emphasis on reflective learning and assessment, *Portfolio Keeping* reviews ways for students to practice reflection, organize a storage system, choose entries, and plan navigation systems. This guide is intended for writing classes that invite paper or electronic portfolios (or a combination of the two) as well as process or best-works portfolios, as a culmination of the writing process.

For this second edition, reviewers wanted the same slender volume — its brevity one of its best features — but also much more information on electronic portfolios. To help strike this balance and bring the book in line with twenty-first-century technologies, Rich Rice agreed to coauthor the new edition. We have tried to retain the conciseness of *Portfolio Keeping,* making it affordable for and accessible to students. The book is intended to complement other writing textbooks, especially process rhetorics or readers and handbooks. These other textbooks cover certain rhetorical strategies much more thoroughly than this volume does; but *Portfolio Keeping* gives more attention to reflection and assessment, for example, through the eleven Taking Stock activities in the text — three of them new to this edition and the rest updated for a variety of tools and types of portfolios. Most of the Taking Stock exercises can be completed in class in fifteen minutes or so, and most combine an individual writing task with a collaborative-learning discussion or follow-up. Organized around the rhythm and pace of a typical process writing course, *Portfolio Keeping* should be a quick and easy reference for students working independently or in a workshop setting.

In assigning *Portfolio Keeping* to your students, you have two equally good options. Students can benefit from reading the entire volume early in the course and then reviewing each chapter as appropriate later in the term. Or you can assign the first part, "The Process of Portfolio Keeping," during the first two or three weeks of the course, and the second part, "From Process to Product — Preparing for Assessment," during the final few weeks. With either approach, the portfolio is the heart of the course. Because many students will be able to read the entire volume in approximately two hours, assignments from *Portfolio Keeping* should fit easily into your course schedule.

A companion volume, *Portfolio Teaching: A Guide for Instructors,* addresses the design and orchestration of a portfolio writing course in some depth, with chapters on course planning; the collection and selection of artifacts for all types of portfolios, including teachers' portfolios; teaching reflection; and evaluating and grading portfolios. Meant to be flexible, not prescriptive, *Portfolio Teaching* is especially useful for new teachers and for instructors new to the portfolio method of teaching and assessing writing. The companion volume also includes an annotated bibliography on teacher-graded classroom portfolios.

ACKNOWLEDGMENTS

We were fortunate to have a number of outstanding reviewers on this project: Rick Dollieslager, Thomas Nelson Community College; T. Kenny Fountain, Yeshiva College; Rick Kemp, University of Miami; T. Shane Peagler; Donna Reiss, Tidewater Community College; and Donna H. Winchell, Clemson University.

Chuck Christensen, the founder and former president of Bedford/St. Martin's (now retired), and Joan Feinberg, the company's current president, made this book possible. John Sullivan offered expert advice for the first edition, and Amanda Bristow helped gather books and reviews for the second. Bridget Leahy expertly guided the manuscript through production, and Barbara Bell copyedited the manuscript with care.

Contents

Preface for Instructors   v

Introduction: Understanding Writing Portfolios   1
 Types of Writing Portfolios   3
  Portfolios for Learning   4
  Portfolios for Evaluation   4
 Forms of Portfolios   5
 Principles of Portfolio Keeping   5
  Choice   5
  Variety   6
  Reflection   6
 Taking Stock   7
  TAKING STOCK 1: Establishing Expectations   7

PART ONE
THE PROCESS OF PORTFOLIO KEEPING   8

1. Setting Goals and Planning Ahead   8

2. Staying Organized and Keeping a Working Folder   11
 Staying Organized   11
 Keeping a Working Folder   12
  Labeling and Saving Your Files   13
  Tracking Readers' Comments   15
  Managing Your Time   16
  TAKING STOCK 2: Getting Organized   16

3. Becoming a Reflective Learner   17
 Practicing Reflective Learning   17
 Journals and Blogs   18
  TAKING STOCK 3: What Is Reflective Learning?   19
 Postwrites   20
  Using Postwrites to Get More Out of Peer review   20
  TAKING STOCK 4: Composing Your Own Postwrite   22
 Midterm Self-Assessments   23

4. Keeping Company and Working with Others   24
    TAKING STOCK 5: Assessing Peer Response   25

5. Keeping Up and Getting Unstuck   27
   Getting Started   27
   Planning and Drafting More Efficiently   28
   Seeking Out Other Readers and Learning about Resources   29
   Finding Good Readers   30
    TAKING STOCK 6: Finding Readers or Help   31

PART TWO
FROM PROCESS TO PRODUCT—
PREPARING FOR ASSESSMENT   32

6. Understanding Assessment   32
   Assessment from the Writer's Perspective   32
    TAKING STOCK 7: Determining Your Program's Values   34
   Assessment from an Instructor's Perspective   36
    TAKING STOCK 8: Reviewing Your Working Folder   39

7. Putting It Together: Selecting and Arranging Artifacts   40
   Starting the Selection Process   41
   The Navigational Scheme   41
      Metaphorical Thinking   42
      Presentation Tools   42
   Choosing the Entries   44
   Storyboarding   45
    TAKING STOCK 9: Getting Help Choosing Artifacts   47

8. Preparing to Write the Introduction
   and Other Reflective Components   48
    TAKING STOCK 10: Revisiting Your Expectations   48

9. The Final Stages: Revising,
   Editing, and Proofreading the Entries   53
   Revising   53
    TAKING STOCK 11: Assessing Revision   54
   Editing   54
   Proofreading   55

10. Portfolio Keeping Continued: Re-Visiting Your Learning   58

PORTFOLIO KEEPING

A Guide for Students

Second Edition

INTRODUCTION

Understanding Writing Portfolios

You're enrolled in a writing course that uses portfolios to organize and share your writing. *Portfolio Keeping: A Guide for Students* will help you feel more confident with the portfolio process. This booklet introduces you to a variety of strategies for making sound decisions, for learning something meaningful, and for presenting your best final product.

You may recognize the term *portfolio* from art or finance: Artists keep samples of their best works in a portable case or folder, pieces that represent their interests, their potential, or their development. They show their portfolios to instructors, gallery owners, their peers (a jury of other artists, for example), or potential employers. In finance, a portfolio is a record of stocks, bonds, mutual funds, and other investments that is reviewed periodically and updated as needed. Professionals in many other fields also compile portfolios, records of their accomplishments that they can use to apply for a promotion or a new job. In all of these examples, the work is not static: It changes with the portfolio keeper's new achievements, new ideas, and new interests.

A *portfolio* is a meaningful collection of selected artifacts or documents. What is a writing portfolio specifically? A *writing portfolio* consists of artifacts, pieces, or entries that demonstrate a writer's thinking and learning processes or that showcase a writer's best work. Collected over time and across interests, a writing portfolio displays a writer's talent and effort, and his or her ability to make thoughtful choices about content and presentation. In its final form, it is also a product meant to be shared with others. Writing portfolios often are designed to be assessed by an instructor or another trained evaluator, to be read by prospective employers, or to be enjoyed by friends and family. Keeping a portfolio will help you pay attention to both the processes and products of writing. It also will help you track the evolution of each writing project and your development as a writer. In starting your own writing portfolio, you join many other writers and learners.

Portfolios provide a structure that helps students practice reflective learning. *Reflective learning* means to think consciously or deliberately about how you learn best or what is most meaningful to you about what you've learned. When you practice reflective learning, you focus on your own writing and learning patterns, habits, and preferences. The goals are to identify what doesn't work well for you, repeat what does, and develop strategies for addressing or overcoming the parts of writing that are frustrating or puzzling. By the end of this course, you will have a record of your writing process for each major project, a meaningful collection of your work, and a better understanding of both useful writing strategies and ways you learn best. All of this should help you become a better writer, reader, and thinker.

Portfolios can be created in a variety of educational situations and for assessment or employment purposes. Not all portfolios emphasize writing, but the writing portfolio has become a popular method of assessment in college classes and in many other environments. And in recent years, educational technologies have increased exponentially the possibilities for collecting, designing, and presenting the artifacts, materials, and projects produced in a class or degree program. That is, in many majors and disciplines, keeping an electronic portfolio gives students a meaningful tool that can be used in job searches. Although it may take more time to develop an e-Portfolio than a paper-based portfolio the payoffs make the extra time worthwhile: Electronic portfolios can be updated, maintained, and distributed more easily; and they offer more flexibility for making connections between entries.

Throughout *Portfolio Keeping,* you'll get good advice for constructing an e-Portfolio. For example, you'll learn about the importance of creating a navigational scheme that is straightforward, that helps your readers move through the document. We do not concentrate on sophisticated Web design in this volume: Our focus here is on the substance of portfolios—careful reflection and good writing. But this book does teach principles of arrangement and navigation.*

What access do you have to reading and writing tools at school, at work, or at home? *Common-tools portfolios*—a focus of this guide—are built from tools that both writers and their readers have in common and use regularly. Common tools for reading and writing include older technologies as well as newer ones: pencils, pens, sheets of paper, legal pads, spiral-bound notebooks, three-ring binders, photographs, index cards, word-processing programs and files, internal and external drives, CDs, uploaded files, Web pages, digital videos, databases, and more. What makes a tool common is simply its availability and familiarity to both you *and* your audience. You may be familiar with Flash, digital video, and database structure, but if your audience isn't, then these tools may not be the best ones to use in your work.

Designs vary, as do writing programs and requirements. The first step is to determine what type of portfolio you are being asked to produce. Is your portfolio going to demonstrate your learning process? Will it showcase your best works? Will it combine both process and product? How will

---

*Some examples of good online-publishing design can be found through the companion Web site, bedfordstmartins.com/portfolio.

it be evaluated? Should you connect the entries using a central theme? a metaphor? a story? Will you be able to use your portfolio in other classes or later on as part of your résumé? These are questions your instructor can help you answer. Your instructor may ask you to include informal writing (journal or blog entries, for example), as well as drafts and the final version of several writing projects; or you may be required to submit a collection of your best writing only. In either case, the portfolio is likely to make up a large percentage of your course grade. Keep a list of the artifacts you've been asked to include, as well as specific notes from your instructor.

Your course emphasizes the writing process, especially revision, and portfolios provide a context and good reasons to revise. The demands of presenting your best work, for example, can help you begin to understand the number of drafts that may be required for a piece of writing to become focused, organized, and developed. Because writing is a very complex act — it's one of the most challenging and sophisticated activities human beings engage in — writers need time to improve and time to build confidence. The portfolio process, which begins on the first day of class and continues over the term, creates more opportunity for writers to practice before both writing process and writing product are evaluated. Grades on individual projects and assignments may be postponed, for instance, giving you time to develop your work.

Portfolio Keeping will help you through the steps of collecting, selecting, and presenting your work, all the while emphasizing reflection. You will examine each assignment and project and make many complex and subtle decisions. Throughout this guide, you will find advice and strategies to help you keep track of your learning and to make reasoned choices about the content and appearance of your portfolio. Your tasks as a portfolio keeper will include tending to your developing ideas, keeping watch over your own learning patterns, helping your peers or collaborators, and being responsible for the final product. Save all of your drafts and notes in a paper or electronic working folder — a storage system for organizing all of your collected work — and keep track of your choices and changes.

In the following sections, you'll find descriptions of the two main types of writing portfolios and their various uses and a description of the forms contemporary portfolios take. Also here is a discussion of the principles of writing portfolios, the characteristics that should underlie every writing portfolio, whatever its type or form. Understanding these principles and the importance of reflective learning will give you a good start toward building your portfolio.

TYPES OF WRITING PORTFOLIOS

Although they share many characteristics, writing portfolios can vary considerably in type or purpose. The purpose of a portfolio defines its audience and, ultimately, the materials that go into it. Our focus in *Portfolio*

Keeping is on writing portfolios. There are two broad types of writing portfolios: learning and evaluation. The former focus on the learning experience; the latter, on the product of that experience.

PORTFOLIOS FOR LEARNING

A *learning* or *process portfolio* asks you to demonstrate your learning. It should reflect the journey more so than the destination.* Your instructor will ask you to collect or create artifacts—essays, photographs, journal or blog entries, charts, letters, video clips, Mp3 files, and so on—that best represent your learning experiences and your engagement with the learning process.

One of the most challenging components of creating a writing process portfolio is selecting the artifacts to include. Your instructor will probably give you a large degree of freedom, which means you're going to have to make reasoned choices from all the possible materials. Apple has a software product called iLife. In theory, you could put your whole life into a portfolio. But would that be appealing to readers? More important in this context, would it serve the purposes of creating a portfolio for a writing class? You have many other means for recording your life experiences: Perhaps you keep a journal or scrapbooks or photograph albums; or maybe you maintain a home page or a blog. But in your record of this class—in your writing process portfolio—the focus should be on your writing and learning.

Although you can expect your process portfolio to be evaluated, you should understand that you have been invited to create and keep the portfolio for your own benefit, not necessarily to prove to your instructor (or coach or supervisor) that you should pass this course (or receive an award or get a promotion). Your thoughts on and understanding of the learning process, and the degree to which your portfolio reflects them, in large part form the basis for assessing your work.

PORTFOLIOS FOR EVALUATION

An *evaluation portfolio,* like a learning portfolio, promotes and sustains learning. But it shifts attention at a certain point from the learning process to the product of that process. This type of portfolio has many variations, but in all of them, the primary goals are to show the reader what you have learned and to convince the reader of your achievements, abilities, and talents. For instance, an artist puts together a portfolio to show her work to a gallery owner or to a potential client; or a writing major creates a portfolio to show his writing samples to an editor or to some other prospective employer. Similarly, students often keep portfolios to show their instructor and classmates, at the end of the term, what they have learned from the course.

---

*Depending on the instructor's purposes, after keeping a process portfolio for several weeks, you may be asked to reshape it into a presentation portfolio.

Evaluation portfolios are often called *best-works portfolios:* From a number of pieces or projects, students choose the best for inclusion in their portfolio. They also are called *presentation portfolios* because the emphasis is on presenting a set of polished products. Evaluation portfolios usually do not include notes, outlines, journal or blog entries, drafts, or other materials that helped you create your final drafts.

FORMS OF PORTFOLIOS

Your instructor may give you a choice of creating a paper portfolio or an electronic one, or some combination of the two. The primary advantage of a paper document is that anyone can read it: It requires no special understanding or access to technology. But assuming that common tools are available to writer and reader, the e-Portfolio offers much more flexibility than a paper portfolio does.

We noted above that electronic portfolios are easier to update, maintain, and distribute. Through hyperlinks, they also make navigating the portfolio easier; and hyperlinks allow the writer to make connections beyond the materials in the portfolio to any materials that are available on the Web. Although a paper portfolio can include photographs and other visual elements, the e-Portfolio allows for the use of a variety of media types. Consider, too, the portability of the e-Portfolio. It can be created and stored and presented online, which makes it readily accessible whenever and wherever you want to work on it. Even if you choose to prepare and store your work on a USB drive or a rewritable CD, when your portfolio is ready for evaluation or presentation, all you have to do is upload it to the Internet.

Once the form of the portfolio is decided—by you or your instructor—you should begin to think about how your reader will navigate through the document. Will there be a table of contents? Will there be hyperlinks on your e-Portfolio home page to connect the reader to other pages on the site?

PRINCIPLES OF PORTFOLIO KEEPING

Are you planning to compose a learning or an evaluation portfolio? a paper portfolio or an electronic portfolio? Whatever the type or form, you must consider the principles of choice, variety, and reflection.

CHOICE

Portfolio keepers need room to choose what to include and how to arrange and present each artifact. If they are simply told what to include, where to do so, and in what form, portfolio keepers won't learn much beyond following directions. Writers make many choices, selections, or decisions at every stage of the writing process, but they are not always conscious of those choices; the portfolio method makes them more aware of their decision making. No matter what type of portfolio you'll be keeping for this writing course, you will need to choose your artifacts carefully and wisely. The guide you are reading now will help you make these important decisions.

VARIETY

Portfolio keepers have different strengths and different interests, and their portfolios should cultivate and celebrate these differences. A writing portfolio invites you to show off your writing ability and the ways you think about different kinds of assignments for different audiences. So, you might include samples of informal writing (journal or blog entires, a paragraph written in class), as well as samples of projects you've spent a great deal of time revising, editing, and polishing. You might demonstrate, for example, how different amounts of time spent on each entry impacts the diversity of your work. Variety is one of the reasons that portfolios are considered a more valid measure of a person's writing ability, especially when compared with a timed multiple-choice test that can only measure grammar, style and usage, punctuation, and mechanics. When your instructor sees your portfolio, he or she is seeing more than one example of your writing, pieces written at different times and for different audiences.

REFLECTION

The portfolio process lets you look at your writing differently, as a whole rather than as a series of separate assignments. The choices you make in building your portfolio will demand that you practice reflective learning, or self-assessment. You will be asked to take a careful look at your work to identify your patterns, strengths, and preferences for negotiating writing tasks, for learning new skills, and for putting those skills into practice. You must go beyond just stringing the pieces of your portfolio together: You need to be able to articulate *why* you made certain choices or *what* those choices are meant to convey. Educational theorists use the word *metacognition* to describe the ability of students to think about their own thinking. *Meta-* means "after," "behind," or "beyond"; *cognition* means "the act or process of knowing." *Metacognition,* then, is the ability to "know beyond one's knowing," or to think about your own thinking.

The "Taking Stock" exercises provided in each chapter ask you to practice reflection, or the important skill of thinking about your own thinking. As you complete each one, save what you have written. Your responses to the "Taking Stock" prompts will give you material that you may want to use in your portfolio.

TAKING STOCK

What has your instructor asked you to create? Are you working on a process or a best-works portfolio? Are you expected to submit your portfolio on paper or electronically? Now that you have a better understanding of how portfolios can differ and how they often are used in writing courses, you're ready to begin portfolio keeping. There is much information you will want to capture during your class that you can't go back and get later. But before you read on, take stock of where you are right now.

TAKING STOCK 1: Establishing Expectations

Examine your syllabus for the course and the required textbooks. Pay close attention to course policies, procedures, assignments, and expectations. Now, in a journal or a blog, write one or two paragraphs about your experiences with portfolios and how you expect to do in this course. What assignments or activities do you think you will do well on? Why? What assignments or activities do you think will be difficult for you? Why? What parts of your reading and writing history make you confident about some parts of the course and hesitant about others? Check with your instructor about whether to turn in this piece. If not, give it a title and/or file name and store it in your working folder; it may come in handy later.

THE PROCESS OF PORTFOLIO KEEPING

—1—
Setting Goals and Planning Ahead

By the end of the first week of class, you should understand your instructor's plan for the portfolio method. Will your portfolio focus on process or product? Should your portfolio be a paper document or an electronic one? Which tools will you have access to? Will the portfolio be checked or assessed before the final evaluation? Will you get to choose any or all of the artifacts you'll include? As early in the course as possible, make sure that you know the answers to these questions, and try to spend some time imagining what your portfolio might look like. Portfolio designers often storyboard the structure of their work on paper, much like a writer might use clustering or mapping (see Figure 7.1 on p. 46 for a sample storyboard). That's a great approach. The sooner you begin to imagine your portfolio's purpose and appearance, making it your own, the sooner you can begin to get the work done.

What are some of the possibilities for arranging and presenting artifacts? Consider the tools that you have access to, the software and hardware you already know how to use or would like to learn, and the experiences you've already had with writing texts or creating documents. Do you know how to change fonts? how to add clip art? how to add and reference pictures from the Internet? how to create graphs? how to insert footnotes? how to add sound or video clips to an electronic file? You do not have to use state-of-the-art technologies to create a state-of-the-art portfolio, of course. Content and reflection are more important than design in this course. But think about your talents or strengths for now. Do you enjoy telling stories? Do you have a good sense of direction? Can you read a map really well? Do you like to read texts on a computer screen, or do you prefer to see them printed on paper? Your final portfolio will reflect much about you as a writer, thinker, and learner.

If your instructor wants your portfolio to be electronic, you will be given very specific directions about which tools to use. You might use a program like Microsoft FrontPage, Netscape Composer, or Macromedia Dreamweaver to build your portfolio as a Web page. You might use other programs to work on artifacts in your portfolio—Apple iMovie or Microsoft Movie Maker for video clips, or Macromedia Flash for more-advanced synchronized multimedia. A common-tools approach is also perfectly appropriate for developing your portfolio: Use tools that you use everyday in your writing class or in other classes, tools like Microsoft Word and PowerPoint. Other common tools might include an online writing tool like Bedford/St. Martin's Comment. If your instructor has asked for an electronic portfolio, you need to know if it needs to be prepared and submitted online, or if it can be submitted offline, on a CD, DVD, USB drive, or another media storage tool. Think carefully, too, about the computers your audience will have access to when reading your portfolio. If readers do not have high-speed access to the Internet, for instance, you should consider incorporating fewer or smaller graphics, sounds, or videos. Similarly, monitors are different sizes. How will your portfolio look on a smaller or larger monitor? Will the font types you have chosen display on most computer monitors? These are some of the variables you must consider when planning the design of your e-Portfolio.

But for now, as you imagine your portfolio, think about the people you know will be reading it and your potential audience, and what they might need in order to understand, appreciate, and navigate through your portfolio. The ability to anticipate readers' needs and expectations is at the heart of good writing. You might pretend you are taking your readers with you on a trip, but they don't know the way—only you do. Show them how to navigate through their journey. Or think of your portfolio as a movie in production, and you are the director, setting up each scene and making connections between things. Writing and directing have much in common.

Remember the three principles of portfolio keeping: choice, variety, and reflection. Some of the questions below will help you think about how you want to achieve choice, variety, and reflection in your portfolio, and how you might want to present yourself as a writer. Write down the answers to these questions, and be prepared to discuss them in class.

- Do you want to show progress—how much your writing and thinking have improved? How might you do that?
- Do you want to show persistence—your ability to stick with a project for a long period? How?
- Do you want to show your abilities as a designer of Web-based materials? Why?
- Do you want to show flexibility—the ability to write in different styles or voices?

- Do you want to show creativity—how you have made the assignments your own? How could this be accomplished?
- Do you want to show independence—revising well beyond your peers' and your instructor's suggestions?

Your answers to these questions may change later, but having goals to help shape your portfolio is a good idea. Your instructor may help you address these questions once the class settles into a routine and as soon as at least one writing project has been taken through each stage of the writing process. Some writing instructors use contracts to help students set and meet certain goals; these contracts are tailored to students' writing strengths, but they also address weaknesses head-on. In the following list, check off what you would like to accomplish in the course. What is important to you?

- ❏ I hope to keep up with all assignments and stay on top of things, not fall behind.
- ❏ I want to become more comfortable with sharing my writing with others.
- ❏ I want to learn more about writing with computers.
- ❏ I'd like to organize my thoughts better.
- ❏ Sometimes when I write, I know what I want to say, but it doesn't come out the way I want it to. I'd like to know how to fix that.
- ❏ I'd like to be able to take constructive criticism without feeling defensive.
- ❏ I want to find out if my writing skills are strong enough to do well in college or to choose a career that involves writing.
- ❏ I want to write forceful arguments that convince people without offending them.
- ❏ I'd like to be able to read over a draft and know what to do to make it better.
- ❏ I want to try to write every day in a journal.
- ❏ I want to figure out why some of my essays go so smoothly and some are so difficult.
- ❏ I want to be proud of my portfolio and do the best work I can.

In addition, see if you can answer each of the following questions. Keep these questions and your answers handy, perhaps in your journal or blog. You will need to review them throughout your portfolio keeping process.

1. Is my portfolio supposed to show development, best works, or some combination of the two?
2. Do I make all of the choices about what to include, or will the instructor or guidelines tell me what to include?
3. How many artifacts or entries can be included? What kind? Can I include work from other classes? work I've produced for a job? pictures, maps, or other graphics? sound clips or other multimedia files?

4. Do all of the entries I include need to be revised and polished? If so, what level, quality, or extent of revision is expected?

5. How much of the course grade is determined by the portfolio grade?

6. Are the different artifacts or entries assessed separately? Or does the entire portfolio receive one grade?

7. Who will be grading my portfolio?

8. What writing will I have to do specifically for the portfolio? Will I need a cover letter or introductory essay? Does each entry need a separate introduction? Is reflection or self-assessment expected, or are description and explanation adequate?

—2—
Staying Organized and Keeping a Working Folder

Once you begin to see how you will construct and present your portfolio, as well as how it will be assessed, and once you have established goals for yourself, you are ready to begin keeping your working folder. Don't wait long to begin this step. You'll have a better experience with portfolio keeping if you take some time in the first or second week of class to begin your working folder. If your portfolio is electronic, you should keep an electronic working folder. Some students use USB drives, rewritable CDs, a blog, a Web space, or their e-mail accounts to store their electronic working folders.

STAYING ORGANIZED

Organized people generally have an edge in portfolio keeping. If you aren't as organized as you would like to be, there's still hope. Start thinking about how organized you usually are, or write a short piece in your journal or blog about what you usually do to try to stay organized. Do you keep a personal digital assistant (PDA) or day planner, carry it with you, consult it, and record appointments and due dates regularly? Do you keep separate notebooks or folders for each class? When you sit down to study for a test or to write an assignment, are you generally able to locate everything you need, or do you spend a lot of time looking for and gathering materials? Depending on how organized you are, you may have to give more or less attention to your working folder.

The first rule is keep everything. When you're building a portfolio, you can't discard papers your instructor has graded and returned even if the project is finished. When they don't expect to work on something again, students might put a returned essay in the back of a spiral notebook, on a shelf of a bookcase, in a stack on a desk, or in a locker or car or closet, and then throw it away during the next cleaning binge. Sound familiar? To discard old papers is understandable, but keeping a portfolio means becoming a saver. For every paper document you keep, make sure that you also have an electronic copy of it. With good storage habits, drafts should be easy to find at a later date. What would you do if you needed to demonstrate what you have learned but couldn't show where you started, or how peer and instructor responses and drafting helped you improve, or where you ended up in your revision work? Again, *keep everything*.

Store your stuff in your working folder (paper, electronic, or some combination of both) so that you can sort through all of your work when the time comes. Nothing is too small or irrelevant if it serves to illustrate your writing and thinking processes. You might want to show how you jotted down an idea for your portfolio introduction on a napkin while catching lunch in the student union, developed that idea with an outline, and then got some more ideas from your peer response group. It may be that writing the introduction took you in a completely different direction, that what was a tangent became the topic of the essay. You might want to show this process in your portfolio. Being organized—keeping your work or files in order—might not come naturally to you, but it can help tremendously when you're building a portfolio.

Keeping is the name of the game, so don't throw away or delete anything. Keep all of your notes, lists, drafts, outlines, clusters, responses from readers, photocopied articles, and references for Works Cited pages. Your assignments may be returned with comments and/or grades, but that doesn't mean the process is over. So that all of this keeping doesn't get out of control, you need to design a storage system that helps you identify and locate particular items, to know what's what. You need to devise a system for storing and locating things quickly.

KEEPING A WORKING FOLDER

A working folder houses all the work that you do before you select the pieces for your portfolio. A portfolio, after all, is a collection of selected work. If you're going to rely on a number of paper documents, you may need a three-ring binder or an accordion file folder to hold all your work. Invest in a good organizer or notebook that will withstand the wear and tear of backpacks or book bags and your busy life. Use the folder just for this course. You'll need the space because you're going to end up with a number of items: all the assignments and handouts from class; your outlines, notes, and drafts; and peer responses and instructor feedback. Even if you are building an electronic portfolio, if you think hard copies will help you stay organized, then print out your work and file it in a paper folder. Many writers, including those who can't imagine writing without a keyboard anymore, edit and revise best on hard copy. You also might print hard copies after you make significant changes to a paper. Printing your drafts regularly can help you see your writing differently; it also expedites portfolio keeping. If your instructor runs a paperless classroom, if all feedback and peer response is electronic, make sure you buy a storage device that you can take with you wherever you go and use on whichever computers you have access to throughout the day.

LABELING AND SAVING YOUR FILES

Whatever your storage system, your goal is to make it easy to find a specific draft or returned paper. Label everything with a date, and make sure that each pocket or file folder has a name. Here are several examples of labels:

- Discovery drafts of first paper
- Notes from field observation
- Summary of *New York Times* article, returned with comments
- Peer response forms—Argument
- Draft of complaint letter
- Ideas for Web page design

Other logical ways of organizing your working folder include labeling or sorting according to (1) chronology, (2) topic, or (3) your own level of interest in each project. Table 2.1 shows examples of each.

The way in which you label the contents of your working folder is up to you, but some kind of labeling and regular reorganizing will help you

TABLE 2.1. SAMPLE LABELS

CHRONOLOGICAL LABELING	TOPICAL LABELING	INTEREST LABELING
• Project 1, drafts and notes • Project 1, instructor comments • Project 2, outline • Project 2, peer response • Project 2, instructor comments	• Literature review for research project • Analysis of three shows • Informed argument about talk radio shows	• Favorite paper so far (Project 3) • Papers I could revise • Papers I don't like

enormously. It is time well spent. And if you are enrolled in a writing class that depends on computers, or if you have been asked to produce an electronic portfolio, you should make sure your working folder is part electronic, as well. Still, it may help to keep your work in both printed and electronic form. You would then have a backup, and it is often easier to see the connections you need to make between artifacts when you can see your work in hard copy.

Electronic portfolio keeping requires very careful saving, file naming, and storage. It's important, for instance, to use a medium for saving your work that is suited to the computers (all of them) on which you might do your drafting or composing. You might have a CD burner on your computer at home, but if there's not one on the computers at school, you won't be able to update your electronic working folder there. Keeping your work on a public computer is not a good idea unless your school requires you to log in to use it. Your work could be removed or copied by anyone. So protect your work, and never leave it on a public computer. Instead keep your portfolio on a personal computer, and back up to a USB drive, a rewritable CD, a writable DVD, or an online space that your school provides. Some students use their e-mail accounts to hold all their files. This is a good backup, but here, too, space can be an issue: You may run out of room. Find a reliable portfolio keeping space, and back up your work, regularly, to another space.

Try to remember these three important points:

1. Store all of your work in the same place, a folder on your computer, for example. The folder can have multiple subfolders, but everything should be in the same place. If you already have a folder labeled *Composition*, create a new folder there and label it *101* or whatever the course number is; then use that folder to create a subfolder for each assignment and all the associated files.

2. Make sure that you can copy all of your work, regularly, from your portfolio keeping space to a backup space that is accessible at school and from the computer where you do most of your work. Be careful not to overwrite newer files with older ones. Develop your own system.

3. Label your work clearly and consistently. If your instructor gives you guidelines, follow them. Otherwise create your own file-naming convention.* For example, you might name a file *Last3B.rtf*, where "Last" is your last name, "3" denotes the third paper you wrote for a particular class, and "B" refers to the second draft of that paper. If a peer or the instructor offers comments on your draft, you could call it *Last3B-Peer.rtf* or *Last3B-Instructor.rtf* where *Peer* or *Instructor* would be the last name of the responder.

---

*Remember that some operating systems do not like spaces in file names.

Practice naming a file here with your name and your instructor's name:

_____.

Toward the end of the course, when you're getting ready to submit your portfolio, you will be able to find the files you need quickly if you have a clear and consistent file-naming convention. Your instructor and peers, too, will know exactly which paper you're sharing. And again, back up your work frequently. It is easy to overwrite files, forget a password, lose a CD, or catch a computer virus on a file.

It's easy, too, to lose your writing when you're working on a computer. Someone kicks the plug; there's a power surge; your word-processing program freezes; or the computer crashes. As you're working, then, save your work often. After you write a great sentence, save your work. After you move a paragraph from the last page to the second page, save your work again. After you painstakingly enter a series of statistics, save your work again. If you are e-mailing your work, be sure to save it first. And at the end of a drafting or revising session on the computer, save your work and then back it up. Finally, if you really want to be safe, make a backup of your backup. The ultimate backup is a printed copy of your electronic work.

TRACKING READERS' COMMENTS

The portfolio method for writing courses relies on a system of tracing writers' progress or charting writers' improvements. Learning to use electronic technologies simplifies your record keeping, saves you time, and helps you present a quality product at the end of the course. This is especially important when it comes to keeping track of the comments and responses you have received on your work.

Your readers — your instructor, peer reviewers, friends, roommates, family members — influence the portfolio process and the final product immeasurably. When someone reads one of your drafts, quickly or carefully, as a favor or as an assigned activity, it is important to track his or her reactions, comments, and suggestions. If you wait until it's time to choose which projects to revise and to submit, you won't remember what your readers said about the piece unless you have recorded their comments. For example, student writers often find themselves in the following situation: The instructor returns an essay with comments and suggestions for revision, but class is almost over, and people are packing up and getting ready to leave. The temptation is to stuff the paper in a folder and rush out, but this is a good time to see if all of the instructor's comments make sense. If the handwriting isn't legible, if it would be hard to make a suggested change, or if the suggestions aren't clear, it will be difficult to know how to improve the paper when it comes time to work on it. If time is short, make an appointment with your instructor during office hours or make a note to send the instructor an e-mail so that he or she can help to clarify the comments.

In any case, before you label or name the project notes and file them away, make sure you understand the comments. And before the opportunity passes, make some changes in response to the suggestions right away, while the ideas are fresh. Chris, for example, gets her paper back and reads the following comment her instructor has written: *"Perhaps you could introduce your grandfather sooner, giving you opportunities to connect this trip to happy childhood memories."* Chris isn't sure where to introduce her grandfather before the ninth paragraph, near the end of the piece, and she also doesn't want her paper to concentrate on childhood memories. Chris stops by her instructor's office later that day to ask for clarification. With the paper in front of them, the two have a conversation about the grandfather reference and where it fits best, if at all. Between the two of them, they decide that Chris should either introduce the connection to her grandfather much sooner or drop it completely because it is just left hanging in this draft. Chris doesn't decide yet; but before leaving her instructor's office, she makes notes that will help focus her revision if she decides to include the paper in her portfolio. As Chris did, wait to file the paper away until you are clear about the comments, and write down your ideas for revision. When you're ready to work on the piece again, you will have both a plan and some fresh insight.

MANAGING YOUR TIME

In addition to saving copies, making backups, and practicing good record keeping, you can also stay organized by managing your time wisely. If time management is a challenge, consider scheduling a block of time (for example, Wednesday nights from 8:00 P.M. to 11:00 P.M.) to work on your writing and portfolio keeping. Even if you have a paper due or another reading assignment you have to get done, you must still take time to review your returned drafts, to make notes that will help you reflect on your writing process, and to work on organizing your materials. Such time is very well spent because you'll be able to present a well-developed portfolio later.

TAKING STOCK 2: Getting Organized

After you have started your working folder, meet with a small group of classmates or consult with them online to compare working folders and ideas for staying organized. How have group members designed their storage systems? What strategies do they use to keep track of drafts and assignments? Which of their "get-organized" techniques are new to you or different from what you're doing? Borrow good portfolio keeping strategies, and incorporate them into your process. Write them down, and put them into your working folder. Ask yourself if your system is logical enough so that you can sustain it for the rest of the course.

—3—
Becoming a Reflective Learner

Consider a lighthouse keeper, a groundskeeper, a timekeeper. What do they have in common? Keepers keep watch. The reflective portfolio method asks you to keep watch over your own work and your own learning, and to pay close attention to your strengths and weaknesses, including your preferences as well as your best and most limited practices for effective writing. Understanding more about yourself as a writer, reader, and thinker helps you make sound choices for your portfolio.

With practice, you'll notice patterns or preferences in your learning. Reflective learners develop the ability to identify and discuss their choices, strengths, and learning processes. In most process and presentation portfolio designs, writers are expected to include a reflective essay or introduction — a preface to the portfolio that, most importantly, identifies what they have learned from collecting, selecting, and revising the entries. A reflective introduction outlines the choices and changes you made in preparing the portfolio for readers or evaluators. Is this something you need to do? It's better to begin developing your reflective-thinking skills now than right before your portfolio is due.

PRACTICING REFLECTIVE LEARNING

Step back and evaluate your performance: What do you do well? What do you need to do better to improve your writing? Maybe you have great ideas but find it difficult to organize them. Maybe you write provocative thesis statements but run out of things to say in their support. Maybe you feel anxious about finding and correcting errors. If you can identify your writing attitudes and habits, you've made a great start toward practicing reflective learning.

You've made a start, too, if you wrote in response to Taking Stock 1 (p. 7). Try to cultivate the habit of writing down, at least once a week or so, some thoughts about your learning in the course. Ask questions like these: What am I learning? How am I learning it? What is or isn't making sense? coming together? clicking? Remember: You can do this with a pen in a journal or in the margins of your work, or on a computer in a blog or a file of notes to yourself. Write and reflect on your writing, and then store your reflection in your working folder.

If you get into the habit of recording details about your class and your learning experiences, you will have considerable materials to draw upon later in the course.

- Write informally about the material in the week's classes and assignments. What do you remember?
- What do you understand, or what could you explain to others?
- In just one or two paragraphs, track your successes and failures.
- Record your observations about the pace and quality of the course and your role in it.
- Did you say something in class that made others think?
- Did someone else say something that made you think?
- What are your goals for next week?

It may seem like busywork, but this kind of writing will help you compose a first-rate portfolio. For instance, you can use this reflective writing as a springboard to the more formal self-assessment that your instructor might ask for later. It's difficult to go back when the class is nearly over and trace what you were thinking in the second week of class. Keeping watch now of your writing process may lead you to an idea for a navigational scheme in your portfolio, to a design framework, or to a holistic and unifying metaphor for your learning in the course.

To make sure you are practicing reflective learning throughout the course, to help you keep watch, your instructor may assign one or more of the following reflective-writing tasks:

- Making regular entries in a writing journal or blog
- Writing postwrites
- Carrying out a midterm self-assessment

If you're not assigned one of these writing tasks, do at least one anyway on your own. (There are several writing prompts in Taking Stock 3, on p. 19.) Keeping watch clearly can help you in the long run, and writing informally is a good way to learn material, rehearse main ideas, reinforce classroom discussion, and respond to class reading material. *Writing to learn* is the popular name for this kind of activity, and reflective learners depend on it.

JOURNALS AND BLOGS

Journals or blogs can take many forms — a personal diary, a travel narrative, a professional record. Generally, a journal can contain anything its keeper chooses to record; but for the purpose of becoming a more conscientious student of writing, keep a writing journal in which you work through the decisions you're making for this course. Track ideas, questions, problems, and triumphs; jot down possible titles, your writing schedule, outlines, and lists. And writers tend to record how their projects are developing or changing, too. Record your learning evolution.

If you're not familiar with blogs, visit http://blogger.com or the companion Web site to this book. A blog* is very convenient because you can access your blog from any computer that is connected to the Internet. If your instructor requires a blog, there may be specific questions you need to answer; however, what makes blog writing effective is the immediacy of the ideas. When you think of something, blog it now. Don't wait until next week. Later you can spend time reviewing your blog. You also can copy and paste links to Web pages you want to look at later into your blog, and use it as a research log, too. Some students, in fact, use their blog as their working folder or even as an electronic portfolio tool itself: You can link all of your artifacts through your blog. (Keep in mind, however, that your blog may be accessible to anyone.)

Read Taking Stock 3, and answer the questions in your journal or blog.

TAKING STOCK 3: What Is Reflective Learning?

Here's an entry from Maria's writing journal:

> I think I'm trying to do way too much in this version. By the time I get to the conclusion, I'm having to summarize too much and cover the same territory again, which may be a sign that I've been over-ambitious. Vicky [a peer reviewer] hinted that my thesis was too broad, but I didn't want to hear it because I was still very excited about the ideas and still finding plenty to say. Now that I've found more examples and developed most of the major points, I see that I need to go back and sharpen the thesis by dropping my reference to the past views of computers and education. I think the paper will work better without the historical overview, and I'll just concentrate on current uses of computers in education. It seems as though I've done a lot of writing on the history part for nothing, but maybe I can use it for another essay later if I stay interested in it.

What evidence do you find here that Maria is a reflective learner? How does this entry move her writing process forward? In your journal or blog, answer the following questions:

- At what time during the day do you write best or have the most concentration?
- Where do you do your best work? Why is that place helpful or inspiring?
- What tools, objects, or things do you like to have around you when you write? When or how did these preferences become apparent to you?
- What do these habits or preferences say about you as a writer? as a learner?

---

*The term derives from the words *Web* and *log*.

POSTWRITES

Writers often are able to write their way to a solution or to a valuable insight. *Postwrites,* also called *writers' memos* or *writing reviews,* are one of the best ways to practice reflective learning for writing classes. Like other forms of reflection, postwrites ask you to write about the writing you're currently doing. In other words, in a postwrite you'd write to a reader about how the writing is going or what you've written so far or what's not going so well. You can write a postwrite at any point in the writing process. Some writers use postwrites between drafts to help sharpen the focus of the writing or to help figure out the most effective organizational structure. Other writers find it helpful to write a postwrite as a way of preparing to share a draft with readers.

Here's how the postwrite works. Before asking other people to read your draft and offer feedback, answer these questions about your draft in writing: How do you feel about it? What shape do you think it's in? What questions do you have for readers about the piece? In other words, do some work judging your own writing before you ask others to judge, and do it in writing. It's not enough to think about your answers to these questions: The process of writing your answers gives you more insight.

The questions in Figures 3.1 and 3.2 were designed by an instructor for students to answer about their own essays, the processes they went through to write the papers and their thoughts on the feedback or advice they received from readers. (Postwrites help writers and readers get more out of the response process, as we discuss below.) You might use the sample questions here as prompts for your own reflection.

Using Postwrites to Get More Out of Peer Review

Postwrites, because they give your readers direction and focus, help move the peer response process along in ways that you need them to move. Composing a postwrite helps you identify areas in a draft with which you feel dissatisfied, even if you cannot quite name, let alone fix, the problems. Alerting readers to these areas will help them help you; that is, a postwrite can focus readers on what you feel your writing needs. It also leads to more thoughtful responses. Without postwrites, readers often give generic, unfocused commentary. How many times has a classmate read a paper of yours and said, "I like it; it's good," and nothing more? When you reply, "Are you sure?" your reader finds a spelling mistake, but that's about it. Reading a postwrite first helps readers know where to look and encourages them to give considered and thorough feedback.

When you compose a postwrite, usually you describe your writing process, identifying the steps you took or a strategy that proved fruitful. These descriptions — one account for each paper you write — provide a record of how you felt about each work before readers saw it. This is an

FIGURE 3.1. POSTWRITE FOR YOUR PERSONAL NARRATIVE

To:

From:

Re:

1. Summarize your paper in two or three sentences.

2. What key decisions or choices did you make?

3. In organizing your narrative, where do these decisions show up in your text?

4. Of the following narrative techniques—showing versus telling, pace, characterization, dialogue, time sequence, a twist or surprise—pick one and explain how and where it works especially well in your piece.

5. What did your readers say about your title? your introduction or lead? your conclusion? your transitions or the flow of your writing? Relate some good advice that you received (and who gave it), and how you used it to improve your text.

6. How can I [the instructor] help you most in my response to this piece? Be specific about the parts or passages that you still aren't satisfied with, or a decision you made that you want me to comment on.

excellent form of directed reflection. Postwrites concentrate the reader's attention on your focus, support, or organization, for example, so that they have more to say to you about what works and what needs work in your draft. If you don't use postwrites in your class, then for each paper you share in a peer response group, or for each paper your instructor collects, compose a journal or blog entry about what you think the paper does well and what it still needs.

In your notes, keep track of the process you went through to plan, research, and draft each paper, as well as where you got stuck and where things clicked. These notes help jog your memory and provide you with phrases to use when you are asked to explain your writing process in your portfolio. Keep postwrites in your working folder, and review them frequently to move in directed ways on your revisions. The two postwrite examples in Figures 3.1 and 3.2 illustrate how the questions should change according to the assignment and what you've already written in the course.

FIGURE 3.2. POSTWRITE FOR YOUR PROPOSAL

Name:

Title:

1. What problem or issue are you addressing in your proposal, and how did you come up with this topic? If you changed topics along the way, when did you switch and why?

2. What exactly are you proposing — a solution or change in policy, procedure, or attitude? Who will be interested in this proposal?

3. What is the most important piece of research that informs your proposal? Summarize the author's argument in two or three sentences.

4. Name three specific ways that your paper has changed since our last workshop. If you wish, identify someone who was very helpful in guiding those changes.

5. How can I [the instructor] help you most in my response to this draft? Be specific about parts or passages that you think still need work or that you want me to look at carefully. What questions do you have for me as a reader?

TAKING STOCK 4: Composing Your Own Postwrite

Review the sample postwrites in Figures 3.1 and 3.2, and then draft three or more postwrite questions for the writing assignment you're working on right now. Your questions should ask where you have been in your writing and where you need to go. Answer your own questions in your journal or blog. You might also do an Internet search for blogs that reflect on writing in progress to get some ideas for your postwrite questions.

MIDTERM SELF-ASSESSMENTS

It is very important to keep watch over your work at midterm. The class is in a routine by this time, and certain concepts should be familiar to you. If you've missed a class that covered something important, or if you don't quite understand a term, concept, or assignment, there's still time to catch up, clarify, or ask for extra help. If you don't get help in a timely way, you may not have a chance to learn from the task you were assigned and apply your learning to what comes next in the course.

Plan to take stock, then, of how you're doing in the class at around midterm. Examine what strategies are or aren't working for you, and what you need to concentrate on for the remainder of the course. Your instructor may design a type of midterm portfolio or exam that asks you to conduct an inventory of your working folder for your portfolio, to look both forward and backward at your progress in the course, and to write some sort of self-assessment or reflective piece. This is good practice for the reflective piece you'll need for your portfolio, and it helps your instructor determine your midterm grade. Even if your instructor doesn't require this type of reflection, it's an excellent idea to review your working folder at midterm and spend at least thirty minutes writing your own self-assessment. Answer questions you have about your writing process, about your strengths as a writer, and about your preferences and writing habits.

In writing their self-assessments, students often discover something about their writing patterns that they had not noticed before, and sometimes they find areas where they need to work harder. Aisha, for example, describes her typical writing process: "I tend to write one draft, bring it to the workshop, then edit that one draft a little and hand it in as a final draft. I never spend a lot of time writing things over or revising my papers. This is a habit I still have from high school classes." Troy sees a lack of development: "I find that in my writing I have good ideas, but I don't develop them enough. I feel all my papers are good, but they need more." And Elsa admits that she isn't giving readers enough help: "I tend to leave things unclear. I assume because I know what I'm talking about that my readers should also." Each of these students identifies areas where his or her writing could use work, and recognizing problem areas is a great place to start. Because these students took stock of their work at midterm, they can benefit from their self-assessment over the rest of the course.

Journals, postwrites, and self-assessments are just three ways of keeping watch over your own learning. Your instructor will likely have other ideas, too. Practicing reflection throughout this course, using any method that works for you, makes your learning more meaningful and increases your chances of pulling together a first-rate portfolio.

—4—
Keeping Company and Working with Others

Writers might work alone at a keyboard or in a secluded corner of a library; they may need privacy and concentration to think. But that doesn't mean that writing is a solitary activity. Writers get their ideas from their environment, and they write with an intended audience in mind. Writers write to be read. In other words, writing is not done in a vacuum; projects grow from ideas that are planted or watered by others through social interactions that may be educational, professional, or recreational. The actual physical activity of writing may take place in what appears to be a closed environment, but the mental activities involved in writing are heavily influenced by society and culture.

Recognizing that writing — making meaning — is a social process helps you make your imagined readers real. You are writing to your instructor and your classmates, of course, but you also are writing to an intended audience. Perhaps you're writing to convince decision makers to adopt a particular policy, or perhaps you're writing to persuade a prospective employer to hire you. What audiences have you written to during this course? Keep in mind that if you're saving postwrites or other work online, your writing may be read out of context by an audience you weren't originally targeting. You have to be aware of all possible readers.

Classes that emphasize discussion, participation, and group work often foster a reflective community of learners. You are part of a subculture, in effect, with shared experiences, vocabularies, and concerns. And a writing class that relies on group work offers distinct privileges: You're aware of the history of the class, along with its inside jokes and stories; you know who is most helpful and whom to ask for help; and you know you'll be missed if you're absent. Any group that meets regularly and has a common goal or mission is bound to establish patterns of communications and relationships. Familiarity and shared experiences, however, cut two ways: Communities offer a sense of belonging, but they also insist on responsible membership.

Being a responsible member of a writing team, response group, or workshop classroom means being prepared to do your share of the work. You need to be ready to help others by meeting deadlines, for example. You also can practice responsible group membership by paying close attention to how your group works and how it might work even better.

TAKING STOCK 5: Assessing Peer Response

Analyze your most recent peer response session; that is, take it apart to see how it worked. Who participated? Did each member contribute? How? If you've worked with the same group before, what rules have been established, formally or not, about how group members are expected to work together? What patterns of communication have developed? What ritual activities does your group engage in? If you've recently joined a new group, what went well in the process of communicating? What didn't? Did everyone participate equally?

Write two or three paragraphs in response to these questions. Share your response with your group members, and then formulate a set of goals for improving your next peer response session.

The writing process is perhaps most social when it involves sharing your drafts with others and receiving their feedback. Writing courses that include portfolios tend to offer many opportunities for this kind of sharing and response, and you are expected to seek and to offer peer response. Even if there's not enough class time to allow for adequate responses, and even if you're not required to do postwrites, you should be a responsible learner and group member, sharing your postwrites and asking classmates to exchange responses, perhaps via e-mail.

There are many ways to offer comments on your peers' work. If your instructor has asked you to follow a particular strategy, you'll want to go with that. If not, here are some ideas for reviewing classmates' electronic drafts:

- You can offer your comments at the top of the draft or in a reply e-mail.
- You can work in the file in your word-processing program, using Track Changes to show your comments, or inserting your remarks in a color, in brackets, or in all caps. Or you might use the program's comment feature.
- Bedford/St. Martin's Comment site offers secure online storage and tools for reviewing classmates' work.* Ask your instructor if this tool is available to you.
- Many students find hyperlinking helpful for commenting, too. If you check out the companion Web site or do an Internet search on "online writing lab," you'll find a list of portals that have a number of valuable handouts about writing. Your instructor may have a list of online handouts, too. You could copy a relevant URL, select a word or phrase in a peer's paper, and insert the link, and then add a comment if you like.

---

*For more on Comment, see the companion Web site.

When your classmate gets the paper back, he or she has a link to a handout that gives particular guidance.

Whatever tool and technique you use, be specific and, where you can, phrase your comments as questions. By asking rather than stating, you are offering advice that keeps on giving. That is, your questions may apply to more than just one point in the paper. Help your classmates develop a plan for their revision. Without a plan, the response you offer — or receive — may be too vague or take too long to be useful.

Becoming a good reader for developing writers takes practice, and many students new to peer response groups struggle with what to say. The sentence openers in the following list assume that you are sitting with a small group of writers discussing your drafts, or that you're at a computer with a classmate's draft on the screen. It will help the discussion and your commentary if you can point to specific passages to illustrate your point. Try using some of these phrases as starters to break the ice in your next peer response group or to begin a comment that you find difficult to express:

- "I like the way you . . ."
- "What strikes me most about your essay is . . ."
- "Why did you decide to . . . ?"
- "This part made me [smile, wonder, feel sad]."
- "I wonder if you should move this part to here so that . . ."
- "I get lost here when . . ."
- "I am surprised by this conclusion because I expected . . ."

Sharing your work and giving helpful feedback will get easier as the course progresses, and you'll learn the benefits of working with others to improve your writing.

The next time you ask a friend or roommate to read a draft for you, even casually or quickly, use the guidelines below, or refer to the sample postwrites in Figures 3.1 and 3.2. It takes extra work to be a good reader for others, but it shows that you respect the process and respect others' ideas if you can engage in a sincere and intelligent conversation. When a friend or peer reviewer just says "It's good," you may be pleased initially. But you need to know why it's good. If you don't, you haven't really learned anything. By the same token, you may think you're being kind by writing "It's good, no problems" on a classmate's work; but this kind of response lacks depth and doesn't help writers improve or realize the true effect of their words. Instead, be honest and give constructive criticism, the kind of criticism that's intended to help.

Readers can only be as helpful as writers want and expect them to be, of course. Here are some questions that might help shape your next peer response session. Ask your next reader to answer these questions for you about your draft:

1. If you read it quickly, can you read it again before we talk about it?
2. What part stands out most for you? What do you remember most about it?
3. Do you think my ideas are in the best order?
4. Where should I add another example or a fact or an illustration?
5. The assignment requires _____. Do you think I've done that?
6. Can you point out one sentence that you stumbled over or had to reread?
7. Is my essay important? How can I make it more significant?
8. Are there places I can be more concise or precise?
9. Do you know of any good Web sites or key terms that I should use to search for sites that might help me think about my paper in a different way?
10. What about the style of my writing: the tone? the sentence variety? the word choice?

—5—
Keeping Up and Getting Unstuck

As you know, much of the work in your course happens outside of class. You often must face the page alone. You may have left your peer response meeting with a list of suggestions from your readers, but late at night in front of the screen, with no one else around, you have to make decisions; you have to keep the process moving. Sometimes, though, you can't. Even the most experienced writers get stuck now and again. When you don't have the option of putting the text away until next week or next month or however long it takes for inspiration to strike, you need to develop strategies that can help you make steady progress or at least keep you from falling hopelessly behind. Read the following three scenarios and think about what you would do if you were stuck in the same way.

GETTING STARTED

On a typical Wednesday during Daria's first-year writing course, the class spends twenty minutes or so discussing a new writing assignment: *Write a review of a book, movie, restaurant, performance, or exhibition for a specific type of publication.* Daria's instructor emphasizes the importance of following certain criteria for the review, and the class generates a list of criteria for reviewing both a restaurant and a horror movie. Students ask questions about length and what newspapers or magazines would be acceptable to target, and then class time is up. Daria is expected to report orally on her ideas for this review in class on Friday, in just two days, and she'll need to have an initial draft for Monday's peer response workshop. But Daria is stuck. She prefers assignments that are more specific and that give her few options; for example, she would feel more confident if the assignment was to review a specific movie for a particular publication. She doesn't know where to begin.

What are Daria's choices? Here are some ideas: She can hope that inspiration strikes in the next forty-eight hours. Or she can stay a few minutes after class to ask the instructor for help. She can e-mail the instructor later that day, or she can call or stop by the instructor's office for a quick appointment. She also can stop by or contact the writing center, to see if a tutor has time to help brainstorm ideas.

Like Daria, if you leave class without fully understanding an assignment, you're going to have to figure it out somehow. Take advantage of any available class time to ask for clarification. If you're confused in class but aren't sure what to ask yet, make sure you have the instructor's e-mail address and office hours, and ask as soon as possible later in the day. Or if class time runs out and your question wasn't answered, stick around to ask the instructor your question, or see if a classmate has time to discuss the assignment. Maybe the assignment seems clear in class but gets murky when you first sit down to work on it. To sort through what's being asked, circle or underline the key words or phrases that signal exactly what's expected. Pay special attention to the verbs. Look for key words like *analyze, explain, illustrate, argue, support, show,* and *discuss.* For terms you don't understand, check the dictionary or textbook, and be sure to ask about them during the next class if you're still unsure.

Getting started with ideas and narrowing the writing task may take considerable time, but if that first step goes well, chances improve that the other steps will also go well. There might not always be enough class time for you to plan your paper or get ideas from others. But if you feel all alone in getting started, find ways to reach out for help.

PLANNING AND DRAFTING
MORE EFFICIENTLY

Antonio is in the same course as Daria. He is trying to develop better habits for writing essays. In many of his classes, Antonio has been able to get by writing papers pretty much the night before they were due. He would write some notes and a quick outline on paper, and then he would write the first draft on his computer. He'd run the spell-checker, change a few sentences around, print the document out, and turn it in. But Antonio realizes that his "system" really isn't going to work anymore. For one thing, the assignments give him so much freedom that he can't just answer the question. He has to find his own subject and narrow the focus. In addition, the instructor expects him to explore other invention strategies besides outlining and to show these strategies in a working folder.

In an effort to break his just-in-time writing habits, Antonio tries several new strategies. He starts carrying a small notebook and pen in his backpack, so that he can jot down ideas when they come to him. Some writers, especially those who commute by car, carry a tape recorder or speech-to-text handheld device so they can talk through ideas while they're driving, using time on the road to get the thinking component of the writing process done. Once Antonio experiences a productive writing session, he takes a few minutes to figure out why he thinks it went so well. He can then try to duplicate the components of a productive writing session if he gets stuck later. And when he's stuck, he feels free to stop for a while; he knows that many writers, when they get stuck, put the draft away or turn to another project to give them some mental distance. Antonio also tries a technique for getting started again later: Some writers stop writing in the middle of a sentence so they will have a specific place to start the next day or in the next writing session.

Antonio also begins to depend on readers for his earliest drafts, sometimes called *discovery drafts* or *zero drafts,* to help him decide which direction to go in or which parts are the most interesting. He learns that readers are useful, not only for fixing errors he didn't see, but also for being a sounding board for his ideas.

SEEKING OUT OTHER READERS AND LEARNING ABOUT RESOURCES

Jasper begins his creative writing class concerned about whether his writing skills are good enough. He's worried that his work won't be up to par. Struggling alone with the first assignment, he wishes he had some way of knowing if he is on the right track. Then, during the second week of class, a tutor gives a brief presentation about the campus writing center's services. She says they take walk-ins on a first-come, first-served basis, but that appointments are also available. For those who cannot always get to the center, some information (handouts on avoiding plagiarism, for example) is available on the writing center's Web site. The tutor recommends that Jasper and his classmates come prepared to the writing center with a copy of the assignment, with any notes or drafts, and/or with a paper returned from an instructor. In response to a question about a typical session, the tutor clarifies that every session is different depending on where students are in the writing process, what they need to work on, and what they bring to the session. Tutors are trained to focus the session in productive ways. Finally, the tutor announces that "we will not proofread your papers," but she also explains that tutors will teach students strategies for finding and correcting their errors.

Jasper learns that the writing center is a place where writers meet to talk about their work with other writers, and that most colleges and universities have writing centers. These places are friendly and informal, with an atmosphere defined by the idea that "everyone is learning to write." Writers at all levels and in all disciplines are welcome. It's not unusual on a given day to find a graduate student writing a thesis in microbiology, a budding poet working on verse for a creative writing course, a communications major getting help with a required course, and a senior working on a résumé. Jasper learns that writing tutors are often students, too, studying writing every day, and that most colleges and universities offer other tutoring or support services, usually paid for by tuition and fees. Even if he just wants to use a computer or have someone explain MLA documentation style, Jasper can visit the writing center and find someone to talk to about his writing.

FINDING GOOD READERS

Daria, Antonio, and Jasper got stuck at different points in the writing process, something that happens to all writers, especially when they are writing on a deadline. Finding a good reader is often the solution to getting unstuck. Ever hear an instructor tell you to read your work aloud or have someone else read your work aloud to you? Writing often can be improved through listening.

Who is a good reader? Good readers can be found in many places, in class and out. Even though your peer response group is the most obvious place to find readers, it's often a good idea to seek the advice of other readers whose judgment you can also trust, especially if you prepare that person well with your postwrite questions. A spouse, friend, roommate, classmate in another course, and tutor in the writing center can be good readers, too.

After sharing a draft with someone, ask yourself these questions:

- Do I want to work on this again? Can I imagine a starting place for revision?
- Do I know exactly what my reader suggested?
- Did the reader's reaction confirm my suspicions or reinforce what I think my paper needs?

If the answer to these questions is yes, then you've found yourself a good reader for your work now and in the future, even if that person is not enrolled in your class.

TAKING STOCK 6: Finding Readers or Help

Locate your campus writing center or learning center, or go online to the school's Web site for help. Find out where it is, and go there! Take notes or collect a brochure or pamphlet that explains its purposes and procedures. In a short paragraph, describe what you found when you got there, whom you talked to or corresponded with, and what you found out about the help that's available to you. Then write clear directions for students or visitors who have just arrived on your campus or who are just learning their way around the school's Web site. Be sure to put what you've written into your working folder.

You might also find credible writing help online through an independent service. Take a look at the services listed at the companion Web site to this book. How do you know the information one or more of these sites offer about writing and writers is legitimate? What kind of help do you think a service could give you and other writers in your class?

FROM PROCESS TO PRODUCT—PREPARING FOR ASSESSMENT

—6—
Understanding Assessment

You are producing a portfolio suited to the purposes of your course. It should be a project that you enjoy putting together, but in most college writing courses it also includes an assessment component. The portfolio method tries to make the assessment process more meaningful to you. Anticipating the final evaluation of your portfolio, then, we turn to analyzing and preparing for the completion of your portfolio keeping and its assessment. You must keep the end in mind as you maintain your working folder and compose your portfolio.

ASSESSMENT FROM
THE WRITER'S PERSPECTIVE

To begin, you must analyze the situation you're in as a writer and decide, accordingly, how to present yourself and how to best reach and most effectively engage your reader. For the assessment of this portfolio, you are trying to convince an audience that you have met certain expectations or criteria, including evidence of your learning. Because you are faced with assessment, the impression you make on your audience has measurable stakes. Through a whole series of decisions, with every sentence you edit and every example you include, you are affecting the outcome.

Although this picture may be intimidating, try to think of your portfolio as a situation that can be analyzed, broken down into parts, and managed. Rhetoric gives us the tools for just this purpose. *Rhetoric,* the study of effective communication, helps writers analyze communication that involves complex human behaviors — like preparing a portfolio or assessing students' writing. We wouldn't really need rhetoric if human beings were always rational and logical; if people didn't have memories, feelings, or associative thoughts; or if language was not often loaded, ambiguous, or dense. We use rhetoric when we think or write on topics about which there can be disagreement. The skeletal system of a rat is not really a rhetorical topic; but whether a politician is a rat is.*

The study of rhetoric teaches us the importance of *situation* and tries to break down the concept of situation into manageable parts. First, effective communication doesn't really begin until someone has identified a reason to communicate and feels compelled to act on it. When people feel the pull or need to say something, they take the first step toward engaging in a rhetorical act. The second step is to recognize at least some of the constraints involved — the obstacles, sensitive areas, or differences that can impede communication. The third step is to shape the form of the communication (tone, voice, word choice) in light of its purpose, its audience, and any constraints on the situation.

For portfolio assessment, your purpose is fairly clear: You need to convince your reader and/or evaluator that your portfolio represents your best work for this course, that you have succeeded in becoming a reflective learner, and that you have demonstrated writing abilities that fit with the highest standards of the course.

Whether this portfolio represents your writing process or your best works, whether it is produced electronically or with more traditional tools, your target audience is one of the most important elements of the rhetorical situation. Obviously your audience in this rhetorical situation is the reader and/or evaluator of your portfolio. If the audience is your classroom instructor, you have an advantage. You've spent time with this person; you have read the course outline and assignments; you have listened to lectures and explanations; and you have participated in activities that this instructor designed and conducted. You probably have determined something about this person's values, preferences, sense of humor. It is especially important, however, to judge your audience, not by stereotypes or careless assumptions, but, whenever possible, by concrete evidence. Based on evidence from the syllabus, assigned readings, in-class activities, and writing assignments, then, what information have you collected about the intended reader?

Indeed, you may be asked to write for an audience other than your instructor, even though your instructor will be evaluating your work. Sometimes portfolio assessments involve instructors from other classes as well. That is, often portfolios are assessed by a team of instructors. If the audience is unknown to you, your decisions will be more difficult, but you can ask questions about your audience; and if you can make safe rather

---

*In some circles the term *rhetoric* carries a negative connotation because of its association with politicians and their "empty rhetoric." Actually, everyone uses rhetoric in order to convince others, understand arguments, analyze problems, or recognize language patterns.

TAKING STOCK 7: Determining Your Program's Values

Knowing something about the values of the writing program at your college or university will help you prepare a portfolio targeted specifically to its readers. If your college writing program has a brochure, pamphlet, or Web page that states the policies, expectations, and aims of the writing program, study that publication carefully to determine what the program values. Those values are the basis on which your portfolio will be evaluated. For example, a writing program that states an emphasis on classical forms of argument is going to read portfolios differently from a writing program with a focus on personal writing and self-disclosure. Determine what qualities of good writing your writing program values or is most likely to reward. In your journal or blog, rank those qualities in order of importance, and write a brief rationale for each; then share your list with your workgroup or the entire class.

than careless assumptions, you can work with those. Is it safe to assume that your portfolio's evaluator will be an instructor of writing, rhetoric, English, or communication?* Yes. Will your work be evaluated by a member of the larger academic community at your college or university? Sure. But what you cannot assume is personal information about your reader; for instance, how long your evaluator has been an instructor or his or her favorite movies. Instead, imagine a reader who has a certain level of education, appreciates reading and writing, and is part of the writing or composition community at your school.

Once you understand what your audience values, you can choose how best to appeal to your audience's sense of reason or emotion and how to establish your own credibility. You will have to decide which appeals are most appropriate given the purpose of your portfolio and whether you are emphasizing process or products. Once you have envisioned your audience, you can choose how best to approach that audience through your voice, or your self-presentation. What image of yourself do you want to convey? Self-presentation is obvious when you give a speech. Speakers make careful choices about their appearance depending on the audience and the formality of the gathering. In a portfolio, your careful choices show up in your language choices and design choices.

How does your language reflect your understanding of your audience, of the situation, and of the course material? First, you can demonstrate that you have successfully adopted the vocabulary of your course. If your

*Remember: Your portfolio may be evaluated by more than one person.

course has emphasized *audience, context, focus, invention, genres,* and *revision,* your evaluator might expect you to use these terms in your discussion of writing. Many readers value strong vocabulary and precise word choices, as well, a way of using language often called *style.*

To present yourself as a careful writer, find an appropriate level of formality in your language and become comfortable with it. Are you typically formal and reserved in your academic work? Your language might reflect that. If you are an easygoing, casual person at school, your language can reflect that too. Your decisions about tone and level of formality show up not only in your word choices but also in your use or avoidance of the first-person point of view.

One way to think about language, tone, and self-presentation is to ask yourself how much distance you want to put between yourself and your writing. Do you want to set yourself apart from your words? Do you want to own your words, to stand behind them? Experienced readers—like your instructor and/or your evaluators—are able to tell if your language sounds hollow or forced, so try as much as possible to be yourself even while acknowledging the needs of your audience.

Most students understand the art of appearing studious or serious, and eager or engaged. Your language must convey sincerity, however, because an experienced reader—and your reader will be experienced—can easily detect overblown claims and pretension. Along these lines, watch your dependence on thesaurus words: You want them to sound natural. Unless you also consult a dictionary to double-check the words you choose, you could easily misuse them.

No matter how carefully you attend to tone and vocabulary and try to match your language to both your personality and the context, a rhetorical situation can be more complicated than you might expect. No matter how well prepared a writer might be, some elements of the context are simply unknowable or may change. Your task is not to try to hold the situation still but to learn to recognize and then negotiate the changes. That is, understanding how rhetorical situations evolve and change, and how complex they are, can help you know when and how to intervene. Unfortunately it is impossible to know everything about the situation surrounding the assessment of your portfolio. You cannot know if your evaluator is going to get enough sleep the night before the evaluation, or if she shares experiences similar to those you discuss, or if he knows more than you do about your research topic. The idea is not to guess your readers' backgrounds, beliefs, politics, or personal lives. Instead you need to learn to make appropriate judgments about your readers as educated, intelligent, aware people who value reading, writing, and fresh ideas.

With an e-Portfolio you might also think about how to present yourself through the usability of your design; that is, the functionality of your portfolio design also provides insight into who you are and how you think. Consider, for example, all the Web pages out there and how you relate to them differently because they use colors, fonts, graphics, and navigational tool sets differently. How will your readers navigate your work? Doesn't the organization of your work say something about its quality?

ASSESSMENT FROM AN INSTRUCTOR'S PERSPECTIVE

Most writing instructors know, from their experiences both as writers and as instructors, how complex assessing portfolios can be.* Testing specialists, composition researchers, and instructors on all levels find writing assessment to be one of the most challenging areas of their profession. Most writers, however, value assessment of their work in the form of feedback, response, report, or even criticism if it is offered in the right spirit and if it helps them improve a piece or recognize patterns in their writing.

In environments other than school where writing is produced and published, grades are not relevant to the writing process; in fact, they seem almost unnatural. But grades are a very real part of your current writing situation. Grades are a necessary evil, and portfolios must be graded, too, when the time comes.

Still, many students associate writing classes with being graded on every piece. After collecting a number of red-inked or highlighted comments on assignments, students begin to believe that instructors just love grading students' written work, that they relish circling or correcting errors, and that their sole mission is to show students where they are wrong. This may be true in rare cases, but most writing instructors don't fit this stereotype; in fact, they often struggle because assessment is such a challenging and complex component of writing instruction. Examine the following myths about grading in light of your thinking and experiences. How many of these statements have you believed? What are your instructor's views on these myths?

Myth 1. Instructors love giving grades on written work; they find it easy to decide what the letter grade should be on any particular essay, story, or exam. Actually, many instructors hate giving grades for writing assignments and often find it difficult to decide whether an essay should receive, say, a B– or a C+. Teaching students to write better is not like teaching them human anatomy, where all the body parts have a name and where test answers are either right or wrong. Writing is a rhetorical situation: It has many shades of gray; and there are many right ways to succeed at a writing task. Every reader experiences a written text differently; even the same reader, on a different day, may respond to something that went

---

*Evidence comes from the Education Resources Information Center (ERIC) database done in 2005. A search on the keywords *writing assessment* produced 7,455 articles and papers on the subject.

unnoticed before. It's very difficult, in fact, to get instructors to agree on a single score for a paper; that's why a divergence of one score is acceptable in large-scale assessments conducted by the Educational Testing Service for exams like the SAT.

Myth 2. Instructors value only error-free prose. When they read, they look mostly at commas and spelling. All readers, even instructors, are interested first in a writer's ideas; then they look to be pulled in by the language and the train of thought. This is what instructors want, too: to be engaged in the ideas, the voice, the anecdotes, the examples, the pace. Instructors are readers first and foremost. They love to read and want to read something good. If the writing is lively and intelligent, an instructor isn't going to notice mechanical lapses. But if the writing is predictable, undeveloped, or unpersuasive, then reading is going to be stalled by grammatical, spelling, and punctuation errors. Errors show up more when the text is unfocused or poorly organized.

Myth 3. Instructors spend most of their free time correcting students' work. It's useful to remember, as you analyze your portfolio assessment, that the instructor reading your work is a person, too, with a wide variety of interests and a number of responsibilities. Besides leading full personal lives, college or university instructors also teach other courses, conduct research or write for publication, serve on department committees and national boards, and do other professional work. When your instructor sits down to read and evaluate a stack of portfolios at the end of a term, many other tasks are waiting. This doesn't mean that you and your portfolio aren't important, but it does mean that you need to make an impression within a very small window of opportunity.

Myth 4. A letter grade is the only way or the best way to assess students' writing performance. In your experience with school writing, you might have received letter grades more than any other kind of response, but there are other ways to assess writing, particularly writing in progress. Most common are notes written in the margins or at the end of paper documents, or inserted as comments in an electronic document. Some instructors type their comments on a separate sheet, without marking the printed or digital text at all. Other means of assessment include having a conversation about the writing—what some instructors call a *conference*—in the classroom, a hallway, or the instructor's office. Conversations can also take place online, over the phone, or via e-mail, fax, or voicemail. And some instructors record their responses on a cassette or in an audio file that students can listen to at their leisure. Whatever the method, effective response needs to be a dialogue, an exchange of ideas. The instructor may offer advice, but the decision to accept it and implement it is the student's. Letter grades really don't initiate the kind of dialogue that's essential to the assessment of a work in progress; they are much more appropriate for finished work.

Myth 5. Instructors are autonomous and independent, and can do whatever they want. Instructors are not autonomous, even if they pretend to be. In obvious and subtle ways, their efforts are shaped and controlled by a number of institutional codes, rules, or guidelines. Instructors are not free to inflict any kind of torture they dream up on students, and they have to satisfy certain requirements, cover specific material, and undergo annual reviews. If instructors were autonomous, most would not give letter grades, knowing that the instructional value of grades is so questionable. But almost all colleges and universities require that instructors give a single letter grade at the end of a term. That alone limits the procedures an instructor can use for assessment.

Myth 6. The evaluation of writing is purely subjective, and everyone is entitled to his or her opinion. Because writing is such a complex act and language can elicit very different responses from people, it is easy to think that evaluators are being subjective when they decide that an essay is excellent, average, or poor. Readers do not develop their criteria for good writing in a personal way, however. Opinions come from somewhere: from one's experiences, from mentors, or from the media. In an academic setting, most judgments rely on evidence or support; therefore, writing is judged not from personal opinion but from a shared understanding of the characteristics of strong, effective prose. Instructors and evaluators of writing have developed a sense of good writing from years of reading in their field, from listening to and working with colleagues, and from writing their own texts. Although the criteria for good writing vary across fields and in different situations, those criteria are shaped over many years of subtle negotiations and implicit social contracts. Even when it's difficult to identify the criteria or to know how to measure the success of a piece of writing, a trained reader relies on shared or community-based criteria. Readers from any background rely on judgments that are neither purely objective nor purely subjective, but a little of both.

Myth 7. Electronic portfolios with hyperlinks, lots of graphics and a great design, and sound and video clips are always better than paper versions. Bells and whistles might attract readers, but to sustain readers' interest, your portfolio will need focused, interesting, lively writing. After all, you've been assigned the work of producing a portfolio in a writing course. You cannot depend on technological savvy to secure a good grade. If you've developed an e-Portfolio, you must take care not to assume that technology can replace thoughtfulness or mask carelessness. Your instructor will know to focus on your reflective and critical thinking.

Myth 8. Instructors are the only audience students need to think about. Particularly if you're working electronically, your classmates and others may have access to your work. In some cases, your portfolio may be shared, both in draft and final forms, with a number of people in your class and perhaps in other writing classes. You need to write for those audiences as well as for the evaluator or evaluators.

There are more myths about writing instructors and writing assessment, but keep these in mind as you prepare your portfolio. They address a dilemma that instructors struggle with every day: how to encourage their students to develop their strengths and have a positive attitude toward writing despite the fact that their work is going to be corrected and critiqued.

Often instructors resolve this dilemma by making a distinction between reading and grading, between response and evaluation. When instructors first sit down with students' writing, they are *readers*. They are looking at where the text engages them and where it doesn't, where it's entertaining and where it's not. For most writing teachers, the primary goal is to give students the feedback and advice of a more experienced reader. This kind of reading response requires evaluation of what is and is not working in the text. Not all forms of evaluation, however, include response. An instructor could, for example, slap a big red C on the project and be done with it. The letter grade would serve as evaluation but not as response: Most writing instructors agree that oral and written commentary is more instructive than a letter grade. Distinguishing between response and evaluation is tricky because some theorists claim that every encounter with a text or artwork is evaluative; we are constantly evaluating the things we encounter. Still, acknowledging the differences between response and evaluation might help you assess the stakes involved in different situations. Is your reader going to respond, to evaluate, or both?

Understanding the elements of assessment should help you make reasoned choices based on what you know and what you can safely assume. Rhetoric can inform those choices by giving you a set of tools with which to analyze the context or situation and to respond appropriately, reasonably, or judiciously. You demonstrate your rhetorical understanding with each set of decisions you make about your portfolio, beginning with your choice of artifacts to include in your portfolio and how they should be arranged, and your recognition of how that choice can influence your readers' experience.

TAKING STOCK 8: Reviewing Your Working Folder

Review your working folder and record your first impressions of your work to date. Taking notes at this point can help you begin to think about the reflective essay or introduction your instructor may have assigned. This is a good opportunity to record some of your observations or impressions. What surprises you? What patterns do you see? What would you want your instructor to know about the work you've done that may not be clear in each artifact?

—7—
Putting It Together: Selecting and Arranging Artifacts

How many potential portfolio entries have you created so far in this course? Have you kept track of your choices and decisions as you composed each piece? What have you produced that you'd like to keep working on? Which artifacts are you going to finish, now that the due date is looming?

Even if your instructor has assigned the number of entries you are required to include, you still must choose which artifacts and decide how much revision each one needs. Can you include multiple drafts of the same assignment to demonstrate your revision skills? Does your instructor prefer to see the final revisions first and then previous drafts, or something chronological? Even in writing classes with very structured portfolio requirements, you'll need to make a number of choices about what types of changes to make and how to present the materials.

In the section titled "Setting Goals and Planning Ahead," you were asked to define your goals for the course as well as for your portfolio (see pp. 8–11). Did you write them down in your journal or blog? This is the ideal time to review what you've written along these lines and to see how your portfolio addresses or reflects your goals. It's also time to confirm answers to questions that you may have had when you started the course:

- Can I include brief response pieces, blog entries, position papers, e-mail, or chat transcripts? Can I include journal entries or impromptu or timed writings done in class?
- How polished, finished, or different do the artifacts or entries need to be?
- How much time do I have at this point to revise and put together my portfolio?
- Do I have the technological know-how I need?
- Does everything I include have to be revised, edited, or both? Can entries be in their "original" state if I include an explanation of why I chose not to revise them?

You might write down what you plan to include in your journal or blog. Meanwhile, in consultation with your instructor and classmates, make sure you understand the scope of your portfolio and what it can include:

- Written text in terms of pages or number of words
- Bulleted lists (like this one)
- Photographs that you've taken or found online
- Clip art
- Charts and graphs
- Audio and video clips
- Hyperlinks to internal files offline and to external files on the Internet

Ask yourself what purpose each artifact serves. Your instructor will examine the choices you make very closely, so you want to think through and be able to explain your decisions. The more content you can include, of course, the more difficult and time-consuming your choices. So find out as soon as possible what kind of entries and how many of them your instructor is looking for.

STARTING THE SELECTION PROCESS

Once you're clear about what you can include in your portfolio, and once you have a general image in mind of the content and design of your portfolio, set aside time for initial planning and storyboarding. (See the sample storyboard in Figure 7.1 on p. 46.)

If you're creating a print portfolio, sit down with your working folder in a place where you have plenty of room to spread out the folder's contents and sort through them. If you are using an electronic folder, label each file clearly first and then open as many files as possible and try to arrange them so that they are all partially visible onscreen and can be easily minimized and restored. Here's where keeping an organized working folder pays off. (If you haven't kept up with labeling and sorting, now is definitely the time to do it.) As you pull labeled pieces out of your working folder, remind yourself what each piece is about and do some initial sorting. Think of three piles: pieces you plan to include, pieces you don't plan to include, and maybes. If you are sorting through electronic files, create three folders and label them something like, "For Portfolio," "Not for Portfolio" and "Maybe for Portfolio." Then move into those folders the relevant files. We talk more about the selection process below. It is not uncommon in a writing course to have as many as fifty pieces of information to sort through at this point.

THE NAVIGATIONAL SCHEME

If you're creating an e-Portfolio, it's now time to settle on a navigational scheme. Readers of print-based portfolios may follow a table of contents, but they move through a portfolio mostly by turning pages, typically in order. In an electronic portfolio, the writer can set up a navigational scheme that links each section, or node, in the portfolio. By clicking on an icon or other hyperlink, readers can move through the work in different sequences. So one reader may choose to review the portfolio in chronological order, while another may choose to start with the final artifact and its process components and then move to another entry. The e-Portfolio writer can create multiple sequences; conversely, the writer can set up a navigational scheme that directs all readers to specific artifacts. Whereas the print portfolio allows readers to flip through pages as they will, the e-Portfolio writer can control page flipping if it makes sense to do so. One thing that is especially convenient, too, is that the navigational scheme can be placed on every section simply by copying and pasting. Readers can see the links *to* all sections *from* all sections.

Although they can be used for both print and electronic portfolios, metaphors are especially meaningful in e-Portfolios because of the graphical user interface. Instead of using words as links to different sections, you can create icons. An *icon* is a pictorial symbol, in this case of the content in a section of the portfolio. Like the topic sentence of a paragraph, an icon needs to tell the reader what to expect when he or she clicks on it. Choosing or creating an icon requires writers to consider their readers: What will my audience think this picture means? In a good navigational scheme, the icons representing each section should all be related. In other words, you should think of an overarching metaphor that symbolizes the work and your efforts in the course, and then develop a series of related icons.

METAPHORICAL THINKING

What word or phrase best describes your work in this course? If, for instance, *growth* encompasses much of your success in this course, then the metaphor of a garden might be appropriate. The icon for one section could be a seed; the icon for another, a sapling; the icon for still another, a fruit-bearing tree. Or suppose *new understanding* captures your progress well. You might explore how the metaphor of a person climbing a mountain symbolizes your work. It's a long path and a difficult struggle through "course" terrain; but as you climb, what's below becomes clear. If you think metaphorically and holistically, your ability to make connections between ideas and artifacts in your portfolio will increase. See the companion Web site for types of symbols and metaphors often used in e-Portfolios; these might spark an idea for you.

PRESENTATION TOOLS

There are three types of presentation tools used to create e-Portfolios, and each has its benefits and limitations (Table 7.1). The type of presentation tool you use plays a significant role in the type of navigational structure you can develop. Ask your instructor which type of presentation tool you

TABLE 7.1. PRESENTATION TOOLS FOR E-PORTFOLIOS: BENEFITS AND LIMITATIONS

PRESENTATION TOOLS	BENEFITS	LIMITATIONS
Common tools: Using a combination of Microsoft PowerPoint and Microsoft Word, for example.	• You do not necessarily have to upload your work online. • You are already very familiar with these programs, and much of your work is ready to go. • Hyperlinking is very easy once you put all of your files into the same folder. • These tools lend themselves to creativity. • It is easy to add animation if you want it.	• Your work isn't as portable. You will need to save it on a USB drive, a network drive, a CD, or some other system for submission. And you probably won't be able to e-mail your e-Portfolio. • Working from multiple computers is difficult unless you save all of your work to a medium that is compatible with each computer. • You can store your work online, but the files will be relatively large.
e-Portfolio program: Using Mosiac, for example.	• Free programs are available and accessible through the companion Web site. • Your instructor may be using a program like Blackboard, WebCT, or TaskStream, which has e-Portfolio tools built in. • Your work is online and easy to update and access from multiple computers.	• Your school may not have ready access to these programs. • Hyperlinking can be a challenge in some of the programs. • The program may limit your ability to personalize your e-Portfolio.
Web page–building program: Using FrontPage or Dreamweaver, for example.	• Your work will be scalable and can grow as you read, write, and think about concepts during and after the course. • Your navigational tool set can include useful mouseover effects • You can share your work with family and friends by sharing your Web site address.	• You may be tempted to spend too much time on the design and look of your e-Portfolio at the expense of reflection and work on its content. • It can be confusing to upload work to an online space. • It is easy to get links wrong. • It is difficult to troubleshoot.

can use: common tools, an e-Portfolio program, or a Web page model. If the presentation tools are up to you, read through Table 7.1 carefully and weigh the advantages and disadvantages of each type.

CHOOSING THE ENTRIES

To begin choosing the entries for your portfolio, consider both the focus of the course and the principle of variety. Review the handouts, assignment sheets, and other course materials to determine which qualities of writing the class has emphasized, and to choose pieces that best illustrate those qualities.

Then consider the variety of the pieces. Which pieces best demonstrate your learning? Your writing ability? Will those pieces also illustrate variety? Try sorting your possible entries by, for example, audience. In your working folder, how many different audiences have you addressed or invoked? Can you demonstrate your ability to write a number of different pieces for different purposes? Sort your entries again chronologically—from those you wrote first to those you wrote most recently. Could you make a case for variety by including entries from early, middle, or late points in the course? Depending on the assignments you've been given, you may think you don't have a variety of work, but consider several options. For example, could you condense one entry and develop another so that your portfolio pieces demonstrate a variety of lengths?

Reread or skim enough of your writing to remember what each piece is about. Then quickly reread your instructor's comments and peer reviews, to remember as much of the context of your original draft as possible. Once you have reread all of your essays or projects, you might want to begin a process of exclusion by creating a storyboard (see the following section).

Some students find it easier to identify the pieces they don't want to include than to pick those they do. You might start by setting aside the essays, projects, or pieces that you cannot imagine working on again. These are the ones for which you have very little enthusiasm, for whatever reasons. Maybe you didn't make good choices to begin with, or you lost interest somewhere along the way. Perhaps it's a project that always frustrated you and never did quite come together, or maybe the piece was timely two months ago but now seems dated. Maybe you've become bored with the topic, or perhaps you think that you still have a lot to learn about the issue before you can write convincingly. In any case, how you feel about a project is extremely important, and only you can determine that.

If you begin with the definite no entries, turn next to the definite yes candidates. Which pieces please you, make you feel satisfied, or still interest you? Which ones do you catch yourself rereading from start to finish? Naturally you may be tempted to ask, "Which one did my instructor like best?" However, the projects you like best are better choices because your instructor isn't the one who is going to be taking the entry through the revising, editing, and polishing stages. Because you have to live with this piece for the next two or three weeks, make sure it is a project that genuinely interests you.

The definite yes and no candidates are the easiest to identify, but your maybe pile is likely to be the biggest of the three. How do you decide among the possible entries in the maybe pile? Perhaps most important, you'll need to envision what each maybe entry would look like in final form. A maybe piece doesn't have to be in excellent shape right now because there's still time to revise, edit, and polish — and that could be exactly what's expected. Your instructor has intentionally designed this course to give you time near the end of the term to revisit the writing process with each of your essays or projects that show the most potential, and to finish them now. Try sorting through the maybe pile with these options in mind:

- Choose a piece that shows promise or potential but that still needs quite a bit of work; the revised work will demonstrate your ability to finish a promising piece.
- Choose a piece that offers an interesting contrast to one or two of your other entries, a piece that adds variety to the portfolio.
- Choose a piece that ties together two or three other entries, that provides a thread or common theme to your portfolio.

In general, use your own instincts and reactions to a piece to judge whether or not to include it. If you can't get excited about a piece, how will you make your reader like it? If you're bored with it, your boredom is going to show. Readers can sense how you feel about your work, so choose examples that get your writing juices flowing. In addition, choose entries about which you have something to say. If you can readily think of points you want to make about a project — about the writing process and how the essay evolved, or about why you wrote the essay, or about what you think its strengths are — then it may be an excellent choice for inclusion. After all, you need to revise each entry, but you also must be able to discuss why you chose it and what it demonstrates about your learning or your writing ability.

STORYBOARDING

A *storyboard* is a series of drawings that depicts a sequence of events. Directors use storyboards to plan their shots in the scenes of a movie, for example. (Sometimes the director's storyboards are included in the bonus material on a DVD.) In effect, storyboarding is similar to clustering or mapping. When you have a handle on what you want to include in your portfolio, stop and plan how you want to organize the entries *before* you begin building. Too often, students spend far too much time at this stage paying attention to the look and design of their portfolio (especially their e-Portfolio) when they should be focusing on the content. Hours or even days later, they may have found the right font or color but do not have a dominant structure or see the relationships between artifacts clearly. Your instructor will evaluate your work primarily for the reflective and critical thinking it demonstrates, and a storyboard can be an enormous help here.

Figure 7.1 is an example of a storyboard. You can draw your own on paper or use a computer program to diagram the structure of your portfolio. Begin with an introduction that leads into your artifacts. You may want to give your readers the opportunity to read through your journal or blog for the course, or you might include the instructor's and your classmates' feedback. In any case, your task is to demonstrate the relationships between and among the artifacts. Think about the lines between each piece here as a contextual reflection, that is, a connection you will have to make in tracing your development from one artifact to another.

As you make your choices and prepare to revise and edit each piece, consider which piece might work best first or last, and how the placement of each entry affects the whole. We know that first impressions are very important and sometimes lasting, so the first few pages of the portfolio are crucial to establishing your credibility as a strong careful writer. Research, in fact, has found that portfolio readers in large-scale assessments make their judgments very early in the process of reading a portfolio, and that

FIGURE 7.1

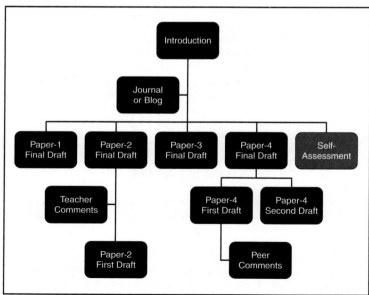

entries in the middle or at the end do not much alter their evaluation.* This finding emphasizes the importance of a well-crafted introduction and suggests that your best entry should follow the introduction. Remember, however, that the study was conducted in large-scale assessments, which means that hundreds of portfolios were being evaluated in one session. If your situation differs, so might the outcome. You need to decide, of course, on the best order, and you may want to address the reasons for the order in the introductory piece. Whatever your decisions, your job in the introduction is to give some of the reasons behind them.

TAKING STOCK 9: Getting Help Choosing Artifacts

Who can help you choose? The people who know your work best include the instructor, of course, but also (and perhaps even more so) the classmates with whom you've collaborated in this course. Without giving them any hints or showing them your writing folder, ask your peer response group members which of your pieces they remember best. Their answers can tell you a lot about which of your essays had an impact. You can ask the same question of your instructor: "Without looking at my writing folder, what did I write that you really remember?" Your instructor might be willing to answer that question, but many instructors will want you to make your portfolio choices independently, without prodding or direction from them.

If all of your sorting and rereading still leaves you uncertain, talk to your instructor about other options. Maybe you want to write one of the projects or assignments again, which would mean an entirely new draft. Your instructor might approve of that, but be sure to check first. Some instructors do not want any surprises in the portfolio, or they might need evidence that you have taken the entry through all of the stages of the writing process.

---

*This reader-response study was conducted at the University of Michigan. See Liz Hamp-Lyons and William Condon, "Questioning Assumptions about Portfolio-Based Assessment." *College Composition and Communication* 44.2 (May 1993): 176–190.

—8—
Preparing to Write the Introduction and Other Reflective Components

---

TAKING STOCK 10: Revisiting Your Expectations

Review your answers to Taking Stock 1, where you practiced reflection. Reread what you wrote about your expectations for this course and about the areas in which you thought your strengths would help you. Do you still agree with what you wrote? How did your expectations match up with the reality of the course? What parts of this exercise can you use in writing your reflective introduction or cover letter?

Reflection can and should take place throughout your portfolio keeping experience, but at some point it's important to make the reflection more formal, to present and discuss evidence of your learning in a formal piece of writing. Before you begin, be sure you understand how the reflective elements in your portfolio should function.

Clarify with your instructor if you are expected to write a reflective opening statement—a cover letter, an introduction, a preface, an essay.* If you are not being asked to preface the portfolio with a reflective introduction, are you expected to describe your entries or introduce your choices in some other way? In other words, there can be two types of reflection: (1) an introduction to the portfolio, and (2) short pieces that introduce each artifact. If your instructor has not assigned a reflective opening statement, he or she may be expecting accounts of your choices or descriptions of your process to appear throughout the portfolio. Ask your instructor if each entry should have a preface. Although the reflective essay does not have to be the first entry in a paper portfolio, it often is, owing to its role in establishing a relationship with your readers and evaluator. If its placement is not specified in your syllabus or the portfolio assignment sheet, check with your instructor.

---

*Your instructor may also refer to this reflective statement as the *introductory slide,* the *jump-off point,* or the *first node.*

In deciding where to place reflective elements in the portfolio, an e-Portfolio offers you additional options. For example, you can insert links that let readers move through the portfolio in different sequences or that they follow a particular sequence in certain places. It makes sense to have them read the reflective introduction first, for example. So, on your portfolio's home page, you might insert just one link, to the introduction. Then, on that page, you can give readers the option to go to any artifact next. Of course readers can skip around in a paper-based portfolio too; but traditionally they read one page at a time in sequence. (By limiting the links you insert in each section, you can achieve the same effect in an electronic portfolio.) If you have posted a reflective essay, but it can be read at any time, provide links to it from each of your other pages.

A good rule of thumb with e-Portfolios is that the reader should be able to get *to* anyplace in your work *from* anyplace in your work. Keep your navigational tool set the same by copying and pasting it on each artifact or on each page of your portfolio Web site. Many e-Portfolios are designed so that readers have to click on the reflective elements before reading the artifacts themselves. This ensures that readers will at least have the opportunity to understand the context of each entry, how and why the artifact was created.*

Whatever form your reflective elements take—a letter to your reader, an essay, a set of paragraphs introducing each artifact, or all of the above—the reflective writing you do could well be your most important writing in the course. Reflective components show your ability to be a reflective learner and to analyze a rhetorical situation effectively. They explain your choices in compiling the portfolio and demonstrate your thinking about your learning. One demonstration of reflective thinking is being able to identify important features or patterns in your writing process. Think of it this way: Readers of your portfolio—even your instructor—cannot see your entire writing process. If you've done most of your composing alone at the keyboard, your readers have not watched you write or watched you do online research; they haven't participated in your peer response groups; they haven't seen all of your notes, drafts, and other evidence of your evolving ideas. They won't know what your friend suggested about the anecdote that opens your argument essay, and they won't know how hard you've worked on adding transitions between paragraphs. Readers will be aware only of what you share with them in the reflective elements. In fact, it is for this reason that many students like to use digital video in their e-Portfolios: to show themselves writing. You can find a few examples of these kinds of clips through the companion Web site.

If your portfolio is a best-works portfolio, the reflective introduction or other elements function as a type of final exam—the ultimate test of what you've learned about the qualities of good writing, about anticipating

---

*Miles A. Kimball, *The Web Portfolio Guide: Creating Electronic Portfolios for the Web.* New York: Longman, 2003: 11–12.

readers' needs, and about the importance of details. If you think of those elements as a final examination, you begin to see the importance you should place on them. Sometimes students work throughout the course very diligently on their assignments and projects, and then spend twenty minutes on a reflective piece. That's simply not enough time for what is a critical component of your portfolio.

You have many options in writing an effective introduction or other reflective element, but you will need to demonstrate reflective learning or self-assessment. In other words, you must show that you can evaluate the strengths and weaknesses of your writing, that you understand what you do well and what you still need to work on. Instructors are not looking for perfection; they are looking for writers who are insightful, conscientious, and engaged in learning.

If you have maintained a working folder and have managed to save, label, and file all of your work for this course in print, in electronic form, or in some combination of the two, here comes the payoff. Retrieve all of the notes, postwrites, and journal or blog entries in which you've recorded something about your writing process, your struggles and triumphs, the adjustments you've made. With these materials, you should be ready to begin drafting your reflective introduction. Have you ever written an essay and then written your introduction or title for the essay? This is a similar process.

As you reflect on your learning, think of a vivid or memorable way to represent that learning to your readers. Most portfolio evaluators are looking specifically for an indication that you can name your learning and identify its significance. Ultimately, this course is about teaching you how to make good writing decisions in the future, not simply about writing individual essays right now. To demonstrate their learning, many portfolio keepers find it valuable to use a powerful theme or rich metaphor to tie the contents of their portfolio together. We've talked a bit about metaphor above; but you may actually find it easier to develop a unifying metaphor *after* you've chosen your artifacts and articulate how each piece contributes to the whole.

- Tam, for example, describes her portfolio as the Boston T, with each artifact a stop along the way between where she boards the subway and her destination. Looking out the window as a passenger, you see a flurry of objects whizzing by you; but when you stop, you understand where you've been.
- Diego chooses a baseball theme. There are nine innings in the game, and different events happen in each of them. A run in the third inning may or may not be significant; it's impossible to know until later, when an analysis of the entire game clarifies its importance.
- Frank, a student who grew up helping on his family farm, uses cropping corn as a metaphor. You have to have the right tools and equipment; you

have to apply your experience to choosing the right week to plant and the right week to harvest; and you have to have luck with the weather. In much the same way, to write well you need to have good tools and the ability to reason based on experience; and, of course, you need a situation that encourages quality writing.

What you see in these examples is a deep connection between the students' personal experiences and their new writing experiences. These students have a better understanding of writing because they are able to see how it works as a whole. The sum can be worth far more than its individual parts. That, in effect, is a primary value of portfolio keeping. The navigational scheme you develop may or may not include a unifying metaphor. Regardless, the scheme should both inform your reflection in the introduction and provide context for each artifact. The navigational scheme helps your reader move through your work, but it also helps you understand the connections you've been making between your world and the writing you've produced in this course.

In the reflective element(s) of your portfolio, especially if yours is a best-works portfolio, you might try some of the following:

- Discuss your best entry and why it is your best.
- Detail the revisions you've made and the improvements and changes that you want readers to notice.
- Demonstrate what this portfolio illustrates about you as a writer, student, researcher, or critical thinker.
- Acknowledge the readers-respondents who have influenced your portfolio pieces and describe how.
- Reflect on what you've learned about writing, reading, or other topics of the course.
- Include specific examples or passages from your working folder.

If you are working on a process portfolio, in addition to some of the points above, you may want to consider these ideas for developing the reflective portion(s) of your portfolio:

- Outline the process you went through to produce one or more of your entries.
- Acknowledge your weaknesses, but show how you've worked to overcome them.
- Discuss each piece of writing you've included, touching on its strengths.

And here are several points to consider in planning and writing your reflective introduction or essay:

- Who will be reading this piece? Is the evaluator reading to suggest changes? to assess your work and make a decision about your effort and talent?

- What is the situation surrounding this reading?
- What will the outcome of the reading be? Can you influence it? If so, how and how much?
- What qualities of writing does your reader value?

Your instructor no doubt will add other points to consider that you need to examine carefully. Be sure to look back over the comments on and responses to your returned projects, and review the course syllabus and assignments. What patterns do you see in your instructor's concerns or directions? Use what you've learned about your instructor's values as a reader to compose a convincing, well-developed reflective introduction or essay. It's doubtful that your instructor is looking to be flattered, and asking for an A is probably not the best strategy, but humor, liveliness, or anecdote might be very effective.

If your evaluators are unknown — that is, if a team of instructors will be reviewing your portfolio — ask your instructor to give you some information about them so that you can decide which logical, ethical, or emotional appeals might be most effective. In this scenario, you won't know your readers personally (and they won't know you at all). Still, it's safe to assume that your evaluators will be trained in portfolio assessment and will share many of your instructor's ideas about good writing. If your college writing program has a set of guidelines or policies and grading criteria, consult it for information as you begin composing.

If your classmates also will be reading your portfolio and perhaps contributing to its assessment in some way, gather as much feedback as you can and make use of it, immediately, in the work itself. It makes sense that your portfolio would be shared with the people who have read and responded to your writing for the entire term, and you may be asked to make your classmates or peer response group your audience. In some classes, the sharing is just that; but in others, your peers may be asked to evaluate the portfolio. Because your instinct would probably be to write more informally for your peers than for an instructor, find out what level of formality is expected, and what uses of language would be most appropriate.

How long should the reflective introduction or reflective essay be? Again, check with your instructor for these types of details. Remember, however, that you need to develop your ideas or support your claims as you would in any effective piece of writing. In this situation, you are trying to convince your reader that you have learned the course's subject matter and also that you have chosen wisely, revised judiciously, and edited carefully. If you are asked to write a letter, follow the format for a business letter (check your style and usage handbook), and include the date and inside address, as well as an appropriate salutation and closing. Above all, remember how important first impressions are: It is critical that you take this piece through the same stages of the writing process that each of your entries has undergone.

—9—
The Final Stages: Revising, Editing, and Proofreading the Entries

Once your reflective elements are in good shape, it's time to turn to the final stages of preparing each portfolio entry. Although most stages of writing tend to overlap, revising, editing, and proofreading should be treated as discrete processes for improving the text: That is, you might find it helpful to honor the differences among these three methods for improving a text. Because it is so important to make a good impression with each of your portfolio entries, this section gives you strategies for sharpening your skills of rereading the text and finding places for improvement. One principle to remember is that any revision you do will create the need for more editing, and any editing you do will require proofreading. Each time you tinker with a piece, you need to attend to all three procedures.

REVISING

To *revise* literally means "to see again." The idea is to view your writing differently, from a different angle or through a different lens. When writers revise, they make global, wholesale, or fundamental changes in a text—big changes, not sentence-level stuff. For example, Farah drafts a proposal to state lawmakers about raising the legal drinking age. When the members of her peer response group agree that lawmakers are not going to be convinced and that her points are too general, she revises the proposal by altering both the audience and the purpose. In her revision, she addresses the university's president directly and proposes a tightening of drinking rules on campus. While the genre or type of writing remains a proposal for change, and its topic is still raising the drinking age for college students, Farah's shift from lawmakers to the university's president allows her to be far more specific and to cite examples from the campus community that her peer reviewers and the president will recognize and understand. Her proposal has become more specific and more immediate; and because its purpose has shifted—from a legislative change at the state level to a rule change locally—she has added to the proposal's credibility and its potential for success. As Farah has discovered, revision is bigger and more involved than sentence-level changes: For her proposal, revision meant writing an entirely new introduction to set a different tone, restating her purpose (or thesis), and adding far more examples. Although she was able to save many of her sentences about responsible drinking, Farah's revising activities included frequent rereading, writing new copy, deleting old copy, and moving or rearranging sentences and paragraphs.

Revision begins with the first reader, and that's you. Every time you read through a passage or paragraph, listening for places where you need to say more or say it differently, you are revising or considering ways to make the text more focused, coherent, and crisp. You may revise naturally and automatically as you compose because composing involves a series of pauses and rereadings. Each time you reread, you may find something to change, move, or clarify. Even though other readers — your instructor, your peer reviewers, your friends — will recommend certain changes, you should develop independent revising habits. Try to read as a reader, not as the writer, and anticipate where readers are going to have questions or are going to want more explanation.

Many students consider revision one of the most challenging tasks in a college writing course. Many have not been asked to revise before, only to edit and proofread for errors. However, because revision is the foundation of portfolio writing courses — giving students time and opportunity to present their best possible work — understanding and practicing revision are key to your success. There's a good chance that your instructor chose to assign portfolios because they invite revision, almost insist on it, by providing a context for the revision — that is, the end-of-course assessment.

TAKING STOCK 11: Assessing Revision

Review your working folder for evidence that you have practiced revision as it has just been defined or described — that is, making global or large-scale changes involving adding, deleting, or moving chunks of text. Where can you demonstrate your effort to revise? Write a short response to share with others about your understanding of revision, the efforts to revise that you found in your working folder, and your goals for revising your portfolio entries.

EDITING

Editing is another part of the writing process that you should be able to do independently although you also will benefit from the fresh eyes of other readers who may catch lapses in syntax or usage that you don't see. *Editing* means working through the text in a systematic way, looking for places to tighten the prose and clarify the ideas with more-precise word choices and punctuation, and to add emphasis with varied sentence patterns. It's important to remember that editing is about making choices, not necessarily about following rules. When writers edit, they make conscious choices to achieve a certain style or tone, for example, or to make certain features of the text consistent with their purpose or thesis. Editing is usually not as extensive as revision: Revision typically involves adding, deleting, or moving sections of text, while editing makes the revised text smoother, more polished, and more cohesive. Editors often add keyword transitions or cut unnecessary repetition. A good handbook can help you with editing techniques, and some of the strategies listed in the proofreading section below also can help with editing. The key to careful editing (and careful proofreading too) is to read differently from the way you read for content. Editing (and proofreading) requires that you *see* the text differently. One way to do that when you're editing on-screen is to change the background color and the color of the text. If you've been writing an essay using black letters on a white or gray ground, change to white letters on a purple background. This kind of change can give you a fresh perspective on the piece.

PROOFREADING

It's time for proofreading after you have revised and edited a text many times and your best judgment says that the text is finished, or you've simply reached a deadline for delivering the piece to others. By the time proofreading is needed, however, you may have memorized the paragraphs and sentences. Therefore, the key to good proofreading is finding ways to see and hear the text differently or to break up the way you usually read, especially when you have read the text from beginning to end dozens of times. Although "seeing the text differently" may sound much like revision and editing, *what* you're trying to see changes: When you proofread, you are looking for mistakes and errors and flaws in formatting. That's it. The most straightforward of the three stages, proofreading asks you to find what's wrong that might make readers stumble while they are trying to concentrate on your ideas with your essay or its formatting. When students talk about fixing a paper, they usually are referring to proofreading because the solutions to proofreading problems don't involve making choices. In contrast to editing, which is all about choices—to improve the style, tone, order, or coherence of a written work—proofreading is about following conventions. You don't have to make choices, but you do have to either know the rules or know where to find them.

With proofreading, then, your job is to find mistakes and errors. There is a difference between the two. Mistakes are easier to find and to fix because you recognize that something must be done as soon as you see them—"Oops, I meant *their,* not *there*"—and then you make the correction.

Errors are more challenging because you often don't recognize them as readily: You may sense that something is amiss, but you can't identify it.

Mistakes are accidental; errors show a lack of understanding or a lack of information. You never did understand the rule for using the possessive apostrophe with a plural noun ("the commuters' lounge"), for example, so you've omitted the apostrophe entirely. Errors and mistakes can be tackled through the same techniques, but rooting out the errors will take more time and diligence and maybe a helpful proofreading partner.

Here are some techniques that may help when it's time to edit and proofread the final entries for your portfolio:

- *Work on a hard copy of the document, essay, or project.* Writing does not look the same on-screen as it does on a page. After revising and editing on-screen, printing out a hard copy is another way of altering the appearance of a familiar text so that you can see things you might be missing. Mark up the hard copy with changes that you can later enter on the computer.

- *Read aloud.* Try reading the piece aloud, as though you are reading to an audience. Stand up, project, and enunciate. How will this help when there's a good chance that anyone who sees you will think you're crazy? Reading aloud helps you hear the words, not just see them. Reading aloud helps clarify your decisions about sentence length and punctuation. Because reading your essay aloud is just plain different from reading it silently, your perspective will change—and that's all that many writers need to enable them to make improvements.

- *Read backwards.* Read backwards? Not word by word, of course, but line by line. This is very unnatural, and that's precisely the point. Because you've probably read your piece dozens of times from beginning to end, you are so familiar with the ideas and the sentence order that you are only skimming the text. You have, in fact, probably memorized the paper, which means you know what comes next, and that doesn't help you find errors and mistakes. Begin reading backwards from the last sentence of the piece. Read up the last page and up the next page, sentence by sentence. The last sentence you proofread will be the first sentence of the document. Why does this method help? When we read, we don't process every word; instead we process chunks of meaning. Our familiarity with written documents gives us powers of prediction—we know what to expect—and the repetition of language patterns make it easy to skim and comprehend long passages without necessarily remembering every keyword or phrase. For proofreading, however, you need to be able to see every word, every mark of punctuation. Proofreading requires a different kind of reading, something that becomes easier with practice. (And you'll discover why publishing companies hire good proofreaders.)

- *Cover up parts of the text.* Covering up some parts of the page to concentrate on others is a strategy similar to reading backwards: It breaks up the normal reading pattern and forces you to zero in on particular passages or paragraphs. For this technique, you need two blank sheets of paper. Lay them lengthwise, one at the top of the page you are proof-reading and the other two or three lines down. The blank pages should cover up most of the lines on the page, leaving only a few lines showing. As you proofread, move the blank pages down to keep as much white space as possible and to isolate the lines you're reading. How does this help? The marks on a page that constitute writing often begin to blur and run together, especially when a reader is tired or intimately familiar with the text. This technique of covering up parts of the text reduces the lines of type a reader can see and creates more white space, which highlights the lines that are visible. Again, this changes your normal view of the text and therefore changes the way you see it.

Finally, as you proofread, don't forget to attend to all of the details that will direct your readers' attention to what it is you want to emphasize, not to mistakes and errors. For a paper portfolio, you should check your page numbers and headers. If you have provided a table of contents, be sure the titles and page numbers are correct, and that the format is easy to follow. Consult a good handbook for proofreading guidelines, or ask your instructor. For an e-Portfolio, you want to be sure all of the links work. Also check that you have provided enough headings, titles, and signposts to help your readers navigate easily.

On every page or for every artifact, your portfolio should meet high standards. It should be a set of documents ready for public presentation, a product in which you can take pride. Taking pride in your work means concentrating on revising, editing, and proofreading in the last days before the portfolio is due. In addition, some students find creative ways to give their portfolio that final touch or distinctive feature; for example, they have their paper portfolio bound or do a collage on the cover. For this assessment situation, however, it's important to remember that a cool video stream, sounds between your slides, or a great color scheme cannot make up for weak writing or careless editing; and neither can a cheerful cover, photographs, or a fancy binding. Check with your instructor about the extent to which you should spend time on the technical or artistic aspects of your portfolio. Some instructors may actually object to this sort of adornment, so ask questions about any creative touches you want to add. In general, you can make the best impression by following the instructions and guidelines you are given, by investing time and care in your portfolio entries, and by making the most of the help, advice, and instruction you have received throughout the course.

—10—
Portfolio Keeping Continued: Re-visiting Your Learning

Your first-year writing class is not the only time you'll be asked to keep a portfolio of your work or to practice reflective learning. In fact, portfolios are an obvious choice to enhance student learning and to tap into the capabilities of electronic storage and delivery systems. For instance, you may be required to produce a portfolio for your major. You may be required to produce one as part of a capstone course for your university. What about making the portfolio for this course an artifact in a larger portfolio for another course or project? Considering grad school one day? You might use a portfolio as part of your application. And, of course, portfolios are very useful as a sampling of your ability when you start looking for a job. Or you can maintain this portfolio on your Web site with a link from your home page. It's likely that you can reuse or retool much of the reflective learning you have produced here. Of course, when the rhetorical situation changes—because the audience and purpose are different—so too must the writing. Thus, portfolios are never static; they must change with the context.

If portfolios are fairly new to you, it might help you to know that students in a number of different majors, and in a variety of learning situations, are being required or encouraged to keep portfolios and to maintain or update an already established portfolio. In some schools, every artifact composed in every class is uploaded to a central location called a *course management system*. Students then give various types of evaluators access to the specific work each one is in charge of evaluating. For instance, an advisor for a major might see all work for that major; a recruiter for a specific job might see all work that prepares prospective employees for that specific job; or an evaluator of work toward specific licenses or certificates or degree plans may be given access to specific types of artifacts.

Students in accredited degree programs are expected to produce portfolios as evidence that they are ready to work as professionals in nursing, business, engineering, pharmacy, or education. Students in instructor certification programs, almost without exception across the country, are being asked to create portfolios that demonstrate mastery of standards or proficiencies, and that are targeted to an audience of educators or departments of education. As the reliance on portfolio assessment grows in a number of fields, your ability to see your work as a whole, and how your work both fits into and prepares you for larger projects and initiatives, is crucial.

Portfolios are increasingly being used in large-scale assessment situations, in which hundreds of students have their writing evaluated via the portfolio method. Some colleges and universities are using portfolios for long-term assessment measurements, or to test students' competence (perhaps as an exit examination to the composition courses). For example, the first-year writing program at New Mexico State University requires students to submit a portfolio that includes five samples of their writing: a self-critique, a writing within the major, a research essay, an editorial, and an argumentative essay. The portfolios are assessed by faculty members who teach the first-year course, and the results are used to evaluate the writing program and its effectiveness. Kalamazoo College in Michigan requires a portfolio for graduation. Members of the class of 2000 were the first to begin keeping an electronic portfolio in their freshman year; they maintained their portfolio work through four years of college, sharing it with advisors once a quarter and using it for reflection and decision making. Because the portfolios are maintained entirely online, students get experience with both electronic communication and portfolio learning.

Other forms of portfolios are increasingly popular at all levels of education. Graduate students earning master of arts degrees in English or other disciplines often have the option of compiling a portfolio in lieu of writing a thesis or taking a reading-list examination, and instructors-in-training or newly hired instructors often keep teaching portfolios that track their progress as teachers. When faculty members apply to different institutions or are reviewed for promotions or tenure, they often submit a portfolio of their accomplishments in the areas of research, teaching, and service, accompanied by a narrative or rationale for each portfolio artifact.

Because portfolios allow for making connections across the curriculum, students increasingly are being asked to create portfolios that link their work from a number of different courses and contexts. Internships, study abroad, cocurricular activities, service learning, and volunteer work all provide excellent material that can be integrated with your academic work in a portfolio. For example, during her senior year, Amanda enrolls in an internship program sponsored by the university. In addition to working at a local television station, Amanda attends weekly meetings with a mentor that prepare her for transferring the skills she has learned in college to the workplace. Portfolio keeping is an important part of this internship. By the end of the semester, Amanda has collected and arranged for credit in her internship course a portfolio that contains a copy of her current résumé, evaluations by her supervisors, journal entries about her experiences at the television station, an essay that makes connections between her academic coursework and her work at the station, and a brochure written to attract other students to the internship program. If you do an internship or spend a semester studying abroad or participating in a community service program, save artifacts of your work while you are producing them because it's difficult to go back and gather them. You may well have an opportunity to share what you have learned as you prepare a portfolio to meet a graduation requirement, to apply for graduate school, or to find work.

We noted above that the portfolio you've created for this course might also be used as an artifact in another portfolio. Sometimes that other portfolio is someone else's. For example, to demonstrate the quality of his or her teaching, your instructor might ask to use your portfolio in a teaching portfolio. Your instructor's portfolio might then circulate through wider networks and ultimately be part of a university's portfolio for accreditation. This kind of retooling is happening at Portland State University in Oregon (see http://portfolio.pdx.edu). In this model, all work falls into one of five themes or areas for improvement — communication and interaction are two examples. These are themes that you can probably see in some way in your portfolio keeping. And even this institutional portfolio project is part of a larger project, the Urban Universities Portfolio Project (http://www .imir.iupui.edu/portfolio).

In the event that your portfolio is retooled, to scale and sustain your work you must maintain its structure. Your working folder — in print or electronic form, or both — must be very well organized. If you are asked to put together a portfolio for your undergraduate work, you would be well prepared if you are a habitual saver of documents, artifacts, notes, and drafts. In particular, as time passes, it's difficult to recapture your thinking and your writing processes. In effect, you must become a researcher of your own learning. Because good reflection is in the details, practice keeping track of those details through a system that makes the most sense to you.

As institutional, educational, and professional uses for portfolios increase and change, you may decide to keep your own portfolio for your personal development as a writer and to track your learning or to record different stages of your development. Perhaps the self-motivated portfolio is the best kind because you create for yourself the opportunity or reason for portfolio keeping, and you become the best judge of your reflective learning. Whatever the purpose of your portfolio, good luck with it and all of the hard work and learning it will represent.

Revision Symbols

Some instructors use these symbols as a kind of shorthand to guide you in revision. The numbers refer to a chapter number or a section of a chapter.

abb	abbreviation **46a–g**	*//*	faulty parallelism **8e, 27**
ad	adjective/adverb **35**	*para*	paraphrase **17d, 18**
agr	agreement **33, 34f**	*pass*	inappropriate passive **28c, 32g**
awk	awkward		
cap	capitalization **45**	*ref*	unclear pronoun reference **34g**
case	case **34c–d**		
cliché	cliché **11a, 23d**	*run-on*	run-on (fused) sentence **37**
co	coordination **25a**	*sexist*	sexist language **21b, 34f**
coh	coherence **8e**	*shift*	shift **28**
com	incomplete comparison **26e**	*slang*	slang **23a**
		sp	spelling **23e–f**
concl	weak conclusion **8f, 19b**	*sub*	subordination **25b**
cs	comma splice **37**	*sum*	summarize **17d, 18, 62b**
d	diction (word choice) **23**	*t*	tone **10d, 17c, 23a, 23d**
def	define **8c**	*trans*	transition **8e, 30b**
dm	dangling modifier **36c**	*u*	unity **8a**
doc	documentation **49–55**	*vague*	vague statement
emph	emphasis unclear **25**	*verb*	verb form **32a–d**
ex	example needed **8b–c**	*vt*	verb tense **32e–h**
frag	sentence fragment **38**	*wv*	weak verb **32**
fs	fused sentence **37**	*wrdy*	wordy **29**
hyph	hyphen **48**	*ww*	wrong word **1, 11a, 23a–b**
inc	incomplete construction **26**	*,*	comma **39**
		;	semicolon **40**
intro	weak introduction **8f, 19b**	*. ? !*	period, question mark, exclamation point **41**
it	italics (or underlining) **47**		
jarg	jargon **23a**	*'*	apostrophe **42**
lc	lowercase letter **45**	*" "*	quotation marks **43**
lv	language variety **22**	*( ) [ ] —*	parentheses, brackets, dash **44a–c**
mix	mixed construction **26a**		
mm	misplaced modifier **36**	*: / ...*	colon, slash, ellipsis **44d–f**
ms	manuscript form	*∧*	insert
no ,	no comma **39j**	*∼*	transpose
num	number **46h–j**	*⌒*	close up
¶	paragraph **8**	*X*	obvious error

Contents

How to Use This Book iii

Preface xi

Writing for College and Beyond

1 The Top Twenty 3

2 Expectations 12

3 Multimodal Assignments 20
- STUDENT PRESENTATION

4 Writing to Make Something Happen 36
- SAMPLE WRITING

The Writing Process

5 Rhetorical Situations 48

6 Exploring Ideas 58

7 Planning and Drafting 64

8 Developing Paragraphs 75

9 Making Design Decisions 90

10 Reviewing and Revising 100

11 Editing and Reflecting 112
- REVISED STUDENT DRAFT
- STUDENT STATEMENT

Critical Thinking and Argument

12 Critical Reading 123
- STUDENT CRITICAL READING

13 Analyzing Arguments 136
- STUDENT ANALYSIS

14 Constructing Arguments 151
- STUDENT ESSAY

Research

15 Preparing for a Research Project 175
a Analyze assignment
b Formulate hypothesis
c Plan research
d Set up research log
e Draft working thesis

16 Doing Research 180
a Kinds of sources
b Start with the library
c Library resources
d Internet
e Field research

17 Evaluating Sources and Taking Notes 193
a Purpose of sources
b Working bibliography
c Evaluate
d Read and interpret
e Synthesize
f Take notes and annotate

18 Integrating Sources and Avoiding Plagiarism 211
a Quote, paraphrase, or summarize
b Integrate text
c Integrate visuals
d Excessive use of sources
e Why to acknowledge sources
f Which sources to acknowledge
g Avoid plagiarism

19 Writing a Research Project 220
a Refine plans
b Organize and draft
c Incorporate sources
d Get responses
e Revise and edit
f Prepare source list
g Create final copy

Language

20 Writing to the World 231
a What is "normal"
b Clarify meaning
c Meet expectations

21 Language That Builds Common Ground 236
a Unstated assumptions
b About gender
c About race and ethnicity
d Other kinds of difference

22 Language Variety 241
a Standard varieties
b To evoke a place
c To build credibility
d Other languages

23 Word Choice and Spelling 245
a Appropriate formality
b Denotation and connotation
c General and specific words
d Figurative language
e Spell checkers
f Spelling rules

24 Glossary of Usage 256

Sentence Style

25 Coordination, Subordination, and Emphasis 269
a Relate equal ideas
b Distinguish main ideas
c Opening, closing positions

26 Consistency and Completeness 275
a Faulty sentence structure
b Subjects and predicates
c Elliptical structures
d Missing words
e Comparisons

27 Parallelism 279
a With items in a series
b With paired ideas
c With necessary words

28 Shifts 281
a In verb tense
b In mood
c In voice
d In person and number
e Direct, indirect discourse
f In tone and word choice

29 Conciseness 284
a Unnecessary words
b Redundant words
c Empty words
d Wordy phrases
e Sentence structure

30 Sentence Variety 288
a Length
b Openings

Sentence Grammar

31 Basic Grammar 294
- PARTS OF SPEECH
- PARTS OF SENTENCES
- TYPES OF SENTENCES

32 Verbs 311
a Verb forms
b Helping verbs
c Regular, irregular verbs
d *Lie, lay; sit, set; rise, raise*
e Tenses
f Sequence
g Active, passive voice
h Mood

33 Subject-Verb Agreement 323
a Third-person singular
b Subjects separated from verbs
c Compound subjects
d Collective-noun subjects
e Indefinite-pronoun subjects